NORTH AFRICAN POLITICS

In the aftermath of the turmoil that shook North Africa in late 2010 and early 2011, commentators and analysts have sought explanations to the factors that triggered the uprisings and to understand why a region, seemingly characterized by relative stability for decades, would suddenly erupt in convulsions. Had an underlying dynamism in the region overwhelmed what were ostensibly stable authoritarian regimes? What were the connections to events and dynamics beyond the region, such as countries in the Middle East, international commodity markets, and environmental factors, amongst others? Why had allies abetted authoritarianism for so long, and what were the implications for such alliances?

North African Politics: Change and continuity brings together experts to explore these questions, providing in-depth analyses of important developments in the region, which build upon and complement the 2008 companion volume, *North Africa: Politics, Region and the Limits of Transformation*. This 21-chapter volume is a key contribution that responds to the need in the Anglo-American sphere for sustained, critical studies on North Africa and examines political, economic, security, social and military aspects of the region. Focused studies on individual countries allow detailed discussion of regional factors. The book also examines extrinsic, trans-regional dynamics, such as North Africa's influential interdependencies with the Levant and the Gulf, Europe, Sahelian and sub-Saharan Africa, and North America. Its innovative approach provides new perspectives on North Africa, extending its research scope to include Egypt and exploring China's evolving role in the region.

Providing an important contribution in the assessment of the ever-shifting political and social tectonics within and beyond North Africa, *North African Politics* is an essential resource for students, scholars and policymakers in Middle Eastern and North African Studies, and beyond.

Yahia H. Zoubir is Professor of International Relations and International Management and Director of Research in Geopolitics at KEDGE Business School, Marseille, France.

Gregory White is the Mary Huggins Gamble Professor of Government at Smith College and co-editor-in-chief of the *Journal of North African Studies*.

NORTH AFRICAN POLITICS

Change and continuity

*Edited by Yahia H. Zoubir
and Gregory White*

Routledge
Taylor & Francis Group

LONDON AND NEW YORK

First published 2016
by Routledge
2 Park Square, Milton Park, Abingdon, Oxon OX14 4RN

and by Routledge
711 Third Avenue, New York, NY 10017

Routledge is an imprint of the Taylor & Francis Group, an informa business

British Library Cataloguing-in-Publication Data
A catalogue record for this book is available from the British Library

Library of Congress Cataloging-in-Publication Data
    North African politics : change and continuity / edited by Yahia H. Zoubir and Gregory White.
        pages cm
    1. Africa, North—Politics and government—21st century.   2. Arab countries—Politics and government—21st century.   3. Africa, North—Foreign relations—21st century.   4. Arab countries—Foreign relations—21st century.   5. Arab Spring, 2010–   I. Zoubir, Yahia H.   II. White, Gregory, 1960–
    JQ3198.A58N68 2016
    320.961—dc23
    2015011831

ISBN: 978-1-138-92294-5 (hbk)
ISBN: 978-1-138-92296-9 (pbk)
ISBN: 978-1-315-68541-0 (ebk)

Typeset in Bembo
by Apex CoVantage, LLC
Printed in Great Britain by Ashford Colour Press Ltd, Gosport, Hampshire

MIX
Paper from
responsible sources
FSC
www.fsc.org   FSC® C011748

To Tricia, Emmett, and Sydney for their love.

—G.W.W.

To my grandson Haizam, who has brought so much happiness to my life; to my family for its enduring support; and, to my friends and colleagues worldwide who have believed in me.

—Y.H.Z.

CONTENTS

PREFACE AND INTRODUCTION

Yahia H. Zoubir and Gregory White

In the aftermath of the turmoil that shook North Africa in late 2010 and early 2011, commentators and analysts have sought explanations to the factors that triggered the uprisings. Why would a region that was seemingly characterized by relative stability and status quo for decades suddenly erupt in convulsions? Had an underlying (and underplayed) dynamism in the region overwhelmed what were ostensibly stable authoritarian regimes? What were the connections to events and dynamics beyond the region – e.g., to countries in the Middle East, to international commodity markets, to environmental factors, and so on? Why had allies abetted authoritarianism for so long, and what were the implications for such alliances?

This volume endeavors to fill a crucial gap in the literature. It seeks to build on and deepen the analyses of a 2008 companion volume, *North Africa: Politics, Region, and the Limits of Transformation.*[1] Moreover, it is part of an ongoing effort to overcome the relative neglect of North Africa in the Anglo-American academy. The reasons for this long-standing inattention are complicated, but may include a perception that North Africa is somehow part of the European and especially French spheres of influence and, therefore, not of particular interest or relevance to North American scholars. Additionally, and on a related note, the Levant and the Gulf region – the Arab-Israeli conflict, the instability in Lebanon and Syria, petro-politics, and the Gulf wars – have long attracted greater attention because of their obvious geostrategic importance. To be sure, there are crucial exceptions to the general lack of attention to North Africa.[2] Nonetheless, there is no denying the need for sustained, critical analyses of the region writ large, especially as time offers the opportunity to reflect on 2011.

Despite the limitations of area studies, as Peter Katzenstein instructs, paying attention to a regional grouping such as North Africa makes good sense.[3] Obviously, regions are significant actors geostrategically, historically, culturally, and economically. What is striking about North Africa, however, is that its framing remains ever open to interpretation. In part this is because it is sometimes lost between sub-Saharan Africa, the Middle East, and even the Mediterranean in area studies conceptualizations. The three central countries of Morocco, Algeria, and Tunisia are often called the Maghreb – Arabic for "where the sun sets" or the west. To confuse matters, Morocco is known in Arabic as *al Mamlakah al Maghribiyah*, or the Kingdom of the Maghreb. For their part, Libya to the east and Mauritania to the south are sometimes considered as part of a Greater Maghreb, especially since they joined a February 1989 pact with Morocco, Tunisia, and Algeria to establish the Arab Maghreb Union. Known in French as *l'Union du Maghreb arabe*, the French acronym "UMA" evokes the Arabic word for *Umma*, or community of believers. Certainly, the UMA never came close to its professed goal of fostering regional cooperation, and it is now effectively moribund.

An additional conceptual question is whether to include Egypt in North Africa. One crucial innovation of this volume is Egypt's inclusion. A glance at the map might suggest that it would seem immediately reasonable to include Egypt in North Africa. Yet the country has long been set aside in North African and/or Maghrebi studies and more typically assumed to be part of the Middle East. One might argue that including Libya is a stretch enough since it is east of the Atlas Mountain range and experienced a strikingly different historical legacy as an Italian colony. Reaching east to Egypt seems to stretch still further.

Yet, Egypt's connections to the rest of North Africa are obvious throughout history. It is impossible to consider Egypt separate from North Africa during the Roman era, the Islamic expansion, Ottoman imperial tutelage, and 19th- and 20th-century European colonialism. Moreover, the influence of Egypt in the post-independence era is undeniable given the influence of Nasserism and the country's geostrategic heft. In fact, the Arab League relocated to Tunis after the signing of the 1979 Camp David Accords. Finally, and most centrally for purposes of this volume, the fall of Zine al-Abidine Ben Ali in January 2011 was closely implicated in affecting the subsequent fall from power of Hosni Mubarak. And Egypt's political experience since 2011 has been deeply affected by and has affected other North African countries. We argue that including Egypt makes strong sense conceptually and analytically. The fallout of the uprisings, notably the emergence of armed militias in Libya and their connections with groups in Tunisia and Egypt, has definitely compelled countries like Algeria, Tunisia, Egypt, and Libya to reconsider their political and security relations.

With all that stipulated, even as the volume focuses on North Africa as a geographical space, it is also committed to examining extrinsic, transregional dynamics, such as North Africa's crucial, influential interdependencies with the Levant and the Gulf, Europe, Sahelian and sub-Saharan Africa, and North America. Often, of course, these interdependencies are asymmetrical. Yet, the geostrategic stakes are profound. The Western Sahara remains a central destabilizing issue in the region, hampering any process of regional integration. Similarly, the French intervention in Mali in January 2013 was connected directly to the influx of deadly arms from Libya after Muammar Qaddafi was overthrown by a NATO-led intervention.

Uprisings that toppled long-standing dictators, such as Ben Ali and Mubarak, mutually informed and inflamed similar protests in Yemen, Bahrain, and Syria. The post-2011 election of Islamist parties in Tunisia, Morocco, and Egypt was a closely watched regional dynamic – one that remained no less salient after the Egyptian military engineered a coup against Mohamed Morsi's elected government in July 2013. And the emergence of the Islamic State (known in Arabic as *al-Dawla al-Islamiya fi Iraq wa ash-Sham*, or "Daesh") in 2014 further implicated the Maghreb; various cells were suspected and/or apprehended in Maghreb countries, with frequent reports of Maghrebis traveling to Iraq and Syria to fight with Daesh.

North Africa's geopolitical dimension and stakes has expanded profoundly in recent decades, and the interests and presence of external actors will only grow. In addition to the treatment of Egypt, a second innovation of this volume is the attention to China's increasing role. China and Algeria have long had close diplomatic relations, stemming in large part from their respective roles in the Non-Aligned Movement; China and Egypt, too, have a deep history of bilateral relations. Nonetheless, China's economic emergence in the 1990s and 2000s only served to deepen its strategic calculations in the region, and China–North African relations have been understudied. Whether China's role in the region will conflict with other external actors remains to be seen.

Above all, the abiding theme of this volume is one of dynamism and profound change. The shifting political and social tectonics within and beyond the region remain hard to assess. As the old saying goes, it might be easier to paint a moving train than to analyze what is happening right now, never mind speculating on future trends. It is truly challenging trying to trace the changing subtleties of the various facets of political Islamism; the encrustation of military and/or monarchical authoritarianism in Algeria and Morocco; the tender and fragile stability that emerged with Tunisia's parliamentary elections in October 2014; Mauritania's profound fragility and its crucial position to the south of Western Sahara and adjacency to Mali; Sahrawis' ongoing rejection of Moroccan occupation, as well as protests against the current leadership of the POLISARIO Front in refugee camps in Tindouf (Algeria); and the profound instability and lack of central authority that wracks Libya (with profound implications for its neighbors in the region and in Europe). Yet, one thing we know is that the French phrase "plus ça change, plus c'est la même chose" – the more things change the more they stay the same – may not only be cynical; in many ways it is wrong. In the case of North Africa, things *have* changed. They are decidedly not the same. Our task is to understand this better or, at least, inform ourselves of the nature of the dynamism.

Perhaps one constant is that people in the region seek human dignity (*karama* in Arabic) and good governance, as do other peoples across the globe. North Africans have challenged incumbent authoritarian regimes at great risk. They faced brutal repression and death with unbelievable determination. The bravery of the masses that rose up to demand change compelled the armed forces in Tunisia and Egypt to abandon dictators in 2011. Bearing this in mind must inform the scholarly community's work.

Organization of the volume

The book is divided into three parts: the drivers of change in contemporary North Africa; internal dynamics; and North Africa in world affairs. Contributors have endeavored to examine recent developments within the region, all the while paying attention to a complicated historical backdrop. In most, if not all, instances, the contributors focused on past dynamics. Readers will understand that, as the volume came to fruition and events on the ground changed rapidly, it became difficult if not impossible to include all recent developments.

In Part I, Gonzalo Escribano analyzes the limits of political reform in the absence of economic development and human security, with an attention to the challenges underdeveloped political institutions face in managing economic change. Mark Tessler and Jennifer Miller-Gonzalez turn their attention to the crucial role that youth play in North African society, again focusing on the changes over the decades in post-independence North Africa. In separate chapters, Miloud Chennoufi and Eduard Soler i Lecha each pay careful attention to security matters. Chennoufi focuses on the crucial question of civil-military relations in two countries, Algeria and Egypt, finding that the appropriate balance between civilian control and military capacity bedevils all countries, but in North Africa it is especially problematic. Soler, for his part, examines all six countries and the complicated interplay of military, police, and intelligence ministries, the same civil-military balance, the role of the military in the economy, and so on. Michael J. Willis' contribution goes to the very heart of a crucial problem in referring to 2011 as "the Arab Spring." After all, a significant portion of the North African population is *not* Arab. The events themselves, understood within the context of a complicated Berber/Amazigh identity, take on a whole new meaning. Stephen Zunes delves into the impressive and abiding pursuit of non-violent change in the region. He highlights the role that gender plays, and offers a view that non-violent pursuit of justice remains a crucial piece of future change. Lina Khatib examines the ways in which men and women in the region used social media as a vector for transnational political activism, civic engagement, and good, old-fashioned reporting. Finally, Alice Wilson closes the first part with a treatment of the Western Sahara. While noting that the conflict is seemingly intractable, it is no less necessary to examine the Western Sahara in the context of the 2011 conflict since it, in many ways, is central to intra-regional politics. One may argue that Western Sahara, not Tunisia, is where the first popular uprising in the region occurred.

Part II turns to the ostensibly internal dynamics of North African states – "ostensible" because the analyses are fully cognizant of external influences on a country's domestic politics. The chapters seek to update the 2008 volume; they delve directly into issues such as state-society relations, economic conditions, gender issues, emerging actors and parties, and, of course, foreign policy. It is at the country level that analyses truly demonstrate the dynamism of the region. Even in countries such as Algeria and Morocco – as Ahmed Aghrout and Yahia H. Zoubir, and Azzedine Layachi examine, respectively – the state apparatus' effort to maintain the status quo is fraught with constant change. Other countries such as Egypt, Libya, Mauritania, and Tunisia have, quite obviously, experienced sharp change. Arguably the most successful in engineering a stable, positive change, as Emma Murphy instructs, has been Tunisia. Ibrahim Awad, Alison Pargeter, and Abdoulaye Diagana unpack the challenging cases of Egypt, Libya, and Mauritania, respectively.

Finally, Part III elevates North Africa qua region into a broader global and systemic level of analysis. Miguel Hernando de Larramendi and Irene Fernández Molina offer a synthesis of the countries' foreign policies, serving as a useful segue into the final section. Yahia H. Zoubir and Stephen Zunes examine the preponderant role of the US in North Africa, and the complicated ways in which North African countries engage the US. In turn, George Joffe offers a trenchant critique of the European Union's engagement with North Africa since the 1995 Barcelona accords. As noted earlier, Imen Belhadj and Degang Sun treatment of China's strategic interaction with North Africa is a unique focus for such a volume. Not to be underestimated in terms of its value-added is Elena Maestri's plumbing of the crucial and also under-examined role of the Gulf Cooperation Council (GCC) in North Africa. Finally, Hakim Darbouche and John Hamilton proffer an outlook for the crucial role of the North African hydrocarbon sector; it is a sector that has buoyed respective economies, even as it undermines sustainable long-term development and reinforces asymmetrical interdependencies with the global economy.

Notes

1. Yahia H. Zoubir and Haizam Amirah-Fernández, eds., *North Africa: Politics, Region, and the Limits of Transformation* (New York: Routledge, 2008).
2. Regional analyses include Bruce Maddy Weitzman and Daniel Zisenwine, eds., *The Maghreb in the New Century: Identity, Religion and Politics* (Gainsville: University of Florida Press, 2007); Phillip Naylor, *North Africa: A History from Antiquity to the Present* (Austin: University of Texas Press, 2010); and Michael Willis, *Politics and Power in the Maghreb: Algeria, Tunisia, and Morocco from Independence to the Arab Spring* (New York: Oxford University Press, 2014).
3. Peter Katzenstein, *A World of Regions: Asia and Europe in the American Imperium* (Ithaca, NY: Cornell University Press, 2005).

PART I
Drivers of change in contemporary North Africa

1

A POLITICAL ECONOMY PERSPECTIVE ON NORTH AFRICAN TRANSITIONS

Gonzalo Escribano

Summary

Following the Arab Spring, Egypt and Tunisia face very difficult economic situations that risk affecting the economic viability of their political transitions. Morocco and Algeria, meanwhile, have both experienced rioting and there is growing uncertainty as to how their economic policies might evolve in the future. This is especially so in Morocco, where tough economic decisions are almost as urgent as in Tunisia and Egypt. Libya faces the distinct challenge of managing its resource wealth from a ground-zero institutional setting. Mauritania is following a different political economy path and will therefore not be analyzed here. From the point of view of political economy, a crucial point is whether the wave of popular revolts that overthrew the incumbent regimes will consolidate into economically viable liberal democracies, and in what economic direction Algeria and Morocco will move since to date they have been spared the enormous fiscal cost of regime change. In other words, the question is whether democratization can be maintained (or continue to be pursued) under current political economy conditions, with the full array of economic structures, institutions, interests and preferences of the various players in society at play.

Introduction

The classic modernization argument regarding political economy preconditions for democratization includes attaining an economic development threshold, education, the emergence of a middle class, the decentralization of economic power, a Weberian bureaucracy and Schumpeterian entrepreneurs, among others (Lipset, 1959, 1994; Rostow, 1960). To these conditions, economic demography added the modernization impact of demographic transition (Bloom *et al.*, 2003) and economic institutionalism as a set of basic economic institutions (North, 1990). While such a theory of modernization has been largely discredited in the Arab World, perhaps in hindsight it might prove not to have been so wrong after all. This formula depicts quite well what actually happened in Tunisia – the 'Tunisian Paradox' (Martínez, 2011); the more modern socio-economic system was the first to revolt. This does not imply that all of the aforementioned preconditions need be in place or that modernization must develop in a predetermined chronological order to reach the final stages and qualify for democratization (Carothers, 2007). Political transitions are seldom ordered, gradual, and sequenced, nor are they suited to a one-fits-all model. For instance, the propensity to revolt tends to increase when the opportunity cost of revolting is low, which makes countries with high inequality or low economic opportunities more prone to revolution (Acemoglu & Robinson, 2001).

In any case, it might be useful to remember the usual set of political economy preconditions for democratization in order to gain some insight into its long-term viability in North Africa. Admittedly more sophisticated versions of these theories have been used in the wake of the Arab Spring to try to explain (however ex post facto) the economic causes of the revolts that overthrew the Egyptian, Libyan and Tunisian dictatorships and seriously challenged the Algerian and Moroccan regimes. Recent analyses point to education coupled with low employment opportunities (Campante & Chor, 2012), the birth of the individual due to demographic transition (Fargues, 2012), inherited institutional deficits (Chaney, 2012), the expansion of entrepreneurship and the private sector (Escribano & Lorca, 2012), and the overall lack of sustainability of the state (Colombo & Tocci, 2011).

The present chapter argues that changing political economy balances have been a significant driver for transformation, and that they remain a key factor in the future economic viability of democratization. The following chapter starts by presenting the evolution of the North African countries' economic situations and policies, and a brief assessment of the economic impact of the Arab Spring. It then analyzes the different players, old and new, in a rapidly changing economic and political arena, highlighting the impact of modernization and diversification in the emergence of a middle class which is not necessarily modeled on Western bourgeoisie. The chapter concludes with a warning against the temptation of addressing legitimate social justice demands through short-term populist economic policies instead of building a consensus for more inclusive patterns of growth.

The economy

As shown in Table 1.1, the North African countries have attained a medium level of economic development, ranking in the high to medium segment of the 2011 Human Development Index (HDI): Libya at 64th; Tunisia, 94th; Algeria, 96th; Egypt, 113th; and Morocco, 130th. All components of the HDI have improved in the region, which is now above the average Medium Human Development and Arab State figures, with the sole exception of Morocco. Life expectancy has greatly increased over the last decades, and the region benefits from higher than average

TABLE 1.1 Human development indicators

	HDI 2011	HDI Rank 2011	Life expectancy at birth, 2011	Expected years of schooling 2011	Gross national income (GNI) per capita, 2011 (PPP 2005 US$)	HDI Rank change 2006–11	GDP per capita average annual growth rate (%) 1970–2008 US$1	Poverty rate[2,3] Under US$1.25	Poverty rate[2,3] Under US$2.75	Quintile Income ratio (top 20% over bottom 20%)[3,4]	Income Gini Coefficient[3,5]	Average % shortfall in minimum dietary energy requirements[1] 1990–92	Average % shortfall in minimum dietary energy requirements[1] 2004–06
Algeria	0.698	96	73.4	13.6	7,658	2	1.1	–	–	6.1	35.3	10	10
Egypt	0.644	113	73.2	11.0	5,269	2	2.5	3.4	43.7	4.6	32.1	10	13
Libya	0.760	64	74.8	16.6	15,521	-5	-1.3	–	–	–	–	7	4
Morocco	0.582	130	72.2	10.3	4,196	0	2.4	2.5	29.6	7.4	40.9	11	13
Tunisia	0.698	94	74.5	14.5	7,281	3	3.1	2.5	25.2	8.0	40.8	7	10
Arab States	0.641	–	70.5	10.2	8,554	–	-1.1	–	–	–	–	–	–
Medium HD	0.630	–	69.7	11.2	5,276	–	2.7	–	–	–	–	–	–

(1) HDR 2010.

(2) UNDP, Arab Development Challenges Report 2011.

(3) Most recent year available.

(4) An income quintile divides the population into five income quintiles (from lowest income to highest income) such that 20% of the population is in each group. A 6.1 quintile income ratio implies that the richest 20% have 6.1 times more income than the poorest 20%: the higher the ratio, the more unequal the income distribution.

(5) The Gini coefficient measures the extent to which the distribution of income among individuals within an economy deviates from a perfectly equal distribution: A Gini coefficient of 0 represents perfect equality, while an index of 100 implies perfect inequality.

Source: UNDP, Human Development Report 2011.

figures for both Medium Human Development countries and Arab States. Schooling has also improved, but there are significant differences across the region, with Algeria, Libya and Tunisia well above the average expected years of schooling of Arab States and Medium Human Development countries. Morocco and Egypt, on the contrary, are at the average of both country groups.

The dispersion of HDI levels is due to significant differences between countries in education, health and income per capita, with Libya benefiting from its hydrocarbon revenues and a relatively small population. Table 1.1 shows how income per capita ranges from over US$15,000 (2005 PPP) in Libya to almost US$4,200 in Morocco and US$5,300 in Egypt. Algeria and Tunisia are in between, at over US$7,000. GDP per capita growth has been much higher in resource-poor than in resource-rich countries, with Libya even reducing it in the last 30 years in line with the aggregate figures for Arab States; Algeria also shows a disappointing per capita growth figure. On the other hand, Egypt, Morocco and especially Tunisia registered significant GDP per capita growth figures, similar to those of Medium Human Development country averages.

After the 2011 revolts, several analyses identified poverty, inequality and even food scarcity as drivers of popular discontent. While human development rapidly increased during the last two decades, the pace of improvement slowed down in the second half of the past decade, when only Algeria, Egypt and Tunisia modestly scaled up the HDI rank. Notwithstanding the region's harsh economic and social realities, a more careful analysis shows the need to qualify such arguments. Income inequality is not extreme: Algeria has a Gini coefficient similar to Spain, Morocco and Tunisia are similar to the US, and Egypt is close to Canada. These are lower figures than for emerging countries like Brazil (53.9), Russia (42.3) and China (41.5). The quintile income ratio is 8 in Tunisia and 7.4 in Morocco, figures comparable to those for the US and the UK. It is 6.1 for Algeria (a similar ratio to Spain and lower than Italy), and 4.6 in Egypt (comparable to Germany's 4.3). Nuancing the extent of inequality is important because highly unequal societies are less likely to see their democracies consolidated (Acemoglu & Robinson, 2001).

The region also has lower than expected poverty levels considering its income level. The poverty rate for a population under the US$1.25 poverty line is 3.4% in Egypt and 2.5% in Morocco and Tunisia. These rates compare well with poverty rates in other emerging countries like Brazil (3.8%), Mexico (3.4%), China (16.2%) and India (41.6%). When the poverty line is raised to US$2.75, poverty rates increase steadily to 43.7% in Egypt, 29.6% in Morocco and 25.2% in Tunisia. These figures do not compare so well with those for Brazil (16.4%) and Mexico (14.4%), but are far below China (53.8%) and India (88.6%). They are also below average poverty rates for the developing world (23.6% under the US$1.25 line and 60.5% under the US$2.75 threshold), and somewhat lower than for Arab countries as a whole, where they reach 3.9% and 40.0%, respectively. In both cases the region has experienced a significant decrease in poverty rates, with the sole exception of Morocco for under US$1.25 rate, which stagnated between 1991 and 2007.

Poverty is mainly a rural phenomenon, but there are also some peri-urban poverty neighborhoods that tend to be more visible.

While 'bread revolts' due to food subsidy reductions have been common in the past and have been one of the components of recent demonstrations, it does not seem from nutritional data that access to food is a significant problem for these countries, with average shortfalls similar to those in Poland and Romania. However, the trend differs between countries, with Egypt, Morocco and Tunisia experiencing a clear deterioration in their nutritional figures. Algeria has stagnating figures and only Libya registered a decrease in malnutrition data. This picture may not do justice to the significant number of people that are still suffering from deprivation in North Africa, but it points to the fact that the socio-economic situation alone probably cannot account for the revolts of 2011. In fact, they have been more violent in Libya, the richest country, and most successful in Tunisia, which comes second in the North African HDI rank.

It has been argued that North African figures on poverty and inequality are underestimated, and that they do not reflect the socio-economic penuries afflicting the region (UNDP, 2011). While there is evidence that such a problem with North African statistical figures may exist, accounting for this discrepancy does not significantly change the picture as recognized by its proponents; compared to most other developing regions North Africa suffers from low levels of poverty. However, it is equally true that in the recent past, progress in reducing poverty has been amongst the slowest rates of any region and cannot be expected to increase significantly in the coming future (UNDP, 2011, p 24). A more sophisticated argument regarding the economic causes of the Arab revolts is precisely that modernization and social transformation outpaced the North African regimes' capacity to deliver on socio-economic demands. In other words, the economic legitimacy of autocracy was increasingly challenged by broader and more demanding middle classes: the cost of autocracy simply no longer compensated for the meager economic benefits delivered by North African governments.

Regarding macroeconomic figures, stability and macro-prudency (with the eternal Libyan exception) over the last two decades have stabilized North African economies and provided the basis for sustained growth in the last decade as well as increased resilience to external shocks. As shown in Table 1.2, during the 2000s economic growth has stabilized after decades of volatility and even in the midst of the crisis remained at relatively high levels. While growth in Algeria and especially Libya remained heavily dependent upon hydrocarbon prices, Morocco and Tunisia have seemingly achieved a more sustainable growth path. Inflation also remained under control, but at the cost of lowering prices through food and energy subsidies. To a great extent, Algeria – and to a lesser extent Libya – succeeded in stabilizing huge hydrocarbon revenues, and the macroeconomic mismanagement that led to past Dutch Disease episodes did not materialize.[1] Morocco and Tunisia have lower inflation records, but their vulnerability to energy and food international prices in 2008 are detailed in Table 1.2.

TABLE 1.2 Selected macroeconomic indicators

	Average 2000–05	*2007*	*2008*	*2009*	*2010*	*2011*	*2012*[1]
	Real GDP growth (%)						
Algeria	4.5	3.0	2.4	2.4	3.3	3.9	2.6
Egypt	4.4	7.1	7.2	4.7	5.1	1.8	2.0
Libya	4.3	6.4	2.4	−1.4	3.7	−59.7	121.9
Morocco	4.4	2.7	5.6	4.9	3.7	4.9	2.9
Tunisia	4.4	6.3	4.5	3.1	3.1	−1.8	2.7
	Consumer price inflation (%)						
Algeria	2.3	3.6	4.9	5.7	3.9	4.5	8.4
Egypt	5.1	9.5	18.3	11.7	11.4	9.9	9.7
Libya	−3.3	6.2	10.4	2.4	2.5	5.6	6.0
Morocco	1.5	2.0	3.9	1.0	1.0	0.9	2.2
Tunisia	2.7	3.4	4.9	3.5	4.4	3.5	5.0
	Government fiscal balance (% GDP)						
Algeria	6.6	4.4	7.6	−6.4	−2.3	−0.2	−3.9
Egypt	−6.8	−7.5	−8.0	−6.8	−7.8	−9.9	−11.1
Libya	12.6	24.0	25.1	−3.0	16.7	−27.7	19.4
Morocco	−5.2	−0.1	0.7	−1.8	−4.4	−6.9	−6.1
Tunisia	−2.6	−2.8	−0.7	−2.6	−0.9	−3.1	−6.4
	Current account balance (% GDP)						
Algeria	14.0	22.8	20.1	0.3	7.5	10.0	6.2
Egypt	1.6	1.7	0.5	−2.3	−2.0	−2.6	−3.4
Libya	18.9	43.8	42.3	14.7	19.8	1.3	21.8
Morocco	2.2	−0.1	−5.2	−5.4	−4.3	−8.0	−7.9
Tunisia	−3.0	−2.4	−3.8	−2.8	−4.8	−7.3	−7.9

(1) Projections.

Source: IMF, *Regional Economic Outlook, Middle East and Central Asia*, October 2010 and 2012.

Fiscal balances also improved during the 2000s compared with the huge deficits and external debts of the past. However, the fiscal balances of Morocco and Tunisia remained fragile and fiscal policy space was limited and proved to be vulnerable to external shocks. Algeria has more fiscal space due to the cancellation of most of its external debt and to its high level of reserves, but remains vulnerable to oil prices (to which gas prices are indexed), meaning that a share of fiscal revenues is illusory, while growing current expenses are not. The external balance started to deteriorate in the second half of the 2000s partly due to external shocks such as increases in oil and food prices. Significant current account surpluses in Egypt and Morocco turned into deficits in the second half of the 2000s and became increasingly subject to stress in both countries. Resource-rich countries experienced a reduction in their current account surplus. In Algeria the high surpluses of the recent past have been greatly reduced due to lower oil prices and reduced gas exports. The World Bank (2010) estimates that the change in the import bill due to a 50% increase in wheat prices accounts for as much as 0.4% of GDP for Morocco, Tunisia and Algeria. Libya has traditionally maintained a comfortable fiscal and external financial position built on hydrocarbon revenues and foreign exchange reserves.

But this generally positive outlook changed dramatically with the Arab Spring, which exacerbated the already slowing economic growth due to the international financial crisis and the Euro crisis. As shown in Table 1.2, in 2011 growth rates diminished most dramatically in the countries experiencing regime change. Egypt recorded a meager growth rate of 1.8% in 2011 compared with 5.1% in 2010, and IMF projections were not much more optimistic for 2012. In 2011 Tunisia registered its first year of recession in the last two decades, with GDP decreasing 1.8% and gloomy prospects for 2012. Strikes and other disruptions in economic activity seriously affected growth and exports, and the collapse of foreign sources of income, like tourism and investment, deepened the economic cost of the revolts. The Libyan disruption of oil production and exports caused the country's growth rate to decrease by almost 60% in 2011, but its fast recovery is expected to boost GDP growth in 2012.

Morocco was also affected through deteriorating external inflows, mainly tourism and foreign investment, and rising uncertainty on the domestic political repercussions of the events in Tunisia and Egypt. But the country weathered the tension in 2011 quite well, achieving 4.9% GDP growth in 2011 due to fiscal countercyclical measures and a rainy agricultural season. Political uncertainty was reduced with a new government led by the *Parti de la Justice et le Développement* (PJD), committed to economic orthodoxy termed as 'pragmatism'. But sluggish demand in Europe and a more prudent fiscal stance was expected to reduce GDP growth for 2012 to below 3%. In Algeria growth continued to be dependent on hydrocarbon prices and production.

The impact of the crisis has also been reflected by worsening macroeconomic balances. Fiscal income fell while expenses were increased by attempts to prevent both social unrest and the deepening of the economic downturn. Rising subsidies, public wages and public jobs translated into growing fiscal deficits in Egypt, Morocco and Tunisia for 2011 and 2012. Algeria also adopted a more proactive fiscal policy that deteriorated its fiscal balance in 2012, but allowed it to maintain a far greater fiscal policy space than its neighbors, with the exception of Libya, whose huge fiscal deficit in 2011 was rapidly reverted to an almost 20% surplus in 2012. In spite of weak demand conditions and price repression, inflation remained at relatively high levels in Egypt and, to a lesser extent, in Tunisia.

In Morocco inflation has been kept under control, but the easing of price repression (reduction of fuel subsidies) and fiscal deficit pressures is projected to double inflation in 2012. In Algeria, fiscal expansion and a less restrictive stance towards the sterilization of hydrocarbon income are expected to double inflation in 2012. The Egyptian, Moroccan and Tunisian external balances have also experienced a marked deterioration during 2011 and 2012. The most pressing situation is the Tunisian and

Egyptian lack of foreign reserves, accounting at the end of 2012 for barely three months of imports; Morocco is also under pressure, with reserves for around six months of imports. Algeria enjoys a comfortable current account surplus, as does Libya after recovering from the 2011 oil export disruption.

North African economic policies have been criticized on the grounds that structural reforms, including institutional ones, have lagged behind macroeconomic stabilization (Escribano & Lorca, 2008). Some microeconomic and institutional reforms have been carried out during the past decades, but implementation has been slow, fragmented and sometimes inconsistent. Trade liberalization, reduction of domestic entry barriers, privatization and the upgrading of the business environment, among other measures, resulted in the diversification of economic activities, an increase in private-sector dynamism and a more open economic system. In the wake of the 2011 revolts, several reforms that awaited their turn for years, such as subsidy and fiscal reform, seemed to be on track. But one of the main (intangible) results of the Arab Spring is the discrediting of the overthrown regimes' economic policies, including much needed microeconomic and institutional reforms. In this context, the economic evolution of North African countries remains uncertain. Before addressing its reconfiguration after the Arab Spring, the following section analyzes the new political economy balances emerging across the region in order to try to capture their influence in the process of economic policy formulation.

A shifting political economy balance

The emergence of North African political economy balances is well documented in the region's political economy literature, which describes how economic transformations have shifted economic influence from colonial to national entities, from rural landlords to urban elites, and from import substitution to export-oriented sectors. Colonial structures shaped regional and economic balances and, after independence, state-led growth and import substituting strategies generated an extractive class of public company managers and rent-seeking entrepreneurs (Richards & Waterbury, 2007). The model collapsed for the first time in the external debt crisis of the 1980s. The stabilization and liberalization policies that followed remained subject to the economic elite's preferences, which, thanks to its political connections, captured a large share of the rents derived from the reforms, including privatizations, public works and services contracts, trade liberalization, etc. (Heydemann, 2004). This changed the rent-seeking model but basically let corporatist capitalism, together with privilege and cronyism, become the main entry barrier into the political economy space. The North African political economy has traditionally been based on the incumbents' political networks of influence, exploiting economic reforms and renewing rent-extractive strategies (Greenwood, 2008).

In Egypt and Tunisia, Mubarak and Ben Ali knitted well-known business architectures to extract rents from their countries (Anderson, 2011). A cable revealed by WikiLeaks showed that in 2006 the US ambassador to Tunisia reported that more than half of Tunisia's commercial elites were personally related to Ben Ali through an extractive network known as 'The Family'. In Egypt, the network was based on the business connections of Mubarak's son Gamal, which was somehow competing with military economic interests. In Morocco, the *makhzen* constitutes a network of influence around the Palace's economic preferences and interests, including a network of businessmen that transit from the public to the private sector (Catusse, 2006). In Libya, the Gaddafi family directly appropriated oil income, and there were no economic reforms comparable to those implemented in other countries in the region. Libyan reforms remained limited to the opening of the hydrocarbons sector to foreign investment, leaving political economy balances unchanged (St John, 2008). As a result, the private business fabric remained weak, and the economy is still completely dominated by the control of oil resources. In Algeria, rent-seeking strategies are also centered on the capture of hydrocarbon wealth by *le Pouvoir*, an opaque body of generals, politicians and politically connected businessmen (Martínez, 2010).

For sure, there are significant cross-country differences in the political economy weight of other traditional actors, such as the military and trade unions (Catusse, 2006). The economic influence of the military is mostly restricted to Egypt, where they control around one-third of Egypt's GDP and conduct important economic activities in strategic sectors such as the iron and steel industry, construction, tourism and agro-food, among others. As a result, they oppose economic liberalization and private sector growth because these threaten its economic power, a position that was highly influential in the Egyptian provisional government (Anderson, 2011). The Algerian military exert control over hydrocarbon resources, opposing any effort to further open the sector to foreign investment, fearing it will weaken its political pre-eminence (Martínez, 2010). Trade unions are a powerful actor in Tunisia, as shown before, during and after the removal of Ben Ali, although their influence is much lower elsewhere in the region.

Even if slow and sometimes reluctant, these economic reforms have slightly shifted the political economy equilibrium in favor of new actors, like small and medium enterprises (SMEs), foreign companies and professionals. Social change has also empowered other actors, like the youth, Islamist political parties and women. Both economic and social transformation offer opportunities to forge new alliances between new actors, or between new and traditional ones. For instance, diversification and export orientation have created a new class of entrepreneurs integrated in transnational industrial networks, which coexist with a more traditional class of small and very small merchants and traditional services providers. While both groups differ in their approach, they share similar concerns regarding economic policy preferences. The economic elites may decide to accompany the emerging middle class and start to get rid of regime compliance costs when they start to exceed expected returns from rent-seeking.

A growing segment of the middle class are liberal professionals that when underemployed add to the 'middle class' poor. Another emerging economic actor is the informal sector, which accounts for a significant part of GDP and employment and is made out of a heterogeneous mix of micro-entrepreneurs in different sectors.

Its role is ambiguous, acting as a driver of diversification and de-concentration of economic power, but at the same time reproducing traditional social mechanisms (Hibou, 2010). In this regard, the main influence that new entrepreneurs can have in promoting political change is the widening of a middle class with preferences different from those of the economic elites.

Big industrial firms dominate industry and older firms are disproportionally represented, showing they are able to survive any reform. The age of local manu-facturing firms in MENA averages 19 years, the same as mature OECD countries, and twice the figure in East Asia and Eastern Europe (World Bank Enterprise Surveys, 2005–2014). This makes the renewal of the industrial structure slower than elsewhere. The subsequent absence of renewal in the business elite, together with low mobility within companies, echoes what has been written regarding political elites by political scientists. However, firm creation has greatly increased in coun-tries such as Morocco and Tunisia, while Algerian and especially Egyptian figures display very low firm renewal, reflecting differences in the degree of economic opening and business environment improvement. It also shows that when entry barriers are lowered, new economic actors enter the market, altering political econ-omy balances (Escribano & Lorca, 2012). However, its impact has been limited by path-dependent institutional constraints (Kuran, 2010).

Foreign investors have shown mixed behavior: when confronted with local economic and political elites they have had to choose between accommodation and defiance. In the first and most common case, they clearly became a part of the status quo. The clearest example has been the entrenched network of interest forged by EU companies with Tunisian companies closely related to the Ben Ali clan (Hibou, 2010), but similar cases can be found in most countries in the region. When foreign companies' interests conflict with the ruling elites, they adopt exit strategies to optimize their investment returns. Foreign companies have certainly helped to modernize the economic system, but have not significantly altered politi-cal economy balances. Multinationals in the Middle East tend to show a clear lack of commitment to the promotion of democracy (Youngs, 2011).

Youth is another new driver of change, especially in the economic realm. North Africa has a wide economic generation gap. As with politicians and high officials, businessmen tend to be older than in other developing regions (14 years of aver-age experience compared with eight in Latin America and South Asia). This is especially frustrating in countries where youth account for a large proportion of the population. In addition, the level of education of the region's businessmen is also lower (World Bank Enterprise Surveys, 2005–2014), explaining the wide-spread feeling of exclusion among better prepared young graduates who cannot gain access to influential positions in either the public or private sectors.

The role of women in the public domain has also been slightly altered, but their voice in economic issues remains marginal, as is that of young people. While men have somehow been able to capture part of the benefits of gender equal-ity measures, this kind of gender-based rent-seeking is increasingly challenged by businesswomen. They face additional entry barriers, but once these barriers are either relaxed or painfully surmounted these women play a more significant transformative role in both the economic and political arenas than is the case for businessmen (Paciello & Pepicelli, 2012). Both youth and women asking for economic autonomy and a political voice are powerful agents of change, but their influence risks being limited in a political context marked by the rise of religious conservatism, where the economic voice of young people tends to be subordinated to that of their elders and that of women to men's.

This leads to the last of the new economic actors considered in this section, Islamist political parties and their domestic economic support base. Regarding its theoretical base, Islamic economics is so vague that almost any school of economic thought can find the way to defend its position. It is a normative corpus based upon a strong sense of social justice, which includes merit and protection of property rights. As in any other society, redistribution can be attained in different ways that are most usually explained by political economy balances rather than religious beliefs. In short, there is a political economy of Islamism which entails its own internal actors and balances.

The transformative role of Islamic Economics and its business dimension is ambivalent. The promotion of honesty, transparency and business success as self-accomplishment constitutes a vigorous driver for change. But other preferences can lead to unrealistic social demands which pursue social justice by means of unsustainable populist policies. This can cause fiscal volatility and difficulties in consolidating democracy (Acemoglu & Robinson, 2001). Some authors have argued that Islamist policies can consist of a combination of economic liberalism with social conservatism (Roy, 2012). Such a mix offers uncertain results if social conservatism harms tourism, foreign investment or trade. It has been argued, from an economic institutionalist perspective, that popular support for Islamist groups can undermine democratic efforts by concentrating political power in their hands in the absence of checks on their power from other interest groups, such as labor unions and business interests (Chaney, 2012).

This appraisal disregards the fact that Islamists themselves have commercial interests, and ignores the entrepreneurial dimension of Islam. Islamic entrepreneurs have their own Schumpeterian attributes within a set of values influenced by Islam rather than Protestantism (Adas, 2006). They have grown considerably over the last decades, especially in Turkey, but also in some North African countries. They may turn out to be the most effective barrier to populist economic policies and the best positioned to balance the trade-offs between religious values and a functioning market economy. They are also the main source of local financing for Islamist movements, potentially reinforcing their influence in economic policy-making. With all these elements in mind, the final section of this chapter tries to explore the prospects for economic policy-making in the region in the coming years.

Economic policy prospects

The previous section described the significance of the economic impact of the revolts; the main question now is how long its negative economic effects will last. Uncertainty has deeply affected economic activity: Tunisia and Egypt have lost more than half of their tourism revenues; foreign investment, which was already low due to the international crisis, has simply halted; government packages to increase wages and subsidies have already been implemented at a high fiscal cost. Other impacts have been more short-lived, like logistical chain disruptions in Tunisian and Egyptian industrial international networks, oil and gas supply disruptions in Libya, capital flight or the decrease of remittances to Tunisia and Egypt. But on the whole, short-term economic prospects for the region look rather gloomy. Coping with increasing social pressures to raise social expenses and mounting political uncertainty in a context of macroeconomic fragility and international crisis is not going to be easy. This is especially so for non-oil exporters, but in the long term also for Algeria. In Libya, the economic evolution will depend on the governance of oil and gas production and exports. Both countries face the distinct challenge of escaping both Dutch Disease and Resource Curse in a more demanding political context.

After the Arab Spring, all North African (and most Arab) countries increased public wages and employment, food and energy subsidies, and public works. These measures have been presented as a commitment to advance social justice and to signal that policies have changed toward a more inclusive pattern of redistribution and growth. Plausible political economy scenarios are not, however, uniform across the region, because countries' trajectories widely differ. Libyan and Algerian political economy balances are determined by a huge and highly centralized hydrocarbon rent, and consequently by a lower degree of diversification and influence of private actors. In principle, oil and gas rents raise their regimes' propensity to fierce political economy bargaining and are therefore more conflict-prone. Algeria is far more diversified than Libya and is much more advanced in economic reforms. But even rentier economies able to provide stability through broader redistribution measures have developed an unsustainable political economy balance which will create pressure for the inclusion of new societal actors (Ross et al., 2011). Tunisia and Morocco have attained a higher level of diversification and middle-class autonomy from the state, with rents being transferred in a manner that is more diffused and difficult to capture. They also count on relatively better management skills, both public and private. Tunisia and Libya are relatively small countries, while Morocco and Algeria host significant populations and have a greater geopolitical and geo-economic role to play. But, to a different extent, all of them are still facing the challenge of state sustainability (Colombo, 2011; Paciello, 2011).

From a political economy perspective, the main contribution of past economic reforms to political change has been facilitating social mobility and diversifying economic power by expanding the middle class and slowly enhancing the power of economic and business elites. This has helped to alter the political economy balances within societies by favoring the decentralization of economic power away from big entrepreneurs and public companies that tend to support the regimes in place. This has gradually eroded the elites' capacity to exert social control through patronage and nepotism, lowering the opportunity cost of revolting. However, the region's institutional framework is clearly deficient, with high levels of corruption and low efficiency in public and private management. Entry and exit in private and social activities is difficult and costly, limiting social mobility and lowering the pace of elite renewal. Institutional and microeconomic reforms remain a key factor in opening the economic policy space while reducing its volatility.

Finally, perhaps the most pressing obstacle relates to short-term economic challenges, which may prove to be very costly politically. This includes rationalizing food and energy subsidies by implementing social targeting, continuing external liberalization, maintaining a prudent macroeconomic stance and resisting fiscally unsustainable – however socially praiseworthy – political demands. Some Islamist-led governments, like Morocco's, have seen progress in this domain, containing the fiscal deficit and rationalizing fossil fuel and electricity subsidies. This proves that, within Islamist parties, pragmatism can overrule populism, greatly contributing to the viability of democratic transitions. Islamists are aware that they have to deliver in the economic domain, but also that their results cannot be short-lived. They also know that part of their constituency, such as the pious middle class, watch their economic interests closely and will not tolerate a populist stance.

However, the populist scenario remains a risk, especially if the legitimacy gained by elected governments begins to be eroded by conflict between internal actors. Economies in political transition tend to be difficult to manage, all the more so during an international economic crisis. The region is exploring its economic options and realizing that its policy space is much reduced. Islamic normative economics do not provide answers to the pressing problems of transition, and it is urgent for North African governments to present a credible and sustainable economic model to their constituencies. For sure, the mixed picture presented in this chapter does not represent the modernist ideal of a harmonious and diversified society, with innovative entrepreneurs being managed by Weberian-ethics bureaucrats, strong institutions that protect property rights and provide checks and balances against social dominance, and a large educated middle class that has attained a homogeneous and secular life-style. Not all of these elements are perfectly aligned and in place to offer this ideal model of democratic transition, and the combination of these factors certainly varies across countries. But it would be wise to let North African societies make their evolving political economy balances work in order to develop an economic model they can recognize as optimal for their needs.

Note

1. Dutch disease is the damaging effect on an economy as a result of the exploitation and export of natural resources (also used nowadays to refer to the effects of other inflows such as a rise of remittances or foreign aid), which causes currency appreciation, de-industrialization, and the expansion of the public sector. When the political effects are also considered (centralized income, clientelism, patronage, etc.) the literature usually refers to the resource curse.

References

Acemoglu, D., & J.A. Robinson (2001), 'A Theory of Political Transitions', *American Economic Review*, vol. 91, nr. 4, pp. 938–963.

Adas, E.B. (2006), 'The Making of Entrepreneurial Islam and the Islamic Spirit of Capitalism', *Journal for Cultural Research*, vol. 10, nr. 2, pp. 113–137.

Anderson, L. (2011), 'Demystifying the Arab Spring. Parsing the Differences Between Tunisia, Egypt, and Libya', *Foreign Affairs*, vol. 90, nr. 3, pp. 2–7.

Bloom, D.E., D. Canning & J. Sevilla (2003), *The Demographic Dividend: A New Perspective on the Economic Consequences of Population Change*, Santa Monica, CA: RAND, www.rand.org/pubs/monograph_reports/MR1274.html.

Campante, F.R., & D. Chor (2012), 'Why Was the Arab World Poised for Revolution? Schooling, Economic Opportunities, and the Arab Spring', *Journal of Economic Perspectives*, nr. 26, pp. 167–188.

Carothers, T. (2007), 'How Democracies Emerge – The Sequencing Fallacy', *Journal of Democracy*, vol. 18, nr 1, pp. 12–27.

Catusse, M. (2006), 'Ordonner, classer, penser la société: Les pays arabes au prisme de l'économie politique', in E. Picard (Ed.), *La Politique dans le Monde Arabe*, Paris: A. Colin, pp. 215–238.

Chaney, E. (2012), 'Democratic Change in the Arab World, Past and Present', *Brookings Papers on Economic Activity*, vol. 42, nr. 1, pp. 363–414.

Colombo, S. (2011), 'Morocco at the Crossroads: Seizing the Window of Opportunity', in S. Colombo & N. Tocci (Eds.), *The Challenges of State Sustainability in the Mediterranean*, Rome: Nuova Cultura-Istituto Affari Internacionali, pp. 161–192.

Colombo, S., & N. Tocci (2011), *The Challenges of State Sustainability in the Mediterranean*, Rome: Nuova Cultura-Istituto Affari Internacionali.

Escribano, G., & A. Lorca (2008), 'Economic Reform in the Maghreb: From Stabilization to Modernization', in Y. Zoubir & H. Amirah-Fernández (Eds.), *North Africa: Politics, Region, and the Limits of Transformation*, London: Routledge, pp. 135–158.

Escribano, G., & A. Lorca (2012), 'Modern Commercial and Social Entrepreneurship as a Factor of Change', in C. Merlini & O. Roy (Eds.), *Arab Society in Revolt: The West's Mediterranean Challenge*, Washington, DC: Brookings Institution Press, pp. 96–122.

Fargues, P. (2012), 'Demography, Migration, and Revolt in the Southern Mediterranean', in C. Merlini & O. Roy (Eds.), *Arab Society in Revolt: The West's Mediterranean Challenge*, Washington, DC: Brookings Institution Press, pp. 17–46.

Greenwood, S. (2008), 'Bad for Business? Entrepreneurs and Democracy in the Arab World', *Comparative Political Studies*, vol. 41, nr. 6, pp. 837–860.

Heydemann, S. (Ed.) (2004), *Networks of Privilege in the Middle East: The Politics of Economic Reform Revisited*, London: Palgrave.

Hibou, B. (2010), 'Discipline and Reform – I', *Sociétés politiques comparées*, vol. 22, February, www.fasopo.org.

IMF (2010), *Regional Economic Outlook, Middle East and Central Asia*, October. Washington, DC: US Government Printing Office.

IMF (2012), *Regional Economic Outlook, Middle East and Central Asia*, October. Washington, DC: US Government Printing Office.

Kuran, T. (2010), 'The Scale of Entrepreneurship in Middle Eastern History: Inhibitive Roles of Islamic Institutions', in W. Baumol, D. Landes & J. Mokyr (Eds.), *The Invention of Enterprise: Entrepreneurship from Ancient Mesopotamia to Modern Times*, Princeton & Oxford: Princeton University Press, pp. 62–87.

Lipset, S. M. (1959), 'Some Social Requisites of Democracy', *American Political Science Review*, vol. 53, nr. 1, pp. 69–105.

Lipset, S.M. (1994), 'The Social Requisites of Democracy Revisited', *American Sociological Review*, vol. 59, nr. 1, pp. 1–22.

Martínez, L. (2010), *Violence de la rente pétrolière: Algérie, Irak, Libye*, Paris: Presses de Sciences Po.

Martínez, L. (2011), 'La Leçon Tunisienne', *ISS Opinion*, January, www.iss.europa.eu/uploads/media/La_lecon_tunisienne.pdf.

North, D.C. (1990), *Institutions, Institutional Change and Economic Performance*, Cambridge, MA: Cambridge University Press.

Paciello, M.C. (2011), 'Egypt: Changes and Challenges of Political Transition', in S. Colombo & N. Tocci (Eds.), *The Challenges of State Sustainability in the Mediterranean*, Rome: Nuova Cultura-Istituto Affari Internacionali, pp. 101–160.

Paciello, M.C., & R. Pepicelli (2012), 'The Changing Role of Women in Society', in C. Merlini & O. Roy (Eds.), *Arab Society in Revolt: The West's Mediterranean Challenge*, Washington, DC: Brookings Institution Press, pp. 53–75.

Richards, A., & J. Waterbury (2007), *A Political Economy of the Middle East*, 3rd edition, Boulder, CO: Westview Press.

Ross, M., K. Kaiser & N. Mazaheri (2011), 'The "Resource Curse", in MENA? Political Transitions, Resource Wealth, Economic Shocks, and Conflict Risk', World Bank Policy Research Working Paper 5742, July.

Rostow, W.W. (1960), *The Stages of Economic Growth: A Non-communist Manifesto*, Cambridge, MA: Cambridge University Press.

Roy, O. (2012), 'Islamic Revival and Democracy: The Case in Tunisia and Egypt', in C. Merlini & O. Roy (Eds.), *Arab Society in Revolt: The West's Mediterranean Challenge*, Washington, DC: Brookings Institution Press, pp. 47–52.

St John, R. Bruce (2008), 'Libya: Reforming the Economy, Not the Polity', in Y. Zoubir & H. Amirah-Fernández (Eds.), *North Africa: Politics, Region, and the Limits of Transformation*, London: Routledge, pp. 53–70.

UNDP (2011), *Arab Development Challenges Report 2011. Towards the Developmental State in the Arab Region*, Cairo.

UNDP, "Human Development Report 2010: The Real Wealth of Nations" (New York: United Nations Development Program, 2010)

World Bank (2010), *Sustaining the Recovery in Times of Uncertainty, Middle East and North Africa Regional Economic Outlook*, Washington, DC: US Government Printing Office.

World Bank Enterprise Surveys, 2005–2014, http://data.worldbank.org/data-catalog/enterprise-surveys (Accessed January 13, 2014)

Youngs, R. (2011), 'Misunderstanding the Maladies of Liberal Democracy Promotion', FRIDE Working Paper 106, January.

2

MAGHREBI YOUTH IN THE WAKE OF THE ARAB SPRING

General observations and evidence from Tunisia and Algeria

Mark Tessler and Jennifer Miller-Gonzalez[1]

A concern for youth and generational change in the Maghreb and broader Middle East is not new. As early as 1976, I wrote about the factors that in Tunisia, as elsewhere, were giving the young men and women then reaching adulthood a character that distinguished them from previous generations (Tessler 1976). Prominent among these factors was the size of the new generation, giving rise to an increasingly important "youth bulge." This spectacular population growth was driven by a birthrate that at the time approached 3 percent and meant, as a result, that within a few years the attitudes and values of young adults would begin to displace those of older Moroccans, Algerians and Tunisians and to define the mainstream normative and behavioral orientations of these countries.

The emerging generation differed in qualitative as well as quantitative terms. Raised in the post-independence period, or perhaps during the war for independence in Algeria, young Maghrebis grew up and acquired their first views about politics and culture largely free from whatever influence, either positive or negative, life under colonialism exerted. On the contrary, the environment in which these young Tunisians, Algerians and Moroccans acquired many of their basic views about politics differed greatly from that prevailing when their fathers, mothers and older siblings experienced the transition from adolescence to adulthood. Thus, as research on political generations elsewhere has shown, and as has been demonstrated by empirical research in the Maghreb as well (Tessler, Konold and Reif 2004), there was a strong possibility that this post-independence generation would look at the world of politics in a way that was different, perhaps quite different, than did their parents.

Finally, relatively high levels of education distinguished this post-independence generation, especially in Tunisia and Algeria. Although the quality of schooling varied and opportunities to go beyond primary school remained limited in some areas, especially for girls, both Tunisia and Algeria made education a national priority after independence. As a result, school enrollments soared and, despite the educational gaps that remained, by the mid- to late-1970s Maghrebi youth were, on average, far more educated than were their older countrymen. This trend continued in the years that followed, with gains registered in Morocco as well as in Tunisia and Algeria, and with more and more girls getting an education in all three countries, further widening the educational divide between young people and the generation of their parents (Austin 2011; Campante and Chor 2012).

Taken together, by the late 1960s and during the 1970s these trends appeared to portend significant and, for the most part, hopeful transitions associated with generational change. There was uncertainty as well, to be sure, but many observers assumed that generational replacement would bring important changes of at least some sort. A study of political generations in the Arab world in 1970 thus characterized the emerging cohort as a "critical mass." Looking toward the coming decade, the author of the study wrote that "the young Arabs approaching adulthood, the critical mass of the 1970s, will increasingly determine the outcome of competing trends." Further, he added:

> In addition to employment, the new generation will be seeking social status and a meaningful identity as Arabs. As they take their place in Arab society, there may well be conflicts and eruptions, and new political movements could arise, based on this class of young adults. Whether they will eventually turn out to be bridge or blockbuster in the national culture, cement or tinder in the fabric of the nation, their impact on the Arab world, its culture and development, will be critical (Mattson 1971, p. 13).

While the preceding analysis proved to be prescient, at least to a degree, the years that followed neither fully fulfilled the aspirations of Maghrebi youth nor in any country brought a national consensus on questions of politics and culture. By the 1980s, there were mass protests in all three countries of the Maghreb. Although discontent was by no means limited to young people, unfulfilled expectations of meaningful employment, or, in many cases, at least some employment, along with mobility blocked by corruption and favoritism, especially among young men and women who were better educated – the so-called *chômeurs diplômés* – were among the most important factors fueling public anger. Young people were also particularly sensitive to the growing authoritarianism in all three countries of the Maghreb and this, too, contributed to alienation among the youth. According to a study based on surveys of Moroccan students conducted shortly before the first of a series of riots that shocked the country during the 1980s, young Moroccans tended to view the state as "omnipotent and omnicompetent," both fearing but also resenting it, if not in fact hating it. As reported by the author, the regime was "widely recognized as not representative of the people," and this, in turn, produced two main reactions: "either complete apathy or at least passivity, sometimes [mistakenly] viewed as acceptance, or alienation and activism in some anti-establishment form or medium" (Suleiman 1987, p. 113; also Bourgi 1989).

Writing about Algeria a few years later, an Algerian newspaper editor offered the following description of the situation in his country to explain the origins of the widespread rioting that took place in Algiers, Oran and other cities in 1988:

> Out of the entire population of this country, there are barely one million per-
> sons with a civilized cycle of life, in the sense that they have good jobs, collect
> a reasonable salary, deal with banks and sometimes take vacations. The rest of
> the country lives at subsistence levels or below (Quoted in Ibrahim 1991).

With respect to politics and culture, the dominant ideology during the first years of independence was one of essentially secular nationalism. In Tunisia and Algeria in particular, although to a significant degree in Morocco as well, socialism and Nasserism, inspired by the revolution in Egypt, captured the imagination of young people in the Maghreb, although not only young people. Personal religiosity was not necessarily in decline, but the most highly valued formulae for political and societal development were not derived from Arab and Islamic traditions but rather borrowed from Western Europe or Communist countries and understood as the best path forward for all "Third World" countries. Over the course of the 1970s and 1980s, however, these models increasingly lost their appeal as development lagged and many young people turned to Islam for solutions to the problems described above. Islamist movements accordingly attracted increasing numbers of young men and women and became important political actors, exerting their influence both in debates about governance and in the lifestyle choices of many individuals.

The origins and implications of the Arab Spring may be understood against this background, as may be the patterns that characterize the present-day orientations of younger North Africans and their older countrymen. The protests that shocked the Arab world at the end of 2010 and into 2011, and that brought regime change in Tunisia and Islamist electoral victories in Tunisia and Morocco, were fueled by many of the same grievances that had earlier produced disturbances: unfulfilled aspirations, corruption and favoritism in the determination of those who were able to advance, and, above all, governments that seemed to disrespect their citizens and care only about themselves and their friends. Expressed as a demand for dignity, which emerged particularly clearly in Tunisia, as it did in Egypt and later in other countries in the Arab east, these accusations against the regime were both articulated and translated into action by young people who, as it was described in Egypt, had "crossed the barrier of fear" in their determination that there would be no return to business as usual.

Anger and resentment directed at the political and economic status quo were by no means limited to young people. Nevertheless, as elsewhere, and as most clearly evident in Egypt and Tunisia, young people were in the forefront of what in at least some countries can only be described as a revolution. As observers have noted, the youth did not form the vanguard of these protests solely because their griev-ances were the most intense. While this was almost certainly a contributing factor, so too, apparently, were the perspective, efficacy, media savvy and communication networks of young people, considerations that distinguished them from their elders. As one sometimes heard in analyses of Egypt, only partly in jest, these are the young men and women who taught their parents "to use the remote control."

Similar aspirations and complaints notwithstanding, the political situation in the wake of the Arab Spring differs significantly in Tunisia, Algeria and Morocco. In Tunisia, as noted, the regime collapsed and the Islamist Ennahda party prevailed in the elections of October 2011. At the other end of the spectrum is Algeria, where protests were less widespread and readily contained, with grievances continuing to simmer but, in the end, the situation looking pretty much like it did before the events of the Arab Spring. In between is Morocco, where the monarchy responded to protests by implementing some, although comparatively modest, constitutional reforms and where the Islamist Justice and Development Party scored a victory in the elections of November 2011. Thus, despite clear parallels in their post-independence political evolution and in the underlying political and economic problems facing the three countries, each emerges from the revolutionary events of the Arab Spring on, at least for the present, a different trajectory.

Comparing the generations in Tunisia and in Algeria

Data collected in nationally representative political attitude surveys in Tunisia and Algeria in 2011 may be used to examine the views of younger men and women and to compare these views to those of older individuals. The surveys were conducted as part of the second wave of the Arab Barometer, which also sought but was unable to carry out a representative survey in Morocco. The Tunisian survey was conducted in September and October 2011 and the Algerian survey was conducted in April and May of 2011. Both were thus carried out after the fall of the Ben Ali regime in Tunisia and the Mubarak regime in Egypt, events critical to the timeline of the Arab Spring, and in the Tunisian case just before the Ennahda electoral victory. The surveys in both countries are based on samples of adults aged 18 and older and both used multi-stage area probability sampling to select respondents. The Arab Barometer survey instrument was administered in each country through face-to-face interviews. Additional information about the second wave of Arab Barometer surveys, as well as country reports summarizing major findings from the 12 Arab countries in which surveys were carried out, can be found on the Arab Barometer website (www.arabbarometer.org).

For purposes of the present discussion the views of three age cohorts in Tunisia and Algeria are considered and compared: 18–24, 25–34 and 35 and older. The analysis also considers sex-linked differences by comparing the attitudes and orientations of men and women both across and within each of the three age groups. The number of respondents possessing each combination of age and sex is given in the appendix. In describing and then comparing attitudes and orientations across and within age cohorts, the topics listed below are considered. Taken together, these topics provide a reasonably broad cross-section of the way people of different ages see the world, particularly those aspects of political and policy relevance.

- Democracy
- Islam's political role
- Women's status and gender equality
- Interpretations of Islam
- Interpersonal trust
- Institutional trust
- Political interest
- Personal religiosity

The Arab Barometer interview schedule contains many questions dealing with most of the topics listed above. Only one or two have been selected in each case for inclusion in the present analysis, however, with the criteria for inclusion being an item's inherent interest or its utility in representing a response distribution characteristic of a larger battery of items. In most cases, items present respondents with a statement and then ask them to indicate whether they strongly agree, agree, disagree or strongly disagree. In order to maximize clarity and parsimony in the presentation of the findings, response distributions have been dichotomized by combining the categories of strongly agree and agree and the categories of disagree and strongly disagree. Accordingly, the tables presenting responses to each item for each country contain eighteen cells and show the percent agreeing and the percent disagreeing for all respondents, for male respondents and for female respondents in each of the three age cohorts.

Not every cell in every table is discussed, or can be discussed. Rather, first, in the pages immediately following, general summaries are offered and patterns that seem particularly instructive are identified. Beyond this, it is left to readers to consult the tables in which they have a particular interest and to derive whatever additional insights they find useful and instructive. Thereafter, following these summaries, the inter-connections among key generational differences are considered and some possible explanations and implications associated with these patterns are suggested.

Democracy. The following two items present Tunisian and Algerian attitudes toward democracy. Each asks respondents whether they strongly agree, agree, disagree or strongly disagree with the statement.

- Democracy may have problems but it's better than any other form of government.
- Citizens in the country are unprepared for the democratic system.

Findings are presented in Tables 2.1a and 2.1b, and it is immediately apparent that there is widespread support for democracy: 89.5 percent of all Tunisian respondents and 84.3 percent of all Algerian respondents agree that democracy, whatever its limitations, is better than any other form of government. These numbers are consistent with findings from other empirical studies in undemocratic or quasi-democratic countries, and in the Arab world in particular (see, e.g., Inglehart 2003; Robbins and Tessler 2012).

TABLE 2.1A Tunisian views about democracy by age cohort and gender

Democracy may have problems but it's better than any other form of government

	18–24			25–34			35 and Older		
	All	*Male*	*Female*	*All*	*Male*	*Female*	*All*	*Male*	*Female*
% Agree	87.6	91.8	83.8	92.7	92.7	92.7	88.7	89.8	87.1
% Disagree	12.4	8.2	16.2	7.3	7.3	7.3	11.3	10.2	12.9

TABLE 2.1B Algerian views about democracy by age cohort and gender

Democracy may have problems but it's better than any other form of government

	18–24			25–34			35 and older		
	All	*Male*	*Female*	*All*	*Male*	*Female*	*All*	*Male*	*Female*
% Agree	77.5	75.0	80.2	86.7	86.2	87.1	86.0	86.6	85.4
% Disagree	22.5	25.0	19.8	13.3	13.8	12.9	14.0	13.4	14.6

While support for democracy is high across all three age cohorts in both countries, there is a modest but notable generational difference in Algeria, with 77.5 percent of respondents aged 18 through 24 agreeing with the statement compared to 86.7 percent of those between 25 and 34 and 86.0 percent of those 35 or older.[2] Although this hardly constitutes a rejection of democracy among young Algerians, it does challenge the view that youth are in the forefront in the struggle for democracy. Additional detail emerges when sex-linked generational differences are considered. In Algeria, the previously noted generational difference is more pronounced among men than among women. In Tunisia, by contrast, women aged 18–24 are less likely than older women to hold favorable views toward democracy to a degree that is, again, modest but nonetheless notable. Interestingly then, although it remains high overall, support for democracy is lowest among young men in Algeria and among young women in Tunisia.

While the first item measures support for democracy, the second asks whether respondents believe their fellow citizens will be able stewards of democracy. As Tables 2.2a and 2.2b demonstrate, responses to the second item diverge sharply from those to the first. The percentage of individuals who agree that citizens in their country are unprepared for democracy is 53.4 percent in Tunisia and only 33.2 percent in Algeria. In Tunisia, aggregate cohort differences are small and in all three age cohorts men are somewhat more likely than women to believe that their fellow citizens are unprepared for democracy. In Algeria, differences across cohorts and between sexes within cohorts are small as well, although among respondents

TABLE 2.2A Tunisian views about democracy by age cohort and gender

	Citizens are unprepared for the democratic system								
	18–24			25–34			35 and older		
	All	*Male*	*Female*	*All*	*Male*	*Female*	*All*	*Male*	*Female*
% Agree	55.2	59.2	51.4	54.9	59.0	50.8	52.0	54.7	48.0
% Disagree	44.8	40.8	48.6	45.1	41.0	49.2	48.0	45.3	52.0

TABLE 2.2B Algerian views about democracy by age cohort and gender

	Citizens are unprepared for the democratic system								
	18–24			25–34			35 and older		
	All	*Male*	*Female*	*All*	*Male*	*Female*	*All*	*Male*	*Female*
% Agree	29.7	28.4	31.1	36.1	38.0	34.1	33.1	35.9	29.7
% Disagree	70.3	71.6	68.9	63.9	62.0	65.9	66.9	64.1	70.3

aged 35 and older, and, to a lesser extent, among those aged 25 to 34, men are again more likely than women to believe that their country's citizens are not prepared for democracy.

Political Islam. Although there is widespread support for democracy in Algeria and Tunisia, it remains unclear whether the form of democracy that respondents have in mind includes or excludes a role for Islam. To explore this question, the following item is used to assess attitudes toward Islam's role in government and political affairs. Again, respondents were asked whether they strongly agree, agree, disagree or strongly disagree with the statement presented to them.

- Religious practice is a private matter and should be separated from socio-political life.

As Tables 2.3a and 2.3b show, the vast majority of respondents in both countries favor the separation of religion and politics. Fully 81 percent of respondents in both Tunisia and Algeria agree that religious practice is a private matter and should be separated from socio-political life. Interestingly, this represents a significant departure from findings based on the 2006–2007 wave of Arab Barometer surveys, which found a deep division of opinion about the political role that Islam should play (Tessler 2010, p. 226).

In Tunisia, the distribution of responses does not vary across age groups, either in the aggregate or by sex. Nor does it differ by sex within any of the three age cohorts. In Algeria, younger male respondents are somewhat less likely than their

TABLE 2.3A Tunisian views about political Islam by age cohort and gender

	Religious practice is a private matter and should be separated from socio-political life								
	18–24			*25–34*			*35 and older*		
	All	*Male*	*Female*	*All*	*Male*	*Female*	*All*	*Male*	*Female*
% Agree	79.9	80.6	79.2	83.3	83.3	83.2	80.6	80.3	81.0
% Disagree	20.1	19.4	20.8	16.7	16.7	16.8	19.4	19.7	19.0

TABLE 2.3B Algerian views about political Islam by age cohort and gender

	Religious practice is a private matter and should be separated from socio-political life								
	18–24			*25–34*			*35 and older*		
	All	*Male*	*Female*	*All*	*Male*	*Female*	*All*	*Male*	*Female*
% Agree	78.2	78.2	78.3	80.2	78.1	82.5	84.1	85.5	82.5
% Disagree	21.8	21.8	21.7	19.8	21.9	17.5	15.9	14.5	17.5

older male countrymen to favor a separation of religion and politics, although the difference is only 6 percentage points, ranging from a low of 78.2 among those under 25 to a high of 85.5 among those 35 and older.

Women's status and gender equality. In light of the consistently high and diffuse support for democracy in the Middle East and North Africa, the heretofore persistence of authoritarianism, considered "the region's political hallmark" (Bellin 2012, p. 127), may seem puzzling. Among the explanations offered for this incongruity is a lack of broad public support for the principles and practices of gender equality (Fish 2002; Inglehart and Norris 2003; but see Donno and Russett 2008). Yet, according to some analysts, budding youth-led movements have accommodated women's rights (Austin 2011, p. 86), and the participation of young women in these movements has been notable. For instance, "in Tunisia's Jasmine Revolution, women did not hesitate to participate in masses in order to make sure that their demands would be taken into account, and that they would be represented in the post-revolutionary government" (Austin 2011, p. 91).

Against this background, the following two items have been used to assess attitudes toward women's status and gender equality, with respondents again asked whether they strongly agree, agree, disagree or strongly disagree with each statement.

- A woman can be prime minister of a country.
- A university degree is more important for a boy than a girl.

Tables 2.4a and 2.4b present the Tunisian responses to both items. The proportion of individuals who believe a woman can be prime minister of a country is

67.4 percent, and 63 percent do not think that a university degree is more important for a boy than a girl. These views are broadly held by members of all three age
cohorts, with no important age-related differences on either item.

In Algeria, the proportion of individuals who believe a woman can be prime
minister is 60.5 percent, while 70.5 percent of the respondents do not think that
a university degree is more important for a boy than a girl. Yet, although levels of
support are high and broadly similar to those in Tunisia, cohort differences, particularly among women, are somewhat larger in Algeria on the question of woman
serving as prime minister, as shown in Table 2.5a. Specifically, 78.2 percent of Algerian women aged 18–24 believe a woman can be the prime minister of a country, whereas the percentages are only 64.9 and 69.7, respectively, among Algerian
women in the two older age cohorts.

The one additional finding pertaining to women's status and gender equality
concerns differences associated with sex. On the question about a woman serving as prime minister, the findings are not unexpected but striking nonetheless.
In both countries and in all three cohorts, woman are much more likely than
men to agree that a woman can be a prime minister, although differences are
larger in Algeria than Tunisia and in Tunisia the difference between men and
women under 25 is statistically significant only at the .10 level. There are also
significant sex-linked differences, but only in Algeria, on the question pertaining
to a university education. In Tunisia, by contrast, perhaps surprisingly, there are
no sex-linked differences in the two youngest age cohorts. Even in the oldest
cohort, where the 7.7-point difference between and women is significant, the

TABLE 2.4A Tunisian views about women's status by age cohort and gender

	A woman can be prime minister of a country								
	18–24			*25–34*			*35 and older*		
	All	*Male*	*Female*	*All*	*Male*	*Female*	*All*	*Male*	*Female*
% Agree	68.9	62.4	73.9	66.8	59.4	72.2	67.1	60.0	73.7
% Disagree	31.1	37.7	26.1	33.2	40.6	27.8	32.9	40.0	26.3

TABLE 2.4B Tunisian views about women's status by age cohort and gender

	A university degree is more important for a boy than a girl								
	18–24			*25–34*			*35 and older*		
	All	*Male*	*Female*	*All*	*Male*	*Female*	*All*	*Male*	*Female*
% Agree	35.8	36.6	35.1	36.5	36.7	36.3	37.5	40.9	33.2
% Disagree	64.2	63.4	64.9	63.5	63.3	63.7	62.5	59.1	66.8

TABLE 2.5A Algerian views about women's status by age cohort and gender

	A woman can be prime minister of a country								
	18–24			*25–34*			*35 and older*		
	All	*Male*	*Female*	*All*	*Male*	*Female*	*All*	*Male*	*Female*
% Agree	65.3	51.3	78.2	57.8	49.1	64.9	60.2	48.2	69.7
% Disagree	34.7	48.8	21.8	42.2	50.9	35.1	39.8	51.8	30.3

TABLE 2.5B Algerian views about women's status by age cohort and gender

	A university degree is more important for a boy than a girl								
	18–24			*25–34*			*35 and older*		
	All	*Male*	*Female*	*All*	*Male*	*Female*	*All*	*Male*	*Female*
% Agree	31.3	45.7	12.7	31.2	42.6	18.9	27.9	41.7	13.7
% Disagree	68.7	54.3	87.3	68.8	57.4	81.1	72.1	58.3	86.3

gap in opinions is far smaller than any of the sex-linked differences in Algeria. It thus appears that there is much more of a national consensus on the question of women's education in Tunisia than in Algeria, with support in this area as high among men, especially younger men, as among women. Nevertheless, the latter finding from Tunisia notwithstanding, the tables show that, overall, the distribution of attitudes toward women's status and gender equality is characterized by a gender divide but not a generational divide.

Interpretations of Islam. Another important question is the degree to which particular interpretations of Islamic law vary as a function of age or gender. The differential levels of rights accorded to men and women in Islamic law would suggest that this may be the case, especially for women since feminism appears to be growing even among Islamist women in the Maghreb (Archer 2007). To gauge popular thinking about what Islam requires, responses to the following two questions are examined:

> Today as in the past, Muslim scholars and jurists sometimes disagree about the proper interpretation of Islam in response to present-day issues. For each of the statements listed below, please indicate whether you agree strongly, agree, disagree or disagree strongly.
> • Islam requires that in a Muslim country the political rights of non-Muslims should be inferior to those of Muslims.

- In Islam a woman should dress modestly, but Islam does not require that she wear a *hijab*.

In both countries and on both items, a majority of the respondents endorse a more liberal or contextualized interpretation of Islamic law. The proportion of respondents who reject an interpretation of Islam that assigns inferior political rights to non-Muslim citizens is 77.2 percent in Tunisia and 71.4 percent in Algeria. Similarly, substantial majorities in each country hold the view that Islam does not require that a woman be veiled or at least wear a head scarf, with 89.3 percent and 70.1 percent of respondents in Tunisia and Algeria sharing this view, respectively.

In Tunisia, as shown in Tables 2.6a and 2.6b, the youngest individuals are slightly more liberal than the oldest individuals on the question of non-Muslim rights, and, in both cases, women are slightly more liberal than men, although these differences are too small to be statistically significant. Cohort and sex-linked differences are, for the most part, even smaller on the question of women's dress. There is, however, a notable cohort difference among men; 93.4 percent of Tunisian men aged 18–24 believe that Islam does not require women to wear the *hijab*, compared to only 86.5 percent of the Tunisian male respondents aged 35 and over. Despite these differences, it is clear that there is broad support for liberal interpretations of Islam in Tunisia and fewer differences associated with either age or gender than might have been expected.

Tables 2.7a and 2.7b present the response distributions for Algeria. With respect to the question about non-Muslim rights, younger and older Algerians tend to have

TABLE 2.6A Tunisian views about interpretations of Islam by age cohort and gender

	Islam requires that in a Muslim country the political rights of non-Muslims should be inferior to those of Muslims								
	18–24			*25–34*			*35 and older*		
	All	*Male*	*Female*	*All*	*Male*	*Female*	*All*	*Male*	*Female*
% Agree	21.1	23.5	18.4	16.9	20.4	12.9	26.1	27.8	23.9
% Disagree	78.9	76.5	81.6	83.1	79.5	87.1	73.9	72.2	76.1

TABLE 2.6B Tunisian views about interpretations of Islam by age cohort and gender

	In Islam a woman should dress modestly, but Islam does not require that she wear a hijab								
	18–24			*25–34*			*35 and older*		
	All	*Male*	*Female*	*All*	*Male*	*Female*	*All*	*Male*	*Female*
% Agree	91.7	93.4	90.1	89.6	88.4	90.8	88.2	86.5	90.2
% Disagree	8.3	6.6	9.9	10.4	11.6	9.2	11.8	13.5	9.8

TABLE 2.7A Algerian views about interpretations of Islam by age cohort and gender

Islam requires that in a Muslim country the political rights of non-Muslims should be inferior to those of Muslims

	18–24			25–34			35 and older		
	All	*Male*	*Female*	*All*	*Male*	*Female*	*All*	*Male*	*Female*
% Agree	27.4	33.3	21.2	33.3	36.8	29.5	26.4	27.4	25.4
% Disagree	72.6	66.7	78.8	66.7	63.2	70.5	73.6	72.6	74.6

TABLE 2.7B Algerian views about interpretations of Islam by age cohort and gender

In Islam a woman should dress modestly, but Islam does not require that she wear a hijab

	18–24			25–34			35 and older		
	All	*Male*	*Female*	*All*	*Male*	*Female*	*All*	*Male*	*Female*
% Agree	74.3	71.8	76.7	73.3	67.2	79.3	66.2	67.5	64.8
% Disagree	25.7	28.2	23.3	26.7	32.8	20.7	33.8	32.5	35.2

similar views in the aggregate, but there is a substantial sex-linked difference in the 18–24-year-old cohort, with 78.8 percent of the female respondents rejecting the proposition that Islam requires that the political rights of non-Muslims be inferior to those of Muslims compared to only 66.7 percent of the male respondents rejecting this proposition. This difference is statistically significant at p = 0.07. On the question of women's dress, younger respondents hold more liberal views than older respondents, with 74.3 percent of those aged 18–24 compared to 66.2 percent of those aged 35 and older believing that Islam does not require women to wear the *hijab*. There are also sex-linked differences on this question in Algeria, but they are substantial only among respondents in the 25–34 age cohort.

Consistent with some of the findings presented earlier, age cohort and sex-linked differences are limited in Tunisia, suggesting something of a national consensus on questions pertaining to Islam and to women's status. In Algeria, by contrast, liberal views on these questions, while broadly characteristic of the population as a whole, are at least somewhat more pronounced among younger respondents and among women.

Interpersonal trust. In this section, we investigate the extent and distribution of interpersonal trust in both countries. Trust has long been considered critical for an effective democracy (see, e.g., Almond and Verba 1963, 1980; Putnam 1992). Yet one of the consequences of living under a repressive regime is its toll on interpersonal trust (Hardin 1996). One young Tunisian described himself in this connection as "being a teenager in a police state," adding that "We never knew our neighbours, never said hello in the entrance hall, for fear everyone was spying and an informer. You trusted no one."[3] To what degree is this observation indicative of a larger trend? And is the youthful population more distrustful than its elders? To answer these questions, the following item is examined, with the focus on the percentage rejecting the proposition that most people cannot be trusted:

• Generally speaking, would you say that most people can be trusted, some people can be trusted and some people cannot be trusted, or most people cannot be trusted?

Table 2.8a displays the results across age and gender categories in Tunisia. An overwhelming majority of respondents do not believe that other people can be trusted. While low levels of trust characterize each cohort, the proportion of respondents expressing misgivings about other people is higher among the younger Tunisians, with levels of trust decreasing monotonically across the three age cohorts: 41.4 percent of those 35 and older, dropping to 32.0 percent among those between the ages of 25 and 34, and finishing at a low of 24.4 percent among those under 25. These inter-cohort differences characterize both sexes but are most pronounced among women, with only 19.8 percent of the female respondents under 25 rejecting the proposition than most people cannot be trusted.

Table 2.8b compares Algerian responses by cohort and gender. The sheer lack of trust among Algerians is striking – a full 92.1 percent believe "most people cannot be trusted." This is significantly higher than in Tunisia and may be due, in part, to the violence that Algeria has experienced in recent decades. In fact,

TABLE 2.8A Tunisian views about interpersonal trust by age cohort and gender

	Generally speaking, would you say that most people can be trusted?								
	18–24			*25–34*			*35 and older*		
	All	*Male*	*Female*	*All*	*Male*	*Female*	*All*	*Male*	*Female*
% Can be trusted	24.4	29.5	19.8	32.0	32.8	31.2	41.4	42.5	40.0
% Cannot be trusted	75.6	70.5	80.2	68.0	67.2	68.8	58.7	57.5	60.0

TABLE 2.8B Algerian views about interpersonal trust by age cohort and gender

	Generally speaking, would you say that most people can be trusted?								
	18–24			*25–34*			*35 and older*		
	All	*Male*	*Female*	*All*	*Male*	*Female*	*All*	*Male*	*Female*
% Can be trusted	6.8	10.7	2.7	4.4	3.8	5.0	10.3	11.1	9.6
% Cannot be trusted	93.2	89.3	97.4	95.6	96.3	88.9	89.7	88.9	90.4

however, the level of distrust is almost exactly the same among younger Algerians, most of whom did not live through the violent convulsions of the 1990s, as it is among older respondents; and this suggests, as in Tunisia, that the explanation for the high level of distrust probably lies elsewhere. Sex-linked differences in Algeria are not consistent across the three age cohorts. Strikingly, 97.4 percent of the female respondents under the age of 25 believe that people cannot be trusted, compared to 89.3 percent of the younger male respondents. By contrast, men are less trusting in the 25–34 age category and there are no sex-linked differences among the oldest Algerians.

Institutional trust. Having investigated patterns of interpersonal trust, we now examine whether and how popular trust in political institutions varies in Tunisia and Algeria. We use the following items, focusing on the percentage expressing a great deal of trust or quite a lot of trust:

> I'm going to name a number of institutions. For each one, please tell me how much trust you have in them. Is it a great deal of trust, quite a lot of trust, a little trust, not very much trust, or none at all?
> *   The prime minister
> *   The courts/justice system

As Table 2.9a demonstrates, a majority of Tunisians place "a great deal" or "quite a lot of trust" in the prime minister, but this varies significantly as a function of age. This level of confidence is expressed by 58.7 percent of respondents between 18 and 24, by 63.2 percent of those between 25 and 34, and by 70.8 percent of those 35 and older. These inter-cohort differences are initially evident only among men, as evidenced by the 16.2 percent gap between the youngest and oldest age cohorts, but a significant difference also emerges among women if the youngest cohort is compared to the two older cohorts combined. Specifically, 61.4 percent of the youngest women express trust in the government compared to 70.1 percent of the older women, a difference that is statistically significant at p = 0.07.

The table also reveals some within-cohort sex-linked differences in trust in the prime minister, with women significantly more trusting than men in the

TABLE 2.9A Tunisian trust in the prime minister/government by age cohort and gender

	How much trust do you have in the prime minister/government?								
	18–24			*25–34*			*35 and older*		
	All	*Male*	*Female*	*All*	*Male*	*Female*	*All*	*Male*	*Female*
% A great deal/a lot	58.7	55.7	61.4	63.2	55.0	70.9	70.8	71.9	69.6
% Very little/none	41.3	44.4	38.6	36.7	45.1	29.0	29.1	28.1	30.4

25–34 age group. With respect to trust in the courts, as shown in Table 2.9b, aggregate trust is somewhat lower and inter-cohort differences are negligible. At the same time, there are inter-cohort differences between women 18–24 and women 35 and older, with over 10 percentage points separating the proportion in each group expressing at least some trust in the courts. Finally, sex-linked differences in this case involve a higher level of trust among women than men in the 25–34 and the older than 35 age cohorts. It is surprising, and for reasons not immediately apparent, that the overall level of trust is higher in the prime minister than in the judicial system and that trust levels vary in different ways for the two political institutions.

Findings about institutional trust in Algeria are presented in Tables 2.10a and 2.10b. With respect to the prime minister, trust is much lower than in Tunisia; about one-quarter of the respondents under 35 have little or no trust in the prime minister, and levels are only slightly higher, at 31.4 percent, for those aged 35 and over.

TABLE 2.9B Tunisian trust in the courts/justice system by age cohort and gender

| | How much trust do you have in the courts/justice system? | | | | | | | | |
| | 18–24 | | | 25–34 | | | 35 and older | | |
	All	Male	Female	All	Male	Female	All	Male	Female
% A great deal/a lot	51.4	52.4	50.5	56.2	51.5	60.7	57.4	52.9	62.6
% Very little/none	48.6	47.6	49.5	43.8	48.5	39.3	42.6	47.1	37.4

TABLE 2.10A Algerian trust in the prime minister/government by age cohort and gender

| | How much trust do you have in the prime minister/government? | | | | | | | | |
| | 18–24 | | | 25–34 | | | 35 and older | | |
	All	Male	Female	All	Male	Female	All	Male	Female
% A great deal/a lot	27.2	28.0	26.3	23.8	20.7	26.9	31.4	32.6	30.2
% Very little/none	72.8	72.0	73.7	76.2	79.3	73.1	68.6	67.4	69.8

TABLE 2.10B Algerian trust in the courts/justice system by age cohort and gender

| | How much trust do you have in the courts/justice system? | | | | | | | | |
| | 18–24 | | | 25–34 | | | 35 and older | | |
	All	Male	Female	All	Male	Female	All	Male	Female
% A great deal/a lot	44.0	44.4	43.6	36.0	31.9	40.0	48.0	49.7	46.3
% Very little/none	56.0	55.6	56.4	64.0	68.1	60.0	52.0	50.3	53.7

Inter-cohort differences are small, with only 4.2 percentage points separating the youngest and oldest respondents, and, on the whole, this is the case for both men and women. The only notable exception is among men in the 25–34 age group. With the lowest level of trust of any subset of respondents, at only 20.7 percent, these men differ from men in other age cohorts and from women in their own cohort. Trust in the courts is somewhat higher overall, the opposite of the pattern observed in Tunisia; it ranges from 36 percent among Algerians aged 25–34 to 48 percent among Algerians aged 35 and older. As in the case of the prime minister, trust in the courts is lowest among men in the 25–34 age group, at 31.9 percent, meaning, again, that the most important inter-cohort and sex-linked differences are between these men and men in other age cohorts and women in the same age cohort.

Political interest. There not only may be variation in the way that different generations perceive and evaluate political institutions but also in their levels of interest in all things political. The events of the Arab Spring would suggest that young people are more interested and engaged in political affairs, but this proposition remains to be tested by systematic empirical research. To assess levels of political interest, the item below is considered. Response options include very interested, somewhat interested, not very interested and not at all interested. In describing and comparing responses, two categories are used: very interested or somewhat interested and not very interested or not at all interested.

• Generally speaking, how interested would you say you are in politics?

Table 2.11a compares Tunisians' level of interest across age cohorts and sex. It is immediately apparent, somewhat surprisingly, that the majority of respondents in each age cohort are not very interested in politics, and that those aged 18–24 are the least interested. Only 32 percent of these young Tunisians are even somewhat interested in politics. The other cohorts are more engaged, but only slightly, and not to a degree that is statistically significant, with 36.3 percent among those aged 25–34 and 38.6 percent among those aged 35 and older expressing an interest in political affairs. Inter-cohort differences are most pronounced among men, with the youngest men being the least interested. There are sex-linked differences in the two older age cohorts, with men being more interested in politics than women by

TABLE 2.11A Tunisian interest in politics by age cohort and gender

	How interested would you say you are in politics?								
	18–24			*25–34*			*35 and older*		
	All	*Male*	*Female*	*All*	*Male*	*Female*	*All*	*Male*	*Female*
% Very/somewhat	32.0	32.1	31.9	36.3	45.9	27.5	38.6	47.9	28.2
% Not very/not at all	68.0	67.9	68.1	63.7	54.1	72.5	61.4	52.1	71.8

a margin of almost 20 percent in both cases. Thus, while political interest in Tunisia appears to be low overall, which is surprising given that the survey was done in the months following the departure of Ben Ali, is it particularly low among men under 25 and among women in all age categories.

Table 2.11b presents the Algerian responses to the item about political interest. Levels are even lower than in Tunisia, and they are low in every age cohort in Algeria. In all three age groups, the aggregate percentage of those who are at least somewhat interested in politics hovers around 20 percent. There are a number of sex-linked differences both across and within age cohorts. Although it remains low overall, political interest increases somewhat as a function of age among men while among women it is lowest in the oldest age cohort. As a result, among Algerians aged 35 and older, but only for this cohort, interest is measurably higher among men than among women.

TABLE 2.11B Algerian interest in politics by age cohort and gender

| | *How interested would you say you are in politics?* | | | | | | | | |
| | *18–24* | | | *25–34* | | | *35 and older* | | |
	All	*Male*	*Female*	*All*	*Male*	*Female*	*All*	*Male*	*Female*
% Very/somewhat	19.2	18.3	20.1	20.0	21.6	18.6	21.3	27.0	15.8
% Not very/not at all	80.8	81.7	79.8	80.0	78.4	81.4	78.7	73.0	84.2

Personal religiosity. There are a large number of items measuring personal religiosity in the Arab Barometer interview schedule. These items ask about religious observance and practice, but since they reflect different levels of religious intensity, no single item gives a complete picture. For purposes of the present discussion, which is concerned primarily about similarities and differences across and within age cohorts, it will be sufficient to examine responses to a question about the frequency of reading the Quran or other religious books. Three response categories are considered: every day or almost every day, sometimes, and rarely or never.

Table 2.12a presents the findings from Tunisia and shows that most Tunisians are religious to the extent that they at least sometimes read the Quran. Tunisians in the 18–24 age category are the least religious. They are significantly more likely than their counterparts in the middle and oldest cohorts to report rarely or never

TABLE 2.12A Tunisian religiosity by age cohort and gender

| | *How often do you read the Quran?* | | | | | | | | |
| | *18–24* | | | *25–34* | | | *35 and older* | | |
	All	*Male*	*Female*	*All*	*Male*	*Female*	*All*	*Male*	*Female*
% Daily/almost daily	44.2	29.9	57.3	54.9	50.0	59.3	58.5	57.1	60.0
% Sometimes	38.8	52.3	26.5	35.7	38.6	33.1	30.9	32.4	29.2
% Rarely or never	17.0	17.8	16.2	9.4	11.4	7.6	10.6	10.5	10.8

TABLE 2.12B Algerian religiosity by age cohort and gender

	How often do you read the Quran?								
	18–24			25–34			35 and older		
	All	Male	Female	All	Male	Female	All	Male	Female
% Daily/almost daily	25.3	28.0	22.5	30.8	27.6	33.8	29.3	34.8	24.0
% Sometimes	33.5	35.2	31.7	30.1	35.5	25.0	35.3	33.1	37.3
% Rarely or never	41.2	36.8	45.8	39.1	36.8	41.2	35.4	32.1	38.7

reading the Quran, even though 44.2 percent do read it every day and another 38.8 percent read it sometimes. Among older Tunisians, 54.9 percent of those aged 25–34 read the Quran every day or almost every day, and among respondents aged 35 and older 58.5 percent do so. These conclusions might be somewhat misleading, however, since they are due in large part to the much lower proportion of men in the 18–24-year-old cohort who read the Quran or other religious books every day or almost every day. This is the case among only 29.9 percent of these younger men, which may be the most interesting finding to emerge from Table 2.12a. If men aged 18–24 are not considered, differences in religiosity across and within cohorts are much smaller.

As shown in Table 2.12b, religiosity levels are much lower in Algeria, with the proportion of those who rarely or never read the Quran or other religious books ranging from 35.4 percent among the oldest respondents to 41.2 percent among respondents in the 18–24 age category. Interestingly, and in contrast to Tunisia, it is women, not men, who are least likely to be even somewhat religious by this measure. This is the case for both the youngest and the oldest age cohorts. Thus, while it is the low percentage of the youngest men who are religious that stands out in Tunisia, it is low religiosity among the youngest women that stands out in Algeria.

Key generational differences and some possible explanations

The summary of findings provided in the previous section identifies the most important patterns to emerge from the Tunisian and Algerian Arab Barometer surveys. It does not try to discuss every finding that might be of interest. As stated earlier, there are likely to be additional elements on which individual readers will wish to focus their attention, and the data are provided, in part, with this possibility in mind. Nevertheless, the preceding discussion offers an account of what the authors believe to be the most instructive patterns revealed by the data. And these patterns show that there sometimes are and sometimes are not inter-generational differences, and these differences, when they occur, sometimes do and sometimes do not vary by sex.

Against this background, the present section draws upon the more detailed information contained in the tables and discussion above to provide a summary of what the authors believe to be the most important ways in which men and/ or women in the youngest age cohort differ from their older counterparts, and from one another. The goal is to shed light on whether and how the generation of Tunisians and Algerians now reaching adulthood is likely to carry distinctive atti- tudes and orientations into the mainstream of their societies and, if so, to stimulate reflection and invite speculation about the possible causes and implications of any generational shifts that appear to be taking place. To the extent that some of the interpretations presented by the authors constitute informed speculation that go beyond the data, readers are encouraged to offer their own assessments and to share in advancing inquiry aimed at a fuller understanding of Maghrebi youth.

Turning first to men in the 18–24 age cohort, Table 2.13 lists the ways in which these young men differ from men in one or both of the two older age cohorts. In this table and the ones that follow, differences are statistically significant at a 0.05 level or below unless it is indicated that significance is at the 0.10 level.

Turning next to women in the 18–24 age cohort, Table 2.14 lists the ways in which these young women differ from women in one or both of the two older age cohorts.

Finally, sex-linked differences for the 18–24 age cohort are shown in Table 2.15. This table lists any sex-linked opinion cleavages within the younger generation of Maghrebis.

TABLE 2.13 Major differences between men aged 18–24 and older men

Tunisia	Algeria
Islam does not require *hijab*: Slightly more likely to agree (p<0.10) Interpersonal trust: Less trusting Trust in prime minister: Less trusting of prime minister Political interest: Less interested Read the Quran: Less likely to read Quran	Support for democracy: Less supportive Political Islam: Somewhat more supportive (p<0.10) Political interest: Slightly less interested (p<0.10)

TABLE 2.14 Major differences between women aged 18–24 and older women

Tunisia	Algeria
Support for democracy: Less supportive Interpersonal trust: Less trusting Trust in prime minister: Less trusting Trust in courts: Less trusting Read the Quran: More likely to read Quran rarely or never	A woman can be prime minister: More likely to agree Islam does not require *hijab*: More likely to agree Interpersonal trust: Less trusting Read the Quran: Less likely to read the Quran daily or almost daily

The following discussion, based on these three tables, considers each country in sequence. Beginning in Tunisia, the Arab Barometer data, somewhat surprisingly, paint a portrait of an alienated generation – alienated from politics, others and religion. Young men are much less trusting of other people, especially compared to members of the oldest age cohort. Further, this lack of trust applies not only to interpersonal relations but also extends to the political sphere, with male members of this generation equally distrustful of the government and the justice system, although it is only with respect to the former that they differ from their elders. Such distrust does not suggest a generation sharply engaged in politics – the politically conscious and efficacious youth that accounts of the Arab Spring describe as having crossed the barrier of fear. On the contrary, coupled as it is with their uniquely low levels of political interest, the emerging picture is one of alienation, perhaps even anomie, rather than the kind of militancy and commitment to change that might give rise to political action.

The finding that young men appear to be similarly disengaged from Islam is consistent with a reading of the data that emphasizes disaffection. Young men are much more likely to report that they rarely or never read the Quran, and much less likely to report reading it everyday. Thus, at least relative to older men, religion does not reduce alienation by providing a tie to the broader society. The lack of support for a more conservative interpretation of Islam also sets these young men apart from their elders, and it suggests as well that their disaffection with the political system does not in most cases lead to an embrace of political Islam. This, again, points to an alienation that tends toward withdrawal and anomie rather than one that tends toward militancy and engagement.

Turning to women in this age cohort, the table above shows that, much like their male counterparts, younger Tunisian women are alienated from others, politics and religion. Compared to older Tunisian women, they exhibit significantly lower levels of trust – both interpersonal and political – and they are also less likely to believe that democracy is the best form of government. The latter finding should be interpreted with caution since, as among all categories of Tunisians, support for democracy among younger women remains high in absolute terms. It is

TABLE 2.15 Major differences between men and women aged 18–24

Tunisia	Algeria
Support for democracy: Women slightly less likely to agree (p<0.10)	A woman can be prime minister: Women more likely to agree
Women prime minister: Men slightly less likely to agree (p<0.10)	University degree more important for a boy: Men more likely to agree
Interpersonal trust: Women slightly less trusting (p<0.10)	Islam requires inferior rights for non-Muslims: Women somewhat less likely to agree (p<0.10)
Read the Quran: Men less likely to read Quran daily or almost daily	Interpersonal trust: Women less trusting

nevertheless significantly lower than in any other category of Tunisian respondents and this finding, coupled with low interpersonal trust, suggests a lack of confidence, at least in relative terms, in the broader mainstream of Tunisian society. Like their younger male peers and consistent with an interpretation that suggests disaffection, the disengagement of younger Tunisian women is not limited to the political and interpersonal realms but rather extends to the religious sphere as well; they are significantly more likely than older Tunisian women to report that they rarely or never read the Quran.

As the preceding suggests, younger Tunisian men and younger Tunisian women differ from their older counterparts in very similar ways, suggesting tendencies that are characteristic of the 18–24 age cohort as a whole, at least at the time the survey was conducted in mid-2011. Yet there are some ways in which these men and women differ from each other. These differences are not large, for the most part being statistically significant only at the 0.10 level. Nevertheless, they shed light on what may be the somewhat different dynamics operating among the two sexes. Interpersonal trust and support for democracy are lower among women than among men in this age category, suggesting, as proposed above, that their disaffection derives from a lack of confidence in ordinary citizens. Further, a relatively greater lack of confidence in ordinary citizens among younger women may itself derive, at least in part, from the greater social constraints that society places on women and the fact that women face obstacles to social, personal and professional advancement beyond those faced by men. The likely explanatory power of considerations associated with the position of women in society, real or at least perceived, is also suggested by the greater likelihood of younger women to believe that a woman can be prime minister of a Muslim country.

To the extent that these interpretations of the data are correct, the conclusion to be drawn is that, in spite of the country's image as the "standard-bearer for the emancipated women in the Arab-Muslim world" (Tchaïcha and Arfaoui 2012, p. 16), and also in spite of the fact the participation of women is one of the notable features of the Jasmine Revolution (Austin 2011), there are some unsettled issues with regard to the opportunities available to women and these issues almost certainly play a role in fostering disaffection among the cohort of Tunisian women now entering adulthood. On the one hand, gains notwithstanding, women are seriously underrepresented in political affairs. On the other, Ennahda's post-Arab spring electoral victory and the subsequent push by Salafis for more restrictive laws and policies have probably led women to worry that new limitations might be placed on their rights and freedoms. Given the timing of the Arab Barometer survey in Tunisia, in fall 2011, these latter developments may be particularly important in helping to explain the sex-linked differences among young Tunisians.

The remaining sex-linked difference in the 18–24 age cohort is the relative lack of religiosity among men. Religiosity, as measured by frequency of reading the Quran or other religious books, is low among both younger men and younger women compared to their older countrymen. But it is much lower, to a degree that is dramatic and more than just large enough to be statistically significant, among younger men. Interestingly, a more recent survey in Tunisia found very similar results with respect to lower levels of religiosity among younger Tunisians in general and younger Tunisian men in particular (Ghanmi 2012).

One explanation for this, although not one that is entirely persuasive, is to be found in modernization theory, which posits that younger generations will be less religious compared to their older counterparts and that men are more likely than women to be exposed to the agents of modernization. Given the extent of education in Tunisia, however, and also the absence of sex-linked differences in attitudes toward the importance of education for women, it seems doubtful that a differential experience with modernization accounts for more than a modest amount of the observed sex-linked variation. More plausible is the likelihood that the greater disaffection among younger men results from the absence of meaning-ful job opportunities. Linking this to a lower level of religiosity requires a causal story that is not self-evident, but one possibility is the somewhat counter-intuitive but nonetheless empirically supported proposition that, in the present-day Tunisian context, blocked aspirations produce movement away from, rather than toward, an attachment to religion.

Algeria differs from Tunisia in numerous respects: history, economy, political system and demographic character. Its experience with the events and conse-quences of the Arab Spring are also very different from those of Tunisia. But there are a few notable similarities as well, particularly widespread unemployment and underemployment and a mass elite gap, fueled to a considerable extent by favoritism and corruption, that come together to foster discontent among the public in general and among young people in particular. It is almost certainly for this reason, at least in part and as in Tunisia, that Algerian men in the 18–24 age cohort are less interested in politics than are their older male countrymen. Even though they are not also lower in political and interpersonal trust, as are their Tunisian counterparts, this suggests a measure of political disaffection. A level of support for democracy that is lower than that of older Algerian men suggests this as well. Algeria held a number of elections during the last decade, but these were not always fair and free, and even to the extent that some were better they had no perceptible impact on the performance of the political system. Democracy, in other words, has done little to inspire confidence in Algeria, and the doubts about democracy resulting from this experience are disproportionately likely to be held by younger Algerian men.

The disaffection of Algerian men now reaching adulthood is neither as broad nor as deep as that which the data suggest characterizes young Tunisian men. They are not alienated from others or from religion, at least no more alienated than are older Algerian men, but they do, presumably for the reasons suggested above, have less concern for political affairs and less confidence that democracy is the best political system. Associated with this outlook is a somewhat greater tendency to favor a political system in which Islam plays a political role, at least in part, presum-ably, because Islamist political movements have often been more attentive to the welfare of ordinary citizens than has the government (Charrad 1997). While the

difference between younger and older Algerian men is only statistically significant at the 0.10 level, and while these younger Algerian men do not appear to be
broadly alienated, in contrast to those in Tunisia, the Algerian experience has led
younger men to hold views about democracy and political Islam that differ from
those held by older Algerian men. The significance of this finding should not be
over-emphasized. Support for democracy remains high in absolute terms and support for political Islam remains low in absolute terms among men in the 18–24 age
cohort. Nevertheless, there is a measurable and potentially consequential difference
in the way that younger and older Algerian men think about how their country
should be governed.

While *political* attitudes distinguish the men of the youngest age cohort in Algeria, *social and religious* orientations set the women in this cohort apart from their
older female countrymen. Younger Algerian women are disproportionately likely
to espouse more progressive views on gender equality and to support less conservative interpretations of Islam than their elders, as measured, in the latter case, by
agreement with an interpretation of Islam that does not require a woman to cover
herself. Unlike their male peers, they also differ from older women in their religiosity, being less likely to read the Quran on a daily basis. Thus, in relative terms,
the cohort of Algerian women now reaching adulthood is socially progressive and
secular in orientation. These young women are not more critical of democracy
and they are not more likely to favor a political role for Islam, even though they
are confronted by the same unfavorable political and economic circumstances as
younger men. One reason for this may be, as reported in one study, that most Algerian women "have not had the opportunity to enter the work force and become
contributing members of society" (Sinha 2012, p. 154), and they are thus less sensitive to and less concerned about broader issues of political economy. As a result,
what sets younger Algerian women apart from older Algerian women is not a
preoccupation with the way their country is governed but rather with their status
and opportunities as women.

This interpretation of the data, if correct, may also help to explain the lower
level of interpersonal trust among women in the 18–24 age cohort. Interpersonal
trust is low among all sectors of Algerian society, remarkably low, in fact, and this
undoubtedly reflects the uncertainty and violence that has marked recent Algerian
history. But it is lowest of all among younger women, being nearly universal, and
so something additional is undoubtedly operating in this instance as well. The best
guess, analogous to what appeared to be the case in Tunisia, is that women who
are more progressive and more concerned about their status and opportunities as
women will, quite logically, be more concerned about the social constraints that
a conservative society places on women and for this reason be less trusting of the
ordinary citizens that make up the mainstream of that society.

Sex-linked differences within the 18–24 age cohort in Algeria reflect the dissimilar ways that younger men and younger women are distinguished, respectively, from their older countrymen of the same sex. Younger men have more

distinguishing political orientations and it appears that material considerations are prominent among the factors shaping their views. Younger women, by contrast, are distinguished by their social and cultural orientations, which appear to be influenced by considerations of personal status, particularly those pertaining to women. Accordingly, among Algerians in the 18–24 age group, women are much more likely than men to support gender equality and to agree with less restrictive interpretations of Islam. More specifically, they are more likely to believe that a woman can be the leader of a Muslim country, to reject the proposition that education is more important for a boy than a girl, and reject the proposition that Islam requires inferior rights for non-Muslims. It is also the case that younger women are significantly lower in interpersonal trust, and not only than older Algerian women but also than men of their own generation. One reason for this, consistent with the proposition offered above, may be that persons with more progressive social and cultural orientations will feel less comfortable and secure, and hence less trusting of others, in an essentially conservative society.

Time-specific age cohort studies are forced to leave unanswered the question of whether any distinctive attitudes and values held by a generation of persons entering adulthood will in significant measure persist during the years ahead or whether, alternatively, through a combination of maturation and new experience, they will change in the future and reduce the degree to which the cohort is distinctive. Nevertheless, for the present, regardless of whether or not cohort differences persist, Maghrebi men and women coming of age during the first and second decades of the current century do differ from their older countrymen in some ways that are thought-provoking and appear to be significant. In highlighting these differences and offering informed speculation about their origins, the present study seeks to encourage reflection and further inquiry into the factors shaping political and social orientations and, equally important, into the implications for Tunisia and Algeria as these young men and women become an increasingly important part of the adult population of their respective countries.

Notes

1. The authors acknowledge with thanks the valuable bibliographic assistance of Nora Sandvik Ling and Hanaa Ziad.
2. Unless otherwise indicated, these and all subsequent reported differences are statistically significant at the 0.05 level or lower.
3. "Young Arabs Who Can't Wait to Throw off Shackles of Tradition," *The Guardian*, 14 February 2011.

References

Almond, Gabriel and Sidney Verba. 1963. *The Civic Culture*. Princeton: Princeton University Press.
———. 1980. *The Civic Culture Revisited*. Boston: Little and Brown.

Archer, Brad. 2007. "Family Law Reform and the Feminist Debate: Actually-Existing Islamic Feminism in the Maghreb and Malaysia." *Journal of International Women's Studies* 8(4): 49–59.

Austin, Leila. 2011. "The Politics of the Youth Bulge: From Islamic Activism to Democratic Reform in the Middle East and North Africa." *SAIS Review* 31(2): 81–96.

Bellin, Eva. 2012. "Reconsidering the Robustness of Authoritarianism in the Middle East." *Comparative Politics* 44(2): 127–149.

Bourgi, Albert. 1989. "Etudiants: où Mènera la Désespoir." *Jeune Afrique* 1519, February: 38–42.

Campante, Filipe R. and Devin Chor. 2012. "Why Was the Arab World Poised for Revolution? Schooling, Economic Opportunities, and the Arab Spring." *Journal of Economic Perspectives* 26(2): 167–188.

Charrad, Mounira.M. 1997. "Policy Shifts: State, Islam, and Gender in Tunisia, 1930s–1990s." *Social Politics* 4(2): 284–319.

Donno, Daniela and Bruce Russett. 2008. "Islam, Authoritarianism, and Female Empowerment: What Are the Linkages?" *World Politics* 56(4): 582–607.

Fish, M. Steven. 2002. "Islam and Authoritarianism." *World Politics* 55(1): 4–37.

Ghanmi, Monia. 2012. "Religiosity on the Rise in Post-Revolution Tunisia." *Magharebia*, August 3.

Hardin, Russell. 1996. "Trustworthiness." *Ethics* 107: 26–42.

Ibrahim, Youssef. 1991. "In Algiers, Curfew and Threats of Worse." *The New York Times*, June 7.

Inglehart, Ronald. 2003. "How Solid Is Support for Democracy and How Can We Measure It?" *PS: Political Science & Politics* 36: 51–57.

Inglehart, Ronald and Pippa Norris. 2003. "The True Clash of Civilizations." *Foreign Policy* 135 (March–April): 62–70.

Mattson, James. 1971. "Development in the Arab World." In Mark Tessler, ed., *A New Look at the Middle East*. Milwaukee: University of Wisconsin–Milwaukee.

Putnam, Robert. 1992. *Making Democracy Work: Civic Traditions in Modern Italy*. Princeton: Princeton University Press.

Robbins, Michael D.H. and Mark Tessler. 2012. "The Effect of Elections on Public Opinion Toward Democracy: Evidence from Longitudinal Survey Research in Algeria." *Comparative Political Studies* 45(10): 1255–1276.

Sinha, Sangeeta. 2012. "Arab Spring: Women's Empowerment in Algeria." *Journal of International Women's Studies* 13(5): 144–159.

Suleiman, Michael W. 1987. "Attitudes, Values and Political Progress in Morocco." In I. William Zartman and Mark Habeeb, eds., *State and Society in Contemporary North Africa*. New York: Praeger.

Tchaïcha, Jane D. and Khedija Arfaoui. 2012. "Tunisian Women in the Twenty-First Century: Past Achievements and Present Uncertainties in the Wake of the Jasmine Revolution." *The Journal of North African Studies* 17(2): 215–238.

Tessler, Mark. 1976. "Political Generations." In Russell Stone and John Simmons, eds., *Change in Tunisia: Essays in the Social Sciences*. Albany: State University of New York Press, 1976.

———. 2010. "Religion, Religiosity and the Place of Islam in Political Life: Insights from the Arab Barometer Surveys." *Middles East Law and Governance* 2(2): 221–252.

Tessler, Mark, Carrie Konold, and Megan Reif. 2004. "Political Generations in Developing Countries: Evidence and Insights from Algeria." *Public Opinion Quarterly* 68 (2): 184–216.

Appendix. Maghrebi youth in the wake of the Arab Spring

**DISTRIBUTION OF RESPONDENTS ACROSS
CATEGORIES OF AGE AND SEX**

Tunisia	*18–24*	*25–34*	*35+*	*TOTAL*
Men	109	135	358	602
Women	119	149	326	594
TOTAL	228	284	684	1196

Algeria	*18–24*	*25–34*	*35+*	*TOTAL*
Men	133	166	305	604
Women	125	170	317	612
TOTAL	258	336	622	1216

3

CIVIL-MILITARY RELATIONS IN ALGERIA AND EGYPT

A comparative analysis

Miloud Chennoufi

More than in any other country in North Africa, the military has played a leading political role in Algeria. Civil-military relations are essential to an understanding of the political evolution of Algeria and should not be considered in isolation of the broader historical context, since independence in 1962. At no time have Algerian officers assumed political power as military personnel. They have either allied themselves with civilian figures, or swapped uniforms for civilian clothes at the very moment they entered political office. The political history of independent Algeria is one of a balancing act of solidarity and competition among three centers of power: the presidency, military command and intelligence services. At no point, however, has the competition among these centers of power resulted in one undermining the others; they share an organic solidarity vis-à-vis the political class and civil society. But this solidarity does not mean systematic consensus, hence the perpetual balancing act that, according to circumstances, marginalizes a particular center. Thus both stability as well as deadlocks in contemporary Algeria stem precisely from this dynamic.

The lack of democratic legitimacy casts doubts on the durability of the entire system overall. To predict its imminent end, however, is a fool's errand, one that prudence does not allow. The Arab Spring, by contagion, could have precipitated a radical change in Algeria, but did not. Indeed, since 2011 the Arab Spring highlighted an additional source of political deadlock in the Arab world already experienced in Algeria in the 1990s, one not the responsibility of impugned regimes, that is, the pre-existing strong ideological polarization between Islamists and secularists. It is precisely this polarization that rehabilitated the Algerian three centers of power. At the dawn of the Arab Spring, some believed that the tragic prior experience of Algeria would force political actors in the Arab world to combine an ethics of conviction with an ethics of responsibility.[1] In effect, religious and secular values would be addressed in various reform efforts by taking into account probable consequences, such that systematic exclusion and concomitant ideological polarization would be abandoned in favor of the kind of dialogue necessary to build stable institutions. Political, military and constitutional deadlocks in Arab Spring countries stem from the fact that this promise failed to be kept. And now it is these obstacles, not the optimistic promises of change, which delineate the horizon of the Arab Spring. For this reason, the Arab Spring can hardly represent a promising alternative for an Algerian population already battered by their own recent conflict.[2]

A critical reflection on civil-military relations in Algeria must therefore be accompanied by a reflection on the foundational conditions of pluralistic political practice. This reflection is not needed in Algeria alone; it is needed in the Arab world as a whole. A comparative approach is therefore essential. This chapter is an attempt to provide a comparative analysis of civil-military relations in Algeria and Egypt. Implicitly, analysis will serve as a touchstone for a foundational reflection on the broader political practice in the Arab world. The aim is to show that reform of civil-military relations – in the sense of the primacy of civilian authorities over the military – is a necessary but not sufficient condition for democratization. It is imperative that this reform effort includes a deeper reform of the vision that the current political protagonists have of their own political practices.

The choice of Egypt as a comparator is not accidental. Both the Algerian and the Egyptian militaries as we know them today were born in the struggle against foreign domination. The National People's Army, the official name of the Algerian military, was established in 1963, and is neither more nor less than the institutionalization of the National Liberation Army (ALN)[3] who fought against French occupation during the war of independence (1954–62). The modern Egyptian military is the result of a long struggle on the part of Egyptian officers to transform the military from a praetorian guard dominated by a body of foreign officers in the service of a monarchy subservient to British interests, to a military whose first objective was to put an end to this domination.

Yet in Algeria and Egypt, the state relied on the power of the military to implement an ambitious modernization strategy. The failure of this strategy had a positive structural effect on civil-military relations, for example, political positions were civilianized within the state apparatus and processes of professionalization took place inside the military. The same failure also led to a greater openness to political opposition and civil society, but with no serious effort to engage in a genuine democratization process. Pluralism was tolerated in an overall undemocratic framework. Still, in both countries, the military remained the ultimate decision-maker. In fact, it is because the Egyptian military decided that President Hosni Mubarak must depart office that his regime ultimately collapsed. Also, the opponents of the Muslim Brotherhood would have never toppled president Mohamed Morsi without the military's decisive action during the summer of 2013. Similarly, the considerable power available to current president Abdelaziz Bouteflika in Algeria is dependent on a permanent transactional relationship with the military command and the intelligence services.

Finally, and most fundamentally, both countries face a common present reality: military reform, understood as subordination of the military to civilian authorities, is unavoidable in any future democratization process, often obscuring a deeper problem, that of ideological polarization in the civilian political field.

A genealogical examination of the political dynamics in Algeria and Egypt, through an analysis of historical political practices, will illustrate the existence of three binary oppositions that in turn illuminate the current state of political deadlock in both countries. As well, a normative perspective is offered for how to overcome these deadlocks. These binary oppositions are: an ethic of conviction versus an ethic of responsibility; foundational violence versus regulatory violence;[4] and political dynamics of exclusion versus inclusion.

This study does not extend to other countries in North Africa. Specifically, the histories of civil-military relations in Libya, Tunisia and Morocco are not ideal foundations upon which to reflect on the current state of their affairs. Qaddafi might have been a military officer, for example, but his regime was not empowered primarily by a strong military institution. The Ben Ali regime in Tunisia relied more on the police force than it did on the military. As for Morocco, the monarchy has always dominated the armed forces; it therefore had to find support elsewhere to establish its authority.

The task-achieving strategy and the limits of authoritarianism

The three centers of power structure described earlier (the presidency, the military command and the intelligence services) have characterized the Algerian political system since independence. As the country was gaining independence, Houari Boumediene, head of the military command, was able to marginalize the civilian Provisional Government and the civilian leaders of the war of independence. He could not, however, seize power as a military man because he was little known outside military and political circles, and therefore had no other claim to legitimacy other than through force. The alliance he formed with Ahmad Ben Bella, a civilian and well known leader, served as a temporary solution to the problem of revolutionary legitimacy. Ben Bella was deeply convinced that being a charismatic leader benefiting from the support of a single party (the National Liberation Front – FLN[5]) would be enough to generate a successful modernization strategy. However, he was unable to grasp the danger associated with sharing power with a highly politicized military command in a context where military coups were still common in the Arab world.

More fundamentally, he did not understand that through the liquidation of pluralism and the persecution of his former civilian revolutionary companions, he was perpetuating a cycle started during the liberation war in which civilians sought the support of the military against other civilians, and in so doing empowered the military in the belief that political power must belong to them. Ben Bella had no way to avoid being the victim of the logic behind this cycle: he was removed from power in a military coup led by Houari Boumediene in June 1965, and then spent the following 15 years in prison. His allies in the National Liberation Front were powerless against the deployment of military force. Moreover, Houari Boumediene had also secured the support of the intelligence services in charge of surveillance and internal security.

Ben Bella referred to the founding violence of the war of independence in order to legitimize his own resort to political violence, liquidation of pluralism and brutal exclusion of political opposition. The basis for the order he helped create could not transform the founding violence into a more benign regulatory violence through the creation of the legitimate institutions of a modern state. The use of political violence by the military command, with Ben Bella's support, against other civilian revolutionary forces remained a common practice until the day he fell himself as one of its victims. In short, the 1963 constitution could not save him. Article 8 provided that the military would participate in the political, economic and social situation through the party structures. Hence, this constitutionally blurred boundary between the political and the military, a legacy of the war of independence that played in favor of Ben Bella at an earlier point, was maintained. But in the same constitution, article 23 gave the president and the FLN broad powers.[6] This would have been enough to prevent the coup if only two additional conditions were met: the non-politicization of the military command and the presence of an institutional vehicle for regulatory violence. Yet it is precisely the absence of these conditions that allowed Ben Bella to become president with the help from the military command in the first place. The conditions for his success also allowed for his subsequent removal, both at the behest of the military.

The three centers of the power structure were maintained under a different configuration during the presidency of Boumediene (1965–78). The apparent balance in the previous period gave way to a structure centered around the presidency, or more precisely around the figure of Boumediene.[7] As a charismatic, ambitious and austere leader, Boumediene was probably the most complex personality to preside over Algeria. He was also the only president to successfully impose an unquestionable authority on both the military command and the intelligence services. But because the rejection of pluralism and political exclusion were consolidated after the 1965 coup, to the point that the FLN was itself marginalized,[8] Boumediene had no other alternative but to rely on the military and the intelligence services.

Unlike Ben Bella and because he was a politicized officer, Boumediene understood that the stability of his regime required the marginalization of other politicized officers. Professionalizing the military command was clearly a necessity. Less politicized, but with a sense of *raison d'état*, leaders of the intelligence services showed a deep loyalty and admiration for Boumediene. They were in charge of the repression; the political assassinations they committed during the 1960s and 1970s served as a warning to all those who doubted the eagerness of Boumediene to use political violence in order to maintain his regime.

At this time, Boumediene did not want to dominate the presidency for the sake of political power alone. Boumediene's ethics of conviction were centered on an ambitious project of socio-economic modernization. The reigning calculation was that the lack of political freedom and the exclusion of any opposition could be a problem for some segments of the elite, but in the end industrialization, the spread of education and the fight against poverty through a proactive strategy of socialist inspiration could secure popular legitimacy. Therefore an ambitious task-achieving agenda was the main source of legitimacy for the system. Nobody can say exactly which direction Algeria would have taken if Boumediene did not pass away prematurely. However, the events that followed his death show that as his task-achieving agenda had not yet reached a point of no return, and because the system was based on force, the entire system depended on the personality of Boumediene himself. Thus his death meant the disappearance of the entire project.

The project was furthermore weakened by the fact that faith in a socialist option was not widely shared within the system.[9] This is also why the actual interface between the regime and the population was not the party but the intelligence services. By their nature and because their mission was not limited to intelligence and counterintelligence, they were acting through control and repression.[10] All of this was a necessary evil according to Boumediene's ethics of conviction; the nobility of purpose authorized such excess. But the indefinite suspension of institution building and the absence of the rule of law, along with the reference to founding violence, resulted in both symbolic and physical violence as the system's actual regulatory mode. It is therefore not surprising that, at Boumediene's death, the most stable institutions were the military and intelligence services.

The dynamics of the system were maintained in the early 1980s under a new president, a soldier who, for the occasion, left his military command post. The choice made to appoint Chadli Benjedid as president was a victory for those who, within the system, did not share Boumediene's ideological predilections. Chadli lacked his predecessor's charisma and ambitions; he was perceived by the military command and the secret services as malleable enough to maintain the power structure while gradually allowing the country to drift away from the previous collectivist economic options. But as it is always the case, the presidency empowers the president. In the Algerian case, such empowerment helps the president turn the dynamics of balancing and competition in his favor. Chadli was probably convinced of the need for a gradual liberalization of the economy and a rapprochement with the United States, abandoning the Boumediene years of economic voluntarism and Third-Worldism. This alone probably increased his chances of being selected as the new president. But once president, he refused to be confined to an executive role and managed to establish himself as the center of the system.

Boumediene controlled the military command and used the intelligence services as an interface with the public. The strong presence of the latter inside the machinery of government and in all sectors gave them disproportionate power. This is why Chadli joined forces with the military command to fundamentally restructure the intelligence services. The loyalty of his military command was secured by patronage and the distribution of economic benefits given to senior officers who, even when they had not demonstrated absolute submission, agreed nevertheless to keep silent in a comfortable life of retirement.

Resorting to repression remained systematic, but the past radical rejection of dissent was slightly abandoned. Therefore fear was no longer enough to secure the loyalty of the state bureaucracy, leading the way to corruption becoming the system's overall regulatory mode. The replacement of the task-achieving strategy with a resource-based economy without any clear strategic vision, led to a crisis of political legitimacy, not only in the eyes of the elite, but most importantly in those of ordinary citizens as well. Exclusion was deeply felt by opposition groups; they were reduced to exile or forced to go underground. The system was more self-centered than ever, concerned only with its own self-preservation, using either means of repression or corruption, or even the manipulation of religious and cultural symbols. A sort of instinctive Machiavellianism generated a broad gap between rulers and ruled. Riots during these years culminated in the popular uprising of 1988 that led to the first attempt – and for the moment the only – of democratic reform and thus a profound change in civil-military relations.

Unlike Algeria, Egypt has experienced a blunt seizure of power by the military who governed by themselves almost without any civil façade until the mid-1960s.[11] President Abdelnasser (the historic leader of the Free Officers) was animated by an ethic of conviction similar to Boumediene's: modernization needed to be undertaken under the aegis of the military given its institutional competence, discipline and operational efficiency. At the time, this belief was widely held, not only in military circles, but also in some political circles and in academia.[12] The unfortunate corollary was that all conventional political parties were excluded and repressed. This was the case for liberal nationalists, communists and the Muslim Brotherhood. Moreover, in the name of social justice, modernization resulted in the adoption of a socialist collectivist economy. The nationalization of private economic interests and land reform translated into further exclusion and in some cases the persecution of the bourgeoisie that had formed before the 1952 revolution.

However, this strategy was not entirely implemented against the popular will.[13] The new military leaders-turned-statesmen were credited with putting an end to a corrupt monarchical system and, more importantly, with having liberated the country from foreign domination. The charisma of President Abdelnasser, triumphant after the Suez crisis in 1956, and his support for decolonization, are all factors that added to the popularity of the regime. Civilians were confined in the role of popular mobilization around a single party (the Arab Socialist Union) and technocratic responsibilities, primarily in the economy and in public administration.

But when the legitimacy of a regime is based on charisma, ideology and task achievement, the expectations are inevitably excessive and cannot be easily met. The Egyptian experience had definitely put a temporary end to the deep social injustices inherent in the previous monarchy. Considerable progress had been made in education, particularly at the post-secondary level. But the enthusiasm thus created later turned into skepticism and cynicism, when a major event, the defeat in the war against Israel in 1967, exposed the weaknesses of the system and related political and policy choices.

President Anwar Sadat, Abdelnasser's successor in 1970, was also a politicized officer. But in his dealing with the military command, he soon succeeded where his predecessor had failed. Abdelnasser was unsuccessful in confronting officers in the General Staff who denied him genuine authority over the military. He managed to contain their animosity by allowing them to enjoy wide economic privileges and ignoring the systematic clientelism orchestrated by the military utilizing state machinery.[14] Sadat was able to impose his authority on the military without much difficulty by posing as a neutral arbiter in the dispute between the officers who wanted change and those who wanted to remain faithful to Abdelnasser. Once his authority was established, he made the choice to deeply professionalize the military.

Professionalizing the military had two specific strategic objectives. First, the concrete goal was to take back occupied Sinai from Israel. This was achieved thanks to the military offensive undertaken in 1973. For a time, the legitimacy of the entire system was based on this singular achievement. The other objective was to limit the influence of the military. The intention was not to engage the country in a process of democratization since Sadat sought to build the state as a reservoir for his own personal power. The goal was not simply a depoliticized military, but to guarantee military loyalty to the president as a person, not as the head of state. This was an ambiguity, if not an outright contradiction, but one that both Sadat and his successor Hosni Mubarak aimed to sustain. This was even more critical for Sadat given that he committed himself on two controversial issues: a radical economic liberalization and negotiations with Israel. These two issues were at the heart of his ethics of conviction.

But because this ethic of conviction guided his actions in the context of a political system centered on his personal power, political exclusion was impossible to avoid. Certainly, Sadat allowed the return of formerly banned and persecuted movements, but these movements had no chance of gaining power because elections were routinely rigged. Toleration of Islamists and liberals was also a way to counterbalance surviving Nasserites. But persecution never failed to happen when it was required for the preservation of the system. Sadat did not hesitate to order military repression of rioters revolting in 1977 against the social consequences of economic liberalization, or the imprisonment of hundreds of opposition figures, Islamists, liberals and Nasserites, who challenged the rapprochement with Israel in the late 1970s. The exclusion had one further consequence. The weak legitimacy of personal power required corruption as a vehicle to mobilize loyalty. Even greater than previously, endemic corruption morphed under Sadat into the system's regulatory mode, its *modus operandi*.

From reform to revolution

President Mubarak inherited Sadat's legacy, but the system of corruption and loyalty was perfected, with even more sophisticated means of repression. Given Mubarak's military background, it would be easy to conclude that the Egyptian military never ceased to be the decision-maker in the last instance. However, while his military background undoubtedly allowed Mubarak to obtain support from the military, his accession to the presidency owed much more to his role as vice-president under Sadat. His dual capacity, as civil and military leader, was an indication that the weight of the military remained important, though not absolute or unchallenged. For thirty years, Mubarak actually sought to *limit* the influence of the military to maintain his personal power. At the same time, he knew that the military was his option of last resort. The fact that the political fate of Mubarak was sealed by the military command who refused to fire on demonstrators during the January 2011 revolution cannot be explained solely as the military opting for democracy. It was also the product of a civil-military balancing act that had developed during the three decades of President Mubarak's presidency.

This balancing act unfolded in different ways over the years. First came professionalization: timidly begun during the last years of Abdelnasser and deepened by Sadat, the process solidified under Mubarak. It resulted in the modernization of military equipment, training and the system of promotion – eventually to the point where the military only held ministerial positions in security-related portfolios in government.[15] In the 1980s, former senior officers were given an opportunity to join the Egyptian state bureaucracy and run state-owned enterprises.[16] Moreover, as reported by Imad Harb, a law adopted in 1979 enabled the military to create and operate enterprises without any state control. Their products ranged from military equipment (for example, armored vehicles, tanks, helicopters and planes) – destined mainly for export – to civilian infrastructure and industrial or agricultural products. The Egyptian defense industry employed 100,000 people and contributed around $500 million per year to the gross domestic product.[17] Finally, the development of defense and security policy remained strictly the responsibility of the military – yet remained circumscribed by Sadat's choice to opt for an alliance and intense military cooperation with the United States. Mubarak was acutely aware that military aid from the United States left the Egyptian military command with limited scope for political action. He was eventually proven wrong during the Arab Spring. Nevertheless, his alliance with the United States was necessary to hold both the presidency and to continue exercising personal power.

In addition to US aid, Mubarak's authority was based on an approach to system regulation that combined repression, corruption and the depoliticization of political positions in favor of technocrats. Political repression was not entrusted to the military; rather the entire repressive apparatus was under the auspices of the Ministry of the Interior and the intelligence services. Mubarak understood that the safest way to keep the military under control was to *not* let it play the role of a political referee. The depoliticization of political positions was made possible by the employment of technocrats who were in turn appointed ministers or senior bureaucrats. Technocrats did not represent a political threat because of their lack of a political base. Finally, corruption escalated to extravagant proportions, becoming an integral part of the daily life of the Egyptian population. But it was corruption at the highest level that resulted in predatory behavior in the largest and most lucrative economic projects (such as resorts, privatization and in real estate development) and that in turn created a social class whose extraordinary prosperity depended on its unconditional loyalty to Mubarak's personal power.[18] This social class constituted the main source of support for Gamal, Mubarak's son, who was being groomed to inherit the presidency.[19]

Such a system could not have any other ethics of conviction than self-preservation, which did not leave room for any kind of strategic vision, and further reduced politics to the balancing practices described above. The ensuing system generated large-scale, systematic exclusion that carried on for at least two reasons. First, Mubarak managed to convince the opposition that his political power was limited by the influence of the military; he was also able to instil fear of a military-imposed repressive regime by making the opposition believe that, should he proceed to allow for more political freedom, he would not be able to contain the anger of the military command nor prevent it from taking radical action.[20] Second, Mubarak took advantage of the ongoing ideological polarization of the political scene. He presented his regime as the *only* actor animated by an ethic of responsibility – in comparison with a probable and predicted theocracy should a process of democratization be unleashed. The assassination of President Sadat by an Islamist commando in 1981, the wave of terrorist attacks against foreign tourists and Egyptian Intellectuals in the 1990s, the so-called Algerian "problem"[21] and the events of September 11 all combined to provide evidence to support his point of view. But this point of view did not make any distinction between or among the different factions of the Islamist movement, that is, those who advocated and practiced armed violence and those who rejected it. This lack of nuance and analytical precision, which effectively functioned to exclude Islamists, was supported by one side of the liberal opposition that promoted an ethics of conviction centered on a Jacobin conception of secularism. But the other side of the liberal camp, while sharing the concern for secularism, did not buy into this simplistic equation and refused to give the Mubarak regime the status of responsible savior. This opposition group was also repressed, and under the approving eyes of some Islamists, whose implicit support to Mubarak's regime on this issue can be explained by their ethics of conviction centered on a theological conception of the state which sees any form of secularism as heresy. In sum, the processes of exclusion practiced by the Mubarak regime were fed by the exclusions inherent to his opponents' ethics of conviction.

From aborted reforms to status quo management

In October 1988, for the first time in the history of independent Algeria, the Algerian military was deployed in the streets to deal with rioters. Deaths were recorded. The rioters, mainly young people, attacked the symbolic representations of the ruling party frustrated by corruption and economic deadlock. The FLN had never been anything but a bureaucratic apparatus whose mission, albeit with mixed success, was to be a mass organization. Yet it is against the FLN, not against the military nor the intelligence services, that the rioters focused their energy. Their elders had a clearer idea of the oversight role played by the intelligence services, but again, they were seen as a tool in the hands of the power embodied by the FLN. It is because the population did not have a clear idea of the three power center structure of the tripartite regime, that president Chadli could aspire to lead the democratic transition with the support of the military and the intelligence services. Chadli, who had secured the support of these two actors over the years, consolidated his position by playing the dynamics of competition and balance, by effectively agreeing to become the front of the system and assume responsibility for both past failures (including repression during the riots) and promises of democratization. Had democracy succeeded, civil-military relations in Algeria would have experienced a concomitant reform, in which case the military would not have had any other choice but to accept being subordinate to democratically elected civilian authorities.

The logic of the president was to find a new source of legitimacy for the regime once the previous task-achieving strategy had been deliberately abandoned. Moreover, the military command and intelligence services were not against this development. They were therefore in favor of a liberal economy and had no choice but to accept some degree of political liberalization in return. Fundamentally, neither the military command nor the intelligence services were willing to take power directly. They felt it was more convenient to leave the field of political initiative to the president.

Following the adoption of a new constitution in 1989, the military was no longer represented in the Central Committee of the FLN. Article 24 referred to the military only in relation to its defense prerogatives, without any reference to other responsibilities, whether political, economic or social. However, Article 162 stipulated the existence of a High Security Council, in which the Minister of Defence participated.[22] The general feeling was that the military had returned to barracks. That being said, as soon as a multiparty political system emerged, the opposition started to denounce the political police and call for its dissolution. The target was, in fact, the intelligence services, now called the Department of Intelligence and Security, which, unlike the military, had not retreated, but maintained the same level of influence.

The years of democratic reform, from March 1989 to January 1992, revealed the existence of a deep ideological polarization between the three currents of the opposition. First, the Islamists, particularly the radicals, mobilized around an ethics of conviction centered on the establishment of a theocracy whose openly-stated goal was to put an end to democracy. Second, a group of left-wing and anti-Islamist liberal parties, whose ethics of conviction revolved around the establishment of a republican regime inspired by French Jacobinism. By definition, their approach excluded religious political movements even when they were committed to democracy and pluralism. Third, another group of anti-Islamist parties downplayed the risk of religious extremism and focused on the necessary liquidation of the old system.

For their part, civilian members of the system, who gravitated around the presidency, were hoping that the opposition's strong polarization would help them be perceived as a safe alternative by a population alarmed by the intransigence of these three currents. But they were underestimating the strength of people's opposition to the system; they were also forgetting that political polarization had ended up dividing the population against itself. The ethics of conviction in the political field was mirrored by a strong dogmatism and systematic rejection of the "Other" in the Algerian population. It is under these conditions that the first multiparty elections took place in Algeria in 1991: conditions that hid a dangerous paradox. The elections were not seen as a step towards democratic reform, but as a means to change the regime according to the exclusivist convictions of each of the various groups. A spirit of subversion and revenge overtook the spirit of reform. Not surprisingly, the outcome of the elections was the overwhelming victory of the radical Islamists. A deep political crisis ensued, so deep that it ended up breaking the balance of the tripartite system, which until then had remained favorable to the president.

President Chadli thought he would be able to force radical Islamists to uphold the constitution – and he was wishing to collaborate with them. But no more than in previous years were the Islamists willing to adopt a discourse of reconciliation. Their attitude was defiant and they categorically rejected the constitution that the president wanted to impose upon them. The intent of the president was to proceed with some form of cohabitation. For their part, the radical Islamists, in their desire to establish a theocracy, overlooked the fact that a democratic transition could alter Algerian power's tripartite structure only by remaining faithful to the spirit of gradual reform. Moreover, the military and intelligence services' commitment were willing to back the process launched by the president on this basis. But the prospect of a theocracy followed a totally different logic that could only result in the destruction of the system. Unlike the Arab Spring in Tunisia and Egypt, Islamism in Algeria was not dominated by the Muslim Brotherhood and their moderate approach, but by the Salafists whose rhetoric and violent acts eventually reversed the balance of power in favor of the military. The military forced the president to resign, cancelled the elections and banned the Salafist Islamic Salvation Front party (FIS).[23] This series of decisions made in 1992 transformed the threat of violence from the Salafist groups into a real campaign of terrorism that bloodied Algeria for a decade. This series of events constitutes the famous "Algerian scenario" that the Arab regimes have used as a scarecrow to limit democratic reform.

At the same time, the military were neither prepared nor willing to govern directly. They were not even prepared to fight against terrorism since the processes of professionalization had only prepared them for a conventional war, not for guerrilla warfare. They therefore attempted to produce a new configuration of the old tripartite structure. They had the support of the Jacobin movements which, by ethics of conviction, thought this was an opportunity to liquidate all Islamist movements, including those that had not joined the armed insurgency, and even those that, like the Muslim Brotherhood, had supported the decision to stop the elections.

The political polarization of the democratic transition had thus been transformed into an armed polarization after the cancellation of elections. The founding violence, upon which the Algerian regime had established its legitimacy, had become a fundamental component of political culture over the years, including that of the opposition. The primacy of regime change over reform resulted in the desire to exercise violence not only against the regime, but also against other opposition groups. As a result, exclusion manifested itself in the regime's political practice *and*, after pluralism was established, in the political rhetoric and actions of the opposition as well.

The approach of the armed forces was also paradoxical. They knew that cancelling the elections and ensuing instability would deepen the crisis of legitimacy. This is the reason why they needed a president whose credibility could alleviate this problem. Yet they had a strong desire to limit the power of the presidency in general. In early 1993 they chose Abdelaziz Bouteflika, a former Minister of Foreign Affairs and a close associate of Boumediene. Bouteflika declined the offer and continued to do so until 1999. We now know that, during the years when the presidency was entrusted to the retired general Liamine Zeroual, there was a debate within the regime, but not about the merits of the armed fight against radical Islamism. Rather, the debate focused on whether the fight should be limited to a security dimension or whether it should have a political dimension as well. Zeroual, supported by the intelligence services, was in favor of the latter. The military command held the opposite view. The debate culminated with the resignation of Zeroual. But it was precisely his departure which helped reorient the entire tripartite structure according to the option he had favored. In a vacuum, the military command could no longer deny Bouteflika the power he was claiming. Bouteflika, who shared Zeroual's vision, became president in 1999 with the support of the intelligence services.

So after ten years, the Algerian regime had returned to a tripartite structure; the games of balancing and competition were in favor of the presidency with the support of one of the two centers of power, the intelligence services. Today, civil-military relations are clearly in favor of a civilian president. This consensus is expressed in various ways. For example, military Chief of Staff Mohammed Lamari made an unusual public statement in 2003 that the military would not support any presidential candidate in 2004, signalling that he was no longer involved in the political arena. Indeed, he resigned when Bouteflika got re-elected. The current Chief of Staff, General Salah Gaied, is known for his loyalty to Bouteflika, and to whom he owes his promotion.[24] This is part of a thoroughgoing reform movement, with the military command oriented towards greater professionalization.[25] Bouteflika understands the threat that a highly politicized military command poses.

Should we then conclude that the military is subject to civilian authority and that civil-military relations in Algeria are close to those that exist under a rule of law regime? This is doubtful, given that the intelligence services have yet to be touched by reform. The fact that the general in charge of the Department of Intelligence and Security, Mohammed Mediene, appointed in 1992 by President Chadli, is still in office is particularly telling. Better yet, under Bouteflika, the intelligence services have become autonomous from the military command, which tipped the balance of power in their favor.[26] Some think it is only a matter of time, that reforming the intelligence services is part of Bouteflika's agenda, because he does not want to share power with any other actor.[27] Another explanation is that Boute-flika's alliance with the intelligence services is absolutely critical to his own power base in the tripartite structure that has always characterized civil-military relations in independent Algeria. The system continues to rely on the strong presence of the intelligence services in various fields of activity, from security services to economy, media and universities. It is not at all certain that Bouteflika can impose his authority without the support of the intelligence services.

The Arab Spring, professionalization and democratization

The political choices made by Sadat in the 1970s gradually removed any reference to the founding violence in the narrative of legitimization. The system that President Mubarak had set up and run for the following three decades could not institutional-ize regulatory violence because it lacked democratic legitimacy. This vacuum was then filled by a façade of pluralism controlled by state violence, backed up by a num-ber of agents whose loyalty was obtained through corruption. Strong polarization in the political field was used by the regime to warn against the founding violence that Islamist movements were determined to trigger in case of change. But this system was faced with the issue of succession. The initial intent was to replicate the Syrian model, thus ensuring the transmission of the presidency to President Mubarak's son Gamal, a scenario rejected by the military. But thanks to its alliances – internally with the intelligence services, the security services of the Ministry of the Interior and the economic elites – and externally via unconditional submission to the United States, the Mubarak government managed to contain the influence of the military. Moreover, the military was politically paralyzed by processes of professionalization as well as their strong dependence on American military aid. Besides, the military's eventual return to the political front stage would not have received the consent of the opposition, whose factions also rejected hereditary succession to the presidency.

Only a major and unexpected and significant event could change the balance of power within the system. The Arab Spring represented such an event. The sheer magnitude and peaceful nature of the early Arab Spring demonstrations quickly exposed the limits of what intelligence and security services could do alone. Mubarak's personal power now rested on the military whose political role Mubarak had himself undermined through professionalization. The military chose not to fire on the crowd and Mubarak's regime fell apart.

The Egyptian case shows, firstly, that professionalization alone does not mean democratization. However, if the conditions are ripe for a large, inclusive and peaceful popular protest, it is difficult, if not impossible, to bring a professionalized military to carry out indiscriminate violence against the population. Profession-alization in Egypt, but also in Tunisia, has prevented the military from inheriting the patrimonial character that can be found in Syria, Libya and the Gulf states. It is their non-patrimonial nature that explains why the military sided with protesters in Egypt and Tunisia, but not in Syria, Libya or Bahrain. The crucial difference in these latter cases is that the patrimonial military associates with the political ruler instead of identifying their primary role as the service of the state. The professionalization of the military is an integral part of the institutionalization of the regulative violence, preventing them from exercising violence against the population.[28]

We can now make the following assumption. As long as the Algerian regime will not have to contain a large and peaceful popular protest, civil-military relations will continue to evolve according to one of the tripartite structure configurations that have always been determinative. The contagion of the Arab Spring has not reached Algeria precisely because of the vivid memory of the deadly confrontation of the 1990s. But this does not mean that the system has a broad popular legitimacy – evidenced by significantly lower voter participation (around 25%) in the 2012 parliamentary elections. This rate also reflects a deep cynicism towards political parties unable to mobilize the population through polarized ideological discourse as they did in the 1990s. Yet polarization still exists, premised on continuing regime exclusion, and cynicism is profound. Moreover, the reputation of opposition parties, both secular and Islamist, has been tainted for two reasons: a series of corruption scandals and moral corruption stemming from participation in rigged elections and ensuing governments. This being said, their participation has always remained symbolic at best because the regularity of elections in Algeria is doubtful.

The risk of imminent contagion of the Arab Spring is even lower now that the experience of states such as Egypt demonstrates that the withdrawal of military rule solves *only* the classic problem of civil-military relations (domination of politics by the military), while creating a situation of deadlock for which civilian political parties are solely responsible. The polarization between contrasting ethics of conviction perfectly illustrates this dilemma. The Muslim Brotherhood, however much more moderate than the radicals who came close to grabbing the power in Algeria, has so far shown by its actions, specifically regarding the debate over the Egyptian constitution, that it considers its relatively small majority as a popular mandate to implement an exclusive ideological project. An ethics of responsibility should have brought the Muslim Brotherhood, in the constitutive moment made possible by the revolution of 2011, to act jointly with other political forces to lay the foundations for a common arena of political action to build institutions, immune from political games inherent in diverging ethics of conviction. The Muslim Brotherhood has shown a clear desire to dominate the institutions of the *ancien régime*. Their actions have caused a backlash from the other side, which found in their opposition a source of legitimacy for their own ethics of conviction. This dynamic generates another form of exclusion, expressed by calls for the removal of Muslim Brotherhood's Mohammed Morsi, even though he was democratically elected to the Egyptian presidency. From a normative point of view, the Egyptian blockage does not allow either Algerian political actors or the Algerian population to see the Egyptian scenario as a credible alternative. It is all the more true now that the Egyptian military has toppled President Morsi, banned the Muslim Brotherhood Organization and is dominating the Egyptian state once again.

In the short term, the real challenge for the Algerian political system will be the succession of Bouteflika. As the configuration of the tripartite structure is highly dependent on the personality of Bouteflika himself, his departure may trigger a change, and give rise to all the risks that such instability entails. Because, in the end, the issue is that of stability. It is indeed the need for stability that helped Bouteflika run for president a fourth time in 2014. It should be noted, though, that paradoxically the intelligence services did not approve this nomination, mainly because of the very fragile health of the president. But it was the president who finally triumphed. This triumph can be explained by the fact that even though as a person Bouteflika is not irreplaceable, the center of power he created around his presidency is not easy to replace. It is based on a strategic depth in the heart of civil society through a patronage system which ensures the support of an opportunistic economic elite and power-hungry politicians. This mechanism is made possible thanks to the distribution of oil revenues; it made part of the population dependent on and in some way satisfied with the system. Added to this is the control that the presidency has established on military command so that the struggle of intelligence against Bouteflika's candidacy was a lost battle. Nevertheless, even if the last presidential election helped buy time, it has not resolved the problem of succession. As the opposition – haunted and paralyzed by his eternal polarization – still fails to offer a credible alternative, the eventual disappearance of the president will cause a new crisis. Unless the whole system collapses, plunging the country into a persistent chaos, the crisis will require a reconfiguration of the three centers of power structure.

Conclusion

For a long time it was believed, not without reason, that the influence of the military in Algeria and Egypt prevented democratization of their respective political regimes. The relatively rapid political withdrawal of the Egyptian military during the Arab Spring has effectively enabled the democratic election of the first civilian president in Egypt. The same thing happened in Algeria when the withdrawal of the military led to the first, and so far the only, democratic elections. But these two experiments show that if the withdrawal of the military is a necessary condition, this condition is far from sufficient. This is why the debate on civil-military relations in Algeria and Egypt must happen *within* the context of a broader foundational reflection. This reflection should focus not only on the political practices of the current regimes, but also on that of the opposition parties presenting themselves as credible alternatives. The reason is that political actors, each led by their ethics of conviction, do not consider responsibility for the consequences of their ethics of conviction, namely the practices of violence and exclusion they justify. As long as this situation lasts, the political systems, as well as civil societies in the Arab world, will remain blocked.

Notes

1. The ethics of conviction/ethics of responsibility dyad is drawn from the thought of Max Weber (Weber 1919, p. 83). The ethics of conviction refers to a set of beliefs and values by which the morality of political action is judged. The ethics of responsibility is to bring the morality of political action not only to compliance with one's convictions; it also

means that possible consequences are considered, including negative consequences on political opponents.
2. Other factors (relative political liberty and freedom of speech, the redistribution of oil revenues, etc.) helped mitigate the effect of the Arab Spring on Algeria. See, in this regard, Dris-Aït Hamadouche (2012).
3. Armée de Libération Nationale.
4. The founding violence is that which is the very foundation of the state, one that establishes sovereignty over a territory with the implicit promise to guarantee freedom to citizens. Regulatory violence is the regulating force that the legitimate institutions of the state use in the administration of justice. It should not be confused with arbitrary violence under authoritarian regimes, police brutality, etc. In the words of Jacques Derrida, ". . . there is the distinction between two kinds of violence . . . : the founding violence, the one that institutes and positions law, . . . and the violence that conserves, the one that maintains, confirms, insures the permanence and enforceability of law, *law preserving violence.*" Derrida (1992, p. 79).
5. Front de Libération Nationale.
6. For an analysis of the military's status in the various Algerian constitutions, see Collombier (2012).
7. Quandt (1998, p. 126).
8. Saidaoui (2012, p. 10).
9. Saidaoui (2012, p. 13).
10. "Intelligence services heavily infiltrated areas of economic, social and even cultural activities. Offices for information and monitoring were created within organizations and companies. Security officers holding these offices received wide prerogatives and power. They even sat on university scientific boards." Saidaoui (2012, p. 12).
11. Harb (2003, pp. 278–280).
12. For example, see Pye (1962), Levy (1966), Shils (1962).
13. Beattie (1988, p. 210).
14. Harb (2003, p. 280).
15. Beattie (1988, p. 223).
16. Aclimandos (2012, p. 2).
17. Harb (2003, pp. 285–286).
18. On the high level of corruption during the Mubarak years, see Kandil (2012, pp. 332–380).
19. On Gamal Mubarak's presidential ambitions, see Collombier (2011).
20. Beattie (1988, p. 223).
21. See *infra*.
22. Collombier (2012, p. 3). It is precisely this structure, the High Security Council, that would serve as a cover to stop constitutional elections in 1992. See below.
23. Front Islamique du Salut.
24. Telemçani (2007, pp. 1–2); Mesbah (2011, p. 7).
25. Mesbah (2011, p. 8).
26. Mustapha (2012, p. 6).
27. Mesbah (2011, p. 9).
28. This paragraph is inspired by Bellin (2012) and Lutterbeck (2012).

References

Aclimandos, T. (2012). "The Army and the Constitution in Egypt: The Current State of Affairs." Arab Reform Initiative. ARI Projects, www.arab-reform.net/army-and-constitution-egypt-current-state-affairs.
Beattie, K.J. (1988). "Egypt: Thirty-Five Years of Praetorian Politics." In C.P. Danopoulos (ed.), *Military Disengagement from Politics*. New York: Routledge, pp. 201–230.
Bellin, E. (2012). "Reconsidering the Robustness of Authoritarianism in the Middle East." *Comparative Politics*, vol. 44, no. 1, pp. 127–149.

Collombier, V. (2011) "Gamal Moubarak et le parti national démocratique ou la stratégie du désastre. Comment ceux qui prétendaient préparer la succession présidentielle ont précipité à la chute du régime." *Outre-Terre*, vol. 3, no. 29, pp. 333–345.

Collombier, V. (2012). "The Military and the Constitution: The Cases of Algeria, Pakistan and Turkey." Arab Reform Initiative. ARI Projects, www.arab-reform.net/military-and-constitution-cases-algeria-pakistan-and-turkey. Accessed December 14th, 2012.

Derrida, J. (1992). "Force of Law: The *Mystical Foundation of Authority*." In D. Cornell, M. Rosenfeld, D.G. Carlson (eds.), *Deconstruction and the Possibility of Justice*. New York: Routledge, pp. 3–67.

Dris-Aït Hamadouche, L. (2012). "L'Algérie face au *printemps arabe*: L'équilibre par la neutralisation des contestations." *Confluences Méditerranée*, vol. 2, no. 81, pp. 55–67.

Harb, I. (2003). "The Egyptian Military in Politics: Disengagement or Accommodation?" *Middle East Journal*, vol. 57, no. 2, pp. 269–290.

Kandil, H.K. (2012). *Power Triangle: Military, Security, and Politics in the Shaping of the Egyptian, Iranian, and Turkish Regimes*. PhD Dissertation. University of California-Los Angeles.

Levy, M.J. (1966). *Modernization and the Structure of Societies: A Setting for International Affairs*. Princeton: Princeton University Press.

Lutterbeck, D. (2012). "Arab Uprisings, Armed Forces, and Civil-Military Relations." *Armed Forces and Society* (article published online), 13 April, pp. 1–25. http://afs.sagepub.com/content/early/2012/04/11/0095327X12442768. DOI: 10.1177/0095327X12442768. Accessed December 2, 2012.

Mesbah, M.C. (2011). "L'armée algérienne face au défi de la transition démocratique." *Seminario Internacional sobre Seguridad y Defensa en el Mediterráneo. Fuerzas Armadas y Transiciones Democráticas en el Mediterráneo*. CIDOB y Ministerio de Defensa. Barcelona. June 13th, 2011.

Mustapha, M. (2012). "État, sécurité et réforme, le cas algérien." Arab Reform Initiative. ARI Projects, www.arab-reform.net/sites/default/files/SSR_Alg%C3%A9rie_M.Mustapha_May12_Final_Fr.pdf. Accessed December 14th, 2012.

Pye, L. (1962). "Armies in the Process of Political Modernization." In J. Johnson (ed.), *The Role of the Military in Underdeveloped Countries*. Princeton: Princeton University Press, pp. 69–89.

Quandt, W. (1998). *Between Ballots & Bullets. Algeria's Transition from Authoritarianism*. Washington, DC: Brookings Institution Press.

Saidaoui, R. (2012). "The History of the Algerian Military Secret Services. From Boussouf to Mediene." (Arabic) *A-Hewar*, www.ahewar.org/debat/show.art.asp?aid=300712. Accessed December 14th, 2012.

Shils, E. (1962). *Political Development in the New States*. Gravenhage: Mouton.

Tlemçani, R. (2008). "Bouteflika and Civil-Military Relations: Civil Strife and National Reconciliation." Carnegie Papers, No. 7, February 2008, http://carnegieendowment.org/publications/index.cfm?fa=view&id=19976&zoom_highlight=arabic. Accessed January 25th, 2013.

Weber, M. (1919). "Politics as a Vocation." In D. Owen, T.B. Strong (eds.), *The Vocation Lectures*. Indianapolis: Hackett Publishing Company (2004), pp. 32–94.

4

SECURITY SECTOR REFORMS IN NORTH AFRICA

Eduard Soler i Lecha[1]

Introduction

The Great Arab Awakening of 2011, often referred to as the "Arab Spring", engendered a debate about reform that had previously been unthinkable. Security Sector Reform (SSR) entered the reform agenda, and sensitive issues such as the powers and privileges of the army, the role of police and internal security forces, the functioning of the penitentiary system and the scope of military justice were all to be reconsidered (Tanner and Ould Mohamedou 2012). Before the uprisings, only a few organizations – like the United Nations Development Program (UNDP), the Geneva-based Democratic Control of Armed Forces (DCAF) and the Arab Reform Initiative (ARI) – pointed to SSR as one of the main challenges for North Africa and the Middle East (Luethold 2004; Sayigh 2007). Nevertheless, its importance has become increasingly apparent.

The success or failure of SSR in the coming years will have a critical impact on the political evolution of this region – that is, whether it moves towards new forms of authoritarianism or if it has a chance for real democratization. This is so for three different reasons. Firstly, SSR is an indispensable ingredient in any democratization process and a fundamental step to rebuilding confidence between the people and state institutions. Secondly, since 2011 the actions and inactions of the security forces (including the regular army, the police, intelligence organizations and paramilitary forces) have either precipitated or prevented the fall of well-established regimes and, consequently, their attitudes are likely to shape the transition period. Thirdly, SSR has not only become central in the reform process but also a politically sensitive issue that contributes to the polarization and fragmentation of North African societies.

The aim of this chapter is to highlight that SSR is necessary for the consolidation of democratic openings in North Africa and that SSR will only be possible in a context of ambitious political reforms. This chapter sheds some light on the specificities of six countries: Morocco, Algeria, Tunisia, Libya, Egypt and Mauritania. It elucidates the differences among these six cases regarding aspects such as the position of security forces in the power structure, their role during the 2011 uprisings, and whether and how SSR has become part of the reform agenda in those countries where changes are actually taking place.

Security forces and authoritarianism in North Africa

Until 2011, many scholars had attempted to provide an answer to why Arab countries were not affected by previous democratic waves. Some maintained that the region lacked the prerequisites for a democratic transition and identified factors such as religion (Islam) and culture (Arab traditions) as elements hampering democracy in the region (Lewis 2002; Sharabi 1988). Other contributions refuted the controversial essentialist explanation and referred instead to the rentier factor as an element impeding any substantive democratization (Beblawai and Luciani 1987; Herb 1999; Ross 2001). More recently, some authors have argued that, rather than trying to understand why democracy has failed in this region, social scientists should try to explain why authoritarianism has succeeded (Albrecht and Schlumberger 2004; Bellin 2004). Some of these authors pointed to the role of security forces and the disproportionately coercive apparatus as two of the elements explaining why authoritarian regimes had been so resilient and able to keep control over dissident voices within their countries.

During the 2011 popular uprisings, the behavior of the army, the police, the presidential guards and the intelligence services became central for understanding, on the one hand, the capacity of a regime to withstand the protests and, on the other, the degree of violence and repression used to suppress the demonstrations. The decision to "shoot or not to shoot" was critical in explaining this course of events. Several authors (Bellin 2012; Droz-Vincent 2011; Sayigh 2011; Soler i Lecha 2011; Szmolka 2012; Gaub 2014) have shown that the choice of the security establishment corresponded to a structural factor: their degree of institutionalization and, a vital concern, whether their core interests depended on the survival of the regime.

In order to understand the durability of authoritarian regimes in North Africa, the circumstances that provoked the collapse of some of these regimes in 2011, and the elements that will shape their political evolution in the years to come, attention should be paid to two main factors: the role and resources of the coercive apparatus, and the inclusionary/exclusionary mechanisms of the North African political regimes. Reforming the security sector in these countries is not only a technical issue but also a very political one. It means shaking the power balance, contesting legitimacies, and reviewing established privileges.

Egypt: Civil-military relations in the forefront

If there is one country in North Africa where civil-military relations are at the core of the political agenda, it is Egypt. The Egyptian army has been a fundamental pillar of Egyptian politics since Nasser's times. Until the election of Mohamed Morsi in 2012, all presidents came from military ranks and, according to the 1971 Constitution, the army was the ultimate guardian of the state, which meant that it was also "the last recourse in maintaining public order" (Aclimandos 2011). The senior officer "caste" was given numerous privileges and controlled a significant portion of the state economy (Sayigh 2012). The Egyptian army also benefited from substantial US military aid and equipment to maintain a huge army of 438,500 active soldiers and 479,000 more in reserve. Despite all the changes that occurred in Egypt since February 2011, the army's prominent role in the political system remains unchallenged and confirmed by the 2014 Constitution. As said by Ibrahim el-Houdaiby (2014: 3), "different alliances of power (including, at certain points, the Islamists, before the security establishment went back to repressing them), have succeeded in protecting the security establishment from serious reforms".

Under Mubarak's rule, internal security forces increased their power and privileges. The police had the reputation of being the backbone of Mubarak's regime, which relied on the State Security Investigations Services (SSI) and the Central Security Forces (CSF) to repress political opponents and crush popular protests (El-Hennawy 2011). As in other Arab countries, the *Mukhabarat* – the intelligence services – were instrumental in keeping the situation under control and were asked to identify and combat internal enemies. As Omar Ashour (2012: 7) states, "if the SSI was the brains protecting the regime, the CSF was its muscle and iron fist".

In parallel, both military and police commanders became active in the economic field. High-ranking officials took advantage of the privatization process initiated in 1991; some accounts point out that the military economy's share could represent up to 15 per cent of Egypt's GDP (Chams El-Dine 2013: 3). Yet, it had to compete with other agents linked to Mubarak's political party, the NDP, and the business elite that surrounded the president's son, Gamal. Indeed, the competition among the armed forces and other elites played a key role in the "conflicting polyarchy" of institutions that partially explain the collapse of the regime (Sayigh 2013).

Thus, it became increasingly difficult for Mubarak to assure the loyalty of the armed forces as evidenced in the massive demonstrations of early 2011. The president had to rely on the riot police and other internal security units to repress the massive demonstrations of January and February 2011. The army, through the Supreme Council of the Armed Forces (SCAF), a governing body of 21 senior officers of the Egyptian army, then headed by the Field Marshall Mohamed Hussein Tantawi, kept a more neutral position; it did not contest the regime, but it did not shoot at the civilians either. By defending the state's core institutions, while safeguarding its own interests, the army was able to keep control of the situation once Mubarak was forced to step down.

The election of a civilian president, Mohamed Morsi, in June 2012 was supposed to put an end to these exceptional circumstances, but some political activists claimed that their revolution was victim of a double hold-up: by the military, on the one hand, and by the Muslim Brotherhood, on the other. The temporary alliance between these two forces, exemplified by their joint support for the March 2011 constitutional reform, was seen by leading activists as the largest obstacle for completing the goals of the revolution.

Civil-military relations quickly became a hot topic in the first stages of the Egyptian transition, revealing four different tensions. The first was the aforementioned clash between revolutionary forces and the security establishment. The military trials of civilians and the continued repression of popular demonstrations were seen as the clearest examples that authoritarianism and repression had not ended with the resignation of Hosni Mubarak. The second was the fight for political hegemony confronting elected politicians and state institutions (including SCAF). Significant episodes of this confrontation were the decision by the Constitutional Court to dissolve the parliament controlled by Islamist parties two days before the presidential elections; the re-activation of the National Defense Council under SCAF; Morsi's military overhaul in August 2012, forcing Field Marshal Hussein Tantawi and several senior generals into retirement; and Morsi's presidential declaration on 22 November 2012, which immunized his actions from any legal challenge. The third tension was the growing discontent in the security apparatus because of Morsi's seemingly flexible attitude towards the increasing Jihadist activities in the Sinai region, coupled with his tougher line towards the security apparatus, capable of contending with these Jihadist forces. The fourth cause of tension was linked to foreign policy choices and their impact for national security in issues such as the support given by President Morsi to Hamas in Gaza and the Muslim Brotherhood in Syria. For instance, a controversial statement by Morsi stating that the Egyptian army will not leave the Syrian people alone in their struggle against Bashar al-Assad (a remark he made without prior consultation with military leaders) significantly strained relations between the president and the Armed Forces (El-Kouedi 2013).

As a consequence of these growing tensions the Egyptian transition entered a critical point. The mentioned temporary alliance between Morsi and the Egyptian army came to an end. Massive demonstrations broke out across the country, in response to the campaign launched by Tamarod and several opposition parties against Morsi's presidency. The result of this was the overthrow of Mohamed Morsi as the Egyptian president, the persecution of the Muslim Brotherhood members, the closure of Islamist media and the suspension of the Constitution approved in December 2012.

Since the military takeover, the country has been divided among those who read these events as a new episode of the 2011 revolution, and those who believe Egypt is experiencing the restitution of old regime practices. Violence has spilled all over the country and a state of emergency was reinstated by the Interim President Adly Mansour. Later on, the Minister of Defence and architect of the coup, General Abdel Fattah el-Sisi, decided to run for president and became the sixth president of Egypt after winning presidential elections in May 2014 with 96.9 per cent of the votes.

In this context, the SSR is likely to remain a sensitive topic in Egypt. Among the many issues at stake, we should mention that the autonomy of the army and its traditional capacity to interfere in civilian affairs have been referred to and, therefore, legitimized in the 2014 constitution. This could have a significant effect on more specific issues such as the transparency of defense budgets, the parliamentary oversight on security affairs, immunity of security officials, transitional justice and the continuity of the army's economic privileges and social status. The fact that it is again a military official who occupies the presidency of Egypt, together with the growing insecurity perception among ordinary Egyptians, are likely to hamper a democractic governance of the security sector and a civilian control of armed forces.

Internal security will also have a prominent role in any proposed reform affecting the security sector. According to Tewfick Aclimandos (2012), Mubarak's regime was a police state more than a military one. Morsi's attempts at restructuring the security sector failed despite the removal of hundreds of officials and changes in the commands of the presidential guard, the military police, the Central Security Forces and the Cairo Security Directorate and, in fact, some reports on the final days of Morsi in power show that the police and the Ministry of Interior have been a key force behind the removal of Egypt's first elected president (Alsharif and Saleh 2013; El-Houdaiby 2014). Moreover, after six months of the coup, 3,143 Egyptians were killed, where 2,588 of those were civilians and 18,977 were arrested for political involvement (Dunne and Williamson 2014). In addition, one year after Morsi's ousting, Amnesty International denounced on a press release that "there have been at least 16,000 detained and at least 80 deaths in custody recorded in the past year, torture and other ill-treatment in detention continues unabated, and fair trial standards routinely flouted" (Amnesty International 2014). That shows that the internal security apparatus is at its full capacity. In these circumstances, the incumbent and future Egyptian governments are not expected to tackle a serious reform of the internal security apparatus and, most likely, will try to tie an alliance with these forces to remain in power.

Libya's post-revolutionary security vacuum

Under Gaddafi, the Libyan security sector was the result of a divide and rule strategy. Gaddafi, who seized power after a coup d'état in 1969, always feared he could be the next victim of a military takeover. Thus, the Libyan president weakened state institutions, including the army, in order to have full and direct control of the country. Gaddafi created paramilitary forces which were much more powerful and better equipped than the regular army. Some of these forces were under the control of Gaddafi's sons, Mutassim and Saadi, other members of his tribe and political allies. In contrast, the regime had no particular interest in weakening or dividing the police forces, which were mostly in charge of traffic and civilian tasks and whose image remained fairly positive among the population (Salem and Kadlec 2012: 10).

Unlike Egypt and Tunisia, the fall of Gaddafi's regime was the result of a conflict that lasted eight months, provoked thousands of casualties and required the intervention of foreign actors. During the armed struggle, some high-ranking officials and entire units of the army and police joined the rebel camp. The National Transition Council, with the support of NATO, tried to coordinate the war efforts and created the National Liberation Army, whose task was bringing together defected members of the regular armed forces and civilians to fight against those segments of the armed forces and the paramilitary groups loyal to Gaddafi. Yet, in some parts of the country rebel militias were relatively autonomous. This is the case, for instance, of the rebels of the Nafusa Mountains, whose actions were decisive in the fall of Tripoli.

The political leaders of post-Gaddafi Libya have been struggling to cope with their transition roadmap, which includes major political reforms, institution-building, national reconciliation and pacification of the country. While in other North African countries civil-military relations are the main focus of the debate, Disarmament, Demobilization and Reintegration (DDR) is rightly perceived as a pre-condition for a successful SSR in Libya.

Since the fall of Gaddafi's regime, Libyan politicians have affirmed that rebuilding and reforming the security sector is one of its top priorities. This would include substantive political and legal reforms, starting with the draft of a new constitution, an agreement about transitional justice, the integration of old regime institutions and the inclusion of new units composed mainly of rebel groups into the army. Some decisions have been very controversial and have only made the situation tenser. This is the case of the approval, in June 2013, of the "Political Isolation Law" that sought to disqualify those who held political office between September 1969 and October of 2011 and those who were against the February revolution of 2011 from holding high positions in the post-Gaddafi government for a period of ten years. Its approval raised doubts about the direction of the political transition because it reinforced the sense of vengeance and mistrust already sprouting in Libyan society and because it can deprive Libya of experienced professionals and the necessary structure that is needed to assure a more stable political transition (Amirah-Fernández 2013).

In addition, one of the most delicate issues has been the relation with the militias that were empowered in the fight against Gaddafi. Compared to other North African countries, Libya is the case in which these groups are stronger and elected institutions weaker. Although at the end of Gaddafi's rule the militias contributed to maintaining security, some of these militias have become a focus of insecurity (Gaub 2013a). This became evident with the assassinations of military figures of Gaddafi's era, the loss of control of certain parts of its territory, the takeover of oil refineries by militias in August 2013 and Ali Zeidan's kidnapping in October 2013. In order to avoid the risk of quasi-autonomous organizations eager to maintain their parcels of power or to get involved in criminal activities, the transitional government had appointed some of its commanders into ministerial positions, while at the same time reintegrating some officials from Gaddafi's era. This process, which took place at all levels, was also visible in the establishment of a new Libyan army. In parallel, the interior and defense ministries constituted the Supreme Security Committee, tasked with coordinating those militias that had not yet been demobilized (Garrigues 2013).

There have been repeated episodes of clashes among different militias, which have increasingly been interpreted as an expression of a secular versus Islamist cleavage. The emergence of a new actor in the Libyan scene, Khalifa Hiftar, a former general in the Libyan army with strong connections in Washington and Cairo, accentuated this dynamic. Hiftar launched the offensive "Operation Dignity" in May 2014 against the Misrata camp, whose members were leading the General National Congress, comprised of some Islamist groups, and were "united by an agenda of purging the elites of the old regime and promoting the former revolutionary forces as the core of a new army" (Wehrey and Lacher 2014).

The fact that Hiftar's allies – eastern tribes, Zintan's militias, federalist militias, disaffected military units and established elites – won the June 2014 elections to the House of Representatives led the Misrata camp to launch a counteroffensive named Operation Dawn that forced the "elected" government to flee Tripoli and establish themselves in Tobruk. Both camps did not recognize the other and claimed to be the legitimate representative of the Libyan people. The situation degenerated into a second civil war making the SSR even more difficult and conditional to a previous process of national reconciliation

More than in any other North African country, Libyan SSR will also mean the maintenance of public order. Firstly, there will be a need of keeping armed militias under control and subsequently disarming, demobilizing and reintegrating part of them into the Libyan security apparatus. Second, the reinforcement of a single national army and police is important in order to prevent part of the territory from becoming a safe-haven and a crossroad for radical groups along Mali, Niger and eastern and southern regions of Libya. And, finally, there is a need to control Gaddafi's era armament so as to stop the illicit traffic of Libyan armament through the Sahel and the Middle East. Despite the role that international actors played in the fall of Gaddafi's regime and the limited resources of the Libyan government to carry out all these reforms, for the moment international assistance in this particular sector has been quite ineffective.

Tunisia: Exception or example?

Despite brutal human rights violations and the repressive character of Ben Ali's political regime, Tunisia was often depicted as an exception in its regional context in terms of modernization and social reforms. It was also presented as an example for other Arab countries in many domains (women's rights, education system, economic openness, etc.). After 2011, many regarded Tunisia as a country that could undergo a successful democratic transition which could inspire its Arab neighbors. This transition will certainly require a substantive reform of Tunisia's security sector.

Tunisians often refer to the Armed Forces as "la grande muette" (the big silent one), part of a long tradition of not interfering in civilian affairs. This is not only the result of the army's will, but also a deliberate attempt by successive Tunisian governments to prevent the military from becoming involved in politics. This process began in 1962, when the authorities denounced a conspiracy involving several military officers who contested the authority of Habib Bourguiba. Ben Ali followed the same policy. In Springborg's (2011: 398) view, "Tunisia's military was essentially placed on ice". The result was that in 2011 Tunisia had one of the smallest armies in the region (35,800 soldiers) and a modest defense budget at only 1.44 per cent of its GDP in 2010 (The International Institute for Strategic Studies 2012: 351).

Ben Ali relied on the Internal Security Forces to protect the regime. No reliable data exists on its size and budget under Ben Ali. Yet, Mohammad Lazhar Akremi, then minister delegate to the Minister of Interior, numbered the Internal Security Forces as 49,000 (Hanlon 2012: 6). As explained by Derek Lutterbeck (2012: 9–10), this figure is far from previous calculations that suggested the policemen numbered between 130,000 and 200,000, and this exaggerated perception shows the extent to which Tunisians perceived police "as practically omnipresent". The intelligence services, which are part of the Internal Security Forces, were at the pinnacle of this coercive and repressive strategy of the regime. Their main goal was to fight against internal enemies and become the real armed branch of the regime, having a solid infrastructure and full access to power. Responsible for serious human rights violations, both the police and the *mukhabarat* were feared and unpopular among Tunisians, while the image of the army was far more positive.

In response to the massive demonstrations of late 2010 and early 2011, the regime used its Internal Security Forces as the main tool of repression. The brutality it used in protests within the center-west regions contributed to the increase in popular outrage and helped spread the protests all across the country. Recent reports suggest, nevertheless, that part of the ISF were also active in overthrowing Ben Ali and detaining members of the presidential family (Belkhodja and Cheikhrouhou 2013). In contrast, the army, which had no visible role in the repression and whose chief of staff, Rachid Ammar, became a visible figure after the collapse of the regime, was acknowledged for having behaved as a republican army and successfully keeping public order during the chaotic days that followed the flight of Ben Ali. As Badra Gaaloul (2011) states, "Ben Ali's strategy of marginalizing the military had the unintended consequence of facilitating the transition from his rule".

Military officers, however, made clear that they did not intend to play a political role during the transitional phase and expressed their will to return to the barracks as soon as possible. Thus, compared to the Egyptian case, civil–military relations are not a major challenge for the consolidation of democracy in Tunisia and, during the transitional phase, what has been taking place is the transformation from an authoritarian to a democratic control of the armed forces.

The reform of internal security forces is even more important. This became quite evident a few weeks after the fall of the regime, when a recently appointed Minister of Interior, Farhat Rajhi, had to escape from the ministry headquarters when more than 2,000 young protesters seized the building with the complicity of some police commanders who remained loyal to the old regime. As an immediate response, Rajhi fired 42 high-level officials. Yet more structural reforms were needed to prevent new incidents of this kind. Thus, before October 2011, Fouad Mebazaa, Tunisia's interim president, along with the Ministry of the Interior, released a document entitled *Security and Development: A White Paper for Democratic Security in Tunisia*, focusing on how to transform a police order into a "police service that can respond urgently to the new challenges of crime". This document failed to intro-duce much-needed reforms, partially because, as pointed out by Querine Hanlon (2012: 8), Ennahda leaders considered this roadmap a product of the "old regime". Nevertheless, Jebali's government continued to seek the support and advice of international organizations, like the Geneva Centre for the Democratic Control of the Armed Forces (DCAF), which even opened an office in Tunisia and carried out numerous cooperation initiatives with the Constituent Assembly, the Ministry of Interior and the Ministry of Defence, among others.

Together with the technicalities of the reform agenda, the Tunisian transition faces four main challenges in the field of security. The first challenge is the imple-mentation of the constitution and how future legislation can make security agencies accountable to the government, parliament and judiciary, especially knowing that "the constitution did not explicitly include transparency and accountability among the principles that govern the work of the security establishment, but instead pro-vided only a few detailed provisions for the functions and roles of the security and military establishment" (Ben Mahfoudh 2014). The second challenge is the reorga-nization and training of the internal security forces in order to clear their image and regain the trust of the Tunisian society. Third, there is a persistent need to address the problem of transitional justice, which on the one hand will mean meting out punishment to those guilty of human rights violations committed during Ben Ali's regime, while at the same time avoiding the exclusion of large segments of society from the political process due to their participation in old regime structures. An example of this dilemma was the preliminary draft on the "Law on the Political Immunization of the Revolution", which provoked harsh partisan clashes in 2013. Fourth, there is a need to preserve the monopoly of legitimate use of violence and maintain public order, as several incidents have shown how insecurity can put addi-tional stress on Tunisia's transition (Ghilès 2013). This was the case of political assas-sinations (Chokri Belaid in February 2013 and Mohamed Brahmi in July that year) presumably by Salafist radicals, and growing activity by terrorist groups in Mount Chambi and the South of the country, which is still a persistent threat to national security. All in all, despite the complexity of this agenda and the persistent security threats, Tunisia is the country where SSR has advanced the most and is likely to achieve more results in the years to come.

Algeria: The black box of power

Algeria has one of the largest armies in North Africa (130,000 active soldiers) and it spends a significant amount of its budget on defense (US$ 8.61 billion, in 2011, representing around 4.4 per cent of its GDP) (The International Institute for Strate-gic Studies 2012: 316). Size matters, but the power of the Algerian army as an insti-tution has more to do with its historical legacy in the war of independence, with the army's involvement in the internal conflict in the 1990s, and with the central position held by some old-guard generals and some "new guard generals" in both political and economic affairs.

The Algerian army has been a powerful institution, stemming from its role during the independence struggle. The *Armée Nationale Populaire* (ANP), formerly *Armée de Libération Nationale* (ALN), was a decisive force in the struggle for independence and, next to the *Front de Liberation Nationale* (FLN), was one of the two pillars around which the new republic was created. Tensions between political and military leaders, but also between different clans or factions, shaped political developments in the country until the 1965 coup d'état. Former president Ahmed Ben Bella was deposed by a bloodless coup organized by the then Minister of Defense, Houari Boumediene. In other words, civil-military relations and the interference of the army in civilian affairs has been a constant feature of contemporary Algerian politics.

The Algerian army is often described as the institution that effectively holds the reins of power, being *le pouvoir* itself. After the 1999 elections, in order to increase his political autonomy, President Bouteflika attempted to diminish the army's involvement in politics, stating that it must be under the president's authority. The resignation in August 2004 of the top military leader General Mohamed Lamari – replaced by Bouteflika's ally Major General Ahmed Salah Gaid – was perceived as a critical moment in this power struggle (Roberts 2007: 11). This was proof of presidential autonomy but, according to some authors, it was also the result of ongoing frictions and negotiations among different regional clans (Bustos and Mañé 2013: 51). More recently, the appointment in summer 2013 of a Vice-Minister of Defence and the transfer of some strategic prerogatives from the Department of Intelligence and Security (DRS) to the military staff (État-major) has been interpreted as a reaction to the new security challenges illustrated by the terrorist attack on the In Amenas gas field but is also regarded as an attempt to reinforce the power of the presidential clan.

In fact, along with the armed forces, intelligence services have played a predominant role in Algeria. The Military Security (MS) – later renamed the Department of Intelligence and Security (DRS) – is a Soviet-style secret police, which still holds enormous power and influence in the political apparatus of the country. General Mohamed Médiene, called "Toufik", the director of the DRS for more than 20 years, has been portrayed as the key actor inside Algeria's "black box" of power. The intelligence services were subjected to several reorganization processes under Colonel Chadli Bendjedid during the 1980s, with the aim of limiting their powers and level of political involvement. However, they regained significant power after the cancellation of the 1992 elections and, according to Mustapha Mohamed (2012: 5), the intelligence services increased their autonomy and even their hegemony over the armed forces and the regime since the 2004 elections.

The role of security forces and the configuration of the Algerian political system is key to understanding why the 2011 protests did not have a significant political impact in Algeria. In parallel with the popular uprising in Tunisia, major protests broke out in Algeria during January 2011 (Dessì 2011; Zoubir and Aghrout 2012). As protests were organized in the capital of Algiers and all across the country, the government reacted by deploying police forces, numbering 30,000 units, blocking roads leading to the center, suspending trains linked to the capital and arresting and dispersing protesters. The strategic deployment of security forces prevented people from attending demonstrations and reduced the scope of these protests, thus avoiding large numbers of casualties. The ability of the coercive apparatus to keep the protest under control is certainly one of the elements that explains why Algeria did not experience a revolution in 2011. Other factors to take into account were the strong memories of the civilian struggle of the 1990s, the capacity of the government to introduce measures to ease the political and social tension, the disunity of the opposition, and the cohesion of the core elites.

In order to ease the tensions, the first reaction of the Algerian government was the announcement of a decrease in food prices, an increase in wages and the promise of new public investments. Another important measure was the lifting of the 1992 emergency laws in February 2011. However, the police continued to legitimize its behavior on the basis of the anti-terrorism laws and the laws on public gatherings imposed in 2001 (Human Rights Watch 2012). Some months later, Bouteflika announced a constitutional reform, the renovation of the electoral code and party law, and the relaxation of stringent media laws. Afterwards, the president instructed a technical constitutional commission to consult with political parties and the civil society. Nonetheless, no timeframe was set for its work, so Algerian activists remained suspicious about the real impact of these reforms.

In other words, the program of political and socio-economic reform does not tackle civil-military relations in any substantial way and it is not likely to promote a democratic control over security forces. A major reason for this is that the army and the internal security forces do not base their power on a legal or constitutional framework, thus rendering a reform of the security sector through legal and constitutional means impossible. As suggested by Mustapha Mohamed (2012: 8), SSR in Algeria would require reforming the Algerian state; the acceptance of constitutional rule by the military would amount to a revolution. Difficulties towards such changes lie, on the one hand, in the reluctance of the security apparatus to undermine its own dominant role in the regime and, on the other hand, in the deterioration of regional security and lack of progress in resolving long-lasting disputes with Morocco. One of the few elements that could represent an opportunity for reform from the inside is the consolidation of a new generation of liberalizing officers which, since 2000, have reached decision-making positions (Mesbah 2011: 11). Yet, this will ultimately depend on the success of a broader political reform process and the evolution of security threats at a regional scale.

Mauritania: A powerful army in a weak state

Since the first coup d'état in 1978, the military has been a major political force in Mauritania, intervening regularly in the decision-making process. Military coups have in fact been the main driver of political change in the country, starting with a series of coups between 1978 and 1984, the last of which led Maaouiya Ould Taya to power. Taya was subsequently ousted in 2005 by Colonel Ely Ould Mohamed

Vall, the head of the Military Council for Justice and Democracy. After a transitional period that culminated with credible legislative and presidential elections in 2007 and the victory of the democratically elected President Sidi Ould Cheikh Abdallahi, a new coup brought General Ould Abdel Aziz to power in August 2008, putting an end to the constitutional regime. A new High State Council composed of military officers has ruled the country since then. In 2009, Abdel Aziz stepped down from the military-led Council in order to participate as a civilian candidate in subsequent presidential elections (Boucek 2009). Abdel Aziz was elected president of the country, and his political party, the *Union pour la République*, dominated the National Assembly and the Senate. In this model, replicated in other African countries, "a military coup is staged, followed by a tactical withdrawal to hold elections that are 'won' by a recently retired military officer" (Houngnikpo 2012: 2).

Protests in Mauritania began when a middle-aged businessman set himself on fire in front of the Presidential Palace on 17 January 2011, initiating a round of peaceful demonstrations in the capital demanding better salaries, jobs and lower food prices. In mid-February, a coalition of youth and student activists created several Facebook groups with the aim of triggering a mass protest (Lum 2011). On 25 February 2011, protesters gathered under the 25th February Movement and drafted a list of 28 points of social and political reforms. Core demands included the establishment of a national agency to combat slavery, constitutional reforms affecting the electoral system, media law reforms and improved transparency. Nonetheless, the protesters' top demand concerned civil-military relations and the withdrawal of the military from politics (Lum 2011). Numerous demonstrations spread throughout the country during the following year, including mass protests by black Mauritanians, students and young professionals. The regime relied on police and security forces to respond to demonstrations with force and repression, firing tear gas to disperse the crowd, and beating, arresting and clashing with protesters.

In October 2011, pro-government parties and some opposition groups signed an agreement expressing the need for political reforms in the following areas: the judiciary, the statute of opposition parties, the electoral code and the role of the army. In addition, the Mauritanian Parliament adopted some constitutional amendments, including a provision prohibiting the perpetration of coups d'état. In fact, as stated by Cédric Jourde (2011: 3), "factions within the military forms perhaps the most important type of political organizations which the head of state has to look after" since all former coups d'état have been perpetrated by the military and president's closest men. That is why when President Abdel Aziz was shot by accident by a Mauritanian soldier, all sorts of rumors spread about a failed coup d'état. Despite the fact that the president himself met with the press to reassure that this was just an unfortunate incident, the main opposition forces asked daily reports on the health of the president and, by doing so, contributed to raising doubts about the official version of the event.

Although Mauritanian security forces are relatively small and under-equipped compared to neighboring countries such as Morocco and Algeria, they still play a central role in the power structure of the country and have constantly intervened in civilian affairs. One of the peculiarities of Mauritania is that the country is confronted by increasing security threats and the government has, on occasion, been unable to fully control its own territory. The lack of capacity of the Mauritanian armed forces, combined with their interference in domestic and regional politics, contributes to the country's image as a fragile state, suffering political instability, institutional weakness, increasing levels of insecurity, radicalization and cross-border criminal activities (Boukhars 2012: 3).

In any attempt to consolidate Mauritania's precarious democracy, SSR will play a central role. Despite the constitutional and legal reforms, the country is still dominated by the military, acting as a veto-player and preventing the civilian political actors from any alternation in power (Jourde 2011: 1). Furthermore, the political opposition in the country is weak and Abdel Aziz has insisted that, despite the protests, he will not resign from power, allowing individuals and clans supported by the military to control the most important sectors of the economy along with the judiciary (Ojeda García and López Bargados 2013).

Morocco: The weight of history

In order to understand the role of security forces in Morocco, and the priorities and feasibility of any SSR agenda, it is worth mentioning three types of historical dynamics. The first is the country's persistent territorial tensions with its neighbors, Algeria and Spain, since independence in 1956 and especially since the Western Sahara conflict in 1975. These open or protracted conflicts have justified the huge size of the armed forces and particularly the army's ground troops, and the existence of 30,000 Auxiliary Forces in charge of maintaining security in the northern and southern regions and surveying the country's borders. According to data provided by the International Institute for Strategic Studies (2012: 339–341), Morocco has 195,800 active soldiers and 150,000 in reserve. In addition, the Gendarmerie Royale, with 20,000 members, is also a well-organized and loyal force that is responsible for maintaining order and exerts a semi-civilian, semi-military control over significant parts of the territory.

The second historical dynamic to bear in mind is the two failed coups d'état and attempts to assassinate Hassan II in 1971 and 1972, the latter carried out by the king's right-hand man, General Oufkir. In response, Hassan II lost trust in the army and undertook its full reorganization, abolishing the Ministry of Defense and replacing it with an administration with limited power. Since then, the palace has exerted total control over the army; the Deputy Minister in charge of Defense has focused on administrative issues and has not been involved in policy making. As explained by Abdallah Saaf (2012), the palace has intervened in internal issues of the army, using the same patterns of control that were applied in the civilian domain. That is, Hassan II and his son, Mohammed VI, serve as the supreme commander of the armed forces, granting officers certain privileges and material advantages to assure their loyalty and thereby balancing out the respective political weights of the army and the Interior Ministry. Thus, the issue in Morocco is not the level of control of the Armed Forces but the type of control, which is not a democratic one and lacks transparency and parliamentary oversight. Moreover, for decades reform of the armed forces has been restrained by modernization and the support of international actors, mainly Europeans, who had an interest in increasing the effectiveness of Moroccan Security Forces in the fight against drug trafficking, irregular migration, organized crime and terrorism.

The third dynamic is the memory of the so-called "years of lead". Throughout the 1970s and 1980s, Hassan II's regime incarcerated and tortured political dissidents and even killed some of them, such as the prominent socialist leader, Mehdi Ben Barka. Under the ruthless control of former Interior Minister Driss al-Basri, members of the opposition suffered arbitrary arrests and torture. The level of violence was particularly high in regions that contested the king's authority, such as the Rif (in the north) and the Western Sahara following Morocco's annexation of this territory in 1975. According to Hanspeter Mattes (2009: 143), during the last years of Hassan II's reign, a "new concept of authority" was introduced that altered the relationship between the state and the citizens. Hassan II wanted to leave behind the leaden years and rebuild a new legitimacy through political liberalization. His son, Mohammed VI, continued this policy and, when the new king acceded to the throne in 1999, he dismissed Basri. In 2004, he created the Equality and Reconciliation Authority (*Instance Équité et Réconcialiation*, IER) to investigate all past human rights violations that occurred between independence and 1999. Among its conclusions, the report requested a clarification of the decision-making processes and the organization of the security apparatus. The IER also called for introducing a system of monitoring and evaluation for all of the security forces. While there have been substantial efforts to investigate past crimes and compensate the victims, reforms remain piecemeal; the mid-2000s reform of the Intelligence Services allowed for the nomination of a civilian head but remained far out of the reach of any legislative or judiciary control (Saaf 2012: 5).

The climate of political agitation in 2011, with the demonstrations organized by the 20th February Movement, the king's initiative to launch a constitutional reform, and the legislative elections in November 2011, opened new spaces for political liberalization. However, SSR has not been at the core of the constitutional reform, and the king's control of the military and security organizations remains intact. Mohammed VI has preserved three areas of "his exclusive domain: religion, security issues and strategic major policy choices" (Ottaway 2011). Article 53 of the reformed constitution stated that: "The King is the Supreme Chief of the Royal Armed forces. The monarch appoints the military forces and can delegate this right". The National Defense remains a royal prerogative and neither the government nor the Parliament has a say in this area. Even the newly created Supreme Council of Security, aiming to consult internal and external security strategies and to supervise the institutionalization of norms of good governance in security issues, remains under the king's control, according to article 54 of the constitution.

However, in Morocco public debate on security issues is growing and SSR is no longer a taboo. Discussions on these topics are rightly associated with broader discussions on the political system and respect of human rights. Unless Morocco moves towards a more ambitious democratization process, structural reforms of the security sector are unlikely. The existing territorial disputes with Spain and Algeria, the conflict in the Western Sahara, and growing instability in the Sahel area can also hinder a comprehensive reform of Morocco's security sector.

Conclusions

SSR has become a hot topic in the ongoing discussions of political reform in North Africa. This has been accelerated by three reasons. First, by the critical role played by security forces in the popular uprisings of 2011. Second, by the growing problem of maintaining public order in several countries, with a particular concern about the role of more or less robust militias and their interference in ongoing political transitions. And, third, because of the significant role that the security forces have and will play regarding the insecurity that links the Sahel and the North African region and the need of a regional coordination in the fight against transnational terrorism, among others.

In this context, SSR has become a popular concept that includes burning issues such as civil-military relations, the involvement of the army in the economy, police reform, the role of intelligence services and transitional justice. Yet, the intensity of the debates and the possibility of carrying out substantial reforms depends on the role of the security forces in the power structure, their attitude vis-à-vis social and political protests, the scope and depth of the ongoing political reforms and the broader regional (in)security environment. As said by Florence Gaub (2013b: 3–4), some of the common challenges for a SSR agenda in the region are political polarization, internal resistance, limited resources, weak democratic institutions, limited knowledge of SSR, incomplete DDR and regional turmoil.

And yet, the differences among the six North African countries are very telling. In Tunisia these reforms are an essential part of the ongoing political transition; in Egypt, the overthrow of President Morsi by the military apparatus has confirmed the importance of civil-military relations and the ongoing capacity of the army and police officials to interfere in civilian affairs; in Libya, the debate about the Demobilization, Disarmament and Reintegration of the militias is a burning issue which could derail the whole transitional process; in Morocco, the issue is not about the level but the type of civilian and democratic control of the security apparatus; in Algeria, there is permanent tension between formal reforms and informal power; and, in Mauritania, the army remains a powerful actor in a weak state.

Note

1. This chapter was written with a research grant from el Ministerio de Economía y Competitividad: "Authoritarianism persistence and political change processes in North Africa and Middle East: Consequences on political regimes and the international scene" (CSO2012–32917). The author thanks Jordi Quero, Anna Lavizzari, Ana Mihaljevic,

Blanca Burillo, Héctor Sánchez and Paula de Castro for their support and assistance. He also thanks Mona el-Kouedi, Jonas Loetscher, Louisa Dris Aït-Hamadouche, Juan Garrigues, Florence Gaub, Francis Ghilès and Yezid Sayigh for their advice and review of specific parts of this chapter.

References

Aclimandos, T. (2011). 'Reforming the Egyptian security services. A review of the press, conventional wisdom and rumours', *ARI Thematic Study: Security Sector Reform*, Arab Reform Initiative.

————. (2012). 'Healing without amputating – Security reform in Egypt', *Arab Securitocracies and Security Reform*, Arab Reform Initiative.

Albrecht, H. and Schlumberger, O. (2004). '"Waiting for Godot": Regime change without democratization in the Middle East', *International Political Science Review*, 25 (4): 371–392.

Alsharif, A. and Saleh, Y. (2013). 'Special Report – The real force behind Egypt's revolution of the state', *Reuters*, 10 October. Available from: http://uk.mobile.reuters.com/article/topNews/idUKBRE99908720131010?i=2 [Accessed: 15 October 2013].

Amirah-Fernández, H. (2013). 'Libya and the problematic Political Isolation Law', *Analysis of the Real Instituto Elcano (ARI)*, 20, Real Instituto Elcano.

Amnesty International. (2014). 'Egypt: Rampant torture, arbitrary arrests and detentions signal catastrophic decline in human rights one year after ousting of Morsi', 3 July, Press Release. Available from: https://www.amnesty.org/en/latest/news/2014/07/egypt-anniversary-morsi-ousting/. [Accessed: 4 November 2013].

Ashour, O. (2012). 'From bad cop to good cop: The challenge of security sector reform in Egypt', *Paper Series*, no. 3, Brookings Doha Center–Stanford Project on Arab Transitions.

Beblawi, H. and Luciani, G. (eds.) (1987). *The rentier state. Nation, state and integration in the Arab world*, New York: Croom Helm/Istituto Affari Internazionali.

Belkhodja, A. and Cheikhrouhou, T. (2013). *14 janvier, l'enquête*, Tunis: Apollonia.

Bellin, E. (2004). 'The robustness of authoritarianism in the Middle East: Exceptionalism in comparative perspective', *Comparative Politics*, 36 (2): 139–157.

————. (2012). 'Reconsidering the robustness of authoritarianism in the Middle East', *Comparative Politics*, 44 (2): 127–149.

Ben Mahfoudh, H. (2014). 'Security sector reform in Tunisia. Three years into the democratic transition', *Security in Times of Transition*, Arab Reform Initiative.

Boucek, C. (2009). 'An election to consolidate the Mauritanian coup', *Carnegie Endowment for International Peace*, 5 May. Available from: http://carnegieendowment.org/2009/05/05/election-to-consolidate-mauritanian-coup/b23i [Accessed: 20 September 2012].

Boukhars, A. (2012). 'The drivers of insecurity in Mauritania', *The Carnegie Papers*, Carnegie Endowment for International Peace, 30 April. Available from: http://carnegieendowment.org/2012/04/30/drivers-of-insecurity-in-mauritania [Accessed: 9 June 2015].

Bustos, R. and Mañé, A. (2013). 'Algeria: Post-colonial power structure and reproduction of elites without renewal', in F. Izquierdo (ed.), *Political regimes in the Arab world*, New York: Routledge.

Chams El-Dine, C. (2013). 'The military and Egypt's transformation process', *SWP Comments*, 6, German Institute for International and Security Affairs.

Dessì, A. (2011). 'Algeria at the crossroads, between continuity and change', *IAI Working Papers*, 1128, Istituto Affari Internazionali.

Droz-Vincent, P. (2011). 'Authoritarianism, revolutions, armies and Arab regime transitions', *The International Spectator*, 46 (2): 5–21.

Dunne, M. and Williamson, S. (2014). 'Egypt's unprecedented instability by the numbers', *Carnegie Endowment for International Peace*, 14 March. Available from: http://carnegieen dowment.org/2014/03/24/egypt-s-unprecedented-instability-by-numbers/h8mb [Accessed: 4 November 2014].

El-Hennawy, N. (2011). 'Police cleansing no substitute for reform, activists say', *Egypt Independent*, 14 July. Available from: www.egyptindependent.com/news/police-cleansing-no-substitute-reform-activists-say [Accessed: 17 September 2012].

El-Houdaiby, I. (2014). 'Changing alliances and continuous oppression: The rule of Egypt's security sector', *Debating Egypt*, Arab Initiative Reform.

El-Kouedi, M. (2013) 'The curious case of the Egyptian armed force', *NDC Research Report*, NATO Defence College, 31 July 2013. Available from: www.ndc.nato.int/research/series .php?icode=3 [Accessed: 9 June 2015].

Gaaloul, B. (2011). 'Back to the barracks: The Tunisian Army post-revolution', *Carnegie Endowment for International Peace*, 3 November. Available from: http://carnegieen dowment.org/2011/11/03/back-to-barracks-tunisian-army-post-revolution/6lxg [Accessed: 16 September 2012].

Garrigues, J. (2013). 'In militias we trust: Libya's conundrum', *Opinión – Seguridad y Política Mundial*, 174, Barcelona: CIDOB.

Gaub, F. (2013a). 'Libya: The struggle for security', *EUISS Brief*, no. 25. Available from: www .iss.europa.eu/publications/detail/article/libya-the-struggle-for-security/ [Accessed: 9 June 2015].

————. (2013b). 'Reforming Arab security sectors', *EUISS Brief*, no. 48. Available from: www.iss.europa.eu/publications/detail/article/reforming-arab-security-sectors/ [Accessed: 9 June 2015].

————. (2014). 'Arab armies: Agents of change', *EUISS Chaillot Paper*, no. 131. Available from: www.iss.europa.eu/publications/detail/article/arab-armies-agents-of-change-before-and-after-2011/ [Accessed: 9 June 2015].

Ghilès, F. (2013). 'Still a long-way to go for Tunisian democracy', *Notes Internacionals*, 73, Barcelona: CIDOB.

Hanlon, Q. (2012). 'Security sector reform in Tunisia – A year after the Jasmine Revolution', *Special Report*, 304, United States Institute of Peace.

Herb, M. (1999). *All in the family: Absolutism, revolution, and democracy in the Middle Eastern monarchies*, Albany: SUNY Press.

Houngnikpo, M.C. (2012). 'Africa's militaries: A missing link in democratic transitions', *Africa Security Brief*, 17, African Center for Strategic Studies.

Human Rights Watch (2012). 'Algeria: Crackdown on protest as election nears'. Available from: www.hrw.org/news/2012/05/09/algeria-crackdown-protest-election-nears [Accessed: 17 September 2012].

Jourde, C. (2011). 'Mauritania 2010: Between individual willpower and institutional inertia', *IPRIS Maghreb Review*, March, Portuguese Institute of International Relations and Security.

Lewis, B. (2002). *What went wrong? Western impact and the Middle Eastern response*, Oxford: Oxford University Press.

Luethold, A. (2004). *Security sector reform in the Arab Middle East: A nascent debate*, Geneva: Geneva Centre for the Democratic Control of Armed Forces (DCAF).

Lutterbeck, D. (2012). 'After the fall: Security sector reform in post-Ben Ali Tunisia', *Arab Securitocracies and Security Reform*, Arab Reform Initiative.

Lum, K. (2011). 'Mauritania's days of rage', *Carnegie Endowment for International Peace*, 18 May. Available from: www.carnegieendowment.org/.2011/05/18/mauritania-s-days-of-rage/6b7r [Accessed: 20 September 2012].

Mattes, H. (2009). 'Morocco: Reforms in the security sector but no SSR', in H. Born and A. Schnabel (eds.), *Security sector reform in challenging environments*, Geneva: Geneva Centre for the Democratic Control of Armed Forces (DCAF).

Mesbah, M.C. (2011). 'L'armée algérienne face au défi de la transition démocratique', paper presented at X *International Seminar on Security and Defense on the Mediterranean (SED-MED)*, Barcelona, 13 June. Available from: www.sedmed.org/analisis_ssm/documents/semX/mohamed_chafik.pdf [Accessed:16 September 2012].

Mohamed, M. (2012). 'State, security and reform: The case of Algeria', *Arab Securitocracies and Security Reform*, Arab Reform Initiative.

Ojeda García, R. and López Bargados, A. (2013). '¿E pur si muove? Logics of power and the process of transition in the Islamic Republic of Mauritania', in F. Izquierdo (ed.), *Political regimes in the Arab world*, New York: Routledge.

Ottaway, M. (2011). 'The new Moroccan Constitution: Real change or more of the same?' *Carnegie Endowment for International Peace*, 20 June. Available from: http://carnegieen dowment.org/2011/06/20/new-moroccan-constitution-real-change-or-more-of-same/5l [Accessed: 19 September 2012].

Roberts, H. (2007). 'Demilitarizing Algeria', *The Carnegie Papers*, Carnegie Endowment for International Peace, 8 May. Available from: http://carnegieendowment.org/2007/05/08/demilitarizing-algeria [Accessed: 9 June 2015].

Ross, M. (2001). 'Does oil hinder democracy?', *World Politics*, 53: 327–328.

Saaf, A. (2012). 'Democratic governance of security in Morocco', *Arab Securitocracies and Security Reform*, Arab Reform Initiative.

Salem, P. and Kadlec, A. (2012). 'Libya's troubled transition', *The Carnegie Papers*, Washington, DC: Carnegie Endowment for International Peace.

Sayigh, Y. (2007). 'Security sector reform in the Arab region: Challenges to developing an indigenous agenda', *Thematic Papers*, Arab Reform Initiative.

———. (2011). 'Roundtable: Rethinking the study of Middle East militaries', *International Journal of Middle East Studies*, 43: 391–407.

———. (2012). 'Above the state. The officers' republic in Egypt'. *The Carnegie Papers*, Washington, DC: Carnegie Endowment for International Peace.

———. (2013). 'Morsi and the Egyptian military', *Carnegie Endowment for International Peace*, 8 January. Available from: http://carnegie-mec.org/2013/01/08/morsi-and-egypt-s-military/f0mv [Accessed: 19 February 2013].

Sharabi, H. (1988). *Neopatriarchy, a theory of distorted change in Arab society*, New York: Oxford University Press.

Soler i Lecha, E. (2011). 'Security forces and Arab revolts', *Opinion – Mediterranean and the Middle East*, 107, Barcelona: CIDOB

Springborg, R. (2011). 'Economic involvements of militaries', *International Journal of Middle East Studies*, 43: 397–399.

Szmolka, I. (2012). 'Factores desencadentes y proceso de cambio politico en el mundo árabe', *Documentos – Mediterráneo y Mundo Árabe*, 19, Barcelona: CIDOB.

Tanner, F. and Ould Mohamedou, M.-M. (2012). 'The imperative of security sector reform after the Arab Spring', *EuroMeSCo Brief*, 43, EuroMeSCo and IEMed. Available from: www.euromesco.net/images/briefs/euromescobrief43.pdf [Accessed: 15 November 2012].

The International Institute for Strategic Studies (2012). *The military balance 2012*, London: Routledge.

Wehrey, F. and Lacher, W. (2014). 'Libya's legitimacy crisis: The danger of picking sides in the post-Qaddafi chaos', *Foreign Affairs*, 6 October. Available from: www.foreignaffairs.com/articles/middle-east/2014-10-06/libyas-legitimacy-crisis [Accessed: 9 June 2015].

Zoubir, Y.H. and Aghrout, A. (2012). 'Algeria's path to reform: Authentic change?', *Middle East Policy*, 19 (2): 66–79.

5

BERBERS IN AN ARAB SPRING

The politics of Amazigh identity and the North African uprisings

Michael J. Willis

The dramatic series of events that unfolded across North Africa in the opening months of 2011 and that saw large crowds descending onto the streets of the region's major cities to demand political change rapidly became commonly known as the "Arab Spring." This was despite the fact that a significant percentage of the population of the region would not describe itself as Arab, but rather as Berber or Amazigh, to use the term increasingly used by many Berbers themselves. The popular uprisings that occurred across the region did, though, have a noticeable impact on the issue of Berber/Amazigh identity, mainly through the shaking up or remaking of existing political configurations within the states of the region that allowed for the issue of Amazigh identity to have a newly raised political profile.

The rise of groups and organizations advocating greater rights for and stressing the importance of the specificities of Berber populations had become a noticeable feature of the political landscape in the two states with the largest Berber language speaking populations in North Africa – Algeria and Morocco – from the beginning of the 1980s. The rise of these forces and the concessions made to them by the Algerian and Moroccan states have been discussed elsewhere.[1] The uprisings of 2011 had an impact on the evolving political discussion and dimensions relating to Amazigh identity in both Algeria and Morocco, but both states were the least affected in North Africa – certainly in the shorter term – by the popular tumult elsewhere: their existing regimes and political systems remaining largely intact.[2] To their immediate east, by contrast, Tunisia and Libya became the two North African states to be most affected by events with the overthrow of the long entrenched regimes of Zine al-Abdine Ben Ali and Muammar Qaddafi. Both Tunisia and Libya contained populations that identified themselves as Amazigh, which, although much smaller than those in Algeria and Morocco, began to rise to a new political prominence in the wake of the revolutions in the two countries.

Tunisia: Coming in from the margins

Tunisia's Berber-speaking population had historically maintained a profile close to invisible within national political life. This was largely due to its small size – accounting for the conventional estimate of 1 per cent of the national population – and its concentration in the remote rural south of the country, far from the influential cities of the north. Its marginal status was also due to the degree of suspicion with which post-independence governments had regarded discussion of distinct Berber identity, fearing that it would prove divisive, especially following the events of the "Berber Spring" in Kabylia in next door Algeria in 1980 and again in 2001. Attempts to form an Amazigh cultural association were made in the 1980s but were strongly opposed by the regime, which kept a close eye on the small number of activists involved. Those expressions of Berber identity that were allowed consisted mainly of those employed in the tourist industry where, like Morocco, the government recognized the particular fascination and exoticism that the term "Berber" seemed to evoke with tourists from Europe, whose visits to the country made an increasingly important contribution to the national economy.[3]

The overthrow of the Ben Ali regime at the beginning of 2011 removed the suffocating constraint that had been placed over political, cultural and social life for most of the period since Tunisia had gained its independence. Alongside the liberals, Islamists and leftists that moved to take full opportunity of this liberalization to organize and express themselves freely for the first time were Amazigh activists. Already in contact with each other online, several associations were formed in the weeks and months that followed, some uniting into the Amazigh Cultural Association, formed in August 2011. They received early support from the much larger and more established Amazigh associations in Algeria and Morocco and in the international diaspora, notably through the decision of the World Amazigh Congress (WAC) in February 2011 to host its next congress in Tunisia. The sixth congress of the WAC duly took place in October 2011 in Djerba, the first time ever on Tunisian soil.

The emerging Amazigh movement also began to involve itself and contribute to the vibrant political debate that was developing in Tunisia over the country's post-revolutionary future. Following the election of a National Constituent Assembly in October 2011, charged with the specific task of drawing up a new constitution for Tunisia, several Amazigh associations organized a demonstration in the capital, Tunis, on 25 December to call for the Amazigh language to be recognized as a national language in the forthcoming constitution. They also demanded for the first time that the language be formally taught in schools in Amazigh regions and at universities and that Tunisians be able to give their children Amazigh names.[4] The fear of these activists was that, without constitutional recognition, and thus protection, Amazigh language and identity would continue to be marginalized to the point of extinction in Tunisia. The demand was not, though, universal from all Amazigh associations, some of whom believed that it was unrealistic to ask for constitutional recognition for a language spoken by such a small minority in the country.[5] The response of those supporting the demand echoed those of fellow activists in other countries in asserting that Amazigh was not a minority identity given the fact that most Tunisians were genetically of Amazigh origin.[6] As one leading activist, Hajer Welhezi, stated, "Only the Amazigh language is a minority; not the people."[7]

Concern for the future status of Amazigh identity in post-revolutionary Tunisia was sharpened somewhat by the rise to political power of the Islamist An-Nahda party, which became the dominant partner in a coalition government formed after the election of the National Constituent Assembly. Amazigh activists feared that the antipathy shown towards the Amazigh movement's demands in other North African states would be replicated in Tunisia, despite the ostensibly more moderate caste of An-Nahda. In July 2012, some activists accused the Ministry of Culture of deliberately replacing the term "Amazigh" with that of "Mountain Villages" in the official description of a festival that took place in Gabès, in the south of the country, that month.[8]

Far more evident hostility to the Amazigh movement came from more hardline Islamist groups and elements that grew in size and influence in the wake of the revolution. Rim Saaidi, a television presenter, claimed she had received death threats after stating in a televised debate in 2011 that she was proud to be Amazigh.[9] Islamists protested against the use of *tifinagh*[10] characters and Amazigh flags at a cultural festival in Tamezret in August 2012, accusing Amazigh activists of "collaborating with foreign entities and of serving a western, secular agenda hostile to the Islamic identity of Tunisia."[11] Although the pressure did not prevent the festival from going ahead, it did lead to the postponement of a conference, due to take place alongside the festival, which sought to bring together and unite six different Amazigh associations.[12]

More dangerous, though, than hostility to the presence of the Amazigh movement and its agenda, was undoubtedly indifference. Few of the main political parties paid any attention or made any reference to the issue of Amazigh identity, reflecting a broader lack of interest in rural Tunisia.[13] As Tunisia confronted the significant political and economic challenges involved in the transition from the longstanding authoritarian regime overthrown in January 2011, the issue of Amazigh rights and identity risked being sidelined and neglected.

Libya: From "enemies of the people" to stalwarts of the revolution

The uprising against the regime of Muammar Qaddafi that erupted a few weeks after the ousting of the Ben Ali regime in Tunisia had a similar, yet even more dramatic, effect on the Berber population of Libya.

Concentrated in the far west of the country, Libya's Berber-speaking populations form a slightly larger percentage of the national population than those in Tunisia. The exact size of that population is, however, unknown largely due to the refusal of the Qaddafi regime to acknowledge their distinct existence after it seized power in 1969. During the period of Italian colonial rule (1911–1943), the Berber populations had been given a degree of judicial and religious autonomy due to their adherence to Ibadi Islamic practices rather than their linguistic distinctiveness, but were otherwise treated on a par with other Libyans. The monarchical Sanusi regime (1951–1969) guaranteed freedom of language in its constitution and made no attempt to enforce the use of the Arabic language.[14]

All tolerance of expressions of distinct Berber identity ended with the accession of Muammar Qaddafi to power. His highly personalized ideology of Arab nationalism did not simply seek to marginalize and minimize the presence and significance of Berber identity, but sought also to deny its very existence. "We in North Africa are Arabs and North Africa is 100 percent Arab," he declared, arguing that Berber identity was simply an invention of European colonialism.[15] According to some accounts, he urged Libyan historians to produce new texts demonstrating that Berbers were really Arabs.[16] To underline this view, Qaddafi sought to repress those expressions of Berber identity that did exist. In 1973 he consciously chose the coastal city of Zuwara, one of the few in the country to have a Berber-speaking majority, to promote his ideological blueprint for Libya contained in his famous Green Book using the occasion to condemn Berber identity as "the enemy of the people."[17] Books on Berbers were burned along with other texts deemed reactionary in the "cultural revolution" that took place later in the decade. The first Berber cultural associations that had begun to emerge in the early 1970s were also crushed, notably the *Rabita Shamal Afriqiya*, whose members were arrested on charges of *hizbiya* (formation of political parties).[18] The regime was also accused of the physical elimination of Amazigh activists, both inside the country and in exile.[19]

The impossibility of activism and the harsh repression within Libya led activists to set up structures outside of the country, specifically the Libyan Tamazight Congress in London, which called for an end to the suppression of rights and the recognition of *Tamazight* – the term given to the Amazigh language – as both a national and official language. The expansion of the use of the Internet gave Libyan Amazigh activists the sort of platform and forum that activists elsewhere in North Africa had begun to make use of in promoting their ideas. Foremost among these was www.Tawalt.com, launched in 2001.[20]

It was the effectiveness of this Internet activism that perhaps led to a softening in the regime's approach to the Amazigh movement. Like the regimes in Tunisia and Morocco, the Qaddafi government had already recognized the benefits of permitting certain cultural expressions of Berber identity in order to attract foreign tourists. This led to its renovating noted examples of Berber architecture. A more concerted conciliatory push occurred from 2007 onward when the Libyan authorities lifted the ban on the use of Amazigh names, allowed the use of signs in Tamazight at government-sponsored events and even organized the first "Amazigh Congress" to discuss education and social integration. Several high profile figures, including Prime Minister Baghdadi Mahmoudi and Qaddafi's son and periodic heir apparent, Saif-al-Islam, made visits to the Berber-populated regions for the first time, and attempts were made to open negotiations with exiled activists.[21]

This rapprochement came to a sudden end in late 2008 when the regime returned to its strategy of repression. Several hundred members of the Libyan Revolutionary Committees and the "Libyan Tomorrow" group, close to Saif-al-Islam Qaddafi, descended on the town of Yefren in the predominantly Tamazight-speaking region of the Nefusa mountains in the west of the country, close to the Tunisian border. They surrounded the house of relatives of the founder of the Tawalt.com website, Mohammed Umadi, shouting slogans that included "the Revolution will not stop" and the "Amazigh entity shall be destroyed." Death threats were painted on the walls of the house and a number of stones were thrown at it. The crowd accused the house's owner of maintaining ties with the World Amazigh Congress (WAC), which they claimed spread ideas that undermined Libya's unity. A list of Libyan Amazigh activists who had attended the most recent WAC in Morocco earlier that year was read out, accusing them of being separatist traitors working for "Western and Zionist imperialism."[22]

The exact reason for the abrupt *volte face* by the regime towards the Amazigh movement is unclear. The targeting of a house owned by relatives of Mohammed Umadi was a clear indication of the concern the regime had about the influence of Tawalt.com. The calculated intimidation paid off when Umadi closed the site in early 2009, despite the fact that he himself lived in exile. There was clear concern also about the international and transnational links, and dimension of the movement. In November 2009, the deputy head of the WAC was deported from Libya on his arrival from his native Morocco to attend the funeral of a well-known Libyan Amazigh figure. A year later, two researchers from the Moroccan *Institut Royal de la Culture Amazigh Marocain* (IRCAM) were arrested along with two local Amazigh activists.[23] It is also very possible that the change in approach, like the original rapprochement and much else that passed as government policy in Libya, was simply a product of the whim of Muammar Qaddafi himself. Earlier in 2008, on a visit to the Berber-dominated Nafusa mountains, the "Brother Leader" had declared: "You can call yourselves whatever you want inside your houses – Berbers, Children of Satan, whatever – but you are only Libyans when you leave your homes."[24]

The Qaddafi regime's renewed antipathy for the country's Amazigh regions was fully reciprocated with the launching of the uprising in early 2011. Zuwara, the town Qaddafi had chosen to promote his Green Book and castigate the notion of distinct Amazigh identity in 1973, was one of the first to rise up in February 2011. Similarly, the Nefusa Mountains became a major center of armed resistance as the rebellion gained momentum. Although these regions were manifestly far from being alone in revolting against Qaddafi's long and often brutal rule, the extensive use of both graffiti in the Tifinagh script and the distinctive Amazigh flag in Zuwara and the Nafusa Mountains indicated the importance of the assertion of Amazigh identity to the revolt in these places. As the regime's forces were progressively pushed out of the Nafusa Mountains, Tamazight began to be taught in schools and appear in local newspapers. This importance was acknowledged with the inclusion of an Amazigh news program on the rebel-supporting *Al Ahrar* television channel that began broadcasting from Doha in March 2011.[25]

The significant contribution made by the Amazigh areas to the struggle against Qaddafi was recognized by the revolutionary forces and transitional authorities following the final fall of Tripoli and the death of the former leader in the fall of 2011. Tifinagh began to feature on official banners, and Amazigh flags and banners not only festooned towns, such as Zuwara, but also appeared in Tripoli and many traditionally Arab regions where they appeared to be welcomed by fellow revolutionaries. In November 2012 local groups, supported by the Ministry of Culture, organized a Festival of Amazigh Culture in the Nafusa Mountains that was attended by an estimated eight thousand people, including government ministers and foreign ambassadors; the event was covered by national television.[26]

In spite of this acceptance and recognition, Amazigh activists pushed for more tangible gains in the aftermath of the revolution and as the new post-Qaddafi state was slowly put together. There was unhappiness at the absence of any reference to Tamazight in the constitutional declaration of August 2011, which, despite guaranteeing cultural rights and national languages for "all the components of the Libyan society," specifically affirmed Arabic as Libya's official language. Activists organized a large demonstration at the government headquarters in Tripoli the following November in response to the failure to secure an agreement from the National Transitional Council chairman, Mustafa Abdul Jalil, regarding their demands. These demands urged that Tamazight be awarded official status alongside Arabic, as well as the appointment of two ministers from Amazigh regions in the transitional government.[27]

Algeria: The beginning of the end of the national paradigm?

Algeria was the first country in North Africa to witness the emergence of a significant Amazigh movement inside its borders with what was then termed the "Berber Spring" of protests and demonstrations that took place in Kabylia in 1980. A further period of unrest beginning in April 2001 in Kabylia was seen as reviving the issue of Amazigh identity after a long period where national attention was largely focused on the rise of the Islamists and the violence of the 1990s that confronted armed groups against security forces. Although the unrest and protest were primarily concerned with political and social rights in Algeria as a whole, the issue of Amazigh and Kabyle identity came to dominate the popular movement – the Coordinations Movement – that emerged from the events. This was due in great part to the Algerian government's adept strategy of focusing on the parts of the protest movement's agenda that did focus on Amazigh identity to avoid support for the movement spreading to the majority of the Algerian population that was not Kabyle or Berber. The approach proved hugely successful, splitting the protest movement into warring internal factions of *accommodationists* and hardliners. The Algerian regime's decision to concede the one demand in the Coordinations Movement's al-Kseur Platform that related to Berber culture and identity – that Tamazight be recognized as a national language – greatly aided this process, as it encouraged elements within Kabylia to push more heavily on this issue and demand Tamazight's recognition as an official language alongside Arabic. More significantly, conceding this demand permitted the regime the opportunity to portray the unrest as essentially ethnic and particularist in nature and thus prevent the unrest and protests spreading to non-Kabyle areas of the country.[28]

The Amazigh movement in Algeria had always traditionally seen itself as a specifically national one, with an agenda for the whole of Algeria rather than just for Kabylia and Algeria's other Berber-speaking areas, notably the Shawi-dominated regions around the Batna-Khenchla region in eastern Algeria. It viewed itself and Kabylia more generally as having consistently been at the vanguard of positive change in Algeria from the resistance to the French in the colonial period through to the human rights and democratization movements of the post-independence years.[29] Yet despite the continuation of this national orientation in the demands of the movement that emerged from the unrest of 2001, the period witnessed the first signs of a rival, more regionalist trend. In August of that year, the veteran Kabyle singer and cultural rights campaigner Ferhat Mehenni announced the creation of the Movement for the Autonomy of Kabylia (MAK). Mehenni explained his decision to launch the new movement as a result of his conclusion that the Berberist movement had failed in its attempts to change and reform the Algerian state, as well as that the logical course of action was to try to implement these changes inside Kabylia's own borders within the context of regional autonomy.

In addition to the manifest failure of Algeria to democratize, Mehenni also pointed to the clear failure of the two most popular parties in Kabylia, the *Front des Forces Socialistes* (FFS) and the *Rassemblement pour la Culture et la Démocratie* (RCD), to attract non-Kabyle support.[30] He was joined by the Kabyle intellectual Salem Chaker who argued that "one can have no doubt that the 'Algerianist' strategy of the Kabyle political elites has shown itself to be a path that has not brought and will not bring democracy to Algeria, nor freedom and security to Kabylia." This was because, Chaker argued, the Algerianist strategy ignored the fact that the majority of Algerians were Arabophones and could not relate to the references of the Kabyles or Berbers.[31] This reference to differences in outlook between Arab speakers and not simply Kabyles, but Berbers as a whole, marked not just a significant break with the national vision of the leaders of the Berber Cultural Movement established in Kabylia in the 1980s, which Chaker had himself hitherto endorsed,[32] but also represented an adoption of a potentially more ethnic view of politics. Nevertheless, the focus of the MAK was to be on Kabylia. In the view of the International Crisis Group, this marked an abandonment of a vision for not just Algeria, but also of Berber-speakers beyond Kabylia.[33] As Mehenni himself concluded, "there is only one solution: that Kabylia ceases to demand for others what it wants for itself. Its grievances must be applied only within its own natural frontiers."[34] The precise strength of this trend was difficult to discern, although it was clear that it enjoyed much greater support amongst some of the Kabyle diaspora than within Kabylia itself, where the majority of Kabyles still identified with Algeria rather than Kabylia as their state. Nevertheless, the MAK received significant attention from the regime, which has traditionally been wary of secessionist tendencies. This was almost certainly because the MAK's regionalist agenda dovetailed perfectly with the regime's desire to portray the Kabyle movement of 2001 as an ethnic and regionalist one rather than one that articulated issues that were of concern to all Algerians.[35]

A further boost to the case for Kabyle regionalism came in September 2005 with President Abdelaziz Bouteflika's statement that "the Arabic language will remain the national language and the only official language of Algeria (. . .). There is no country in the world that has two official languages [*sic*][36] and this will never be the case in Algeria where the only language, established by the Constitution, is Arabic."[37] This definitively rebuffed a demand from elements of the Coordinations Movement that Tamazight be made an official, as well as a national, language. Whether part of the conscious official policy to play up the MAK or, more likely, a populist gesture to Algeria's Arabophone majority, in the context of the national referendum on the Charter for Peace and National Reconciliation that initiated in 2005, the effect was the same in further convincing the likes of Mehenni and Chaker of the futility of pursuing their objectives within the framework of the wider Algerian state. Thus, in April 2010, Mehenni announced his intention to create a "Provisional Government of Kabylia" in exile which was formally established in Paris the following June.[38]

The eruption of popular uprisings in the North African states to the east of Algeria in early 2011 gave a fillip to those majority elements of the Algerian Amazigh movement who still viewed their demands as an integral part of a drive for change in Algeria as a whole. In common with Berberist movements in Morocco and Libya, they perceived an opportunity to put pressure on the national regime to liberalize and democratize: a process that would involve the granting of further rights and recognition of Amazigh identity. Amazigh associations featured prominently amongst the main institutionalized coalition of organizations and political parties that sought to pressure the government to reform through street protests. The Coordination Movement, the Algerian branch of the WAC, and the Coordination of Amazigh Associations were all founding signatories of the *Coordination Nationale pour le Changement et la Démocratie* (CNCD) launched in January 2011.[39] In addition to the primary demands of opening up the political system and the lifting of the national state of emergency, the CNCD also called for the "affirmation of the national and official character of the Arabic and Tamazight languages."[40]

In contrast to the protest movements in Tunisia, Egypt and Libya, the CNCD failed to make much headway in pushing the Algerian regime to accede to its demands. This led to Algeria becoming one of the Arab states least affected by the turmoil of what became known as the "Arab Spring." The reasons for this failure lay partly in the adept way in which the Algerian regime responded to the perceived threat of popular protest by drawing on the large revenues accumulated by the long years of high oil and gas prices to dampen public anger through increases in state subsidies and the creation of jobs.[41] More importantly, it benefitted from the wariness of street protests and political upheaval felt by the majority of the Algerian population following the painful experiences of the collapse of the political opening of 1988–1992 and the resultant bloodletting throughout the 1990s. The CNCD also weakened itself by failing to mobilize a genuinely broad coalition of support for its campaign by choosing a relatively narrow ideological base for itself. This was exemplified in the leading role played by the RCD party in the CNCD.[42] The RCD's militantly secularist agenda served to alienate the overwhelming majority of Algeria's population that favored a public role for Islam in Algeria, and who theoretically could have been drawn to support the CNCD. Indeed, Islamist figures who tried to participate in the weekly demonstrations organized by the CNCD were chased away by CNCD supporters in marked contrast to the protest movements in Egypt, Libya and Morocco, where Islamists marched alongside liberals, secularists and members of the Amazigh movement.[43] This failure to unite a broad opposition front demonstrated the highly ideologically divided and sclerotic nature of Algerian politics, of which the Amazigh movement was a part, but also possibly the further tactical nous of the Algerian regime, some observers finding the narrow ideological base of the CNCD to be improbably convenient for the authorities.

The failure of the CNCD to bring change at the national level in Algeria gave succor to those elements of the Amazigh movement who looked to a more Kabyle-based approach to achieve their objectives. On their formation, both the MAK and the Provisional Government of Kabylia had been widely dismissed inside Algeria as the personal projects of Ferhat Mehenni with little support beyond a handful of Mehenni's close friends in exile.[44] Yet, as the CNCD demonstrations in Algiers were beginning to run out of steam in the spring of 2011, the MAK attracted nearly a thousand people to a demonstration in Tizi Ouzou, the capital of Kabylia, in April. The fact that most of those participating were students indicated the potential growth in appeal the MAK had amongst the predominantly youthful population of Kabylia.[45] Official awareness of and concern about this may have been behind a ban imposed by the authorities on a march organized by the MAK to mark the Amazigh New Year in January 2012.[46]

Morocco: A very royal concession

The decade that followed the establishment by King Mohammed VI of the *Institut Royal de la Culture Amazigh* (IRCAM) in 2001 was characterized by a steady, if slow, institutionalization of the monarch's promises to promote Amazigh culture and to introduce teaching of a unified form of Amazigh language into schools in Morocco. Prominent Amazigh activists were invited to join the Institute, but its formation split the Amazigh movement with some seeing it as an opportunity to further their agenda whilst others viewed it as a classical Moroccan regime strategy to co-opt and defang the movement.[47] Consequently, whilst many Amazigh activists accepted the Palace's invitation to work within IRCAM, others kept their distance. Within a short time of IRCAM's establishment, there were complaints from both outside and within the Institute that, despite royal endorsement, the Institute's efforts were being frustrated and delayed by elements of the administration, even at the ministerial level, allied to some of the political parties, notably those parties of an Arab nationalist orientation. In 2005 a number of members of IRCAM left the Institute in protest at what they saw as attempts to block the integration of Amazigh language into education and the media.[48] A unified form of written Tamazight – Tifinagh – was nevertheless formally introduced into a number of Moroccan schools from September 2003 and this was seen as an important step forward and evidence of the political will existing at the top of the state, even if the number (317) and proportion (5 per cent) of schools it was initially introduced into were quite small.[49] Critics, however, pointed out that the reforms were introduced by administrative circular only, and that no changes had been made to either the Education Law or the Constitution to reflect these new initiatives.[50] Significant numbers of activists remained within IRCAM, nonetheless, out of the conviction that the commitment of the king, as the pre-eminent political power in Morocco, would ensure the Institute's ultimate success. It was a perspective that the Royal Palace was fully aware of and sought to exploit to both ensure the loyalty of a large part of an increasingly popular movement that could easily align itself against the regime (as had been the case in Algeria) and even use as ally, bulwark and counterweight to the slowly rising power of the kingdom's Islamists.

Those members of the Amazigh Cultural Movement that had stayed out of IRCAM viewed the problems it encountered as an inevitable result of co-optation. The more radical wing of the movement believed that a more independent and political approach was needed in order to move beyond the cultural dimension within which the Moroccan state wished to contain the Amazigh movement. Since the 1990s there had been talk of the need for the creation of an Amazigh political party. Amazigh activists had an established contempt for the veteran *Mouvement Populaire* party that was strong in rural areas, but which they viewed as a loyalist sinecure to attract Amazigh votes and devoid of any ideology. Some even accused it of being sustained and paid by the Moroccan state to recuperate and thwart the Amazigh elite.[51] In 2005, radical activists announced the intention to create a new party called the *Parti Democrate Amazigh Marocaine* (PDAM). Aware of the legal ban on political parties referring to ethnicity in their name, statutes and agenda, the PDAM sought to get around this by arguing that the party was open to all Moroccans and that, since everyone in Morocco was at least partly of Amazigh decent, the use of the term Amazigh could not be seen as ethnically divisive.[52] This argument was not accepted by the authorities and in April 2008 the Administrative Tribunal of Rabat annulled the constitution of the PDAM because of its formal references to Amazigh identity.[53]

Those Amazigh activists that remained highly skeptical of the regime's commitment to the promotion of Amazigh language and culture participated in significant numbers in a series of popular protests demanding political reform that developed in Morocco in early 2011. Amazigh flags and banners bearing Tamazight and Tifinagh featured heavily in the marches and demonstrations. Like their counterparts elsewhere in the region, Morocco's Amazigh activists viewed thoroughgoing political reform and liberalization as a natural extension and guarantor of their own demand for expanded cultural and linguistic rights and pluralism. As a reflection of this, the fairly heterogeneous and amorphous protest movement that developed and named itself the "February 20th Movement" (after the date of its first major demonstration in 2011) included the call for the recognition of Tamazight as an official language in its set of demands.

Amazigh activists were as surprised as most other Moroccans by the swift and comprehensive way in which the Moroccan regime responded to the protests through a speech by the king on 9 March, which appeared to endorse and promised to introduce most of the main demands of the February 20th Movement. With specific regard to the issue of Amazigh identity, the king pledged to "Enshrine in the Constitution the rich, variegated yet unified character of the Moroccan identity, including the Amazigh component as a core element and common asset belonging to all Moroccans."[54] Although it was unclear how exactly Amazigh identity would be enshrined in the constitution, the commitment to do so represented a break with past constitutions, none of which had made any reference to the subject. Fearing that constitutional references would be limited to being listed as a component of national identity or simply a "national" language, Amazigh activists were keen to push for Tamazight to be recognized as an official language alongside Arabic.[55] They were encouraged by the support of IRCAM, whose Administrative Council had advocated such a reform from 2005, and also from a number of the political parties, none of whom had hitherto supported such a change.

Proponents of Tamazight being made an official language were delighted by the inclusion of a clause to this effect in the text of the new constitution announced by the king on 17 June. This was due mainly to the fact that many of the other reforms the king had pledged in March had been noticeably watered down in the new document. Some noted that original proposals for Arabic and Tamazight to be listed alongside each other as official languages had been modified to refer to the latter as an official language in a paragraph following one stating that "Arabic remains the official language of the State."[56] This was viewed by some activists as suggesting a "definitely hierarchical relationship."[57] Nevertheless, even these skeptics were forced to acknowledge the new text was "certainly a victory" in terms of granting what had been for many years the principal demand of the Amazigh movement.[58]

The granting of official status to the Amazigh language had the effect of weakening the support of Amazigh activists for the February 20th Movement, which viewed the new constitution as a whole as falling well short of its demands. Although some Amazigh associations supported the February 20th Movement's call to boycott the referendum on the new constitution, others did not.[59] This prompted suspicions that the concession on official status had been a deliberate move by the Royal Palace to secure the defection of the Amazigh associations and activists from the protest movement. The February 20th bloc saw support for its marches and demonstrations ebb as the king adroitly took the political initiative away from the street protests with the introduction of the new constitution, which was approved by a huge official margin (98.5 per cent) in the referendum that took place just two weeks after it was unveiled.

The political initiative moved even further away from the February 20th Movement with the scheduling and holding of fresh national legislative elections four months after the introduction of the new constitution. The outcome of these elections posed new challenges for the Amazigh movement since they produced a plurality for the Islamist Party of Justice and Development (PJD), which became the dominant element in the new government. In common with most Islamists, the PJD had an established antipathy to the main thrust of the Amazigh movement's agenda, which it viewed as seeking to undermine the rightful place of Arabic, the language of the Quran and thus Islam, in public life. Although several of its leading figures were Berber speakers[60] and the party had publicly acknowledged the right of a public place for Amazigh language and culture, the PJD had been strongly opposed to Tamazight being granted official status alongside Arabic.[61] In addition to established arguments citing religion and national tradition in support of the retention of the supremacy of Arabic, leading PJD figures had also emphasized the practical difficulties of introducing a new official language.[62] This raised fears amongst Amazigh activists that PJD figures in the ministries and the parliament would use these difficulties as an excuse for the delay and watering down of the introduction of Tamazight. These concerns were only exacerbated by the inclusion of the Istiqlal Party in the governing coalition alongside the PJD. The Arab nationalist ideology of the party, having traditionally been set against the Amazigh movement, led to accusations that its ministers in previous governments had deliberately tried to block and delay reforms, such as the introduction of Tamazight into schools.[63]

The process of introducing the organic law that the king's speech of June 2011 promised would "specify the ways and means of integrating [Tamazight] in teaching and in [the] public sector"[64] did indeed take a long time. The first proposals from the political parties were presented only in the parliament at the end of 2012. This slowness, together with doubts about the commitment of the PJD, the Istiqlal ministers and members of parliament, led to elements of the Amazigh movement launching a campaign for the "real officialization" of Amazigh language in early 2012.[65] Nevertheless, the government did begin a process of consultation with both IRCAM and Amazigh associations and non-governmental organizations (NGOs) over how to introduce Tamazight.[66]

In more tangible terms, official figures released in September 2012 appeared to show that the number of schools teaching Tamazight in Morocco had increased to over 4,000 from an initial 317 in 2003, and that 545,000 children, amounting to 15 per cent of all pupils, had received classes in Tamazight.[67] Moreover, the expected sabotage in parliament of legislation introducing Tamazight looked like it might be countered by significant support from a number of parties in the chamber. This was most dramatically demonstrated by the posing of a question regarding the introduction of Tamazight in schools by a deputy in the Tamazight language itself during a parliamentary session in April 2012. This was presented as support for the speeding up of the introduction of the use of Tamazight in the administration of which parliament was an integral part.[68] A more likely explanation of what was a rather orchestrated piece of political theatre was that the issue of Tamazight was being used by the parties in the formal opposition, to whom the deputy who posed the question belonged, as a stick with which to beat the Istiqlal and the PJD in government. The fact that the deputies who applauded the question most enthusiastically were from parties traditionally close to the Royal Palace indicated that the tacit, yet established, strategy of using the Amazigh movement and issue as a counterweight and check on the Kingdom's Islamists was still very much alive.[69] Indeed, the commitment of the king to the recognition and expansion of Amazigh linguistic and cultural rights remained the deciding factor on the issue as on all others, despite the supposed concessions made by the Monarchy in the new constitution. Amazigh activists publicly acknowledged this fact, pointing out that none of the political parties had called for Tamazight to become an official language before the king's speech of March 2011.[70] Some privately observed that the antipathy felt towards the introduction of Tamazight by Morocco's largest and most popular political parties, the PJD and the Istiqlal, gave them pause for thought about pushing for further political liberalization and democratization, since this process would inevitably result in power being transferred away from their great advocate and protector in the shape of the Monarchy and into the hands of their ideological enemies.[71]

The transnational dimension

The political changes that shook North Africa from the beginning of 2011 also served to strengthen the transnational dimension of the Amazigh movement. The overthrow of the longstanding regimes in Tunis and Tripoli not only allowed Amazigh movements in the two countries to express themselves in ways they had not been able to before, but also allowed them to establish more open links with movements in other states. Such links had already been established thanks to the Internet, and more institutionally through the WAC but, as has been shown, the Libyan regime in particular had worked to frustrate and punish such contact. The decision to hold the sixth WAC Congress in Djerba, Tunisia, in October 2011 was a conscious recognition of the changes that had occurred. Participants at the Congress notably sang the Libyan national anthem in Tamazight.[72]

As well as bringing the Tunisian and Libyan Amazigh movements more fully into the framework of transnational organs such as the WAC, which traditionally had been dominated by Algerians and Moroccans, the events of 2011 also served to bolster and forge new links between the Amazigh communities in Tunisia and Libya. Geographically concentrated on both sides of the Libyan-Tunisian national border, Libyan and Tunisian Amazigh communities not only shared language and culture, but also the Ibadite faith and significant historical contact before the imposition of more rigid state frontiers. These links were rekindled in a very tangible way through the flight of a significant part of the Libyan Amazigh community across the border into Tunisia in the early months of the uprising against the Qaddafi regime. Many relocated to Djerba, where they already had links with the local Amazigh community.[73]

The according of official status to Tamazight in the constitutional changes that occurred as a direct result of the events of 2011 in Morocco encouraged Amazigh movements in other states to push for a similar prize from their own governments. In Algeria, where comparisons with Morocco were always keenly felt, Amazigh activists noted that their movement had not yet achieved "the considerable advances recorded by our brothers in Morocco without having paid the price that we have paid."[74] The newly vocal Amazigh movements in Libya and Tunisia also explicitly acknowledged the example set by Morocco in their own campaigns to have Tamazight recognized as an official language in the new post-revolution constitutions.[75]

Both before and after the uprisings of 2011, Amazigh activists from across the region continued their efforts to have North Africa reconceptualized as a region that was not simply an integral part of what they termed the Arab-Islamic world. This involved not only stressing the Berber aspects of North African history and identity, but also its Mediterranean and European dimensions, which they portrayed as having been neglected through overemphasis by regimes on links with the Middle East. Increasing numbers of activists argued that the heavy official focus on the Middle East had led to the unnecessary importation of that region's problems and conflicts, notably terrorism and religious extremism. Some even argued that the constant attention to the travails of the Palestinians was a deliberate policy by regimes to distract attention from the very significant problems within North Africa itself.[76]

Towards the end of the first decade of the twenty-first century, some of the most radical Amazigh activists were prepared to take a significant step further in not only criticizing support for the Palestinians, but in establishing formal links with the state of Israel. Both Ahmed Adghrini, of the dissolved PDAM party in Morocco, and Ferhat Mehenni, of the MAK in Algeria, led small delegations of Amazigh activists to Israel. They portrayed the visits as part of their broader campaign to draw attention to minority identities within the region which had been marginalized by what they saw as the Arab-Islamic hegemony. Mehenni even compared Israel to Kabylia, arguing that both were in a "hostile environment," but that Israel had managed to achieve a state whereas Kabylia was still to do so.[77]

These initiatives and sentiments were enthusiastically welcomed by elements in Israel that had long encouraged their development as part of a well-established Israeli foreign policy strategy of creating links and nurturing allies with non-Arab groups and states in the wider region. They received a much colder response within North Africa itself where they were widely condemned as lending support to the continued colonization and oppression of the Palestinians by the Israelis.[78] The most vehement condemnation inevitably came from the Arab nationalist and Islamist organizations and parties for whom support of the Palestinians was one of their core principles.[79] The vast majority of the populations in North Africa still, nevertheless, strongly opposed expanding links with Israel, a fact that led one senior member of the Islamist PJD in Morocco to describe, with a broad smile, Ahmed Adghrini's visit to Israel as a "massive strategic error."[80] Indeed, links and friendship with Israel were still opposed not only by most ordinary Amazigh but arguably even by most within the broader Amazigh movement itself: only the most radical wings of the movement participated in and endorsed the initiative.

Conclusions

The surge of popular protest that swept across North Africa in 2011 brought over-all benefit to those groups and organizations that believed there should be more official recognition and a greater place afforded to the language and culture of the Amazigh populations of the region. In Libya and Tunisia these forces were able to organize and express themselves for the first time. In Morocco, what was viewed as the ultimate prize for Amazigh movements everywhere – the according of official status to Amazigh language in the national constitution – was won. All of these things would not have occurred without the popular protest movements which forced political changes from the regimes in the region through either getting them to reform or depart. This created a greater opening of political space which was taken advantage of by a greater plurality of forces, actors and voices than had hitherto been permitted.

The Amazigh movements were, however, only one of a number of forces that were able to express and assert themselves in the new less constricted politi-cal climate that developed across North Africa. The chief political beneficiaries of the changes were, of course, the Islamists, whose organizations rose to new prominence and whose political parties won elections and moved into govern-ment ministries for the first time in both Tunisia and Morocco in late 2011. Long seen as the chief ideological foes of the Amazigh movement, even its nemesis, the rise of the Islamists was regarded with understandable wariness by the Amazigh movement. In some quarters, their rise to political ascendancy was viewed as presaging a frontal assault on the Amazigh movement and its achievements as the Islamists sought to forcibly redefine identity in the region in strictly Arab and Islamic terms, in which Amazigh identity would not only play no part but which was actually portrayed as a dangerous Trojan horse for foreign and western influ-ence. Such an envisaged scenario ignored, however, not only the more pluralist impulses of parties such as the PJD in Morocco and An-Nahda in Tunisia, but also their weaknesses: neither party attracted even close to a majority of the votes in the elections of 2011.

The opening up of the political environment also strengthened countervailing forces, not least amongst the Amazigh movement itself, which in Morocco, in par-ticular, saw steady growth in popular support especially amongst students and youth in the southwest of the country. More generally, the changed political atmosphere brought about by the events of 2011, with ordinary North Africans energized by the influence they had been able to exercise over what had been considered as unmovable and unassailable political leaderships, suggested that populations were unlikely to support or indeed tolerate a return to an authoritarian and ideologi-cally exclusive political system. Nevertheless, the regimes in the two states with the largest Amazigh populations, Algeria and Morocco, had once again demonstrated during 2011 their proven ability to respond and deal with any potential political threat coming from their respective Amazigh movements by resorting to the tried and tested tactics of, respectively, divide-and-rule and co-optation.

Notes

1. See Michael J. Willis, "The Politics of Berber (Amazigh) Identity: Algeria and Morocco Compared," in Yahia H. Zoubir and Haizam Amirah-Fernández (eds.), *North Africa: Politics, Region, and the Limits of Transformation*, London: Routledge, 2008, pp. 227–242.
2. On Morocco, see Abdeslam Maghraoui, "The Perverse Effect of Good Governance: Lessons from Morocco," *Middle East Policy*, 19, 2 (Summer 2012): 49–65. On Algeria, see Yahia H. Zoubir and Ahmed Aghrout, "Algeria's Path to Reform: Authentic Change?" *Middle East Policy*, 19, 2 (Summer 2012): 66–83.
3. "Tunisian Amazighs Face Islamist Harrassment," *Magharebia*, 31 August 2012.
4. "Manifestation pour la reconnaissance de Tamazight le 25 décembre en Tunisie," Tunisie-Amazigh.com, 24 December 2011.
5. "Tunisian Amazighs Face Islamist Harrassment," *Magharebia*, 31 August 2012.
6. "Tunisian Amazigh and the Fight for Recognition," *Tunisia Live*, 13 October 2011.
7. "Tunisian Amazighs Campaign for Equal Rights," *Magharebia*, 6 July 2011.
8. "Tunisian Town Celebrates Amazigh Cultural Heritage," *Tunisia Live*, 22 August 2012. The Minister of Culture, Mehdi Mabrouk, was not, however, himself a member of An-Nahda.
9. "Tunisian Amazigh and the Fight for Recognition," *Tunisia Live*, 13 October 2011.
10. Tifinagh is a distinct written script that is increasingly used by Amazigh activists in which to write the Amazigh language, which had traditionally been largely only a spoken language.
11. "Tunisian Amazighs Face Islamist Harrassment," *Magharebia*, 31 August 2012.
12. "Tunisian Islamists Oppose Berber Unity," *Nuqudy*, 2 September 2012. (http://english.nuqudy.com/North_Africa/Tunisian_Islamists_-3049).
13. "Tunisian Amazigh and the Fight for Recognition," *Tunisia Live*, 13 October 2011.
14. Aisha Al-Rumi, "Libyan Berbers Struggle to Assert Their Identity Online," *Arab Media and Society*, (Spring 2009): 3–4.
15. Al-Rumi, op. cit., p. 3.
16. "Berbers Can No Longer Be Suppressed in Libya," *The National*, 28 October 2012.
17. "Amazighs Aspire to a 'Brighter Future' in Post-Gaddafi Libya," *Tunisia Live*, 28 February 2012.
18. Al-Rumi, op. cit., p. 4.
19. For details, see Al-Rumi, op. cit., p. 6.
20. Al-Rumi, op. cit., pp. 1 & 5.
21. Al-Rumi, op. cit., pp. 2 & 6.
22. Al-Rumi, op. cit., pp. 1–2.
23. Amnesty International, "Libya: Four Arrested Amid Fears of Amazigh Culture Crackdown," Public Statement AI Index: MDE 19/001/2011, 6 January 2011.
24. Quoted in Lindsey Hilsum, *Sandstorm: Libya in the Time of Revolution*, London: Faber & Faber, 2012, p. 30.
25. "Amazighs Aspire to a 'Brighter Future' in Post-Gaddafi Libya," *Tunisia Live*, 28 February 2012; Hilsum, op. cit., p. 207; "Amid a Berber Reawakening in Libya, Fears of Revenge," *New York Times*, 8 August 2011.
26. "Demonstration for Amazigh Rights," *Libya Herald*, 6 September 2012; and "Amazigh Assert Their Cultural Identity at Jadu Festival as Magarief Expresses Support for Constitutional Recognition of Berber Language," *Libya Herald*, 11 November 2012.
27. "Demonstration for Amazigh Rights," *Libya Herald*, 6 September 2012.
28. Azzedine Layachi, "The Berbers in Algeria: Politicized Ethnicity and Ethnicized Politics," in Maya Shatzmiller (ed.), *Nationalism and Minority Identities in Islamic Societies*, Montreal and Kingston: McGill-Queen's University Press, 2005, pp. 208–211. There were also suggestions that regime manipulation had not been limited to its reaction to the unrest, but had even played a part in provoking it in the first place. One investigation into the outbreak of the protests of April 2001 concluded that outside interference in the police's chain of command had led to the security services being particularly

provocative. International Crisis Group (ICG), *Algeria: Unrest and Impasse in Kabylia*, Middle East/North Africa Report No. 15, 10 June 2003, p. 9.

29. See Michael J. Willis, *Politics and Power in the Maghreb. Algeria, Tunisia and Morocco from Independence to the Arab Spring*, London: Hurst & Co., 2012, pp. 223–224.

30. Ferhat Mehenni, *L'Algérie: La Question Kabyle*, Paris: Editions Michalon, 2004, p. 95.

31. Salem Chaker, "Preface," in Mehenni, op. cit., p. 13.

32. Layachi, op. cit., p. 212.

33. International Crisis Group, op. cit., p. 25.

34. Mehenni, op. cit., p. 95.

35. International Crisis Group, op. cit., p. 25; Layachi, op. cit., pp. 211–218.

36. Switzerland, Belgium and Canada are all examples of countries that contradict Bouteflika's claim.

37. "Après ses déclarations à Constantine sur Tamazight," *El Watan*, 24 September 2005. Despite the rejection of Tamazight ever being an official language, the Algerian government continued to make concessions in the cultural sphere. In 2007 President Bouteflika announced the establishment of an Algerian Academy for the Amazigh Language and also a High Council for the Amazigh Language. Whether these measures were designed to sow further division within the Coordinations Movement, both were presented as the fruit of the long drawn-out negotiations between the regime and the Movement since the unrest of 2001. "Elle sera aidée par un conseil supérieur," *El Watan*, 20 and 21 June 2007.

38. "La Kabylie cherche sa voie vers l'autonomie," *Le Figaro*, 21 April 2010.

39. "La Coordination nationale pour le changement et la Démocratie," *Le Soir d'Algérie*, 24 February 2011.

40. "Elle a rendu publique hier sa plate-forme pour une période de transition," *Liberté*, 28 March 2011.

41. "Conseil des ministres: Des mesures conjoncturelles pour apaiser les tensions sociales," *El Watan*, 23 February 2011.

42. Yahia H. Zoubir, "The Arab Spring: Is Algeria the Exception?" *IMed/Euromesco*, October 2011. Available at: www.iemed.org/observatori-en/arees-danalisi/arxius-adjunts/copy_of_focus-en/61-Zoubir.pdf

43. The former deputy leader of the Front Islamique du Salut (FIS), Ali Belhadj, had been driven away by protestors when he tried to join the demonstration in Algiers on 12 February. "Ali Benhadj indésirable," *El Watan*, 13 February 2011.

44. See, for example, "Il fausse le débat sur la régionalisation: La provocation de Ferhat Mehenni," *El Watan*, 3 June 2010.

45. "Un millier de manifestants à la marche du MAK à Tizi Ouzou," *El Watan*, 21 April 2011.

46. "Tizi Ouzou: La marche du MAK empêchée," *El Watan*, 13 January 2012.

47. Laura Feliu, "Le Mouvement culturel amazigh (MCA) au Maroc," *L'Année du Maghreb 2004*, Paris: CNRS Editions, 2006, p. 281; Ignace Dalle, *Les trois rois: La monarchie marocaine de l'indépendance à nos jours*, Paris: Fayard, 2004, p. 722.

48. "IRCAM, le beau temps après la tempête," *La Gazette du Maroc*, 7 March 2005; Author's interview with member of IRCAM, Rabat, 8 April 2005.

49. Dalle, op. cit., pp. 723–724.

50. Feliu, op. cit., p. 285.

51. Interview with Rachid Raha, President of the World Amazigh Congress, *Maroc Hebdo International*, 29 September 2000.

52. Author's interviews with Ahmed Adghrini, Secretary-General of the PDAM, Rabat, 2 July 2004 and 7 September 2007.

53. "La justice confirme l'illégalité du 'Parti démocrate amazigh,'" *Aujourd'hui Le Maroc*, 21 April 2008.

54. "Speech by King Mohammed VI of Morocco in Rabat," *Agence Maghreb Arabe Presse*, 9 March 2011. Available at: www.al-bab.com/arab/docs/morocco/kings_speech_9_3_2011.htm.

55. "Morocco's Amazigh Push for Language Recognition," *Magharebia*, 22 March 2011.

56. Royaume du Maroc, *Bulletin Officiel*, 30 July 2011. Available at: www.sgg.gov.ma/BO/bulletin/FR/2011/BO_5964-Bis_Fr.pdf.

57. Interview with Meryem Demnati, member of the Observatoire Amazigh des droits et libertés au Maroc (OADL), *El Watan*, 12 September 2012.

58. Meryem Demnati, quoted in "Nouvelle constitution. Oui, mais ..." *Tel Quel*, 2 July 2011.

59. The Tamaynut association, for example, endorsed the boycott of the referendum on the constitution on the grounds of the changed wording of the final version of the constitution's text on the place of Tamazight. "Morocco Debates Constitutional Changes," *Magharebia*, 30 June 2011.

60. The PJD's leader between 2002 and 2008, Saad Eddine Othmani, had been a Berber-speaker from the Souss Valley in southern Morocco.

61. Before the final text of the constitution had been unveiled, the PJD had stated that it was willing to allow Tamazight to become a national language but that it should be written in Arabic script rather than in Tifinagh or Latin script. "L'amazighité, divise toujours les partis," *Le Soir Echos*, 1 April 2011.

62. Lahcen Daoudi, who was to become Higher Education Minister in the new government, had spoken of the problems associated with accommodating the three different regional variations of Berber language in the country and also the task of translating all official documents, which he argued rendered the according of official status as "not practical." "Amazigh Campaigners Challenge Parties," *Magharebia*, 22 April 2011.

63. *Le Soir Echos*, 22 June 2011; *La Vie Eco*, 1 August 2011. Some activists blamed the change in the wording on the issue of official language in between early and final versions of the constitution on pressure from the PJD and the Istiqlal. "Morocco Debates Constitutional Changes," *Magharebia*, 30 June 2011.

64. Text of king's speech of 17 June 2011, *Agence Maghreb Arabe Presse*, 17 June 2011.

65. Interview with Meryem Demnati, *El Watan*, 12 September 2012.

66. "Identité. En avant l'Amazigh!" *Tel Quel*, 16 May 2012.

67. "Diversité linguistique: L'amazigh à "école,'" *Aujourd'hui Le Maroc*, 14 September 2012.

68. "Raïssa Tabaâmrant s'adresse au parlement en tamazight," *Tel Quel*, 8 May 2012.

69. The deputy who posed the question to Fatima Chahou (also known as singer Raissa Tabaamrant) belonged to the RNI party, originally established by the husband of the current king's aunt. She was strongly applauded by members of her own party as well as those of the Party of Authenticity and Modernity (PAM), established by the king's closest advisor. The question was asked of the Minister for National Education, a member of the Istiqlal party, who was obliged to ask for an informal translation.

70. Interview with Moha Ennaji, *Le Soir Echos*, 6 June 2011.

71. Author's interview with member of IRCAM, Rabat, 31 March 2008. One member of IRCAM once observed that, should the constitutional article enshrining the king's status and power be abolished, this would be "the end of IRCAM." Author's interview with member of IRCAM, Rabat, 1 April 2006.

72. "Sixth World Amazigh Congress Opens for First Time in Tunisia," *Tunisia Live*, 3 October 2011.

73. "Tunisian Amazighs Push to Institutionalize Language and Culture in Tunisia," *Tunisia Live*, 8 March 2012.

74. Interview with Arezki Abboute, *El Watan*, 19 April 2012.

75. "Tunisian Amazighs Campaign for Equal Rights," *Magharebia*, 6 July 2011.

76. *Agraw Amazigh*, 4 January 2001.

77. "Algeria's Kabylie Craves Friendship with Israel," *The Jerusalem Post*, 27 May 2012.

78. "Les élucubrations de Ferhat Mehenni," *El Watan*, 31 May 2012; *Alarabiya*, 22 May 2012.

79. The desire to attack the shibboleths of these ideological enemies may not have been entirely absent from the motivations of those Amazigh activists who advocated links with Israel.

80. Author's interview with Lahcen Daoudi, Rabat, 13 April 2010.

6

CIVIL INSURRECTIONS IN NORTH AFRICA

History and prospects

Stephen Zunes

Despite the stereotype of North Africa as an area of violent conflict, many of the most important challenges to authoritarianism and social injustice have included unarmed civil resistance. The dramatic events of 2010–2011 were not the first wave of mass protests to sweep North Africa and force political change. During the Algerian independence struggle there were significant popular protests, strikes, and other nonviolent forms of resistance which complemented the armed revolution. Elsewhere, there were a series of popular protests against conservative autocratic pro Western governments which prompted military coups by left-leaning nationalist army officers in Libya and Egypt. These new regimes partially satisfied the popular yearning for asserting national pride, challenging imperialism, breaking up the old aristocracy, and making modest efforts at pushing wealth downward, but in most cases these nationalist governments also ended up strengthening oppressive state apparatuses and weakening civil society. In the 1980s, mounting foreign debt forced most North African countries, irrespective of their formal ideology, to cut back on subsidies for food and fuel and impose other austerity measures which brought millions of people into the streets. Through various combinations of liberalization and repression, however, the regimes largely survived. Armed uprisings by Islamist extremists in the 1990s, particularly in Algeria and Egypt, resulted in horrific acts of terrorism by insurgents and brutal crackdowns by the state, underscoring the repercussions of using military means to challenge well-entrenched dictatorships.

Another wave of mass protests took place between 2000 and 2003 in response to the second Palestinian intifada and the US invasion of Iraq, though some regimes channeled these into officially-sanctioned marches to focus attention on the foreign occupations of other Arab nations rather than on grievances closer to home. At the same time, some of the activist groups that emerged during this period, such as Kefaya in Egypt, emerged into popular opposition movements focusing on the authoritarianism, corruption, and economic injustice at home.

Major unarmed North African revolts prior to the Arab Spring

Egypt's independence struggle, 1919–1922

North Africa was the location of one of the first mass, largely unarmed civil insurrections in history, predating the "Arab Spring" by nearly a century, in the Egyptian resistance against British colonialism following the end of World War I. Unemployment, inflation, and failed attempts by the British to squelch dissent after the war made the call for independence evolve into a national cause. In March 1919, when efforts by nationalists to make their case for independence were initially rebuffed, they mobilized a campaign of resistance. In response, their leaders were arrested and exiled to the British-controlled island of Malta. This attempt by the British to squelch dissent by deporting these opposition leaders immediately triggered an unprecedented popular uprising that, within three years, led to limited independence. The uprising was notable in that members from all religions and classes of Egyptian society were moved to action. Within weeks, isolated student demonstrations turned into strikes by transportation workers and professionals, which quickly became a national general strike that dragged the economic and social affairs of Egypt to a standstill. Courtrooms were empty of lawyers. Railroad tracks and telegraph lines used by British interests were sabotaged at strategic locations. Largely nonviolent protests broke out throughout the country, though small-scale violence in the form of rioting broke out in some instances, such as in Cairo, Tanta, and in the Asyut Province. Still, the British violently suppressed demonstrations and killed hundreds of protestors. Within weeks, over 10,000 students, workers, and professionals marched on Cairo's Adbin Palace in open defiance of the British crackdown. Thousands more joined them at the scene in what would be the largest demonstration of the uprising. Wives of the exiled nationalist leaders and other women played critical roles in the resistance by organizing strikes and boycotts of British goods and petitioning foreign embassies on behalf of the independence movement. British authorities in Egypt and London understood that they had lost control of the situation by the third week of March. Winston Churchill declared before the British House of Commons that the whole of Egypt was virtually in insurrection. The British released the nationalist leaders and a promise to engage in negotiations in return for an end to the demonstrations.

Talks dragged on through the next year without resolution, as the British insisted on maintaining control of the country's foreign and security affairs, the lucrative cotton industry, and nearby shipping routes. Nationalists then boycotted the talks and protests resumed with renewed strikes, the closing of shops, pamphleteering, and open dissent in the streets. The British then agreed in principle to an end of the protectorate, but their attempt to set up a puppet Egyptian leadership was again met by strikes and demonstrations. A stalemate ensued that led to a compromise that did not fully satisfy the demands of the nationalists, but did result in Egyptian independence in February 1922 with a freely elected parliament.

Sudan's ouster of dictators, 1964 and 1985

Sudan has a much-deserved reputation for the massive violence which has taken the lives of literally millions of people since the country gained its independence from Great Britain in 1956. Yet it was this predominately Arab country which has witnessed two of the world's earliest and most impressive and successful nonviolent civil insurrections against dictatorship. The first major Sudanese pro-democracy uprising took place against the regime of Field Marshal Ibrahim Abboud in October 1964. When authorities tried to suppress the growing public debate regarding the legitimacy of the military government, which had ruled the country since 1958, large protests by a coalition of students, professionals, workers, leftists, nationalists, and Islamists broke out. Within a week, a general strike had shut down the country. On October 28, scores of nonviolent protesters in Khartoum were gunned down by government forces. Politicians and activists, through family and other personal ties, took advantage of a deepening split within the military to convince them to depose Abboud and return the country to civilian governance on October 30. A series of unstable civilian coalitions governed the country for the next five years until the democratic government was deposed by a bloodless military coup in May 1969, led by Colonel Jafaar Nimeiry.

Over the next sixteen years, Nimeiry shifted his ideology from left-wing nationalist to pro-Western anti-communist, and then to Islamist, but never altered his increasingly unpopular and autocratic style of leadership. Early in the spring of 1985, however, there were a series of massive and largely nonviolent demonstrations in the capital of Khartoum and the neighboring city of Omdurman. A general strike called by trade unions and professional organizations paralyzed the country as the pro-democracy movement gained increasing support from a growing cross-section of the population, including the business community. Despite thousands of arrests and scores of shootings, the largely peaceful protests continued, with even the country's judiciary joining the civil rebellion. Protesters shut down pro-government radio stations and occupied airport runways to prevent Nimeiry, who was then on a state visit to Washington, from returning home. On April 6, the military seized power, formally overthrowing the dictator. Pro-democracy activists continued their protests, however, forcing the new junta to allow for an interim civilian-led government followed by democratic elections that gave the Sudanese one of the most open democratic political systems in North Africa.

As with the earlier experiment in democracy, however, the shaky civilian governments that followed were unable to unify the country. A coalition of military officers and hardline Islamists seized power in 1989 and has ruled ever since. The regime of Omar al-Bashir has been more thorough than previous autocrats in terms of the systematic destruction of key civil society institutions, particularly the trade unions, which played a major role in the 1964 and 1985 uprisings. Still, pro-democracy groups like *Girifna* (Arabic for "We are fed up") have continued to organize. In addition to armed regional rebellions in the west, south, and northeast in recent decades, there have also been periodic nonviolent struggles for greater democracy and accountability. In the 1990s, anti-regime protests were gaining traction until the 1998 US bombing of the country's largest pharmaceutical plant (apparently based on erroneous intelligence that it was a chemical weapons factory controlled by Al-Qaeda) enabled the regime to steer popular resentment towards the United States. Another uprising in 2005, centered in the poorer shantytowns of the capital, was violently suppressed. Scattered demonstrations in February 2011 were also crushed.

In June of 2012, and again in September of 2013, a new wave of protests emerged. Despite being met by severe repression, there were impressive innovations by the pro-democracy forces. Recognizing the vulnerability of large concentrations of protesters to the armed forces of repressive regimes, the protests were organized as a series of simultaneous small demonstrations in many parts of the country and various neighborhoods of the capital. The grievances have not been ethnic or even ideological as much as they were a simple demand for an accountable government. Though students, as in the previous uprisings, were disproportionately represented among the protesters, there was also a strong component of poor and working-class Sudanese, as well as older people. Women played an important role as well, with the first protest of the 2012 uprising organized by female students at the University of Khartoum. Just as the movement has been consciously decentralized in terms of protests, it has been consciously decentralized in terms of organization.

Algeria's popular struggles

Algeria's political history has long centered on the armed resistance to French colonialism led by the National Liberation Front (FLN), which has ruled the country since independence in 1962. As Malika Rahal has noted, "This narrative was institutionalized in Algerian academia during the 1970s while state monopoly over book publications, including history textbooks, left no outlet for competing narratives."[1] However, the independence struggle did include significant unarmed resistance against French colonialism for many decades through cultural associations, trade unions, Sufi and family networks, political parties, and other networks. From petitioning to public protests to boycotts to emigration to cultural resistance, Algerians nonviolently expressed their opposition to the French occupation, created autonomous political space, shaped national consciousness, and made the European hold on their country more and more tenuous, even prior to the launch of the armed struggle in 1954. The general strike in April 1952, the indefinite student strike commenced in May 1956, and the eight-day general strike of January/February 1957 helped served notice of popular opposition.

Unfortunately, the brutality of the French occupation and the revolution itself limited the range of collective action. Following independence, the FLN could take advantage of its revolutionary credentials, the country's economic growth, its progressive foreign policy, and relatively good efforts at diversifying the economy and providing social welfare to hold back concerns regarding authoritarianism, arrogance, mismanagement, and corruption. However, the strong secular orientation of the FLN in an Islamic society, as well as the party's estrangement from the masses, made the leadership forget just how strong traditional values remained, particularly among the growing numbers of urban poor. By the 1980s, a whole generation had grown up since the FLN's bloody independence struggle from France and the heroism of the revolution could no longer legitimize rule by a party which was unable to find meaningful opportunities for millions of unemployed and underemployed youth, particularly in the face of declining oil revenues and a growing national debt.

In March of 1980, government efforts to prevent a poetry reading by prominent Berber writer Mouloud Mammeri in Tizi Ouzou prompted protests which turned into weeks of protests in the Kabylia region and in the capital of Algiers demanding an end to repression and the recognition of Tamazight as an official language along with Arabic. The demonstrations were brutally suppressed, but marked the beginnings of organized Berber resistance.

Opposition to FLN rule grew within the Arab majority as well as throughout the decade, as anti-regime protests from Islamist and pro-democracy oppositionists peaked in October 1988, forcing major democratic openings in Algeria, including the scheduling of free competitive parliamentary elections in December 1991 and January 1992. However, when the FLN fared poorly in the first round, with the Islamic Salvation Front (FIS) decisively winning and threatening to win a super-majority in the second round scheduled a few weeks later, the military staged a coup on January 11, cancelling the election and jailing FIS leaders. While the initial resistance was nonviolent, Algeria was soon plunged into a decade-long civil war with horrific mass killings on both sides, particularly from the Armed Islamic Group, which took the lives of over 200,000 Algerians.

Subsequently, Algeria has experienced a gradual liberalization from the top down. Small protests broke out in Algeria in January 2011, particularly in poor urban areas, following the announcement of increased prices on important goods. Because Algeria had been somewhat more open in terms of public protests than most North African countries, and authorities were more used to handling demonstrators, they were able to more effectively suppress the opposition through a combination of repression and compromise. A major series of demonstrations scheduled for February 12 were contained using non-lethal means of crowd control. Only 5,000 turned out for demonstrations the following week and, in a number of cases during this period, security forces decisively outnumbered the protesters themselves.

Meanwhile, Berber protests in 1990, 1994, and 1995 – while often met with serious government repression – nevertheless forced greater recognition of Berber cultural and linguistic rights. Major resistance starting in 2001 and continuing for the next several years scored additional victories. Leading political figures and political parties, once suppressed, now actively engage in government affairs and electoral politics.

Despite its socialist rhetoric and revolutionary heritage, Algerians struggle with many of the social, economic, and political frustrations of other North African countries. However, the long-established oligarchy of the FLN, the military, and business interests has proved more sustainable than the one-man rule which has characterized most of its North African neighbors. More fundamentally, the trauma of the civil war and subsequent fear of any kind of mass disorder has discouraged most Algerians from joining protests.

Moroccan resistance

For different reasons, Morocco has not had a history of mass civil insurrections that have seriously threatened the regime. The ability to personify the state through the monarchy, which still enjoys some popularity in key sectors of the population, has served to limit any threat to the regime since the two attempted military coups in the early 1970s. This has been made possible in part through the relatively progressive and nationalistic persona of King Mohammed V, who helped lead his country to independence from France in 1956. Though his successors have been less popular, they have been shrewd political leaders, who have combined their claims of being a *sayyid* – descendants of the Prophet Mohammed and thereby providing religious legitimacy – with an effective balance of concessions and repression to limit mass dissent.

In addition to scattered acts of armed resistance, there were protests, petitioning, riots, and other forms of unarmed resistance to the French protectorate, particularly in the 1952–1954 period, between the exile of Sultan Mohammed to Madagascar and the French agreement to negotiate independence. Mohammed died in 1961 and was succeeded by his son Hassan II, who suppressed political parties and targeted opponents, though a relatively strong labor movement survived. Following austerity measures in March of 1965, major protests erupted in Casablanca, Rabat, and Fez, leading to widespread repression with as many as one thousand casualties. Ben Barka, the popular exiled leader of the National Union of Popular Forces, which supported the protests, was kidnapped and murdered by the king's security services a few months later. In June 1981 and, in particular, in January 1984, violent protests across the country in reaction to the elimination of food subsidies – imposed by the government in response to demands by the International Monetary Fund – resulted in hundreds of deaths.

Several rounds of peaceful protests emerged in 2011. Protesters had to try to balance showing loyal to the monarchy while expressing anger at endemic corruption, the high costs of living, and lack of political liberties. Major protests were scheduled for February 20, supporters ranging from urban educated youth to the popular al-Adl wa al-Ihsan Islamist movement. The initial turnout was sparse but soon grew dramatically, with demonstrations hitting more than a dozen cities. The protests were peaceful and repression by security forces was minimal, as demonstrators called for democracy, accountability, and the rule of law without directly challenging King Mohammed. The king responded with a speech on March 9 in which he appointed a committee to propose constitutional reforms. Demonstrations continued, peaking on March 20, as tens of thousands hit the streets. A terrorist attack the following month in Marrakesh, despite apparently being unrelated to the protests, gave the regime an excuse to crack down. The brutality of the repression might have led to increased protest, but the king quickly called for a referendum on constitutional changes to be voted upon within weeks which, while maintaining the primacy of the monarchy, did offer some important concessions for a more representative government. The amendments passed overwhelmingly, but most Moroccans have not seen much real change, and scattered protests have continued. Indeed, a culture of resistance has emerged among Moroccan youth, with scores of gatherings – including demonstrations and sit-ins – most weeks, in both urban and rural areas.

Mali's nonviolent revolution, 1991

Opposition to the corrupt and dictatorial regime of General Mousa Traore in Mali grew during the 1980s. During this time, austerity programs imposed to satisfy demands of the International Monetary Fund brought increased hardship upon the country's population while elites close to the government lived in opulence. An opposition movement emerged, led by the Alliance for Democracy in Mali (ADEMA), which was brutally suppressed by the regime.

Starting on March 22, 1991, ADEMA organized mass pro-democracy rallies and a nationwide strike in both urban and rural communities, which became known as *les evenements* ("the events"), or the "March Revolution." In the capital of Bamako, soldiers opened fire indiscriminately on the nonviolent demonstrators. Although the demonstrations were conceived as nonviolent and nonviolent discipline had been maintained up to that point, riots broke out briefly following the shootings. Barricades and roadblocks were erected to protect protesters from soldiers. Traore declared a state of emergency and imposed a nightly curfew. Despite the loss of many lives, protesters continued to come back each day to demand the resignation of the dictatorial president and the implementation of democracy. A total of 300 people are estimated to have died during the four-day protest. By March 26, the growing refusal of soldiers to fire at the largely nonviolent protesters turned into a full scale mutiny, as thousands of soldiers put down their arms and joined the pro-democracy movement. That afternoon, Lieutenant Colonel Amadou Toumani Toure announced on the radio that he had arrested the dictatorial president, Moussa Traore.

Toure then suspended the existing institutions and took the lead in the transitional government, which was initially named the National Council of Reconciliation. He promised he would neither run for president nor take over power once a president was elected in free and fair elections. Renamed the Transitional Committee for the Salvation of People, Toure appointed a civilian prime minister. ADEMA leader Alpha Oumar Konare was elected president soon thereafter. In 2002, Toure came out of retirement and was elected president and was re-elected five years later, though his second term was marred by corruption and inept leadership.

Soon after the March Revolution of 1991, the Malian government negotiated a peace agreement with armed Tuareg rebels in the north in which the insurgents agreed to end their rebellion in return for a degree of autonomy. In March 1996, there was a massive ceremonial burning of the rebels' surrendered weapons in Bamako. Only relative minor flare-ups in fighting occurred over subsequent years until the armed overthrow of the Gaddafi regime in Libya in 2011 resulted in disparate armed groups – including Tuareg tribesmen – gaining access to major stores of armaments. Some of these vast caches of weapons were passed on to Tuaregs in Mali who, now having the means to effectively challenge the government militarily, resumed their long-dormant rebellion under the leadership of the National Movement for the Liberation of Azawad (MNLA). Charging that the civilian government was not being tough enough against the rebels, US-trained Army Captain Amadou Sanogo and other officers staged a coup in March of 2012, ending North Africa's longest democratic experiments. Tuareg rebels, taking advantage of the political divisions in the capital, then consolidated their hold on the northern part of the country by capturing its remaining towns and declaring an independent state. Within weeks, however, radical Islamist militias – including extremists allied with Al-Qaeda – ended up taking over virtually all of the territory that had been initially seized by forces of the over-extended MNLA. Military intervention by France in January 2013 helped drive out the Islamists from populated areas of the north, reuniting most of the country under government control. Meanwhile, as a result of nonviolent resistance by pro-democracy activists, jockeying by political leaders, and international pressure, Sanogo was forced to step down within weeks of seizing power and a coalition government led the country until free elections took place in September 2013, bringing former prime minister Ibrahim Boubacar Keïta to the presidency.

Western Sahara: The struggle against occupation

As happened during the late 1980s in the Israeli-occupied Palestinian territories and in apartheid South Africa, the first decade of the new century saw the locus of the Western Sahara independence struggle against Moroccan occupation shift from the military and diplomatic initiatives of an exiled armed liberation movement to an unarmed popular resistance from within, as young activists in the occupied territory and even in Saharawi-populated parts of southern Morocco confronted Moroccan troops in street demonstrations and other forms of nonviolent action, despite the risk of shootings, mass arrests, and torture. An armed struggle led by the nationalist Polisario Front, based primarily out of Saharawi refugee camps in neighboring Algeria, had battled Moroccan occupation forces from the 1975 Moroccan invasion to the 1991 cease fire, which came about as a result of promises by Morocco that they would allow for a UN-supervised referendum on independence. When Morocco reneged on its promises, and with the kingdom's French and American allies blocking the UN from enforcing its mandate, Saharawis from different sectors of society launched a series of protests, strikes, cultural celebrations, and other forms of civil resistance. Many of these focused on such issues as educational policy, human rights, and the release of political prisoners, but have become increasingly centered on the right to self-determination. They also raised the cost of occupation for the Moroccan government and increased the visibility of the Saharawi cause. Indeed, perhaps most significantly, civil resistance has helped to build support for the Saharawi struggle for self-determination among international NGOs, solidarity groups, and even among the small but growing number of sympathetic Moroccans.

Internet communication became a key element in the Saharawi movement, with public chat rooms evolving into vital centers for sending messages and allowing breaking news regarding the burgeoning resistance campaign to reach those in the Saharawi diaspora and international activists. Despite attempts by the Moroccans to disrupt these contacts, the diaspora has continued to provide financial and other support to the resistance. Though there have been complaints from inside the territory that support for their movement by the older generation of exiled Polisario leaders was inadequate, the Polisario appears to have recognized that, by having signed a cease-fire and then having had Morocco reject the diplomatic solution expected in return, their options are limited. As a result, increasing numbers of Saharawis appear to believe that the only real hope for independence has to come from within the occupied territory, in combination with solidarity efforts from global civil society. There have been some small victories, such as the successful campaign in 2009 which forced Moroccans to allow Saharawi nonviolent resistance leader Aminatou Haidar, whom they had expelled from her country, to return after she engaged in a near-fatal month-long hunger strike at an airport in the Canary Islands.

After Moroccan authorities used force to break up the large and prolonged demonstrations of 2005 and 2006, the resistance opted mainly for smaller protests, some of which were planned and some of which were spontaneous. A typical protest would begin on a street corner or a plaza where a Saharawi flag would be unfurled, women would start ululating, and people would begin chanting pro-independence slogans. Within a few minutes, soldiers and police would arrive, and the crowd would quickly scatter. Other tactics have included leafleting, graffiti (including tagging the homes of collaborators), and cultural celebrations with political overtones. Such nonviolent actions, while broadly supported by the people, appear to have been less a part of coordinated resistance than a result of action by individuals. Still, the Moroccan government's regular use of violent repression to subdue the Saharawi-led nonviolent protests suggests that civil resistance is seen as a threat to Moroccan control.

One of the obstacles to internal resistance is that Moroccan settlers outnumber the indigenous population by a ratio of more than 2:1, and by an even wider margin in the major cities, making certain tactics used effectively in similar struggles more problematic in the case of Western Sahara. For example, although a general strike could be effective, the large number of Moroccan settlers, combined with the minority of indigenous Saharawis who oppose independence, could likely fill the void resulting from the absence of much of the Saharawi workforce. Although that might be alleviated by growing pro-independence sentiment among ethnic Saharawi settlers from the southern part of Morocco, it still presents a challenge that has not been faced by other largely nonviolent struggles in occupied lands, such as those in East Timor, Kosovo, and the Palestinian territories.

Despite this, civil resistance also appears to have forced a shift in Morocco's strategy of maintaining control of the mineral-rich territory. Although the Moroccan autonomy plan for the territory put forward in 2006 is fairly limited in scope and does not meaningfully address Morocco's legal responsibility to recognize the Saharawi's right of self-determination, it nevertheless constitutes a reversal of Morocco's historical insistence that Western Sahara is as much a part of Morocco as other provinces by forcing them to acknowledge that it is indeed a distinct entity. Protests in Western Sahara in recent years have begun to raise some awareness within Morocco, especially among intellectuals, human rights activists, pro-democracy groups, and some moderate Islamists – long suspicious of the government line in a number of areas – that not all Saharawis see themselves as Moroccans, and that there exists a genuine indigenous opposition to Moroccan rule.

In the occupied territory, Moroccan colonists and collaborators are given preference for housing and employment and the indigenous people receive virtually no benefits from their country's rich fisheries and phosphate deposits. In response, a new tactic emerged in September 2010, as Saharawi activists erected the tent city about 15 kilometers outside of El Aioun, the former Spanish colonial capital and largest city in the occupied territory. By November, the nonviolent protest had swelled to close to 20,000 people, which, relative to the population, was much larger than the protests in Egypt's Tahrir Square three months later. Since any protests calling for self-determination, independence, or enforcement of UN Security Council resolutions are brutally suppressed, the demonstrators pointedly avoided such provocative calls, instead simply demanding economic justice. Even this was too much for the Moroccan monarchy, however, which was determined to crush this nonviolent act of mass defiance. The Moroccans tightened the siege in early October, attacking vehicles bringing food, water, and medical supplies to the camp, resulting in scores of injuries and the death of a 14-year-old boy. Finally, on November 8, the Moroccans attacked the camp, driving protesters out with tear gas and hoses, beating those who did not flee fast enough, and killing several. This set off a wave of rioting, which in turn triggered the burning and pillaging of Saharawis' homes and shops, with occupation forces shooting or arresting suspected activists, hundreds of whom disappeared after the outbreak of violence.[2]

Nonviolent resistance by Saharawis has not only occurred in opposition to the Moroccan occupation, but in the refugee camps as well, where nearly half the population lives. The Polisario Front has ruled up to 170,000 Saharawis in refugee camps in the desert of southwestern Algeria since the exodus following the 1975 Moroccan invasion. While Polisario guerrillas waged an armed struggle against Morocco, the Front set up a sophisticated governmental structure in exile independent of Algerian control, calling itself the Saharawi Arab Democratic Republic (SADR), which has been recognized by more than 80 countries and is a full member state of the African Union. Their governance in the refugee camps includes a network of health care centers, cottage industries, agricultural projects, and distribution systems that have won praise from international development agencies. Though Morocco occupies most of the territory, roughly half of the indigenous peoples of this sparsely populated country live in these camps under Polisario control.

Despite these impressive structures, which have ensured a high degree of economic and social democracy, actual political democracy for most of this period was limited. Many Saharawis felt there was too much domination by one element of the Polisario and that there existed serious discrepancies between the movement's egalitarian line and the political reality. On the political level, the Polisario's executive committee, despite the facade of participatory democracy, made all the real decisions; many of the local political leaders were hand-picked by the committee. There were a series of work stoppages and protests in 1988 as democrats pressed for liberalization. Hardliners resisted, arresting democratic opposition leaders. Still facing stiff opposition from the population through ongoing nonviolent resistance, the SADR went through several governments that autumn, but still failed to satisfy the population. Due to continued protests, however, the democrats won a series of victories in 1990–1991 and have subsequently come to largely dominate the movement, with one of the key protest leaders becoming prime minister. Among other reforms, the executive committee and Politburo were replaced by a national secretariat with key positions held by reformers, as well as a new and more democratic constitution and an independent human rights commission. While there are still scattered reports of human rights abuses, the situation is vastly improved compared to the earlier period, and is far better than in the Moroccan-occupied territory.

Undoubtedly the already existing social and economic democracy made possible the transition to a more democratic political system. Yet given the isolation of the camps and the monopoly of the armed force in the hands of the Polisario elite, a more active repression would likely have been attempted had the leadership thought it would work. Indeed, it may be the first time that such a serious division within a national liberation movement was resolved through nonviolent action, avoiding disintegration into armed factions or the establishment of a new rival liberation organization.

Arab Spring uprisings

Tunisian revolution, 2010–2011

After 24 years of rule under the autocratic Zine el Abidine Ben Ali, opposition had been steadily growing, particularly among younger Tunisians, in response to corruption, high unemployment, poverty, and political repression. On December 17, 2010, the self-immolation outside of municipal offices in the central Tunisian town of Sidi Bouzid by 26-year-old Mohammed Bouazizi – a fruit seller whose merchandise had been confiscated following his refusal to pay bribes – sparked a series of demonstrations across the country. Bouazizi's plight was seen as emblematic of the injustice and economic hardship afflicting many Tunisians under the Ben Ali regime. Street protests broke out throughout central Tunisia and were initially disorganized and largely spontaneous, at times deteriorating into full-scale riots, thereby giving the regime the political space for increased repression.

However, by the end of the month, protests became more organized and spread to the capital of Tunis. The pro-democracy movement grew to include the Tunisian Federation of Labor Unions as professional groups, including lawyers, 95% of whom honored calls for a strike on January 6, 2011, to protest brutality by security forces. The following day, the regime arrested a number of prominent journalists, bloggers, activists, and musicians. A series of massacres of demonstrators by security forces between January 8–12 in Kasserine, Mbarki, and Dachraoui resulted in a popular backlash that turned the scattered protests into a full-scale unarmed insurrection

There was little concern expressed in allied Western capitals of the regime's repression. Secretary of State Hillary Clinton instead expressed her concern over the impact of the "unrest and instability" on the "very positive aspects of our relationship with Tunisia," insisting that the United States is "not taking sides" and that she will "wait and see" before even communicating directly with Ben Ali or his ministers.[3] Congress weighed in with support of the regime by passing a budget resolution that included $12 million in security assistance to Tunisia, one of only six foreign governments provided direct taxpayer-funded military aid.

There was little outside powers could do to bolster Ben Ali's flagging rule, however. On January 13, as protests gathered momentum, the authoritarian president announced unprecedented reforms and promised not to seek re-election in 2014, but these concessions failed to quell the insurrection. Indeed, the trade union federation issued a formal call for a general strike. On January 14, the government imposed a state of emergency and banned gatherings of more than three people, threatening that "arms will be used if orders of security forces are not heeded." Tens of thousands of Tunisians ignored the threat, marching upon the dreaded Interior Ministry as the general strike effectively shut down the country. Tunisian army generals, apparently concerned at the willingness of their forces to follow orders to commit such a large-scale massacre, informed the president that they would not obey orders to fire into the crowds. Within hours, Ben Ali resigned and he and his family fled the country.

The prime minister, Mohamed Ghannouchi, then assumed power as interim president, replaced the following day by Fouad Mebazaa, the former speaker of the lower house of parliament. Since both were leading members of the ruling party, the Democratic Constitutional Rally (RCD), protests continued, forcing the inclusion of leading opposition figures in the cabinet. Demonstrators persisted until top government posts were purged of any members of the RCD and other close associates of the former regime on January 27.

Elections in October brought together a broad coalition government, led by the conservative Islamists Ennahda party. During the next two years, concerns about possible restrictions on women's rights and a failure to curb extremist violence led to large-scale protests, resulting in the resignation of the prime minister and the eventual installation of a technocratic government in December 2013. Elections in October 2014 brought to power Nidaa Tounes, a center-left coalition led by secularists, trade unionists, and liberals. A democratic constitution ratified in January 2014 included provisions guaranteeing freedom of speech, freedom of religion, gender equality, and protection of the country's natural resources.

Egyptian revolution, 2011

What has since become known as the 2011 Egyptian Revolution was the culmination of growing popular resistance in the preceding years. During the first decade of the new century, crushing poverty, increasing human rights abuses, rampant inflation, institutionalized corruption, a deteriorating educational system, and high unemployment spawned massive protests, with many thousands taking to the streets in Cairo, Alexandria, and other major cities despite brutal police attacks on demonstrators, widespread torture of detainees, and other repressive measures. Between 1998 and 2010, more than two million Egyptians participated in more than 3,300 strikes, demonstrations, and factory occupations. A 2007 sit-in by 3,000 municipal workers at the finance ministry ultimately won higher salaries and the right to form an independent union. In the spring of 2010, thousands of workers staged rotating sit-ins in front of the parliament building despite efforts by police to disperse them by force. As protests grew, the government announced a freeze on further privatization and gave in on other economic demands.

There had been a dramatic growth in Egyptian civil society during the final decade of Mubarak's rule, with an increasing number of labor strikes and small, but ever-larger, demonstrations led by such youthful, secular pro-democracy groups as Kefaya (meaning "Enough!") and the April 6 Movement (named after a nationwide strike and protest on that date in 2008). Towards the end of 2010, increasing government repression, the murder by police of a popular blogger for exposing government corruption, worsening economic conditions, blatantly rigged parliamentary elections, and the implication of security forces in a church bombing that appeared designed to stoke sectarian tensions, led some activists to believe that popular sentiments against the regime were deep enough and widespread enough that change was indeed possible. The successful uprising in Tunisia made some Egyptians believe a similar uprising might be successful in their country as well.

A demonstration was scheduled for January 25, a national holiday honoring the country's notoriously brutal and corrupt police. Hundreds of feeder marches surged through the back alleys of Cairo, growing block by block, and by the time they fed into Tahrir Square, they numbered in the tens of thousands. Similar scenes unfolded in cities throughout the country. Police responded brutally, but protesters held the square and other key points in cities throughout the country. Two days later, the regime shut down virtually all Internet and mobile phone service, but the crowds continued to swell. While overwhelmingly peaceful, there was some rioting, looting, and vandalism, and the headquarters of the government New Democratic Party was burned on January 28. The police were overwhelmed and withdrew as the army was called in to try to maintain order. A full-scale revolt was in progress.

The regime tried to appease the protesters with minor reforms. Mubarak initially appointed a vice-president and reshuffled his cabinet. Three days later, he announced he would not seek re-election, his son would not succeed him as expected, and he would reform the constitution. By this point, however, it appeared that nothing short of the downfall of the regime would satisfy protesters as the crowds swelled into the millions in cities and towns throughout the country.

Mubarak and the military unleashed thugs to attack not just demonstrators, but journalists and others, in Cairo, Alexandria, and other cities. There was a mass release of criminals from prison and, with the police in disarray, it appeared the government was deliberately sowing enough chaos that Egyptians would demand a strong government crackdown. By this time, the death toll was approaching 1,000 and international criticism – including from the United States, the Mubarak regime's most important foreign backer – was increasing. Despite initial hesitation, the Obama administration began quietly pushing for the dictator to step down. Mubarak resigned on February 11.

While the first round of presidential elections in 2012 resulted in a slight majority for more democratic and secular candidates, the top two candidates who made the runoff represented the military and the Muslim Brotherhood (Ikwan), considered to be the worst possible result by leaders of the pro-democracy uprising, resulting in a narrow victory by Ikwan nominee Mohammed Morsi. While attempting to bring some degree of civilian primacy over the military, Morsi's conservatism and semi-autocratic style alienated millions of Egyptians who, quietly encouraged by the military, engaged in increasingly larger demonstrations. After only a year in office, the massive protests prompted a military coup and brutal crackdown which extended to not just the Brotherhood and other Islamists opponents, but pro-democratic forces as well. Elections in 2014, which were widely considered to not be free or fair, resulted in the election of General Abdel Fattah el-Sisi, who has effectively prohibited protests and banned the leading pro-democracy groups which had led the movement against Mubarak.

Libya's civil war

The significance of the largely nonviolent uprisings that successfully brought down the dictatorships in Tunisia and Egypt is even more pronounced if contrasted with the armed uprisings in Libya, which began through overwhelmingly nonviolent struggles.

In Libya, pro-democracy protests began on February 15 in Benghazi and elsewhere in eastern Libya. In less than a week's time, the initial unarmed insurrection had resulted in pro-democracy forces taking over most of the cities in the eastern part of the country, a number of key cities in the west, and even some neighborhoods in Tripoli. It was also during this period when most of the resignations of cabinet members and other important aides of Gaddafi, Libyan ambassadors in foreign capitals, and top military officers took place. Thousands of soldiers defected or refused to fire on crowds, despite threats of execution. Still, mass killings of unarmed protesters combined with defecting soldiers bringing their weapons soon turned what was initially a largely nonviolent uprising along the lines of Libya's neighbors into a full-scale civil war. Now facing the regime's heavily armed forces on the battlefield, the opposition began losing ground. Following Gaddafi's infamous February 22 speech threatening massacres in rebel strongholds, the United Nations – at the encouragement of the Arab League – passed a resolution declaring a no-fly zone to protect civilians from attack by regime forces. NATO forces went well beyond that mandate to effectively become the air force for the rebels. This initially enabled Gaddafi to rally far more support to his side than he would have otherwise by taking advantage of the nationalist reaction to a European and North American attack on the country. Despite this, Gaddafi was eventually overthrown, though at a horrific human cost. It is important to note, however, that the reason the anti-Gaddafi rebels were able to march unexpectedly into Tripoli with so little resistance in August 2011, instead of the bloody and protracted battle that so many expected, was because of the massive and largely unarmed civil insurrection that had erupted in the city's neighborhoods. Indeed, much of the capital had already been liberated by the time the rebel columns entered and began mopping up the remaining pockets of pro-regime forces.

It raises questions as to whether Gadhafi could have been toppled through an unarmed insurrection in the manner of Ben Ali and Mubarak. As a rentier state, the effectiveness of strikes and other traditional tools of nonviolent resistance would have been more limited. In addition, the regime's dependence on foreign mercenaries would make them less likely to defect and more likely to obey orders to shoot into crowds. Still, by his final years in power, Gadhafi had alienated virtually every sector of Libyan society across the regional and ideological spectrum and the success of largely nonviolent methods of resistance at the beginning and end of the struggle gives some indication that it may have been possible if better planned and there had not been such a rush to arms. Given the lives lost, the physical destruction, and the instability which has followed, the military victory over the Gadhafi regime has come at enormous costs.

Implications for democracy

One advantage of nonviolent resistance is that, in order for an unarmed civil insurrection to succeed, a coalition representing broad segments of society needs to be built; this requires the kind of compromise and cooperation critical for building a democracy. By contrast, armed struggles are centered on an elite vanguard with a strict military hierarchy and martial values, patterns of leadership that often continue once rebel military commanders become the new political leaders. Successful armed revolutions send the message that power comes through an ability to kill your opponent and destroy its assets. This is why – with a number of important exceptions – dictatorships overthrown by nonviolent insurrections usually become stable democracies within a few years, while dictatorships overthrown by armed revolutions are more likely to become new dictatorships, often with continued violence and chaos.[4]

Despite the inevitable political struggles that come with any transition to democracy, Tunisia's democratic evolution has been peaceful, with traditional oppositionists, leftists, moderate Islamists, and others cobbling together a new constitutional order. Contrast this with the violence and chaos – including the extra-judicial killings of Gaddafi and hundreds of his supporters – that took place in neighboring Libya. Since Gaddafi's overthrow, more than 200,000 men in a country of barely six million remain in armed militia groups not under the control of the Libyan government, with radical Islamists with ties to international terrorism controlling large swathes of territory and rival militias fighting for control of airports, seaports, oil fields, and other valuable assets.

The events of 2011 have changed North African society. German anthropologist Samuli Schielke, who was present at the demonstrations in Egypt, observed that the sense of unity and power experienced by the protesters in Tahrir Square and elsewhere was necessarily transient, since negotiations, party politics, tactical decisions, and other processes that have taken place subsequently certainly don't "equal the incredible energy of coming together in the popular contestation of public space and saying 'no!'" However, he observed, "thanks to its utopian nature, it is also indestructible. Once it has been realised, it cannot be wiped out of people's minds again. It will be an experience that, with different colourings and from different perspectives, will mark an entire generation."[5]

Similarly, after covering both the Tunisian and Egyptian uprisings, British journalist Peter Beaumont emphasized the significance of this shift in attitude: "A threshold of fear has been crossed. For what has happened in both countries is that the structures of a police state have been challenged and found, to the surprise of many, to be weaker than imagined." Even before Mubarak was forced out, he noted that "a transition of power is already under way" – not as a result of formal negotiations or diplomatic efforts by the United States or the European Union, but through the people effectively seizing power for themselves. These bold actions by what were once relatively small bands of activists "have been embraced by a wider population no longer afraid to speak or to assemble."[6]

For years, these autocratic regimes offered short-term fixes and various small concessions that failed to pull up the roots of the country's problems. A combination of paternalism and repression by these regimes had fostered an atmosphere of apathy and cynicism. Now, however, a whole new generation has been empowered. Despite the disappointing reversals in Egypt, the chaos in Libya, the ongoing authoritarianism in Morocco and Algeria, and the continued occupation of Western Sahara, the uprisings have demonstrated that the political power of any government rests ultimately upon the willingness of the population to recognize its authority and obey its edicts.

Tunisia's apparently successful democratic transition could serve as a model for the rest of North Africa. The region hosts an increasingly literate population and growing civil society, spearheaded by young people who are tired of the old politics, hungry for social justice, largely secular in outlook, and suspicious not just of the current regimes, but extremist alternative ideologies as well. The best hope for democratic change in North Africa will not likely come from outside intervention, armed revolution, or top-down reform by elites, but rather from civil society employing tools of strategic nonviolent action.

Notes

1. Malika Rahal, "Algeria: Nonviolent resistance against French colonialism, 1930s–1950s," in Maciej Bartkowski, ed., *Recovering Nonviolent History: Civil Resistance in Liberation Struggles*, Boulder: Lynne Rienner, 2013.
2. Stephen Zunes, "Upsurge in repression challenges nonviolent resistance in Western Sahara," *Open Democracy*, 17 November 2010.
3. "Secretary Clinton's interview with Al Arabiya," U.S. Department of State, Office of the Spokesman, Secretary of State Hillary Rodham Clinton with Taher Barake of Al Arabiya, 11 January 2011, http://iipdigital.usembassy.gov/st/english/texttrans/2011/01/2011011 1171532su0.726681.html#ixzz3Hq4fyCjL.
4. Erica Chenoweth and Maria J. Stephan, *Why Civil Resistance Works*, New York: Columbia University Press, 2011.
5. Samuli Schielke, "Some first conclusions from the Egyptian revolution," *An Anthropologist's Diary of the Egyptian Revolution and What Followed*, 6 February 2011, www .jadaliyya.com/pages/index/580/youll-be-late-for-the-revolution-an-anthropologists-diary-of-the-egyptian-revolution.
6. Peter Beaumont, "These are uprisings with all the energy and optimism of a rock festival," *Guardian*, 5 February 2011.

7

SOCIAL MEDIA AND MOBILIZATION IN THE ARAB SPRING AND BEYOND

Lina Khatib[1]

The Arab Spring has become closely associated with social media; initial reports labeled the Arab uprisings as "Twitter" and "Facebook revolutions". Yet, while social media have indeed played an important role in the Arab Spring, they were not the primary catalyst for the Arab uprisings in North Africa. Other communication tools like the mainstream media and mobile phones also played a central role during the uprisings. More importantly, all communication technologies played a supporting role to offline mobilization tools during the Arab Spring. Social media use during the Arab Spring did not emerge overnight; these technologies have their roots in communication processes dating back at least a decade, during which Arab activists honed and adapted their online mobilization strategies as well as ways of organizing and publicizing their efforts. In the context of transition in North African countries, the challenge of social media is to evolve from a tool for activism to a regime building tool. The demands of democratic transition and regime building require interactions, hierarchies, and activist networks that are very different from those used in challenging authoritarian leaders. Although social media have revealed themselves to occupy a much more marginal position in this context, they have already become so firmly connected with youth movements in the Arab world that they have begun to transform the way in which politics is performed by state actors, thereby planting the seed for new political dynamics in the region, albeit dynamics conditional upon changes in offline political activism.

Revisiting social media before the Arab Spring: A revolutionary infrastructure

Before analyzing the role of social media during and after the Arab Spring, it is important to revisit the different ways in which social media were used by activists before the Arab Spring, since those uses became established components of online activism in the region. Particularly in the five years leading up to the first revolution of the Arab Spring, the Arab world witnessed a rise in the use of the online media for political purposes, with Egypt leading the way. The Kifaya movement that began in late 2004 sparked the use of the online media for documentation and self-reporting, which quickly paved the way for their use in popular mobilization. Kifaya, which reached its peak in 2005, was a grassroots movement against the hereditary succession of the Egyptian presidency, and partially relied on social media, and especially blogs, to document and disseminate photographic images of police brutality against protesters, as well as to crowdsource documentation of state fraud in the context of elections. Initiatives like www.shayfeen.com encouraged citizens to monitor parliamentary and presidential elections by using video cameras to record incidents of fraud in voting stations.

Social media as a political platform gained momentum with the establishment of Wael Abbas' Misr Digital blog in March 2005, which became an online political newspaper chronicling Kifaya's activities and the state's violent response through stories often accompanied by photographs, gaining credibility for the blog (Al-Malky 2007). Abbas' pioneering site was notable for helping break the taboo regarding speaking out against regime brutality. His posting of pictures of people who had been attacked by the police encouraged other torture victims to start taking photos and videos of their injuries with their mobile phones and post them on the internet (Younis 2008), and in January 2007 he started uploading mobile phone videos taken by the police as they tortured detained citizens (Radsch 2008). Abbas' Misr Digital catalyzed the rise of self-reporting and political blogging in Egypt, and a new symbiotic relationship between the press and the blogosphere (Gharbeia 2008). Abbas explains that in some cases when the press could not report directly on sensitive stories, they would inform Abbas, who would agree to break the story on his blog, after which the press would simply report his article. This proved a successful method of getting around censorship (Abbas 2008).

Other bloggers began to follow Wael Abbas in using social media sites like Flickr. One such blogger was Hossam el-Hamalawy, whose blog and Flickr Photostream constitute two of the most comprehensive photographic archives of public political life in Egypt since the Kifaya movement (Radsch 2008). This rising prominence of social media was in some part due to Kifaya's activism. As Amr Gharbeia, one of the Egyptian bloggers, explained in 2008, "Kifaya found a space for expression on the internet after being physically restricted on the streets. Before, the police used to surround Kifaya protesters on a given street and no one would know what the police were doing" (Gharbeia 2008). The posting of online images, for example, created visibility about police brutality. In doing so, social media helped push the boundaries of what could be represented in the public domain in Egypt, creating a public (though virtual) space for the expression of dissent, and helping break taboos, including those against criticism of the president.

Social media also helped connect different communities. Kifaya has used the same technique as secular activists influenced by the Muslim Brotherhood, which used such sites to display photographs of Brotherhood prisoners. This strategy allowed the Brotherhood to humanize its prisoners through individual online posters. The Brotherhood went still further by launching one blog for every prisoner, which were usually run by the prisoners' children (Younis 2008). The internet, therefore, facilitated dialogue between Muslim Brotherhood youth activists and their secular counterparts. Not only did secular bloggers support Brotherhood bloggers who had been detained through online banners and other forms of support, they also engaged in debates about their respective visions for Egypt. One such debate was between Muslim Brotherhood blogger Abdul Monem Mahmoud, who ran the popular Ana Ikhwan blog until he left the Brotherhood in 2009, and online activist Ahmed Sherif. In 2008, Sherif created a video in which he argued that Egyptians come from different walks of life, and criticized the Brotherhood for seeking to paint all of them in one color. Mahmoud's response after being sent the video by Sherif was to post it on his blog and ask readers to comment on it. Mahmoud used the video as a tool to publicly ask the questions of whether the Muslim Brotherhood was succeeding in reaching out to different sectors of Egyptian society, what kind of message the Brotherhood was sending society, and whether the Brotherhood was forcing its Islamist "color" on others.

Social media also facilitated reaching out to communities beyond the immediate networks of Egyptian activists. Mobile phones played an important role in this process. Rafael argues that mobile phones "bring a new kind of crowd about, one that was thoroughly conscious of itself as a movement headed towards a common goal" (Rafael 2003: 403). In the Egyptian case, mobile phones allowed activists to engage other activists beyond the online community, but they were also used to disseminate the message of the online media to a wider crowd. Audio recordings meant to be downloaded and circulated via mobile phones, such as those by Mahmoud Tawfic, became a means of reaching out to people beyond the internet. Mahmoud Tawfic's audio pieces mixed actual recordings and satirical commentary to critique issues like Mubarak's landslide victory in the September 6, 2005 election and fraud during the parliamentary elections of November 9, 2005. The pieces pushed boundaries by presenting the voices of the people declaring that "Mubarak is void" and giving eyewitness accounts of the presence of fraud in the elections.

Ahmed Sherif took this further between 2005 and 2008 through videos meant for distribution online as well as via mobile phones. The videos, mainly accompanied by satirical songs, commented on political developments and issues like constitutional amendments and Mubarak's birthday. Explaining the way he distributed the videos, Sherif said in 2008, "When I released the mobile phone videos, I posted them on YouTube but also sent them 'manually' to a large mailing list of friends and sympathizers. I sent them as 3GP files (the appropriate MMS format for cell phones) so they would spread within their own communities". Sherif's motive behind this strategy was twofold. First, as he put it, "I thought the Web 2.0, at large, could be extremely conductive, and serve the voicing of free opinions and even help the migration of free uncensored expression from the Web to other offline and more accessible media (print, radio, mp3 exchange . . .). I always bear in mind that less than 5 or 10% of the Egyptian population has access to the Internet".

Second, "Video, in general (for songs or other purposes) is perfect in a country with so many people who can't read or write. I had always been hoping, from the very beginning, that these videos would reach these populations. It's probably just a dream, but who knows what might happen" (Sherif 2008).

But social media went beyond being tools of documentation or expressing dissent. They also became tools of online and offline mobilization. As Etling et al. write, "Egyptian bloggers frequently use pictorial badges on their sites to show support for various campaigns, such as for freeing bloggers, calling for reform, or promoting social issues" (Etling et al. 2009: 15). Amr and Ahmed Gharbeia were two Egyptian bloggers who started the use of these internet pictorial banners to organize offline protest campaigns, which became a standard mobilizing method. In this way, the Egyptian blogosphere became an example of how technology "reflects and mirrors the culture in which it evolves rather than guiding and directing it" (Barber 2003: 33). A Facebook campaign led by Esraa Abdel Fattah and Ahmed Maher in 2008, for example, called for a national strike in support of workers' rights. The strike and the resulting birth of the April 6 youth movement marked the "discovery" of the internet's potential to support large-scale offline action among Egyptian activists.

A similar trajectory was taking place, albeit on a different scale, in Tunisia. Tunisian opposition and protest websites have existed since 1998, when the "Takreez" distribution list appeared. The Tunisian government's tight control over the internet space as well as the arrest of opposition figures forced much protest activity to be conducted in the diaspora, leading to the establishment of a number of sites like tunisnews.net, an independent news portal set up by Tunisian exiles to report on repression inside Tunisia, and reveiltunisien.org in 2002, a hub for Tunisian and French political activists (Lamloum 2011). As Laryssa Chomiak documents, "In July 2001 . . . the late economist Zoubir Yahyaoui, nephew of oppositional Judge Mokhtar Yahyaoui, created TUNeZine, an online portal critiquing the Ben Ali regime. TUNeZine primarily published articles about the regime's human rights abuses as well as Judge Yahyahoui's infamous open letter to President Ben Ali criticizing the absence of an independent judiciary" (Chomiak, 2014). This online activity continued, and in 2008 worker protests in the Southern town of Gafsa started being covered on Facebook by Tunis-based activists (Breuer 2012). The response of the Tunisian government was to greatly restrict internet traffic and to arrest or harass internet activists within Tunisia, like the blogger Slim Amamou. Undeterred, Amamou and other activists organized a Facebook campaign titled "Tunis in White" in May 2010 in protest of restrictions on internet freedom, which called on Tunisians to protest by wearing white and gathering at Avenue Habib Bourghiba in the capital. The public protest was not successful as the government shut down the Facebook page – but not before activists from the wider community started engaging in debate about political participation, censorship, and political freedom (Chomiak, 2014). Similarly, in Egypt, the death of 28-year-old Khaled Said in June 2010 at the hands of the Egyptian police after he posted on YouTube a video of Egyptian policemen profiting from drug sales catalyzed the creation of a Facebook group, "We Are All Khaled Said". It also became a platform for the expression of political demands, from campaigning against torture and electoral fraud to the lifting of emergency law (Tarzi 2011).

The cases of Egypt and Tunisia in the run up to the Arab Spring illustrate how "the Internet can empower political movements in the region, since it *provides an infrastructure* for expressing minority points of view, breaking gatekeeper monopolies on public voice, lowering barriers to political mobilization (even if symbolic), and building capacity for bottom-up contributions to the public agenda" (Etling et al. 2009: 15, emphasis added). As such, social media became part of a larger revolutionary infrastructure that contained components of internet use that were later utilized during the Arab revolutions of 2011. Mary Joyce (2011) summarizes some of the components as being to:

1. Document: digital content creation
2. Broadcast: information-sharing, no call to action
3. Mobilize: information-sharing, with call to action
4. Co-Create: design and planning
5. Protect: evading censorship & surveillance

Beyond these practical uses of the internet, the revolutionary infrastructure also contained social components strengthened by the use of social media: the creation of a social space to express political dissent; affinity between diaspora and home communities; interactions between communities with different ideological leanings; and support by urban, middle-class communities for grievances of those from working-class backgrounds, thereby strengthening social cohesion. While much attention has been given to the practical components of internet use in the context of Arab activism, the social components are an important dimension that emerged more clearly during the Arab uprisings. What this means is that both micro and macro processes were at play in determining the role of social media before and during the Arab Spring.

Social media and the Arab Spring

During the Arab Spring, social media were used for three main purposes: cyber activism, civic engagement, and citizen journalism. Khamis and Vaughn summarize:

> The role of new media before, during, and after the Egyptian revolution was especially important in three intertwined ways, namely: enabling cyberactivism, which was a major trigger for street activism; encouraging civic engagement, through aiding the mobilization and organization of protests and other forms of political expression; and promoting a new form of citizen journalism, which provides a platform for ordinary citizens to express themselves and document their own versions of reality (Khamis and Vaughn 2011).

Cyberactivism took place before and in tandem with street protest. In Tunisia, the online media were used to disseminate anti-regime material, like the video clip of the song *Rais Lebled* (O country's president) by Tunisian rapper Hamada Ben-Amor, which had been posted online in late 2010, leading to the rapper's arrest (Miladi 2011). It was also used to express outrage at the self-immolation of Mohamed Bouazizi, the young fruit seller who set fire to himself in protest against his maltreatment by the police for operating a street cart without a license, and simultaneously, at the response of Ben Ali, who capitalized on the opportunity to arrange a photo-op while visiting Bouazizi in hospital. While Tunisian online activism played a supporting role to growing street protests, in Egypt, the "We Are All Khaled Said" Facebook group was seminal in rallying online support for a gathering in the streets on January 25. A YouTube video by a young activist called Asmaa Mahfouz – a simple to-camera statement by Mahfouz, asking Egyptians to join her on January 25 in Tahrir Square, using colloquial language that invoked patriotism, chivalry, and women's honor as reasons to join in the protest – was also disseminated online and covered by the mass media. Mahfouz' video is important to reflect upon because it illustrates the role of emotions in mobilization. Recent theory on mobilization emphasizes the role of emotional responses in galvanizing collective action (Goodwin, Jasper, and Polletta 2000); in this line of research, a sense of injustice and anger is considered essential to mobilization. Gamson has argued that an "injustice frame" is built on "the righteous anger that puts fire in the belly and iron in the soul" (Gamson 1992: 32). Research has found that a sense of moral outrage may compel individuals to participate in mobilization efforts without engaging in any rational calculation of benefits to be reaped from doing so. Goodwin, Jasper, and Polleta have coined the term "moral shock" to describe when "an unexpected event or piece of information raises such a sense of outrage in a person that she becomes inclined toward political action, whether or not she has acquaintances in the movement" (Goodwin, Jasper, and Polletta 2001: 16). It can be argued that the deaths of Khaled Said in Egypt and Mohamed Bouazizi in Tunisia were incidents of "moral shock" that social media helped amplify.

The success of the revolutions in Tunisia and Egypt was an inspiration for a group of youth in Morocco who formed the February 20 Movement to call for political reform. Like their Egyptian counterparts, February 20 youth also formed groups on Facebook and disseminated an online video featuring 13 Moroccans from different walks of life speaking in their native Arabic or Berber. "I am Moroccan and I will take part in the protest on February 20," they all say, and then go on to explain their reasons for marching: "freedom, equality, better living standards, education, labor rights, minority rights and so on" (Lalami 2011). However, the Moroccan activists quickly lost momentum and failed to reach out to a wider community, despite initial backing by one Islamist group, al-Adl wal-Ihsan. Their mobilization efforts were further quashed by the cosmetic constitutional reform announced by the Moroccan king in late 2011, which seemed to satisfy Islamists as well as to co-opt civil society groups (Benchemsi, 2014). One factor that may explain the failure of the February 20 movement is that, unlike Tunisia and Egypt, which had contained long-term interactions between different social groups, February 20 youth were largely confined to a limited, new social network without wider ties, and thus without the kinds of macro ties that would give cyberactivism an impact on the ground.

Civic engagement and mobilization soon led to a more practical use for social media. Crowdmapping, the use of online interactive maps to document crisis events through open-source software like Ushahidi, was used to document incidents of abuse as well as to create a visual online history of protests (Samnani and Nur 2011). This kind of dissemination of information plays an important role in mobilization, since the availability of information is the prerequisite for debates that shape people's political opinions. As Shirky argues, the more widely accessible the information, the more people are able to formulate considered perspectives (Shirky 2011). It can be argued that this process of information dissemination and conversation helped the formation of a core group of activists who participated in street protests, and who, through offline networks, were able to reach out to wider members of their communities to engage them in protest.

Social media websites were also used "to transmit information on medical requirements, essential telephone numbers and the satellite frequencies of Al Jazeera" (Sultan Al Qassemi, quoted in Beaumont 2011) and for the dissemination of protest tactics when the channel was being disrupted by the Egyptian government. In Egypt, Google Earth shots were used to direct street protests. These screenshots were distributed online and offline through a 26-page manual titled "How to Protest Intelligently", which contained tactical advice on street mobilization (iRevolution 2011). Such uses of social media, with their awareness of the importance of linking offline and online mobilization, have their roots in earlier experiences of political protest. One such experience was the failed Egyptian strike on May 4, 2008, which, like its April 6 predecessor, was initiated though social media. The failure of the strike sparked activists to think of better ways to translate cyberactivism into offline mobilization. As Faris cites in an article from 2008: "In the aftermath of the failed May 4th follow up strike [which was called for through Facebook that year], Hossam El-Hamalawy lectured his fellow activists and readers that 'this technology should be complimentary [*sic*] and a logistical support for whatever we do ON THE GROUND.' El-Hamalawy argues that 'the general strike is coming, but from below'" (Faris 2008: 9).

Through trial and error over the years, activists learned two valuable lessons. First, that online activism on its own is insufficient and that it has a dialectical relationship with offline activism, with each better suited for different goals according to various circumstances. The most basic illustration of this point was when the Egyptian government shut down the internet for four days during the January 25 Revolution, forcing online activists to rely on other methods to get people to the streets. Secondly, for mobilization efforts to be effective, activists must reach out to communities beyond their own. This point was demonstrated in a number of ways during the Tunisian revolution. The revolution capitalized on the relationship between activists within Tunisia and those in the diaspora, fostered through years of online activism by those in exile. It also capitalized on international support for local activists, as illustrated through the hacking group

Anonymous' crackdown on Tunisian government websites (Allagui and Kuebler 2011). The relationship between middle-class activists in urban areas and those from working-class backgrounds also helped this process of outreach, with this affinity having begun during the worker protests in Gafsa, as presented earlier. Activists therefore learned the importance of creating affinities between disparate communities in the offline world as well as the online world in order to mold individual potential into group action. Howard and Hussain argue that during the Arab Spring, the "digital media helped to turn individualized, localized, and community-specific dissent into a structured movement with a collective consciousness about both shared plights and opportunities for action" (Howard and Hussain 2011: 41). Yet it was not the media that directed this process, but the people themselves, who used the media as one tool for collective action among many other tools. The key enabler, then, is not the media, but the wider dynamic of social cohesion.

Affinities between different communities (rural and urban; home and diaspora) were also projected through citizen journalism. During the Jasmine Revolution, Tunisian activists traveled from urban centers to remote rural areas to document protests using video (Breuer 2012). These videos, portraying protesters attacking government buildings, victims of police shooting, and mass rallies throughout Tunisia, were posted on opposition websites and disseminated through social media, becoming a key source for Al-Jazeera after the Tunisian government blocked the channel's on-the-ground reporting of the revolution. As Miladi points out, it was Al-Jazeera's reliance on videos and images posted on YouTube and Facebook that fueled Tunisians' increased use of social media during the revolution (Miladi 2011). As such, social media content went on a circular journey, from the online to the mass media and back to the online media in the form of the production of more online content. The Tunisian diaspora also helped the dissemination of videos and news to the outside world through Twitter (Poell and Darmoni 2012).

In Egypt, too, citizen journalism increased as the Egyptian government tried to block journalists from reporting on the protests. In addition to ordinary citizens, a number of Egyptian activists were quite sophisticated in their use of recorded video, having completed training abroad and learned from analyzing the experiences of other activist movements, such as the Green Movement in Iran, which offered lessons in what constitutes effective video images (Ishani 2011). The merger of trained activists and ordinary people in the use of ICTs also illustrates the coming together of different networks of people during the Arab Spring who were able to use these technologies spontaneously as well as strategically (Allagui and Kuebler 2011).

Strömbäck argues that "it is possible to reach out to wider audiences through the Internet, but in the absence of coverage in the traditional news media, this possibility is seldom realized" (Strömbäck 2008: 243). Citizen journalism during the Egyptian revolution recognized the importance of "metacoverage" (Gitlin 1980) as footage recorded by protesters in Tahrir Square became a primary form of recorded images of the revolution broadcast on television. In this sense, when analyzing the role of social media in citizen journalism, it is important to think of the roles and interplay of new and old media (Aday et al. 2012). Moreover, far from restricting the understanding of the value of social media to in-country dynamics, one should bear in mind their use for external outreach. As the Blogs and Bullets study of the new media during the Arab Spring shows, the new media played more of a role in disseminating news to outside the MENA region during the Arab Spring, suggesting that the in-country impact of the new media as disseminators of information may have been exaggerated (Aday et al. 2012).

Studies like those by the Dubai School of Government echo this finding about social media tools, suggesting that during the Egyptian revolution, "For many protestors these tools were not central. It can also be argued that Facebook was an instrumental tool for a core number of activists who then mobilized wider networks through other platforms or through traditional real-life networks of strong ties" (Dubai School of Government 2011: 5). This finding echoes the position of Malcolm Gladwell (2010), who argues that political change can only happen through high-risk activism by movements with strong ties and a well-defined group identity. He says that social media, on the other hand, require little sacrifice while making people feel like they have done something meaningful. While this analysis rightly focuses on the circumscribed role of social media and points out certain important dynamics, it nevertheless misses, to a degree, the wider social and political dynamics that impact the lives of those activists using social media.

What these arguments overlook is that online activism in the context of authoritarianism in the Arab world is not a low-risk activity. As presented in the discussion above, activism in a virtual setting can result in arrest and real life intimidation. By prioritizing strong ties, they also miss the role of weak ties in political change. As Etling, Faris, and Palfrey argue, "Political change in consolidated democracies is driven by organizations with strong networks. Political change in authoritarian regimes is more likely to be enabled by more decentralized associations with loose networks" (Etling, Faris, and Palfrey 2010: 38). Studies on the role of networks in political activism have shown that weak ties play a seminal role in this context. In a study from 1993, Denoeux argues that informal associations in Egypt were instrumental for mobilizing popular dissent. In 2008, Lim echoed this finding, arguing that "there is little evidence that strong ties are more effective than weak ties in recruiting activists" (Lim 2008: 961). While those studies focus on weak ties formed in face-to-face settings, social media also encourage the formation of weak ties as activists "meet" others virtually.

Yet these studies on the limited impact of social media rightly point out the importance of offline networks and activism mechanisms. As Ramesh Srinivasan puts it: "By fixating on technologies and the few youth that actively use them, we ignore a much more powerful narrative – the story of how synergies are created between classes to mobilize as a network without depending on social media. In Egypt, these networks may include family connections, neighborhoods, mosques, and historical institutions, such as the previously banned Muslim Brotherhood. New technologies hardly erode or overwhelm these classic models of communication and information sharing" (Srinivasan 2011). As argued earlier in this chapter, the on-the-ground realities in Tunisia and Egypt point to a merger of the two modes of communication, as offline and online tools were used simultaneously and for different purposes. This echoes positions like that of Granovetter, who in 1973 argued that the transmission of mass media information in community organizations is dependent on weak ties. He went on to say that "weak ties, often denounced as generative of alienation . . . are here seen as indispensable for individuals' . . . integration into communities; strong ties, breeding local cohesion, lead to overall fragmentation" (Granovetter 1973: 1378). More weak ties, then, mean more cohesive communities and thus greater ability for collective action. What these debates ultimately tell us is that any meaningful analysis of the role of social media during the Arab Spring must not examine them in isolation from other networks and modes of communication, especially of the offline world, and that we must pay attention to their role within both micro and macro-level social processes.

Conclusion: Social media and democratic transition

If social media ultimately played a limited role during the Arab Spring, is there a role for social media in the processes of democratic transition and state building after the Arab uprisings? The indicators seem to point out a marginal role for the social media in this context. In the period following the uprisings in North Africa, social media continued to be used for a number of purposes, just as they had been before and during the revolutions. In Egypt, they continued to be used for documentation, online videos exposing violence against protesters by the Supreme Council of the Armed Forces were circulated through an initiative called Kazeboon (liars) (Elshami 2012). In Tunisia and Egypt, they also continued to be used to report arrests and police abuse (Global Voices 2012a and 2012e). Social media were also used for a number of purposes that were either new or had become more important since the revolutions. In Morocco, social media were a platform for social protest and were used during the 2012 protest calling for an end to forced marriage after rape (Global Voices 2012c). In Egypt, social media assumed a higher profile as tools for monitoring elections. In Tunisia, they found a new role as civic education tools, used to organize citizenship initiatives (Global Voices 2012d). In Libya, a country with very limited use of social media during the Gaddafi era, social media were used to solicit citizen comments on drafting a new electoral law (Global Voices 2012b). Crowdsourcing also became a central mechanism for initiatives like regional humanitarian assistance, such as for sending humanitarian convoys from Egypt to Libya (iRevolution 2012).

However, these initiatives remain limited in scope and fragmented in nature, led as they are by decentralized actors. It is much easier for such fragmented actors to achieve a specific goal like the departure of a leader than to work on something as complex as formulating policy. The challenge of centralization seen online reflects offline dynamics: The youth who spearheaded the uprisings in Tunisia and Egypt and who called for protest in Morocco have played a limited role in the period immediately following relative regime change or constitutional reform, partly because of their firm commitment to loose, decentralized networks, both online and offline (Benchemsi, 2014). For example, crowdsourcing initiatives regarding constitution drafting in Egypt may have informed a number of (internet-active) youth, but they were not enough to give youth voices weight when an assembly whose membership largely excluded young voices eventually drafted the constitution.

The challenges facing youth in North Africa certainly include the need for group strategies and hierarchies (Gladwell 2010), and necessitate the building of strong ties in face-to-face settings. Social media encourage the formation of weak ties, which are positively correlated to greater likelihood of leaving current groups and joining new ones (McPherson et al. 1992). While this decentralization helped youth evade censorship and arrest under authoritarianism, it does not help the formation of the kinds of stable networks needed to form new political parties and lobbying groups. Moreover, the capacity of social media to be the main tools of collective action is limited. As Diani argues, "It is hard to imagine ICT to operate [*sic*] as a substitute for the ties created by associations and social groups" (Diani 2011: 473) in the offline world. Bellin sums up this argument by saying:

> Even if social media can facilitate contentious collective action that can bring down an authoritarian regime, this media may be less effective at advancing the subsequent process of building democracy. To the contrary, the very qualities that make social media effective at evading authoritarian repression – anonymity, spontaneity, lack of hierarchy – may be precisely the qualities that undermine its ability to help build the institutional foundation of a working democracy. Without hierarchy, institutionalized longevity, or a clear identity, it becomes difficult for activists to identify collective priorities, negotiate compromises, and make credible commitments to those compromises (Bellin 2012: 139).

What adds to the challenge faced by activists is that patrimonial regimes do not leave effective state institutions in their wake, making it doubly hard to form such institutions without effective strategies and hierarchies (Bellin 2004).

One thing social media have had an impact on in the transition period, however, is the style of politics. Presidential candidates during the Egyptian election of 2012 used social media in their campaigns, not only to disseminate electoral platforms (in the case of Mohamed Morsi) but also to project an image of modernity and outreach to Egyptian youth (in the case of Abdul Monem Abul Fotouh). While this stylistic change is largely superficial, the increased use of social media in mainstream political processes is likely to continue into the future. Such changes can play an indirect role in supporting the growth of transparency and demands for accountability from leaders. But this can only happen if offline tools of network formation, political activism, and institution building are put in place to direct the processes of transition.

Note

1. This chapter draws from Lina Khatib, *Image Politics in the Middle East: The Role of the Visual in Political Struggle* (London: IB Tauris, 2013).

References

Abbas, Wael (2008). Interview with the author. Cairo, March.

Aday, Sean et al. (2012). *New Media and Conflict after the Arab Spring*. Blogs and Bullets Report II. Washington, DC: United States Institute of Peace. Available: www.usip.org/files/resources/PW80.pdf.

Allagui, Ilhem and Kuebler, Johanne (2011). Arab Spring and the Role of ICTs: Editorial Introduction. *International Journal of Communication* 5: 1435–1442.

Al-Malky, Rania (2007). Blogging for Reform: The Case of Egypt. *Arab Media and Society*, Spring, issue 1. Available: www.arabmediasociety.com/articles/downloads/20070312143716_AMS1_Rania_Al_Malky.pdf.

Barber, Benjamin R. (2003). Which Technology and Which Democracy? In Jenkins, Henry, Thorburn, David and Seawell, Brad (eds.), *Democracy and New Media*, pp. 33–48. Cambridge, MA: The MIT Press.

Beaumont, Peter (2011). The Truth about Twitter, Facebook and the Uprisings in the Arab World. *The Guardian*, February 25. Available: www.guardian.co.uk/world/2011/feb/25/twitter-facebook-uprisings-arab-libya.

Bellin, Eva (2004). The Robustness of Authoritarianism in the Middle East: Exceptionalism in Comparative Perspective. *Comparative Politics* 36(2, January): 139–157.

Bellin, Eva (2012). Reconsidering the Robustness of Authoritarianism in the Middle East: Lessons from the Arab Spring. *Comparative Politics* 44(2, January): 127–149.

Benchemsi, Ahmed (2014). Morocco's Makhzen and the Haphazard Activists. In Khatib, Lina and Lust, Ellen (eds.), *Taking to the Streets: The Transformation of Arab Activism*. Baltimore: The Johns Hopkins University Press.

Breuer, Anita (2012). *The Role of Social Media in Mobilizing Political Protest – Evidence from the Tunisian Revolution*. Bonn: German Development Institute.

Chomiak, Laryssa (2014). Architecture of Resistance in Tunisia. In Khatib, Lina and Lust, Ellen (eds.), *Taking to the Streets: The Transformation of Arab Activism*. Baltimore: The Johns Hopkins University Press.

Diani, Mario (2011). Networks and Internet into Perspective. *Swiss Political Science Review* 17(4): 469–474.

Denoeux, Guilain (1993). *Urban Unrest in the Middle East: A Comparative Study of Informed Networks in Egypt, Iran, and Lebanon*. New York: State University of New York Press.

Dubai School of Government (2011). *Arab Social Media Report* 1(2). Available: www.dsg.ae/portals/0/ASMR2.pdf.

Elshami, Nancy (2012). Grassroots Mobilization, Social Entrepreneurship, & the Future of Egypt. *Muftah*, March 30. Available: http://muftah.org/grassroots-mobilization-social-entrepreneurship-the-future-of-egypt/.

Etling, Bruce et al. (2009). *Mapping the Arabic Blogosphere: Politics, Culture, and Dissent*. Internet & Democracy Case Study Series, Berkman Center Research Publication number 2009–06. Berkman Center for Internet & Society. Available: www.alhaqqsociety.org/research/MappingTheArabicBlogosphere.pdf.

Etling, Bruce, Robert Faris, and John Palfrey (2010). Political Change in the Digital Age: The Fragility and Promise of Online Organizing. *SAIS Review*, Summer–Fall, 37–49.

Faris, David (2008). Revolutions Without Revolutionaries? Network Theory, Facebook, and the Egyptian Blogosphere. *Arab Media and Society*, Fall, issue 6. Available: www.arabmedia society.com/articles/downloads/20080929153219_AMS6_David_Faris.pdf.

Gamson, William (1992). *Talking Politics*. Cambridge: Cambridge University Press.

Granovetter, Mark S. (1973). The Strength of Weak Ties. *American Journal of Sociology* 78(6, May): 1360–1380.

Gharbeia, Amr (2008). Interview with the author. Cairo, March.

Gitlin, Todd (1980). *The Whole World Is Watching*. Berkeley: University of California Press.

Gladwell, Malcolm (2010). Small Change. *New Yorker*, October 4. Available: www.newyorker .com/reporting/2010/10/04/101004fa_fact_gladwell.

Global Voices (2012a). Arab World: Technology in the Time of Revolution, April 17. Available: http://globalvoicesonline.org/2012/04/17/arab-world-technology-in-the-time-of-revolution/.

Global Voices (2012b). Libya: Draft Electoral Law Criticized, January 10. Available: http:// globalvoicesonline.org/2012/01/10/libya-draft-electoral-law-criticized/.

Global Voices (2012c). Morocco: Protest to End Forced Marriage after Rape, March 16. Available: http://globalvoicesonline.org/2012/03/16/morocco-sit-in-planned-to-raise-awareness-about-the-plight-of-rape-victims/.

Global Voices (2012d). Tunisia: The New Phase of Social Media, March 13. Available: http:// globalvoicesonline.org/2012/03/13/tunisia-the-new-phase-of-social-media/.

Global Voices (2012e). Tunisia: Online Platform to Monitor Police Abuse, July 10. Available: http://globalvoicesonline.org/2012/07/10/tunisia-online-platform-to-monitor-police-abuse/.

Goodwin, Jeff, Jasper, James M., and Polletta, Francesca (2000). The Return of the Repressed: The Fall and Rise of Emotions in Social Movement Theory. *Mobilization: An International Quarterly* 5(1): 65–83.

Goodwin, Jeff, Jasper, James M., and Polletta, Francesca (2001). Introduction: Why Emotions Matter. In Goodwin, Jeff, Jasper, James M., and Polletta, Francesca (eds.), *Passionate Politics*, pp. 1–26. Chicago: University of Chicago Press.

Howard, Philip N. and Muzammil M. Hussain (2011). The Role of Digital Media. *Journal of Democracy* 22(3): 35–48.

iRevolution (2011). Civil Resistance Tactics Used in Egypt's Revolution #Jan25, February 27. Available: http://irevolution.net/2011/02/27/tactics-egypt-revolution-jan25/.

iRevolution (2012). Crowdsourcing Humanitarian Convoys in Libya, April 6. Available: http://irevolution.net/2012/04/06/crowdsourcing-convoys-libya/.

Ishani, Maryam (2011). The Hopeful Network. *Foreign Policy*, February 7. Available: www .foreignpolicy.com/articles/2011/02/07/the_hopeful_network.

Joyce, Mary (2011). *7 Activist Uses of Digital Tech: Popular Resistance in Egypt*. International Center for Nonviolent Conflict. Available: www.nonviolent-conflict.org/images/stories/ webinars/joyce_webinar.pdf.

Khamis, Sahar and Vaughn, Katherine (2011). Cyberactivism in the Egyptian Revolution: How Civic Engagement and Citizen Journalism Tilted the Balance. *Arab Media and Society*, Summer, issue 13. Available: www.arabmediasociety.com/?article=769.

Lalami, Laila (2011). Arab Uprisings: What the February 20 Protests Tell Us about Morocco. *The Nation*, February 17. Available: www.thenation.com/blog/158670/arab-uprisings-what-february-20-protests-tell-us-about-morocco#.

Lamloum, Olfa (2011). *Al-i'lam al-ijtima'i wa thawrat al-jeel al-arabi al-jadid*. Al-Jazeera Research Center. Available: www.aljazeera.net/NR/exeres/AC7A8E0B-9952–435F-9A6C-6D0 25279CC8E.htm.

Lim, Chaeyoon (2008). Social Networks and Political Participation: How Do Networks Matter? *Social Forces* 87(2): 961–982.

McPherson et al. (1992). Social Networks and Organizational Dynamics. *American Sociological Review* 57(2): 153–170.

Miladi, Noureddine (2011). Tunisia: A Media Led Revolution? *Aljazeera.net*, January 17. Available: http://english.aljazeera.net/indepth/opinion/2011/01/2011116142317498666.html.

Poell, Thomas and Darmoni, Kaouthar (2012). Twitter as a Multilingual Space: The Articulation of the Tunisian Revolution Through #sidibouzid. *European Journal of Media Studies* 1. Available: www.necsus-ejms.org/twitter-as-a-multilingual-space-the-articulation-of-the-tunisian-revolution-through-sidibouzid-by-thomas-poell-and-kaouthar-darmoni/.

Radsch, Courtney (2008). Core to Commonplace: The Evolution of Egypt's Blogosphere. *Arab Media and Society*, Fall, issue 6. Available: www.arabmediasociety.com/articles/down loads/20080929140127_AMS6_Courtney_Radsch.pdf.

Rafael, Vicente L. (2003). The Cell Phone and the Crowd: Messianic Politics in Recent Philippine History. *Public Culture* 15(3): 399–425.

Samnani, Hina and Nur, Lolla Mohammed (2011). Crowdmapping the Arab Spring – Next Social Media Breakthrough? *Voice of America News*, June 28. Available: www.voanews.com/english/news/middle-east/Crowdmapping-Arab-Spring-Next-Social-Media-Breakthrough—124662649.html.

Sherif, Ahmed (2008). Email interview with the author. April.

Shirky, Clay (2011). The Political Power of Social Media: Technology, the Public Sphere, and Political Change. *Foreign Affairs*, January/February. Available: www.foreignaffairs.com/articles/67038/clay-shirky/the-political-power-of-social-media.

Srinivasan, Ramesh (2011). London, Egypt, and the complex role of social media. *Washington Post*, August 11. Available: www.washingtonpost.com/national/on-innovations/london-egypt-and-the-complex-role-of-social-media/2011/08/11/gIQAIoud8I_story.html.

Strömbäck, Jesper (2008). Four Phases of Mediatization: An Analysis of the Mediatization of Politics. *Press/Politics* 13(3): 228–246.

Tarzi, Fadl (2011). Arab Media Influence Report 2011 – Social Media and the Arab Spring. *News Group International*. Available: http://newsgroup.ae/amir2011/amir-march-29.pdf.

Younis, Nora (2008). Interview with the author. Cairo, March.

8

WESTERN SAHARA

Change under the radar

Alice Wilson[1]

Each passing year seems to confirm the intractability of the conflict, ongoing since 1975, over Western Sahara, the UN's last decolonization case in Africa. Sovereignty over the desert territory of 266,000 km² (roughly comparable to the size of the United Kingdom or the state of Colorado) is disputed between Morocco and Western Sahara's liberation movement, POLISARIO Front. That the conflict has fallen into the grip of an apparently irreconcilable political stalemate suggests that for each party the status quo is something between tolerable, at least preferable to the likely alternatives, and for some perhaps even desirable. Yet the costs are also high. In human terms, thousands of Sahrawis (a contested term)[2] are either living in what a recent report described as a "state of fear" in Moroccan-controlled Western Sahara (Robert F. Kennedy International Delegation 2012) or as refugees in the harsh *ḥamāda* desert near Tindouf, in southwest Algeria. The costs are also regional, as the unresolved conflict impedes North African integration (Zoubir 2010). There are likewise financial costs, not least for the international community. The latter is responsible not only for much aid to the refugees,[3] but also for the annual multi-million dollar costs of the UN mission to Western Sahara (MINURSO).[4] For Morocco, a country with challenging human development indices,[5] the opportunity to exploit the phosphate and fishing resources of Western Sahara may nevertheless be outweighed by the significant resources needed for supporting the military presence in Western Sahara and subsidizing the civilian settler population.[6]

This chapter describes the status quo for which these costs are borne before going on to contrast it with an alternative view that, under the radar of formal politics, the conflict has undergone dynamic change in recent years. If, politically and diplomatically, the conflict over the *territory* is at an impasse, then the conflict over the *people* of Western Sahara has recently seen game-changers. The people of Western Sahara are mobilizing in new ways; they are taking novel and groundbreaking stances challenging both Morocco and POLISARIO; and they are literally on the move in new migratory patterns across the territory. If these changes pass all too easily under the radar of formal politics, this is one of many means by which the people of Western Sahara have been all too often overlooked in their own conflict. The irony of this tendency is poignant, given that, at least in international law, the Western Sahara dossier hinges upon the right of the people of Western Sahara to self-determination. After considering recent changes on the ground for the people of Western Sahara, the chapter concludes by relating these shifts to the regional context in the wake of the Arab Spring, and the prospects for conflict resolution.

Western Sahara and the status quo

The conflict over Western Sahara took shape in the mid 1970s as the UN increased its pressure on Spain to decolonize the then Spanish Sahara. Spain agreed to conduct a plebiscite in which the territory's people would decide their political future. The UN visit to the territory in May 1975 found overwhelming local support for independence and the liberation movement, POLISARIO, formed in May 1973, which had been leading armed resistance to the Spanish colonial presence. Yet following the International Court of Justice's Advisory Opinion, which found that the claims to Western Sahara presented by Morocco and Mauritania did not obviate the right of the people of the territory to self-determination, in November 1975 Morocco mobilized Moroccan civilians to march into and "reclaim" Spanish Sahara. Although the incursion of these civilians into the territory was brief, the Green March was politically and symbolically potent. It increased the pressure on Spain to renege on its original decolonization plans. A few days later that month, Spain, Morocco and Mauritania signed the Madrid Tripartite Accords (MTA), which arranged for Spain to hand over the administration of the territory to Morocco and Mauritania.[7] Following Spain's withdrawal, Morocco and Mauritania partially annexed the territory. Thousands of civilian Sahrawis fled the territory, and from early 1976 were settled in refugee camps near Tindouf, Algeria. POLISARIO fought against the annexing powers, assumed (with Algerian consent) the leadership and governance of the refugee population, and on 27 February 1976 proclaimed the Sahrawi Arab Democratic Republic (SADR). Mauritania's withdrawal in August 1979, and subsequent recognition of the SADR, left POLISARIO and Morocco vying, to this day, for sovereignty over the territory.

The conflict hinges upon both a divided territory, and a division between annexed and exiled populations. In the 1980s, Morocco built a military wall as a defense against POLISARIO. Often known as the "berm", it divides the territory between a westerly portion, larger and richer in resources, under Moroccan control, and an easterly portion, without coastal access, under the control of POLISARIO. A fusion of POLISARIO and SADR operates as a government-in-exile from the refugee camps near Tindouf, and governs the exiled population. The size of this (and other) Sahrawi population(s) is disputed; in the late 2000s the refugees may have numbered between 100,000 and 160,000.[8] Other Sahrawi communities in southern Morocco, northern Mauritania, as well as migrant communities in Europe, live in varying degrees of contact with the annexed and/or exiled populations.

Some commentators apprehend the conflict over Western Sahara as a dispute between Morocco and Algeria, with POLISARIO as the latter's stooge. Nevertheless, Algeria has never made a claim on Western Sahara. It has been argued that the tensions and rivalry between Morocco and Algeria would not end if the Western Sahara conflict were resolved (Willis 2012; Zoubir 2001; Zunes and Mundy 2010). Conversely, some analysts have suggested that if Morocco and Algeria were to resolve their own differences, this would not bring an end to the question of Western Sahara, where the nationalism of the people of Western Sahara, which cannot be reduced to a question of Moroccan–Algerian relations, is at stake (Zunes and Mundy 2010). Seeing the conflict in terms of Morocco and Algeria exacerbates the tendency to overlook the people of Western Sahara in their own conflict.

Analysts of Western Sahara agree that the conflict is at a stalemate (Dunbar 2000; International Crisis Group 2007; Jensen 2005; Theofilopoulou 2006; Zoubir 2007; Zunes and Mundy 2010). The UN-brokered ceasefire of 1991, which brought 16 years of military confrontation to a halt, has arguably transferred the conflict from military to non-military fronts (Zunes and Mundy 2010). These new fronts include the corridors of the UN, non-violent protests in Moroccan-controlled Western Sahara, and a discursive and political battle between Morocco and POLISARIO to be recognized as a legitimate actual and potential government for the people of Western Sahara (cf. Clarke 2006; Messari 2001). Just as the military battle could not be won outright by either party (Zunes and Mundy 2010), nor, it would seem, can any of these new arenas of conflict.

One of the major erstwhile proposed solutions to the conflict, a referendum on self-determination, has likewise fallen into a dead-end. The UN's plans for a self-determination referendum are perhaps now virtually reduced to a rhetorical presence in the name of the UN mission for a "referendum" in Western Sahara (MINURSO). The revised plans of the UN Secretary General's former Special Envoy to Western Sahara, James A. Baker, for a referendum, even one that gave a vote to Moroccan citizens continuously resident in the territory since 1999, ended in deadlock. Morocco refuses a referendum that would include independence as an option, and POLISARIO insists on the inclusion of independence as an option.[9]

There is also a deadlock pitting rhetoric against realpolitik. The official raison d'être for the conflict has always hinged upon the right of the people of Western Sahara to self-determination. This right arises from the UN's designation of the territory as non-self-governing, and was confirmed in the International Court of Justice's Advisory Opinion of 1975. UN Security Council (UNSC) resolutions continue to observe the language of the fulfillment of the right to self-determination of the people of Western Sahara. But resolutions also repeat the need for a mutually acceptable political solution. This entrenches the stalemate, because the political agendas of parties to, or influential in, the conflict are either not always, or only potentially, compatible with self-determination.

On the side of POLISARIO and its allies, POLISARIO claims to prioritize self-determination. If it also combines that priority with others, such as independence and POLISARIO's own survival as a liberation movement, then these priorities are at least potentially compatible with self-determination. Algeria's discourse about the conflict also emphasizes its support for self-determination. Its continued support may in fact have much to do with its own fears of, and wishes to contain, Morocco's potential expansion (Willis 2012: 274); but, for the moment, these interests are, again, compatible with support for self-determination. But notably, Algeria's and POLISARIO's broader political agendas are only compatible with self-determination interpreted as a choice made by, rather than for, the people of Western Sahara.

On the side of Morocco and its allies, in contrast, the self-determination of the people of Western Sahara is only compatible with broader political agendas if self-determination is curtailed to preclude any option that leaves Western Sahara not internationally recognized as part of the Kingdom of Morocco – in other words a choice already made for the people of Western Sahara. Thus, Morocco has supported self-determination to the extent that it believed its fulfillment would affirm the territory's status as part of Morocco. In the 1950s Morocco was supportive of the decolonization of the former Spanish Sahara through a referendum on self-determination (Willis 2012: 270–271). Later, Morocco claimed that an act of self-determination of the people of Western Sahara, confirming Moroccan sovereignty, had already occurred through the vote of a minority of the members of Spain's *djemaa*, or Council of *Shuyukh* [tribal leaders], in 1976. This vote was not recognized by the UN or Spain as fulfilling self-determination (Hodges 1983: 235). It has been argued that driving Morocco's tenacity in its position on Western Sahara, however, is a concern not for self-determination, but rather the regime's conviction that, through the cause of the "Moroccan Sahara", it can unite its own fractious political scene and keep threats to the monarchy in abeyance (Willis 2012: 272). Similarly, Morocco's closest Western allies on Western Sahara, France and the United States, are arguably not motivated in that support by a concern for self-determination, or even a view of the validity of Morocco's claims to the territory. Instead, it has been claimed, their support is based on the view that if the monarchy loses the Sahara, it might lead to the collapse of one of the West's closest allies in the Maghreb (Zunes and Mundy 2010).[10]

Not only is the self-determination of the people of Western Sahara not a political priority for Morocco and its allies, then, but in fact their actual priorities seem in direct conflict with self-determination understood as a choice made by the people of Western Sahara. That UNSC resolutions insist on both self-determination and a mutually acceptable political solution, when there is incompatibility between the political agendas of the parties to or influential in the conflict and their approaches to self-determination, predisposes the conflict to remain trapped in the status quo.

The incompatibility at the heart of UNSC resolutions projects onto the face-to-face meetings and negotiations between Morocco and POLISARIO. These resumed in 2007, also the year in which Morocco presented an autonomy proposal for Western Sahara. But with each side continuing to attend to its own political priorities, incompatible with those of the other, each round of meetings ends with no breakthrough.

The formal politics of the Western Sahara conflict are at a standstill. This status quo is not only a reproduced effect, but is also active in quashing potential new developments in formal politics. For instance, there have been calls from human rights NGOs (Human Rights Watch 2008, 2012) and from the UN commission on torture (United Nations Committee against Torture 2011) for investigations into alleged human rights abuses by Morocco against pro-independence Sahrawi political activists in Moroccan-controlled Western Sahara. Nevertheless, when the MINURSO mandate is renewed by the UNSC, requests for the peacekeeping mission in Western Sahara to include human rights monitoring (as most other UN peacekeeping missions include) are vetoed by Morocco's allies at the Security Council or dropped.[11] When a pre-released version of the 2012 UN Secretary General's report on Western Sahara was critical of Morocco for compromising the neutrality of the UN, and explicit in suggesting MINURSO's role to implement self-determination, it was later edited to produce a final report that was less critical of Morocco, and referred to MINURSO's role to implement UNSC resolutions (What's in Blue 2012). Thus, the status quo blocks potential new developments in formal politics.

Despite the ongoing lack of, and obstacles to, any breakthrough in formal politics in recent years, affairs on the ground have been far from static. In fact, the more the stasis takes hold of formal politics, the more that shifts on the ground seem to intensify.

New developments under the radar

Popular mobilization

A major development on the ground in recent years has been the proliferation and intensification of popular political mobilization amongst Sahrawis, directed at both Morocco and POLISARIO. Neither of these trends is without precedent, but both forms have manifested themselves in new ways since 2005.

If Sahrawi popular political mobilization against Morocco was for a long time centered in POLISARIO's leadership in exile, then from 1999, when Sahrawis in the annexed territory began non-violent demonstrations of resistance against Morocco (see Shelley 2004), the role and profile of the annexed population in anti-Moroccan mobilization has grown. In 2005, annexed Sahrawis became the new, or at least rival, center of gravity in the Sahrawi pro-independence movement. Protests by annexed Sahrawis against Morocco intensified, becoming what both annexed and exiled Sahrawis came to call their "Intifada" (Mundy 2006). In 2010, annexed Sahrawis' protests reached an unprecedented level.

From 9 October to 8 November 2010, Sahrawis set up tents to form protest camps in the desert near El 'Ayoun, at a place called Gdeim Izik. The Moroccan authorities highly restricted access to the protest camps for outsiders. They suspended the Moroccan office of *Al Jazeera* news channel on 29 October 2010 (*The Guardian* 2010). With the exception of one international security officer being allowed in on 4 November, Morocco otherwise prevented UN monitors from accessing the site (United Nations Security Council 2011). European and Moroccan press coverage has stressed economic aspects of protestors' demands, such as demands for jobs and homes (e.g. BBC 2010; Bennani 2012; Radio France Internationale 2010). Video footage from the protest camp, though, stresses political dimensions and opposition to Moroccan control over the territory (Sahara Thawra 2010).

The protest camp grew quickly in size. The number of protestors may have reached as many as 20,000 by 8 November (Verdier 2010).[12] Tensions between protestors and the Moroccan authorities grew quickly too, especially after Moroccan security forces shot and killed a 14-year-old Sahrawi boy who was trying to join the encampment on 24 October (Radio France Internationale 2010). On the morning of 8 November, "Moroccan auxiliary forces and police officers forcefully dispersed the protesters and destroyed the camp using tear gas, water cannons, batons and loudspeakers mounted on vehicles and helicopters. There is no evidence that live ammunition or other lethal means were used" (United Nations Security Council 2011). In the clash, both sides claimed fatal casualties, eleven on the side of the Moroccans, and four on the side of the Sahrawis. After the dismantling of Gdeim Izik, further violence ensued in the city of El'Ayoun, where it was reported that Sahrawis attacked public and private property, and Moroccan settlers attacked Sahrawi private property (United Nations Security Council 2011). Many Sahrawis were arrested in connection with Gdeim Izik. In 2013, 24 were condemned by a military court to sentences ranging from life to two years (*Al Jazeera* 2013).[13]

Gdeim Izik, and especially its dénouement, attracted international attention and criticism of Morocco's handling of the protests. But the international attention brought to it was proportionate to general international levels of interest in Western Sahara — that is to say, it was scant and short-lived. This continued to be the case, even when, a few weeks after Gdeim Izik, political and economic protest took off in Tunisia, spreading to Egypt and then across the Arab world. Some Sahrawis (cf. Lewis 2011), and some observers, such as Noam Chomsky (Democracy Now! 2011), claim annexed Sahrawis' protests as the first in the Arab Spring. The Arab world (Morocco excepted) generally paying little attention to Western Sahara, it seems unreasonable to claim that Tunisians, Egyptians or others took inspiration from Western Sahara, as so many in the Arab world took inspiration from Tunisia and Egypt. Yet the absence of a causal relationship between Gdeim Izik and other uprisings does not preclude there being other connections between the Sahrawis' largest protest to date – perhaps, as a proportion of the total population, one of the largest protests in the Arab world since 2010[14] – and protest movements in Tunisia, Egypt and beyond (see Wilson 2013).

If Gdeim Izik made little international impact, there can be little doubt that it was a game-changer in relations between annexed Sahrawis and Moroccans, both settlers in Western Sahara and the authorities. The violence between Sahrawis and Moroccans that followed the dismantling of the protest camps laid to rest the "myth" of peaceful cohabitation between the two groups in the troubled region (Bennani 2012). Indeed, since then there has been further violence; the initial death of one Sahrawi in violence after a Dakhla football match in September 2011 led to further clashes between Moroccan settlers and Sahrawis (United Nations Security Council 2012). When visiting Moroccan-controlled Western Sahara in 2012, I asked some Sahrawi women how they dressed and spoke when they visited cities in the north of Morocco. They told me that before Gdeim Izik, they had worn a *melh.fa* (style of dress favored by Sahrawi and other hassanophone women) and had not disguised their Hassaniya dialect. In the wake of Gdeim Izik, though, they preferred to change their dress and speech when going north to avoid attracting negative reactions if they were recognized as Sahrawis.

If ordinary Moroccans were shocked about the violence in which the protests had ended (violence for which they held Sahrawis responsible), then the authorities seem also to have been disturbed by the scale of the protest. In the wake of Gdeim Izik, for the first time ever, a Sahrawi, rather than a Moroccan, was appointed to the position of governor of El 'Ayoun (Bennani 2012). The new constitution of 2011, put forward by the monarchy in response to the 20th February movement, Morocco's Arab Spring protest group, included recognition for the first time for what is named in the constitution as the "Hassani" language. Such recognition remains firmly within Morocco's framework of cultural and linguistic diversity within the perceived national territory, but was perhaps an attempt to concede something in the face of the largest Sahrawi protest to date.[15]

It is not only in annexed Western Sahara that Sahrawis have recently intensified their popular political mobilization. Mobilization demanding political change is reported across several sites, targeting not Morocco but POLISARIO. Like the mobilization of annexed Sahrawis against Morocco, recent mobilization targeting POLISARIO is not without precedent. In 1988 there were protests in the refugee camps calling for internal political reforms (Zunes 1999). In 2004 a movement claiming to be both within POLISARIO and yet critical of it went public, later adopting the name *khaṭṭ ashshahīd* (the line of the martyr). It called for internal reforms within POLISARIO, criticized its alleged corruption, nepotism and tribalism, and advocated a return to war (Campbell 2010). The change in recent years is that it now seems routinized for popular political mobilization in the refugee camps, and, reportedly, amongst Sahrawis elsewhere, such as in Spain and even annexed Western Sahara, to direct demands for change and reform against POLISARIO (cf. Gómez Martín and Omet 2009). Curiously, these demands simultaneously reaffirm support for POLISARIO – a political dynamic which leads Gómez Martín and Omet (2009) to dub these movements "non-dissident dissidences".[16] This is an interesting notion with which to critique the Euro-American expectation that formal political opposition should take the form of rival political parties.

Demonstrations in the refugee camps demanding political reforms of POLISARIO have been reported on a "small scale" on 5 March 2011, in late 2011 and March 2012 (United Nations Security Council 2011, 2012). In fieldwork in the refugee camps in September 2011 and February 2012, interlocutors discussed not only the aforementioned demonstrations of March and late 2011, but also further "demonstrations" in the refugee camps in the wake of Gdeim Izik demanding a return to war, as well as incidents, in summer 2011 and early 2012, of public protest against particular policies. In February 2012, I observed two Sahrawi women refugees, who discovered that they were not registered to vote in the SADR Parliamentary elections, confront a male officer of POLISARIO, saying "We won't accept this. We'll demonstrate". On that occasion, the officer established a dialog with the women, who eventually accepted that their absence from the refugee camps in the period prior to the elections had prevented their registration. The women departed on good terms with the officer.[17] Dialog and negotiations were also the means with which, in the third party reports I collected, actual rather than threatened demonstrations were met. This reported series of demonstrations in the refugee camps, and the readiness with which a vocabulary of demonstrations came to the lips of those confronting an officer of POLISARIO, suggest not so much that the refugees are becoming increasingly "ungovernable", but rather that governance in the refugee camps is not threatened by the expression of dissent in the public domain, and that it is now an established feature of political life in exile that frustrations can be made public through collective action. The readiness of a language and practice of demonstrations of dissent is also surely a sign of the increasingly high levels of frustration amongst the exiled population – frustration not only with POLISARIO, but also, ultimately, with the international community and its status quo.

Moving to take a stand

In parallel to new popular mobilizations, several individuals from Western Sahara have used movement in and out of the conflict's key zones to establish novel political platforms. In a highly ironic twist, given that a demonstration of up to perhaps 20,000 Sahrawis was overlooked by most of the world, the actions of one woman brought Western Sahara briefly to the attention of the Western media in 2009. Human rights activist Aminetou Haidar, from annexed Western Sahara, was denied entry to El 'Ayoun by Moroccan authorities on 13 November 2009 when she refused to register her nationality as "Moroccan" on her entry card. Expelled to Lanzarote airport (Canary Islands), she staged a hunger strike there. Under pressure from its allies, France and the United States, the Moroccan authorities relented and allowed her to return on 17 December (Rainsford 2009).

Seven other Sahrawis from annexed Western Sahara and southern Morocco, dubbed the "Casablanca seven", used movement to and from the refugee camps to foreground political protest. They made an openly declared visit to the Tindouf refugee camps before returning to Casablanca airport. Ordinarily, Morocco only tolerates persons it claims as its own citizens to visit the refugee camps openly through the UN organized visits to reunite family members separated by the conflict. (Families operate various clandestine means to find other ways of meeting up with relatives outside these UN visits, discussed below.) The seven were arrested on their return to Casablanca airport on 8 October 2009, accused of threatening the security of the Moroccan state, and their case was sent to a military court. One was freed in January 2010, three in May 2010 and three in April 2011 (Amnesty International 2011).

A third case of interest is that of POLISARIO police officer Mostapha Selma Sidi Mouloud. There is a long history of exiles leaving the refugee camps for annexed Western Sahara as a one-way trip, interpreted by POLISARIO as defection, and by Morocco as acquiescence to Moroccan claims over Western Sahara.[18] In contrast to such one-way trips, more recently Sahrawi refugees have come to make unofficial short-term visits to annexed Western Sahara before returning to the refugee camps, round trips which are tolerated by POLISARIO (see below). During one such visit, however, Sidi Mouloud made a public endorsement of Morocco's plan for autonomy for Western Sahara before setting off to return to the refugee camps. The politics of his movements between the conflict's divided areas thus invert those of the "Casablanca seven". Before reaching the refugee camps, Sidi Mouloud was arrested by POLISARIO on 21 September 2010 (Human Rights Watch 2010), and then released on 2 December 2010 (*Alarabiya* 2010).

Each of these three cases of movement on an individual level resulted in new political platforms: Haidar's because of the international reaction she garnered, and the latter two cases because of individuals' unprecedented, and to date still unique, use of movement to provoke a reaction from a party to the conflict. In an international climate of stalemate where nothing seems to change, individuals on the ground are forging their own new political terrains.

Moving to beat the system

The final case that I consider of change under the radar of formal politics is popular, and thus somewhat akin to the popular mobilizations examined above. It also concerns movement between the conflict's zones, and is therefore analogous to the case of individuals taking a stand through movement. But unlike either of the previous cases, this new development seeks to avoid rather than provoke a reaction from one of the parties to the conflict. After years during which the movement of annexed and exiled Sahrawis between the spaces of annexation and exile was impeded by war, closed borders and politics, the situation eased somewhat after the ceasefire and the opening of the land border between Morocco and Mauritania. During fieldwork in the refugee camps in 2007–2009, I not infrequently met annexed Sahrawis who were informally visiting the refugee camps with the full knowledge of the refugees and POLISARIO, but without that of Morocco. Exiled Sahrawis also made informal visits to the annexed areas, which they distinguished from "defections" by disguising their identities in various ways from Moroccan authorities (although they did not disguise these visits from POLISARIO). In this context of increased and more relaxed access, in 2010, by several accounts, there was a boom in "defections" from the refugee camps (Filali-Ansary 2010).[19] "Defectors" at the time received a house and monthly maintenance allowance from the Moroccan authorities, to the tune in the late 2000s of 1,250 dirhams (115 euros) (Soudan 2010). Some Moroccan accounts questioned the motives of the 2010 rush of defectors, many of whom were single young men (Soudan 2010). Exiled Sahrawis had their own ideas as to the reason for the "boom". They explained that "defectors" claimed benefits from the Moroccan state, sold them on and then returned, suitably enriched, to the refugee camps. I met people who had successfully completed this circuit, and my interlocutors could name more. After Gdeim Izik, Morocco's policy changed, and houses were only given to family groups of defectors. The "boom" desisted. Though apparently short-lived, the "defection boom" saw some Sahrawis on the ground improvise a means of manipulating the presumed political phenomenon of defections for quite other purposes.[20]

Western Sahara beyond the Arab Spring

The situation on the ground in Western Sahara in the last few years has been far from "more of the same". The people of Western Sahara have been mobilizing and migrating in new ways that challenge both Morocco and POLISARIO. But if Western Sahara's formal politics seem to be "business as usual", year after year, even at a time when the Maghreb has seen the most radical political change in decades, then does this merely suggest that Western Sahara is the misfit in the Maghreb? In the light of the internal and external threats brought by the Arab Spring, Maghreb states have reissued calls for unity and cooperation (Zoubir 2012). Even when this has concerned Morocco and Algeria directly, though, it has left the issue of Western Sahara (and closed land borders between Algeria and Morocco) unmentioned (Zoubir 2012: 97). Given the entrenchment of the status quo, it is hard to imagine how Western Sahara could come to fulfill its alleged potential as a driver for deeper integration in the Maghreb (cf. Zoubir 2012).

I suggest that, far from being a superfluous and awkward piece in the Maghreb jigsaw, Western Sahara sits on the very fault line that has so recently reconfigured the Maghreb. The Arab Spring took so many people and governments by surprise because the uprisings appeared to be indigenous movements, and it had long been assumed that there could be no change there without external support (Willis 2012: 332–333). If such assumptions have been shaken elsewhere in the Maghreb, Western Sahara is surely one of their last strongholds. A conviction that political change cannot be achieved without external support enables and dictates the ease with which the people of Western Sahara are routinely overlooked in their own conflict. Yet indigenous political mobilization in Western Sahara cannot be reduced historically to mere dependence on external support. Algerian support for POLISARIO came after POLISARIO's foundation, and after Algeria's initial support for partition between Morocco and Mauritania and cold shoulder to POLISARIO (Willis 2012: 273–274, 277). Algeria's subsequent support for POLISARIO, especially in providing a safe haven during the war, was crucial (Willis 2012: 277); but in today's context of transnational civil society solidarity for self-determination in Western Sahara, and remittances from Sahrawis' international migration, it is not clear that the future of nationalism in Western Sahara relies on the support of external state actors. Recent developments on the ground indicate that indigenous political mobilization is strengthening and solidifying, not dissolving. This raises questions about the potential effects of indigenous mobilization on the conflict and its stalled resolution.

In formal circles, the notion that indigenous mobilization could shake the stalemate is receiving increasing attention. The UN Special Envoy to Western Sahara, Christopher Ross, calling in November 2012 for the stagnant formal negotiations to be suspended, advocated not only "quiet shuttle diplomacy" between the parties, but also an increase in contact between the divided Sahrawi populations, citing the potential of such contact "to change perceptions even in the absence of movement in the negotiating process" (Ross 2012). On the other hand, fears that Sahrawis' frustrations may transform into radicalization are also cited as a reason to shake the status quo (e.g. Ross 2012). The evidence for existing radicalization amongst Sahrawis is elusive, though. The kidnapping in October 2011 of three European humanitarian workers in the refugee camps – the first such incident to take place in the refugee camps – was claimed by the extremist Mali-based Movement for Oneness and Jihad in West Africa. If policy-makers focus on questions of security that neglect the concerns raised in actual, rather than potential, indigenous mobilizations, this may ultimately reproduce in a new form the familiar overlooking of the people of Western Sahara in their own conflict. Finally, indigenous mobilization has raised the international profile of the Western Sahara conflict, and the opportunity to address an international audience only strengthens indigenous mobilization. This makes it all the less likely for a solution to achieve popular acquiescence unless that solution addresses the concerns around which people are mobilizing. It seems that intensified indigenous mobilization gives grounds for both optimism that the stalemate could be shaken, and caution that an increasingly mobilized indigenous population will resist all the more any political solution in which the people of Western Sahara have been overlooked.

Notes

1. I thank George Joffé, Michael Willis, Yahia Zoubir and an anonymous reviewer for their constructive comments on earlier drafts. Responsibility for views, and any errors, remain mine alone. I am grateful to the representation of Polisario in the UK for facilitating research access to the refugee camps in Algeria, and to Morocco's Agence du Sud for facilitating research access to the Moroccan-controlled areas of Western Sahara. Fieldwork was made possible by support from the UK's Economic and Social Research Council (Algeria 2007–2009), Prométée research project on the legal anthropology of property (www.cjb.ma/205-andromaque-et-prometee/212-le-projet.html) (Algeria in 2011 and 2012), and the British Council in Morocco, the Prince Alwaleed Bin Talal Centre for Islamic Studies at the University of Cambridge, and Homerton College, University of Cambridge (Moroccan-controlled Western Sahara in 2012).
2. The people of Western Sahara use "Sahrawi" to refer to their national identity, but the term also has a wider, non-specialist meaning in Arabic of "pertaining to the desert". For a discussion, see Zunes and Mundy 2010: 92–95.
3. The number of refugees for which aid is provided has fluctuated, exacerbated by controversy over the size of the population resident in the refugee camps (see note 7 below). Zunes and Mundy (2010: 127–128) write that "[f]ollowing reports and studies indicating widespread malnutrition, aid was increased to 155,000 persons in 2000 and again to 158,000 in 2004. In 2005, however, the UNHCR and World Food Program reduced the number to 90,000 persons". This reduction in aid was presented in terms of the aid agencies seeking to help the most vulnerable refugees. A recent report highlights high rates of malnutrition, as well as obesity, amongst the Sahrawi refugee population (Grijalva-Eternod et al. 2012).

4. The UN Mission for a Referendum in Western Sahara, MINURSO, has been running since 1991; the approved budget for MINURSO for July 2012 to June 2013 was $60,796,600 (United Nations General Assembly 2012).
5. In the 2011 UNDP Human Development Ranking, Morocco ranks 130 of 187 countries (UNDP 2011).
6. Morocco's revenues from the exploitation of resources in Western Sahara, and the costs of supporting a Moroccan military and civilian presence there, are not transparently documented in the public domain. For an argument that the financial costs of annexation outweigh the financial gains of resource exploitation, see Shelley 2004.
7. Of two UN General Assembly resolutions passed on 10 December 1976 in the wake of the MTA, resolution 3458 A called for a popular referendum on self-determination, without acknowledging the MTA, and resolution 3458 B took note of the MTA whilst still calling, beyond the content of the MTA, for a popular consultation on self-determination (Ruíz 2008: 12).
8. In 2000, the numbers of Sahrawi adult voters approved by the United Nations Mission for the Referendum in Western Sahara (MINURSO) were 41,150 for Moroccan-controlled Western Sahara and 33,998 for the refugee camps (Zunes and Mundy 2010: 214). For a discussion of population figures for the refugee camps, see Chatty, Fiddian-Qasmiyeh and Crivello 2010: 41.
9. For a discussion of Baker's two referendum plans, see Zunes and Mundy 2010.
10. For further discussion of third parties' interests in the Western Sahara conflict, see Darbouche and Zoubir 2008.
11. In April 2012 France opposed the proposed inclusion of human rights monitoring in the MINURSO mandate (What's in Blue 2012). In April 2013 the United States initially proposed to include human rights monitoring in MINURSO, following which Morocco cancelled joint military exercises with its ally (USA Today 2013). The United States then dropped the proposed inclusion of human rights monitoring (What's in Blue 2013).
12. The UN estimates 6,610 tents at Gdeim Izik, suggesting "over 15,000" demonstrators (United Nations Security Council 2011: 1).
13. On the Gdeim Izik protest, see Murphy and Omar 2013 and Wilson 2013.
14. If protestors did indeed reach some 20,000 people, then, given an adult annexed Sahrawi adult population of 41,150 in 2000, this was, in local context, a markedly high rate of participation in a protest.
15. For a discussion of how the Moroccan constitution of 2011 maintained authoritarian powers in the hands of the monarchy, missing the opportunity to introduce real changes that could favor a resolution for the conflict on Western Sahara, see Theofilopoulou 2012. For a discussion of the place assigned to Sahrawis in official Moroccan nationalism, see Deubel 2012.
16. All translations are mine, unless otherwise stated.
17. For further discussion of elections in the refugee camps, see Wilson 2010.
18. For a discussion of exiles who leave the refugee camps to live in Moroccan-controlled Western Sahara, see Hernández 2001; Wilson 2014.
19. Refugee interlocutors also recalled 2010 as a time of a boom in "defections".
20. On migration movements to and from the refugee camps, including the "defection boom", see Wilson 2014.

References

Al Jazeera (2013). 'Morocco court sentences West Sahara activists'. Online. Available: www.aljazeera.com/news/africa/2013/02/2013217135233700377.html (17 February 2013) (accessed 18 February 2013).

Alarabiya (2010). 'Polisario releases detained former security chief'. Online. Available: www.alarabiya.net/articles/2010/12/02/128197.html (2 December 2010) (accessed 5 June 2012).

Amnesty International (2011). 'Morocco royal pardon an encouraging step'. Online. Available: www.amnesty.org/en/library/asset/MDE29/002/2011/en/41ece1b7–0bf5–40fc-b9c9-bc39e9ff7a5d/mde290022011en.pdf (15 April 2011) (accessed 14 November 2012).

BBC (2010). 'Deadly clashes as Morocco breaks up Western Sahara camp'. Online. Available: www.bbc.co.uk/news/world-africa-11710400 (9 November 2010) (accessed 7 March 2012).

Bennani, D. (2012). 'Sahara. La bombe à retardement', *Tel Quel* (29 February). Online. Available: www.telquel-online.com/content/sahara-la-bombe-%C3%A0-retardement (accessed 15 March 2012).

Campbell, M.O. (2010). 'Dissenting participation: Unoffical politics in the 2007 Saharawi General Congress', *Journal of North African Studies*, 15: 573–580.

Chatty, D., Fiddian-Qasmiyeh, E. and Crivello, G. (2010). 'Identity with/out territory: Sahrawi refugee youth in transnational space', in Chatty, D. (ed.), *Deterritorialized Youth. Sahrawi and Afghan Refugees at the Margins of the Middle East*, Oxford: Berghahn Books.

Clarke, K. (2006). 'Polisario: Resistance and identity', *L'Ouest saharien*, 6: 129–140.

Darbouche, H. and Zoubir, Y. (2008). 'Conflicting international policies and the Western Sahara stalemate', *The International Spectator*, 43 (1): 91–105.

Democracy Now! (2011). '"The genie is out of the bottle": Assessing a changing Arab world with Noam Chomsky and Al Jazeera's Marwan Bishara'. Online. Available: www.democracynow.org/2011/2/17/the_genies_are_out_of_the (17 February 2011) (accessed 6 March 2012).

Deubel, T. (2012). 'Poetics of diaspora: Sahrawi poets and postcolonial transformations of a trans-Saharan genre in northwest Africa', *The Journal of North African Studies*, 16 (4): 295–314.

Dunbar, C. (2000). 'Saharan stasis: Status and future prospects of the Western Sahara conflict', *Middle East Journal*, 4: 522–545.

Filali-Ansary, H. (2010). 'Comment les ralliés du Polisario vivent leur retour au Maroc', *La Vie Eco*. Online. Available: www.lavieeco.com/news/politique/comment-les-ralliés-du-polisario-vivent-leur-retour-au-maroc-16319.html (4 April 2010) (accessed 7 March 2012).

Gómez Martín, C. and Omet, C. (2009). 'Les "dissidences non dissidentes" du Front Polisario dans les camps de réfugiés et la diaspora sahraouis', *L'année du maghreb*, 5: 205–222.

Grijalva-Eternod, C.S., Wells, J.C.K., Cortina-Borja, M., Salse-Ubach, N., Tondeur, M.C., Dolan, C., Meziani, C., Wilkinson, C., Spiegel, P. and Seal, A.J. (2012). 'The double burden of obesity and malnutrition in a protracted emergency setting: A cross-sectional study of Western Sahara refugees', *PLoS Med*, 9: e1001320. Online. Available: http://dx.doi.org/10.1371%2Fjournal.pmed.1001320 (accessed 15 November 2012).

Hernández, A. (2001). *Sáhara: Otras voces*, Málaga: Algarazara.

Hodges, T. (1983). *Western Sahara: Roots of a Desert War*, Beckenham: Croom Helm.

Human Rights Watch (2008). *Human Rights in Western Sahara and in the Tindouf Refugee Camps*, New York: Human Rights Watch.

———. (2010). 'Polisario arrests rare dissenter'. Online. Available: www.hrw.org/news/2010/09/22/algeria-polisario-arrests-rare-dissenter-refugee-camps (23 September 2010) (accessed 15 November 2012).

———. (2012) *Morocco and Western Sahara*, New York: Human Rights Watch.

International Crisis Group (2007). *Western Sahara: Out of the Impasse*, Middle East/North Africa Report N°6611. Online. Available: www.crisisgroup.org/en/regions/middle-east-north-africa/north-africa/western-sahara/066-western-sahara-out-of-the-impasse.aspx (11 June 2007) (accessed November 15 2012).

Jensen, E. (2005). *Western Sahara: Anatomy of a Stalemate*, Boulder, CO: Lynne Rienner Publishers.

Lewis, A. (2011). 'Morocco still provoking resistance on Western Sahara', BBC. Online. Available: www.bbc.co.uk/news/world-africa-16186928 (22 December 2011) (accessed 6 March 2012).

Messari, N. (2001). 'National security, the political space, and citizenship. The case of Morocco and the Western Sahara', *The Journal of North African Studies*, 6: 47–63.

Mundy, J. (2006). 'Autonomy & Intifadah: New horizons in Western Saharan nationalism', *Review of African Political Economy*, 108: 255–267.

Murphy, J. and Omar, S. (2013). 'Aesthetics of resistance in Western Sahara', *Peace Review: A Journal of Social Justice*, 25: 349–358.

Radio France Internationale (2010). 'Au Maroc, le traitement de faveur dont bénéficient les "ralliés" sahraouis suscite des convoitises'. Online. Available: www.rfi.fr/afrique/20101026-maroc-le-traitement-faveur-dont-beneficient-rallies-sahraouis-suscite-convoitises (26 October 2010) (accessed 15 March 2012).

Rainsford, S. (2009). 'Hunger striker Aminatou Haidar returns to W Sahara', BBC. Online. Available: http://news.bbc.co.uk/1/hi/world/africa/8421107.stm (18 December 2009) (accessed 15 November 2012).

Robert F. Kennedy International Delegation (2012). 'Preliminary observations'. Online. Available: www.frontlinedefenders.org/files/preliminary_report_on_western_sahara_by_rfk_centre.pdf (5 September 2012) (accessed 12 November 2012).

Ross, C. (2012). 'Briefing to the Security Council'. Online. Available: http://sahara-panorama.blogspot.co.uk/2012/11/rosss-brienfing-to-sc-november-2012.html (28 November 2012) (accessed 8 January 2013).

Ruíz Miguel, C. (2008). 'Spain's legal obligations as administering power of Western Sahara', *Group for Strategic Studies*, 311: 1–21.

Sahara Thawra (2010). 'Campamento Gdeim Izik'. Online video posting. Available: www.youtube.com/watch?v=O6HcTyI7_-U&NR=1&feature=endscreen (3 November 2010) (accessed 15 March 2012).

Shelley, T. (2004). *Endgame in the Western Sahara. What Future for Africa's Last Colony?* London: Zed Books.

Soudan, F. (2010). 'Les ralliés de Sa Majesté', *Jeune Afrique*. Online. Available: www.jeuneafrique.com/Articles/Dossier/ARTJAJA2577p022–030.xml0/algerie-maroc-mauritanie-refugieles-rallies-de-sa-majeste.html (9 June 2010) (accessed 15 March 2012).

The Guardian (2010). 'Morocco bars al-Jazeera for "unfair" coverage'. Online. Available: www.guardian.co.uk/media/2010/oct/29/morocco-al-jazeera (29 October 2010) (accessed 16 June 2012).

Theofilopoulou, A. (2006). *The United Nations and Western Sahara: A Never-Ending Affair*, Special Report, United States Institute of Peace. Online. Available: www.usip.org/files/resources/sr166.pdf (accessed 15 November 2012).

———. (2012). 'Morocco's new constitution and the Western Sahara conflict – A missed opportunity?', *The Journal of North African Studies*, 17: 687–696.

United Nations Committee against Torture (2011). 'Concluding observations of the Committee against Torture. Morocco'. Online. Available: http://www2.ohchr.org/english/bodies/cat/docs/CAT.C.MAR.CO.4_en.pdf (accessed 6 April 2012).

United Nations Development Programme (2011). *Human Development Report 2011. Sustainability and Equity: A Better Future for All*, New York: Palgrave Macmillan.

United Nations General Assembly (2012). *Financing of the Support Account for Peacekeeping Operations*. Online. Available: www.un.org/ga/search/view_doc.asp?symbol=A/C.5/66/17 (12 June 2012) (accessed 15 November 2012).

United Nations Security Council (2011). 'Report of the Secretary General on the situation concerning Western Sahara'. Online. Available: www.un.org/ga/search/view_doc.asp?symbol=S/2011/249 (1 April 2011) (accessed 15 November 2012).

———. (2012) 'Report of the Secretary General on the situation concerning Western Sahara'. Online. Available: www.un.org/ga/search/view_doc.asp?symbol=S/2012/197 (5 April 2012) (accessed 15 November 2012).

USA Today (2013). 'Morocco cancels war games with U.S. overnight.' Online. Available: www.usatoday.com/story/news/2013/04/16/morocco-cancels-war-games-with-us-over-rights/2089089/ (16 April 2013) (accessed 29 August 2013).

Verdier, M. (2010). 'Le devenir des Sahraouis s'assombrit sur fond de violence', *La Croix*. Online. Available: www.la-croix.com/Actualite/S-informer/Monde/Le-devenir-des-Sahraouis-s-assombrit-sur-fond-de-violence-_NG_-2010-11-09-558616 (9 November 2010) (accessed 15 March 2012).

What's in Blue (2012). 'Western Sahara consultations'. Online. Available: http://whatsinblue .org/2012/04/western-sahara-consultations.php (16 April 2012) (accessed 17 June 2012).

———. (2013). 'Western Sahara mission mandate renewal'. Online. Available: www.what sinblue.org/2013/04/western-sahara-mission-mandate-renewal.php (24 April 2013) (accessed 2 September 2013).

Willis, M. (2012). *Politics and Power in the Maghreb: Algeria, Morocco and Tunisia from Independence to the Arab Spring*, London: Oxford University Press.

Wilson, A. (2010). 'Democratising elections without parties: Reflections on the case of the Sahrawi Arab Democratic Republic', *The Journal of North African Studies*, 15 (4): 423–438.

———. (2013). 'On the margins of the Arab Spring (Western Sahara)', *Social Analysis*, 57 (2): 81–98.

———. (2014). 'Cycles of crisis, migration and the formation of new political identities in Western Sahara', in Pérouse de Montclos, M., Petit, V., Robin, N. (eds.), *Crises et migrations dans les pays du sud*, Paris: Harmattan.

Zoubir, Y. (2001). 'Algerian-Moroccan relations and their impact on Maghrebi integration', *Journal of North African Studies*, 5 (3): 43–74.

———. (2007). 'Stalemate in Western Sahara: Ending international legality', *Middle East Policy*, 14: 158–177.

———. (2010). 'The Western Sahara conflict: Regional and international repercussions', *Bulletin of Concerned Africa Scholars*, 85: 72–77.

———. (2012). 'Tipping the balance towards inter-Maghreb unity in light of the Arab Spring', *The International Spectator: Italian Journal of International Affairs*, 47: 83–99.

Zunes, S. (1999). 'Unarmed resistance in the Middle East and North Africa', in Zunes, S., Kurtz, L.R. and Asher, S.B. (eds.), *Nonviolent Social Movements: A Geographical Perspective*, Malden, MA: Blackwell.

Zunes, S. and Mundy, J. (2010). *Western Sahara: War, Nationalism and Conflict Irresolution*, Syracuse: Syracuse University Press.

PART II

Internal dynamics of North African states

9

ALGERIA: REFORMS WITHOUT CHANGE?

Ahmed Aghrout and Yahia H. Zoubir

Introduction

Depicted as the 'Third Wave of Revolution' in the Arab world, the popular uprisings that have swept through this region in recent years had already shaken a number of entrenched authoritarian regimes. These 'bottom-up' uprisings have hitherto led to the downfall of four long-reigning authoritarian leaders in Tunisia, Egypt, Libya and Yemen.[1] This movement is still ongoing in other countries, and even turning into chaos and bloodshed as in Syria. Although the reasons which prompted these protests vary from country to country, they are, by and large, the result of popular frustration and disillusionment with political regimes that have become increasingly less responsive to the legitimate aspirations – be they socioeconomic, political or all together – of their respective societies. While the ramifications associated with this 'Arab Awakening' are still unfolding, the fact remains that, besides unseating some long-serving dictators, the upheaval across the region has also pushed other regimes into promising reforms and/or actually carrying them out. Well before the recent Arab uprisings, Algeria did experience a major popular unrest in October 1988. But this time Algeria has thus far been immune from the massive popular revolts that have gripped several other Arab countries. Surely these are very challenging times, yet the Algerian regime steadfastly avoided embracing a radical approach to change. Instead, it decided to settle on the less costly option, combining redistributive transfers and a raft of concessions in the political realm. The various elections held so far (legislative, local and presidential) and their outcomes were undeniably a litmus test of how genuine the current regime is in its reform plans to promote real political change. Yet they proved to be no more different from past elections, thus ensuring a continuation of the country's political, economic and institutional stagnation.

With this in mind, this chapter proposes to briefly review the background leading to, and the scope of, the proposed reform agenda. It analyzes those elections and their significance for the country's political development. It contends that these elections, being at best a 'democratic farce', are perpetuating the status quo and, as a result, enabling the regime to maintain itself. The growing challenges – social discontent, corruption scandals, political and economic decline – are all ingredients fueling uncertainty as to the country's future.

The process inducing the reforms

The popular uprisings of October 1988 in Algeria prompted the move towards political pluralism.[2] This opening of the political system also eased the restrictions on freedom of expression, association and organization. In short, these transformations were regarded as a milestone on the road to democratic rule.[3] In spite of optimistic expectations, the changes turned out to be just a short-lived experience of political liberalization. Indeed, the civilian-military coup in January 1992, by canceling the electoral process, brought to an end what might have been a first democratic attempt in the country's history. A state of emergency was decreed and several constitutional rights were suspended. The resulting political stalemate was to herald a phase of brutal conflict and violence, plunging the country into instability.[4]

From the mid-1990s, however, Algeria's political development was to be marked by the provision of a degree of an incipient multiparty political system due to the reinstatement of the institutional process through the holding of regular local and national elections. Yet, one must point to the fact that this was paralleled with government restrictions, ranging from crackdown on, and judicial harassment of, the media to limitations to freedom of assembly or association. For these reasons the resumption of the electoral process could not be acclaimed as a sign of democracy, but only served to maintain an authoritarian rule legitimizing itself through a 'democratic façade' or 'new authoritarianism'.[5] F. Volpi is correct in pointing out that 'Algeria illustrates a type of authoritarian resistance to popular challenges that is based on pseudo-democratization, redistributive patronage, and an effective use of the security apparatus'.[6] For their part, people have become increasingly disillusioned and disengaged from politics as reflected in the low level of electoral turnout in various elections. The widespread belief is that these elections have made no difference to the way the country is governed – perceived as synonymous with maintaining the political status quo and keeping the patron-client regime in place. Until today, this depoliticization of the citizenry has in fact served the interests of the regime, which could obviously respond better to socioeconomic demands – through redistribution of the oil-rent – than political calls for genuine change.

Intermittent and localized strikes, protests and riots have become an integral part of Algeria's social landscape for a number of years. The more violent protests were those of early January 2011, coinciding with comparable events in neighboring Tunisia. These protests had more to do with socioeconomic deprivation than a well-articulated list of political demands.[7] Soon after, nevertheless, this protest movement took a new turn with the formation on 21 January of the *Coordination Nationale pour le Changement et la Démocratie* (National Coordination for Change and Democracy, CNCD).[8] Its initiators intended to bring the 'democratic opposition' together and unite the forces for democratic change to enable Algeria to emerge from its 'sclerotic situation' and 'continuous shrinking spaces for freedom'.[9] The removal of the country's 19-year-old state of emergency, the lifting of restrictions on the media and political participation, and the release of the people arrested as a result of popular protests were among its immediate key demands. Nonetheless, in its endeavor to organize protest marches, the CNCD failed to gain the same momentum as did other protest movements in the Arab region. In addition to the fact that it was torn by internal divisions,[10] it also faced government crackdown. As a corollary, its protest marches were suspended on 23 June after more than 15 vain attempts.

It was not only Algeria's traumatic memories – war of independence (1954–1962) and a decade-long internal conflict (1990s) – and the presence of a weak and divided opposition which have prevented the development of a large protest movement.[11] The government's handling of the situation, resorting to redistributive transfers and promising further political reforms, including the lifting of the state of emergency, also enabled it to ward off the threat of a mass unrest. The reforms, which President Bouteflika pledged in a long-awaited speech on 15 April 2011, were chiefly concerned with the electoral system, women's representation in elected bodies, cases of incompatibility with the parliamentary mandate, political parties, associations and information.[12] The Council of Ministers, in its meetings held on 28 August and on 11–12 September 2011, endorsed a series of proposed pieces of legislation relating to these issues. After that these legislative texts were debated and approved by both houses of the parliament during their autumn session, which started on 4 September 2011 and closed on 2 February 2012.[13]

It is worth pointing out that within its reform agenda, the government adopted a raft of measures, some of which were intended to ensure a 'free, fair and transparent poll'. The *Assemblée Populaire Nationale* (National Popular Assembly)[14] was enlarged from 389 to 462 members.[15] Two commissions were established: *Commission Nationale de Supervision des Elections* (National Commission for Election Supervision), composed exclusively of judges appointed by the President; and *Commission Nationale Indépendante de Surveillance des Elections Législatives* (Independent National Commission for the Surveillance of Legislative Elections, CNISEL), made up of representatives of political parties and independent candidates.[16]

The reform agenda

In an interview to the French daily *Le Monde* (4 July 2012), on the occasion of the fiftieth anniversary of Algeria's independence from France, President Bouteflika asserted that the package of political reforms is intended to 'deepen the democratic process in the country'. In this regard, it must be pointed out that what might have been an ordinary process of legislation was acclaimed by the regime as a milestone towards democratic change. With the exception of two new legislative bills, women representation in elected institutions and cases of incompatibility with parliamentary mandate, the substance of the other texts (electoral code, political parties, associations and information) was already covered in existing legislation that has been there for more than two decades.

What marked the proposed package of reforms was the lack of any public debate about them. However, it did trigger a 'heated' parliamentary debate which brought to notice differing partisan predilections amongst the major political forces – this was particularly the case when the first batch of legislative acts were debated. The proposed draft electoral bill was decried by the FLN, especially in its stipulations relating to 'prohibition of political nomadism' and 'conditions for cabinet ministers running for election'. The irony is that this same text and others, including the one on women's political representation, had previously been approved (28 August 2011) by an FLN-dominated cabinet government. The FLN, backed by its ally in the ruling presidential coalition, the RND, succeeded in getting the bill passed in parliament with both provisions dropped. The provision stipulation prohibiting 'crossing the floor' (changing party affiliation) was championed by several opposition parties, such as the *Parti des Travailleurs* (Workers' Party, PT) and the FNA, which suffered the majority of the defections during the 2007–2012 legislature, mostly to the governing parties, the FLN and the RND. These parties also opposed the proviso requiring ministers, wishing to stand for election, to resign from their positions three months before elections. This was seen by the opposition as favoring the ruling parties whose ministers could make use of government machinery during electioneering. Even after the adoption of the electoral law, the PT's leader, Louisa Hanoune, continued to call for ministers standing for election to resign from the cabinet prior to the campaign for the legislative elections.

The draft law on increasing women's political representation proposed, in its original version, electoral list quotas for women of 33 per cent.[17] Yet again the two ruling parties (FLN and RND) were able to introduce amendments setting variable quotas of between 20 per cent and 40 per cent in the final text of the bill, a percentage that is directly proportional to the number of seats in each electoral constituency. Such amendments were seen as a real setback for women's rights to an enhanced political representation, and which the original draft bill sought to attain through what may be termed as 'affirmative action'. Reacting to this, Halima Lakehal, an FLN MP, avowed that 'the President's text has been deprived of all meaning compared with the original bill'.[18] In the same context, Amina Gharbi Bounab, another FLN MP, stated that 'this law is nationally and sexually discriminatory towards women'.[19] The *Ligue Algérienne pour la Défence des Droits de l'Homme* (the Algerian League for the Defense of Human Rights), in a critical report (April 2012) pertaining to the political reform legislation package, contended that the law intends neither to ensure equal representation between women and men in elected assemblies nor to promote women's full participation in the country's political and public life.

The adoption of the reform legislation paved the way to the legalization of a multitude of new political parties. The new law on political parties, adopted in January 2012, revoked the previous 13-year-long ban on their creation.

Over a short period of time (26 February–21 March 2012), 21 political parties were granted legal status ahead of the legislative elections. Scores of these political formations were set up by dissidents from established political parties, such as the *Front de Libération Nationale* (National Liberation Front, FLN), *Rassemblement National Démocratique* (National Democratic Rally, RND), *Front National Algérien* (Algerian National Front, FNA), *Rassemblement Culturel et Démocratique* (Rally for Culture and Democracy, RCD) and *Mouvement de la Societé pour la Paix* (Movement of Society for Peace, MSP). This proliferation of new political parties continued as the country prepared for the local elections of 29 November 2012. Nonetheless, it should be borne in mind that a good number of these new formations are far from being the result of the failure of old parties to integrate new societal demands or issues. Many of these new parties, comments an observer, are serving solely as vehicles for their respective leaders' personal ambitions and as such have 'no charisma, no political programme or militant base'.[20] Furthermore their proliferation has contributed to the fragmentation of the country's political landscape, something which has, undeniably, played a part in decreasing the willingness to vote for an already disaffected electorate. Commenting on their proliferation, the former Minister of Interior, Daho Ould Kablia, was reported to have said that 'If it were up to me, I would have refused, but one must apply the law scrupulously. Why create parties when many of them have no popular support or anchoring in society'.[21] Whatever the truth underlining this comment, the fragmentation was in fact a blessing for the regime – if not of its own making – for this fragmentation prevented the emergence of a strong, popular party, such as the FIS in 1989–1992 – which could contest the hegemony of the FLN/RND.

Elections as a litmus test

The three-week parliamentary electoral campaign was officially launched on 15 April and involved some 44 political parties – of which 21 were newly created parties – and 185 lists of independent candidates. By and large, the campaign went off without any major incident. Of the minor incidents that occurred one can cite the display of electoral posters at unauthorized places. Other incidents included cases of election posters torn down or defaced with messages reflecting the daily hardship faced by average citizens, especially the soaring prices of staple foods. In other words, the electoral 'billboards have become for them a forum for expression', wrote the French-language daily-newspaper, *l'Expression*.[22] Yet one major feature that particularly marked this campaign was the widespread voter apathy. There were reports of meetings and rallies canceled, some of which for the reason that they drew only small numbers of voters. There were also allegations of parties and candidates bribing people to attend these rallies and meetings. All things considered, the campaign seemed to have had no significant effect on the lethargic mood of the electorate. Amongst the main recurrent themes touched upon during the campaign were unemployment, declining purchasing power, shortage of affordable housing, insecurity and need for change. Yet what almost continually 'haunted' most, if not all parties and candidates, as well as the authorities throughout the campaign, was the specter of low voter turnout. For that reason, it became imperative that this key issue had to be addressed by both sides of the political spectrum to tackle public apathy and encourage turnout. In the run up to Election Day, for instance, the government spared no effort in resorting to various measures to appeal to citizens to vote in large numbers. In addition to television adverts and posters, the ministry of interior launched its campaign through mass texting, telling voters that 'voting is both an act of citizenship and a duty'.[23] Even President Bouteflika, in his successive speeches since mid-April, urged people to go to the polls and vote en masse. In one televised speech, he equated the independence struggle with the national duty of citizens to vote. Also the invitation of about 500 foreign observers – from the United Nations (UN), European Union (EU), African Union (AU), Arab League (AL) and Organization of Islamic Cooperation (OIC) – to monitor the vote was intended to provide some kind of guarantee that the elections will be fair, free and transparent. From the Algerian authorities' point of view, these elections were regarded as the initial step in the process of implementing the range of political reforms the country had embarked upon in the wake of the so-called 'Arab Spring' or 'Arab Awakening'.

With almost 25,000 candidates competing for the enlarged 462-member assembly (389 members previously), the elections took place on 10 May 2012 as scheduled. They were conducted at an estimated 48,878 polling stations and saw the mobilization of some 300,000 members of staff. Out of more than 21.6 million registered voters, only about 9.3 million cast their vote, that is, an official voter turnout rate of 43.1 per cent – this obviously includes the vote of the diaspora whose electorate numbered almost a million.[24] There is no doubt this was a satisfactory figure for the authorities, compared to the 35.7 per cent obtained in the previous legislative elections of 2007. In spite of that this turnout must be approached with caution since it does include the invalid votes, the largest proportion of which was more likely to be intentional spoiling. In this respect, this represented over 18 per cent of the total vote (more than 1.7 million). When this is taken into account as a form of protest vote – which was clearly the case – the voter turnout would stand at about 35.3 per cent only. Whatever the case, people interviewed for this research all concurred that the polling stations were practically empty and that the only visible voters were the elderly who responded to Bouteflika's appeal, using a nationalist slogan reminiscent of the call for the rising up against colonial France on 1 November 1954.

Contrary to expectations, these elections allowed the FLN – the party in power since independence in 1962 – to register the greatest gains, by garnering 221 seats of 462 seats in the lower house of parliament. Even though this represents almost 48 per cent of the total seats, the FLN only managed to receive 17.3 per cent of the total valid votes (over 7.6 million). The RND, of the then Prime Minister Ahmed Ouyahia (2008–2012) and an ally of the FLN in the ruling coalition, came second with 70 seats. The other party that did relatively well in these elections was the *Front des Forces Socialistes* (Socialist Forces Front, FFS), the country's oldest opposition party. After more than a decade of boycott of national elections, the FFS decided to return and contest the elections. It succeeded to secure 21 seats. Obtaining 17 seats, Louisa Hanoune's party, the PT, performed slightly less than in the 2007 legislative elections. But the big loser of these elections was the *Alliance Verte* (Green alliance, AV) – consisted of three Islamist parties, the MSP, *El Islah* (Islamic Renaissance Movement) and *Ennahda* (Movement for National Reform) and formed in March 2012 to compete in the elections as a common list – which got 47 seats. Much to their chagrin, the alliance could not replicate the electoral success attained by the Islamists parties across the region (Egypt, Morocco and Tunisia) as the results bucked their early expectations. In reaction, the AV accused the government machinery of manipulating these elections with the intention to favor the ruling parties, the FLN and RND. Its leader, Bouguerra Soltani (2003–2013), contended that the results were 'illogical, unreasonable and unacceptable' and that they signaled 'a return to single-party rule'.[25] Moreover, the newly elected MPs from the AV and other smaller Islamist parties walked out of the inaugural session of the newly elected legislature on 26 May 2012 to denounce what they claimed were fraudulent elections.

In a similar vein, Mohamed Seddiki, the chairman of the CNISEL, stated in a press conference on 3 June that the elections were 'devoid of legitimacy'.[26] His organization, he maintained, recorded in its 30-page final report 'several violations and breaches of the electoral process' which tarnished the 'credibility and transparency' of these elections. It ought to be mentioned that the representatives of the FLN and the RND, the two ruling parties and main winners of these elections, refused to sign the final report – a copy of which was handed over to the Presidency and the Ministry of Interior.

Even though, statistically speaking, the FLN came out with the largest number of seats, it did so without attracting much of the votes – just over 1.3 million votes (17.3 per cent). It is clear that a number of considerations combined together made it possible for this political party to realize such electoral success. Many people of the old generation interpreted President Bouteflika's calls on two symbolic dates (24 February and 8 May 2012) as appeals to vote for the FLN. Also several parties, notably the newly established ones, were unable to obtain the 5 per cent of votes cast to be eligible for proportional distribution of seats, something which clearly benefited established parties, principally the FLN. Those who voted for the FLN opted for continuity rather than change, which, in their view, would be tantamount to an adventurous undertaking in these times of uncertainty in the Arab region.

Although the election results 'saw the regime tighten the grip on power', the international reaction to these was, on the whole, encouraging. Whether the EU, the AL, the AU, or the OIC, they all maintained that these elections were 'free, transparent and organized in a peaceful way'. The United States Secretary of State, Hillary Clinton (2009–2013), was quoted as having said that 'these elections – and the high number of women elected – are a welcome step in Algeria's progress toward democratic reform'.[27]

Notwithstanding these different reactions, the fact remains that a 'new government' was formed four months (4 September 2012) after poll results; a period which fueled a great deal of speculation about the possible tensions taking place between the critical power brokers in the political system. And when this much-awaited government was unveiled, it turned out to be a 'ministerial reshuffle' rather than the formation of a new government cabinet. Even if the reshuffle witnessed the departure of a number of important members, such as Prime Minister Ouyahia, who was replaced by Abdelmalek Sellal, as well as Yazid Zerhouni and Hamid Temmar, who were considered part of Bouteflika's inner circle,[28] half of the ministerial departments remained in the same hands – including key ones such as foreign affairs, finance, interior and energy. Also, with only three women in the 36-member cabinet, this reshuffle was far from reflecting their representation in the new legislature, having won almost a third of seats (143 out 462 seats).[29] In a nutshell, neither the legislative elections, obviously together with their outcome, nor the named 'new government' seem to suggest a genuine commitment and strong determination to further the crucial political changes the country needs. Such state of affairs can only mean one thing: the whole process has only served to maintain the status quo whilst giving the impression that things are changing. This was confirmed by the April 2014 presidential election, which enabled Bouteflika to secure a fourth consecutive term in office in spite of his poor health condition.

Bouteflika, the presidential clan and the problematic of a transition

The 'Constitutional Coup' orchestrated by Bouteflika in 2008, which lifted the limitation of presidential mandates, allowed him to seek, and obtain, perennial power no matter his age and/or his ability to perform his presidential functions due to his illness. While his supporters' argument that 'it is not Bouteflika, who needs Algeria, but it is Algeria, which needs Bouteflika' is far from reflecting genuine support for the president and his alleged superlative credentials, it does in fact highlight a few paramount issues: the continued crisis of the system and its inability to initiate a genuine transition. Bouteflika and the so-called 'revolutionary family' believe that they constitute the force that secured the country's independence and, as such, are entitled to rule the country until their death. This quasi 'aristocracy' refuses to hand over power to the new generations and has been unsuccessful in promoting a productive economic system, relying instead on the oil rent which they can use as laegitimizing tool. Thus, the legislative elections and the local elections of November 2012, which gave the FLN/RND 48 per cent of the votes, had little impact on the country's political landscape. Official figures reported 44.3 per cent participation for the municipal election (APC) and 42.8 per cent for the departmental (APW) seats. The only importance of these elections is that they were the prelude to the presidential election. The biggest question was whether the president would be a candidate for a fourth mandate. The stroke he suffered on 27 April 2013 and his long hospitalization in France resulted in divisions among those inside and outside the regime, including senior retired officers, who wished for him to retire and those who wanted him not only to continue ruling, but were also pushing for his running for a fourth term. Upon his return from France, Bouteflika – some might say his clan – appointed to key ministerial positions, such as the Interior and Justice, and the Constitutional Council, individuals who are very close to him and made important changes within the military hierarchy and within the powerful intelligence powerhouse, the Department of Research and Security (DRS), which lost a few of its traditional prerogatives. The objective has been to reduce the power of the head of the DRS, who had been an ally of Bouteflika in the past.[30]

Given the notorious opacity of the Algerian political system, the reasons for confronting the intelligence services are not very clear. However, one can surmise that the investigations about the high corruption in the national oil company, SONATRACH, and other ministries, that involved senior officials close to Bouteflika, like Chakib Khelil, might have been the trigger for such restructuring of the intelligence services. Another reason might have been Bouteflika's desire to control some institutions in order to secure his reelection. Indeed, many of the former prerogatives of the DRS have now come under the direct control of the presidency.

Having established the hegemony of the presidency, Bouteflika was certain of his reelection on 17 April 2014, an election which many parties boycotted. The main contender, Ali Benflis, a former prime minister and close associate of Bouteflika before 2004, stood no chance despite his appeal to the youth and his promises of change. Bouteflika could not even run a campaign – his Prime Minister Abdelmalek Sellal and other ministers campaigned on his behalf. The opposition denounced the reelection as a violation of the Constitution – since the president cannot perform his duties – but their divisions and lack of anchorage within a depoliticized society elicited contempt from the regime, which accused them of being anti-nationalists seeking to destabilize the country.

Conclusion

The Algerian regime under Bouteflika's rule has been able to maintain itself in power. It did this thanks to the oil rent, which it uses to mute discontent within society and to co-opt a divided opposition, often led by former members of the regime who do not have the trust of a population, particularly the youth, who see little hope for the future. The regime believes that the seeming stability the country currently enjoys is everlasting. Officials raise the specter of destabilization such as happened in Libya and Syria should Bouteflika and his cohorts leave office. They also believe that their being at the forefront on the war against terrorism in the neighborhoods gives them broad international legitimacy. At the moment, the regime is seeking a replacement for Bouteflika, one who could safeguard the enormous interests they have accumulated since 1999. While the Algerian population has bought into the 'stability' belief and is content with seeing some of its socio-economic grievances addressed, a big drop in the price of oil would jeopardize one of the bases of the regime's legitimacy, that is, rent redistribution, which may have unforeseen consequences.

Notes

1. Zine El-Abidine Ben Ali (November 1987–January 2011), Hosni Mubarak (October 1981–February 2011), Muammar Gaddafi (September 1969–October 2011) and Ali Abdullah Saleh (May 1990–February 2012).
2. For an account, see Keith Sutton, Ahmed Aghrout and Salah Zaimeche, 'Political Changes in Algeria: An Emerging Electoral Geography', *The Maghreb Review*, vol. 17, nos. 1–2, 1992, pp. 3–27; Keith Sutton and Ahmed Aghrout, 'Multiparty Elections in Algeria: Problems and Prospects', *Bulletin of Francophone Africa*, vol. 1, no. 2, 1992, pp. 61–85.
3. Yahia H. Zoubir, 'Stalled Democratization of an Authoritarian Regime: The Case of Algeria', *Democratization*, vol. 2, no. 2, 1994–1995, pp. 109–139.
4. Yahia H. Zoubir, 'The Failure of Authoritarian Developmentalist Regimes and the Emergence of Radical Protest Movements in the Middle East and Africa: The Case of Algeria', *Journal of Third World Studies*, vol. 13, no. 1, Spring 1996, pp. 127–184.
5. Stephen King, *The New Authoritarianism in the Middle East and North Africa* (Bloomington, Indiana: Indiana University Press, 2009).
6. Frédéric Volpi, "Algeria versus the Arab Spring', *Journal of Democracy*, vol. 24, no. 3, July 2013, pp. 104–115.
7. They are usually referred to as the 'oil and sugar riots'.
8. Founded as a loose umbrella rather than an alliance, it incorporated diverse opposition groups: political parties, civil society organizations and independent trade unions. For a full list of the CNCD founding members, see the *Ligue Algérienne pour la Défence des Droits de l'Homme* (the Algerian League for the Defense of Human Rights) website (www.la-laddh.org/?lang=fr).
9. Ait Ouarabi Mokrane, 'Vers l'élargissement du front pour le changement', *El-Watan* (daily newspaper), 24 January 2011.
10. The divisions that surfaced within the CNCD regarding its *raison d'être* caused it to split into two distinct factions: CNCD-political parties and CNCD-civil society. It was the first faction which vowed to continue its protest campaign.
11. This conflict is estimated to have claimed between 150,000 and 200,000 lives and the forced disappearance of over 7,000 people.
12. An institution, the Commission Nationale de Consultations sur les Réformes Politiques (National Commission for Consultations on Political Reforms, CNCRP) was established to gather views and suggestions on this proposed package of reforms. For a month (21 May–21 June 2011), the CNCRP collected the suggestions of over 250 statesmen, political party members, and leaders from state associations. Following the conclusion of its consultation work, a final report was handed over to President Bouteflika.
13. These texts were published in the *Journal Officiel de la République Algérienne (JORA)*, vol. 51, no. 1, 14 January 2012, pp. 4–39, available at: www.joradp.dz/FTP/JO-FRANCAIS/2012/F2012001.pdf, accessed 10 April 2013; and vol. 51, no. 2, 15 January 2012, pp. 5–34, available at: www.joradp.dz/FTP/JO-FRANCAIS/2012/F2012002.pdf, accessed 10 April 2013.
14. The assembly is elected through a closed-list proportional representation system to serve five-year terms.
15. Ordonnance no. 12–01, déterminant les circonscriptions électorales et le nombre de sièges à pourvoir pour l'élection du Parlement, 13 February 2012, *JORA*, vol. 51, no. 8, 15 February 2012, pp. 4–5.
16. Loi organique no. 12–01, relative au régime électoral, 12 January 2012, *JORA*, vol. 51, no. 1, 14 January 2012, pp. 8–31.
17. By way of illustration, their under-representation was reflected in the fact that only 7.7 per cent of women sat in the 389-member *Assemblée Populaire Nationale* (National Popular Assembly) and less than 5 per cent in the 144-member *Conseil de la Nation* (Council of the Nation).
18. 'Algérie: vote d'une loi accusée de limiter la représentativité féminine', *Jeune Afrique* (online), 4 November 2011, available at: www.jeuneafrique.com/Article/ARTJA WEB20111104091148/, accessed 25 April 2013.

19. *Ibid.*
20. Nacerdine Djabi, 'Les petits partis, incapables de franchir le seuil des 7% aux élections locales', *Algérie Presse Service*, 10 August 2012, available at: www.aps.dz/Les-petits-partis-incapables-de.html, accessed 26 May 2013.
21. "Daho Ould Kablia évoque les échéances électorales" Liberté (daily newspaper), 5 August 2012, http://www.liberte-algerie.com/actualite/daho-ould-kablia-evoque-les-echeances-electorales-84383/, accessed on August 14, 2015.
22. Nadia Benakli, 'Devant une campagne more, l'abstention ravive l'inquiétude', *L'Expression* (daily newspaper), 23 April 2012.
23. Yahia Bounouar, "Elections : panique au sommet, les citoyens harcelés," Le Quotidien d'Algérie, 20 February 2012, http://lequotidienalgerie.org/2012/02/20/elections-panique-au-sommet-les-citoyens-harceles/ (accessed 10 March 2012).
24. Figures in this section are derived from the *Journal Officiel de la République Algérienne*, vol. 51, no. 32, 2012, pp. 4–22, available at: www.joradp.dz/FTP/JO-FRANCAIS/2012/F2012032.pdf, accessed 22 October 2014.
25. 'L'AAV choquée par ses résultats aux élections législatives', *Algérie 360°* (online), 2012, available at: www.algerie360.com/algerie/l%E2%80%99aav-choquee-par-ses-resultats-aux-elections-legislatives/, accessed 15 March 2013.
26. Synthèse APS, "CNISEL : Adoption du rapport ," El-Moudjahid, 3 June 2012, http://www.elmoudjahid.com/pdf-elmoudjahid/669 (accessed 5 June 2012).
27. US Department of State, 'Algerian Elections', *Press Statement*, 12 May 2012, available at: www.state.gov/secretary/rm/2012/05/189811.htm, accessed 23 March 2013.
28. There were also other important departures such as the long serving Aboubakr Ben-bouzid (1993–2012) and Abdelaziz Belkhadem, Prime Minister (2006–2008) and then Minister of State and Personal Representative of President Bouteflika (2008–2012).
29. 'Nouveau gouvernement algérien: la continuité . . . sans grand changement', *Jeune Afrique* (online), 5 September 2012, available at: www.jeuneafrique.com/Article/ARTJAWEB20120905085803/, accessed 9 May 2013.
30. Boualem Ghamrassa, 'Algeria: The Bouteflika Spring?', *Ashark Al-Awsat*, (online), 9 November 2013, available at: www.aawsat.net/2013/11/article55321769, accessed 21 October 2014.

10

THE MAKING AND UNMAKING OF THE 2012 CONSTITUTION IN EGYPT

Ibrahim Awad

Introduction: The erosion and collapse of the Mubarak regime

The active movement that ate away at the foundations of the Mubarak regime until its fall can be considered to have started in 2004. During that year, *Kifaya*, a group that brought together liberals, Nasserites, leftists and Islamists, emerged. *Kifaya*, Arabic for "enough", staged demonstrations in public spaces that were modest in magnitude but significant in meaning. They expressed their rejection of both the extension of Mubarak's rule and of the so-called inheritance project in which Gamal, the president's second son, would take over as head of state when his father stepped down. At the beginning, *Kifaya* was met with skepticism, yet it proved such skeptics wrong when a number of rejectionist groups emerged in its wake, such as the 9 March Movement, founded at Cairo University by a number of academics. This group had the same political convictions of *Kifaya*, but naturally emphasized academic freedoms and denounced the systematic interference of state security in university life. Several groups that followed, such as Writers Against Inheritance and The Egyptian Campaign Against Inheritance, focused solely on one objective: resisting the inheritance project. In 2009, the National Association for Change became the standard bearer of the wish to put an end to the Mubarak regime.

Beginning with a protracted strike in 2008 at the important textile industry city of Mahalla Al Kubra, Egypt began experiencing industrial actions as it never had before (Amer 2012). The neo-liberal economic policies put in place since 2004 had accelerated the liberalization and deregulation begun a decade earlier, resulting in wide income gaps, job insecurity and expanding poverty. Strikes and sit-ins multiplied: instances of industrial action jumped from 266 in 2006 to 614 in 2007 to 1,900 in 2009 (ACPSS 2010). In 2010, protest reached the central seats of government. Sit-ins by precariously employed, poorly paid or fired workers were staged in the vicinity of the office of the prime minister and of the People's

Assembly. Economic protest was at the origin of the emergence of further activism for change; the youth who founded the April 6 Movement took its name from the date that workers in Mahalla Al Kubra had started their strike. The first independent trade union, Employees of Real Estate Taxes, applied for legal recognition soon after. This union would years later give rise to the Egyptian Federation of Independent Trade Unions (EFITU). Established earlier, the Center for Workers and Trade Union Services (CWTUS) continued calling for freedom of association, denouncing government policies and educating workers about their rights.

In the meantime, the virtual world was increasingly populated by youth groups airing their discontent and protest. Like other opposition actors, they decried corruption and repression and called for freedoms and democracy. Egyptian State Security could not keep up with the technological savvy of these groups, and in the buildup to 25 January 2011, these virtual groups called on their members to take to the streets. Their calls were realized as many gathered in the streets of Cairo and other cities, embarking on an action of great magnitude. Eighteen days later, Mubarak and many top figures of his regime had been toppled.

The foundations of the constitutive process

Three weeks later, the first step was made in the process of drafting a new Egyptian constitution. The Supreme Council of the Armed Forces (SCAF), to which Mubarak had surrendered power, appointed a committee to propose amendments to the 1971 Constitution that it had earlier suspended. This constitution would be reinstated until a new one was adopted. The committee proposed the election of the two houses of parliament, which, in turn, would select a 100-member constituent assembly. A president would be elected afterwards, to whom the military would hand over power, returning to their barracks by September, with the president overseeing the drafting and adoption of the new constitution. SCAF submitted the proposed amendments to referendum. Secularist political forces campaigned for their rejection. The amendments had not touched the devastating powers of the president, precisely those against which Egyptians had risen, they argued. Secularists considered that a new constitution needed to be adopted before any elections took place. Candidates for the presidency also needed to know whether they would exercise power in a presidential or semi-presidential system, or would be reduced to symbolic representation under a parliamentary one. Islamist forces, including the Muslim Brotherhood and the *Salafis*, who made on that occasion their first appearance on the political scene, came out in full support of the amendments. The Islamists claimed that the reinstatement of the 1971 Constitution would preserve Article 2, which provided that the principles of the Islamic juridical system, *shari'a*, would be the principal source of legislation.

In fact, secularists had not put the inclusion of Article 2 in question. Muslim Brotherhood and *Salafis* insisted that they had and used their vast organizational and financial power to mobilize for the approval of the amendments. Although they never referred to it, the time factor was certainly on the minds of the Muslim

Brotherhood. Because of their solid organizational structure, elections in a matter of a few months would be in their favor. The office of the president as well as a majority in parliament would then allow them to imprint the new constitution with their symbolic ideals. The secularists meanwhile must have thought that their lack of organization would put them at a disadvantage in any early voting. The divide between Islamists and secularists around the constitutional amendments marked the first political alignments in post-Mubarak Egypt. The amendments were approved by 77 percent of the voters. SCAF considered the vote an expression of support for their plans for the future. The 1971 Constitution was not reinstituted and a constitutional declaration of 62 articles was promulgated instead, which included all the provisions approved by referendum except one (SCAF 2011). By freezing the distribution of power, the vote was an invaluable push for the Islamists (Awad 2013).

The symbolic ideals of the Muslim Brotherhood concerned bringing political and religious spaces closer together; Islamic ethics and morality would guide the social and political system. Existing laws did not submit to the tenets of *Shari'a* and they had to conform to them. If ethics, morality and *Shari'a* were respected, the problems of society would be solved. *Salafis* went further: they emphasized the Islamic identity of Egypt, which should override all other political considerations. For secularists, *Shari'a* had not been infringed upon but respected. Egypt's problems were of a political, economic and social nature and should be treated as such. Their solutions were the objectives of the 2011 revolutionary movement.

The assertion in this chapter is that the contrasting Islamist and secularist prescriptions for Egypt's future shaped both political alignments and the constitutive process from its foundation until the 2012 Constitution was adopted. Various actors proposed divergent prescriptions, which resulted in contentious constitutional provisions. After the Constitution entered into force, these provisions continued to be challenged. On their part, both the exercise of power and the socioeconomic environment generated new political alignments. The interaction between challenges to constitutional provisions and the new political alignments was to determine the fate of the new Constitution and of the political order it had put in place.

Actors in the constitutive process

As the constitutive processes began, three groups of actors could easily be identified: political Islamists, secularists and youth groups. The military, which launched the process and had interests of its own to preserve, should also be added. These actors are briefly reviewed below:

i. The military

The military was the foundation and the spinal cord of the Egyptian authoritarian system for six decades. Mubarak's surrender of power to SCAF was an expression of their tacit agreement on the continued role of the military in the political system.

This role had a natural corollary: the autonomy of the military and its lack of accountability to a civilian power, even a democratically elected one. This role did not emerge from any constitutional text, but grew from the metamorphosis of the July army movement into an authoritarian regime. Preserving this principle of autonomy would later weigh heavily on the constitutive process.

ii. Political Islam

The Muslim Brotherhood, the *Salafis* and former *Jihadists* are the three components of political Islam in Egypt. Varied references to Islam and to religious values as a framework for political action unite them.

The Muslim Brotherhood is the most significant actor among them. Since its establishment in 1928, the Muslim Brotherhood has considered the adoption of Islamic ethics and morality as the path to Muslims' renaissance. A return to the Islamic juridical system, *Shari'a*, after decades of legal modernization was another means to bring about this desired awakening. Renewal and awakening also required the reunification of Muslims under a caliphate. The fall of the Islamic caliphate in Istanbul in 1924 was considered the ultimate sign of decline and submission. This attachment to transnational political organization, however, created doubt as to the Muslim Brotherhood's adherence to the modern territorial nation-state, the only political construction where democracy has been practiced. Nonetheless, the Muslim Brotherhood announced their faithfulness to democratic principles at the beginning of the transitional process. Electoral mechanisms of democracy were politically favorable to them; their vast and tightly knit organization and the extensive network of social assistance that they had developed ensured them a considerable advantage before any competitive pluralistic process started. To engage in the new political system, the Muslim Brotherhood set up *Al Huriya wal 'Adala* (Freedom and Justice) party.

The *Salafis* are a movement composed of different organizations, essentially active in charity and in advocacy for the purity of the early days of Islam. The movement does not have a central organ with authority over its component groups. It has historically kept away from politics, advocating obedience to the ruler, and this was the *Salafis'* attitude towards both Mubarak and his opponents until his last days in power. Because it was not mentioned in the Quran, some *Salafis* denounced democracy as heresy. *Salafis* claim they are more numerous than Muslim Brotherhood, and, reflecting the non-centralized character of their movement, *Salafis* formed several political parties in order to take part in the transition, the most important of which is *Al Nour* (Light).

The *Jihadists* were a serious enemy for the Mubarak regime in the 1990s; in 1981, *Jihadists* had assassinated Sadat. Two *Jihadist* organizations existed: the *Jama'a Islamiya* and the *Jihad*. They were especially violent in Upper Egypt, where they attacked symbols of the State, and in the heart of Cairo, where they targeted tourism. For these acts *Jihadists* were systematically rounded up and judged, executed or jailed for long terms. *Jihadists* were acting against an unjust and corrupt regime which, moreover, did not follow Islamic precepts. They were concerned with the religious foundations and legitimacy of the exercise of violence to dislodge the ruler. In the 2000s, many incarcerated *Jihadists* had major ideological reconsiderations and announced their abandonment of armed struggle. Indeed, after Mubarak's fall, some among them felt that they should join the new open political process. To do so, a faction of former *Jihadists* set up *Al Bena' wal Tanmiya* (Construction and Development) party.

iii. The secularists

The secularists are united by their defense of the principles of liberal democracy, including the separation of political and religious spaces; protection of the rights of association, expression and belief; equality and non-discrimination; and free elections. Secularists reached the transition after decades of systematic antagonism from the successive stages of the July regime. In addition, the three Mubarak decades saw an open and increasing hostility and misinterpretation of secular precepts and ideas by components of the religious movement. Secularists were branded as non-believers and accused of being against religion. In fact, Egyptian secularism was never hostile to religion. Prominent secularists included pious believers and biographers of the prophet. In an increasingly conservative society, with the State silent if not active in the accusations, this intimidation bore fruit. To stave off the attacks to which they were subjected, the secularists surrendered. They abandoned the term *'almaniya* (secularism) and declared their defense of the *madaniya* (the civilian character) of the state. Secularists were also themselves divided. First, there was a liberal vs. left divide. Then, there were subdivisions representing the different shades of each. Divisions reflected the different priorities given to respecting the processes of democracy, as opposed to reaching its real values. Economic and social concerns faced those of procedure. At the beginning of transition, it seemed that liberals and the left had not realized that a far more existential struggle than that over their own differences awaited them.

One considerable burden secularists carried, and which was held against them, was the fact that their ideals of liberal democracy were also those of the colonial and imperial countries responsible for decades of subjugation and for Palestinian dispossession. One important point scored by secularists as they approached transition was the adherence to their ranks of Nasserites, defenders of the modern state but previous adversaries of liberal democracy. This was only reasonable after the left had unified to unequivocally support the same democratic ideas. Most importantly for the transition, secularists not only defended the separation of political and religious spaces, but also called for the supremacy of elected civilian political authorities over the military.

Divisions and subdivisions were manifested in the many parties in which liberals and the left joined the transition. Some of these parties, like the neo-Wafd for the liberals and the *Tagamo'* for the left, had existed under Mubarak and compromised with his regime. New parties were now legally recognized, such as the Al Dostour; Liberal Egyptians; The Egyptian Social Democratic Party (ESDP); Freedom's Egypt; Ghad Althawra, for the liberals; and the Socialist and People's Alliance, for the left. Also on the left, the active Revolutionary Socialists, a Trotskyite party, emerged from the underground. Along with other unrecognized minor organizations, such as the Socialist and Communist parties, Revolutionary Socialists did not ask for legalization.

iv. Youth groups

Youth groups triggered the immediate protests that developed into a revolutionary movement in January 2011. In the real and virtual world, these groups, which spanned the political spectrum, multiplied. They worked together well during the protests; A Coalition of Youth for the Revolution was formed in early February 2011, bringing together nationalist, liberal, Islamist and leftist groups. The youth of the Muslim Brotherhood had worked hand in hand with those of other political orientations. Socialized to the idea of pluralistic action, part of the young Muslim Brotherhood eventually broke with their mother organization. The April 6 Movement, the Mohamed Elbaradei Campaign, the Coptic Union of Maspero Youth, the Justice and Freedom, and the Young Socialists, in the real world, and *Kollona Khaled Said* (We are all Khaled Said), in the virtual world, are some of the best known youth groups. Great expectations were placed on the revolutionary youth groups, which shared with secularists their support of separation of political and religious spaces. The reality was that they neither had a developed vision for the future nor ambitions to take political power. The transition period would show that their strength lay in protest and the refusal to submit, a power that should be neither underestimated nor overvalued. Some youth group members also joined the newly created parties or became active in the political process as independents.

In a country where 60 percent of the population is under the age of 30 years and where unemployment and poverty for youth are well above the national average, youth groups and activism are of the utmost significance.

Launching the constitutive process and the formation of the constituent assembly

The constitutive process could not respect the timetable set in the March 30 Constitutional Declaration; it formally started in November–December 2011. The results of the elections to the People's and the *Shura* assemblies in November and December 2011 and in February 2012 determined the composition of the constituent assembly. In the People's Assembly, Islamists gained a total of 61 percent of seats, 41 percent for the Muslim Brotherhood and 20 percent for the *Salafis*. In the *Shura* Assembly they secured 83 percent of seats in the absence of interest and engagement by secularists (Carnegie Endowment for International Peace 2012). Islamists maintained that the constituent assembly should reflect the composition of the two houses of parliament. Secularists insisted that the constitutive process should be consensual. Finally, Islamists reserved for themselves 65 percent of seats, making a disingenuous concession: when consensus could not be reached, provisions would be adopted by 67 percent of votes in the assembly in a first round of voting. But in a second round, the required majority was 57 percent of votes only, below the Islamists' representation in the assembly (Abdelzaher, Nour, and Fakhry 2012). The composition of the assembly was challenged before the Constitutional Court, which did not take long to decide that it was indeed unconstitutional. The rationale of the Court's decision was that the two houses had selected a number of their members to sit on the constituent assembly and that the constitutional declaration had only provided for members of parliament to select the constituent assembly, not to sit on it themselves (She'irah 2012). The two houses of parliament quickly embarked on selecting a second constituent assembly. Islamists and Secularists disagreed again on the representativeness of the assembly and on convergence in drafting the Constitution. A compromise was finally reached: the Islamist and secularist sectors would each have 50 percent of the membership. But when it came to selecting the members, Islamists insisted that representatives of Al-Azhar, of the Egyptian Churches, of the State and of professional bodies be counted in the secularist quota (Abdelmeguid 2012), leaving the secularists with much less than half the assembly membership. The second assembly still ended up with some parliamentarians among its members, even if they were fewer than in its predecessor, and its composition was thus also challenged before the Constitutional Court.

Secular party representatives and independent members attended meetings of the first assembly. Despite its unbalanced composition, they hoped to reach an understanding on procedures with Islamists that would make compromise possible. The Islamist alliance was clear but non-formalized and the secular parties, in contrast, consulted together but did not act as a unified alliance. It is noteworthy that some secularists, such as the Wafd and Ghad Althawra parties, Nasserites, and independent members had joined the Muslim Brotherhood and *Salafis* in a Democratic Alliance to prepare for the legislative elections.

Because of the "agreed" rules for the Islamist-secularist distribution of seats and for the adoption of constitutional provisions, some secularists, such as the ESDP representatives, declined membership in the second assembly. Other members did not occupy their seats. Despite withdrawals from the Democratic Alliance, a number of secular members persisted in trying to weigh in on both the discussions and the final product of the assembly. Political scientist and secularist Wahid Abdul Majid was even designated as a spokesperson.

The assembly set up five substantive committees: the State and Essential Foundations of the Egyptian Society; Rights, Freedoms and Public Duties; the System of Governance and Public Authorities; the Independent and Supervisory Apparatuses; and Proposals, Dialogues and Societal Communication. A general Drafting and Research Committee was established to receive texts agreed upon in the substantive committees and to reformulate them into the technical language of constitutional law. It was also assumed that this body would reconcile texts and eliminate contradictions.

During the summer of 2012, in the shadow of the first weeks of Muslim Brotherhood President Mohamed Mursi's term in office, suspicions of unconstitutionality notwithstanding, the second assembly started its work. News of its proceedings filtered out, but neither public opinion nor political parties paid much attention. Debates looked unruly and no systematic and discernible communication existed with the outside world.

Intensification of the process and realignment of actors

Interest in the constitutive process was rekindled when the press published reports about issues and provisions that were discussed in the assembly. To external observers, the process looked quite untidy. Reportedly completed texts were contradictory. When published texts were met with outrage, voices quickly retorted that they were proposals yet to be discussed. Substantive committees often disowned texts that the drafting committee had consolidated and informally leaked and denounced the drafting committee as interfering in their substantive jobs. Fighting between assembly committees further regenerated interest in the constitutive process. Finally, unfinished versions of the draft constitution were published on the website of the constitutive assembly in October and November 2012. Provisions in the October version were an improvement on the texts leaked in the previous weeks. The November text benefited from comments on the previous version and the discussions it occasioned. Yet, great divergences persisted over the same bones of contention. Outside the assembly, secular political forces and observers disapproved the published provisions. They reiterated their calls for a consensual constitution and on the president to appoint a new, more representative, assembly (Khaled 2012).

Discrepancies were also registered within the assembly between the Islamists and the secularists who had remained on its membership. As discussions progressed and texts were drafted, secularist members realized that their views were largely disregarded. Two non-secularist members were appointed as co-spokespersons with the secularist member, who eventually resigned. Other secularist members also successively withdrew from the assembly. They quickly joined the meetings and consultations that liberals, Nasserites and leftists who had never joined the assembly were holding. The first contours of secularist realignment were being drawn up. Only a few members who could not be counted either as *Salafis* or Muslim Brotherhood remained on the assembly. They gave a pluralistic semblance to the process led by the Muslim Brotherhood.

On November 21, 2012, President Mursi published a new complementary constitutional declaration which was to extend the mandate of the constituent assembly to February 2013 and deprive the Constitutional Court of the authority to adjudicate the constitutionality of the constituent assembly and of the electoral law that presided over the elections of the *Shura* Assembly. Several declarations complementing the March 30 Constitutional Declaration had been published in 2011 and 2012. One provision in the November Declaration had resulted in the changing of the public prosecutor, which had been an objective of the president, the Brotherhood and some revolutionary groups.[1] Most bewilderingly, the new declaration shielded laws, measures and decrees adopted by the president against any appeal. This provision certainly had no precedent even in the most authoritarian regimes Egypt had previously endured.

The extension of the duration of the constituent assembly, intended to allow it to finish its work, was neither accompanied by measures to address the withdrawal of a good part of its members nor to balance out its composition, as the secularist camp had repeatedly requested. Depriving the Constitutional Court of a most important part of its responsibilities was meant to preempt its decision in respect of the constituent assembly expected for December 2. Young Muslim Brotherhood and *Salafis* joined action against constitutional provisions by besieging the building of the Constitutional Court to keep judges from entering and meeting in session.

The new declaration was met with an uproar. It was on this occasion that secularist movements, parties and independents, from the liberals to the left, formally coalesced around its rejection into the National Salvation Front (NSF). The far left Revolutionary Socialists did not join the front. Neither did youth groups.

In contrast, Islamists closed ranks behind President Mursi, but never formalized their alliance. The rationale was not that function is more important than structure; in fact, the Muslim Brotherhood is a compact organization, a source of strength unavailable to the *Salafis*. Formal leadership of the Muslim Brotherhood would relegate *Salafis*, who consider themselves more numerous than their partner, to a secondary role. This adds to tension over differences in religious interpretations, with the *Salafi* interpretation more extreme, roadblocks to a formal alliance between the two groups.

Alarmed by the reaction to his November 22 Declaration, the president backtracked, formally abiding by the recommendations of a sham National Dialogue. He abolished the declaration and promulgated a new one, in which the most important provision related to the Constitution was the extension of the duration of the constituent assembly for three months, until March 15, 2013.

The abolition of the November 21 Declaration decreed that its legal consequences would still stand. This meant that the substitution of the public prosecutor and a restrictive law decree "to protect the revolution, promulgated between adoption and abolition", would remain valid. The break between secularists and the Muslim Brotherhood was consummated.

The constituent assembly did not benefit from the extension of its mandate. On November 29, it held a marathon 18-hour session, discussing provisions with which it had never dealt before, and ended up adopting the draft constitution. The speaker of the assembly dashed to the presidential palace and submitted the draft to President Mursi, who immediately convened a referendum to approve it. The rush was aimed to preempt both a possible overruling by the court judges and a probable decision of unconstitutionality of the assembly. This rush deepened divisions between Islamists and secularists, but the latter were encouraged by public rejection of the November 21 Declaration and of the way the draft constitution was passed.

Bones of contention and the adoption of the new Constitution[2]

Several provisions in the draft epitomized the differences between Islamists and the NSF and other secularists. The campaign before the referendum and the reactions after the Constitution was eventually adopted reinforced these differences, which evolved around the relationship between political and religious spaces, equality and non-discrimination, civil and political rights, the powers of the president, the status of the military and the effective exercise of economic and social rights.

i. Relationship between political and religious spaces

The formulation of Article 2 of the 1971 Constitution was maintained: principles of *shari'a* were kept as the principal source of legislation. However, two new articles on the subject were added. Article 219 defined what the principles of *shari'a* were in a way that might have put at risk their established interpretation by the Constitutional Court. The Court had ruled that principles of *shari'a* are those provisions that contribute to the realization of its objectives: the protection of religion, life, reason, honor and property (HSC 2004). The new article referred in an ambiguous formulation to "fundamental and doctrinal rules", when the fact is that the undisputed provisions of *shari'a* are very few. Other provisions are controversial and disputed in the doctrine, with interpretations varying from the tolerant and sophisticated to the most extremist and fanatic. Article 4 was the other addition. It provided for consulting "the commission of supreme Ulemas of Al-Azhar in affairs concerning Islamic *shari'a*".[3] Even if not binding, the opinion of Al-Azhar would not have been ignored in any lawmaking process. Secularists considered that this provision placed state institutions under the jurisdiction of a religious one, thus threatening legal and social stability and interfering with the premises of democracy. They also suspected that this was a first step to be followed by a takeover of Al-Azhar by the most extremist Ulemas, who would then change the legal character of the State and impose a theocratic order.

Another provision with possible consequences for the separation of political and religious spaces was Article 76, which, in a unique departure from legal principles, provided that crimes could be established and penalties leveled on the basis of a constitutional text. In other words, the legal principle that no crime exists without having been spelled out in a law was blatantly ignored. This was considered to open the door for judges to establish that crimes have been committed and to decree corporal punishment on the basis of constitutional provisions on *shari'a* without a need for a backing from criminal law. This was all the more worrisome since criminal law is subject to control by the Constitutional Court, whereas constitutional provisions are not.

ii. Equality and non-discrimination

During the marathon session in which the draft was approved, the formulations of certain articles in previously published versions suddenly changed. One example was Article 33, which provided that citizens were "equal in rights and obligations, with no discrimination between them". The reference to sex, origin, language, religion or belief as inadmissible bases of discrimination, which had figured in all previous Egyptian constitutions, were dropped in the last minute. An obligation on the State to actively combat discrimination and religious hatred did not figure in this article or any other, and protection of cultural diversity was not envisaged either. Secularists suspected that, as formulated, this article could justify the adoption of discriminatory laws. Whether justified or not, suspicions widened the distance between the two opposing camps.

Another infringement of equality and non-discrimination can be found in Article 3, which provided that the *shari'as* of Christian and Jewish Egyptians are the principle sources of legislations governing their personal matters and religious affairs, and the choosing of their spiritual leaders. For drafters of the Constitution, this provision balanced Article 2 and proved their generosity towards Christian and Jewish Egyptians. In fact, a question arose as to the rights of Egyptians who did not follow any of the three Abrahamic religions. Additionally, this text was a response to a request which had never before been made. In Egypt, Christians and Jews have always been governed in their personal and religious affairs by their own legislations. In fact, this article seems to have been introduced in order to balance the shrinking gap between political and Islamic religious spaces. Moreover, singling out a group of citizens according to their religious affiliations is discrimination in and by itself.

Neither did the Constitution include provisions intending to prevent discrimination against women. It did not protect them against violence nor ensure the effective exercise of their inheritance rights. It is no surprise, then, that the Constitution did not envisage an active policy to ensure women's equality.

iii. Civil and political rights

It is striking that the title of Part I in the new Constitution was "Foundations of State and Society", and Part II, "Social and Moral Foundations". In this chapter, Article 10 provided that "State and society preserve the authentic character of the Egyptian family". In Article 11 "the State sustains ethics and morality", among other values. Society thus subjected itself to the control of the State rather than surrendering powers to it and setting rules for the exercise by the State of these powers. The most conservative interpretations of authenticity, ethics and morality could be invoked under these provisions. They could result in restricting creativity. They could also infringe on all women rights. This misgiving was justified: Article 81 provided that rights and freedoms are exercised in a way that does not contravene the foundations mentioned in Part I of the Constitution. Reading simply the final text of the Constitution does not, of course, reveal the proposals that the negotiating process ignored; the adopted text is expressive of the intentions of the drafters of the Constitution.

Article 70 did not set a definition of childhood in terms of age, only addressing child labor by stating that children should not be employed in inappropriate occupations before the completion of obligatory schooling. Finally, the new Constitution did not retain proposals prohibiting imprisonment for crimes related to the exercise of freedom of the press, not did it prohibit the suspension, closure or seizure of media. The freedom to establish written media was guaranteed. But setting up radio, television and digital media was left unprotected constitutionally and regulated only by law, which could result in greater restriction. The Constitution did not introduce either an article prohibiting human trafficking or child marriage.

The sudden introduction of Article 231, which did not figure in any of the published drafts, was bewildering. This article provided that the first parliamentary elections after the adoption of the Constitution would reserve two-thirds of seats to electoral lists and one-third to independents, with political parties and independents having the right to slate candidates in both categories. This was precisely the system declared unconstitutional by the Constitutional Court, which resulted in dissolving the People's Assembly in June 2012. The inclusion of this procedure, usually dealt with by law, was considered a manipulation of the Constitution in order to circumvent the ruling of the Constitutional Court.

iv. Powers of the president

To bring evidence to their claim that the new Constitution limited powers of the president, supporters pointed out Article 141, which provided that the president exercised his powers through the president of the Council of Ministers, his deputies and his ministers. The opposition retorted that this same provision provided for various exceptions, which added to the powers reserved for the president in other articles. The president was the chief of the executive branch, appointed the prime minister, not necessarily from the majority party, and formulated the general policy of the State. Exceptions in Article 141 provided that his direct prerogatives included defense, national security and foreign policy affairs. He presided over the Council of Ministers when he wished, appointed civil servants and members of the military and dismissed them, may declare a state of emergency, may pardon convicted criminals and reduce sentences, convened referenda, appointed 10 percent of members of the *Shura* Assembly, appointed judges of the Constitutional Court, appointed heads of supervisory bodies, and presided the Council on National Security. With respect to the appointment of heads of supervisory bodies, opponents dismissed the significance of the conditioned approval of the majority of the *Shura* Assembly, as no weighted majority was required. Challengers brought further evidence in support of their argument about the vast powers of the president in the new Constitution, which the revolutionary movement had sought to reduce. Article 151 reserved few subordinate prerogatives for the government that the prime minister presided. This article provided that the government only participated with the president in formulating the general policy of the State and in supervising its implementation. The government oriented activities of ministries and its dependent bodies and coordinated with them, and whereas parliament could withhold confidence from the prime minister or ministers, challengers added, the president was politically unaccountable.

v. Status of the military

The Constitution innovated in comparative constitutional law by explicitly stipulating that the Minister of Defense would be appointed from officers of the armed forces. In no other country does the Constitution provide that the Minister of Defense must come from the ranks of the armed forces. Contrary to long-standing demands, Article 198 allowed the trial of civilians before military courts for crimes of "harming" the armed forces, and left it to law to define these crimes. The same provision declared that law would determine other competencies of military courts, which opened the door for the expansion of their jurisdiction. Discussing the budget of the armed forces was left to the Council of National Defense, in which the majority of members were military. The sensitivity of balancing national security considerations with the people's right to control state finances had been recognized and earnestly discussed. The adopted text completely deprived parliament of the right of controlling the military. The provisions on the military, taken together, thus amounted to granting them special status and autonomy.

vi. The effective exercise of economic and social rights

Chapter 3 in Part II treated economic and social rights. All such rights were mentioned but no mechanism or rules were envisaged to operationalize these obligations of the State. Articles on "high quality education", "scientific research" and "health care" provided that the State would allocate "sufficient resources" to them. "Sufficient" was a subjective assessment – no objective yardstick or recourse against the State should it fail in meeting these obligations was included. The example exists of a constitution that has set percentages of state budget to specific rights. This may be a rigid approach but it is the case of Article 212 of the Brazilian Constitution that allocates 43 percent of tax revenues for education. In another constitutional order, social and economic rights can be adjudicated in courts. Articles 32–35 of the Indian Constitution guarantee the right to constitutional remedies for violation of individuals' bill of rights. In a developing country, such as Egypt, where poverty is widespread, education and health care services are of deficient quality, and illiteracy still affects over a quarter of the population, the guarantee of economic and social rights and their effective exercise are a moral challenge. But they also constitute a political question of primary significance that threatens stability and may disrupt efforts to establish a durable and viable new political system. Absorbed in their symbolic and ethical preoccupations, drafters of the Constitution seem not to have realized that.

Bones of contention in the draft constitution deepened the cleavage separating religious and secularist groups. The former commended the draft and called on the electorate to approve it. Approval, they claimed, was a vote for stability and for resumption of normal life. Secularists were undecided. Reflecting different opinions within the coalition, the NSF wavered between boycotting the referendum and participation with rejection of the text. Only a few days before the first stage of the referendum on December 15, 2012, the front finally threw all its weight behind rejection. The referendum further consolidated the NSF. Strands that had led the modern Egyptian state at different times overcame their differences and coalesced in its defense. The objective alliance of the religious groups around the constitution remained informal. Other secularist groups, outside the NSF, joined the front in rejecting the draft. Amid accusations of interference in the voting process, results of the referendum were announced: 63.7 percent of voters supported and 36.3 rejected the text, the participation rate reaching 33 percent only. The Constitution was adopted, but only with the support of 21 percent of eligible voters. It is difficult to imagine how this low support could augur stability. The drop in support to Islamist themes from the height of 77 percent in the March 2011 referendum is especially noteworthy. Considered with President Mursi's slight majority in the May–June 2012 presidential elections – 51.73 percent to Shafik's 48.47 percent – this score may be interpreted as general fluidity in the electorate, to be contrasted with the polarization of political actors.

The new Constitution and the political system

Constitutional provisions are not alone in fashioning the political system; political situations and policies also transform it. They can even affect the fate of constitutional provisions and their sustainability.

The adoption of the new Constitution should have been a harbinger of a new political system that reestablished the authority of a democratic state at the service of its citizens and ensured the resumption of economic growth with a just distribution of its fruits. This did not happen. Demonstrations and protests against the new order continued. The NSF called on its supporters to demonstrate their continued opposition to the Constitution and their rejection of the "brotherization" of the State. But the streets of Cairo and other Egyptian cities were not exclusively the territory of the NSF. The Revolutionary Socialists also continued demonstrating against the Constitution and the new order that was shaping up. A new Anarchist Group emerged, especially in Alexandria; the Black Blocks, which claimed intellectual links with similar groups in industrialized countries, all of a sudden became active in squares and streets of various cities and espoused violence against the State and its institutions. Some consider that Black Blocks is only a tactic and the organization behind them to be the Anarchist Group. The anarchist language of the hooded Black Blocks lends a degree of credibility to this contention. Street children and youth vented their anger against the socioeconomic order that had ignored them and appeared destined for stasis. Anomic groups formed and disbanded to protest against the deteriorating economic situation, lack of fuel, "brotherization", verdicts against football supporters and a host of other motives of discontent. Clashes erupted and new victims were killed. Supporters of the president also mobilized. Observations of the second anniversary of the January 25 uprising witnessed especially violent confrontations. Loyalists accused the NSF and its leaders of being responsible for the disorder. In fact, they gave the NSF more credit than it deserved. The accusation also hid from them the real origins of the problems that seriously affected President Mursi's attempts at ruling the country.

In the first two months after the adoption of the Constitution, the economy further deteriorated. The Egyptian pound lost in value, falling from $1=5.7LE in December 2010 to $1=6.74LE by December 2012, with annual inflation at 6.3 percent (Gamal El-Din 2012). Later on, the inflation rate jumped to 9.75 percent in June 2013 (Central Bank of Egypt 2013). The Central Bank announced rules for the use of foreign exchange, which amounted to setting an order of priorities in imports and restricting them. Tourism, the second most important source of foreign exchange, could not be expected to pick up again amidst violence and turbulence in the country. A serious crisis of fuel erupted, which affected transportation, consumer prices and the generation of electricity. Faced with opposition from youth groups and the left, the government could not make a decision with respect to the protracted negotiations over an International Monetary Fund (IMF) loan destined to assuage the serious foreign exchange crisis and to restore investors' confidence in the Egyptian economy. Instances of religious extremism were registered.

To make things worse, a draft electoral law was discussed in the *Shura* Assembly, which held legislative power until the Representatives Assembly were elected. The draft designed electoral districts with widely varying representative-to-population ratios and with population mixes that made them favorable to the Muslim Brotherhood. For the opposition, this was manipulation aimed at ensuring an absolute majority victory for the Liberty and Justice Party. In accordance with the new Constitution, the draft was referred to the Constitutional Court for prior constitutionality control. A draft law on civil society organizations was also discussed in the *Shura* Assembly. Human rights organizations denounced the restrictions this imposed on civil society and demanded its withdrawal. The same organizations revealed increasing cases of arbitrary detention, by the police as well as by non-state actors, and severe torture that at times resulted in death (CIHRS 2012).

The president convened a national dialogue to find a solution to the impasse. He renewed his offer to discuss amending the controversial provisions in the newly adopted constitution. The president invited members of the Islamist alliance and its affiliated parties and members of the NSF, but not the Front as such. NSF members declined the invitation. They demanded a clear agenda and a commitment to implement decisions. Active groups such as the April 6 Movement and the Revolutionary Socialists were not invited. A Front of National Conscience, made up of individuals who are members of Islamist and affiliated parties, with the exception of *Salafis*, and independents, was established. An Alliance of National Forces, in good part constituted by former supporters of the Mubarak regime, emerged.

Despite these regroupings, the Muslim Brotherhood, *Salafis*, especially the Noor Party, and the NSF remained the main actors on the political stage. On the streets, the April 6 Movement and similar youth groups, the Revolutionary Socialists, anomic youth formations and the discontented crowds were actors to reckon with, especially if no progress was going to be made on the economic and social fronts. The discrepancy between actors ready to discuss policy around a negotiating table and those using street action to negotiate was noteworthy. It looked like the failure of the former could leave the latter alone in the fray, further radicalizing them. Condemnation and repression would not be effective given the numbers involved and their geographical spread. Even if these actors were only a minority, their pressure on the streets could keep the new constitutional arrangements from settling.

A major development in the political process was the initiative launched by Noor Party *Salafis* to bridge the gap between the president and the NSF. The initiative envisaged a change of government, guarantees for clean parliamentary elections and the removal of the public prosecutor appointed by the president in November 2012, a demand made by various opposition groups and members of the judiciary. The initiative was well received by the NSF and the two parties met to discuss it. In contrast, the president and his party did not like that the Noor behaved as an autonomous actor. They overtook the initiative when the party's chair paid a visit to two leaders of the NSF to discuss the best conditions for holding a useful dialogue. This was indicative of how the Muslim Brotherhood looked at an Islamist alliance: other parties should be subordinate to them and should not be permitted to act on their own account. In any case, the whole idea of a dialogue was aborted when the president, with no prior consultations and without addressing the opposition's demands, convened, in the third week of February, parliamentary elections for the end of April 2013. On the same day, the draft electoral law was amended by the *Shura* Assembly, after the Constitutional Court had declared a number of its provisions unconstitutional. Analysts remarked that not all the Court's observations had been addressed, which opened the door to declaring the next Representatives Assembly unconstitutional. Constitutional uncertainty thus extended from Mubarak to the military through the Muslim Brotherhood. The haste with which the draft law was amended was similar to that which presided over the adoption of the draft constitution at the end of November 2012.

The fall of the 2012 Constitution

The parliamentary elections never took place. The amended electoral law had to be submitted to the Constitutional Court, which took time to decide on its constitutionality. But tensions mounted in the spring of 2013. The president and his supporters went on denouncing the "deep state", which kept them from carrying out their revolution. It is noteworthy that the "deep state", signifying the entrenched institutions and interest groups, not only of the state but also of the economy, was a concept imported from the literature of the Turkish Justice and Development Party (AKP), a brother party to the Brotherhood and its Freedom and Justice Party. On its part, the opposition continued denouncing the brotherization of public administration and the poor conduct of the affairs of the state. The president provided them with abundant evidence to support their claims. For example, he appointed a number of governors among which were several Muslim Brotherhood members. These appointments included one where provocation was added to awkward judgment. One of the leaders of the *Jama'a Islamiya*, the group held responsible for the massacre of 58 tourists in 1997 in Luxor, was appointed governor of this leading touristic city in Egypt (Kingsley 2013). The president kept refusing to change the government and the public prosecutor. The *Shura* Assembly legislated at a frenetic pace, the opposition objecting that the legislative powers of the upper house of parliament were only temporary until the election of the Representatives Assembly and, therefore, limited to essential laws that could not wait. In May, the country was mobilized to loudly denounce the temporary deviation by Ethiopia of the course of the Blue Nile, part of the process of construction of the Renaissance Dam. Building the dam had been a subject of negotiations for many years without definitive agreement about it. But the temporary deviation was a technical measure known to Egyptian water and dam specialists, who did not consider that it had any practical negative significance. In June, the president invited key political figures to a meeting destined to discuss the "threats to national security" that the deviation and the Renaissance Dam represented for Egypt. Only leaders of Islamist and other small parties allied to the Muslim Brotherhood attended the meeting. Discussions, offensive to Ethiopia and deprived of any professional, diplomatic or political sense, were broadcast live on television without informing participants (El-Behairy 3 June 2013). The opposition considered that the language used in the discussions, and their unprecedented live broadcasting, were the real threats to national security. On June 16, a rally of solidarity with Syria was convened at the Cairo indoors sports stadium. In front of an audience of some 20,000 supporters, Mursi not only expressed support to the fighting opposition in Syria, he also pledged the participation of Egyptian armed forces. Spokesmen of Islamist parties and groups took the floor, with several *Salafis* interpreting the Syrian conflict in a purely sectarian perspective. Without any reaction from the president or his aides, either during or after the rally, they ferociously attacked *Shi'a Muslims* and threatened them with *annihilation* (El-Behairy 4 June 2013). Two days later, four citizens, from the tiny Egyptian *Shi'a* community, estimated at between 20,000 and 60,000 individuals in an 85 million population, were lynched and killed in a village south of Cairo.

Parallel to the accumulating manifestations of what was considered poor governing, a new youth movement, *Tamarrod*,[4] came into being. Its sole purpose was to collect signatures on a petition calling on the president to step down and to call for early presidential elections. Its aim was to collect 15 million signatures. Surprisingly, in a matter of a few weeks, *Tamarrod* announced that it had met its target. A short time later, it declared that signatures reached the number of 22 million (Rizk 2013). To back up its demands, *Tamarrod* called on the population to stage demonstrations on June 30, the first anniversary of the inauguration of Mursi as the Egyptian president.

On June 23, the Minister of Defense, General Abdel Fattah El Sisy, who was appointed to his post by Mursi in August 2012, publicly called on all political forces to reach an agreement within a week in order to spare the country political instability (Kamel 2013). On June 30, General El Sisy's request was formulated in the language of an ultimatum to the president: if he did not reach an understanding with the opposition within 48 hours, the armed forces would intervene (Saleh and Fick 2013). The millions who took to the streets of cities, towns and villages of Egypt on that day were seen as lending legitimacy to any move by the military in respect of Mursi's presidency.

Mursi did not budge. On July 3, General El Sisy convened a meeting with the leaders of the two highest religious institutions, Al-Azhar and the Christian Orthodox Church, and with representatives of the most prominent secularist parties and *Tamarrod*. Only one Islamist party, the *Salafi El Noor*, was represented in the meeting. The participants agreed on a road map. It included the deposition of Mursi and launching a process aimed at setting in place a new political order. Most importantly, and in conformity with this aim, the agreed road map announced to the population by General El Sisy, provided for the appointment of the president of the Constitutional Court as provisional president and for the suspension of the Constitution adopted six months earlier and its amendment (BBC 2013). Most participants had wished to abolish the Constitution altogether. The representative of the *El Noor* party had joined the meeting precisely to defeat this purpose. The so-called identity provisions and Article 219 were the achievements of the *Salafis* in the 2012 Constitution. They wanted to preserve them. The forces behind the July 3 event, particularly the military, wished to have an Islamist cover to their interference with the constitutional process. On July 8, Adly Mansour, the provisional president issued a Constitutional Declaration, which described how a six-month process of amending the Constitution, followed by parliamentary and presidential elections would unfold (State Information Services 2013). A 10-member technical committee of jurists would propose amendments within a month from its formation. These amendments would be submitted for debate to a 50-member commission representative of the population. Professional and academic bodies and civil society organizations would select their representatives, to whom the government would add ten public figures. The draft to be adopted by the Commission within two months would be submitted by the provisional president to a referendum within another 30 days.

In the last week in August 2013, the technical committee finished its work. It proposed amendments and deletions that affected 198 from among the 236 articles of the constitution. In addition to enlarging freedoms and spelling out the unacceptable grounds of discrimination, the committee proposed the removal of identity provisions and the deletion of Article 219 (Essam El-Din 2013). It also deleted from Article 4 the provision on involving Al-Azhar in the legislative process. In sum, the technical committee meant to reinforce freedoms and the principle of non-discrimination and to enlarge the distance between the political and religious spaces that the Constitution of 2012 had seriously reduced. However, the committee did not touch the structure of the Constitution. Article 4 on Al-Azhar was kept, but without its involvement in the legislative process. Article 3 on the *shari'as* of Christian and Jewish Egyptians was also maintained. This meant that three out of the first four articles in the amended draft of the Constitution had religious undertones, which had never been the case in Egyptian constitutions previous to the one drafted by Islamists in 2012. If this structure is maintained at the end of the amendment process, a question may be legitimately raised: have Muslim Brotherhood and other Islamists left an indelible imprint on the Egyptian constitutional order in only one year in power?

When the 50-member Commission was formed in the first week of September, all Islamist parties, except *El Noor*, declined to be represented. The distribution of the membership looked clearly in favor of forces attached to the separation of political and religious spaces, and opposed to the identity provisions and to article 219 (Ahram Online 2013). The knots with which Islamists had thought they would commit Egypt to *stasis* did not look tightly tied.

The military's position tipped the balance against President Mursi and his Islamist supporters. Besides choosing to side with the population, this position deserves further interpretation. After all, the 2012 Constitution recognized privileges to the armed forces as no Egyptian basic law had done before. Why, then, did the armed forces revolt against the political order that made this possible? In fact, the constitution is not alone in determining the attitudes of political actors anywhere. The Egyptian armed forces were for 60 years used to being the first political force in the Egyptian state. They seem to have estimated that the political practice of President Mursi, of the Muslim Brotherhood and of their other Islamist supporters weakened the Egyptian state and changed its character. What good was it to be the first political force in a weakened state, which, in addition, was going to be different in nature to the one they dominated for so long? The pledge by Mursi to involve the Egyptian military in the Syrian conflict without consulting them was said to have been the straw that broke the camel's back.

Concluding remarks

Two opposing perceptions of the constitutive process were at play in Egypt since it was initiated by the military shortly after Mubarak stepped down. Two years later, Islamists considered that the Constitution adopted in December 2012, where their symbolic ideals were addressed, was a precious foundation on which to build their political edifice. This should be done through elections, in which their solid organization, in addition to their assumed popularity, would give them an advantage. The constitution and parliamentary majority should thereafter be the base of undisputed political action. Political, economic and social challenges would then be addressed. This was particularly the perspective of the Muslim Brotherhood, to which they expected *Salafis* to subscribe. *Salafis* were not necessarily entirely in agreement. The non-formal alliance between the two components of political Islam during the constitutive process was not indissoluble with contact to the concrete realities of political life.

Secularists questioned the constitutional text and gave precedence to challenges. They particularly emphasized that the Constitution ignored or restricted some rights and did not appropriately provide for addressing political challenges. For secularists, these rights and challenges were the reasons that Egyptians had risen against the Mubarak regime. Solutions in the Constitution and in policy were the objectives of the revolutionary movement. Narrowing the gap between political and religious spaces, the *raison d'être* of the Muslim Brotherhood, and recovering ancient sources of identity, a fixation of *Salafis*, might have received the consent of a good number of citizens at a specific point in time. This consent could not necessarily extend indefinitely. The exercise of power after the adoption of the Constitution could reveal the consequences of these two determinants of the new constitutional order.

Having adopted the Constitution that they wished, the Muslim Brotherhood could have then listened to the concerns of secularists and given them partial satisfaction. Rather than doing that, they appended other Islamists and exercised power alone. The Muslim Brotherhood continued to use their symbolic agenda and to "brotherize" the state. Socioeconomic concerns were relegated to a secondary order of priority.

The practice of political power brought the opposition together. It also revealed to a citizenry used to a certain distance between political and religious spaces what bringing these closer to each other meant in real life. On their part, the military saw the state being weakened and discovered an intention to involve them in an external conflict without consulting them. The alliance between the organized opposition, large and diverse sectors of the citizenry, and the military brought down the political order put in place by the Muslim Brotherhood and the Constitution that they had drafted.

Practice of political power will also determine the fate of the constitutional order that will emerge from the constitutional amendment process. The opposition and the citizenry are diversified. In order for any new order to be sustainable, constitutional provisions and, particularly, political practice need to take account of this diversity. The cost of ignoring it will be political and constitutional instability.

Notes

1. However, this review only deals with the provisions of the November Declaration with a bearing on the making of the new constitution.
2. The Constitution of Egypt 2012 is available in English at http://niviensaleh.info/constitution-egypt-2012-translation/, and in Arabic at www.egypt.gov.eg/arabic/laws/download/Current_Constitution_20121225.pdf. This review of contentious articles of the new 2012 constitution benefits from Zulficar, 2012 and Bahaa Eddine, 2012.
3. Al-Azhar is a most respected religious institution in Egypt and the whole Islamic world.
4. Arabic for *Rebellion*.

References

Abdelmeguid, Wahid (21 June 2012), "The full story of the constituent assembly's battle", *Al-Shoruk News*. Online at http://shorouknews.com/columns/view.aspx?cdate=21062012&id=e0f322e9-e17c-42fa-89c0-39057201e099.

Abdelzaher, Nermine, Ali Nour, and Noura Fakhry (11 June 2012), "The People's Assembly finally approves the bill on the constituent assembly standards" (translation added), *Al Youm Al Sabe'*. Online at www.youm7.com/News.asp?NewsID=702918.

Ahram Online (26 August 2013), "Strong Egypt Party refuses to join Egypt Constitutional Committee", *Ahram Online*. Online at http://english.ahram.org.eg/News Content/1/64/79991/Egypt/Politics-/Strong-Egypt-Party-refuses-to-join-Egypt-Constitut.aspx.

Al Ahram Center for Political and Strategic Studies (ACPSS) (2010), "Arab strategic report", 365–366, Cairo.

Amer, May (3 January 2012), "Al Mahala Al Kubra workers: We started the revolution early" (translation added), BBC Arabic. Online at www.bbc.co.uk/arabic/middleeast/2012/01/120103_egypt_mahala_workes.shtml.

Awad, Ibrahim (2013), "Breaking out of authoritarianism: 18 months of political transition in Egypt", *Constellations*, Volume 20, Number 2, 275–292.

Bahaa Eddine, Ziad (4 December 2012), "Ten reasons to reject the draft constitution", *Al-Shoruk News*. Online at www.shorouknews.com/columns/print.aspx?cdate=05122012&i.

BBC (4 July 2013), "Egypt crisis: Army ousts President Mohammed Morsi". Online at www.bbc.com/news/world-middle-east-23173794.

Cairo Institute for Human Rights Studies (CIHRS) (21 February 2012), "Egypt: 8 months after Dr. Mohamed Morsi assumed the presidency, the rapid deterioration of the state of human rights in Egypt must be halted". Online at www.cihrs.org/?p=5954&lang=en.

Carnegie Endowment for International Peace (29 February 2012), "Results of Shura Council elections". Online at http://egyptelections.carnegieendowment.org/2012/02/29/results-of-shura-council-elections.

Central Bank of Egypt (2013), "Headline and core inflation – June 2013". Online at www.cbe.org.eg/NR/rdonlyres/C4D84EEF-2169-47C7-AAAD-A94BDCFBE868/1964/Monthly_Inflation_June2013.pdf.

El-Behairy, Nouran (3 June 2013), "Morsi meeting discusses effects of dam", *Daily News Egypt*. Online at www.dailynewsegypt.com/2013/06/03/morsi-meeting-discusses-effects-of-dam/.

El-Behairy, Nouran (4 June 2013), "Morsi forms committee on dam, meeting mistakenly televised", *Daily News Egypt*. Online at www.dailynewsegypt.com/2013/06/04/morsi-forms-committee-on-dam-meeting-mistakenly-televised/.

Essam El-Din, Gamal (20 August 2013), "Updated: Amended draft of constitution passed to president", *Ahram Online*. Online at http://english.ahram.org.eg/newscontent/1/64/79525/egypt/politics-/updated-amended-draft-of-egyptian-constitution-pas.aspx.

Gamal El-Din, Yousef (7 September 2012), "Egypt's pound at fresh lows: An opportunity?" CNBC. Online at www.cnbc.com/id/48937951/Egyptrsquos_Pound_at_Fresh_Lows_an_Opportunity.

High Constitutional Court of Egypt (HSC) (19 December 2004), "Case no 119 legal year 21". Online at http://hccourt.gov.eg.

Kamel, Nasser (24 June 2013), "Egyptian army will remain neutral in June 30 protests", *Al-Monitor*. Online at www.al-monitor.com/pulse/politics/2013/06/egypt-army-neutral-june-30-demonstrations-morsi.html#.

Khaled, Ahmad (7 November 2012), "40 parties and political movements demand the reformation of the constituent assembly" (translation added), *Al-Misriyun*. Online at http://almesryoon.com/permalink/47252.html#.US5JIJr8Iyk.

Kingsley, Patrick (17 June 2013), "Egypt's Mohamed Morsi appoints hardline Islamist to govern Luxor", *The Guardian*. Online at www.theguardian.com/world/2013/jun/17/morsi-appoints-islamist-governor-luxor.

Rizk, Mariam (5 November 2013), "Tamarod: From rebellious youth to political actors", *Ahram Online*. Online at http://english.ahram.org.eg/NewsContent/1/151/85217/Egypt/Features/Tamarod-From-rebellious-youth-to-political-actors.aspx.

Saleh, Yasmine and Maggie Fick (1 July 2013), "Egypt army gives Mirso 48 hours to share power", Reuters. Online at www.reuters.com/article/2013/07/01/us-egypt-protests-idUSBRE95Q0NO20130701.

She'irah, Wafaa (10 April 2012), "Merits of the invalidity of the constituent assembly: All the Assembly Members have to be chosen from outside the Parliament" (translation added), *Al-Badeel*. Online at http://elbadil.com/organizations/2012/04/10/41175.

State Information Services (8 July 2013), "Interim president issues constitutional Declaration for Transitional Period". Online at www.sis.gov.eg/En/Templates/Articles/tmpArticles.aspx?CatID=2666#.VYakWlVViko, accessed on June 21, 2015.

Supreme Council of Armed Forces (SCAF) (2011), *Constitutional Declaration*. Online at www.egypt.gov.eg/arabic/laws/constitution/default.aspx.

Zulficar, Mona, (7 December 2012 and 10 December 2012), "Q&A about the draft of the new Constitution" (in Arabic), *Almasry Alyoum*. Online at www.almasryalyoum.com/node/1294961.

11

LIBYA: FROM 'REFORM' TO REVOLUTION

Alison Pargeter

Of all the states in North Africa, Libya has arguably experienced the most profound political, economic and social transformation since the unleashing of the Arab Spring. Not only was Libya's the most protracted and bloody of all of North Africa's revolutions, but the toppling of its leader, Colonel Muammar Qadhafi, resulted in the opening up of the largest power vacuum in the region. Along with its leader, almost all of the vestiges of the former regime and, more importantly, the unique and bizarre state that Qadhafi created, were swept away almost overnight. Indeed, given the peculiarities of his *Jamahiriyah* (State of the Masses) when Qadhafi collapsed, the state collapsed with him.

As a result Libya has had to rebuild itself almost from scratch. Qadhafi's Libya was a country without proper functioning institutions, without opposition or civil society, and without any real political culture. Qadhafi's was also a regime that thrived on chaos and for which state building was always secondary to the pursuit of ideological ambitions. As a result, the reformatory task facing the country's new rulers and political actors following the revolution has been gargantuan.

Initially Libya seemed to make serious strides in pulling itself through the transition to the post-Qadhafi era. It defied expectations by holding its first national elections in July 2012, less than a year after the country was fully liberated, and by putting in place an interim government and an elected General National Congress as parliament. This was an extraordinary feat for a country in which political parties had been banned and membership of any organization outside of the framework of the state had been punishable by death. It also elected a sixty-member Constituent Assembly tasked with drawing up a new constitution.[1] Moreover, within one year of liberation, oil production was almost back to pre-war levels of 1.6 million bpd.[2] The government also launched a series of initiatives to get the country's militias to hand over their weapons and to integrate themselves into the country's official security organs.

However, beyond these achievements, the country has struggled against the most enormous challenges, posing serious questions about whether it will be able to transform itself into a functioning modern democracy. Some of these challenges are the by-product of the way in which the revolution unfolded, with each area forming its own militias to fight against the former regime, and others are the result of the country's geography and particular historical experience. Yet many of these challenges are the direct legacy of over forty years of rule under Qadhafi. Indeed, the vast chasm that has opened up with the collapse of the political center has facilitated the rise of local power brokers ranging from militia leaders to towns, tribes and Islamist groups, including those of a militant bent. The presence of these forces has left the new authorities with no real power base of their own and with little choice other than to rely on goodwill and appeasement as means of trying to propel the county forward.

This chapter traces the main internal drivers that fuelled Libya's revolution, examining in particular the consequences of the Qadhafi regime's failed reformist project, which by the end of the 2000s had dwindled to almost nothing. It will then go on to address the key internal challenges facing the country in the post-Qadhafi phase and that are hampering its transition to a modern, functioning democracy. The chapter covers the period up to the end of 2013.

Drivers for change: Failed reform

The reasons why Libyans followed their Tunisian and Egyptian counterparts and took to the streets in February 2011 were not difficult to fathom. Like their neighbors, they were frustrated at the years of political and economic marginalization, the brutal repression and the endemic corruption. They also feared that dynastic rule was taking hold. Just as in Egypt, where it was feared that Gamal Mubarak was set to take over from his father, there was a growing unease in Libya that Qadhafi was grooming his son, Saif Al-Islam, for power.

However, there were other specifically Libyan reasons why people were prepared to risk their lives for change. There was a particular frustration in Libya at the fact that Qadhafi had spent the past four decades using the country as a vast laboratory for his bizarre political and economic experiments.[3] In his bid to create the ultimate stateless society and to achieve perpetual revolution, the Libyan leader had ravaged the country, frittering away its oil wealth on pet projects and destructive foreign policy adventures, while creating a domestic polity and economy that was utterly dysfunctional. Despite the country's plentiful energy reserves, most ordinary Libyans were struggling to make ends meet, doing at least two jobs to survive and lacking the most basic of services and infrastructure. In frequent visits to Libya between 2004 and 2010, many Libyans lamented regularly to the author that the country should have been another Dubai. Or, as one popular joke that made the rounds after Libya agreed to relinquish its weapons of mass destruction programs in December 2003 went, 'When the weapons inspectors arrived in Libya they expected to find weapons of mass destruction, but all they found was mass destruction!'

To make matters worse, the colonel subjected the population to his personal whims with a particular contempt, blaming them when his policies went wrong for not having implemented his ideas properly. He even insisted that he was not the country's ruler, but simply the 'Leader of the Revolution' or 'Brother Leader.' Such an approach bred a certain sense of humiliation in some Libyans. As one Libyan diplomat described, "Since the uprisings, this is the first time I can walk down the street without feeling ashamed of being Libyan. I can now hold my head high."[4] Thus, the particular hatred for Qadhafi, which was later expressed through both the brutality of his killing in October 2011 and the queues of Libyans who lined up in Misrata to view his rotting corpse, was another driver for internal change.

Furthermore, it was no coincidence that the uprisings began in Libya's second city of Benghazi and spread quickly through the east of the country. It was in the east that marginalization had long been acutely felt. While many areas outside of the capital were left neglected and starved of proper infrastructure, it was in the east that this marginalization held particular symbolism. This was drawn in part from the fact that Benghazi had been Libya's capital during the time of the monarchy, which itself had its roots in the Senussi religious order that was centered in the east. Thus there was a feeling that by moving the capital of his new revolutionary state to Tripoli, Qadhafi had stripped Benghazi of its rightful role.

More importantly, however, after the regime uncovered the existence of militant Islamist networks in the east in the late 1980s and again in the mid-1990s, Qadhafi determined to punish the region. The area was turned into a kind of security zone. Families were forced to take part in combing operations in the mountains in the hunt for suspects, and thousands of Islamists and suspected Islamists from Benghazi and other towns in the east were arrested and detained in the notorious Abu Slim prison in Tripoli. It was in this prison that a grisly massacre took place in 1996, in which hundreds of Islamist prisoners were summarily executed, the majority of whom came from the east. The regime's continued unwillingness to even inform the families of those who were killed of how their relatives had died bred a particular resentment in Benghazi, where there were few families left untouched by the regime's brutality. It was the protests by the Abu Slim victims' families and the arrest of their lawyer, Fathi Terbil, in Benghazi on 15 February 2011 that first sparked the uprisings and propelled Libya into the Arab Spring.

Yet there was another ingredient in this potent mix. By the end of the 2000s, the Libyans had become utterly frustrated by the failed reform project that the regime had launched following its rehabilitation into the international community.[5] In a bid to demonstrate to the world that Libya was changing internally as well as externally and that it was worthy of the foreign investment it desperately needed to kick start its energy sector, the regime began to talk about the need for reform, particularly in the economic sphere. Qadhafi – a long-time proponent of radical Socialist-style economics – took to speaking of the need to diversify the economy away from its reliance on oil and gas and to attract foreign investment.[6] In 2003, Qadhafi also parachuted in the reformist-minded General Secretary (Prime Minister), Shukri Ghanem, a known advocate of free market economics, who began talking about modernization, privatization and the paring down of Libya's burdensome state sector. After decades under a closed and suffocating economic system, made worse by the international sanctions that were imposed from 1992 until 1999, some Libyans saw in this project the possibility of real change and of the chance to take advantage of the new opportunities afforded by Libya's reintegration into the international community.

Even more electrifying was the talk of political change. The political reform debate was personified in the figure of Saif Al-Islam, Qadhafi's eldest son by his second wife, who took on the mantle of arch reformer. Saif Al-Islam stunned Libyans by launching a series of human rights initiatives, such as an anti-torture campaign in which he encouraged victims of torture to come forward and seek redress against the security services. Saif Al-Islam also threatened to bring those members of the security services and revolutionary committees found to have committed torture to justice and encouraged the families of the victims of the Abu Slim prison massacre to pursue their rights. He began challenging the regime's hard-core ideologues, especially members of the feared Revolutionary Committees, by accusing them of holding the country back. Indeed, the leader's son took on the role of defender of the ordinary people against the excesses of the state.

At the same time, Saif Al-Islam launched a series of 'independent' media outlets, such as the *Cornia* and *Oea* newspapers, which, while clearly part of the regime, at least provided space for Libyans to complain about the government and to express their frustrations with the shortcomings of the state. It became increasingly commonplace in the years leading up to the revolution for these outlets to publish articles by Libyans bemoaning the state of the economy or complaining about corruption. Sometimes these articles went too far for the state to stomach. In May 2008, Benghazi academic Dr Fathi Al-Baja wrote a piece that was published in the *Corina* newspaper titled, "Where is Libya Heading?" in which he complained about inefficiency, nepotism, the slow pace of reform and the curtailment of freedoms. Al-Baja was hauled in by the security services after his article appeared and was accused of inciting public opinion and of raising doubts about Qadhafi's revolution. Al-Baja and Izzadine al-Awaj, the editor-in-chief of the newspaper, were ordered to go and sign in at the state security offices every week.[7] However, in January 2009 Saif Al-Islam stepped in and forced General Prosecutor Mohamed al-Misrati to cancel all procedures against the men. He also told Al-Baja to continue writing and expressing his opinion without restriction.

Perhaps most controversially, however, Saif Al-Islam launched a project to draw up a constitution. In 2004, he tasked groups of Libyan academics and legal specialists, supported by international experts, to draft a new constitution that would not simply constitutionalize the *Green Book* – Qadhafi's famous political, economic and social treatise that formed the basis of his Jamahiriyah system – but that would shake up Libya's political structures.[8] Given that since the *Green Book's* introduction in the late 1970s, Libya's complex political system had been based on Qadhafi's unique (and in his mind perfect) creation, the idea of altering it was a radical departure.

By the late 2000s, however, the constitution project was all but dead in the water. Despite its initial optimism, the committee tasked with drafting the new document soon came to the realization that Saif Al-Islam had lost interest in the initiative and that, in fact, he had never had any real commitment to the details of the project. As one member of the committee recalled, "He was always busy. He never responded to us, not once. Saif Al-Islam was not interested in details, problems or challenges."[9] The committee became so disillusioned that by the summer of 2008, they handed over the draft they had been working on and washed their hands of the whole project.

Yet Saif Al-Islam was not the only obstacle to the constitution project. Qadhafi was outraged at his son's efforts to tamper with the political system that had underpinned his regime for almost forty years and after a draft of the constitution was leaked to the media in 2008, he put a stop to the initiative. Saif Al-Islam was so upset that he stormed off abroad, announcing that he was withdrawing from public life.[10] Despite his behavior, however, it was dawning on Saif Al-Islam, just as it was on those Libyans who had put their faith in the reformist project, that there were always going to be limits to what this project could achieve. This is not to suggest that Saif Al-Islam had any real reformist vision that would turn Libya into a modern functioning democracy. Despite his repeated talk of "participatory democracy" and transparency, it is debatable whether he had any vision at all. As Al-Baja once complained, "Saif al-Islam's vision is incomplete and inadequate. It pays much attention to the skin of reform and not the meaning or the real scientific content of reform."[11]

However, by the late 2000s it was becoming clear that even the limited changes that Saif Al-Islam had been trying to achieve were always going to be constrained by his father and the system that had underpinned his rule for the past four decades. Indeed, the fate of the constitution was symptomatic of the problems facing the reformist project more broadly. For all that Qadhafi was prepared to allow some opening up and some superficial changes, he was not going to countenance anything that might threaten the stability of his regime. As Saif Al-Islam himself acknowledged in August 2007, there were four lines in Libya that could not be crossed: Islam and the application of sharia law; the security and stability of Libya; national unity; and, most importantly, Muammar Qadhafi.[12]

Moreover as international companies returned to the country to invest in the energy sector, there was less pressure to reform. As money flowed back into the regime's coffers, the regime sat back even more comfortably on its laurels, dealing with the mounting public frustration by trying to fob the masses off with promises of wealth distribution schemes. Indeed, the late 2000s saw the Qadhafi regime initiate several schemes to give money directly to the people or to issue interest-free loans. One such scheme involved the Libyan Economic and Social Development Fund distributing assets directly to the people by giving individuals shares in state companies.[13] However, this and other similar schemes became utterly bogged down in the bureaucracy and corruption that enveloped public life, meaning that it was those with links to the regime rather than ordinary Libyans who benefitted.

Thus the reformist project came to be associated with unfulfilled promises as the succession of reformist initiatives petered out into nothing. At the same time, by the late 2000s, Saif Al-Islam appeared increasingly to be replicating his father, creating a kind of personality cult of his own. He took to holding his own annual celebration on 20 August, and just as Qadhafi insisted he had no formal position in the state, Saif Al-Islam maintained that he was simply leader of Libya's civil society. This personality cult became all the more pronounced on 20 August 2009, when Saif Al-Islam accompanied convicted Lockerbie bomber Abdelbasset Al-Miqrahi back home from the UK following his release from prison on compassionate grounds, declaring, "I told them that I would get Abdelbasset out on the 20th August and I told them that if he left the prison on the 20th August this would be a sign from Allah that I am walking on the right and correct path. . . . Even this date is a message from Allah."[14] Indeed, the whole reform project had become so personalized that without Saif Al-Islam, it had no momentum of its own.

It would be wrong to suggest that there were no changes at all during this period. The country had certainly moved on from the acute repression that had characterized the 1980s and 1990s. Although anyone suspected of disloyalty to the state was still at severe risk, there was a degree to which people could express their frustrations, if not with the regime itself, at least with the state and its institutions. Saif Al-Islam also succeeded in securing the release of hundreds of militant Islamist prisoners who had signed up to a series of revisions written in August 2009 by the imprisoned leadership of the Libyan Islamic Fighting Group (LIFG) and who were released in waves until the time when the uprisings broke out in 2011. However, there was some justifiable cynicism about the leader's son's motivations for this initiative. The fact that the releases were high profile media events to which international media were invited; that the revisions were sent to prominent Islamic scholars around the world; that they were translated into numerous foreign languages in glossy publications; and that the leaders of the militant groups were forced to undertake 'road shows' around the country, declaring their support for Saif Al-Islam and the project, left many Libyans wondering about the true motivations behind this scheme. Moreover, dealing with the LIFG and other militants in this way was a sure way of neutralizing the few opposition currents that had ever succeeded in taking hold in the country. Indeed, this initiative was arguably more about security than human rights.

Furthermore, it is undeniable that Libya's rehabilitation into the international community had precipitated, in Tripoli at least, the mushrooming of new retail outlets, smart cafes and five star hotels. The Tripoli of the eve of the revolution was a very different place to that of 2008. However, most of the economic opportunities afforded by this opening were being seized by those with links to the upper echelons of the regime, most notably Qadhafi's own family. Although Saif Al-Islam had gained popularity by railing against Libya's 'Fat Cats' – corrupt officials who were using public money to line their own pockets – the leader's son and his siblings had amassed enormous fortunes through a mind boggling array of business ventures, from the health sector to the aviation industry to the energy sector. Some of these ventures included the signing of contracts for projects that were totally unsuited to Libya. As former Transport Minister Mohamed Zeidan reflected in 2011, in relation to Saif Al-Islam's plans to build an enormous new airport in Tripoli the capacity of which would far exceed the country's needs, "The important thing was to sign the contract . . . the bigger the contract, the bigger the commission."[15] Thus, while Qadhafi retained a kind of purity through his attachment to his Bedouin roots and his revolutionary ideals, by the eve of the revolution he had allowed his children to create a kleptocracy of staggering proportions.

Meanwhile, most Libyans were still struggling just to get by and much of the country remained bereft of proper services and infrastructure. As one Libyan commented after Saif Al-Islam initiated a highly publicized and ill conceived scheme to provide one million laptops to school children, "I don't think a Libyan needs a mobile or a laptop whilst his feet are wading through sewage."[16] To make matters worse, the gap between rich and poor was widening. Meanwhile, despite the loosening up of the system, the basic fundamentals of the state, both repressive and dysfunctional, remained the same.

As a result, those Libyans who had placed their hope in reform, viewing it as the best alternative in an otherwise bleak landscape, had come to the bitter realization that this program was little more than a sham aimed primarily at enhancing Libya's international reputation. As one of Saif Al-Islam's own advisors, who was part of the reformist current, ruefully reflected when the leader's son made a hawkish speech against those who had risen up in Benghazi in February 2011, this was "the final chapter in the comedy that was reform."[17]

The dashed expectations associated with this realization only increased resentment against the regime. Yet this resentment was mixed with a new boldness. For all that the reformist project had been little more than an exercise in cosmetics, the limited opening up that had accompanied it seemed to have prompted a new kind of willingness among Libyans to challenge the status quo. Strikes and small scale localized protests over issues such as the lack of basic services, the appropriation of public land by officials and the non-payment of salaries became an increasingly regular occurrence. One typical example occurred in the eastern town of Derna in October 2008, when angry inhabitants of a dismal shantytown on the outskirts of the city staged a protest outside a block of newly built flats after heavy rain had caused the structures in the shantytown to collapse.[18] The new flats outside of which they were protesting had originally been earmarked for the poor of the town. However, as was typical of housing schemes across the country, the flats were being taken by officials. Indeed, just prior to the revolution, there were many newly built and half-built housing blocks intended for the poor that were either empty or commandeered by those with links to the regime.

However, the regime was left particularly shaken in August 2010 after a delegation of protestors marched on Qadhafi's Bab Al-Aziziya barracks following a large scale demonstration outside the Workforce, Training and Employment Office in Tripoli's Al-Jumhouriya Street. Angry public sector workers vented their fury at the fact that they had not received their salaries, in some cases for several months.

Taking the protest to Qadhafi's door was something new in the Libyan context. Indeed, it was a widely held belief in Libya at the time that simply approaching the Bab Al-Aziziya complex was enough to get you shot.[19] Even more ominous for the regime were the little-reported protests that broke out in January 2011 in response to events in neighboring Tunisia. In unprecedented scenes, Libyans went in the thousands to occupy empty and half-finished blocks of flats in government housing projects across the country and to vent their anger not only at housing shortages but at the regime's failure to allocate the units in a fair or timely manner.[20]

As such, the regime's flirtation with reform had only served to heighten frustrations and to embolden people to the point where, once the fear had been broken by events in Tunisia and Egypt, Libyans in the east felt compelled to rise up to oust their own tyrant. Even Qadhafi and his hardnosed son, Moatassim, are reported to have lashed out and blamed Saif Al-Islam at the time when the uprisings broke out, accusing him of having upset the balance in the country with his 'western ideas.'[21] Moreover, many of those engaged in the revolution had been either linked to Saif Al-Islam's reformist current or had been somehow emboldened by it. This includes the families of the Abu Slim massacre victims who had sparked the uprisings by their protests against the regime, the released Islamists militants who had been freed by Saif Al-Islam and who went on to fight on the rebel frontlines, and the academics and technocrats who had supported Saif Al-Islam's project and who were driving efforts to form a government in waiting in Benghazi. Thus, while external events were a major contributing factor to the revolution, by launching and then failing to make good on its reformist project, the regime had sown the seeds of its own undoing.

However, contrary to events in neighboring Tunisia and Egypt, the uprisings that began in Benghazi in February 2011 did not engulf the whole of the country. Qadhafi dug his forces in in his main power base of Tripoli and refused to step down. As a result the uprisings mutated into a kind of civil war as Qadhafi employed his forces to try to quash the unfolding events. Indeed, the Libyan leader believed that if he could hold on to the capital, it would only be a matter of time before he could re-organize his forces and re-establish control across the rest of the country. His confidence was born partly out of the well-founded assumption that unlike in Tunisia and Egypt, where the army had taken the side of the people and been pivotal in forcing Presidents Ben Ali and Mubarak out of power, the Libyan army was in no position to be able to force anything. Qadhafi had always kept the army purposefully weak, relying instead on a myriad of security forces that he knew would remain loyal.

However, this confidence was soon to be shattered when the West entered into the fray. The United Nations Security Council voted for the imposition of a no-fly zone over Libya and the authorization of the use of military action, including against tanks and heavy artillery on the ground, in order to protect civilians. The Arab League also backed these calls and on 12 March 2011, nine out of the league's twenty-two members called on the UN Security Council to impose a no-fly zone in order to protect civilians from air attack. On 19 March, under the leadership of the United States, France and Britain flew sorties over Libya. Then, at the end of March, NATO took over responsibility from the United States for the enforcement of the no-fly zone and the arms embargo. Although the events of the ensuing conflict are outside the scope of this chapter and have been covered in detail elsewhere,[22] it is reasonable to assert that without NATO intervention the Qadhafi regime may well have survived, certainly in the west of the country. However, the combination of outside intervention and the push on the ground from Libyan rebels resulted in the collapse of Tripoli in August 2011. This was followed by the final capture of Qadhafi himself in October 2011 when he was killed at the hands of a group of rebels from Misrata.

Post-revolution: Collapse of the center

The final collapse of the Qadhafi regime in October 2011 opened up a vast chasm. Gifted with enormous wealth and a small population, Qadhafi had crafted one of the most personalized and centralized states in the world. Despite the complex political and economic structures that made up his Jamahiriyah, in reality all power lay with the colonel and his coterie of advisors and close family members. While this power was predicated upon the foundations of an efficient and multilayered security apparatus, drawn largely from loyal tribes and vast patronage networks, the center was Qadhafi. So much so that aside from the energy sector, which Libya needed to survive, Qadhafi stripped the country of all functioning institutions. The colonel refused to countenance the existence of any institution or body that could serve as a focus for dissent.

As a result, those institutions that did exist were little more than facades. This included the army, which Qadhafi kept purposefully weak and ill equipped; the religious establishment, which was turned into little more than a propaganda machine for Qadhafi's quirky ideology; and even the state bureaucracy and civil service, which served primarily as a means of absorbing the thousands of Libyans who needed jobs in the state sector. Thus, whereas in neighboring countries undergoing revolutions at the same time there was at least a state left behind when the ruling regimes fell, in the Libyan case, when Qadhafi was toppled, the state went with him.

Meanwhile, Qadhafi's banning of political parties and his utter intolerance of any kind of political or civil society activity outside of the Jamahiriyah meant that Libya was left devoid of a political culture. Thus when the regime fell, there were no political parties, organizations or even civil society movements that could step in to fill the power vacuum. While Egypt's Muslim Brotherhood, which although banned under successive regimes was able to operate semi-clandestinely, moved in to become the dominant new power, Libya had no political force that could do the same.

With no single current or entity having enough of a power base to garner any real centralized control or legitimacy, Libya experienced the emergence of local power brokers. These power brokers ranged from the militias and revolutionary brigades that had formed during the struggle to oust the Qadhafi regime to local councils established in the main towns and cities to tribes that came to greater prominence in the absence of other social mechanisms and to extremist Islamist groups, such as Ansar Al-Sharia. Indeed, the center fractured into a myriad of small local powers for which local interest has superseded national interest.

In many ways, Libya's new centralized ruling bodies became a reflection of this new localism. The National Transitional Council (NTC), established during the revolution and the main ruling power after liberation until the holding of national elections in July 2012, was little more than a collection of appointed representatives of different towns. Moreover, the way in which the election law was structured only served to enshrine localism within the new polity. The law ruled that only 80 out of the 200 seats in the General National Congress were to be contested by political parties, with the remainder going to individual candidates. The individuals elected in July 2012 comprised an array of local notables, tribal sheikhs and local religious figures elected largely because of their local reputations rather than for their political platforms. Furthermore, the majority of the political parties that contested the elections failed to achieve any genuine national spread. The Muslim Brotherhood's Justice and Construction Party, which took seventeen seats in the congress, was the main party that succeeded in having a national reach and an ideology, although this was still limited. Although Mahmoud Jibril's National Forces Alliance took thirty-nine seats across the country, this alliance can hardly be considered a truly national political party given that it is a coalition of over fifty parties and NGOs, most firmly rooted in their own localities.

Yet despite their local flavor, Libya's new ruling bodies continued to find themselves largely at the mercy of more powerful local actors. This is particularly true in the case of the thousands of militias and revolutionary brigades that proliferated during and, in some cases, after the revolution, many of which have a special legitimacy and heroic status born out of their struggle against the former regime that far outstrips that of the ruling elite.

The NTC and its Executive Board, both of which comprised technocrats, many of whom had either returned from exile abroad or who were members of the former regime before defecting to join the revolution, could never match these revolutionary elements in terms of having clout on the ground. As former head of the Executive board Mahmoud Jibril complained in October 2011 when he announced his resignation, "I resigned because I felt I had no influence i.e. we make decisions that are thrown in the rubbish bin. . . . The NTC has a formal legitimacy – however there is another legitimacy on the ground that decides whether or not to execute the instructions of the NTC or the Executive Board."[23]Although the National General Congress had a greater legitimacy than the NTC given that its members were directly elected, it still struggled to have anything like the validity of the revolutionary elements. The same was true of the government, headed by Prime Minister Ali Zidan, as evidenced by the fact that in October 2013 Zidan himself was kidnapped from his Tripoli hotel room by members of the Libya Revolutionaries Operations Chamber.

Bringing these revolutionaries into line has been particularly challenging. While successive ruling authorities have done their best to integrate revolutionary elements into official state security structures, their attempts have born little fruit. At the end of 2012, for example, the newly appointed Interior Minister, Ashur Al-Shuwail, announced his determination to integrate the Supreme Security Committee (SSC) – a powerful collection of militias which answer nominally at least to the Interior Ministry – into official state structures, including the police. However, while some SSC elements were persuaded to sign up, the majority, including its leadership resisted. The same is true of the Libya Shield Brigades – established in 2012 as a parallel defense force answering nominally to the Ministry of Defence. Despite the state's efforts to bring these revolutionary brigades into line, the Libya Shield Brigades have continued to operate as near independent bodies. Indeed, spread across the country, they are some of the most powerful military brigades operating in Libya. In addition to these forces, there are hundreds of other brigades, militias and armed groups – many of them Islamist in orientation – that are operating completely beyond state control.

That is not to say that the state has done nothing to try to force these brigades to dissolve themselves. Following the events of Bloody Friday in Tripoli in November 2013, when a revolutionary brigade from Misrata opened fire on a crowd of protestors demanding its dissolution, the state tried to capitalize on the resulting public anger by renewing its calls for the militias to be disbanded. On 16 December the Congress passed a new law criminalizing the illegal possession of weapons. It also announced its intention to apply Congress Decision 27 (passed in March 2013) to clear Tripoli of all illegal armed militias and Congress Decision 53 to dissolve all illegal armed groups and integrate them into official security structures.

However, given its weakness, the government has been unable to apply these decisions in any meaningful way. Although some militias, namely those from Misrata, withdrew from the capital following Bloody Friday and a handful of others handed over their bases to the authorities, others simply switched locations or stayed put. As one Libyan official commented in early December 2013, "Many of these forces have moved to different locations and haven't actually left the capital. . . . Despite the government's talk about taking measures to activate Decision Number 27, some of the evacuations and relocations of these forces are still questionable."[24]

The failure on the part of the new authorities to dissolve the militias and replace them with a strong national army and police force is partly because the enticements that the government is offering are not appealing enough. Moreover, with few alternative lifestyles on offer, many of these revolutionaries are unwilling to give up their newfound power and status. More importantly, however, these institutions are still tainted by their association with the past. The Libyan army in particular, and, to a lesser extent, the police, are deemed by many revolutionaries to be too strongly linked to the former regime. Islamist political elements, including the Libyan Muslim Brotherhood's Justice and Construction Party have also shied away from rebuilding the army given its links to the past, arguing instead that the Libya Shield forces should form the backbone of the country's security forces. Thus, there is a strong resistance by many revolutionary elements, as well as by their political allies, to the country's national forces being rebuilt.

This lack of a strong centralized military force has left Libya's new rulers with no option but to rely upon these militias and brigades to help provide security and to contain the outbreaks of unrest that have become a feature of the post-revolutionary landscape. In 2012 for example, the government sent units from the Libya Shield to try to quell clashes that had erupted in the southern town of Kufra between Arab and Tebu tribes there. In the event, the intervention of this militia only served to inflame local tensions as the Libya Shield forces took sides and began indiscriminately shelling ethnic Tebu areas in the town. One Tebu tribal chief in Kufra complained in January 2013, "We want the army to secure Kufra, and not a group of civilian revolutionaries who have no military principles."[25] Likewise the central authorities have had to rely upon revolutionary forces to secure the country's borders. Following the crisis that erupted after the Ain Amenas gas plant attack in Algeria in January 2013, and with concerns that militant elements might try to do the same in Libya, the government was forced to rely upon the powerful Zintani brigade to secure the country's borders.[26]

This reliance on these revolutionary elements has only served to entrench their power even further. Indeed, such is their control that the central authorities have on occasion found themselves forced to give political endorsement to their actions. In October 2012, revolutionaries from Misrata launched a siege on the town of Bani Walid after the town refused to hand over a group suspected of abducting Misratan hero Omran Shaaban, the young revolutionary who killed Qadhafi. While the case of Omran Shaaban was certainly a catalyst for the attack, the rivalry between Misrata and Bani Walid stretches back over generations. Moreover, Bani Walid was one of the main strongholds of the former regime and was one of the last towns to fall to rebel forces during the revolution. As such the Misratans had long been seeking the opportunity to take their revenge for the particularly brutal siege imposed upon them by the Qadhafi regime during the revolution. Thus, after the elders of Bani Walid refused to hand Shaaban's abductors over, Misratan revolutionaries launched a bloody assault on the town, claiming that it still contained Qadhafi loyalists.

Faced with a fait accompli, the Congress, unable to control and negotiate with the Misratan militias that had turned back a delegation, had little alternative but to support them. The Congress issued law number 7, authorizing the use of force; it sent some of its troops to the town, essentially legalizing and giving its blessing to the assault. It also tried to rationalize its failure to control the militias by giving credence to the idea that former high ranking regime elements were present in the town. The head of the Congress, Mohamed Al-Magarief, even went as far as to declare on the anniversary of Qadhafi's death, "The campaign to liberate the country has not been fully completed."[27]

It is not only on the security front that Libya's new political bodies have become hostage to the revolutionaries. Revolutionary brigades and militias have also taken to storming the Congress headquarters or staging protests and sit-ins at oil facilities and ports as a means of forcing the government to respond to their demands.

While these demands have, for the most part, been related to personalized matters such as accessing medical treatment abroad or the payment of compensation, they have also centered on governance issues. In November 2012, for example, angry revolutionaries stormed the Congress to object to some of the choices that the newly appointed Prime Minister, Ali Zidan, had proposed for his new cabinet. Revolutionary forces also intimidated the Congress into passing the controversial Political Exclusion Law, a law aimed at purging the political establishment and the administration of elements linked to the former regime. Armed elements disrupted Congress sessions, threatened and attacked Congress members, and eventually put a number of government ministries under siege until the Congress agreed in May 2013 to pass this draconian law. The legislation prohibits anyone with the slightest link to the former regime from holding senior public office, meaning that by voting in its favor many Congress members ended up excluding themselves from public life. Even the first head of the Congress, Mohamed Al-Magarief, had little choice but to quit his post on account of the legislation despite his having been one of the most prominent of all Qadhafi opponents since the early 1980s, due to the fact that in the early years of the former regime he had served as Ambassador to India.

Thus the authorities have found themselves locked into a pattern of reactive policymaking, appeasing revolutionaries and other local power brokers at every turn rather than focusing on progressing the transition or fixing the day-to-day problems of ordinary Libyans. As a result, the legitimacy of both the legislative and executive powers has been seriously undermined, hampering the transition to democracy even further.

The rise of regionalism

If the lack of a center is one of the main challenges facing post-Qadhafi Libya, another is the enduring issue of regionalism that has been catapulted to the fore in the post-revolutionary phase. Although this chapter is not the place for a detailed analysis of the origins of Libya's regional divisions, the country has always comprised three distinct regions – Tripolitania in the west, Cyrenaica in the east and Fezzan in the south – with three distinct identities. For all that a national consciousness developed in Libya after it became a single country at the time of independence as well as during the Qadhafi years, regional identity always played a major role. In addition, as explained above, during the latter years of his rule in particular, Qadhafi accentuated these regional divisions, marginalizing the east in particular.

Thus, following the revolution, the east and south, which perceived themselves to have been excluded from the political and economic arena by the former regime, believed that the new Libya would represent a more equitable distribution of power and resources. This belief had a particular poignancy in the east, which, as the birthplace of the uprisings, felt a strong sense of ownership of the revolution. However, as the country has lurched through the transition there is a growing feeling in both the east and the south that the country's new rulers are perpetuating the former regime's exclusionist policies.

Anger at this perceived exclusion has been voiced repeatedly in the many demonstrations that erupted against the new ruling authorities, particularly in the east. In November 2011, for example, Benghazi residents took to the streets, calling for the revolution to be corrected and protesting at the region's underrepresentation in the newly formed cabinet. Indeed, while the new authorities have sought to appease the various new local power brokers by giving a broad regional balance to many of the country's new political institutions, many easterners have viewed this as a deliberate attempt to marginalize them. As one Benghazi lawyer, Tahini Al-Sharif, complained at the end of 2011, "The regime has not changed. It is the same which oppresses and marginalizes cities."[28] The authorities' failure to resolve the security crisis in the east, or to clamp down on the assassination campaign against security figures there, has only fuelled perceptions in the region that the country's new powers are indifferent to their situation.

While the failure to invest more heavily in the east may be more a reflection of the central authorities' preoccupation with more pressing priorities rather than any lack of political will, it has served to consolidate the view that the east is still Tripoli's poor relation. This ongoing sense of marginalization has given rise to an increasingly vocal federalist movement that is calling for some sort of autonomy in the east. This movement still has a limited support base, in part because the term 'federalism' is so fraught with negative connotations linked to 'colonialist plots.' The federalist current is also countered by the presence of powerful Islamist militias in the east, including those of a militant bent, which remain avowedly opposed to the federalist project. It is also not a unified current. Indeed, the federalist movement in the east has fractured into competing currents that are focused around certain tribes and cities. The most important of these currents is led by Ibrahim Jedhran, from Ajdabia, who is from the powerful Margharba tribe.[29] Jedhran, who is head of the politburo of the self-appointed Cyrenaican Transitional Council, spearheaded the protests that began in the summer of 2012 and that crippled Libya's eastern oil ports for a year. Jedhran, supported by certain key sheikhs and elders from his tribe, linked these protests, which were staged by his supporters in the Oil Facilities Guard, to his federalist demands, including that the east be given greater control over the resources located there. Jedhran also tried to sell oil from the eastern ports independently of the government. Yet for all that it may be fractured and still limited in size and support, the federalist current continues to be a force in both the political arena and on the ground.

However, Libya's traditional east-west division has been superseded by another more complex form of regionalism with various towns and areas now competing for dominance and power. Most notably the town of Misrata has emerged as a new power center that has sought to dominate in the capital and beyond. Misrata proved itself militarily during the revolution by defeating the regime's forces after a particularly bloody three-month siege on the city. The town also gained enormous symbolic legitimacy after Misratan forces captured and killed both Qadhafi and his son, Moatassim. Since the revolution, Misratan revolutionary forces, including the Libya Shield Central Brigade and other brigades from the city, have proved particularly potent and through these brigades the town has sought to assert its dominance in the political arena.

Likewise Zintan, an unremarkable town in the western mountains, is also jostling for power in the new Libya. Zintani fighters were instrumental in breaking Qadhafi's hold over the capital in the summer of 2011 and also gained kudos from capturing Qadhafi's son, Saif Al-Islam, as he tried to flee the country. After the fall of the Qadhafi regime the various revolutionary brigades from both Zintan and Misrata remained in the capital, each controlling different areas, as well as key strategic facilities in the city. The Zintani brigades, for example, controlled Tripoli International Airport while the Misratans took control of key camps and neighborhoods.

The situation has been made more complex by the fact that other smaller towns and areas in the west of Libya have lined up between these two emergent powers. In addition these powers have themselves backed different political factions, with the Misratans taking the side of the Islamist political current and the Zintanis siding with the liberal bloc. Hence Libya has fragmented into an array of different towns all competing for dominance both politically and on the ground.

This rise in regionalism has been accompanied by a growing reassertion of the role of the tribes. Under Qadhafi the tribes were largely contained and their power relegated to the social sphere, where they were encouraged to act as social mediators in disputes. They were also used as a mechanism of control with Qadhafi ensuring that they kept their members in line, threatening them with collective punishment if any tribal member dared to challenge the state. Since the revolution these tribes have continued to play a mediating role, stepping in to try to resolve disputes and protests and engaging in local reconciliation efforts. Tribal elders have been used repeatedly to bring together warring factions, especially in the south where inter-communal violence between Arab and Tebu and Tuareg tribes has persisted. However, some tribes have become increasingly assertive in the political arena. The Margarba tribe, for example, has become linked with the federalist project in the east through Jedhran, who is from the tribe. More importantly, some tribes have become military forces in their own right. The Wershefana in the west and Awlad Suleiman in the south, for example, have become tribal militias.

However, it should be noted that so far the country's most important tribes have refrained from taking sides or from engaging in the political or military arena. Some of the most powerful tribes, such as the Werfella and the Miqraha, both of which had strong links to the Qadhafi regime, are refusing to engage and are sitting on the sidelines. This is primarily because they still feel as though they are being scapegoated for their past. Indeed, Libya's failure to embark upon any serious national reconciliation process is serving to deepen divisions, including on a tribal level.

Libya is also grappling with tensions related to its ethnic minorities. This includes not only issues related to the Tebu and Tuareg tribes, but also to the country's Amazigh population. Libya's Amazigh are mostly located in the western mountains in the towns of Nalut, Yifren and Jalu. Qadhafi refused to recognize that Libya had any ethnic minorities at all, this being at odds with his Arab nationalist vision. Libya's Amazigh were prohibited from using their language, naming their children Amazigh names or engaging in any kind of activism that promoted Amazigh culture or rights. After the revolution, groups of Amazigh have become more politically active and have started to demand certain cultural and linguistic rights such as requesting that the new constitution recognize Amazigh as an official language. The Amazigh boycotted the elections to the Constituent Assembly (the committee tasked with drawing up the constitution) in February 2014 after their demands that their linguistic and cultural rights be guaranteed in the document were not met. Although the Amazigh question is still relatively contained and marginal to the larger challenges facing the country, it could evolve into a more serious issue in the future.

These challenges are clearly proving difficult for Libya's new ruling powers to overcome and the country is slipping deeper into the quagmire. As the various local power brokers continue to fight it out for control, state building has been relegated once again. Issues such as rebuilding infrastructure and providing jobs, services and opportunities have all had to take a back seat as successive ruling bodies have been too wrapped up in trying to bring some semblance of order and security to the country. The situation has been made worse by the repeated disruptions of the energy sector as revolutionaries, frustrated oil workers and oil security guards, as well as disenfranchised local youth, have taken to staging sit-ins and strikes at oil fields and ports to get their demands met. This action has all but crippled the economy.[30] Thus, despite the fact that with its vast energy resources and tiny population Libya had the potential to become the success story of the Arab Spring, the country's inability to grapple with these seemingly insurmountable challenges is taking it ever closer to becoming a failed state.

Notes

1. Although this Constituent Assembly that is located in Al Baida in the east of the country has been working to draw up a new constitution to replace the Constitutional Declaration that was issued in August 2011, progress has been slow and largely eclipsed by the problems that have engulfed the country.
2. "Oil Production Boosts Libya Economy, Instability Hampers Reconstruction". AFP. 20 October 2012.
3. For a detailed picture of Qadhafi's rule, see Alison Pargeter, *Libya: The Rise and Fall of Gaddafi*, Yale University Press. 2012.
4. Telephone interview with Libyan diplomat. March 2011.
5. Libya's rehabilitation began after Qadhafi finally agreed to hand over the Lockerbie suspects in April 1999, opening the way for the suspension of UN sanctions. However, it became more sustained following the country's agreement to relinquish its WMD program in December 2003.
6. In September 1999 Qadhafi told a group of foreign businessmen attending a Symposium on Prospects for International Investment and Trade in Libya, "If you want to invest in Libya, you are welcome" (Paul Rivlin, "Economic Developments in the Middle East and North Africa 1999". Middle East Contemporary Survey, Volume 23; Volume 1999. The Moshe Dayan Center for Middle Eastern and African Studies, p. 409). He reiterated

these sentiments at another investment conference in 2000 where he noted, "Libya wants to encourage foreign capital investment and partnership. . . . We will create the right atmosphere for the investor" ("Libva – Moammar Mohammed Abdel Salam Abu Minyar Al Qadhafi". Oil Diplomacy. 29 July 2002. Available on www.thefreelibrary.com/LIBYA+-+Moammar+Mohammed+Abdel+Salam+Abu+Minyar+Al+Qadhafi.-a089807455.)

7. Libya Focus. January 2009. Menas Associates. Subscription only publication available at www.menas.co.uk.

8. "An Interview with Dr. Yousif Sawani, Part 1". Sharq Al-Awsat Newspaper. 8 October 2011. Available on www.aawsat.com/details.asp?section=4&article=644004&issueno=12002.

9. "An Interview with Dr. Yousif Sawani, Part 1". Sharq Al-Awsat Newspaper. 8 October 2011. Available on www.aawsat.com/details.asp?section=4&article=644004&issueno=12002.

10. "Saif Al-Islam Al-Qadhafi Calls for Further Reform, Threatens to Withdraw from Politics". Passed to the *Telegraph* by WikiLeaks. 31 January 2011. Available on www.telegraph.co.uk/news/wikileaks-files/libya-wikileaks/8294857/SAIF-AL-ISLAM-AL-QADHAFI-CALLS-FOR-FURTHER-REFORM-THREATENS-TO-WITHDRAW-FROM-POLITICS.html.

11. "Libya Al-Youm Fi Hewar Khass Ma'a Al-Doctour Fathi al-Ba'aja" [Libya al-Youm has special interview with Dr Fathi al-Ba'aja]. Libya Al-Youm. 19 August 2007. Available in Arabic on www.libya-alyoum.com/look/article.tpl?IdLanguage=17&IdPublication=1&NrArticle=9994&NrIssue=1&NrSection=14.

12. Libya Focus. September 2007. Menas Associates. Subscription only publication available through www.menas.co.uk.

13. Libya Focus. May 2010. Menas Associates. Subscription only publication available through www.menas.co.uk.

14. "Said Saif al-Islam Muammar Qadhafi: al-Ifraj Aan Al-Meghrahi Munasaba Tariqiya Fi Hayat al-Libeen" [Mr Saif al-Islam Muammar Qadhafi: The release of Al-Meghrahi is a historical occasion for the Libyans]. Oea. 22 August 2009. Available in Arabic on www.oealibya.com/front-page/local-news/5266–2009–08–22–00–46–36.

15. "Mohamed Zaidan: Kadnahtaj Dictator Akhar" [Mohamed Zaidan: We may need another dictator]. Al-Majalla. 25 August 2011.

16. Quoted in Alison Pargeter, "Reforming Libya: Chimera Or Reality", Mediterranean Paper Series. October 2010.

17. "An Interview with Dr. Yousif Sawani, Part 3". Sharq Al-Awsat Newspaper, 10 October 2011. Available on www.aawsat.com/details.asp?section=4&issueno=12004&article=644297&search=الصواني%20يوسف&state=true.

18. Libya Focus. October 2008. Menas Associates. Subscription only publication available through www.menas.co.uk.

19. Conversations with Libyans during numerous visits between 2000 and 2010.

20. The Kawarsha project in Hay Al-Fatah in Benghazi comprising some 800 housing units, for example, was broken into and occupied. In Al-Medina Jadida near Tajoura, a 10,000-unit project was occupied despite the fact that the buildings were still under construction and did not have electricity or water supply. A 608-flat project in Badia that was run by Aisha Qadhafi's Al-Watassimu charity was also occupied, as was one of Saif Al-Islam's projects in Derna.

21. Author interview with Noman Bin Othman, London. April 2011.

22. See Alison Pargeter, *Libya: The Rise and Fall of Gaddafi*, Yale University Press. 2012.

23. "Dr Mahmoud Jibril Reveals to Al-Sharq Al-Awsat Qadhafi's Plan to Return to Power". Al-Sharq Al-Awsat. 18 October 2011. Available on www.aawsat.com/details.asp?section=4&issueno=12012&article=645603#.UslxRECYYiQ.

24. Quoted in Libya Focus. December 2013. Menas Associates. Subscription only publication available at www.menas.co.uk.

25. "Tribal Clashes in Libya's Kufra 'kill 4'". AFP. 9 January 2013.

26. "Libya Reinforces Border, Oilfields after Algeria Attack". Reuters. 23 January 2013.
27. Libya Focus. October 2012. Menas Associates. Subscription only publication available at www.menas.co.uk.
28. Libya Focus. November 2011. Menas Associates. Subscription only publication available at www.menas.co.uk.
29. The other main currents comprise that led by Ahmed Zoubair Senussi, who heads the Cyrenaican Transitional Council and whose main support is in Benghazi, and that led by former Deputy Defence Minister Sadiq Al-Ghaithi, whose main support base is in Tobruk.
30. The cost of the year-long strike staged by Jedhran from August 2013 that paralyzed four eastern oil ports cost the country an estimated US$14 billion in lost oil revenues ("Libyan Rebels Agree to End Oil Terminal Siege". Al-Jazeera. 6 April 2014. Available on www.aljazeera.com/news/africa/2014/04/libyan-rebels-agree-end-oil-terminal-seige-201446215231852735.html).

Bibliography

Pargeter, A. Reforming Libya: Chimera or Reality? German Marshall Fund. Mediterranean Paper Series, October 2010.
Pargeter, A. *Libya: The Rise and Fall of Gaddafi*. New Haven: Yale University Press. 2012.

Newspapers and other publications

AFP
Al-Majalla
Al-Sharq Al-Awsat Newspaper
Libya Focus. Menas Associates. Subscription only publication.
Reuters

Websites

Libya Al-Youm (website discontinued)
Libya: News and Views. www.libya-watanona.com
Majalla. www.majalla.com/arb/
Oea Libya (website discontinued)
Telegraph Online. www.telegraph.co.uk
Veotgate. www.vetogate.com

12

POLITICAL CHANGE IN MAURITANIA: DESPERATELY SEEKING ITS 'ARAB SPRING'

Abdoulaye Diagana[1]

Introduction

Geographically set in the Sahara-Sahel, Mauritania is politically caught in the opposing winds blowing from North Africa and Sub-Saharan Africa. The political upheavals of its neighbors to the north and south have made this double identity palpable once again. While the repercussions of the fall of the Berlin Wall and subsequent changes in the international order led to political convulsions in Sub-Saharan Africa, they have barely changed the course of Mauritania's politics. The country's 1991 political reforms did what they were designed to do: entrench the regime, which cannily seized the moment to set itself more deeply within the geopolitical sphere of Arab countries through the Arab Maghreb Union (UMA). Later, when Mauritania withdrew from the West African Economic Community (ECOWAS), it clearly showed its determination to adopt a national identity that was not that of a Sub-Saharan African country. Withdrawing from ECOWAS membership and anchoring itself in the UMA allowed Mauritania to take advantage of a context where the slogan, "sacred national union," would serve as a pretext for a range of policies that tended to gloss over its cultural, political and – less widespread – religious diversity.

The events redefining the geostrategic balances in the Arab world are part of the debate concerning Mauritania's national cohabitation and identity. At first glance, the demands and aspirations of the populations living between the Sahel and the Sahara appear to overlap. They include profound political reform and the introduction of open, democratic, fair and transparent elections for winning, managing and transmitting political power. Similarly, the demonstrations across the region reflect the populations' pressing demand for transparent economic governance, an end to corruption and socioeconomic measures that lead to more equitably shared wealth. Overall, the goal is to put an end to the spiral of poverty and unemployment that is hitting younger generations hard and forcing them, increasingly, to lower their professional aspirations (Zoubir 2012).

Demonstrators dissatisfied with an authoritarian police state are also demanding greater public freedoms. Mauritania's decentralization process began in the mid-1980s (Diagana 2010) and the process of political liberalization undertaken in the early 1990s (Diagana 2011; Diagana 2013) never truly opened up the country's political arena. Wherever they look, Mauritanians seeking political change share these aspirations with other populations like them in North Africa and the Middle East.

The various political movements in Mauritania are as diverse as they are divided about their objectives. *La Jeunesse du 25 février* (Children of February 25), whose leaders follow satellite images night and day, sees itself as part of the tradition of Arab revolutions. The *Coordination de l'Opposition Démocratique* (Democratic Opposition Coordination Group, COD) offers itself as a political alternative by demanding that the current government quit. If there is any link at all between these two groups, it is not obvious. Facing off against these reformist groups, the majority is mocking their demands for change: "these new revolutionary old guys . . . have systematically pillaged the country's wealth and citizens' sources of income and used demagoguery and abusively exploited modest, good-hearted Mauritanians, and they have the nerve to hypocritically call for reform and reconstruction."[2] For its part, the Islamic Party, Tawassoul, has declared its readiness to come to power, but is incapable of shaping the course of events in any fundamental way (cf. note 6).

Two other groups complete the team. The abolitionist group[3] focuses on the aftermath and realities of slavery. Activists from the abolitionist group were constantly harassing Ould Abdel Aziz; six IRA *(Initiative pour la résurgence du movement Abolitioniste)* militants were arrested after an *autodafé* of Malekite books in April 2012.[4] The second group was created in response to a government census that the black population rejected violently, seeing in it a plan to minimize their demographic weight in Mauritania. During the last mobilization, the army fired real bullets at young demonstrators in the south.[5] Spearheaded by the *Touche Pas à Ma Nationalité* (TPMN, Keep Your Hands off My Nationality) collective, this particular battle had lost momentum after internal squabbles ultimately divided the collective's ranks. Regrouping, the TPMN is once again consolidating, particularly after Mauritanians living in France demonstrated against being forced to show their French visa to sign up for the national census. In July 2013, violent demonstrations broke out in Kaédi, a city in southern Mauritania, after the rape of a local woman by a northern merchant. The Mauritanian authorities were so threatened by the situation that they rescheduled municipal and parliamentary elections several times.[6]

Finally, Mauritania must cope with the crisis on its borders with northern Mali. The Islamic groups taking control of the areas to which the Tuareg rebellion lays claim seem to embody the failure of Nouakchott's frontal approach to its border wars against terrorist groups laying siege to the no man's land of the Sahel-Sahara between Algeria, Mali and Mauritania. Ould Abdel Aziz's regime felt obliged to get involved and quite publicly harbored several leaders of the National Movement for the Liberation of Azawad[7] in Nouakchott despite the serious risk of spillover from the Malian conflict. However, the French Operation Serval, supported by MINUSMA,[8] will not include any Mauritanian troops.[9]

Rather than re-joining ECOWAS and pulling its weight in the geopolitics of Sahel, Mauritania sought to find in the reactivation of the UMA an opportunity to reenergize its diplomacy, a "spring" unlike those reshaping the geopolitics of the Arab world.

Given this, is it reasonable to attribute the failure of the movement in Mauritania, even partially, to this particular situation of being torn between African-ness and Arab-ness? What are the elements for analyzing the failure of the Arab Spring in Mauritania?

A chaotic general protest

Of the demonstrations that are shaking the Arab world, those in Mauritania's capital, Nouakchott, have only been somewhat disruptive. Unlike the other Arab protests, those in Mauritania have not managed to develop sufficiently to shape any major political events. The goals of the various groups are occasionally incompatible. *La Coordination de la Jeunesse du 25 février* first appeared on the streets on February 25, 2011, after an anonymous group used social networks to call for demonstrations. It is pursuing the path of the other Arab revolutions, riding on the successful protests in Egypt and Tunisia, to demand that the government be dissolved, that the prices of basic goods be lowered, that the right to congregate/demonstrate be officially recognized, and that President Ould Abdel Aziz, who came to power on August 6, 2008, in a military coup against a democratically elected civilian government, step down. The Coordination offered to demand "the rights that have been taken from the population and from young people [and] thoroughgoing reforms [by mobilizing large numbers of] pupils, students, graduates, unemployed graduates, workers, consumers, the oppressed, and everyone aspiring to bring real change to Mauritania."[10]

But unlike the protest movements in Tunisia and Egypt, the *Coordination de la Jeunesse du 25 février* never managed to galvanize or to lead the Mauritanian masses.

The Jama'a[11] of Red Blocks Square and the call from Tahrir

One of the common aspects of these Arab revolutions has been the symbolic investment of a public space that is transformed into a rallying place and point of convergence for the longstanding resentment accumulated during years of contested governments. With its predestined name, Cairo's Tahrir (Liberation) Square has become something akin to a Bastille to be stormed, to join the panoply of popular revolutions. Taking a public square makes it possible for a revolt to take shape. The protesters who assemble in it join ranks and forces around a common ideal, despite occasionally irreconcilable differences.

With no liberation square at which to assemble in Nouakchott, the small, diverse and hesitant groups met with no particular organization at Red Blocks Square.[12] The Coordination's improvised leadership had had great difficulty attracting crowds to the square, and started to split apart when some of its leaders suggested moving to a less central square. These same leaders also suggested submitting an authorization to protest to the police, which the radical fringe rejected as unacceptable, seeing it as tantamount to recognizing an administration whose legitimacy it was calling into question. The protests slowly dissipated. From the split a new group, the *Coalition de la Jeunesse du 25 février*, later emerged. After the *Coordination de la Jeunesse du 25 février* met with the president on August 1, 2011, it was never able to restore the confidence of its members. The *Coalition de la Jeunesse du 25 février* saw that meeting as a sign of loyalty to the government. The meeting sounded the death knell for the entire youth movement.[13]

The symbolic dimension of the occupation of a public space was not sufficient to rally the various groups in the protest movement around even the most minimal demands. Some in the Coordination militated for radical change while others were satisfied with reforms to the system – as the government itself was suggesting. At the same time, a third group was ostentatiously distinguishing itself from the first two by issuing categorical demands. Even if there was no *jama'a* in the public space, the protest movement could still bank on mobilizations after Friday prayers, which has worked wherever Arab revolts had taken place.

Joumou'a:[14] Friday on high alert

When countries with an Islamic tradition are in crisis, balances can shift on Fridays. After the traditional 1 p.m. prayers on this sacred day, protesters can manipulate the crowds that have gathered for prayer to pressure the government. In Mauritania, however, the protest movement did not use the multiplying effect of *Joumou'a*, perhaps because the government keeps the country's mosques under surveillance. Some of the most influential imams are paid and attended to by the public authorities, and would not agree to call the government's authority into question. Indeed, their sermons opportunely insist that a faithful Muslim must reject the *fitna*[15] and submit to the Caliph's authority.

Jeich: A faithful army

In Tunisia, as in Egypt, combination of Joumou'a (Friday) and Jama'a (meeting) led to a third J, for *Jeich*, or army, whose role was decisive in each case. In Mauritania, the Great Mute remained loyal to the General Mohamed Ould Abdel Aziz's government even as demonstrators were chanting slogans demanding a regime change. During the many weeks when President Ould Abdel Aziz was forced to remain in France, leaving his country with no news of his health, the uncertainty did not strengthen the opposition, which was demanding a parliamentary investigative commission and declaring a constitutional vacuum.

Mohamed Ould Abdel Aziz was the longtime head of the BASEP (Presidential Security Battalion), the elite unit that is reputedly the country's best equipped and who had sworn loyalty to its General. Moreover, Mohamed Ould Abdel Aziz had been careful to keep officers loyal to him in command positions. It is not therefore surprising that these loyalists were deaf to the protesters' demands.

Islamist youth: A no-show

The leaders of the protest movement had called for revolution but it was immediately obvious that young Mauritanian Muslims were not responding: the leaders had been less subtle than their counterparts in Egypt and Tunisia. During the initial protests at Red Blocks Square, the front ranks included, according to the movement's leaders, well-known individuals belonging or sympathetic to Islamist groups. But when the Coordination indicated that no recuperations would be tolerated, dissensions heightened among the young people who had come to protest. The protesters had little in common. The movement had been launched by secular individuals from well-off families that had held high-level government responsibilities whereas the more structured young Islamist group close to the Tawassoul Party came from modest backgrounds and had experienced persecution, particularly under the dictatorship of Mouawiyya Ould Sid'Ahmed Taya (1984–2005).

Notwithstanding the random organization and diversity of demands, the determination to mobilize against the established order in Mauritania was palpable. But the popular reactions to the protests were thwarted by the lack of clarity among the leaders. Confrontations took the form of barbs between protesters and the police, whom the government had ordered to avoid aggravating the situation. The Mauritanian government had learned from the lessons of Sidi Bouzid, where the Tunisian revolution was ignited.

High-risk survey

The government census begun in May 2011 broke the momentary equilibrium and led to demonstrations. For the country's black populations, the census was an attack on their demographic weight, and they massively rejected it. They mobilized behind a new group led by young members of Mauritania's African community, *Touche Pas à Ma Nationalité*, TPMN.[16] The protest culminated in the destruction of the Municipal Court of Kaédi, the country's largest southern city. A day later in Maghama, 120 kilometers south of Kaédi, the police opened fire on young protesters demonstrating in front of their garrison. Their live bullets killed seventeen-year-old Lamine Mangane and wounded several others; some protesters were shot in the back. For certain analysts, these events may have been a catalyst for unifying ambient anti-government resentment. A structured insurrection could have galvanized its militants against this kind of brutality. Yet these events did not reignite a protest movement in Mauritania. Why not?

A single country, many peoples

To answer the question, we have to assemble the various streams flowing along the fault lines running through Mauritania's populations. The country's three major populations – Arabs, Blacks and Haratines, who are somewhere between the first two – live side by side and mutually ignore one other. The Arabs struggle to keep their stranglehold on the power they have held since 1960, when Mauritania became independent. The Africans denounce racial injustices and demand that wealth and responsibility be more equitably shared among the various groups. The Haratines struggle against their de facto slavery. While slavery was officially abolished and criminalized in 2007, it continues to be a burning issue in Mauritania. The three groups rarely manage to make common cause of their combat without becoming paralyzed by their specific stances. For example, when the secular Hassanophones launched a protest on the heels of the Egyptian and Tunisian revolutions, the African-Mauritanians considered it their responsibility to boycott it as supporting it would have meant legitimating the vision of an Arab Mauritania. The Haratines consider that emancipation and the equitable sharing of political and economic power are the only worthy struggle. And, emancipation necessarily involves combating the country's Arab and Black fiefdoms. That these groups abandoned each other at critical moments is unsurprising. For the Hassanophone population, the shootout in Maghama was not a cause to which they would rally.

With the notable exclusion of the groups largely led by African-Mauritanians (*Alliance pour la Justice et la Démocratie/Mouvement pour la Rénovation*, AJD/MR; the *Mouvement pour la Refondation*, MPR; the Party for Liberty, Equality and Justice, PLEJ), neither the political parties of the majority nor the opposition made much of this incident. The opposition did not know how to seize the moment to put pressure on the majority. For want of a clear position and discourse, its voice was barely audible.

An opposition undone by Byzantine quarrels

Most of today's opposition leaders have been on the political scene since at least the beginning of a controlled democratization, which began in 1992 under Colonel Ould Taya's government. Even when dressed in civilian clothing, the military exercises absolute control over all political power, largely because the opposition leaders are incapable of agreeing on strategies and putting aside their personal ambitions to galvanize the civilian population to join their ranks. Which explains why, when Ould Abdel Aziz's government feared being overwhelmed by the street protests, it called for a national dialogue.[17] The opposition's call for a boycott was undone by a few political movements and individuals who had previously been in the front lines of the protest against the 2008 military putsch: Messaoud Ould Boulkheir,[18] leader of the national assembly (with only 4 of 95 deputies); Boidiel Ould Hoummeid, an emblematic figure during Ould Taya's dictatorship, and the leader of a new political group known as Al Wiam. The picture includes two other parties close to the Arab nationalists, but they lack any real political heft. The most important opposition parties had scrupulously respected the boycott, seeing the majority's call for dialogue as just another ploy to allow Ould Abdel Aziz to retain his grip on power.

The *Rassemblement des Forces Démocratiques* (Rally for Democratic Forces, RFD) presided over by Ahmed Ould Daddah, the leader of the official opposition party, had categorically rejected all dialogue so long as the government refused on a jointly agreed meeting place. The *Coordination de l'Opposition Démocratique* (COD) held the same position. In August 2012, it had adopted a Charter rejecting any election "without guaranteed transparency." The goal of any political dialogue was Ould Abdel Aziz's resignation.

The two opposition parties finally faced off. The ten parties under the COD umbrella wanted to adopt a radical position; the other opposition group wanted to be more accommodating and enter into dialogue with the government. The government agreed to hold discussions with the latter. On paper, there was real progress.[19] In practice, the tensions remained between the government and the boycotting opposition.

Should we conclude that Ould Abdel Aziz's government survived thanks to the dissensions among the political opposition and the tepid mobilization of the masses unconvinced of a credible alternative?

Did the nature of the government play a role?

Contrary to the other governments overthrown by Arab revolutions, the Mauritanian government in Nouakchott is quite recent. Ould Abdel Aziz came to power on August 6, 2008, having organized a coup against Sidi Mohamed Ould Cheikh Abdallahi (2007–2008), the sole civilian to be elected in a free election. He was not a victim of long-lived power. Therefore, Aziz never misses an opportunity to decry Ould Taya's political policies and administration.

Dressing up old ideas in new clothes

Aziz's repeated references to sidelining the leaders of the previous government are leitmotifs in his speeches. During the 2007 presidential campaign, he described the major figures of the Ould Taya era as symbols of mismanagement. Ould Abdel Aziz himself had campaigned in 2009 to combat poverty and mismanagement. His populist discourse so swayed the general population that political players who protest against the legitimacy of his government are often suspected of waxing nostalgic for the days when they could dip into the public till with impunity. As President Ould Abdel Aziz put it: "Who opposes my government these days? Former ministers, governors, and high level civil servants who can no longer stroll down the Champs-Elysées with their families and go shopping in Paris with stolen money."[20]

Ould Abdel Aziz is not what we might call an unstained newcomer to the political arena. He headed Ould Taya's presidential guard, and remained during the military transition led by Colonel Ely Ould Mohamed Vall (2005–2007) and again under Sidi Ould Cheikh Abdallahi (2007–2008). Today's government and high-level civil servants include individuals who are emblematic of the governments that came after the 1978 military coup and are responsible for the many human rights abuses[21] perpetrated under Ould Taya. Even the manner in which the government deals with the opposition's criticisms and demands recalls his era.

From "shut your face" to "keep talking"

Regular media coverage has been critical for the protests shaking the Arab world. Regularly broadcast satellite images have smashed the isolation imposed by the culture of silence that has killed the prospects of many nascent protests whose demise met with general indifference. During Ould Taya's dictatorship, a free – written – press was tolerated insofar as it allowed the government to purchase the image it sought without threatening the system's future with freedom of expression. Today, Ould Abdel Aziz's regular lessons about democracy would be the envy of many established or nascent democracies. From the regime's viewpoint, the fact that journalists can write freely about such sensitive subjects as the army or the fight against terrorism attest to the maturity of Mauritania's democracy. In the same vein,[22] they point to the fact that the opposition and civil society can organize unauthorized marches and sit-ins without undue repression.[23]

Freedom of expression has made great strides since the air and radio waves were liberalized in 2011. Several private radio and TV stations have opened and continue to operate independently today. But the licensing process is far from transparent. Many applications are rejected out of hand, without any valid reason. Those who do get licenses are reputed to be close to the government. Mauritania's audiovisual world is, as a result, relatively homogenous and unrepresentative; there are few or no francophone channels or stations for the country's various ethnic groups.

Are we then supposed to marvel at a mature Mauritanian democracy? In point of fact, the government is multiplying the number of electronic sites and organs that are either sympathetic or merely mercenary in order to blunt the denunciations and revelations in the independent press. It also solicits articles to destroy or tarnish the image of journalists who are often denounced as *peshmergas* or mercenaries.

Having controlled the sole source of national coverage and procured the loyalty of a few local organs, the government can give protests free rein without fearing adverse coverage. News channels now control the public space.

The public realm: The stakes

By contrast to the other dictatorships in the Arab world, the public space in Mauritania is available to protestors as a place for expressing a new citizenship. The square has not showcased the government's military might nor has it been used to promote a personality cult. Surely influenced by its strict form of Islam, Mauritania's political culture erects no statues; it makes no declarations to the glory of an enlightened leader in the capital.

But since the commemoration of the fiftieth anniversary of Mauritania's independence of November 2010, enormous portraits and banners to the glory of President Ould Abdel Aziz festoon government buildings, private buildings and some public spaces, a practice that has intensified since Aziz was shot in October 2012.[24] Political parties, the public administration, some associations and more or less representative NGOs all vie with one other to declare their loyalty and well wishing from the most visible spots in the capital.

Pictures of Aziz are visible everywhere in Nouakchott, even in the squares where anti-government protests are held. It is a little like having Big Brother watching. The posters remain whole, and are neither tagged nor ripped from the walls. As of September 2012, the construction of a new commercial mall has begun on Red Blocks Square. This is one more move to evict the demonstrators from the center of town. As space is mobile (Retaillé 2005), protesters still have a possible future, unless they also drift towards the government, the opposing camp, which is currently betting on its political economy to justify its power.

Infrastructure dressed up as a political program

In the absence of any political progress, Ould Abdel Aziz is proclaiming economic achievement to quell the opposition, despite the dim macroeconomic picture. With a GNP of $1,000 per capita for an estimated population of 3.5 million, Mauritania has moved from number 164 to 167 out of 185 countries ranked on the basis of the ease of doing business in 2012 by *Doing Business*. Transparency International's December 5, 2012, report ranks Mauritania 123 out of 176 countries in terms of corruption. The government points to its large infrastructure and urban multipurpose construction projects.

New cities and infrastructure

On June 22, 2011, the Council of Ministers examined and adopted by decree a series of projects to create new cities considered to have public utility. In Hodh Echargui Province, the government built the city of Mbeyket Lahwach, 1,200 kilometers southeast of Nouakchott and forty kilometers from the Malian border, for a total cost of 565 million Ouguiyas or nearly $190 million.[25] The plans include nearly 2,000 subdivisions that will ultimately become home to 10,000 people.

The new city of Chami, located at kilometer 220 on the road between Nouakchott and Nouadhibou was also approved and similarly declared to be of public utility. The government will pay 250 million Ouguiyas or nearly $90 million to cover the cost of 3.6 kilometers of water pipes that can be connected – for free – to up to 200 homes. The city will have two 30 KVA generators to supply electricity.

How should the government's predilection for building in the middle of nowhere be interpreted? The Council of Ministers issued a communiqué on June 22, 2011, regarding Chami:

> This project fits into our plans of building new cities with considerable potential for being veritable poles of development. The subdivision where we are building Chami, a new city, set on the coast mid-way between Nouakchott and Nouadhibou covers 685 hectares (extendable) with 5,680 housing sites and 805 commercial sites. All public services and administrative buildings will be built.

The same reasons were given for building Mbeiket Lahwach, Termessa (in Hodh El Gharbi Province, east of Nouakchott) and Bouratt, in Brakna Province, south of Nouakchott.

The security crises in the Sahel-Sahara that periodically thrust Mauritania into the international limelight have forced the government to create new cities in strategic locations in the country's vast uninhabited spaces, enabling the authorities in Nouakchott to better monitor the national space. The plan to establish a network of fixed and mobile military garrisons concomitantly with the creation of these new cities will make it easier for the government to maintain its surveillance of the national territory.

Endless modernization projects

In addition to the new cities, the Mauritanian government has also begun to modernize the country's public works infrastructure. Three examples are worth mentioning.

A new international airport is being built twenty-five kilometers north of Nouakchott on 18,000 m² of land that includes 4,800 m² of maintenance hangars. The freight zone will have an annual capacity of two million passengers. The landing runways will be able to accommodate large aircraft, including Boeing 747s and Airbus A380s. The construction is being done by Najah Major Works, a Mauritanian company to which the government is giving 451 hectares of land, two-thirds of which are located in Nouakchott's old airport, and the balance around the new airport. The contract was awarded without any public bidding. The shareholders of this unknown company are assumed to have close ties to the government. The local press carried several diatribes against this procurement that occurred without any calls for tender, to unknown companies, and with suspected close relationships between company shareholders and the government, and lively debates took place in the National Assembly where the opposition lambasted the lack of transparency and denounced the fire sale of the public domain to private interests. In a country where public and private holdings are often chaotically mingled, giving those in some circles the ability to profit from the confusion (Chabal and Daloz 1999), the opposition has an opportunity to attack the government and its allies on the grounds of the unfair advantages and benefits of such transactions.

The second project concerns two new energy plants that are being planned; one to generate 120 megawatts for a cost of €125 million (or approximately $165), financed by Mauritanian and international funds; the second, with a capacity of fifteen megawatts, for a cost of €22.5 million (approximately $30 million), to be financed by the United Arab Emirates. When completed, the large central plant in Banda will run on natural gas and produce 350 megawatts for mining production units in neighboring Mali and Senegal.

There is no mystery about why Nouakchott has been so interested in the Banda project. When President Ould Abdel Aziz returned from an extended trip to France in October and November 2012, he focused on the energy sector as a means of depriving opponents and protesters seeking to fault him for the regular power cuts endured by Mauritanians.

Lastly, to attract investors, the government declared on January 2, 2013, that the country's economic capital, Nouadhibou, would henceforth be a Free Zone (law number 2013–001). Considered a priority development zone, the city has a special regime for customs, taxes, land, social benefits and currency exchange.

As befits a military regime, the government undertook these projects without any preliminary consultation, eliminating the debate before the deliberation that characterizes a true democracy (Sen 2005). In the end, a re-election in the form of a plebiscite took place.

Having succeeded in neutralizing his opposition, President Mohamed Ould Abdel Aziz went into the election year in the best of positions to remain in power. His re-election was all but guaranteed owing to an unplanned gift from his African peers: Mauritania inherited the presidency of the African Union for a year, for the first time since 1972. This was a privileged position for him to boost his international stature. As a fine tactician, he compels the opposition, once again, to make a mistake by rejecting all the proposals they made in order for them to agree to take part in the elections. The political parties and Labor Unions, under the banner of the FNDU, were left with no other choice than to call for the boycott of the election, making things much easier for Mohamed Ould Abdel Aziz. Facing no serious opponent and in an election without much suspense, the incumbent president won with a remarkable 82% score. Following his inauguration on August 2, 2014, he flew to the US to attend the Africa–US summit and thus start in a position of strength thanks both to the legitimacy conferred by his election as President of Mauritania and as President of the African Union.

Conclusion

Can the economy give Ould Abdel Aziz's government a reprieve and a second wind? That's the question being raised after the political protests have lost steam despite political and institutional fragility.

Beyond the internecine struggles undermining the opposition, there are some indications that the lassitude and despair fueling popular uprisings are losing ground in Mauritania.

The activity in the extractive industries and the infrastructure investments denote some dynamism in the Mauritanian economy, which the IMF confirms.

The macroeconomic results of the first half of 2012 were satisfactory. After a year of severe drought in 2011, agricultural production is coming back and the public works sector should stimulate a vigorous recovery in economic growth. Real GNP growth for 2012 is projected to be 6.2%, despite a strong drop in mining production and sluggish demand from Europe. Inflation will be stabilized at 6% (annual rate), thanks in part to government control of prices for certain products.

The IMF emphasizes the "unprecedented room for maneuver" in the budget, particularly given the record level of cash reserves estimated to be about "US$ 750 million, in other words, the equivalent of 5.3 months of imports."

The flattering observation does not, however, shroud the precarious political and socioeconomic realities: high rates of unemployment (31% in 2008)[26] and poverty (43%)[27] and a 5.1% inflation rate in September 2012, according to the National Bureau of Statistics. In light of these figures, the opposition mocks the majority's accomplishments, "you can't eat growth," "you can't eat tar," "why build roads when people can't buy a car?"

Elections are constantly delayed and the opposition is refused any place in the management of public affairs, or at least in the electoral process.[28] This all portends political instability, despite the government's apparent control over the situation.

The risks of popular change in Mauritania seem to have dulled somewhat. No Arab Spring has blossomed. The various political analysts and players can reflect on Habermas (1996: 88).

> Instead of imposing on others a maxim that I would hope to be a universal law, I should submit my maxim to everyone so that they can examine its claim to universality through discussion. A slippage occurs: the center of gravity no longer resides in what each individual hopes to propose as a universal law without contradiction but rather in that which all can recognize as a universal law.

By criminalizing the unconstitutional political changes in early January 2013, Ould Abdel Aziz believes that he can neutralize the army, the only institution truly able to unbalance the current equilibrium. But the true risks facing the country lie on its borders, in the Malian crisis. No law can protect the country against the effects of a war in a neighboring country or the contagion of the international jihad that is taking root in the Sahara-Sahel. As a good military man, General Ould Abdel Aziz has certainly not lost sight of the fact that the military had come to power in 1978 as the direct result of another conflict in the former Spanish Sahara in which the country had gotten involved under its first president, Moktar Ould Daddah.

Notes

1. Translated from the French by Deborah Glassman.
2. Remarks by Mohamed Ould Abdel Aziz, President of the Islamic Republic of Mauritania, during a meeting in Nouadhibou on March 13, 2012, reported by Agence Mauritanienne d'Information.
3. The most important members of this group are El Hor, SOS Esclaves and the IRA *(Initiative pour la Résurgence du mouvement Abolitioniste)*.
4. They were temporarily freed as of 2012. See also Ould Ahmed Salem 2013.
5. On September 27, 2011, in southern Mauritania, the Maghama police shot live bullets at young demonstrators who were demanding a simplification of the census procedure, killing seventeen-year-old Lamine Mangane. Nine others were shot, some in the back.
6. The term of the current national assembly, which began in November 2006, ended in November 2011. The elections were delayed several times, and set for October 2013 and then for November 23, 2013, when they were held. The incumbent UPR made significant strides followed by the reformist Muslim party, Tawassoul, which thus became the second most important party in Mauritania.

7. The National Liberation Movement of the Azawad started the revolt in Northern Mali in 2012. The Mauritanian government's treatment of the rebels led to virulent reactions in the Malian press and among certain political actors who saw it as proof that the Mauritanians were behind the demands for secession. President Ould Abdel Aziz did not attend the official inaugural ceremony of Ibrahim Boubacar Keita, the new Malian President, on September 19, 2013, which rekindled speculation about the disagreement between Nouakchott and Bamako.

8. The multipurpose mission that was part of the UN's efforts to stabilize Mali.

9. Mauritania had promised to send 1,800 soldiers but had vainly requested that they be assigned to the border between Mali and Mauritania. In a public meeting on August 13 in Nema in southeast Mauritania, President Ould Abdel Aziz recalled, "We defined our conditions: we will only get involved if our soldiers are next to our borders [with Mali] and nowhere else."

10. Communiqué of February 25, 2011.

11. Group, community, assembly.

12. There is no resemblance between the color of the stones and the Bolshevik Revolution. The blocks levers were built in the early 1960s to welcome the first civil servants of newly independent Mauritania.

13. The government opportunely presented it as such.

14. Friday collective prayers, depending on the context.

15. Disturbances, revolt, civil war, riots . . . Referring to the consecutive disturbances after the assassination of the Third Caliph of Islam, Osman Ibn Affan, in 656. After the assassination, the Battle of the Camel was waged by the companions of the Prophet Mohamed, who fought around the camel of Mohamed's wife, Aisha. See the Tabari Chronicle, *The History of God's Messengers and Kings*, translated by Herman Zotenberg, corrected by Mohamad Hamadé, Paris: Al Bustane, 2002, p. 868 and *passim*.

16. Mauritanian Africans are Sudanophones, including Bambaras, Peuls, Soninkés and Wolofs. The black Haratines (former slaves) speak the language of their former masters, who speak Hassanyia.

17. Between September 17–19, 2011, in Nouakchott.

18. Following the last legislative elections, M. Ould Boulkheir lost his position as speaker of the National Assembly. President Ould Abdel Aziz appointed him president of the Economic and Social Council. He was not a candidate for the June 21, 2014, presidential election.

19. Constitutional changes include the following: criminalization of coups d'état; making government responsible to Parliament; judicial independence; reforming the status of the opposition, whose leader would henceforth be elected (which is not true for the current leader, Ahmed Ould Daddah); reforming the electoral code and the mission of the CENI, which is now completely responsible for organizing elections from start to finish, that is, from establishing electoral lists to announcing results; and increasing the number of seats in the National Assembly from 95 to 146.

20. Interview with the author, November 23, 2012, in Paris.

21. Ould Taya's long reign is the most decried in the country's history. His violent, repressive government left no quarter free from attack: unions, the press, religions. Most emblematic was the massacre of thousands of Black Mauritanians between 1989 and 1991 under the guise of a border conflict with Senegal. Crimes against humanity are a central part of the political debate about national cohabitation.

22. In response to the author's question, during a show called *Meet the People* in August 2013 in Nema, President Ould Abdel Aziz answered that it was "perfectly normal that workers strike because it wasn't forbidden and that company directors should also listen." This was one way among others to blame companies for the problem.

23. The list of the victims of the repression is starting, however, to grow. Besides Lamine Mangane, the death of Mohamed Ould Mechdoufi during a demonstration of workers at the Copper Mining Company on July 15, 2012, at Akjoujt should be also noted. On November 28 of the same year, a young rap music artist Abou Fall had his hand severed by a grenade thrown by the police. In May 2012, a students' strike was violently repressed.

Some of its leaders were dismissed from the university. A few weeks later, the Secretary General of the Students' Union (SNEM) was brutally assaulted in Kaédi and left for dead. Evacuated to Nouakchott, he now lives in hiding. On March 2, 2014, Ahmed Ould Mahmoud, a young activist against an incident portrayed as Quran profanation in a suburb mosque of Nouakchott, was found dead. In May 2014, the police violently dispersed a peaceful walk organized by hundreds of Black Mauritanian refugee returnees from Senegal after twenty years of exile. The walk started in Boghe on April 25, 2014, and the marchers trekked 300 kilometres. The violent reaction of the police provoked a wave of indignation throughout the country. The Mauritanian Embassy in France was occupied by fourteen Mauritanians. They have been accused of thrashing the office and are now being prosecuted.

24. In the official version of events, this was an accident.
25. 1€ = approximately 400 Ouguiyas. 1$ = approximately 300 Ouguiyas.
26. National Office of Statistics. This is the only figure available and appeared in the July 2012 annual publication.
27. World Bank.
28. After the municipal and parliamentary elections boycotted by the opposition parties grouped under the banner of the Coordination of the Democratic Opposition (COD, without the party Tawassoul, of Islamic persuasion), the presidential election occurred in the same atmosphere. These groupings created a movement called FNDU that was comprised of seventeen political parties, labor unions and civil society organizations (joined this time around by Tawassoul). The FNDU committed to a new dialogue with the government in April 2014 for the organization of a presidential election with mutually agreed on rules. Unable to secure an agreement, the FNDU decided to maintain the boycott. Ahmed Salem Ould Bouhoubeyni, the former chair of the Lawyers' Bar Association, left the race for the same reasons. The candidates for the presidential election were MM. Boidiel Ould Houmeid, Ibrahima Moctar Sarr, Biram Ould Dah Ould Abeid, the incumbent president M. Mohamed Ould Abdel Aziz, and Mrs. Lalla Mariem Mint Moulay Idriss.

References

Chabal, Patrick and Jean-Pascal Daloz. 1999. *Africa Works: Disorder as Political Instrument (African Issues)*, Indianapolis, IN: Indiana University Press.

Diagana, Abdoulaye. 2010. "Le développement local en Mauritanie, Les migrations subsahariennes," in *Hommes et migrations*, 1286–1287, pp. 246–256.

———. 2011. "Transfert de normes et logiques d'acteurs en pays soninké. Quand la décentralisation redistribue les équilibres politiques à l'échelle locale. (Mauritanie, Mali, Sénégal)," Doctoral thesis in Geography; directed by Denis Retaillé, Rouen University.

———. 2013. "Territoires, souverainetés et frontières; Quand les dynamiques réticulaires défient les logiques étatiques," in *Hommes et migrations*, 1304, pp. 103–109.

Habermas, Jurgen. 1996. *Morale et communication. Conscience morale et activité communicationnelle.* Paris: Cerf.

Ould Ahmed Salem, Zekeria. 2013. *Prêcher dans le désert*. Paris: Karthala.

Retaillé, Denis. 2005. "L'espace mobile," in Benoit Antheaume and Frédéric Giraut (eds.), *Le territoire est mort. Vive les territoires! Une (re)fabrication au nom du développement*. Paris: IRD, pp. 175–202.

Sen, Amartya. 2005. *La démocratie des autres. Pourquoi la liberté n'est pas une invention de l'Occident.* Translated by Monique Bégot. Paris: Payot.

Zoubir, Yahia H. 2012. "Tipping the Balance Towards Intra-Maghreb Unity in Light of the Arab Spring," in *The International Spectator: Italian Journal of International Affairs*, 47:3, pp. 83–99.

13

MOROCCO: KEEPING THE REVOLUTION AT BAY WITH AN ENHANCED STATUS QUO

Azzedine Layachi

The westernmost country in North Africa, the Kingdom of Morocco, has known the least disturbance during and since the 2011–2012 period known as the "the Arab Spring." For several reasons, it has managed to keep at bay – and minimized – the contagion effect of the popular upheavals that engulfed the Middle East and North Africa (MENA) region. One of them is not contentment and prosperity across most of the population. In fact, many Moroccans have been quite unhappy with the living conditions, unemployment, poor quality of governance, corruption, and a host of other issues. Yet, they did not rise up and attempt to bring down the monarchical regime that has ruled the country for centuries. However, a protest movement did develop around a series of demands. Known as the "February 20 Movement," this social mobilization of mostly young people prompted a swift response from King Mohamed VI in a March 9, 2011, speech that promised important reforms, including constitutional amendments; these were approved by referendum the following July 1. New parliamentary elections were immediately set and the moderate Islamist Party for Justice and Development (PJD) won the highest number of seats and was allowed to lead a coalition government for the first time. The outcome of this series of state responses, right in the middle of major social upheavals in the region, amounted to a relative pacification of the protest and an effective prevention of social explosion.

In search for the reasons why and how Morocco has avoided a social upheaval similar to those in Libya, Tunisia, Egypt, Syria, Bahrain, and Yemen, this chapter explores, among other things, the nature of the protest that started on February 20, 2011, and the reaction of the monarchy and the government to the "Arab Spring" and the February 20 Movement. It will look at the outcome of the reforms and government actions since 2011. It will also present the overall social and economic conditions against the backdrop discussion on state/monarchy predation in a country that remains generally poor, with a high illiteracy rate, and a rampant corruption at all levels.[1] Throughout this chapter, questions pertaining to the nature of the regime, government–monarchy relations, and the role of the *Makhzen* will be also be addressed.

Before delving into Moroccan politics in the post-"Arab Spring," it is useful to set the context with a general overview of the socio-economic conditions of recent years and the policies enacted to deal with the challenges they posed.

Socio-economic conditions

Morocco has the third largest population in the Arab world, after those of Egypt and Algeria; it stands today at 33.1 million with a growth rate of 1.4%.[2] The kingdom has 75% of the world's known reserves of phosphate rock and is the largest exporter of that commodity. Its biggest industrial development has been in phosphate-related industries.

The agricultural sector, which accounts for 20% of gross domestic product and employs 40% of the labor force, remains highly dependent on rain, which it often lacks. In 2007 droughts caused the worst production in recent history and led to a steep decline of Morocco's GDP growth rate from 7.9% in 2006 to 3% in 2007. However, things improved in 2008 and 2009 thanks to better rain conditions and some reforms. In 2010, due to increasing public expenditures – 6% of the budget went to consumer subsidies – and a challenging global economic environment – especially the sluggish economic growth in Europe – the trade and budget deficits widened and the GDP growth rate fell to 3.2%. However, in 2011, the economy's growth rate was close to 5% but it slipped in 2012 back to 3% and was expected by the IMF to reach 4.5% in 2013. These wide fluctuations are mostly attributed to the performance of the agricultural sector, which in turn depends on rain. The economy continued to be negatively affected in the last two years by the economic slowdown in Morocco's main export market, the European Union, and by an expansion in 2011 of state spending on social programs and subsidies.

The official overall poverty rate for 2012 was 9%, but it jumped to 14% in the rural areas;[3] unemployment stands at 9% (22% for the young, with 100,000 unemployed graduates). These figures constitute a net improvement from ten years ago, but do not truly reflect the vast extent of visible poverty (one in four Moroccans lives in absolute poverty or is under its threat) and unemployment in both rural and urban areas. The illiteracy rate of 55% is the highest in the Maghreb region in spite of important government actions since King Mohamed VI's accession to the throne in 1999.

In its 212 Article IV Consultation report, the IMF, which praised Morocco's "broad macroeconomic stability," warned, however, that the country's economic outlook is undermined by domestic economic "rigidities," and that growth will depend to a large part on "the sustained delivery of reforms."[4] A carefully worded warning stated that "there is increased urgency in moving ahead with the reforms, in particular that of the subsidy system. . . . More investment in human capital and basic infrastructure is necessary to promote inclusive growth."[5]

One of the issues raised by deficiencies in the area of human capital is the high level of youth unemployment, the mismatch between the educational curriculum, and the requirements of employability – especially in urban areas – and the lack of trust in the government to provide solutions to the socio-economic problems faced by many Moroccans. For these and other reasons, many young Moroccans consider migration out of the country as the only hope for better life prospects. Many accept the risk of dying on the high seas while crossing illegally into Europe rather than continuing to live without hope in their own country. Many young people, along with many migrants from Sub-Saharan Africa, constantly try to migrate through the enclave Spanish cities of Ceuta and Melilla by scaling tall border fences or by sea (in February 2014, many drowned when they were shot by Spanish border police as they tried to get around a man-made breakwater that separates Moroccan and Spanish waters).

To deal with the socio-economic conditions described above, the state enacted in recent years several social programs, public sector employment programs (e.g., paid internships), wage increases, and subsidies for basic goods. The government led by the Islamist Party for Justice and Development (PJD) has been contemplating cuts to public spending, including an overhaul of the expensive state subsidies and pension program. However, the high political cost of such polices made these measures almost impossible to materialize. The costs may include the loss of popularity of the Islamist party and social unrest like the one that engulfed the region in 2011.

It is important to note that the social and economic challenges Morocco faces today have their roots in the reign of the previous king, Hassan II, and that the current monarch has so far done more than his father in trying to alleviate some of these conditions. He has directly addressed poverty, illiteracy, and a poor human rights record, among which is women's rights. All of these areas were either neglected by King Hassan II or badly handled during his reign. However, and as will be examined below, recent revelations about Mohamed VI's wealth and that of people close to him, have raised concerns among Moroccan and outside observers.

King Hassan II: "The years of lead"

The rule of King Hassan II (1961–1999) was characterized by an unequivocal authoritarianism (known as the "Years of Lead") that imposed the hegemony of the monarchy over society, controlled the economy from above, monopolized religious leadership, and yet maintained relative peace and stability through an artful combination of repression, co-optation, and occasional accommodation with the opposition. However, the most challenging opposition figures were jailed, pushed into foreign exile, or eliminated; several independent civic and professional associations, student organizations, and unions were disbanded, co-opted, or put under state control; the representative institutions – mainly parliament – were denied power of their own, and the media were under strict state control. After the military was neutralized following two coup attempts in 1971 and 1972, the leftist opposition (National Union of Popular Forces, UNFP, and the Union of Socialist of Popular Forces, USFP) was also rendered ineffective. There developed thereafter an ideological and an institutional vacuum that was easily filled by slogans and networks of grassroots Islam, which offered a radically different social and political project. With the combination of calls for democratization and religious revival, the Islamists pushed for the widening of the arena of political participation by making more people involved. The king and members of the governing elites inadvertently played a facilitating role by manipulating religious groups and symbols. They often used the Islamist sentiment against the secular left and vice versa. However, in the end, the monarchy managed to strike a delicate balance between the two tendencies by way of a constantly shifting game of repression, tolerance, and co-optation of one challenging group at a time, or more at once.[6]

As for the institutional setting, under Hassan II the often-revised constitution provided for an elected legislature and a multiparty political system but the apparent political plurality could not challenge the powerful monarch who was both at the center and above the political system. Hassan II ruled as an absolute monarch who relied on cronies, prominent business families, Sufi orders, powerful members of the Alaoui family (which has controlled Morocco for over 350 years), and prominent Berber leaders. He tended to find these more reliable than the political parties and other formal institutions of representation. Following the two failed assassination attempts against him, King Hassan harshly repressed all political opposition, paid little attention to the alarming socio-economic indicators, and engaged the country in the irredentist invasion and occupation of Western Sahara, starting with the "Green March" of November 1975. At that point, any dissenting voice was deemed unpatriotic and dealt with accordingly if it did not redeem itself by standing behind the monarch.

When society seemed finally pacified, and in response to rising domestic and international outcries against grave human rights violations and lack of freedoms in his kingdom, the king engaged in political reconciliation with the opposition by appointing in 1998 the leader of USFP, Abderrahmane Youssoufi, to the position of prime minister. He also allowed for the first time nine Islamists to join parliament. Hassan II was always wary about political Islam ever since Abdeslam Yassine, a schoolteacher, openly challenged his legitimacy and his policies in 1974. In response to this challenge, King Hassan II outlawed Adl wa Ihsan ("Justice and Charity"), the main Islamist movement in Morocco then and now, and locked its leader away in a mental institution before placing him later under house arrest.

Besides repressing grassroots political Islam, the king, at the same time, worked to revive and enhance a benign official Islam for the purpose of improving the legitimacy of the monarch as "Commander of the Faithful" and reducing the appeal of radical Islamism. It was only toward the end of his reign that King Hassan finally allowed a token representation of Islamism in parliament. His successor son, King Mohamed VI, went further when he legalized the first Islamist party, Justice and Development (PJD), and allowed it to partake in elections in 2002.

Mohamed VI: The pro-active king of the poor . . . and the rich

Mohamed VI began his reign with a promise to improve the human rights condition in the country and to work on alleviating poverty and illiteracy. He publicly admitted the existence of the Tazmamat "death camp" and other prisons in
the Sahara where rebel army officers and political dissidents were jailed for years
without trial or access to their families. The new king established the Equity and
Reconciliation Commission, headed by human rights activist Driss Benzekri, to
investigate rights violations during the "Years of Lead." By April 2005, the Commission had investigated 22,000 cases and compensated the families of the victims
from a fund of $3.8 million. In 2000, the king issued a "National Action Plan for
Human Development" that aimed to alleviate poverty, illiteracy, and underdevelop-
ment; it included several progressive dispositions on women's rights and freedom
of the press.

However, a series of bombings in Casablanca in 2003 attributed to Islamists,
which killed 45 people, provoked a heavy reaction against independent publications
such as *Le Journal*,[7] leading to the arrest and beating of the leader of the Moroccan
Association for Human Rights, and a violent police repression of demonstrations
against new restrictions on freedom. Scores of people were arrested under the suspicion of being connected to radical networks.

In spite of the tough state reaction to the 2003 bombings, which included also
a harsh new antiterrorism law, a new bomb attack occurred on March 14, 2007, in
a Casablanca internet café, which killed only the suicide bomber and injured two
people. On April 28, 2011, a powerful bomb exploded the Jamaa al-Fnaa Square in
Marrakech, killing 15 people, 10 of whom were foreigners. The attack was blamed
on local radical Islamists.

Beyond, the measures noted above, it is fair to say that the relative political
liberalization that was underway was not halted or reversed as a reaction to these
attacks, and that the state did not engage in a wide-scale repression of all political opposition as would have been done during the rule of King Hassan II in
similar circumstances. On the contrary, the 47-year-old monarch pushed for yet
more political reforms and even allowed the Islamists to lead government after the
July 2011 constitutional reform, which slightly altered the monarch's power over
the governing institutions, as will be discussed later.

In July 2001, the king established a Royal Amazigh Language and Culture
Institute in reaction to protests in Berber areas, notably the Rif. The Institute's
goals include the standardization of the Amazigh (Berber) language, which has five
regional variations, teaching it in schools, and developing media programs devoted
to highlighting and preserving the Amazigh culture.

King Mohamed VI's most important social reform effort was the amendment in
2003 of the Family Code known as the *Mudawana*. The reform raised the minimal
marital age for women from 15 to 18 years (the same as for men), made wives
equal to husbands in ownership of property, and allowed them to initiate divorce
proceedings. In the law at least, women can no longer be married without their

own consent. In case of divorce, they would receive custody of the children and the father must pay child support. Also, unilateral repudiation by men was forbidden. The king appointed the first female Royal Counselor and imposed a quota of 30 seats for women in parliament. In the 2009 municipal elections, thanks to a new quota of 12% of the seats reserved for women, 3,406 women were elected, a far cry from 127 only in 2003.

In the 2002 parliamentary vote, the monarch allowed the Islamists to enter the process, for the first time, under their own structure, the Party of Justice and Development (PJD). Their relative electoral success (they earned 42 seats) made them the third party in Morocco after the long-established USFP (50 seats) and Istiqlal (48 seats). In the 2007 parliamentary elections the PJD moved to second place with 46 seats after Istiqlal (52 seats). The USFP ran fifth with 38 seats after the Popular Movement (41 seats) and the National Rally of Independents (RNI) (39 seats). However, the voter turnout was the lowest ever, at 37%, and claims of electoral fraud, vote buying, and manipulation of the results by the state and the monarchy were rampant.[8] In the 2011 parliamentary elections, following the latest constitutional reform, and in the midst of upheaval in parts of the Arab world, the Islamists finally reached the rank of first party by getting the most votes and thus deserving to form and lead a coalition government. They won 107 out of 395 seats (26%), followed by Istqlal (60 seats), and RNI (52 seats). The new pro-monarchy Islamist party Authenticity and Modernity Party (PAM), which fared well in the 2009 municipal elections, did less well in the last parliamentary elections.

Except for the 2011 vote, all initiatives and reforms enacted or promoted by the monarchy and the state prior to the spring upheavals in the region were said to have dampened somewhat the potential contagious effect and helped nurture a prevalent view of the young monarch as a benevolent leader who is eager to enact positive change in the country. On almost all important issues, he acted proactively and pre-emptively by being one step ahead of major social protest or instability. When, early in his reign, the militant Berber movement was gaining momentum in both Algeria and Morocco, he responded by creating in 2001 the Royal Institute of Amazigh [Berber] Culture (IRCAM). "Instead of posing Berber culture as a challenge to national unity, the king promoted embracing it as a necessary step in his project for a 'democratic and modernist society.'"[9] In spite of its shortcomings, this initiative undercut somewhat the momentum of the Berberist challenge.

Similarly, after having inherited from his father's reign contentious human rights issues, Mohamed VI engaged in acknowledging the terrible things (imprisonment, torture, and other atrocities) that were done to people by the state during the "Years of Lead" (i.e., during his father's reign) and proceeded to give monetary compensation to the victims or their families. He did it through the Equity and Reconciliation Commission (Instance Equité et Reconciliation, IER) that he created in 2004. This action was welcomed by many people even though it did not go as far as naming and making accountable those responsible for the human rights atrocities. However, the commission was another proactive response of King Mohamed VI to a persistent domestic and international pressure on the treatment of human rights in Morocco prior to 1999, the year he was enthroned. While the Moroccan environment has become relatively friendlier to human rights, this does not preclude that violations still take place under the new king, albeit not to the same extent as in the past. However, the US Human Rights Report of 2013 relayed a stark picture of major abuses in Morocco proper and Western Sahara.[10]

The young king also faced head on two other important issues that were neglected by his father: illiteracy and poverty. By the second year on the throne, he began a series of activities meant to alleviate both. He had little success in making a serious dent in both, but his hyperactivism in these areas – crisscrossing the country in highly publicized fanfare – earned him the title of "king of the poor." However, since then, his people have also learned that their king was a very rich monarch, who took advantage of his authority to extract substantial wealth from investments in his country's economy. This earned him the title of "Predator King."[11]

A 2008 article in *Forbes* magazine indicated that the young king of Morocco is ranked seventh among the richest monarchs in the world. In 2000, he had a personal wealth estimated at $500 million, which had grown to $1.5 billion by 2008 and $2.5 billion thereafter. He became richer than the emir of Qatar and six times richer than the Kuwaiti King.[12] In 2009, he was ranked among the world's 15 richest royal figures, which is a stunning paradox in relatively poor country. According to a 2013 report of the US Congressional Research Service, the "phosphate industry and much of the economy are dominated by the royal family and associated elites who control large, multi-sectoral, holding companies."[13] Besides the fact that the king himself is a major landowner, the royal family has a majority of shares in the National Investment Company (SNI), which controls substantial assets in Moroccan financial companies, insurance, construction, and commodities.[14]

As a consequence of the widely perceived predatory behavior of the monarchy, conflict of interest is one of the biggest obstacles to sound economic reforms which could lift millions of Moroccan out of poverty. However, and surprisingly enough, the popular protest movement that started on February 20, 2011, while the region was engulfed in unprecedented and simultaneous upheavals, did not target Mohamed VI himself, but the governing institutions below him (parliament, the government, and elements of the shadowy Makhzen[15]), as well as public policies or their absence on certain issues. The protest focused also on the constitutional order and called for the reduction of the monarch's powers and the establishment of a truly constitutional monarchy. However, as discussed below, the monarch, through his now famous March 9 speech, was able to deflect and diffuse the societal challenge by proactively calling for substantial institutional reforms.

The February 20 Movement and regime response

As popular upheavals were spreading fast across the MENA region, large demonstrations started in several Moroccan cities on February 20, 2011. The mostly young protesters demanded political and economic reforms and an end to widespread corruption. This event marked the birth of what became known as the "February 20

Movement"[16] and managed to attract more than 200,000 people in many cities for demonstrations across the country demanding immediate reforms. In spite of the fact that they "lacked the energy and zest of the revolts of Tunisia and Libya and even the much smaller protests in Algeria" in the same period, the demonstrations were effective. "The demands of the demonstrators included a new government, a constitutional reform that would limit the powers of the king, an end to corruption, the improvement of living conditions, and social justice."[17] The protesters did not target King Mohamed VI himself due to his favorable image among a large sector of the population as a reformist who is concerned about the plight of the poor. The Makhzen and the corrupt and inept leaders below him were the actual targets.

The constitutional reform of hope and despair

To preempt a wider and dangerous social upheaval across the kingdom, Mohamed VI announced in his March 9, 2011, speech that a constitutional reform would be prepared by a commission and submitted on July 1 to a referendum. He indicated that the amendments would give more power to parliament and the prime minister and his cabinet and would allow more political freedom. He also promised more job creation for the youth.

The constitutional amendments approved by referendum on July 1, 2011, included the appointment of the prime minister from the party with the largest number of seats (traditionally, the king appointed anyone he wished, even a non-partisan technocrat); the transfer of some of the monarch's powers to the prime minister, including that of dissolving parliament; and the power of parliament to grant amnesty (previously a privilege of the monarch only). The reformed constitution made the Berber language an official language next to Arabic, expanded human rights and political freedoms, and called in Article 19 for the establishment of an "authority in charge of parity and fighting all forms of discrimination."

The constitutional reform was welcomed by many Moroccans and foreign observers. However, it was also criticized for not going far enough in the direction of democracy.

> The political elite of many of the major political parties and factions . . . expressed their strong support. But it is clear that, while the monarchy was explicitly responding to more recent social and political pressures, the drafters of the new constitution were directly responding to the will of the traditional *makhzen* and essentially working in the shadow of a long and well-established authoritarian rule.[18]

The February 20 Movement indicated that the reform failed to establish the constitutional monarchy demanded by the protesters. In fact, the king retained most of his powers, including the leadership of the "Council of Ministers" or cabinet – which makes him the actual head of the executive branch, not the prime minister. He kept the power to appoint the prime minister himself based on electoral results and to dismiss ministers. The king will also head the new Supreme Security Council, which handles domestic and international security and anticorruption measures, and retains "the power to appoint military and civil service personnel, choose ambassadors, ratify international treaties, address the parliament with no right of reply, dissolve the legislature, approve judicial nominations, and declare a state of emergency. He maintains his position as 'Commander of the Faithful,' the kingdom's Islamic spiritual leader."[19] He continues to chair the Council of Ulema (the state's religious scholars), which has extensive oversight on fatwas (religious rulings) and the sermons of Friday prayers in every mosque.

The extensive power retained by the monarchy indicated that it was not willing, or ready, to become a constitutional monarchy that reigns but does not rule. The king today both reigns and rules. This led Freedom House to state in its 2013 report:

> Morocco is not an electoral democracy. Most power is held by the king and his close advisers. Even under the 2011 constitution, the monarch can dissolve Parliament, rule by decree, and dismiss or appoint cabinet members. He sets national and foreign policy, commands the armed forces and intelligence services, and presides over the judicial system. . . . The judiciary is not independent, and the courts are regularly used to punish opponents of the government. Arbitrary arrest and torture still occur, though they are less common than under King Hassan.[20]

To the youth protest movement, the 2011 reforms from above were not expected to bring much change and the push from below for real democracy and its tangible tenets has to continue:

> What is at stake in this unmistakably unequal trial of strength is who will hold the reins of political change and in which direction the country will head: towards a new phase of modernization and authoritarian consolidation – by renewing existing strategies of adaptation to the international environment and reconciliation between monarchy and opposition – or towards genuine democratic transformation?[21]

The new constitutional measures, however, should not be dismissed entirely because they did open the way for some positive variation, and the real test is whether and how they will be implemented and whether key political actors, such as the PJD, would use them to the fullest extent in order to exert meaningful concessions from the mighty monarchy and effect tangible changes in the way the country is governed and the way it responds to the demands and needs of the citizenry.

Keeping the "Arab Spring" at bay

To signal its commitment to change, the monarchy almost immediately after the approval of the amended constitution planned early parliamentary elections for

November 25, 2011. It also took several tangible measures intent on quieting the street protests, including "socio-economic measures such as increased subsidization of basic food products and fuel, salary raises for civil servants, the creation of jobs for unemployed graduates and a subsidy for the unemployed, the establishment of obligatory medical insurance and an expansion of free health care provision."[22] These measures increased the state's budget deficit to 7.5% of GDP (up from 6.8% in 2011) in a context of rising current account deficit (-9.7% in 2012). This led the government to seek the assistance of the IMF, which approved in August 2012 a loan of $6.2 billion in the form of Precautionary Liquid Line.[23] The IMF assistance came with a strong recommendation to cut down on subsidy and other spending which have been used by the government to quiet protest without engaging in serious economic reforms.

The overall unemployment rate has steadily declined in the last two decades. It stands today at around 9%. However, among the unemployed, the youth are particularly affected. Around 50% of the unemployed are between 15 and 24 years old. Also, according to a World Bank survey, 49% of the youth "are neither in school, nor the workforce."[24] In Morocco, which is said to be at the height of its youth bulge, the youth make up 30% of the total population and 40% of the working age population.[25] Many of these young people, who face little prospects of stable employment and better living conditions, have been considering two radical options for the future: illegal immigration to Europe, or joining radical Islamist factions at home or abroad, such as al Qaeda affiliates in either the Middle East, the Maghreb, or the Sahel,[26] or the Islamic State in Iraq and Syria (ISIS).

On the political front, the early parliamentary elections of 2011 produced a coalition government led by the Islamist PJD and which included three other parties: Istiqlal Party (PI), the Popular Movement (PM), and the Party of Progress and Socialism (PPS). Since taking over the control of government, the PJD has had a hard time focusing on any substantial piece of legislation and found itself unable to alleviate some of the key problems faced by the young and the needy sectors of the population. Some of the difficulty may have come from the fact that the Islamists could not adjust from being an opposition force to that of governing and thus taking initiatives rather than waiting for cues from the monarchy or the Makhzen.

Furthermore, most key social and economic areas remained under the control of the monarchy and its shadow cabinet made up of special advisors to Mohamed VI. Also, the much needed stringent economic and social reforms could not even be considered by parliament at a time when the monarchy had to keep the "Arab Spring" contagion at bay with generous subsidies – even if they benefited the better-offs in most cases – salary increases, micro-credits, and public employment for the youth. Much of the promises made by Abdelilah Benkirane, the PJD leader, right after taking over government, have remained elusive, including an economic growth rate of 5.5% for the first four years, a reduction of income inequality, and a fight against corruption. Moreover, his government was placed in the awkward position of having to consider reducing the consumption subsidies as dictated by the IMF. The PJD announced cuts to public spending, including state subsidies for basic goods (6% of GDP in 2011) and pensions, but found it difficult to act on them for fear of popular unrest. This has heightened the PJD's political predicament of wishing to enact reforms but at the same time fearing their consequences.

To make matters worse for the Islamist prime minister, the most important coalition partner, the Istiqlal Party, decided in May 2013 to leave the majority group and pull its six ministers out of the government. That was the culmination of a bitter seven-month animosity between the two coalition partners which was fueled by several factors, including a clash of the personalities of the PJD leader, and the new and controversial head of Istiqlal, Hamid Chabat; fundamental differences on policy matters; and probably the unwillingness of Istiqlal to accept a junior role in a coalition it had hoped to lead itself. While the Istiqlal leader criticized what he called the PJD's hegemonic tendency – with Benkirane acting as head of party rather than head of government – the Islamists party criticized Istiqlal's poor performance in past governments and even accused some of its leaders of funneling money out of the country to purchase apartments in Paris. For some observers, this dispute came down to two factors: the desire of the new Istiqlal leader to impose his control over the party which ended up with a dissident faction, and the inexperience or inability of Benkirane to lead both a government and a governing coalition.

On July 9, 2013, the divorce between the two rival parties was finalized when five out of six Istqlal ministers resigned – the minister of national education, Mohamed El Ouafa, refused to do so then because he disagreed with Chabat. The PJD was then faced with two alternatives: either call for new parliamentary elections or try to form a new majority coalition with other parties. It decided for the latter and asked Salaheddine Mezouar, the leader of the National Rally of Independents to join a new coalition. The RNI, a centrist party with close ties to the monarchy, accepted but at a high cost to the PJD, which had to give several key ministerial posts to the new coalition partner. A new government, with a higher number of technocrats and women than before, was finally formed in October 2013.

This government crisis and other non-essential issues seem to have been consuming the PJD-led governments at the expense of taking advantage of an almost unique opportunity to push for meaningful social and economic reforms, as well as institutional changes that could, in the long term, alter the nature of the regime. The author attended in January 2014 a session of parliament in Rabat, which focused entirely on illicit permits given to contractors to load tons of sand from beaches in contravention of existing environmental laws. The bickering between Istiqlal and PJD parliament members was theatrical but not amusing. It was taking away precious time and energy from much needed efforts to tackle more pressing issues. In a way, this could be playing well into the hands of the monarchy and the Makhzen, which do not wish to see a truly empowered parliament come to life with debates and decisions on the implementation of the new constitutional concessions made by the monarchy, and on issues of social justice, unemployment, corruption, and human rights. Karim Tazi, an industrialist and critic of the regime, suggested that "right now the prime minister and the king are only preventing each other from ruling. The king does not want to give the impression that he is still running the country, while Benkirane is uncertain of his own domain. The country is running on inertia."[27]

The PJD finds itself in a serious predicament: in order to maintain its popular support and legitimacy in the eyes of its constituency and the population at large, it is expected to challenge not only the existing modus operandi but also the institutional setting, including, at one point, taking on the Makhzen and maybe the king himself. However, since the PJD's leader Abdelilah Benkirane is explicitly pro-monarchy, he is unlikely to move beyond what the monarch wishes him to tackle, if anything of substance. This has left him unable – or unwilling – to tackle the major points of contention raised by the February 20 Movement such as the institutional setting, inclusionary economic reforms, job creation, and social justice. The PJD discourse keeps reiterating a commitment to the people's concerns in a frank, clear, and bold way, but its option may be limited to simply comforting the protesters of the February 20 movement which it qualified as a historic movement for democracy.

Once the euphoria of the constitutional reforms waned, the monarchy put the breaks on some of the early concessions it made at the height of the popular upheavals in the region. Now, according to Mohammed Masbah, it aims "to weaken the party while at the same time using it to stabilize the regime. In the short term, and as long as the PJD is able to retain popular support, it will remain in office and retain a limited margin of maneuver for reform."[28]

However, it can also be argued that, in the absence of an alternate political party with a similar popularity, the PJD may be the best option for the monarchy and the Makhzen to ensure social peace now and in the coming years. In spite of its shortcomings, the Islamist party still commands a substantial popular support and as long as it remains in office – whether leading the government or solely being part of it – its constituency might still hope for positive change and would not thus take to the streets to challenge the existing order. However, if the party either proves incapable of delivering on key promises or is thrown out of office (by losing the majority support in parliament, or by not doing well in the next elections), disillusioned supporters may join the ranks of a revived February 20 Movement – or another one – in a street challenge that would be much bigger than the one of 2011 and which may not shy away from questioning the nature of the regime itself.

It appears, thus, to be in the best interest of the monarchy, the Makhzen, and the state, that Benkirane and his party continue somewhat to play the roles assigned to them: appeasement and control of constituents, and serving the monarchy's agenda. The only problem is that in order to continue to perform such functions, they must deliver on some of the promises they made, something that soon appeared difficult because most of the issues they built their reputation on are now controlled by the monarchy or have become key instruments of the monarch's hyperactive populism.

Since the day the Islamists of the PJD and of other formations became popular as tolerated political forces, King Mohamed VI has been actively seeking to upstage them by tackling directly and constantly some of their main issues, such as poverty and social justice. Through his wide campaigns against social ills and poverty, he sought to hinder the Islamists' actions in these areas while trying to reinforce the legitimacy of the monarchy that was tarnished by his father's actions – or lack of action. However, this did not prevent the Islamists from finally establishing their presence in the public sphere and exhibiting their well-entrenched networks in major cities. But, once the PJD was handed the power to lead the government, the Islamists became trapped in the position of having to work with – and sometimes for – the monarchy without advancing their own agenda by one iota. This reminds us of what happened to the socialist opposition that was also handed the power to lead the government at the end of the reign of Hassan II. It, too, suffered the same fate and lost a substantial amount of credibility and legitimacy. They fell right into the trap of co-optation after having realized that their hands were tied in the face of the immense problems the masses suffered from in the late 1980s and throughout the 1990s. Most areas of public policy were handled directly by the monarchy – including structural adjustment policies, foreign policy, justice, and Western Sahara. They ended up failing their constituency and anyone who had placed a little hope in their capacity to change things for the better. The PJD of Benkirane is aware of that possible fate if the rules do not change, but it has proven incapable or unwilling to tackle them:

> The party has opted for a non-confrontational approach, and its leader has tended to be compliant vis-à-vis the monarch. Whatever the motives behind the PJD's behavior – pragmatic or tactical – it is likely to turn out to be a risky business. Recent experiences have shown that the participation of opposition forces in the established institutional framework has contributed toward their being discredited vis-à-vis their social basis.[29]

Now both the monarchy and the PJD are in a bind whereby they need each other but the exigencies of their respective legitimacy might be on a collision course. If the PJD ends up with the same fate as the USFP when it was handed the government by Hassan II, there is no other party and leader likely to serve as moderating relay for protestors and unhappy citizens, that is unless Adl wal Ihsan decides to enter the political field now that its charismatic leader is no longer around to prevent that. However, as it may be hoped by many of its supporters, Adl wal Ihsan may want to see the rules changed before entering the political arena, unlike previous opposition parties which played by the palace's rules and lost.

Notes

1. In 2013, Transparency International ranked Morocco 91 (out of 177 countries) with a corruption index of 35 (out of 100, with 0 for highly corrupt and 100 for very clean). See Transparency International, "Morocco," 2013. Online at www.transparency.org/country#MAR.
2. World Bank Data, online at http://data.worldbank.org/indicator/SP.POP.GROW/countries/MA?display=graph.
3. The data are from the World Bank Data. Consulted on October 30, 2013. Online at www.worldbank.org/en/country/morocco.

4. IMF, "Morocco: 2012 Article IV Consultation [. . .]—Staff Report," April 2013. Online at www.imf.org/external/pubs/ft/scr/2013/cr1396.pdf.

5. IMF, "Morocco . . ." p. 4.

6. For more on this, see Azzedine Layachi and Abdelkader Haireche, "National Development and Political Protest: Islamists in the Maghreb Countries," *Arab Studies Quarterly*, 14: 2/3, Spring/Summer 1992, pp. 69–92.

7. A 2005 document of Reporters Without Borders indicated that 80% of the country's journalists did not feel free to write about many issues, despite the protection presumably afforded by the Action Plan. In the last few years, several journalists were arrested, fined, and even jailed, and some newspapers were shut down, for having published items on sensitive issues.

8. The monarchy's interference with the elections was explained by the usual need to block the rise of a single party and to prevent the Islamists from gaining the upper hand.

9. Paul Silverstein and David Crawford, "Amazigh Activism and the Moroccan State," *MERIP Report*, 233: 34, Winter 2004.

10. US Department of State, "Morocco 2013 Human Rights Report," 2013. Online at www.state.gov/documents/organization/220579.pdf.

11. Catherine Graciet and Éric Laurent, *Le Roi Predateur* (Éditions Du Seuil, 2012). See also Fédoua Tounassi, "Mohammed VI, un roi en or massif," *Courrier International*, 975, July 9, 2009. Online at www.courrierinternational.com/article/2009/07/09/mohammed-vi-un-roi-en-or-massif.

12. David Pendleton, "The Top 15 Wealthiest Royals," *Forbes Magazine*, August 22, 2008. Online at www.forbes.com/global/2008/0901/038.html. See also David Pendleton, "King of Rock," *Forbes Magazine*, June 17, 2009.

13. Alexis Arieff, "Morocco: Current Issues," *Congressional Research Service Report RS21579*, October 18, 2013.

14. Souhail Karam, "Morocco Regulator in Pledge on Monarchy-Owned Firms," *Reuters*, September 30, 2011. Online at www.reuters.com/article/2011/09/30/idUSL5E7KU2 VA20110930.

15. The Makhzen refers today to the king and the informal power holders around him; it is believed to yield more power than the formal institutions of the state and is unaccountable. It includes members of the economic, religious, and military elites who exercise power informally through state institutions and society. The Makhzen is at the heart of the political system. To understand Moroccan politics, it is necessary to be acquainted with it.

16. The movement was a loose coalition of online activists, university and unemployed youth, unaligned Islamists, and members of the Adl wal Ihsan organization; it gained the support of several NGOs, such as human rights associations, some small leftist parties, a number of trade unions, the Berber movement, and some intellectuals.

17. Azzedine Layachi, "Meanwhile in the Maghreb: Have Algeria and Morocco Avoided North Africa's Unrest?" *Foreign Affairs*, March 31, 2011. Online at www.foreignaffairs.com/articles/67691/azzedine-layachi/meanwhile-in-the-maghreb.

18. Mohamed Madani, Driss Maghraoui, and Saloua Zerhouni, "The 2011 Moroccan Constitution: A Critical Analysis," *International Institute for Democracy and Electoral Assistance 2012*. Stockholm, Sweden: International Institute for Democracy and Electoral Assistance. Online at www.idea.int/publications/the_2011_moroccan_constitution/.

19. Emma Hayward, "Morocco's Constitutional Referendum: Context, Content, and Impact," *Morocco Board News Service*, July 1, 2011. Online at www.Moroccoboard.Com/News/5338-Moroccos-Constitutional-Referendum-Context-Content-And-Impact. For a good, yet sharply critical, perspective on the limits of the constitutional reform, see Ahmed Benchemsi, "Morocco: Outfoxing the Opposition," *Journal of Democracy*, 23: 1, January 2012, 57–69.

20. Freedom House, "Morocco," *Freedom in the World*, 2013. Online at https://freedomhouse.org/report/freedom-world/2013/morocco#.VXrJHVVViko.

21. Irene Fernández Molina, "The Monarchy vs. the 20 February Movement: Who Holds the Reins of Political Change in Morocco?" *Mediterranean Politics*, 16:3, 2011, 435–441, p. 435.

22. Molina, "The Monarchy vs. the 20 February Movement . . ." p. 437.
23. IMF, "Morocco – Program Note," April 4, 2015. Online at www.imf.org/external/np/country/notes/pdf/morocco.pdf.
24. The World Bank, "The Challenge of Youth Inclusion in Morocco," May 14, 2012. Online at www.worldbank.org/en/news/feature/2012/05/14/challenge-of-youth-inclusion-in-morocco.
25. The World Bank, "Taking Up the Challenge of Youth Inclusion in Morocco," video data slides, May 14, 2012. Online at www.worldbank.org/en/news/video/2012/05/14/taking-up-the-challenge-of-youth-inclusion-in-morocco.
26. Abdeslam Maghraoui, "Morocco's Youth Problem and Its Global Ramifications" *IslamiCommentary* (The Duke Islamic Studies Center), October 9, 2013. Online at http://islamicommentary.org/2013/10/abdeslam-maghraoui-on-moroccos-youth-problem-and-its-global-ramifications/. See also Imrane Binoual, "Northern Morocco Loses Young Men to ISIS," *The Magharebia*, March 10, 2014. Online at http://magharebia.com/en_GB/articles/awi/reportage/2014/10/03/reportage-01. (Note: *The Magharebia* web site is sponsored by the United States Africa Command.)
27. Karim Tazi, cited in James T. Raub, "The Reform of the King," *Foreign Policy*, October 8, 2012. Online at www.foreignpolicy.com/articles/2012/10/08/the_reform_of_the_king.
28. Mohammed Masbah, "Morocco's Slow Motion Reform Process: The Tug of War Between the Palace and the Justice and Development Party," *Comments 2014/C 06*, German Institute for International and Security Affairs (SWP), January 2014. Online at http://bit.ly/SWP14C06.
29. Saloua Zerhouni "'Smartness' Without Vision: The Moroccan Regime in the Face of Acquiescent Elites and Weak Social Mobilization," *Comments 2014/C 11*, German Institute for International and Security Affairs (SWP), February 2014. Online at http://bit.ly/SWP14C 11.

14

FROM DEMOCRATIC CONSENSUS TO A STRUGGLE FOR POWER

The fragility of transition in Tunisia

Emma C. Murphy

Introduction

In January 2011, Tunisia moved to the Arab centre-stage as a popular uprising forced the aging authoritarian president, Zine el Abidine Ben Ali, into exile and swept away the political and security structures on which he had relied. Enthused by the Tunisians' apparent success in embarking at last upon a genuine and internally generated democratic transition, populations from Rabat to Bahrain, Tripoli to Sanaa, took to the streets demanding a similar lifting of the repressive hand in their own countries. The results have been varied but nowhere has the democratic process been propelled as far as it has in Tunisia. However, the first free and fair elections brought unexpected results and consolidation is still at risk, threatened not only by uncivil and anti-democratic forces but also by the profound economic turmoil that has accompanied the political uncertainties. The Tunisian journey of transition thus far provides us with insights into aspects of the body-politic which have been long suppressed but which are now resurfacing, unveiling the fragility of transition at a moment when the politics of identity prevail. This chapter does not focus on the electoral transformation in 2014 but instead examines the legacy of Ben Ali and the immediate aftermath of his downfall.

The iron grip of Ben Ali

The Tunisian revolution[1] seemed to come from nowhere. The standard view among observers before 2011 was that President Zine el Abidine Ben Ali held the country in a vice-like grip. His regime combined electoral authoritarianism (Haugbølle and Cavatorta, 2011: 326) at the level of institutional politics, with reliance on an extensive and pervasive security apparatus that brutally intimidated, suppressed or eradicated all forms of political protest. Periodic elections for both the two houses of the legislature and directly for the presidency saw repeated overwhelming victories for the president and his party, the RCD. Apart from the very obvious manipulation of results, the elections suffered from tight control over all aspects of the competitive process, from party legalization and candidacy approval, to media coverage and campaigning, boundary gerrymandering, and voting procedures (Alexander, 2010 and 2011; Murphy, 1999). The legal opposition was largely confined to elitist, Tunis-centric off-shoots of the ruling party itself which received occasional ministerial posts (never of the strategic variety) as a reward for assisting in the maintenance of the democratic façade. Any genuine competitors for power were excluded, silenced, imprisoned or exiled via constitutional and judicial manipulations, or a malevolent *mukhabarat*. The Presidential Guard, the National Guard and the various political police forces numbered as many as 130,000 for a total population of just 10.5 million (Schraeder and Redissi, 2011: 6). Often operating outside the remit of the Interior Ministry and the civilian police, they were reportedly supported by funds managed directly from the Palace at Carthage and were infamous for their assaults on human and civil rights. After the brief honeymoon period of the presidency in the late 1980s, during which a National Dialogue and National Pact had suggested that civil society would at last be able to play its full role in leading a democratic transition, the regime had turned against not just Islamist forces but all the civil society organizations such as trade unions, student movements, lawyers associations, journalists and human rights organizations which had been the momentum behind demands for political reform during previous decades. Without an active social base, the opposition parties became lame puppets of the regime regardless of the vocal few. The RCD too was subjected to internal reforms, which made it little more than a mobilization tool for Ben Ali, and power was increasingly concentrated around the figure of the president himself. Having abolished the presidency-for-life when he acceded to power, Ben Ali altered the constitution in 2002 through a referendum to enable himself to repeatedly stand for office. His ministers – increasingly technocrats rather than party men – lacked independent power bases and were frequently rotated to prevent them from developing them. Only a few 'hard-men' from his old career in the security forces were kept close and retained their positions (Alexander, 2010; Murphy, 1999). Meanwhile, drawing on capital accumulated through his own domestic struggle with political Islam, Ben Ali utilized the European and American enthusiasm for the post 9/11 global War on Terror, to complete the securitization of his regime with effective international compliance, if not endorsement.

But if political opposition was constrained by such manipulations, at the same time, Ben Ali was able to skillfully recast the nationalist ideological legitimacy of the early Bourguibist years into a mythology of national consensus. Larbi Sadiki, in the earlier edition of this volume, paid considerable attention to the post-colonial process of identity construction and reconstruction that he described as "a continuous act of adjusting the ethnic imagery to politically value-laden narratives" (Sadiki, 2008: 117). Whilst Bourguiba had asserted a territorially-defined identity that located Tunisian individuals as citizens relative to the state, Ben Ali refined the notion of an ethnic homogeneity to an essentially bourgeois, *sahelian* identity that endorsed the values of political stability, democratic gradualism and laïcité (Cava-torta and Haugbølle, 2012: 189). This was reflected in claims of a national political consensus which consequently supported the secular, even western orientations, of the regime constructed during his predecessor's era, its pursuit of economic liber-alization and its intolerance of Islamist political forces.

Béatrice Hibou has argued that this political consensus was in fact a "power-ful technology of power", designed to discipline and silence Tunisians. It was "an illiberal criticism of pluralism" (Hibou, 2011: 205–6), which – together with dis-courses of Tunisian uniqueness and reformism – served to pacify and subordinate the population to a regime-orchestrated master narrative. Ironically, such articula-tions resonated well with international partners, and serviced the requirements of outward-oriented business elites, but over time they so suffocated expressions of alternative identities that it became almost impossible for both Tunisians and exter-nal observers not to re-mouth, even believe, the spin.

Ben Ali's narrative revolved around the proposition that economic growth and prosperity required political stability above all else. The benefits of a liberal eco-nomic strategy would be lost if democratic reforms allowed self-interested social forces sufficient political space to disrupt them, an argument which was given credibility as the international financial community applauded the controlled budget deficits, sustained and regionally-high rates of GDP growth,[2] rehabili-tated debt profile, managed inflation and progressive privatization of state assets (Murphy, 2012). In its five-year plans, the Tunisian government spoke the lan-guage of private entrepreneurship, industrial quality upgrading and technology investments for the global knowledge economy. At the same time, the country was on course to achieve its Millennium Development Goals in key areas such as education, health, life expectancy, reduced infant mortality rates, and access to services like water, electricity and sanitation. Official figures reported declining poverty levels – only 3.8% of the population was considered to live below the national poverty line in 2009 – and women appeared to enjoy the most progres-sive civil and social rights in the Arab region. It was true that the International Financial Institutions and lenders such as the European Union expressed con-cern over rising unemployment figures, attributed more to the demographic surge then to neo-liberal economic formulations, and the social security system was clearly struggling with an embedded deficit, but Tunisia continued to climb the rankings for governance, international competitiveness and human develop-ment. The urgency of the democratic deficit receded into the shadows cast by macro-economic achievements.

Rumblings of discontent

Behind the projections of economic well-being, however, all was distinctly not well. In 2008 a wave of protests and riots swept through the western region and the mining towns of the Gafsa Basin. The upheavals were sparked by job losses in the Gafsa Phosphate Company as a result of the company's restructuring.

The company was the largest employer in a region that had few other resources, an acutely high level of youth unemployment, and a population convinced that it had been neglected by the political centre. The mobilizations drew in a wide spectrum of the population through local trade unions, students, unemployed graduates, teachers, human rights and women's groups. Their protests were aimed not just at the prospect of even greater regional unemployment, but also at the nepotism and corruption that had infiltrated all aspects of the GPC's operations, including its relations with the largest trade union, the UGTT. As the list of grievances grew, and the protests spread across the region, Ben Ali adopted a carrot-and-stick approach, promising targeted funding for the region and demoting local political officials on the one hand, and unleashing the brute force of the police upon the protesters on the other. Shootings, beatings, arrests, curfews and trials followed, accompanied by a largely successful media blockade designed to prevent contagion (Gobe, 2011).

The Gafsa Revolt provides us with early indications of a number of dynamics that would resurface on a national scale in late 2010. Firstly, the economic liberalization process had a regionally uneven impact. The northern metropolitan and coastal areas that were dominated by the manufacturing sector, tourism and some agriculture, might have been benefitting from increased international trade and commerce, but the southern and western interiors were losing traditional productive activity and witnessing proportionately far higher unemployment and resulting relative poverty. They further suffered from both a lack of investment and development expenditure and political under-representation in the mechanisms of government in Tunis to argue for more. Secondly, unemployed graduates had emerged as a mobilized social force. The expansion of the higher education sector over decades had acted to disguise real unemployment, but as those same graduates entered an over-stocked job market armed with new communicative skills and national networks formed on the campuses, they proved to be a formidable social movement. The Revolt also saw local trade unions and professional associations beginning to act independently of their national leaderships that had been largely co-opted into the regime. They worked closely with national civil society organizations like the LTDH and the Committee for the Defense of Liberties and Human Rights in Tunisia, and as the trials proceeded through the courts system in 2009 and 2010, with the independent media and lawyers associations, the personnel of which were themselves subjected to harassment, intimidation and even legal prosecution. The more tightly the regime sought to contain the fall-out from the Revolt, the more intensive, coordinated and collaborative the social mobilization of regime opponents became. Despite efforts to prevent discussion of the riots and the subsequent incarcerations and abuses on the formal and social media, what had started as a localized set of protests, had become a nation-wide re-awakening of civil society at the grass roots.

The grievances that had been at the heart of the Gafsa Revolt were not unfamiliar to most Tunisians. The official figure for unemployment in 2008 was 14.2% nationally, but in towns like Moularès, M'Dhila and Redeyef it was as high as 38.5%,

28.4% and 26.7%, respectively. Unofficially, estimates were much higher, especially among the young and with graduate unemployment estimated to hover around the 50% mark (Erdle, 2011: 43). As a consequence of a substantial demographic bulge, the Tunisian economy needed to grow by 6.5% just to accommodate new entrants to the labour market (European Union, 2010: 7), but had in fact grown by an average of 5% per annum over the preceding twenty years. The difficulties of resolving this escalating problem of youth unemployment were compounded by a structural mismatch between the demand for labour (which came principally from growth in low-skilled manufacturing sectors like textiles) and the fact that 57% of new entrants held university degrees (IBRD, 2009: 12). Even these dispropor-tionately represented the arts and humanities and the private sector complained of shortages of technical, engineering and business skills. The government's discursive commitments to training the labour force for a knowledge economy had not yet translated into the profound structural change required to reverse a deteriorating employment picture. Moreover, Europe, which remained the destination for 76% of Tunisian exports (Belhassine et al., 2009: 5), was suffering its most profound reces-sion in over thirty years, reducing demand and growth in both the manufacturing and tourism sectors.

A global spike in food and fuel prices that began to tax the pockets of even the wealthier classes compounded the problems of widespread unemployment. Between 2000 and 2011, the prices of oils and fats quadrupled, while cereal and sugars tripled, and dairy and meat products doubled (FAO, 2011). The government operated a targeted subsidy programme for some staple food items and regulated domestic fuel prices, absorbing some of the impact at the expense of a subsidy bill which rose from 4.1% of current expenditures in 2002 to 11.6% in 2009 (Albers and Peeters, 2011). Nonetheless, inflation began to climb, peaking at nearly 5% in 2008 (IMF, 2010). A credit boom which had resulted from liberalization of the financial sector and the availability of new products since the turn of the century had left an estimated 85% of Tunisians living with household debt (Bertelsmann Stuftung, 2011) and few had the margins to accommodate these shocks comfortably. Thus, far from the conventional characterization of a wide-based middle class, Tunisia was riddled with both growing inequality and rising poverty. The officially-set poverty line of TD400 per year was too low to reflect the real point at which the so-called "floating middle classes" (estimated at 45.6% of Tunisians) were liable to slip into vulnerability when struck by unemployment, rising prices and diminishing social transfers (Mubila et al., 2011). In retrospect, the World Food Programme has esti-mated that nearer to 12% of the population were living in poverty at the time of the Uprising (Labidi et al., 2011).

If Ben Ali's social bargain – offering economic prosperity in return for politi-cal acquiescence – was wearing thin, it was made even harder to stomach by the very visible cronyism and corruption that permeated every aspect of Tunisian life. With political control of the country tightly centralized around the figure of the president himself, Ben Ali was able to steadily transfer the resources of the country into his own hands and those of his extended family, including that of his wife Leila Trebelsi. In 2009 a World Bank report noted uneasily that private sector growth was being stymied by corruption, nepotism, bribery, lobbying, tax avoidance and non-transparent governance (Belhassine et al., 2009: 4) but the real scale of cronyist capture of the economy was entirely missed. A relatively small group of individuals, tied by clan, were able to amass vast personal fortunes and business empires. Drawing on informal presidential endorsements and discretion, privileged access to financing and contracts, poor mechanisms for regulation and transparency, and a corrupt and fearful judiciary, *la famille* came to control as much as 30–40% of the national economy (Lewis, 2011: 2). Ben Ali and Trebelsi family companies dominated the private media, cement, petroleum distribution, shipping, construction, car dealership, telecommunications, insurance and air transport sectors. They benefitted from preferential terms in buying state assets, often supported by bank loans which were either under-guaranteed or even supported by the World Bank itself. Their companies were exempted from import duties and frequently enjoyed monopolistic control over domestic markets. They acted as middle-men for foreign investors, creaming off lucrative rents in exchange for 'fixing' deals and buying licenses and, once their fortunes were made, they illegally transferred much of the wealth to private bank accounts and property-holdings overseas. The scale of the pillage was simply extraordinary: by June 2011, Tunisian investigators had tracked down Ben Ali and Trebelsi assets in twenty-five countries with an estimated value of ten billion euros (Magharebia, 2011). But if this came as a surprise to international observers, it was nothing new to Tunisians who witnessed the trickle-down effect of corruption across society. The two agencies responsible for enforcing anti-corruption measures, the National Audit Office and the Disciplinary Financial Court, had been rendered ineffective by the power of the family, its reliance on the repressive security apparatus and the heavy censorship (or indeed acquisition) of the media which might otherwise have called them to account. Consequently, as a now famously WikiLeaks-leaked US Embassy cable recounted, nepotism and corruption spread throughout the economy: the right connections could secure a passport, and a bribe could win a scholarship or a job in the public sector. Parking tickets could be made to disappear and unsecured bank loans could be raised (WikiLeaks, 2008). Moreover, the clans were not shy to display their newfound wealth. Glittering new international brand shops sprang up, contrasting sharply with the decaying *banlieu*; expensive cars sped between the chic residential complexes along the coast into Tunis, unhindered by the police; and imposing sea-side mansions were constructed in prime locations often seized illegally from their previous owners. Leila Trebelsi became famous for her extravagant shopping trips to Europe when an entire aeroplane would be commandeered to carry her purchases, and Ben Ali's son-in-law became known for the tiger he kept in his garden. Tunisia had become a two-faced *Janus*: the international community saw a stable regime, committed to a neo-liberal economic strategy that seemed to be delivering on macro-economic goods, while Tunisians saw a despotic, self-interested regime enjoying the nation's wealth while they themselves were falling backwards into debt, impoverishment and political despair.

Political crisis

Although the revolution itself took the world by surprise, the developing economic crisis did not in fact translate into a political crisis overnight. Subterranean shifts in the structures of power and opposition were beginning to occur since the mid-2000s. The 2004 elections had been boycotted by a number of political parties who proclaimed the electoral process nothing but a sham. After the election, which Ben Ali duly 'won' with 95% of the votes cast, the parties came together in a more formal alliance, the *October 18 Collectif*, the first to combine leftist, democratic secular and Islamist parties. Although it operated essentially in exile due to the illegal status of two of its main partners, the liberal *Congress for the Republic* and the Islamist *Ennahda*, the alliance was active for five years and enabled a dialogue across the ideological divide that resulted in the issue in 2010 of a manifesto of shared principles entitled *Our Way Towards Democracy*. The alliance could not claim to be representative of all Tunisians and it was weakened by unresolved differences and a physical distance from its political base (Haugbølle and Cavatorta, 2011), but it did challenge Ben Ali's claim that Islamists would never sign up to a democratic agenda and demonstrated that the secular opposition was not irrevocably trapped in a cycle of collusion and co-optation with the regime. While the political parties were not the driving force of the 2011 revolution, the dialogues maintained during this period paved the way for their collaboration in sustaining momentum for transition once the regime fell and in establishing the new political structures thereafter.

Ben Ali, meanwhile, stood for a fifth term of office in 2009, winning again with a not very credible 89% of the votes. By now the president was seventy-three years old and, as repeated rumours spread of his ill health, thoughts were turning inevitably to his succession. There was no clear candidate from the ruling party: he had cleansed the RCD top-tier of anyone who might have had an independent base. Instead it looked as if the mantle would be passed through his own family. His son-in-law, Sakher El Materi, owner of the massive Princess Holdings company, had been moved into the RCD Central Committee in 2008 and elected to the Chamber of Deputies in 2009. But more worrying for many were the apparent political ambitions of his much younger wife, made clear through the growing frequency with which the media covered her various charitable activities and public speeches. Rumours abounded that conspiracy was afoot, and that Leila was plotting with sinister presidential advisors like Abdelwahab Abdallah and Abdelaziz Ben Dhia, to force Ben Ali to stand down before the 2014 elections so that she in turn could become the RCD party nominee. Neither alternative had any support beyond the family and the newly-enriched business elites, and as the clock ticked the future political leadership of the country began to look precarious.

A fruit seller can change the world

While the occupants of the Palace in Carthage were pre-occupied with securing their economic and political family fortunes, an unemployed graduate sought to earn a few dinars by selling vegetables from a stall in the rural town of Sidi Bouzid. Lacking an official permit, Mohamed Bouazizi found his cart confiscated by the local police and – in an act of despair he doused himself in paint thinner and set fire to himself on 17 December 2010. His tragic protest caught the imagination of sympathetic town residents and a series of demonstrations swept through the southern towns, much as they had two years earlier. The government responded with much the same strategy as it has used in Gafsa, combining a visit to the area by the Minister for Development, who bore promises of investment and employment programmes, with brutal police beatings. Ben Ali declared the protesters to be 'thugs' and 'terrorists', and the police were ordered to open fire upon them. But this time, protesters were quick to spread video footage captured on mobile phones via social networking sites, preventing the media blackout that had contained the Gafsa Revolt. By 27 December, the demonstrations had spread across the country, reaching Tunis itself and drawing the attention of the international media. Tunisia has one of the highest internet penetration rates in the Arab world and cyber-activists courageously worked to disrupt government efforts at censorship and misinformation, even as mobile telephones and the social media were used to orchestrate the demonstrations and connect activists to the population at large. Protesters were emboldened by images of themselves being broadcast on *al-Jazeera* and soon on local private television stations like *Nessma TV*. The barriers of fear and isolation were broken and, as the fatalities began to mount, outraged Tunisians from all sides of the political spectrum took to the streets.

Three distinct features marked the course of the revolution. Firstly, the protests were not organized by political parties or under ideological banners. They were genuinely inclusive and largely spontaneous. What organization existed was the product of the networks built between the civil society associations during their years of resistance to authoritarian impositions, particularly since the Gafsa Revolt and largely at the local or community level. Associations of lawyers, doctors, human rights activists, students, women, and journalists were quick to express their solidarity with the poor and unemployed who had initially seen Bouazizi's cause as their own, rapidly translating the motifs of economic grievance into a generalized call for political freedom and providing an unexpected middle-class thrust of solidarity. The political parties were barely visible at this stage. Most faced a clear crisis of their own, after decades of collusion with Ben Ali and with little credibility as active opposition. But *Ennahda* too was shy to take centre stage and the discourse of the revolution was clearly one of democracy and not Islam.

A second and more surprising aspect was the inability of the regime to formulate a coherent and effective response. On the one hand, Ben Ali used national television broadcasts to threaten protesters with the full force of the law, declared curfews and a national state of emergency, and unleashed the fury of the security forces at his command. But equally he sought to placate protesters with first the sacking of regional governors and junior ministers, then the entire government, and with promises of new elections within six months. In a final address on 13 January and unusually speaking in colloquial Tunisian rather than formal Arabic, he made unprecedented concessions, promising greater political and media freedoms while declaring he would not himself stand for office again.

By now, the weakness of his political position was becoming clear. Crucially, and a third significant feature of the Uprising, the army Chief of Staff, Rachid Ammar, refused Ben Ali's order that he turn the army against the protesters. The Tunisian army had not been a political player under either Bourguiba or Ben Ali, both presidents preferring to depend on internal security forces under their own direct patronage. Instead, the armed services were kept relatively small (around 35,000 strong) and had been professionalized, not least through their collaborations with the American and European militaries. Unlike the military in Egypt or Algeria, the Tunisian armed forces had not developed their own business empires and had no economic stake in protecting Ben Ali's regime. The defence budget was kept comparatively low (at around 1.5% of GDP; Lutterbeck, 2012: 7), the Ministry of Defence was civilianized, arms purchases were modest and the equipment manifesto was becoming progressively obsolete. Thus the military had no more cause to come to Ben Ali's aid than the RCD political apparatchiks being sidestepped by the ambitious conspirators in the Palace, or the businessmen excluded from opportunity by *la famille* and its cronies. Ultimately, the president had become a liability even to his own power base, a source of political instability and economic impoverishment rather than security and growth. Almost before he knew it, Ben Ali was being bundled onto an aeroplane and out of the country to ultimate exile in Saudi Arabia.

The interregnum

Ironically, Ben Ali was as much a victim of a constitutional coup as his predecessor. His replacement by first Prime Minister Mohammed Ghannouchi and later speaker of the National Assembly Fouad Mebazaa was managed through the invoking of the constitution by the same technocratic elites that Ben Ali had positioned around himself, backed by the army's commitment to secure the streets but make no direct political interventions. Significantly, rather than succumbing to a bloody internal squabble over who should now take power, they fell back on traditions of constitutionalism which go back to 1860, when the first constitution in the Arab world had been promulgated under French protectorate rule. Ghannouchi put together a new government on 17 January, making a gesture of reconciliation towards the protesters by offering cabinet places to leading opposition and civil society figures. But Tunisians were in no mood for compromise and the political figures now holding the reins of power had no power base of their own on which to fall back. Even as Ghannouchi was deploying a new Political Reform Committee (under jurist Yadh Ben Achour) to develop an institutional pathway to political reform, the opposition figures succumbed to pressure from the street, resigned from the government and formed a new Committee to Defend the Revolution. Over the next two months, and under sustained pressure from the organized opposition, intensively mobilized civil society, a media which had finally found its voice, and on-going battles between determined protesters and a heavy-handed police force, Ghannouchi's vision for piecemeal liberalization was forced to give way to a new broad-based consensus in favour of full democratic transition. RCD ministers, including Ghannouchi himself, were forced to first disown the party and then resign their government posts. The RCD was dissolved and the Political Reform Committee was merged into the Committee to Defend the Revolution, now re-named the Higher Commission for the Achievement of the Objectives of the Revolution. Finally, the State Security Division and other branches of political police were dissolved, eliminating the last institutional bastions of the *ancien regime*. All this was managed with the army doggedly remaining on the sidelines, refusing to intervene other than to ensure security for crucial institutional 'moments', such as the holding of the national baccalaureate exams, and new national elections in October (Gaaloul, 2011).

The new political elites represented in the Higher Commission determined that the crucial first stage of the transition would be the full revision of the constitution, addressing the imbalances of power which had so disastrously favoured the president over the legislature. A new legal framework was devised for elections to a Constituent Assembly to oversee this process, initially scheduled for July but later deferred until October (Murphy, 2013). The framework comprised three elements: a constituency-based electoral law based on a 'largest remainder' proportional representation system which favoured smaller parties; the establishment of an independent electoral commission (the *instance supérieur independent pour les elections*) and a set of laws regulating the funding and campaigning of political parties in the run-up to the elections. A heavy representation of lawyers and jurists in the Higher Commission ensured that an overarching concern with visibly-democratic processes prevailed, sometimes at the expense of operational efficiency and in ways which ultimately worked to constrain parties rather than enable them. The massive proliferation of legal parties and electoral lists disguised the advantages given to established party brands which were less in need of severely constrained campaign funding and media coverage. Indeed, with media coverage of the campaigns tightly controlled to ensure equity, the run-up to the elections was dominated less by discussions of policy specifics than by profound questions of identity and the proper nature of the state itself. With protesters still occupying key sites around the city, and with public confidence in the democratic process still fragile and untrusting, it did not take much for these debates to spill over into yet more protests on the streets.

The legalization of the Islamist *Ennahda* party had raised the possibility that the secular basis of the constitution and of the state itself might be challenged following the elections to the Constituent Assembly. *Ennahda* leaders repeatedly affirmed their commitment to the democratic processes and institutions of government, declaring that they would not seek to amend the progressive Personal Status Code, which had afforded Tunisian women a unique (for the Arab region) package of rights, including full equality as citizens. Ardent secularists in turn discounted these claims as disingenuous, and argued that should it come to power, the party would swiftly abandon them in favour of the *shari'ah*-based system advocated by an increasingly vocal *salafist* component. Incidents such as the screening by a private television company of a cartoon depicting God in human form, and the refusal by a university to allow a woman wearing the full Islamic *niqab* veil to register, generated highly-charged demonstrations and counter-demonstrations, with issues of women's rights, freedom of expression and the role of *shari'ah* dominating public discussions above arguably more urgent issues such as reviving an economy devastated first by Ben Ali and then by the uprising which had unseated him.

The bumpy road to Tunisian democracy

Nonetheless, in the end, the election results bore witness to the salience of these debates. Despite some concerns – largely over technical flaws – the elections were judged to be peaceful, free and fair, with vast numbers of Tunisians serving as polling station staff or domestic observers, standing as candidates, or simply voting. The overall turn-out figure of 52% of voters was not high, but in fact 86% of those who registered to vote, did so. Much to the surprise – and consternation – of many, *Ennahda* had won over 37% of the vote and 89 out of the 217 National Constituent Assembly (NCA) seats. The language of a restored Muslim identity, combined with republican politics and a promises of cross-party collaboration for the common good had earned them first place. They were further helped by what amounted to brand-recognition and for having been the most consistent opponents of Ben Ali, as well as by the failures of their secular opposition. The latter had proved unable to overcome their intrinsic elitism and personality-driven divisions to form an effective coalition against *Ennahda*. Those which announced themselves willing to work with *Ennahda* in government (like Moncef Marzouki's Congress for the Republic, which won 29 seats) did better than those which rejected collaboration (including Nejib Chebbi's Progressive Democratic Party). A surprise third place went to a new party, *Aridha Chaabia,* which was headed by a London-based businessman, Hachmi Hamdi. Hamdi had been discounted by many as inconsistent, even a buffoon. At one time a figure in the *Mouvement de la Tendance Islamist,* he had latterly owned a television station which had aired programmes sympathetic to Ben Ali. His campaign had focused on his home region of Sidi Bouzid, appealing to folk sentiments and promising to plough his personal fortune into its rehabilitation. When he appeared to have won a staggering 26 seats, his campaign was investigated and in a bizarrely arbitrary move the ISIE first discounted eight of the seats it had won, and then restored seven of them.

Allegations of illegal financial support for *Ennahda*, vote-buying and double-talk not withstanding, the elections suggested that Tunisians sought a rebalancing of the state to reflect a more culturally-bound Muslim identity than the adamantly secular modernism of Ben Ali. But they also showed that the majority of Tunisians remained wedded to a democratic vision for the future, albeit one marked by cross-party collaboration and ideological moderacy. This was not the mythical national consensus of the *ancien regime*, which privileged gradualism over radical political transformation and a fundamentalist form of *laïcité* over cultural expressions of Muslim identity, but rather a more fluid and pluralist consensus around the need for normative renewal. Tunisian journalist Jamel Dridi explained it thus:

> Under 23 years of dictatorship, Tunisians lost all their points of reference and their traditional and civil values. . . . In the old political system, the people in government behaved as in the mafia. They did not serve the state and its citizens, but rather used the state to rise to wealth on the shoulders of the citizens. . . . Ennahda was immediately perceived as a break with the past. Tunisians no doubt chose Ennahda because it represented the enemy to Ben Ali's regime. However, most of all Ennahda, whether rightly or wrongly, represented in the eyes of some of the population a return to morality, righteousness, and justice. . . . And it's not even a matter of religion, but rather of seeking direction and values (Mahjar-Barducci, 2012).

These are not, however, all-inclusive sentiments and since the elections the democratic transition process has been constantly challenged by a tide of *salafist* activism which seeks a very different future for the country.

Having won the elections, but not a majority, *Ennahda* chose to form a coalition government with its old *Collectif* partner, Moncef Marzouki's CRP, and the social democratic *Ettakatol* (the Democratic Forum for Labour and Liberties), collectively referred to as the Troika. It refused outright to deal with the party in third place, *al-Aridha Chaabia*, which was viewed as a maverick some-time ally of Ben Ali[3] despite Hamdi's populist rhetoric, and elected instead to work with the centre-left in a gesture towards national unity. The three main government posts, President of the Republic, President of the Constituent Assembly, and Prime Minister, were divvied up between them, Marzouki taking the first, *Ettakatol*'s Mustapha Ben Jaffar the second, and *Ennahda*'s Hamadi Jebalia the post of prime minister. Rachid Ghannouchi, the spiritual leader or sheikh of *Ennahda*, declared that he would not himself be seeking office. A speedily-agreed 'mini-constitution' set out the distribution of responsibilities and it was soon clear that, despite its ministerial minority, the Islamists would be gaining from a powerful premiership relative to a largely ceremonial presidency. Immediately *salafist* elements both inside the party and independent of it, began pushing for movement in more radical directions, demanding school and campus segregation, the Islamization of textbooks, harsh punishments for persons deemed to have offended Islam through the media and arts, and even for the implementation of *shari'ah* law. Groups such as *Ansar al-Sharia* and *Hizb al-Tahrir* engaged in targeted intimidation of secular political and media figures, violent demonstrations (which included the raid on the US Embassy in September 2012, in which four Tunisians were killed) and even the unilateral establishment of a 'caliphate' in the rural town of Sejnane.[4] Although analysts declare that such groups have only limited support, and then mostly in conservative rural areas, *Ennahda* leaders proved more ambiguous in their defence of republican values than their coalition partners had hoped. They failed to use the full capacities of the ministries of Religious Affairs, the Interior, and Human Rights and Transitional Justice (all under *Ennahda* ministers) to constrain such activism, largely turning a blind eye, and even seeming at times to endorse it.[5]

The publication of a first draft for the revised constitution, composed by an *Ennahda*-dominated committee, provoked particular outrage among liberals and secularists, with thousands taking to the streets in protest at articles which were deemed to be efforts at introducing an Islamic state through the back door (specifically redefining women as 'complementary' *(takāmul)* rather than equal to men, and threatening to criminalize blasphemy and thereby curtail freedom of expression and the media). Ultimately, however, *Ennahda* consistently chose to appease its coalition partners, withdrawing its enthusiasm for the blasphemy law, ensuring that commitments to women's equality were clear in the draft, and backing away from efforts to define Tunisia as an Islamic state or *shari'ah*-driven. Its leaders, however, defended their efforts to integrate *salafist* elements within educational and religious institutions as a means of moderating them, claiming that the alternative is alienation and greater radicalization.[6] Clearly, the party saw itself as treading a precarious path between the pragmatic demands of government and ideological pressures from below.

The continuing question marks over *Ennahda*'s republican commitments spurred Tunisian civil society and the secular opposition into new life, and at times into direct confrontations with *salafist* opponents. As the government sought to maintain arbitrary authority over the media, and with repeated attacks on the liberal media, striking journalists forced the government to implement Decrees 115 and 116, which guarantee freedom of information, protect the rights of journalists and establish an independent audio-visual commission. The trade union movement was re-invigorated with the election of a new leftist UGTT leadership which did not shy away from organizing strikes in protest at the government's inability to manage the country's economic and social woes. In turn, the UGTT was confronted with challenges from both the establishment of a new alternative Tunisian General Labour Confederation (CGTT) and from elements within the government itself, which mobilized thuggish attacks on union offices across the country in an effort to break leftist solidarities. Suspicions fell on *Ennahda*: as one unionist wrote, and referring to the close financial relations between that party and the Qatari government which many suggest accounted for *Ennahda*'s well-funded electoral campaign:

> Now, once again, the Tunisian regime, this time under the façade of a 'democratically' elected government, has decided to move onto the offensive in an attempt to intimidate its biggest threat: the organised working class. . . . The present government prefers indeed to defend the interests of its Qatari friends than to improve the social conditions of the majority (CWI, 2012: 2).[7]

Meanwhile, human rights organizations, judges unions and lawyers associations, lobbying vigorously for reform of the judicial system and women's organizations, sought to keep the defence of their social and political rights at the forefront of public debate. Political parties also appeared to be learning the lessons of the first elections: the insecurity of the coalition, and the seeming moves to the religious right by *Ennahda*, opened up the middle ground for new parties such as *Nidaa Tounis* (led by former Prime Minster Béji Caïd Essebsi) and alliances of democratic centre-left parties such as the Popular Front and *al-Joumhouri*. These could be seen as evidence not only that secular forces were maturing, overcoming personality-driven divisions and strategizing in advance of new elections, but also that the liberal middle classes were recovering from their post-Ben Ali angst and were reasserting themselves in the political domain.

This reassertion came not only out of concerns for the republican future of the state, but also from the deteriorating economic situation. The immediate fall-out from the Uprising included dramatic falls in tourist revenues and foreign direct investment (Achy, 2011).[8] Large sections of the Tunisian business sector were frozen as assets of *la famille* were seized by the state and temporarily frozen, and unemployment rose accordingly.[9] Caught by both a liquidity shortage and a downgraded sovereign debt rating, the interim government of Essebsi had drawn on international reserves to fund a short-term economic and social programme, which essentially spent public money on job creation and targeted social aid. After a year of close to zero growth in 2011, the *Ennahda*-led government, promising liberal business-friendly policies, also chose to pursue short-term gain over long-term structural reform, creating 25,000 new public sector jobs and deepening food and fuel subsidies in an effort to stimulate domestic demand. Ultimately, this could only scrape the surface of the unemployment crisis, with subsidies still insufficient to offset an inflation rate of over 5% per annum. The strategy came at the cost of a 20% rise in government spending which could not be sustained on the back of the sale of confiscated assets, money from by-gone privatizations, and special donations from abroad. The economy remained in urgent need of structural reforms, as well as the political stability which is needed to encourage foreign investors, tourists and international lenders to return (Achy, 2011). With labour protests and strikes weakening the economy further (El-Issawi, 2012: 4) and the government failing to vigorously pursue the corruption which had eroded investor confidence, the government resorted to an unpopular IMF Stand-by Loan agreement in June 2013.

A momentary whiff of optimism was soon dispelled. As this paper is being written, the summer of 2013 has seemed to all but derail Tunisia's democratic transition. The assassination of one popular leftist politician in February, the subsequent resignation of Prime Minister Hamidi Jebali, and a second assassination in July, have finally snapped many Tunisians' patience with *Ennahda* rule. Many were convinced of *Ennahda*'s complicity in the assassinations, or at least its negligence in containing the activism of Islamist militants behind them.[10] As tens of thousands took part in a general strike and repeated mass demonstrations in Tunis, the *Ettakatol* Party demanded that the government be dissolved and a national dialogue initiated with the intention of creating a new national salvation government. The National Constituent Assembly was dissolved by its president, Mustapha Ban Jafaar, as many of its members walked out, and the constitution-writing business was completely stalled. Meanwhile, the Tunisian army found itself fighting an intense military campaign against al-Qaeda affiliates in the western region along the border with Algeria. The UGTT found a new role for itself mediating between the government and opposition, but weeks of political stalemate and public protest saw the economy begin to nosedive and the introduction of deeply unpopular austerity measures designed to prevent complete budgetary collapse. Finally, on 28 September, *Ennahda* capitulated and the government agreed to resign in favour of a negotiated caretaker government which will see the country through to new elections.

The state we're in

The fragility of Tunisia's democracy today is clear. The deadline set for the agreement of a new constitution has passed and the capacity of a new caretaker government to see elections through is uncertain. The parties in the coalition Troika have indicated that their own partnership will not extend into the new era (al-Monitor, 2012) and the opposition parties now have to adjust their agendas from simply the removal of *Ennahda* to clear programmes for action. Arguably, a maturing pluralism is replacing the consensus-oriented politics which held the state together in the immediate aftermath of the Uprising. But Tunisian parties are still better at articulating what Tunisians *don't* want, than how to achieve what they *do* want.

On the positive side, *Ennahda*'s capitulation to the widespread demands that they hand over power indicates its ultimate commitment to a democratic republic. The argument made by the secular opposition that their secret agenda is one person-one vote-one time loses salience when confronted with a voluntary (if begrudging) withdrawal from government. Tunisia has ultimately navigated a complex and bitter political breakdown, which reflects the deepest ideological and identity-based divisions in society, without resorting to either civil war or military coup.

But the gloves may now be off and, with *Ennahda* on the defensive, will it swap its current alliance for one with more conservative religious, even *salafi*, groups? Will the secular parties recklessly take advantage of this victory to move against Islamist parties of all shades, to exclude them from Tunisia's political future? Put bluntly, the "twin tolerations" of religious citizens towards the state on the one hand and of the state towards its religious citizens on the other, which seemed to determine the success of the October 2011 elections (Stepan, 2012), are no longer secure. The question which Tunisians must now confront is whether there remains any fundamental national consensus or collective identity around which they can build a shared future and, if so, what does it look like?

Notes

1. The use of the label 'revolution' in this context is often contested. It is used here in recognition of the scale of the popular mobilization but acknowledging the theoretical difficulties attached therewith.
2. In 2009, the World Bank's International Bank for Reconstruction and Development noted an average annual growth rate of 5% per annum over the previous twenty years, comparable with other mid-range development stars such as Taiwan, Turkey, Poland and Brazil (IBRD, 2009: 2).

3. After the revolution, the newly-formed Commission for the Investigation of Corruption published a letter dating back to 2009 in which Hamdi wrote to Ben Ali, confirming that he would air a series of programmes on his television channel high-lighting 'democratic' progress under the president in return for financial support.

4. The move to implement *shari'ah* law in the small town of Sejnane was driven by Hichem Merchegui, who is reportedly linked to al-Qaeda. The term 'sejnanistan' has been coined by secularists to describe efforts to impose Islamic dress and standards of behaviour.

5. Incidents have included *salafist* students replacing the Tunisian flag with a black *salafi* flag; demands from women to wear the *niqab* during university examinations; the legalization of the salafist *al-Islah* (Reform Front) party; the attack on the editor-in-chief of *al-Maghreb*, who had supported the owner of *Nessma TV*, Nabil Karoui, when the latter was fined by the courts for his airing of *Persopolis* on the grounds that he disturbed public order and violated sacred values; the sentencing of individuals to heavy prison terms for allegedly "mocking Islam" on social media; the defence of polygamy by Transitional Justice Minister Samir Dilou and his subsequent comments that homosexuality is a "perversion that required medical treatment"; *Ennahda* delegate Souad Abderrahim's comment that single mothers were a "disgrace to Tunisia"; a conference hosted by Hizb al-Tahrir at which delegates denounced women's rights as articulated in secular texts; an attack on a Constitutional Council member in Kelibia; and the gang-rape of a woman by policy who argued that she had been found in an indecent posture with her boyfriend.

6. In October 2012, a leaked video showed Islamist leader Rachid Ghannouchi lecturing *salafists* to be patient, warning them that "the army and the police are not safe" and that the state apparatus is still in the hands of the secularists. Ghannouchi claimed the video was taken out of context, that moderate *salafists* were being demonized, and that doing that would only bring them to power in the long run (Reuters, 2012).

7. According to the CWI, Islamist leader Sadok Chourou, declared in the National Assembly that strikers were "enemies of God", that the best solution for ending strikes was force, and that the Qur'an suggested anything from cutting off a hand or leg to crucifixion was appropriate.

8. Estimates for lost tourism revenues amount to 50% in 2011, with a corresponding 20% decline in FDI. Over eighty foreign companies closed their Tunisia operations.

9. By 200,000 people in 2011 alone according to Achy (2011), or 2% according to the IMF (2012).

10. One of the suspects behind both assassinations and the attack on the US embassy in 2012 had been allowed to roam free round Tunis, orchestrating the activities of *Ansar al-Sharia*, an al-Qaeda affiliated group with – until August 2013 – *Ennahda* protection.

References

Achy, L. (2011), *Tunisia's Economic Challenges*, Washington, DC: Carnegie Middle East Center.

Albers, R. and M. Peeters (2011), *Food and Energy Prices: Government Subsidies and Fiscal Balances in Southern Mediterranean Countries*, European Economy Papers 431, Brussels: European Commission.

Alexander, C. (2010), *Tunisia: Stability and Reform in the Modern Maghreb*, London: Routledge.

Alexander, C. (2011), "A Month Made for Drama", in M. Lynch, S.B. Glasser and B. Hounshell, eds., *Revolution in the Arab World: Tunisia, Egypt, and the Unmaking of an Era*, Washington, DC: Foreign Policy and the Slate Group, pp. 45–49.

Al-Monitor (2012), "Secular Tunisian Party Set to Drop Islamist Ennahda after 2013 Vote", available from www.al-monitor.com/pulse/fr/contents/articles/politics/2012/10/tunisia-secular-party-set-to-drop-islamist-ennahda-after-2013-vote.html, accessed on 16 June 2015.

Belhassine, N. et al. (2009), *From Privilege to Competition: Unlocking Private-Led Growth in the Middle East and North Africa*, MENA Development Report, Washington, DC: World Bank.

Bertelsmann Stuftung (2011), *BTI 2010 Tunisia Country Report*, available from www .bertelsmann-transformation-index.de/145.0.html?L=1, accessed on 27 September 2011.

Cavatorta, F. and R.H. Haugbølle (2012), "The End of Authoritarian Rule and the Mythology of Tunisia under Ben Ali", in *Mediterranean Politics*, 17(2), pp. 179–195.

CWI Committee for Workers International (2012), "Tunisia: Hands off the UGTT Union!", available from www.socialisworld.net/doc/5599, posted on 24 February 2012, accessed on 26 October 2012.

El-Issawi, F. (2012), *The Tunisian Transition: The Evolving Face of the Second Republic*, available as pdf from www2.lse.ac.uk/IDEAS/publications/re, accessed on 31 October 2012.

Erdle, S. (2011), *Industrial Policy in Tunisia*, Bonn: German Development Institute.

European Union (2010), *European Neighbourhood and Partnership Instrument: Tunisia Strategy Paper 2007–2013 and National Indicative Programme (2007–2010)*, available at https://ec.europa.eu/europeaid/strategy-paper-2007-2013-and-national-indicative-programme-2007%E2%80%932010-tunisia_en, accessed on 16 June 2015.

FAO (2011), "World Food Situation", available at www/fao.org/worldfoodsituation/wfs-home/foodpricesindex/en/, accessed on 27 September 2011.

Gaaloul, B. (2011), "Back to the Barracks: The Tunisian Army Post-Revolution" *Sada*, Carnegie Endowment, available from www.carnegieendowment.org/2011/11/03back-to-barracks-tunisian-army-post-revolution, accessed on 7 November 2011.

Gobe, E. (2011), "The Gafsa Mining Basin Between Riots and a Social Movement: Meaning and Significance of a Protest Movement in Ben Ali's Tunisia", available at https://halshs .archives-ouvertes.fr/halshs-00557826/document, accessed on 15 June 2015.

Haugbølle, R.H. and F. Cavatorta (2011), "Will the Real Tunisian Opposition Please Stand Up? Opposition Coordination Failures under Authoritarian Constraints", in *British Journal of Middle Eastern Studies*, 38(3), pp. 323–343.

Hibou, B. (2011), *The Force of Obedience: The Political Economy of Repression in Tunisia*, Cambridge: Polity Press, English edition, first published in French as *La force de 'obéissance* by Editions La Découverte, Paris, 2006.

International Bank for Reconstruction and Development (IBRD) (2009), *Country Partnership Strategy for the Republic of Tunisia*, Washington, DC: The World Bank.

International Monetary Fund (IMF) (2010), *World Economic Outlook 2010*, Washington, DC: IMF, available from www.imf.org?external/pubs/ft/weo/2010/02/weodata/weorept. aspx?sy=2002&, accessed on 18 October 2012.

International Monetary Fund (IMF) (2012), "Tunisia Faces Economic Social Challenges amid Historic Transformation", *IMF Survey Magazine*, available from www.imf.org/ external/pubs/ft/survey/so/2012/car090512a.htm, accessed 31 October 2012.

Labidi, N. et al. (2011), *Food Security in Tunisia: Rapid Assessment Report*, Rome: World Food Programme.

Lewis, A. (2011), "Tracking Down the Ben Ali and Trebelsi Fortune", *BBC News Africa*, 31 January 2011, available from www.bbc.co.uk/news/world-africa-12302659, accessed on 4 October 2011.

Lutterback, D. (2012), *After the Fall: Security Sector Reform in Post-Ben Ali Tunisia*, Arab Reform Initiative, available at www.arab-reform.net/after-fall-security-sector-reform-post-ben-ali-tunisia, accessed on 16 June 2015.

Magharebia (2011), "Ben Ali Trabelsi Assets Found in Twenty-Five Countries", in *Magharebia*, available from http://magharabia.com/en_GB/articles/awi/newsbriefs/general/2011/ 06/02, . . . accessed on 4 October 2011.

Mahjar-Barducci, A. (2012), "Understanding the 'Islamist Wave' in Tunisia", available from www.rubincenter.org/2012/04/understanding-the-%E2%80%9Cislamist-wave%E2% 80%9D-in-tunisia/, accessed on 15 June 2015.

Mubila, M. et al. (2011), *The Middle of the Pyramid: Dynamics of the Middle Class in Africa*, Chief Economist Complex Market Brief, Tunis: African Development Bank.

Murphy, E. (1999), *Economic and Political Change in Tunisia: From Bourguiba to Ben Ali*, Basingstoke: Macmillan.

Murphy, E. (2012), "Under the Emperor's Neo-liberal Clothes: How the IFIs Got It Wrong in Tunisia", in N. Gana (ed.), *Mapping and Remapping the Tunisian Revolution*, Edinburgh: Edinburgh University Press, 35–57.

Murphy, E. (2013), "The Tunisian Elections of October 2011: A Democratic Consensus", in *Journal of North African Studies*, 18(2), pp. 231–247.

Reuters (2012), "Tunisian Islamist Leader Says Salafis Must Not Be Demonized", available on www.reuters.com/article/2012/10/18/us-tunisia-salafis-idUSBRE89HQ920121, accessed on 19 October 2012.

Sadiki, L. (2008), "Engendering Citizenship in Tunisia", in Y. Zoubir and H. Amirah-Fernádez (eds.), *North Africa: Politics, Region, and the Limits of Transformation*, Oxon: Routledge, pp. 109–132.

Schraeder, P.J. and H. Redissi (2011), "Ben Ali's Fall", *Journal of Democracy*, 22(3), pp. 5–19.

Stepan, A. (2012), "Tunisia's Transition and the Twin Tolerations", in *Journal of Democracy*, 22(2), pp. 89–103.

WikiLeaks (2008), *Corruption in Tunisia: What's Yours Is Mine*. Classified cable from Ambassador Robert F. Godec to Secretary of State Washington, DC, Reference ID 08 TUNIS679, EO 12958, 23 June 2008, available from http://wikileaks.ch/cable/2008/06/08TUNIS679. html, accessed on 7 October 2011.

PART III

North Africa in world affairs

15

THE EVOLVING FOREIGN POLICIES OF NORTH AFRICAN STATES (2011–2014)

New trends in constraints, political processes and behavior[1]

Miguel Hernando de Larramendi
and Irene Fernández Molina

One of the least explored aspects of the relationship between foreign and domestic policy, where a static view has generally prevailed, concerns the dynamic effects of institutional change and regime change – discontinuity at the internal level – on the states' foreign policy behavior. Starting from a basic framework of Foreign Policy Analysis (FPA), this chapter will examine how the political transformations in North Africa since the 2011 uprisings affected foreign policy in five countries: Morocco, Algeria, Tunisia, Libya and Egypt. The heterogeneity and asymmetry of the domestic changes that these states have witnessed are recognized from the outset, as is the fluid and open nature of the current situation in the region, which only allows identifying some broad trends and drifts. The main argument defended with this empirical stocktaking, based on press articles and topical analyses, is that these countries' pressing financial constraints and security imperatives in their borderlands ultimately prevented any change of direction or transgression of the existing patterns in their foreign policies, in spite of the accession of some new actors into the decision-making structures. In short, structure prevailed over agency.

The analysis of the recent evolution of these foreign policies will focus on three levels (Hinnebusch & Ehteshami 2002: 1–27; Nonneman 2005: 19–29; Korany & Dessouki 2009: 29–41). The first section addresses the contextual factors or constraints (*why*) in four different settings: international or global, regional, sub-regional and domestic environments. The second section looks more closely at the domestic arena, analyzing changes in policymaking and decision-making (*how*) in a situation where persistent centralization coexists with a relative increase in participation, greater importance of the dynamics of coalition building and cohabitation in power of very different political forces, as well as growing influence of public opinion.

Finally, three tendencies are examined regarding the resulting foreign policy output or behavior *(what)*. The first of them is the continuity in the basic external orientations of each state, including the absence of international normalization or realignment processes. The second is the pursuance of essentially cautious and adaptive foreign policies, as observed at both the regional level (re-composition of alliances, combination of revolutionary solidarity with good neighborliness with the regimes having resisted the wave of protests, temporary perception of encircle-ment of the Algerian regime) and international level (maintenance of previous patterns in bilateral relations with the EU, pragmatism and search for engagement and recognition by mainstream Islamism, two-level games in relations with the United States). The third trend is the ups and downs of regionalism at the mercy of the circumstances, at a time when its resurgence was more rhetorical than effective.

1. Determinants of foreign policy: New constraints and opportunities in the international, regional and neighborhood environments

1.1. Looking desperately for international funding

The international stage on which the political changes of 2011–2014 occurred was, above all, one of global economic and financial crisis. Yet, the baseline structural conditions of North African countries were substantially dissimilar. On the one hand, there were the mixed oil-based economies whose income essentially came from their abundant energy resources (Libya and Algeria), while on the other there were the more open and diversified "semi-rentier" economies (Alissa 2007: 2) of countries that were poor in hydrocarbons, depending more on the export of agri-cultural products and manufactured goods, foreign investment, migrant remittances and tourism (Egypt, Tunisia and Morocco). The common anomaly was – and is – low productivity and a marked external dependence. It was from the outside that the economic shock was transmitted into this area in an indirect (non-financial) fashion, but bearing critical consequences eventually (Mañé 2011).

In a second phase, since mid-2011, the earlier precarious situation was aggravated by additional economic turmoil triggered by ongoing political transformations, especially in countries where they took a revolutionary turn, virtually paralyzing domestic activity for months (Tunisia, Egypt). The downturn in economic growth was accompanied, in most cases, by an ostensible deterioration in macroeconomic balances, both domestic (public accounts) and foreign (balance of payments and foreign exchange reserves). Only the mixed oil-based economies of Algeria and Libya, sustained by their hydrocarbon exports, avoided current account deficits (Escribano 2013).

This economic structure and situation of dependence, uncertainty and vulner-ability, which were considerably more serious in the countries poor in hydrocar-bons, acted as a powerful constraint – probably the most determining one – on the North African foreign policies in 2011–2014. The lack of growth and budget-ary difficulties to face demands for increased public expenditure, a key element of political legitimacy, turned attracting foreign investment and financing into an unavoidable priority. This has forced these countries to be flexible and pragmatic in their relations with the U.S., the European Union (EU) and multilateral financial institutions, while at the same time tirelessly wooing the wealthy Arab Gulf states. Expectations or promises of a more assertive and autonomous foreign policy with respect to the West invariably ran up against this need, albeit not without domestic controversies and negotiations.[2]

The most telling example of this two-level game (Putnam 1988) was the negotiation process between post-revolutionary Egypt and the International Monetary Fund (IMF). In 2011, the growing budget deficit in Cairo coincided with an alarming reduction in the foreign exchange reserves, the result of losses of revenue and the decision not to devalue the pound. In its urgent search for financial assistance, the provisional government of Essam Sharaf initially opted for a policy of "local" borrowing, i.e., drawing on Arab or domestic sources instead of the unpopular international financial institutions. Hence a $3-billion loan from the IMF was rejected in June 2011. Such a risky decision was explained by the Egyptian government's confidence in the alternative financial support, more generous ($10 billion) and subject to less conditionality, from Saudi Arabia, the United Arab Emirates (UAE) and Qatar. However, at the beginning of 2012, not even a tenth of the promised Arab funding had been disbursed.[3]

In these circumstances, the cabinet of Kamal Ganzouri (December 2011–August 2012) had to step back and reopen negotiations with the IMF. However, the members of parliament from the Muslim Brotherhood's Freedom and Justice Party (FJP), who had obtained a large majority in both chambers in the elections held between November 2011 and March 2012, rejected the agreement on the grounds that an interim government should not take such a far-reaching decision.[4] Shortly after being elected president, the also *brother* Mohammed Morsi formally requested a $4.8-billion IMF loan,[5] going back on some of the earlier resistances of his fellow party members. In November 2012, it was announced that an agreement of principles had been reached. Although the deal never materialized in the end, the tug-of-war was protracted between, on the one hand, the preferences of many of the domestic actors and the Islamist rank and file and, on the other hand, President Morsi's pragmatism – and continuity with the orthodox foreign economic policy of ousted Hosni Mubarak.

Egypt was not the only North African country to seek financial assistance from the IMF in these years. In August 2012, the Fund approved a two-year program for Morocco in the amount of $6.2 billion within the framework of the Precautionary Liquidity Line (PLL).[6] The Tunisian government led by Secretary General of al-Nahda Hamadi Jebali considered the possibility of requesting a credit line of $2.5 billion for 2014.[7] In any case, the leaders of both Tunisia and Morocco were sure that the focus of their foreign economic relations would continue to be the EU, for trade, investment and financial assistance alike. This was another essential factor behind the continuity of their foreign relations. Even Morocco was willing to put aside its permanent territory-related tensions with Spain and stage a new bilateral honeymoon in a high-level meeting held in October 2012 for the sake of mutual economic interests.

On the other hand, this almost structural pro-Europeanism did not prevent Tunisia and Morocco from trying to diversify their relationships and, above all, seek alternative sources of funding (Albarracín & Cusí 2012). Beyond the imperatives of geographical contiguity and revolutionary solidarity, this was one of the clearest motivations behind the efforts made by the new Tunisian authorities to strengthen bilateral relations with oil-rich Libya. Indeed, the eastern neighboring country was the destination of the first trip abroad taken by Moncef Marzouki after being elected President of the Republic in December 2011. After the fall of Muammar Qaddafi, the Benghazi-based rebel forces from the Libyan National Transitional Council (NTC) made assurances that they would give priority to Tunisia in their economic deals as a reward for its vital support – and for receiving hundreds of thousands of Libyan refugees – during the civil war against the toppled regime.[8] The potential complementarities or synergies between two neighboring countries with such different economic structures were conspicuous, beginning with the promised participation of Tunisian companies and workers in Libya's post-conflict reconstruction.[9]

But the targets par excellence of the economic courting by Morocco, Tunisia and Egypt were the Arab Gulf countries. Most prominently, after Morsi's military ouster and the electoral confirmation of General Abdel Fattah el-Sisi as the Egyptian president, it was Cairo's "heavy and unprecedented dependence" on mainly Saudi financial assistance that appeared as a major factor likely to shape his foreign policy – for example his stance on the Syrian conflict (Dunne 2014). This brought to the forefront the less privileged states' difficulties in finding a balance between their economic and political imperatives in this context. The best example was the hesitations surrounding the unusual offer made to Morocco to join the Gulf Cooperation Council (GCC). The invitation was extended during a summit of the heads of state of the GCC held in Riyadh in May 2011 and included both the distant North African kingdom – a geographical incongruity – and neighboring Jordan[10] (the difference was that the latter, bordering Saudi Arabia, had asked to join this regional organization 15 years earlier). In Rabat, the proposal was initially received with a mixture of surprise ("avec un grand intérêt") and gratitude.[11]

The explanation for the initial favorable Moroccan reaction lay, above all, in economic interests – in contrast to the motivations of the GCC, which were primarily political and strategic. In addition to attracting more investment from the Gulf States, like that flowing into Morocco since the early 2000s, joining this regional organization would open the prospect of free movement of labor to the markets of its thriving founding members (Achy 2011).[12] The deep economic crisis in the EU and the Eurozone, Morocco's natural economic partner, made it even more advisable to explore this avenue.[13] However, months later significant reservations began to emerge among the authorities in Rabat, who now claimed to prefer an "advanced association" or "advanced status" to full membership of the GCC.[14] Rabat's step back was probably due to the fear that officially entering the club of conservative Arab monarchies most resistant to democratic change would backfire from a political point of view, at a time when foreign and domestic expectations were moving in exactly the opposite direction and major efforts were being made to *sell* the July 2011 constitutional reform in Europe and the U.S. In any case, the plan was definitively aborted shortly afterwards because of a lack of consensus between the members of the GCC and Saudi Arabia's withdrawal of support.[15]

1.2. Security imperatives in the immediate sub-regional environment

Also driven by primarily economic factors, another emerging element in the international context of North African foreign policies in 2011–2014 was China's growing influence in this region (Bregolat Obiols 2010; Nicolas 2011). Likewise, Russia was to seize the opportunity opened by old and new Arab leaders' uncertainty about European and U.S. support, and their desire to diversify their international partners by strengthening relations especially with more status quo-oriented powers. In the broader regional context of the Middle East and North Africa, the leading player at this time was the GCC, both as a block and as a heterogeneous collection of individual states – due to the differences between the interests and the internal dynamics of each regime. Its *rediscovery* and fight for greater influence in North Africa developed on two planes: the political-religious sphere, supporting emerging organizations like the Muslim Brotherhood (Qatar) and the Salafist movements (Saudi Arabia), and the economic sphere, providing generous financial assistance for the reconstruction of the southern Mediterranean economies (Colombo et al. 2012; Tocci et al. 2012; Ayub et al. 2013; Schumacher & Fernández Molina 2013). Its competitors in this domain were Iran and Turkey, two non-Arab powers that had been very active on the regional scene since the end of the Iraq War (2003) and viewed the 2011 political transformations as an unprecedented window of opportunity for their pretensions of leadership (Falk 2012).

In any event, beyond these shared regional trends, the priority for North African foreign policies continued to be constraints arising from the most immediate sub-regional context, i.e., country-specific security concerns due to risks or threats in border or neighboring areas.[16] For Egypt, the main issue of this type was the deterioration in the security situation in the Sinai Peninsula after the fall of the Mubarak regime. The revolution and partial withdrawal of security forces created a dangerous power vacuum in the area, which had already witnessed an increase in criminal activity and Bedouin political violence in previous years (attacks on infrastructure, kidnappings and some terrorist acts). The intensification of these actions and armed clashes with the police raised the specter of Islamist radicalization (Attalah 2012; Goodman 2012).

In the realm of foreign policy, this instability in the Sinai directly affected Egypt's relations with Israel. The need to deploy sufficient police and troops to maintain security in the area was at odds with the appendix to the 1979 bilateral peace treaty that stipulated the demilitarization of most of the peninsula, limiting the presence of armed forces. The demand to pragmatically review this provision, without disputing the treaty as a whole, was subject to growing consensus on the Egyptian political landscape. Leaders in Cairo were also well aware of the advisability of avoiding a military build-up that would threaten the perception of security in Israel – which, in turn, sped up the construction of a protective fence along this 250-kilometer-long border. Substantial divergences persisted, on the other hand, between the approaches of the military and President Morsi on how to cope with insecurity in the Sinai (heavy-handed versus softer tactics), which arguably represented one of the triggering factors for the military ouster of the latter in July 2013 (Aziz 2013). Morsi's military successor, President Sisi, was to put his preference for harsh and expeditious methods into practice in October 2014, when he reacted to a terrorist attack that killed 33 Egyptian soldiers in North Sinai by launching a major military campaign, declaring a state of emergency in this governorate and creating a security buffer zone between the Egyptian side of the border town of Rafah and the Gaza Strip – which required evacuating residents and demolishing houses.[17]

Even more serious was the state of "borderline chaos" (Cole 2012) faced by the new Libyan NTC authorities following the internal conflict underway in 2011. The mismanagement of the 4,300-kilometer-long desert border of this country, in a virtual state of state absence after the collapse of the Qaddafi regime (Wehrey 2013), gave rise to the illegal trafficking of arms, people and narcotics, in addition to the smuggling of fuel and other goods. The security risks inherent in this situation extended far beyond the Libyan territory. Among other things, the uncontrolled circulation and proliferation of arms coming from Libya throughout the Sahel region – along with the return home of hundreds of Tuareg paramilitary forces who had been serving in Qaddafi's Islamic Pan-African Legion – were instrumental in prompting the crisis that unfolded in northern Mali in early 2012.

To deal with this muddle, in December 2012, the Libyan General National Congress decided to provisionally close the borders with Algeria, Niger, Chad and Sudan and declare the country's entire southern region a closed military zone under emergency law.[18] At the same time, Prime Minister Ali Zeidan called for a regional summit on border security to be held without delay. In January 2013, he met in Ghadames with his peers from Tunisia and Algeria, with whom he agreed to form joint patrols to monitor the borders. The EU also offered to send a civilian Common Security and Defense Policy (CSDP) mission to build Libya's capacities for border security and management.[19]

In mid-2014, as security vacuum and factional violence mounted further, developing into a full-blown civil war, it was Libya's big eastern and western neighbors that intervened in different ways. After retired Libyan general Khalifa Haftar launched an anti-Islamist military operation in Benghazi without any authorization from the central government, which was seen as a hardly disguised coup attempt, Sisi's Egypt reportedly supported Emirati airstrikes in eastern Libya with the purpose of assisting the new breakaway faction of the Libyan military. The Cairo government officially denied any direct military involvement, though (Wehrey, Bishop & Alrababa'h 2014). In the following months, in the context of the legitimacy crisis created by two rival governments claiming authority in Libya, Egypt considered as "legitimate" the one based in Tobruk, whose Prime Minister Abdullah al-Thani visited Cairo in October to seek help against "terrorism".[20] Meanwhile, Algeria raised its diplomatic profile as mediator with an initiative to host inclusive inter-Libyan dialogue[21] – rejecting any military solution outright – for which it received praise from the U.S., the UN and the EU in September–October 2014.

In Sahelian Mali, the Tuareg insurrection led by the secular National Movement for the Liberation of Azawad, and the humiliating retreat south of Bamako's army, left the immense northern territory under the control of the rebels, who were progressively displaced by their local Islamist allies (Ansar al Dine) and Al Qaeda in the Islamic Maghreb (AQIM). This evolution set off alarms in the international community, which viewed the new North African failing state as a breeding ground for imminent terrorist and criminal threats. The Economic Community of West African States (ECOWAS) led the mediating efforts to find a negotiated solution, while at the same time preparing for the possibility of an international military intervention to assist Mali's armed forces in recovering control of the breakaway region, supported by the UN Security Council in October 2012 (Resolution 2071, unanimously adopted).

All of this brought to the forefront the strategic role that neighboring Algeria was called on to play in either scenario. The responsibility placed upon this state stemmed from its status as a regional military power and its geographical contiguity with the area in question – sharing a border of more than 1,000 kilometers – as well as the experience of its authorities in fighting Islamist terrorism and its intelligence services' direct knowledge of the organizations operating there. Among other things, in 2006 the Algerian government had already helped to negotiate the so-called Algiers Accords between the Malian government and the Tuareg rebels. Because of this, the country was put under intense diplomatic pressure to become involved in the budding intervention, a possibility that President Abdelaziz Bouteflika and his government rejected outright, holding fast to the doctrine of non-interference in internal affairs (Dris-Aït Hamadouche 2014).

Principles aside, Algiers' real fear was long-lasting destabilization in its historical backyard due to the Western adventure and a spillover of the terrorist threat onto its own territory, at a time of internal political uncertainty, when the main concern was to shield the legitimacy of the regime itself. Neither the actions taken by the ECOWAS, which was seen as an African organization subordinate to French interests, nor the announced participation of Morocco in their plans generated confidence in this country. The Algerian alternative was to increase diplomatic contacts with all the parties in order to find a "political solution" to the conflict, which was still considered feasible (Arieff 2012; Boukhars 2012; Zoubir 2012b; Ammour 2013; Charef 2013). At the same time, what initially appeared to be a burden and a source of political headaches was to become a very effective weapon for enhancing the international profile of this state, which was now energetically cultivated by the U.S., France and other countries (Dennison 2012: 3). The "terrorism rent" (Keenan 2012: 202–204) could once again be exploited successfully, this time in its regional security version. For example, the crisis in Mali was the main focus of U.S. Secretary of State Hillary Clinton's trip to Algiers in October 2012 and of the first visit in history by a British Prime Minister to this capital, made by David Cameron in January 2013.

Finally, the advance of the Ansar al Dine and AQIM militias towards Bamako precipitated French intervention at the request of Mali's president in January 2013, with the backing of the ECOWAS and UN authorization. Amidst internal controversy and some hesitation, the Algerian authorities opted then for a "mix of cautious diplomacy and technical cooperation", "doctrine and pragmatism",[22] which led them to authorize French airplanes to fly over its airspace.[23] This reluctant concession would soon turn against them: it was the pretext used days later by the terrorist group responsible for attacking and taking hostages at the In Amenas gas plant, which resulted in a cumbersome operation by the Algerian army (and more than 60 dead, including 29 of the attackers). More broadly speaking, the French intervention largely spoiled Algiers' enduring approach to security in the Sahel (Nickels 2013b).

Morocco, a non-permanent member of the UN Security Council in 2012–2013, also saw the Mali crisis, from the very beginning, as an opportunity to pursue its own foreign policy interests. The security risks and growing international terrorist presence in the Sahel had long been a recurring theme in Moroccan diplomatic discourse, implicitly or explicitly linked to the failure to resolve the Western Sahara conflict (Desrues & Hernando de Larramendi 2012). Inflating the threat, Rabat sought to draw attention and ensure the great powers' support for its positions on this issue, especially after launching its Autonomy Plan (under Moroccan sovereignty) for the disputed territory in 2007.[24] In 2012, therefore, the Moroccan representative regularly highlighted the Sahel in the Security Council sessions.[25] Although Islamist Minister of Foreign Affairs Saad-Eddine El Othmani claimed to give priority to mediation and a political solution for Mali[26] – as a sample of double discourse or division of roles – Morocco in fact cosponsored the French draft for resolution 2071 (12 October 2012), voted for resolution 2085 (20 December 2012) and expressly supported intervention plans put forward by France and ECOWAS, an organization with which it maintained good relations.[27]

In September 2013, after the election of Ibrahim Boubacar Keïta as the new Malian President, Mohammed VI swiftly ordered the shipment of humanitarian aid and attended the investiture in person, together with his top security advisors, trying to secure that Bamako remained within Morocco's sphere of influence and as far as possible from Algeria and the Polisario Front.[28] Rabat also took advantage of the situation to give fresh impetus to its relations with the Sahel states and the Community of Sahel-Saharan States (CEN-SAD), a 23-member organization founded by Libya, which Morocco joined in 2001, in yet another attempt to compensate for its absence from the African Union (AU),[29] and which it now wanted to lead (Nickels 2013a).[30] All in all, the "enlargement of the Maghreb security complex into the Sahel" entailed increased diplomatic competition and a "policy of mutual institutional exclusion" between Algeria and Morocco (Boserup, Martinez & Holm 2014: 42–44).

Predictably enough, the Western Sahara issue was always at the background of all of these moves.[31] In fact, Morocco had to weather two serious crises on this front in May 2012 and April 2013. The first one arose from its own withdrawal of confidence from Christopher Ross, the UN Secretary-General's personal envoy for the conflict. The decision was officially justified by arguing that negotiations were at a standstill, buried in secondary matters, and Ross' actions had been "unbalanced and partial".[32] However, Rabat had to step back months later, having failed to force the dismissal or resignation of the diplomat, who was firmly backed by Ban Ki-moon and the U.S. administration. The second crisis was triggered by the U.S. attempt to extend the mandate of the UN Mission for the Referendum in Western Sahara (MINURSO) to the monitoring of human rights in both the disputed territory under Moroccan control and the Polisario-ruled refugee camps in Tindouf, Algeria – a scenario frantically rejected by Rabat. This time Morocco's maneuvers were much more successful, as they eventually got the U.S. to take back its original initiative before the final vote at the Security Council (Fernández Molina 2013a and 2013b).

2. Decision-making within uncertain cohabitations

The North African foreign policy decision-making processes continued to be largely opaque at this stage, both in countries engaged in post-revolutionary processes and in those where the status quo in the distribution of power prevailed. The success of Islamist parties at the polls in Egypt, Tunisia and Morocco gave these movements access to governmental responsibilities within the framework of asymmetric cohabitations that differed from case to case. The structure of each of these cohabitations determined the parties' ability to participate in or influence the decision-making processes of foreign and security policies, one of the cornerstones of power that the former regimes' actors were most reluctant to abandon and where Islamist movements lacked proven experience.

In Tunisia, the Islamist al-Nahda party formed a coalition government in December 2011 with two liberal, left-wing groups, agreeing to provisionally share institutional responsibilities until a new constitution could be drafted and presidential and legislative elections held. Hamadi Jebali, Secretary-General of al-Nahda, was to head the interim government while Moncef Marzouki, Secretary-General of the Congress for the Republic (CPR), was appointed President of the Republic, and Mustapha ben Jaafar, Secretary-General of the Democratic Forum for Labor and Liberties (al-Takattul), became chairman of the National Constituent Assembly (NCA). The provisional law organizing public powers assigned responsibility for foreign policy, jointly and by consensus, to the President of the Republic and the head of government (Art. 11).[33] The position of Minister of Foreign Affairs was held between December 2011 and March 2013 by Rafik Abdessalam, a member of al-Nahda and son-in-law of the historic party leader Rached Ghannouchi. This power-sharing created a duumvirate that turned out to be dysfunctional and generated publically visible tensions, for example, when the government unilaterally approved the extradition of former Libyan Prime Minister al-Baghdadi al-Mahmoudi in September 2012. The lack of prior consultation prompted an angry official statement from the President of the Republic that decried the decision as "illegal".[34]

These differences constantly hindered the running of the coalition government at a time when it was worn down by the deterioration in the socioeconomic situation and the increase in political violence. The deep political crisis provoked in February 2013 by the killing of secular leftist opposition leader Chokri Belaid revealed tensions inside the *troika*. Al-Nahda formed a new coalition government headed by Ali Larayedh, but accepted that "sovereignty ministries" (Interior, Justice, Defense and Foreign Affairs) were occupied by technocrats without party affiliation. The foreign ministry was thus assigned to Othman Jarandi, a career diplomat.[35] The murder of yet another opposition leader, Mohammed al-Brahimi, in July 2013, and intensified Jihadist attacks against the Tunisian army on the border with Algeria further destabilized the country, in a regional context marked by the war in Mali and President Morsi's overthrow in Cairo.

The political crisis could be overcome through a National Dialogue promoted by four civil society institutions and chiefly the historic Tunisian General Labor Union (UGTT). The constitution drafting process was accelerated and the establishment was agreed of a caretaker technocratic government, led by Mehdi Jomaa, which was to be in place until the holding of legislative and presidential elections in late 2014. The foreign ministry was assigned to a senior UN official, Mongi Hamdi. The new Tunisian constitution adopted in January 2014 maintained some duality in foreign policy decision-making by assigning to the President of the Republic, elected by universal suffrage, the power to define "the general state policies in the domains of defense, foreign relations and national security".

In Egypt, the process of political transition following the ouster of Mubarak was marked by cohabitation between the army – the real nerve center of the former regime – diverse Islamist groups and the secular forces at the origin of the revolts. The Supreme Council of the Armed Forces (SCAF) controlled the transition process between February 2011 and August 2012, setting the pace and ensuring continuity in foreign and security policy. One day after Mubarak's fall, the SCAF published a statement stressing its commitment to respect "all regional and international obligations and treaties".[36] This declaration sent a reassuring message to the U.S. and Israel that the 1979 peace treaty with Israel would not be questioned, at the same time trying to ensure continuity of the American annual $1.3-billion military aid package, tied to the treaty and earmarked for army use.

The armed forces' decades-long participation in defining the Egyptian foreign and defense policy had been justified thus far with a nationalist discourse that stressed their role in the October 1973 war against Israel. Their influence had increased in the first decade of the 21st century, after diplomat Amr Moussa left the Ministry of Foreign Affairs in 2001 to become Secretary-General of the Arab League. From that moment, it was the General Intelligence Service (GIS), headed by Omar Suleiman, one of President Mubarak's closest advisors, which acquired visible influence over key issues in foreign policy, security and the fight against terrorism (Grimm & Roll 2012).[37] After the fall of Mubarak, the military leadership presided over by Field Marshal Mohamed Hussein Tantawi tried to secure its influence and autonomy in these areas before transferring executive power to civilians. The removal of the SCAF in August 2012 did strengthen the power of the newly elected Islamist President Mohammed Morsi, yet without putting at risk many of the prerogatives accumulated by the armed forces. Tantawi was then replaced as commander-in-chief by General Sisi, who also became Minister of Defense.

The constitution approved by referendum in December 2012 – rejected by the liberal and secular forces – granted the president direct powers with regard to foreign policy, defense and national security (Art. 141) but maintained some of the previous prerogatives of the armed forces. The constitution enshrined the National Defense Council (Art. 197), which had been reactivated by the SCAF in June 2012 before executive power was transferred to President Morsi. This body, in which the military retained the power to block decision-making, was supposed to oversee the military budget and be consulted by the president before declaring war or sending troops abroad (Art. 146).

Between August 2012 and July 2013, the Muslim Brotherhood and the army established a somewhat tense *modus vivendi*. Foreign policy was formulated by the president's office, headed by Rifaa el-Tahtawi, an experienced career diplomat with close ties to the Muslim Brotherhood. The influence of the FJP in the decision-making process was apparent from the ideological and party leanings of the president's advisors: Essam el-Haddad handled international and cooperation issues while Hassan Malek was in charge of relations with the private sector and the internationalization of Egyptian companies. Both were members of the FJP and maintained close ties with Khairat al-Shater, deputy supreme guide of the Brotherhood (Grimm & Roll 2012). Other *brothers* such as Essam al-Aryan also collaborated in defining and implementing foreign policy.

As happened during the final years of Mubarak's presidency, the Ministry of Foreign Affairs continued to play just an implementing and accompanying role, not occupying a central position in the decision-making process (Hillal Dessouki 2009: 182–183). It was President Morsi who took center stage in this arena, actively trying to promote Egypt as a regional power on the international stage during his first months in office.

The armed forces continued to be a key player in relations with Israel through the military intelligence services, while the president handled the dialogue with Hamas, with the participation of members of the Brotherhood. This division of labor allowed President Morsi to strengthen his international image as an honest and committed mediator during the November 2012 Gaza crisis, limiting the impact that resulted from the tacit acceptance of Israel's normalization in the eyes of the ranks of his party. The armed forces maintained autonomous positions in foreign policy issues deemed to affect national security. Evidence of the military establishment's positions prevailing over ideological solidarity between the Muslim Brotherhood and Hamas could be seen in the continued closure of the Rafah border crossing to the passage of goods. The fear that free circulation between the two sides of the border would intensify the climate of insecurity in the Sinai was used to oppose the creation of a free trade zone with Gaza, which Israel could use to absolve itself of its international obligations to the territory (International Crisis Group 2012: 12–17). The army also questioned initiatives for dialogue with the Jihadist groups in the Sinai, taking advantage of the restrictions established in the 1979 treaty for the deployment of Egyptian soldiers along the Israeli border. In November 2012, the army refused to interrupt operations against these groups to facilitate the work of an official delegation sent by President Morsi to talk with representatives of the Jihadist movement in the peninsula (Chams El-Dine 2013: 5–7).

The deterioration of relations between the Egyptian presidency and the SCAF was accelerated by the political crisis around the constitutional declaration issued by Morsi in November 2012, which put the presidency above judicial review. The calls by the military for political dialogue among all parties were not well received by the Muslim Brotherhood. Unrest at the top of the Armed Forces also grew because of the adoption – without prior consultation with the SCAF – of some foreign policy measures allegedly liable to endanger national security (International Crisis Group 2013b: 4). Along with differences over how to manage insecurity in the Sinai (Aziz 2013), a decisive grievance was the decision to break off diplomatic relations with the Syrian regime of Bashar al-Assad. It was announced by President Morsi in mid-June 2013 during a National Conference for the Support of the Syrian Revolution attended by Salafi leaders, who called for the start of a jihad against the "sectarian Syrian regime" and the Shiite infidels.[38] The assignment of management responsibilities to Islamist activists of the Gamaa al-Islamiyya, who were involved in the past in kidnappings or attacks against the Egyptian troops in the Sinai, also helped trigger the army's intervention and the dismissal of President Morsi on 3 July 2013, after the massive demonstrations called by the Tamarod movement. The new government was constituted by interim President of the Republic Adly Mansour; General Sisi took over the vice-presidency in addition to the Defense Ministry, while the Foreign Ministry was attributed to the diplomat Nabil Fahmi, Ambassador to Washington from 1999 to 2008.

The new constitution adopted in January 2014 maintained the central role of the army in the Egyptian political system. The election of General Sisi as president in May 2014 completed the process of reconcentration of control over decision-making processes in foreign policy, security and defense (Lampridi-Kemou & Azaola 2013). The Defense Ministry was occupied by Sedki Sobhi, who became also the chairman of the SCAF, while the Foreign Affairs portfolio was assigned to Sameh Shoukry, a career diplomat who served as ambassador to the U.S. between 2008 and 2012.

In Algeria, where the status quo had prevailed, anti-authoritarian protests did not bring about any important changes in the power structure, yet they brought existing tensions within the regime to the surface. The institutional architecture and formal structures of the political system established in the constitution did not stand in the way of the exercise of real power. Since Houari Boumediene's coup d'état in 1965, that power had been in the hands of an intricate complex formed by the military leadership, heads of the intelligence services and actors in the energy and industrial sectors, which is indeed popularly known as *Le Pouvoir* (Entelis 2013).

Since becoming President of the Republic in 1999 as "the least evil of the candidates" (Zoubir 2004: 180) for the military, Abdelaziz Bouteflika had tried to expand the room for maneuver for civilian power at the expense of his former promoters, who then chose to step away from the political frontlines. Bouteflika used his success in reintegrating Algeria into the international community after the "moral embargo" imposed upon it during the civil war in the 1990s as a lever to gain autonomy, showcasing the experience acquired during his 15 years at the helm of the Ministry of Foreign Affairs between 1963 and 1978. Yet he only achieved a limited autonomy, leaving strategic sectors like national security and the control and exploitation of energy resources beyond his reach.

The hesitations and refusal to support international intervention in Mali once again revealed the contradictions and differences existing within the opaque Algerian power structure. The permission granted, *in extremis*, to French planes to fly over Algerian territory in January 2013 triggered a strong wave of criticism directed at Bouteflika. He was accused of colluding with Paris and supporting the return of French colonialism to the region in a campaign probably promoted by the military intelligence services – the *Département de Renseignement et de la Sécurité* (DRS), led by General Mohamed Mediene – whose clout within *Le Pouvoir* had grown stronger since the 1990s (Addi 2013). The forceful response to the terrorist attack at the In Amenas gas plant a few days after France began its operations in Mali reflected how the balance of power continued to tip in favor of the DRS in security-related issues. Perceiving the attack as a direct threat to the economic bases of the regime and, therefore, to its own political hegemony, the DRS applied an *éradicatrice* solution similar to that carried out during the civil war, resulting in the death of 37 foreign workers and 29 kidnappers.

The hospitalization in France of President Bouteflika between April and July 2013 heightened internal tensions between the presidential clan and the DRS regarding the uncertainty about the succession. During his convalescence, the judicial branch of the DRS launched investigations of corruption among senior officers of the state oil company Sonatrach who were close to the president. After his recovery, Bouteflika tried to strengthen his position by cutting the powers of the DRS and reshuffling the government to promote his allies.[39] The new Foreign Minister Ramtane Lamamra was, however, an experienced technocrat with a significant diplomatic career and higher profile than his predecessors.[40]

In Morocco, the reformist adjustments used by Mohammed VI to defuse pro-democracy protests did not alter the underlying power structure. Although the 2011 constitution relatively expanded the head of government's powers, the king and his opaque circle of advisors continued to play a central role in the processes of policy definition and decision-making, thus creating a parallel government at court. The formation of a coalition government presided over by Abdelilah Benkirane, Secretary-General of the Justice and Development Party (PJD) in December 2012, reestablished an asymmetric cohabitation between the palace and a government tasked with mainly subsidiary functions. The 2011 constitution reduced somehow the power of the king, who would no longer directly appoint the Minister of

Foreign Affairs. However, and although that position was occupied by Saad Eddine El-Othmani, the former PJD Secretary-General, the king appointed Youssef Amrani, a professional diplomat with palace ties who was Secretary-General of the ministry between 2008 and 2011, to be Deputy Foreign Minister.[41] Moreover, at the same time that the PJD came into the power, the Royal Cabinet – working as genuine shadow cabinet – was further strengthened by the inclusion of former Minister of Foreign Affairs Taieb Fassi Fihri, in December 2012.

Prime Minister Benkirane openly recognized and accepted the subordinate position of his cabinet when he said, in May 2012: "In Morocco the head of the government has power, but His Majesty is the supreme master of this power. The king intervenes in the decisions of the head of government and can choose the advisors that he wants".[42] This limited degree of governmental autonomy was made clear after the July 2013 military coup in Egypt. Following the lead of Saudi Arabia and other Gulf countries, Mohammed VI was quick to congratulate the new interim Egyptian President, Adly Mansour. In contrast, Benkirane's cabinet limited itself to take note of topical developments in a neutral statement issued by the Foreign Ministry.[43] The condemnation of the coup was left to the PJD's party organs and members of parliament, as well as connected religious organizations (Parejo & Feliu 2012; Hernando de Larramendi 2013).

The PJD's influence in foreign policy further waned after the cabinet reshuffle provoked by the Istiqlal Party's exit from government in October 2013. The ruling coalition was then joined by the National Rally of Independents (RNI), an old allied party of the monarchy whose leader, Salaheddine Mezouar, became the new Minister of Foreign Affairs. Another RNI member, Mbarka Bouaida, was appointed Deputy Foreign Minister, with Youssef Amrani being transferred to the Royal Cabinet as *chargée de mission*.[44]

3. A not so surprising foreign policy behavior

The foreign policy behavior or output resulting from all of the above-mentioned constraints (international, regional, domestic) and policymaking dynamics comprises the general definition of the agenda and priority objectives that guide each state's conduct as well as the specific actions and discourses. First, on a more abstract level, the national role conceptions (Holsti 1970) rooted in the different North African countries did not vary substantially after 2011, whether because of the high degree of social consensus they enjoy or because of their close connection to structural constraints. For example, one of the aspirational claims most often repeated at this stage – the desire for renewed regional leadership for the post-revolutionary Egypt – was nothing more than the reflection and *updating* of a historical role conception widely accepted both inside and outside the country.

Second, the region did not witness in these years international normalization or realignment processes like those associated in the past with regime changes or democratic transitions in other parts of the world. Arguably, normalization is only necessary for states that have been somehow isolated due to their regime's political-ideological nature or behavior contrary to international norms. This was the case until the end of the 1990s, to varying degrees, in Algeria and Libya, due to the bloody internal conflict underway in the former country and to the UN sanctions imposed after the 1988 Lockerbie bombing to the latter. However, the trend for both regimes during the first decade of the 2000s was accelerated rehabilitation and reinsertion into the international community. After Bouteflika enacted the 1999 Civil Concord Act and joined the "global war on terror" (Keenan 2012), and the EU and the U.S. reestablished relations with the former *rogue state* of Qaddafi,[45] the North African countries' relations with the main powers and participation in multilateral bodies were all full and trouble-free, without exception.

Third, the hypothesis of realignment, both at the international and regional levels, was hinted during the earliest phases of the Egyptian transition. Some observers detected indications of the emergence of a more or less ideological "post-Western" foreign policy (Sasnal 2012) as the Muslim Brotherhood won elections and gained power. The main concern was that the newly-elected Islamist leaders in Cairo might be tempted to denounce the 1978 Camp David Accords and the 1979 bilateral peace treaty between Egypt and Israel, considered by the U.S. as the cornerstone of Middle East regional stability and security. Yet, in fact, the FJP representatives gave assurances from the very beginning that they would respect the international treaties signed by the Egyptian state, even if diplomatic relations with Tel Aviv were downgraded. Months later, in September 2012, President Morsi's speech to the UN General Assembly made it clear that there would be no fundamental changes in the basic orientations of Egyptian foreign policy.

3.1. Adaptation at the regional and international levels

As a result, the general trend of the international behavior of these countries since 2011 was caution and pragmatism. Such an unstable and fluid context could only produce essentially adaptive foreign policies – the exact opposite of "rebellious foreign policies" driven by the rejection of a given international or regional political order (Charillon 2007).[46] The capacity to adapt was simultaneously put to the test on two levels: regional and international. At the regional level, the asymmetry in the domestic political changes witnessed in different states entailed an uncertain re-composition of alliances, as well as a difficult balance between solidarity among revolutionary actors and good neighborliness with the regimes that had resisted the wave of protests. This gave rise to paradoxical and delicate decisions, such as when President Marzouki paid homage to his old Moroccan fellow and human rights activist Abdelhamid Amine (Moroccan Association of Human Rights, AMDH), an incorruptible opponent of a monarchy that the new Tunisian authorities had to work with at the same time.[47]

The clearest sign of the need to swiftly react to regional transformations was the perception of encirclement of the Algerian regime extended in 2011 and early 2012. Although Bouteflika and his supporters were able to weather the domestic storm and defuse the protests organized in different cities around the country as the Tunisian revolutionary virus spread, their new sensation of vulnerability was not dispelled. After keeping quiet about the rapid succession of events in Tunisia, the authorities in Algiers clearly opposed the fall of the Libyan regime, rejecting the international intervention under NATO control and even – according to unproved accusations – providing covert support to Qaddafi's resistance. They also gave asylum to various members of the toppled dictator's family and were the last of the Maghreb states to recognize the victorious NTC.

In a second phase, in the face of potential domestic parallels, Algeria's threat perception increased due to the Islamist election victories in three neighboring countries (Tunisia, Morocco and Egypt) and, even worse, to the U.S. and EU's positive engagement with these new governing parties. This was compounded with the strengthening of bilateral political and economic ties between post-revolutionary Tunisia and Libya[48] and the proposal to extend GCC membership to Morocco, which reinforced Algeria's distancing from this powerful club of conservative Arab monarchies – whose support for Islamist and Salafist forces in various Arab countries was not appreciated either (Darbouche & Dennison 2011; Spencer 2012).

In any case, Algeria's regional isolation was nothing but relative and transitory. Moves to the contrary – conciliatory gestures to build confidence between neighboring countries – included official visits to Algiers by Prime Minister Beji Caid el Sebsi, head of the Tunisian interim government between February and December 2011, and by President Marzouki (Kéfi 2012; Zoubir 2012a: 89–90). In March 2012 in Tripoli, Algerian foreign minister Mourad Medelci gave assurances that the members of Qaddafi's family taking refuge in his country, whose extradition was rejected, would not be allowed to interfere in Libyan affairs[49] (they would eventually leave this country in March 2013). Compounded with the strengthening of cooperation on security matters, this made it easier to break the stalemate in bilateral relations and allowed the NTC President Mustafa Abdul Jalil to travel to Algiers the following month. In December, Libyan Prime Minister Ali Zeidan chose the same destination for his first trip abroad.[50]

Two years later, in view of the deep deterioration of the security situation in Libya, Syria, Egypt and Mali, the Algerian authorities felt internationally courted and reinforced in their original status quo-defending positions, which installed them in a somewhat told-you-so attitude: "Algeria will continue its efforts to stop hegemony, bloodshed and dismantling of regimes, because the stability and security of our country are dependent on the stability of the neighborhood, development and prosperity", said President Bouteflika in August 2014.[51] This discursive focus on stability and security arguably contributed to the mobilization of domestic support in front of external threats and the regime's very endurance (Boserup, Martinez & Holm 2014: 15).

The adaptation needs of North African foreign policies were significantly lower at the international level. Apart from promises for more effective democratic conditionality – in principle a domestic politics issue – the expectations held by Europe and the U.S. about their external behavior had not changed substantially. From the EU point of view, the most advanced partners of the Euro-Mediterranean Partnership

(EMP)/Union for the Mediterranean (UfM) and the southern dimension of the European Neighborhood Policy (ENP) continued to be the same before and after 2011 (Morocco, Tunisia and Jordan). These were first and foremost three countries always ready to cooperate and strengthen relations with Brussels to the extent possible, regardless of the scope or credibility of domestic reforms carried out domestically.

It was the EU's wayward pupil *par excellence*, Algeria, which most clearly made an adaptive shift in its relations with Brussels in 2011–2014. This was the only country in the area that had refused to participate in the ENP, which it considered Eurocentric and lacking co-ownership. Throughout the previous decade, its cooperation had been partial and reticent, "on an occasional, case-by-case basis and as a result of pragmatic cost-benefit analysis" (Schumacher 2012: 89). Analysts attributed this to the country's unusual financial strength (abundance of foreign exchange reserves) coming from its energy resources, but also to a renewed foreign policy assertiveness from a political point of view (the so-called Russian syndrome) (Darbouche 2008; Martinez 2010: 32–33). However, Algeria's new regional fragility gave way to more flexible positions and a more constructive attitude towards Brussels (Darbouche & Dennison 2011). The May 2012 legislative elections were the first for which the Algerian government invited monitors from an EU Election Observation Mission and subsequently accepted their recommendations. These months also witnessed a significant change regarding technical sectorial cooperation, using the EU's twinning instruments. Most importantly, for the first time Algiers expressed its desire to become involved in the ENP, negotiating the corresponding bilateral Action Plan. The first round of talks took place in October 2012, at the same time that the forthcoming conclusion of a memorandum of understanding on the Strategic Energy Partnership proposed by Algeria in 2006 was announced.[52] The solidity of this rapprochement, which was closely connected to the evolution of regional crises, remained still to be seen. The situation in Mali once again placed the European states in a position of *demandeurs*, returning the EU–Algeria balance of power in favor of the latter (Dennison 2012: 3).[53]

In the other North African states, policies towards the EU ranged from temporary paralysis in countries with a serious power vacuum or domestic instability (Egypt, Libya) (Rękawek & Sasnal 2012) to oriented business as usual in old "model students" (Morocco, Tunisia). In December 2011, as part of the strategic response to the Arab Spring, the EU Council agreed to open negotiations on Deep and Comprehensive Free Trade Areas (DCFTAs) to improve the trade conditions of the existing bilateral association agreements with Morocco, Tunisia, Egypt and Jordan. However, the provisional Egyptian authorities preferred not to enter into formal international negotiations – both on this issue and the Mobility Partnership – until the transitional stage was over and an elected government in place.[54] This cautious response contrasted with the determination with which Morocco and Tunisia made progress in both dossiers, despite post-revolutionary uncertainty and the government's temporary nature in the latter case.

The steady pace of the Tunisia–EU relationship was the result of reciprocal interest and political will. Brussels viewed Tunisia as the Arab Spring country with the best prospects for democratization and political stability, and the most likely to serve as an example for the region. For their part, the new Tunisian leaders were anxious to establish themselves as interlocutors and close partners of the EU and its key member states. This led to intense bilateral political contacts, including the launch of an EU-Tunisia Task Force to coordinate support for the Tunisian transition in September 2011 and the deployment of an EU Election Observation Mission to the Constituent Assembly elections held the following month. Of the *troika* formed after these elections, it was Islamist al-Nahda party, long excluded and repressed by the regime of Zine al Abidine Ben Ali, that had the most pressing need for international recognition. Prime Minister Hamadi Jebali visited Brussels in February and October 2012. The culmination of this dialogue, besides increased European financial assistance, was the political accord on the promised EU–Tunisia Privileged Partnership, reached during the 9th Association Council, and resulting in a new bilateral Action Plan in November 2012.[55]

Although the Tunisian transition's image abroad suffered seriously in the following months as tensions grew between the government coalition parties and violent street clashes occurred between Islamist militants and the left-wing secular opposition,[56] the international community welcomed al-Nahda's voluntary exit from government and the formation of a technocratic cabinet in early 2014 as encouraging signs of compromise. The country's first democratic legislative and presidential elections held in October and November 2014 – also monitored by an EU Election Observation Mission – were widely commended as a historic milestone and shot up Tunisia's international standing in a context of despair about the region's democratic prospects.

Anyway, the master in terms of international adaptation continued to be Morocco, which had been already granted a so-called Advanced Status by the EU in 2008 (Remiro Brotons & Martínez Capdevila 2012). The authorities in Rabat were aware of the need to *equate* the regime changes witnessed in other countries with the top-down constitutional reform of July 2011, which actually left the distribution of power and the political hegemony of the monarchy essentially intact. Thus, they paired the constitution drafting process with an ambitious diplomatic campaign intended to *sell* its allegedly democratic results to Morocco's main international partners. This, building on a long background of positive external perception, led the EU to reward the kingdom with political and financial incentives similar to those offered to post-revolutionary Tunisia (Biscop, Balfour & Emerson 2012: 32).[57] Even the success of the moderate Islamists of the PJD in the November 2011 elections further enhanced Morocco's image abroad, serving as a sign of the regime's reformist inclinations and *normalization* within its regional context.

Nonetheless, the EU delegation to Morocco on several occasions highlighted the insufficiency of the reforms made by this country: "less ambitious than expected in a number of sectors receiving budgetary support."[58] The North African kingdom also experienced serious setbacks in the European Parliament, including a rejection of the EU–Morocco fisheries agreement in December 2011 on the legal grounds that its direct benefits for the Sahrawi population had not been satisfactorily demonstrated.[59] A year later, the Parliament expressed "its concern at the deterioration of human rights in Western Sahara"[60] and appointed a *rapporteur* to follow the issue.

3.2. Pragmatism and two-level games in relations with the United States

With regard to the U.S., the great unknown of the new period concerned possible difficulties with accommodating the new Islamist parties that came to power in different countries. Although the debate about the doctrinal specificity of mainstream Islamism in foreign policy and international affairs tilted years ago in favor of the thesis of normalization and pragmatism, so far there had not been many opportunities to test the different hypotheses with effective political behavior (Fernández Molina 2007: 16–19). Indeed, beyond the anti-American notes that sprinkled the electoral platforms and speeches of parties across the political spectrum (Sasnal 2012: 3), the Tunisian al-Nahda, the Moroccan PJD and the Egyptian FJP all appeared interested in establishing themselves as interlocutors of the U.S. administration and generally received a satisfactory response.

Tensions in relations with Washington originated in events like the attacks against the American diplomatic representations in Benghazi, Tunis and Cairo in September 2012 after the release of the Islamophobic film *Innocence of Muslims*. The political consequence was a sensitive two-level game: the new Islamist authorities had to simultaneously deal with, on the one hand, U.S. pressure to speed up the investigation of the events and intensify the fight against terrorism[61] and, on the other, petitions for clemency from Salafist sectors that were becoming increasingly visible in the public space.[62]

In the Egyptian case, besides this, the main bilateral crisis in the wake of the 2011 revolution was provoked by holdovers from the Mubarak regime, such as the Ganzouri government's Minister of Planning and International Cooperation, Faiza Abou el-Naga, who incited a campaign against democracy-promotion NGOs as of December 2011. Four of the five organizations accused of working without a license, receiving illegal funding or engaging in "political activity" – with 43 foreign workers prosecuted – were American.[63] The State Department declared that this was essentially a political dispute that needed to be addressed government-to-government. The trial threatened the continuity of the substantial military assistance provided annually to Egypt by the U.S. ($1.3 billion), since congressional approval of the aid was conditioned on the administration being able to show that the transition government in Cairo was meeting specific political requirements (Project on Middle East Democracy 2012). In the end, it was necessary to invoke a national security waiver for assistance to be resumed. More generally, this episode highlighted the difficulties faced by the Western governments and diplomats when choosing their partners and interlocutors in the midst of such a confusing mixture of new and old actors (Dunne 2012).

The FJP and President Morsi, in contrast, surprised the international community with their marked pragmatism in foreign policy matters. This attitude can be attributed both to the needs for foreign (Western) political recognition of the new leaders, who were facing a persistently turbulent domestic situation,[64] and to the economic constraints examined above in the chapter, without ruling out previous evidences that the originality of the Islamist views on foreign affairs might have been overestimated. Perhaps the most striking feature was the continuity in Egypt's relationship with Israel (Abuel Hassan 2013). After issuing reassuring statements about respecting the bilateral peace treaty, Morsi sent President Shimon Peres a warm formal letter in October 2012, kept Egypt's border with Gaza largely closed and continued to fight smuggling in the tunnels (demolishing or flooding many of them). At the same time, however, he lowered the profile of the bilateral relations with Israel, delegating their management to the security apparatus to avoid being directly involved, and made a display of military force with a counterterrorist offensive in the Sinai in August 2012 that was not coordinated with Tel Aviv.[65] As to the Palestinians, the new Egyptian Islamist leaders adopted a neutral position between Fatah and Hamas, advocating intra-Palestinian unity and reconciliation.

The moment of truth that tested the difficult combination of assertiveness and pragmatism that the leaders of the "new Egypt" needed to show in this regard was the Israeli offensive against Gaza in November 2012. Morsi and his supporters found themselves trapped in the midst of contradictory pressures coming from at least five fronts: first, public domestic opinion, including the Muslim Brotherhood's rank and file, who strove to make their voices heard after the revolution, demanding an attitude towards Israel distinctly different from Mubarak's passivity; second, Hamas and the Palestinians, who trusted in the active solidarity of their Cairo *brothers*; third, other political actors from across the Arab world, also convinced of the need for a new Egyptian leadership; fourth, the U.S. and other Western countries, which were instead concerned about minimizing the regional impact of this outbreak; and fifth, the Egyptian national security establishment, which was the traditional interlocutor with Israel and the U.S. (International Crisis Group 2012: 12–17). The only way to successfully reconcile such different expectations was to opt for mediation.

After withdrawing the Egyptian ambassador to Tel Aviv, Morsi decided to send Prime Minister Hisham Qandil to Gaza in a historical visit, which – as was the case previously with that of the Qatari Emir – broke the Strip's international isolation. In fact, this audacious gesture of autonomy from Washington, which was immediately imitated by the Tunisian Minister of Foreign Affairs,[66] was deep down a way of legitimizing the leading mediating role that Cairo intended to take on (proof of this was that neither the U.S. nor Israel put up any resistance). The objective was to take advantage of Morsi's leverage over Hamas to act as a moderating influence and bring about a cessation of hostilities as soon as possible. Finally, after eight days of war, a truce was reached with Egyptians securing guarantees. The joint press conference where Egyptian foreign minister Mohamed Kamel Amr announced the ceasefire together with the U.S. Secretary of State Hillary Clinton was a representation of the close collaboration between the two governments, also supported in this diplomatic race against the clock by UN Secretary-General Ban Ki-moon. This mediation was a clear success as pertains to the international validation of Cairo's new Islamist leaders, now turned into peace brokers and "responsible partners" of the West, "part of the solution and not part of the problem" (Kinninmont 2012; Makovsky 2012). But more importantly, it did not have any legitimacy cost in the eyes of domestic and Arab constituencies. In fact, quite the contrary: Morsi took advantage of the boost to try to solidify his position domestically, approving by decree a controversial constitutional declaration that safeguarded presidential powers.

The Israeli–Palestinian conflict was not the only Middle East issue where Morsi's Egypt alternated between pragmatism and gestures of autonomy and independence. Another move in this respect that received a lot of attention was the opening to Iran, a regional enemy of Mubarak's regime with which diplomatic relations had been broken since the 1979 revolution. The change in attitude actually occurred before the Muslim Brotherhood came to power – in the summer of 2011 an Egyptian delegation visited Tehran – and was in large part a display of the rupture with the foreign policy of the Mubarak era. However, this was accompanied at all times by guarantees that nothing would be done at the expense of Egypt's special relation with the Gulf States. Morsi maintained the usual cautious approach, dashing Iran's expectations for complete normalization and a potential alliance either at the political level (the creation of a regional anti-Israeli front) or the economic level (the sale of oil to Egypt to compensate for the U.S. and European embargo). The reciprocal historic presidential visits for the summits of the countries of the Non-Aligned Movement (Tehran, August 2012) and the Organization for Islamic Cooperation (OIC, Cairo, February 2013)[67] did not overcome Egyptian resistance to Iran's pursuit at a time when the two states were in opposite camps regarding both regional sectarian Sunni–Shiite rivalry and the Syrian civil war (Ehteshami 2010; Esfandiary 2012; Khalaji 2012). The vicissitudes of the Egyptian initiative for regional mediation in the Syrian conflict, as part of a quartet including Saudi Arabia, Iran and Turkey, illustrated both the potential and the limits of Morsi's proactive approach.

The military coup with wide civilian backing that overthrew Morsi and the Brotherhood in July 2013 provoked new uncertainty and speculations as to the possible reorientation of Egyptian foreign policy. The Minister of Foreign Affairs of the new interim government, Nabil Fahmi, stressed the need for Cairo to regain international status before both the U.S. and the EU, whose attempts to mediate in the deepening internal crisis were domestically perceived as evidence of Egypt's unprecedented weakness. The ensuing diplomatic offensive was aimed above all at seeking international recognition for the new Sisi presidency and containing condemnation over internal violence. The two other stated priorities were Africa – with the purpose of solving the revived dispute over Nile waters with Ethiopia[68] and the suspension of Egypt's membership in the AU that followed the coup – and the Arab countries – among which the new authorities in Cairo wished to rally renewed support after they adopted divergent positions on Morsi's ouster, particularly clear in the Saudi Arabia–Qatar divide.[69] Notwithstanding this, Fahmi's legitimacy and role as representative of the Egyptian state were still denounced by the Muslim Brotherhood in September 2013 during the UN's General Assembly.[70] On the same occasion, Tunisian President Marzouki demanded Morsi's liberation, leading to the withdrawal of the Egyptian and UAE's ambassadors from his country.[71]

President Sisi's own moment of truth in foreign policy was the Israel–Gaza conflict that took place in July and August 2014. Similarly to Morsi in 2012, Sisi engaged in mediation efforts in order to enhance his regime's international standing and to try to get U.S. military assistance restored, but two prominent differences made the two experiences unalike. The first novelty was a new form of *domestication* of Egypt's policy toward Gaza and Hamas, which was viewed by the Cairo military authorities as an extension of the battlefield of the domestic war against the Muslim Brotherhood – with both Islamist organizations being labelled as "terrorist" likewise. This ultimately turned Egypt "from mediator with interests, to interested party that also mediates" (Dunne & Brown 2014), and led it to side with Israel (the enemy of its enemy) even more openly than Mubarak. The second difference, connected to this, was Sisi's decreased leverage with Hamas and inability to fulfill Egypt's traditional broker role in the Israeli–Palestinian conflict, which was based on contacts with all parties. In fact, Egypt initiated dialogue with Hamas only after the latter rejected a first ceasefire proposal that had only been agreed with Israel; this proved to be indispensable to broker an indefinite ceasefire. For the rest, the other North African countries seemed to pay relatively little attention to this bloody Israeli offensive compared to previous similar episodes.

The new pressing regional security issue on which none of these countries could avoid taking a position was the daunting rise of the Islamic State (IS), which seized control of large parts of Syria and Iraq and proclaimed a worldwide "caliphate" in mid-2014. The U.S. decision to assemble a coalition of partner countries to fight this designated terrorist organization as of August 2014 put considerable strain on all the Middle Eastern and North African leaders who were requested to join it. While they generally shared the perception of a major security threat, they also feared that overtly supporting an U.S.-led military intervention in the Middle East would not be palatable to part of their domestic actors and public opinion, and might even backfire from a security perspective provoking terrorist reprisals in their territory. A telling example of the behavior that this two-level game brought about was Rabat's hesitations and ambiguity following the U.S. administration's official announcement that the kingdom would participate in the anti-IS coalition. After three weeks of silence, a communiqué of the Moroccan foreign ministry simply stated that "active support" (military and intelligence) would be provided to the UAE "in their fight against terrorism and for the preservation of regional and international peace and stability".[72] This limited commitment indicated a wish to keep one foot inside and the other outside the budding alliance. Meanwhile, Algeria chose to stay out of military involvement, arguing that it was preferable to concentrate its efforts on diplomatic mediation in Mali and Libya (Roussellier 2014).

At the same time, this international emergency also opened opportunities for Arab regimes that extracted legitimacy and other significant "rents" (Keenan 2012: 202–204) from the fight against terrorism, chief among which at this time was Egypt – the other North African country that appeared on the list of anti-IS coalition members disclosed by the U.S. State Department in mid-September, together with Morocco.[73] Sisi eagerly stated that Egypt was "completely committed to giving support" to this alliance,[74] yet putting emphasis on the connection – or assimilation – between IS and terrorist groups in the Sinai and the Libyan border that were the target of his own counterterrorist campaigns. Arguably, the IS threat was providential for him in order to justify his contested domestic security policies and repression of the Muslim Brotherhood, to gain increased regional leverage and support from his Gulf allies (despite divergences with Saudi Arabia on the Syrian civil war) and to fully recover recognition from the U.S. and the international community (Helmy 2014).

3.3. Regionalism at the mercy of the situation

One final variable of foreign policy behavior that is potentially related to domestic political changes is greater or lesser tendency towards international cooperation. In this respect, the possible dynamics resulting from the Arab Spring include the resurgence of regionalism at different scales among the concerned countries, from the level of Arabism (Phillips 2014) and the role of the Arab League (Pinfari 2012) to smaller sub-regional organizations such as the GCC and the Arab Maghreb Union (AMU).

In fact, in the case of the North African states, the wave of protests and regime changes did give rise to a temporary resurrection of the Maghreb integration project, now under the outstanding leadership of the Tunisian president. During his tour of the region's capitals in February–March 2012, Marzouki tried to inject new democratic blood into the always sluggish AMU, defending the construction of a "Maghreb of freedoms" as a space for fluid exchanges based on the freedoms of circulation, residence, work, investment and property for citizens of member countries (Sayah 2012). The first step, supported by an agreement of principle reached among the five governments, was to organize a summit of the AMU heads of state in Tunisia in the autumn of 2012. The opportunity was also a result of the timely détente between Morocco and Algeria, initially a defensive reaction on the part of both regimes to the shared threat of internal destabilization. In January 2012, in an eloquent gesture of reconciliation, the foreign minister of Benkirane's cabinet, Saad-Eddine El Othmani, chose Algiers as the destination for his first trip abroad. Also the EU backed these moves with a joint communication from the High Representative and the Commission on "supporting closer cooperation and regional integration in the Maghreb".[75]

However, the recurring tensions in the Algeria–Morocco duo quickly dashed the hopes that had been raised. In one of its ritual calls for "normalization", Rabat conditioned its participation in the AMU summit on reopening of the border with its neighboring country (closed in 1994), a linkage that Algiers rejected, arguing that bilateral differences should not interfere with the broader Maghreb process. The conflict in the Western Sahara caused additional frictions in April–May 2012, first when the Moroccan delegation left the funeral of the first president of the Algerian republic, Ahmed Ben Bella, due to the presence of President Mohamed Abdelaziz of the Sahrawi Arab Democratic Republic (SADR), and then when Morocco withdrew its confidence from UN envoy Christopher Ross. In the end, the highly-awaited AMU summit was indefinitely postponed and the regional status quo remained unchanged (Hernando de Larramendi 2008 and 2012). Relations between Morocco and Algeria hit new lows one year later, when tensions around the failed initiative to extend MINURSO's mandate were coupled with the call of the new leader of the nationalist Istiqlal Party, Hamid Chabat, to recover Moroccan territory "usurped" by Algeria in the Tindouf area.[76] The speech delivered by President Bouteflika at the AU supporting the extension of MINURSO's mandate provoked the recall of the Moroccan ambassador in Algiers in November 2013. Bilateral strain grew again during the summer of 2014 following the appointment of former Mozambican President Joaquim Chissano as AU special envoy for Western Sahara. This tense atmosphere led to several incidents along the shared border, closed since 1994, where Morocco started to build a three-meter metal fence between the coastal city of Saidiya and Jerada to allegedly "combat the terrorist threat".

The Tunisian regional leadership also waned as domestic tensions in this country mounted. For example, in 2013 the candidacy of former foreign minister Rafik Abdessalam (December 2011–March 2013) to the position of secretary-general of the AMU was rejected by other Maghreb countries on the grounds that he belonged to al-Nahda.[77] Meanwhile, Mauritanian President Mohammed Ould Abdel Aziz was growing increasingly mistrustful of the Moroccan regime and refused to receive representatives of this country on several occasions, besides getting closer to the Polisario Front.[78] Competition between Algiers and Rabat for France's favors after socialist François Hollande won the presidency was also intensifying. President Hollande's official trip to Algeria in December 2012, which he hoped to use to encourage an unprecedented rapprochement and resolve the historical grievances undermining bilateral relations (even recognizing France's crimes during colonialism),[79] had to be compensated with an almost simultaneous visit by Prime Minister Jean-Marc Ayrault to Rabat, to avoid offending Morocco's sensibilities.[80] At the end of the day, the regionalist tendencies initially fuelled by the 2011 uprisings would find it quite difficult to move from the sphere of discourse to effective action.

Notes

1. This chapter is part of the results the results of the R&D Project: "New spaces, actors and instruments in Spain's International Relations with the Arab and Muslim World" (CSO2011–29438-C05–02), funded by the Spanish Ministry of Economy and Competitiveness.
2. The counterexample is Algeria: "(. . .) Without the significant backing of its hydrocarbon revenues and the tight control exerted over its internal rentier economy, Algeria's uncompromising stances would prove more difficult to sustain" (Spencer 2012).

3. In May 2012, a first Saudi $500-million aid package was received. One year later, Qatar deposited $3 billion in the Central Bank of Egypt after a trip by members of Hisham Qandil's government to Doha (Schumacher & Fernández Molina 2013: 17). However, $2 billion were returned to Qatar in September 2013 amid growing bilateral tensions following the military coup against President Mohammed Morsi – while Saudi Arabia, Kuwait and the UAE pledged $12 billion in grants and interest-free loans. *Reuters*, 19 September 2013.
4. *Oxford Analytica*, 9 May 2012.
5. *Egypt Independent*, 20 August 2012. *Ahram Online*, 22 August 2012.
6. International Monetary Fund, Press Release, 3 August 2012.
7. *African Manager*, 29 November 2012.
8. Estimates of the number of Libyan refugees in Tunisia in 2014 range from 600,000 to one million according to the Tunisian Ministry of the Interior. *Le Monde*, 13 May 2014.
9. *Financial Times*, 4 January 2012. *The New York Times*, 2 November 2011.
10. *Al Ayam*, 16 May 2011.
11. Ministère des affaires étrangères et de la coopération [MAEC, Morocco], Press Release, 10 May 2011.
12. *Al Ittihad Al Ishtiraki*, 13 May 2011. *The Economist*, 19 May 2011.
13. *The National* [UAE], 28 November 2011.
14. *Al Quds al Arabi*, 1 September 2011. MAEC [Morocco], Press Release, 2 November 2011.
15. After Jordan and Morocco's foreign ministers participated for the first time in a meeting with their GCC counterparts (September 2011) and a five-year economic development plan was approved for both countries amounting to $5 billion in total (December 2011), the upgraded relationship between the GCC and the latter was labelled "strategic partnership".
16. On security concerns at the Tunisian borders (organized crime, contraband and illegal trafficking, terrorism), see International Crisis Group (2013c) and International Crisis Group (2014).
17. *Al Hayat*, 29 October 2014.
18. *Libya Business News*, 18 December 2012.
19. *EU Neighbourhood Info Centre*, 31 January 2013.
20. *Al Quds al Arabi*, 8 October 2014.
21. *Middle East Monitor*, 16 September 2014.
22. *Le Figaro*, 24 March 2013.
23. Moroccan and Mauritanian backing for this intervention, which was less uncertain, also caused divisions between political forces.
24. *Al Ittihad al Ishtiraki*, 10 February 2010. MAEC [Morocco], Press Release, 14 January 2008.
25. *MAP*, 28 January 2012. *MAP*, 4 May 2012.
26. *Jeune Afrique*, 25 November 2012. *El Imparcial*, 12 December 2012.
27. *Al Quds al Arabi*, 15 November 2012.
28. *Yabiladi*, 16 September 2013, 19 September 2013.
29. Morocco's African policy in recent decades was marked by the country's withdrawal from the Organisation of African Unity (OAU) after the organization admitted the Sahrawi Arab Democratic Republic (SADR) in 1984.
30. The conspicuous absence in the CEN-SAD was, in fact, Algeria.
31. In February 2013, El Othmani attended a meeting of donors for Mali held at the AU headquarters in Addis Ababa after receiving guarantees that no Sahrawi representative would be present.
32. MAEC [Morocco], Press Release, 17 May 2012.
33. Constitutional Law 6–2011 of 16 December 2011, on the provisional organization of public powers, *Journal Officielle de la República Tunisienne*, No. 97, 20 and 23, December 2011.
34. *France 24*, 26 June 2012.

35. Yet much of the power and the external representation lay in fact outside the formal institutional sphere, as shown in September 2013 by the meeting between the Algerian President Abdelaziz Bouteflika and al-Nahda leader Rached Ghannouchi, who did not hold any official position in Tunisia. See *Huffington Post Maghreb*, 11 September 2013.
36. *The New York Times*, 14 February 2011.
37. Omar Suleiman played a crucial role in Egyptian diplomatic efforts to forge reconciliation between Palestinians from Hamas and from Fatah, although releases of diplomatic documents by WikiLeaks showed that he had worked with the Israelis to try to deny Hamas its electoral victory in Gaza. See *The New York Times*, 19 July 2012.
38. *Al Ahram Weekly*, 19 June 2013.
39. *Jeune Afrique*, 30 September 2013.
40. *Liberté*, 14 September 2013.
41. *Le Soir*, 4 January 2013.
42. *El País*, 20 May 2012.
43. MAEC [Morocco], Press Release, 3 July 2013.
44. *Lakome*, 10 October 2013.
45. In 2006, the U.S. reestablished diplomatic and trade relations and removed Libya from the list of state sponsors of terrorism. The EU offered this country observer status in the Euro-Mediterranean Partnership in 1999 and gave the green light to negotiations for a bilateral framework agreement in 2008 (Sánchez Mateos 2005; Joffé & Paoletti 2010: 24–29; Zoubir 2011).
46. See also Hoyt (2000) and Caprioli & Trumbore (2003).
47. *Lakum*, 10 December 2012.
48. *Financial Times*, 4 January 2012.
49. *Reuters*, 5 March 2012.
50. *Libya Herald*, 8 December 2012.
51. *L'Expression*, 26 August 2014.
52. European External Action Service, Press Release, 8 February 2013. *EU Neighbourhood Info Centre*, 7 December 2012. In early 2013, Algeria also expressed its commitment to Union for the Mediterranean (UfM) projects. See *EU Neighbourhood Info Centre*, 4 January 2013.
53. Unlike in 2012, in April 2014 the EU refused to send an EU Election Observation Mission to the presidential elections in which Bouteflika was reelected.
54. *EU Neighbourhood Info Centre*, 30 November 2012.
55. Left-wing opponents from the Popular Front criticized the legitimacy deficit of this agreement, which was concluded by a provisional government. See *Business News*, 20 November 2012. *Tunisia Live*, 21 November 2012.
56. For example, in December 2012, disturbances in Siliana resulting from strikes called by the UGTT forced President Marzouki to cancel a European tour. Two months later, his visit to Brussels was disrupted by the traumatic assassination of the leftist opposition leader Chokri Belaid – also the source of a brief diplomatic incident with France due to declarations by Interior Minister Manuel Valls about the need to support the Tunisian "democrats" against "Islamic fascism".
57. This meant once again confusing pro-European activism with willingness for real political reform (Behr 2012: 21).
58. *Lakome*, 5 February 2013.
59. Among other economic, environmental and developmental reasons. See European Parliament/Committee on Fisheries, "Recommendation on the draft Council decision on the conclusion of a Protocol between the European Union and the Kingdom of Morocco setting out the fishing opportunities and financial compensation provided for in the Fisheries Partnership Agreement between the European Community and the Kingdom of Morocco", 29 November 2011.
60. European Parliament, "Annual report on human rights and democracy in the world 2011 and the European Union's policy on the matter", 13 December 2012.
61. *Tunisia Live*, 12 December 2012.

62. Generally speaking, in the Tunisian case, "An-Nahda finds itself in an increasingly uncomfortable position, caught between non-Islamists who accuse it of excessive leniency and laxity in dealing with the security threat and Salafis who denounce it whenever it takes a harder line" (International Crisis Group 2013a: ii).

63. National Democratic Institute, International Republican Institute, Freedom House and International Center for Journalists.

64. "In order to have their hands free domestically, the Islamists must make themselves indispensable to the west (. . .)" (Roy 2012).

65. Before Morsi became president, Egypt had launched a similar operation (August 2011) and cancelled the export contract for Egyptian gas to Israel (April 2012) (Trager 2012). In March 2012, the People's Assembly had approved a report tabled by the Arab Affairs Committee defining the "Zionist entity" as Egypt's "number one enemy" and endorsing Palestinian resistance "in all its kinds and forms". It called for the severance of bilateral diplomatic relations expelling Israel's ambassador in Cairo and recalling Egypt's ambassador in Tel Aviv, as well as a return to economic boycott policies and the cessation of gas exports to that country.

66. In an apparent response to this trip to Gaza, in December Israel blocked the Tunisian ambassador to Palestine from returning to Ramallah. See *Tunisia Live*, 6 December 2012. On the other hand, the Moroccan response to this offensive focused on the humanitarian sphere – setting up a field hospital – and avoided an official visit to the strip, disappointing some domestic circles.

67. *Aswat Masriya*, 5 February 2013. Some Salafist organizations in Egypt were particularly critical of the possible Shiite influence that this visit might symbolize. See *Ahram Online*, 5 February 2013.

68. Tension had risen between Egypt and Ethiopia since May–June 2013, after the latter disclosed its plans to build a giant dam (Nahda) on the upper Nile, which were viewed in Cairo with anxiety, as a threat to national water security (Halawa 2013; Blanc 2014).

69. *Ahram Online*, 19 July 2013, 15 August 2013.

70. *Egypt Independent*, 26 September 2013.

71. *Tunisia Live*, 30 September 2013.

72. Ministère des affaires étrangères et de la coopération [MAEC, Morocco], Press Release, 28 October 2014.

73. www.state.gov/r/pa/prs/ps/2014/09/231886.htm.

74. *Ahram Online*, 8 October 2014.

75. European Commission/High Representative of the European Union for Foreign Affairs and Security Policy, "Joint Communication to the European Parliament, the Council, the European Economic and Social Committee and the Committee of the Regions: Supporting closer cooperation and regional integration in the Maghreb: Algeria, Libya, Mauritania, Morocco and Tunisia", JOIN (2012) 36 final, 17 December 2012.

76. *Lakome*, 2 May 2013.

77. *Al Hayat*, 12 September 2013.

78. Some information suggested that Mohammed Ould Abdel Aziz suspected possible Moroccan complicity in the attack that almost killed him in October 2012. See *Demain Online*, 26 December 2012. Many opponents of his regime had moved to Marrakech since 2008. *Yabiladi*, 27 September 2013.

79. *Le Quotidien d'Oran*, 5 December 2012. *Jeune Afrique*, 18 December 2012.

80. *Jeune Afrique*, 12 December 2012. The most serious bilateral crisis between Morocco and France since the early 1990s broke out in February 2014, after a French NGO filed lawsuits for "complicity in torture" of several French citizens (of Moroccan and Sahrawi origin) against Abdellatif Hammouchi, the head of the Moroccan domestic intelligence agency Directorate-General for Territorial Surveillance (DGST), and French police officers went to the very residence of the Moroccan ambassador in Paris to deliver the court's summons without Rabat's diplomacy having been previously alerted. Morocco suspended the implementation of all judicial cooperation agreements with France.

References

Abuel Hassan, Gamal (2013), "Morsi and Netanyahu: Business as Usual", *Al Monitor*, 4 April.

Achy, Lahcen (2011), "Morocco: What a GCC Membership Would Mean for the Economy", *Babylon & Beyond/Los Angeles Times*, 3 June.

Addi, Lahouari (2013), "La crise algérienne au prisme de la guerre au Mali", *Libération*, 3 February.

Albarracín, Javier & Cusí, Paula (2012), "Les agendas économiques des partis islamistes en Afrique du Nord", *Afkar/Idées*, No. 35, Autumn, pp. 58–61.

Alissa, Sufyan (2007), "The Challenge of Economic Reform in the Arab World: Towards More Productive Economies", Carnegie Endowment for International Peace/Carnegie Middle East Center, Carnegie Papers No. 1, May.

Ammour, Laurence Aïda (2013), "Algeria, the Sahel, and the Current Mali Crisis", *Notes Internacionals CIDOB*, No. 67, January, 1–6.

Arieff, Alexis (2012), "Algeria and the Crisis in Mali", Institut Français des Relations Internationales, Actuelles de l'Ifri, 19 July.

Attalah, Lina (2012), "Sinai: The Paradox of Security", *Bitterlemons International*, 29 March.

Ayub, Fatima, Al Omran, Ahmed, Roberts, David, Kareem, Mona & Gengler, Justin (2013), "What Does the Gulf Think about the Arab Awakening?", European Council on Foreign Relations, Gulf Analysis, April.

Aziz, Sahar (2013), "Sinai's Role in Morsi's Ouster", *Sada*, 20 August.

Behr, Timo (2012), "After the Revolution: The EU and the Arab Transition", Notre Europe, Policy Paper No. 54, April.

Biscop, Sven, Balfour, Rosa & Emerson, Michael (2012), *An Arab Springboard for EU Foreign Policy?* Brussels/Ghent: Egmont/Academia Press.

Blanc, Pierre (2014), "De l'Egypte à l'Ethiopie, quand la puissance se déplace en Afrique nilotique", *Confluences Méditerranée*, No. 90, Summer, pp. 123–139.

Boserup, Rasmus Alenius, Martinez, Luis & Holm, Ulla (2014), "Algeria after the Revolts. Regime Endurance in a Time of Contention and Regional Insecurity", Danish Institute for International Studies, DIIS Report No. 15, June.

Boukhars, Anouar (2012), "The Paranoid Neighbor. Algeria and the Conflict in Mali", Carnegie Endowment for International Peace/Middle East, October.

Bregolat Obiols, Eugenio (2010), "China's Influence in the Mediterranean", in *IEMed Mediterranean Yearbook 2010*, Barcelona: IEMed, pp. 23–27.

Caprioli, Mary & Trumbore, Peter F. (2003), "Identifying 'Rogue' States and Testing Their Interstate Conflict Behavior", *European Journal of International Relations*, Vol. 9, No. 3, September, pp. 377–406.

Chams El-Dine, Chérine (2013), "The Military and Egypt's Transformation Process", Stiftung Wissenschaft und Politik, SWP Comments No. 6, February.

Charef, Abed (2013), "L'Algérie et la crise malienne", *Afkar/Idées*, No. 37, Spring, pp. 46–48.

Charillon, Frédéric (2007), "Les politiques étrangères contestataires", *Les Cahiers de l'Orient*, No. 87, September, pp. 25–31.

Cole, Peter (2012), "Borderline Chaos? Stabilizing Libya's Periphery", Carnegie Endowment for International Peace/Middle East, October.

Colombo, Silvia, Coates-Ulrichsen, Kristian, Ghabra, Shafeeq, Hamid, Shadi & Ragab, Eman (2012), "The GCC in the Mediterranean in Light of the Arab Spring", German Marshall Fund of the United States/Istituto Affari Internazionali, Mediterranean Paper Series, December.

Darbouche, Hakim (2008), "Decoding Algeria's ENP Policy: Differentiation by Other Means?", *Mediterranean Politics*, Vol. 13, No. 3, November, pp. 371–389.

Darbouche, Hakim & Dennison, Susi (2011), "A 'Reset' with Algeria: The Russia to the EU's South", European Council on Foreign Relations, Policy Brief No. 46, December.

Dennison, Susi (2012), "The EU, Algeria and the Northern Mali Question", European Council on Foreign Relations, Policy Brief No. 69, December.

Desrues, Thierry & Hernando de Larramendi, Miguel (2012), "Initiatives souveraines, attentisme partisan et protestation au Sahara: une année politique transitoire au Maroc", in *L'Année du Maghreb 2011*, Paris: CNRS, pp. 305–332.

Dris-Aït Hamadouche, Louisa (2014), "L'Algérie et la sécurité au Sahel: lecture critique d'une approche paradoxale", *Confluences Méditerranée*, No. 90, Summer, pp. 105–121.

Dunne, Michele (2012), "Rethinking U.S. Relations with a Changing Egypt", Project on Middle East Democracy (POMED), Policy Brief, 22 March.

Dunne, Michele (2014), "Foreign Policy Shaped by Donors", *Sada*, 3 April.

Dunne, Michele & Brown, Nathan J. (2014), "How Egypt Prolonged the Gaza War", *Foreign Policy*, 18 August.

Ehteshami, Anoushiravan (2010), "Iranian Political Influence on the Euro-Mediterranean Region", in *IEMed Mediterranean Yearbook 2010*, Barcelona: IEMed, pp. 28–32.

Entelis, John P. (2013), "Algerian Crisis: The Primacy of Le Pouvoir", *The Cairo Review of Global Affairs*, 28 January.

Escribano, Gonzalo (2013), "A Political Economy Perspective on North Africa's Transitions", Real Instituto Elcano, Working Paper 3/2013, 30 January.

Esfandiary, Dina (2012), "Iran and Egypt: A Complicated Tango?", European Union Institute for Security Studies (ISS), 18 October.

Falk, Richard (2012), "Turkey's Foreign Policy: Zero Problems with Neighbors Revisited", *Foreign Policy Journal*, 9 February, available at https://richardfalk.wordpress.com/2012/02/08/turkeys-foreign-policy-zero-problems-with-neighbors-revisited/, accessed 15 June 2015.

Fernández Molina, Irene (2007), "Le PJD et la politique étrangère du Maroc: entre l'idéologie et le pragmatisme", *Documentos CIDOB Mediterráneo*, No. 7, May. Barcelona: Documentos CIDOB.

Fernández Molina, Irene (2013a), *La política exterior de Marruecos en el reinado de Mohamed VI (1999–2008). Actores, discursos y proyecciones internas*, PhD thesis, Madrid: Universidad Complutense de Madrid.

Fernández Molina, Irene (2013b), "Breaking the Deadlock in the Western Sahara", *Sada*, 10 June.

Goodman, Joshua (2012), "Shades of the Sinai's Instability", *Sada*, 15 March.

Grimm, Jannis & Roll, Stephan (2012), "Egyptian Foreign Policy under Mohamed Morsi. Domestic Considerations and Economic Constraints", Stiftung Wissenschaft und Politik, SWP Comments 35, November.

Halawa, Abdelmonem (2013), "Morsi Struggles with Policy Toward Ethiopia's 'Nahda' Dam", *Fikra Forum*, 11 June.

Helmy, Abdallah (2014), "Egypt's Sisi Gains Leverage from the Fight Against the Islamic State", European Council on Foreign Relations, Commentary, 2 October.

Hernando de Larramendi, Miguel (2008), "Intra-Maghrebi Relations. Unitary Myth and National Interests", in Zoubir, Yahia H. & Amirah Fernández, Haizam (eds.), *North Africa: Politics, Region, and the Limits of Transformation*, London/New York: Routledge, pp. 179–201.

Hernando de Larramendi, Miguel (2012), "Construction maghrébine après le 'Printemps arabe'", *Afkar/Idées*, No. 36, Winter, pp. 22–24.

Hernando de Larramendi, Miguel (2013), "El islamismo político y el ejercicio del poder tras el despertar árabe: los casos de Egipto, Túnez y Marruecos", *El islamismo en (R)evolución: movilización social y cambio político*, Cuaderno de Estrategia, No. 163, pp. 71–116.

Hillal Dessouki, Ali E. (2009), "Regional Leadership: Balancing off Costs and Dividends in the Foreign Policy of Egypt", in Korany, Bahgat & Dessouki, Ali E. Hillal (eds.), *The Foreign Policies of Arab States: The Challenge of Globalization*, 3rd ed., Cairo: American University in Cairo Press, pp. 167–195.

Hinnebusch, Raymond & Ehteshami, Anoushiravan (eds.) (2002), *The Foreign Policies of Middle East States*, London: Lynne Rienner.

Holsti, Kal J. (1970), "National Role Conceptions in the Study of Foreign Policy", *International Studies Quarterly*, Vol. 14, No. 3, September, pp. 233–309.

Hoyt, Paul (2000), "'Rogue States' and International Relations Theory", *Journal of Conflict Studies*, Vol. 20, No. 2, Fall, available at https://journals.lib.unb.ca/index.php/JCS/article/view/4312/4927, accessed 16 June 2015.

International Crisis Group (2012), "Israel and Hamas: Fire and Ceasefire in a New Middle East", Middle East Report No. 133, 22 November.

International Crisis Group (2013a), "Tunisia: Violence and the Salafi Challenge", Middle East/North Africa Report No. 137, 13 February.

International Crisis Group (2013b), "Marching in Circles: Egypt's Dangerous Second Transition", Middle East/North Africa Briefing No. 35, 7 August.

International Crisis Group (2013c), "Tunisia's Borders: Jihadism and Contraband", Middle East/North Africa Report No. 148, 28 November.

International Crisis Group (2014), "La Tunisie des frontières (II): terrorisme et polarisation régionale", Middle East/North Africa Briefing No. 41, 21 October.

Joffé, George & Paoletti, Emanuela (2010), "Libya's Foreign Policy: Drivers and Objectives", German Marshall Fund of the United States/Istituto Affari Internazionali, Mediterranean Paper Series, October.

Keenan, Jeremy H. (2012), "Foreign Policy and the Global War on Terror in the Reproduction of Algerian State Power", *State Crime*, Vol. 1, No. 2, Autumn, pp. 196–216.

Kéfi, Ridha (2012), "Les nouvelles orientations diplomatiques", *Afkar/Idées*, No. 36, Winter, pp. 18–20.

Khalaji, Mehdi (2012), "The Enduring Egypt-Iran Divide", The Washington Institute, 31 December.

Kinninmont, Jane (2012), "Egypt and President Mohammed Morsi Make a Good Impression on the West", *The Telegraph*, 22 November.

Korany, Bahgat & Dessouki, Ali E. Hillal (eds.) (2009) *The Foreign Policies of Arab States: The Challenge of Globalization*, 3rd ed., Cairo: American University in Cairo Press.

Lampridi-Kemou, Athina & Azaola, Bárbara (2013), "Contemporary Egypt: Between Reform and Continuity", in Izquierdo Brichs, Ferran (ed.), *Political Regimes in the Arab World. Society and Exercise of Power*, London/New York: Routledge, pp. 125–152.

Makovsky, David (2012), "How to Defuse the Israel-Gaza Conflict: Cairo's Crucial Role", *The New York Times*, 20 November.

Mañé, Aurèlia (2011), "¿Ha acabado la crisis global con el contrato social árabe?", *Economía Exterior*, No. 57, Summer, pp. 99–110.

Martinez, Luis (2010), "Algérie: les illusions de la richesse pétrolière", Centre d'Études et de Recherches Internationales (CERI), Les Études du CERI No. 168, September.

Nickels, Benjamin P. (2013a), "Morocco's Engagement with the Sahel Community", *Sada*, 3 January.

Nickels, Benjamin P. (2013b), "Mali's Regional Ramifications", *Sada*, 6 June.

Nicolas, Françoise (2011),"Chine et Inde: deux nouveaux acteurs dans l'espace nord-africain", in Mohsen-Finan, Khadija (ed.), *Le Maghreb dans les relations internationales*, Paris: CNRS, pp. 307–334.

Nonneman, Gerd (ed.) (2005), *Analyzing Middle East Foreign Policies and the Relationship with Europe*, London/New York: Routledge.

Parejo, María Angustias & Feliu, Laura (2012), "Morocco: The Reinvention of a Totalitarian System", in Izquierdo Brichs, Ferrán (ed.), *Political Regimes in the Arab World. Society and the Exercise of Power*, London & New York: Routledge, pp. 70–99.

Phillips, Christopher (2014), "The Arabism Debate and the Arab Uprisings", *Mediterranean Politics*, Vol. 19, No. 1, March, pp. 141–144.

Pinfari, Marco (2012), "A Changing Mediterranean: Regional Organisations and North Africa during the Arab Spring", *The International Spectator*, Vol. 47, No. 1, March, pp. 134–150.

Project on Middle East Democracy (2012), "Backgrounder: The Campaign Against NGOs in Egypt", POMED, 10 February.

Putnam, Robert D. (1988), "Diplomacy and Domestic Politics: The Logic of Two-Level Games", *International Organization*, Vol. 42, No. 3, Summer, pp. 427–460.

Rękawek, Kacper & Sasnal, Patrycja (2012), "Libya's Problems after Qaddafi", Polish Institute of International Affairs, Bulletin No. 94 (427), 2 October.

Remiro Brotons, Antonio & Martínez Capdevila, Carmen (eds.) (2012), *Unión Europea-Marruecos: ¿Una vecindad privilegiada?* Madrid: Academia Europea de Ciencias y Artes.

Roussellier, Jacques (2014), "ISIS, a Game Changer for Algeria", *Sada*, 21 October.

Roy, Olivier (2012), "The Myth of the Islamist Winter", *New Statesman*, 13 December.

Sánchez Mateos, Elvira (2005), "Libya's Return to the International Scene", *Mediterranean Politics*, Vol. 10, No. 3, November, pp. 439–445.

Sasnal, Patrycja (2012), "Egypt's Foreign Policy: Post-Western and Pan-Islamic", EuroMeSCo Brief No. 34, 8 February.

Sayah, Habib (2012), "La Tunisie face aux enjeux régionaux: entre leadership et intégration", Institut Kheireddine, 19 May.

Schumacher, Tobias (2012), "New Neighbors, Old Formulas? The ENP One Year after the Start of the Arab Spring", in Ghali, Amine, et al. (eds.), *The Arab Spring: One Year After. Transformation Dynamics, Prospects for Democratization and the Future of Arab-European Cooperation*, Gütersloh: Bertelsmann Stiftung, pp. 87–104.

Schumacher, Tobias & Fernández Molina, Irene (2013), "EU and GCC Countries' Foreign Policies and the Mediterranean Neighbourhood. Towards Synergetic Cooperation?", Gulf Research Center, Gulf Papers, August.

Spencer, Claire (2012), "Strategic Posture Review: Algeria", *World Politics Review*, 25 July.

Tocci, Nathalie, Maestri, Elena, Özel, Soli & Güvenc, Serhat (2012), "Ideational and Material Power in the Mediterranean: The Role of Turkey and the Gulf Cooperation Council", German Marshall Fund of the United States/Istituto Affari Internazionali, Mediterranean Paper Series, June.

Trager, Eric (2012), "The Gaza Invasion: Will It Destroy Israel's Relationship with Egypt?", *The Atlantic*, 15 November.

Wehrey, Frederic (2013), "Libya's Revolution at Two Years: Perils and Achievements", *Mediterranean Politics*, Vol. 18, No. 1, March, pp. 115–121.

Wehrey, Frederic, Bishop, David & Alrababa'h, Ala' (2014), "Backdrop to an Intervention: Sources of Egyptian-Libyan Border Tension", Carnegie Endowment for International Peace, Article, 27 August.

Zoubir, Yahia H. (2004), "The Resurgence of Algeria's Foreign Policy in the Twenty-First Century", *The Journal of North African Studies*, Vol. 9, No. 2, Summer, pp. 169–183.

Zoubir, Yahia H. (2011), "The United States and Libya: The Limits of Coercive Diplomacy," *Journal of North African Studies*, Vol. 16, No. 2, June, pp. 275–297.

Zoubir, Yahia H. (2012a), "Tipping the Balance Towards Intra-Maghreb Unity in Light of the Arab Spring", *The International Spectator*, Vol. 47, No. 3, September, pp. 83–99.

Zoubir, Yahia H. (2012b), "The Sahara-Sahel Quagmire: Regional and International Ramifications", *Mediterranean Politics*, Vol. 17, No. 3, November, pp. 452–458.

16

THE UNITED STATES AND NORTH AFRICA

Yahia H. Zoubir and Stephen Zunes[1]

Long neglected as a region in U.S. strategic calculations, North Africa has taken on added importance not only since the 9/11 attacks on the United States, but also following the popular uprisings in Egypt, one of the main U.S. allies in the region, and in Libya. What are the United States' interests in North Africa? Is it true that it aims not only at countering terrorism and assisting the countries in the region, but also at countering the growing Chinese and Russian influence in the region? Is it also true that the United States – through various programs, such as the Middle East Partnership Initiative (MEPI) and the Millennium Challenge Account – seeks to undermine European initiatives, such as the Euro-Mediterranean Partnership (Barcelona Process), replaced by the Union for the Mediterranean (UfM) in 2008?

The main argument in this chapter is that U.S. interest for North Africa has grown considerably and that, in terms of regional security, Washington has already consolidated its influence. If in the 1990s, transatlantic relations in the area were more complementary than competitive,[2] it has become evident that the United States now plays a role of leadership in Maghreb-Sahel security. This chapter analyzes the evolution of U.S. policy toward the Maghreb. One of the subsidiary arguments is that President Barack Obama has consolidated the policy that his predecessor, President George W. Bush, pursued toward the region. When Barack Obama became president of the United States in January 2009, there was widespread expectation that he would pursue a less militaristic, more multilateral, and much more cooperative policy than that of his predecessor. There was also the anticipation that he would push for genuine democratization and thus put pressure on authoritarian regimes in the Middle East and North Africa (MENA) region to implement concrete democratic reforms. Following 9/11, the United States urged Arab regimes to democratize, though such pressure was limited and inconsistent. Particularly following Hamas's 2006 democratic electoral victory in Palestine, it became more apparent that the United States, and Europe for that matter, would prefer authoritarian or semi-authoritarian regimes to Islamist-oriented ones. This is why expectations were high in the MENA that Obama's policy would make good governance and democracy an essential part of U.S. foreign policy.

Until the Arab uprisings of 2010–2011, continuity rather than change characterized U.S. policy toward the Maghreb, and security issues continued to predominate over questions of democracy and good governance. In May 2010, the administration unveiled the National Security Strategy, which stated that:

> The United States supports the expansion of democracy and human rights abroad because governments that respect these values are more just, peaceful, and legitimate. We also do so because their success abroad fosters an environment that supports America's national interests. Political systems that protect universal rights are ultimately more stable, successful, and secure. As our history shows, the United States can more effectively forge consensus to tackle shared challenges when working with governments that reflect the will and respect the rights of their people, rather than just the narrow interests of those in power.[3]

Although this statement reflected the hoped-for changes after eight unsuccessful years under the Bush administration, as well as Obama's foreign policy orientation before his election, there was little evidence in the conduct of U.S. policy to support the policy declarations enunciated in the National Security Strategy document. In rejecting the problematic neoconservative ideology of his predecessor, Obama had largely fallen back onto the *realpolitik* of previous administrations – by continuing to support Hosni Mubarak and other repressive allies in the region through unconditional arms transfers and other security assistance. While the Obama administration, like much of the international community, was understandably skeptical of externally mandated, top-down approaches to democratization through "regime change" – a key element in the foreign policy of the outgoing Bush administration – as of the end of the first half of Obama's first term, there appeared to be no alternative policy in place.

Despite this, there was nonetheless a subtle shift in the U.S. government's discourse on human rights when Obama came to office. The Bush administration pushed a rather superficial, structuralist view. It focused, for instance, on elections – which can easily be rigged and manipulated in many cases – in order to change certain governments for purposes of expanding U.S. power and influence. Indeed, Bush praised the fraudulent 2005 presidential elections in Egypt as "important steps" toward freedom and democracy. Obama, by contrast, took on more of an agency view of human rights, emphasizing such rights as freedom of expression and the right to protest, recognizing that true democracy can only come from below and not imposed from above. At the same time, it quickly became apparent that, regardless of the rhetoric about democracy and good governance, security relations remained paramount. For example, military assistance to autocratic North African regimes continued and, in some instances, increased. It is safe to argue at the onset that the continuity in policy reflected Obama's genuine belief in the logic of the Global War on Terror (GWOT), or what the Obama administration soon after its inauguration relabeled "Overseas Contingency Operation."[4] Regardless of which phrase is used, the Obama administration, through its actions, had in many ways, at least until the uprisings, pursued the same strategic logic as that of the second-term Bush administration. In other words, the ideological foundations of U.S. policy had remained basically the same. An analysis of U.S. policy toward the Maghreb and its contiguous region, the Sahel, corroborates this observation, even if some adaptations had to be operated rhetorically, following the 2011 events in Tunisia, Egypt, and Libya. While some calls for greater democratization were ushered, the patterns had remained virtually the same, except perhaps the leniency that the United States showed toward Islamist parties in Tunisia and Egypt – which led to some suspicions in those countries that the United States wished to promote Islamist regimes.

As will be examined in more detail below, the Obama administration's response to popular challenges to allied dictatorships in Tunisia and Egypt was mixed. To its credit, the Obama administration quickly recognized that the pro-democracy revolutions were not seeking American leadership and that any efforts to become too deeply involved would be counter-productive. Criticisms that the United States had not exercised sufficient leadership in more directly supporting the uprisings are seriously misplaced, since to do so would have almost certainly created a backlash that would have harmed these movements. Similarly, the Obama administration correctly realized it could not stop these uprisings either, despite criticisms from the right that they bear responsibility for the downfall of staunch U.S. allies. Indeed, as with former Soviet leader Mikhail Gorbachev in the face of the pro-democracy uprisings in Eastern Europe in 1989, Obama recognized there were limits as to what a declining hegemonic power could control in an increasingly pluralistic and complex region.

There were times when it appeared that President Obama genuinely supported the aspirations of the revolutions,[5] even while recognizing that public opinion in the Arab world – which would matter much more in the case of democratization – was generally less favorably aligned to U.S. policy goals than allied autocratic regimes. However, there were other times when it appeared that his administration was reluctant to end its backing of autocratic allies or support the aspirations of the largely youthful pro-democracy protesters in the streets.

The United States and North Africa: Historical background

While Egypt and Libya had been considered of important strategic significance for the United States, the former French possessions of Tunisia, Algeria, and Morocco were primarily seen as being within the French sphere of influence. Since the late 1970s, however, the entire region has become one of great strategic significance to the United States. Not only has the search for energy become a paramount objective, but the events of 9/11 had played a critical factor in persuading U.S. policymakers to establish a presence in the Maghreb and its neighboring Sahel region.

The expansion, albeit limited, of the Al-Qaeda network into the Maghreb-Sahel region induced the United States to devise a number of security measures to counter the suspected threats emanating from the sizable, vastly barren, not fully controlled area. Indeed, the United States has instituted many security and military arrangements with the local governments to achieve its objectives. Yet, it is still uncertain whether the United States has sought to and/or succeeded in establishing its hegemony in this region as it has in the Middle East. The objective here is two-fold: (a) identify U.S. interests and analyze how Washington has sought to achieve them; and (b) determine how much shift in policy toward the region has taken place under the Obama administration, especially since the Arab uprisings.

Even during the cold war period when the United States in the main paid relatively little attention to the Maghreb, the United States was cognizant of its interests in the region and was certainly not oblivious to events there. Indeed, during certain periods, the United States showed greater economic and political interest. One can cite a few important phases during which the United States became involved in the Maghreb: the Second World War, the decolonization period in the 1950s and 1960s, the conflict in Western Sahara since 1975, the Algerian crisis in the 1990s, the period since 9/11, and, of course, since the upheavals of 2010–2011. In spite of its desire to see the formation of an integrated region in North Africa, the United States seldom viewed the Maghreb as a regional entity, notwithstanding its geopolitical importance; Washington preferred to maintain bilateral relations with each state. Bilateral relations with Morocco and with Tunisia had been close since the independence of these two countries in 1956 and have remained so until today.[6] The Maghreb as a regional entity was significant only insofar as the events in the area could potentially threaten the stability of Southern Europe, NATO's Southern Flank. Throughout the cold war period, the main objective was curbing communist influence, in particular that of the USSR, and promoting Western interests. In spite of close relations with Morocco and Tunisia, Americans relied on France, the old colonial power, to play the dominant role in the Maghreb. Therefore, until the beginning of the 1990s, there was no American regional policy in the Maghreb. However, following the end of the cold war and the collapse of the Eastern bloc, a regional policy (dictated by the global strategy of the unrivaled U.S. superpower), seemed to gradually take shape. Thus, in the 1990s, American policy favored the emergence of a regional entity in the Maghreb, an integrated market economy following the concept of "trading blocs" or trade zones. Although Libya was not included in the plan, the United States considered its eventual integration once relations with that country were completely normalized in 2008. Following full, formal normalization of relations with Libya in 2008, the United States has included Libya in the North Africa Partnership for Economic Opportunity (NAPEO),[7] which replaced the U.S.-North Africa Economic Partnership, launched in 1999, from which Libya had been excluded.

In the post-cold war period, U.S. interest in the Maghreb increased considerably. This resulted from two major factors: (a) the globalization of economic and trade relations; and (b) the events of 9/11, not least because many members of the

Al-Qaeda terrorist network, the so-called "Arab Afghans," are of North African origin. By the end of the 1990s, American policymakers were persuaded that the Maghreb was a promising regional economic entity. However, as we try to show in this chapter, the stalemate in Western Sahara has hitherto precluded regional integration because of the tension over the conflict between the two pillars of the process of integration – namely, Algeria, which supports the independence movement, and Morocco, the occupying power in Western Sahara. Since its inception in 1975, the Western Sahara conflict aggravated tensions in Algerian–Moroccan relations, thus making their economic integration virtually impossible.[8] To this day, the conflict between Morocco and the Sahrawi nationalists remains unresolved. The continued stalemate has not only worsened Algerian–Moroccan relations, accelerated an arms race, and prevented regional integration, but it has also compelled Washington to readjust its policy to adapt to that reality. Although the status quo in Western Sahara has not had a major negative impact on U.S. policy in the region, it has nonetheless severely constrained the security cooperation between Algeria and Morocco, two major partners in the fight against global terrorism.

The issue that has kept the most attention of the U.S. policy in the Maghreb relates to the Western Sahara conflict.[9] Given the cold war context and the U.S.'s traditionally close ties with Morocco, the United States used its power to ensure that Morocco would prevail in Western Sahara. Because Algeria was an ally of the Soviet Union, the United States viewed the conflict from a cold war perspective and left no doubt as to what side it was on, regardless of the fact that the question of Western Sahara was (and remains) a decolonization issue and that Sahrawi nationalism received no support from the Soviet Union.

The United States' bilateral relations with the North African states

Despite their proclaimed statements about building a unified entity similar to the European Union, the Maghreb states have failed to materialize that vision, not even with the creation in 1989 of the Arab Maghreb Union (U.M.A.) and the eventual attribution to Egypt of an observer status. Their differences derive from the ideological, political, and economic orientations that the Maghreb states established following their independence from colonial rule. Morocco and Tunisia, like Egypt, opted for a pro-Western orientation and thus established close security relations with Western countries. For historical reasons, Algeria, though nonaligned, established close political and military relations with the socialist countries. Though also nonaligned, Libya adopted an anti-Western orientation that brought it at loggerheads with the Western world, the United States in particular, while maintaining strong ties with Moscow to offset Western pressure.[10] Enmity between the United States and Libya took on serious proportions in the 1980s, with the United States engaging in a series of air strikes on the country in retaliation for alleged Libyan ties to terrorist groups and disputes over navigation in the Gulf of Sidra.

Morocco

Given their historic ties, coupled with the ideological and political affinities that bound Morocco and the United States, Morocco has always occupied a strategic position in U.S. policy toward the Maghreb. During the cold war, Morocco played a key role as a proxy for U.S. interests in Africa and the Middle East, dispatching its armed forces to troubled areas and giving the Central Intelligence Agency and the National Security Agency (NSA) wide latitude to operate in the kingdom. Notwithstanding the geopolitical transformations that have occurred since the cold war, Morocco has retained its strategic significance for the United States because the monarchy has consistently played a key role on behalf of the United States in various arenas, such as counterterrorism, support for African allies, and a relative openness toward Israel. This explains why, prior to the U.S. occupation of Iraq, it received more U.S. aid than any other Arab country, with the exception of Egypt. This aid, which increased manifold during the war between 1976 and 1991, was instrumental in allowing Morocco to continue its occupation of Western Sahara. The U.S. assistance to Morocco, despite occasional fluctuations, has remained relatively constant. Under the Obama administration, such aid has now extended to yet other allocations, such as the Trans-Saharan Counterterrorism Partnership (TSCTP), through which Morocco receives military and security assistance. U.S. aid to Morocco currently totals over $30 million, with approximately one-third of that military-related. In a reversal of previous policy which forbade Morocco from using U.S. assistance outside its internationally recognized borders, Congress pushed through language beginning in 2011 that aid "shall be made available for assistance for the Western Sahara," which many observers interpreted as an endorsement of Morocco's control over that occupied country. In late December 2009, Lockheed Martin (with Washington's support) secured an $841.9-million contract to finalize production of twenty-four new F-16 fighters for the Kingdom of Morocco, as well as for electronic-warfare gear and support equipment. The contract built on a preliminary $233-million award Lockheed obtained in June 2008 to start off the construction of the airplane.[11] Although it is true that Algeria in 2006 had purchased considerable hardware to replace and/ or upgrade its near-obsolete equipment, the decision of the United States to allow the sale and the financing of sophisticated equipment to Morocco has contributed to the arms race in the region.[12]

American concern with the survival of the pro-Western, "moderate" monarchy – as guarantor of the U.S. and Western presence in the area – has overridden other regional concerns. The U.S. reaction to 9/11 bolstered Morocco's standing in U.S. policy, even though neighboring Algeria, whose security and military cooperation has been very effective, is also now a strategic partner of the United States in the region. One cannot understand U.S. support for Morocco, which has continued under the Obama administration, without comprehending the historic centrality of Morocco in the U.S. policy toward the Maghreb. In the era of globalization, America's support for Morocco is perhaps also related to the acceleration of economic reforms and the liberalization of the market, which included large-scale privatization, an approach which coincides with American ideological objectives. Also significant is the support in favor of Morocco within both parties in the U.S. Congress, in part because Morocco is regarded as less hostile towards Israel than most Arab states. Despite human rights violations, the United States did not change its policy towards Morocco, which it often depicts as a model of democratic reform in the Arab world.

In 2004, the Bush administration designated Morocco as a "major non-NATO ally," a coveted status then granted to only fifteen key nations, such as Japan, Israel, and Australia. The following month, the Senate ratified a free trade agreement with Morocco, making the kingdom one of only a half dozen countries outside of the Western hemisphere to enjoy such a close economic relationship with the United States. The long-standing ties with Morocco explain why the United States has never supported the emergence of an independent Western Sahara, espousing instead Morocco's so-called "autonomy" proposal over a referendum on self-determination as recognized in UN resolutions.[13] In doing so, the United States is effectively supporting the annexation of the territory without an act of self-determination by the people of what is recognized as a non-self-governing territory as required by international law. In November 2013, White House spokesman Jay Carney announced that President Obama believes "Morocco's autonomy plan is serious, realistic, and credible. It represents a potential approach that can satisfy the aspirations of the people in the Western Sahara to run their own affairs in peace and dignity." Morocco also has strong support within the Pentagon and some segments of the State Department.

President Obama and Moroccan King Mohammed VI met in November 2013. Two days before the summit, Human Rights Watch issued a statement calling on the U.S. president to tell the king that "U.S. support for the reform process in Morocco depends on moving beyond rhetoric and making tangible change." Specifically, the human rights group called for "stronger legal protections for rights and an end to impunity for police who use violence and commit other abuses."[14] Instead, according to a White House statement, Obama applauded the Moroccan monarch for "deepening democracy" and "promoting economic progress and human development."[15]

Though there have indeed been at least some modest political openings, along with economic liberalization, within Morocco itself, the United States has failed to publicly acknowledge the seriousness of the human rights situation within the occupied Western Sahara. While the State Department's annual report on human rights acknowledges "limitations on the freedom of speech, press, assembly, and association . . . [and] the use of arbitrary and prolonged detention to quell dissent," the suppression of supporters of self-determination, and the use of "torture, beatings, and other mistreatment of detainees" with impunity,[16] a White House statement following the conclusion of the summit pledged that the United States and Morocco would "work together to continue to protect and promote human rights in the territory."[17]

Algeria

Until the last decade, Algeria's relations with the United States were not all that close, which explains why the regime received little support when it was on the brink of collapse in the 1990s in the face of a violent Islamist insurgency. Due to European concerns, however, the United States became more involved in the region and eventually provided some conditional support to Algeria. By the close of the 1990s and into early 2000, the situation in Algeria had improved considerably. This normalization, coupled with the events of 9/11, resulted in a dramatic rapprochement between Algiers and Washington, most notably in the security and military realms. Algeria has since regularly taken part in joint military exercises. Given Algeria's geographical location and its geopolitical significance, Americans reiterated *ad nauseam* that Algeria is "an exceptional partner of the United States in the global war on terrorism." The United States succeeded in drawing Algeria into a regional security arrangement, which includes not only the Maghrebi countries (Algeria, Mauritania, Morocco, and Tunisia), but also the Sahelian states, such as Chad, Mali, Senegal, Niger, and even Nigeria.

The bilateral military cooperation is evident on the ground as American and Algerian troops work closely together in the Algerian desert.[18] Yet, the amount of U.S. military assistance to Algeria remains relatively insignificant. In 2014, the United States provided Algeria with a modest $1.3 million within the International Military Education and Training (IMET) program for training military personnel in the United States and a similar amount in counterterrorism assistance. The United States no longer seems to make an issue with the obvious resurgence of authoritarianism in Algeria. The strong cooperation in the security field has allowed not only Algeria but also other authoritarian states to collect dividends from their security cooperation with the United States.[19] Under the Obama administration, the United States has been pleased with the leadership that Algeria has taken in promoting regional security cooperation. For instance, on March 16, 2010, Algeria organized a successful ministerial conference in Algiers that brought together the Sahara-Sahel countries, Algeria, Burkina Faso, Libya, Mali, Mauritania, Niger, and Chad. The main objective was to strengthen the war on terrorism in the region and to implement UN antiterrorism resolution 1904 (December 2009),[20] which criminalizes the payment of ransoms to hostage takers who use the ransoms to fund terrorist activities.[21] The United States expressed support for this initiative.[22] In March 2011, the two countries held the first meeting of the Bilateral Contact Group on Algerian-American Counterterrorism and Security Cooperation.[23] From the U.S. perspective, "the launch of the Bilateral Contact Group on Algerian-American Counterterrorism and Security Cooperation represents a historic moment for the development of bilateral security cooperation. This mechanism will give a new qualitative impetus to the U.S.-Algerian strategic partnership."[24] A strategic dialogue was initiated in October the following year.[25]

One should also note that economic relations between Algeria, a hydrocarbons producer, and the United States have also witnessed considerable expansion since

July 2001, when the two countries signed a Framework Agreement on Trade and Investment; the accord instituted a consultative procedure on trade and investment that will eventually result in a bilateral investment treaty, mutual trade benefits, and a double taxation arrangement, and it effectively opened up Algeria's profitable oil and gas resources more broadly to multinational corporations. Bilateral trade between Algeria and the United States has grown continuously; the volume of exchanges has surpassed $12 billion. Given U.S. energy dependence, Algeria will remain, however, a strategic market for the United States for the years to come, since, according to the U.S. Department of Energy, "Algeria holds the world's tenth-largest amount of proved natural gas reserves and the third-largest technically recoverable shale gas resources."[26]

Tunisia

Since its independence in 1956, Tunisia maintained almost unbroken, friendly relations with the United States. Tunisia's pro-Western stance proved extremely attractive, as did its model of political, economic, and social development. In the 1990s, it was common for American policymakers to portray Tunisia as a success story: reforms, market liberalization, secularism, promotion of women's rights, unconstrained use of birth control, and elimination of illiteracy.

The United States and Tunisia conducted joint military operations annually. Owing to its strategic importance and its "moderation," Tunisia had succeeded in escaping, at least publicly, condemnation of its serious violations of human rights. Tunisia was spared because, like Morocco and Egypt, it justified repression in the name of maintaining the stability and the survival of the government against "radical" Islamist forces hostile to the Western world. Tunisia continued to benefit from Washington's leniency and tolerance of its authoritarian regime[27] until the overthrow of President Zine el Abidine Ben Ali on January 14, 2011.

In the years prior to the popular uprising, the United States appeared oblivious to the growing discontent in the country. The U.S. ambassador, in preparation for then-Secretary of State Condoleezza Rice's visit in 2008, spoke in glowing terms about the authoritarian regime of Zine el Abidine Ben Ali. A memo read, "Tunisia styles itself as a country that works," adding, "While Tunisians grumble privately about corruption by the first lady's family, there is an abiding appreciation for Ben Ali's success in steering his country clear of the instability and violence that have plagued Tunisia's neighbors."[28] According to Bush officials, "the lack of Tunisian political activism, or even awareness, seems to be a more serious impediment. While frustration with the First Family's corruption may eventually lead to increased demands for political liberalization, it does not yet appear to be heralding the end of the Ben Ali era."[29]

During the first weeks of the Tunisian protests, rather than praise the pro-democracy movement and condemn the country's repressive regime, Secretary of State Hillary Clinton instead expressed her concern over the impact of the "unrest and instability" on the "very positive aspects of our relationship with

Tunisia," insisting that the United States was "not taking sides" and that she would "wait and see" before even communicating directly with the Tunisian dictator or his ministers.[30] Furthermore, just days after the popular uprising against the Ben Ali dictatorship that began on December 17, 2010, Congress weighed in with support for the regime by passing a budget resolution that included $12 million in security assistance to Tunisia, one of only seven foreign governments provided direct taxpayer-funded military aid.[31]

Along with limited political freedom and government accountability, the poor economic situation in Tunisia was a major focus of the protests, particularly among unemployed educated youth. Secretary of State Hillary Clinton acknowledged this issue on January 11, 2011 – nearly four weeks after the outbreak of the uprising – in noting that "one of my biggest concerns in this entire region are the many young people without economic opportunities in their home countries." Rather than calling for a more democratic and accountable government in Tunisia, however, her suggestion for resolving the crisis was that the economies of Tunisia and other North African states "need to be more open."[32] Ironically, Tunisia under the Ben Ali regime – more than almost any country in the region – had been following the dictates of Washington and the International Monetary Fund in instituting "structural adjustment programs" privatizing much of its economy and allowing for an unprecedented level of "free trade." The United States also backed IMF efforts to push the Tunisian government to eliminate the remaining subsidies on fuel and basic foodstuffs and further deregulate its financial sector. Countries that have adopted this neoliberal model often see increased economic output, but it can also exacerbate inequality. This was certainly the case in Tunisia, where some publically owned enterprises were simply transferred to the family of the president's wife, and the gap in economic opportunity grew between the relatively prosperous coastal areas and the impoverished interior and southern regions, where the protests originated. Indeed, it is probably no accident that the suicide of Mohamed Bouazizi, the unemployed young man from central Tunisia forced to sell fruit on the street, only to be abused by police and have his wares seized, became the spark that led to the revolution.

These policies, which increased rather than decreased unemployment while enriching those close to the country's top ruling families, was privately acknowledged by the U.S. embassy, which labeled the Ben Ali regime as a "kleptocracy." These cables described Tunisia as a "police state, with little freedom of expression or association, and serious human rights problems" and that "President Ben Ali is aging, his regime is sclerotic and there is no clear successor."[33] The country's elites were described as almost Mafia-like in their complex networks of control, stealing enormous wealth from almost every sector of the economy, and a series of WikiLeaks documents vividly described the extravagant lifestyle and related egregious behavior by the families of the president and his in-laws.

Neither the Obama administration nor its predecessors apparently shared its concern over the regime's persistent pattern of gross and systematic human rights violations. Indeed, Tunis became the home of the Middle East Partnership Initiative, a regional office for the State Department's "democratic reform program." U.S. officials justified their support for Ben Ali's dictatorship in the name of the "war on terror," even though radical Islamist movements had been weaker in Tunisia than in practically any other Arab country. Ben Ali's regime assisted the United States in "extraordinary rendition," where suspected Islamist radicals captured by U.S. forces or kidnapped by intelligence services were brought to Tunisia for interrogation and torture. Tunisia was also one of the governments more willing to cooperate with the U.S. Africa Command (AFRICOM) in its efforts to extend U.S. military operations and military relations with African countries.

After official silence following more than two weeks of protests and increasingly severe repression by the government, the State Department began to issue some mildly worded rebukes over the police attacks against demonstrators. Even though most of the protests had been nonviolent, State Department spokesman P.J. Crowley chose to represent the movement as its most unruly components, stating that the Obama administration was "concerned about government actions, but we're also concerned about actions by the demonstrators, those who do not have peaceful intentions."[34]

U.S. policy began to shift as the pro-democracy movement gained momentum, however. Just two days after the interview in which she appeared to back the Ben Ali regime, Clinton took a more proactive stance at a meeting in Qatar, where she noted that "people have grown tired of corrupt institutions and a stagnant political order" and called for "political reforms that will create the space young people are demanding, to participate in public affairs and have a meaningful role in the decisions that shape their lives."[35] Both out of recognition that France still had more influence on Tunisia than did the United States and that events inside the country would ultimately decide the country's fate, the United States recognized there were limits as to what actions could be taken to impact the outcome.

The following day, January 14, as Ben Ali was fleeing the country for exile in Saudi Arabia, President Obama came forward with the most pointed declaration in support of democracy in the Arab world since he became president:

> I condemn and deplore the use of violence against citizens peacefully voicing their opinion in Tunisia, and I applaud the courage and dignity of the Tunisian people. The United States stands with the entire international community in bearing witness to this brave and determined struggle for the universal rights that we must all uphold, and we will long remember the images of the Tunisian people seeking to make their voices heard. . . . [E]ach nation gives life to the principle of democracy in its own way, grounded in the traditions of its own people, and those countries that respect the universal rights of their people are stronger and more successful than those that do not. I have no doubt that Tunisia's future will be brighter if it is guided by the voices of the Tunisian people.[36]

Even after the overthrow of Ben Ali, Tunisia has continued to receive hefty support from the Defense Department, whose officials wish to keep Tunisia on the side of the United States, but also assisting it in defeating the armed Islamist groups who have emerged and garnered support because of the chaotic situation in Libya following the overthrow of Gadhafi in October 2011. Similar to other Arab governments, Tunisia benefited from the events of 9/11 and their aftermath and thus succeeded in obtaining support from the United States through its participation in the GWOT, assistance to Iraq, recognition of the Iraqi Council of government, and participation in peacekeeping operations. Tunisia is also an active member of the Trans-Saharan Counterterrorism Partnership. The security relationship remains paramount; the United States has consolidated its military cooperation with Tunisia, whose armed forces are equipped more than 70 per cent with U.S. military hardware. In 2014, Tunisia received $67 million in U.S. aid, in roughly equal amounts of military and economic aid.

Libya

Following thirty years of hostility, including direct confrontation, the United States and Libya finally normalized their relations in a relatively very short time span.[37] The final settlement in 2003 of the Lockerbie affair (the bombing of Pan Am flight 103 in December 1988 over Scotland, allegedly by Libyan operatives) marked the culmination of a process begun in 1999, followed by Libya's astonishing proclamation on the eve of Christmas 2003 that it decided to dismantle its weapons of mass destruction (WMD) programs and MTCR-class missile systems. On April 22, 2004, President Bush partially lifted sanctions on Libya, a move that allowed U.S. citizens to do business and invest in Libya. Most sanctions were finally revoked in September 2004. This allowed the return of U.S. oil companies; hence, in January 2005, Occidental and Chevron secured 11 of the 15 contracts in Libya's first open competition for oil contracts.[38] In December 2005, Exxon Mobil Corporation signed agreements for the exploration and the production of oil with the Libyan National Oil Company (NOC). After 2006, the United States removed Libya from the list of countries that supported terrorism, and excluded Libya from the annual list of countries not fully cooperating with U.S. antiterrorism efforts. Libya and the United States could then share what some have referred to as "permanent interests," which in the case of U.S.–Libyan relations include counterterrorism, trade, energy, regional stability, nuclear proliferation, Africa, cultural and other initiatives, human rights, and (to a lesser degree) democracy.[39] Condoleezza Rice's trip in 2008 was the first of a U.S. Secretary of State since John Dulles's visit to King Idriss I in 1953. The trip was a way to recompense Libya for abandoning its WMD program and for the Jamahiriya to make final payments to the victims of the Lockerbie incident. Issues of human rights, however, did not make the top of Rice's agenda.

Beginning in 2003, the United States and Libya extended negotiations to widen discussions connected with policies on Africa, terrorism, human rights, and economic reforms in Libya. The discussions on oil and commercial questions resulted in extremely lucrative deals for American companies.

The normalization of relations with Libya confirmed that during Bush's second term the United States was not making democracy a *sine qua non* for its relations with autocratic regimes in MENA. Clearly, the United States resorted to realism by sacrificing human rights principles in exchange for abundant Libyan oil. The Jamahiriya boasts the largest reserves of oil in Africa, estimated by OPEC at 41,464 million barrels, and the eighth-largest reserves in the world. Gas reserves are estimated at 1.419 trillion cubic meters. Given the U.S. thirst for oil, normalization with Libya should have come as no surprise. In any event, Libya's energy resources are considerable, particularly because much of the oil and gas wealth remains untapped. The problem, certainly, is that this wealth, far from encouraging reforms, strengthened the authoritarianism of the regime and provided little incentive for democratization.

The other area of interest for the United States is Libya's role in the so-called War on Terror. Even before 9/11, Libya cooperated with the United States on matters of terrorism,[40] since Libya itself was also confronted by armed radical Islamist groups. After 9/11, Libya's cooperation increased even further. The United States recognized the importance of Libya's cooperation and began co-opting it into the security network that the United States has built in the Sahara-Sahel region and Maghreb-Sahel. Libya became part of the U.S. Africa Command (AFRICOM) Operation Enduring Freedom Trans Sahara (OEF-TS), which provides military support to the TSCTP program.

In January 2009, the United States and Libya signed a historic pact on defense cooperation. The non-binding agreement, signed at the Pentagon, indicated that the two countries now had military-to-military relations and would work together in areas such as peacekeeping, maritime security, counterterrorism, and African security and stability, according to Theresa Whelan, the deputy assistant secretary of defense for African affairs. Whelan anticipated foreign military sales between the countries. However, despite the growing economic and military ties between the United States and Libya, Gadhafi – like the Algerian government – continued to oppose the presence of AFRICOM on the African continent, a suspicion derived from his long-standing anti-colonial sentiments.

Gadhafi's leadership style had always been repressive, impulsive, unpredictable, and seemingly arbitrary. Yet his nationalism, anti-imperialism, and professed socialism led many educated Libyans who formed the backbone of the government to stay loyal despite their misgivings, in large part in reaction to what was seen as the punitive and hypocritical sanctions imposed by Western nations and the constant threat of renewed U.S. air and missile strikes against the country. It was only when the sanctions and threats of war subsided that there began to be a dramatic increase in resignations and self-imposed exile by prominent Libyans who had been members and supporters of the government. In short, the U.S.-led efforts to isolate, punish, and threaten the regime likely contributed to Gadhafi's longevity as dictator. Once relations were normalized and the isolation and threats subsided, Gadhafi was seen less as the strong leader defending his nation against Western imperialism and more as the mercurial and brutal tyrant that he was.

The initially nonviolent anti-regime uprising in Libya in February 2011, like those in neighboring Tunisia and Egypt, took the United States by surprise. When the civil insurrection turned into an armed struggle and regime violence increased, the United States joined Britain and France, along with various NATO and Arab allies, in providing arms and engaging in air strikes in support of the rebels. As an indicator of the extent of antipathy toward the Gadhafi regime, there was a surprising degree of support within Libya and throughout the Arab world for the NATO intervention, even from leftists, nationalists, and Islamists normally opposed to Western intervention. The Arab League, followed by the United Nations Security Council, passed resolutions calling for the enforcement of a no-fly zone to protect the civilian population from Gadhafi's forces. President Obama, noting how – unlike the U.S. invasion of Iraq – there was regional and international support for the intervention and the United Nations had offered legal authority, played a major role in the military campaign. Still, cognizant of the region's sensitivity to the U.S. role in the region, he opted for a policy of "leading from behind," allowing French and British forces to play a more visible role.

NATO went well beyond the mandate provided by the United Nations Security Council to simply protect the civilian population through the establishment of a no-fly zone. Instead, NATO became an active participant in a civil war, providing arms, intelligence, and advisors and conducting over 7,500 air and missile strikes against military and government facilities. Armed units from the Saudi and Qatari regimes contributed to the fighting on the ground. As Arab League secretary General Amr Mussa told reporters, "What has happened in Libya differs from the goal of imposing a no-fly zone and what we want is the protection of civilians and not bombing other civilians."[41]

The U.S./NATO intervention initially appeared to strengthen the Gadhafi regime. Indeed, for a full four months following the NATO intervention, there was a bloody stalemate. The crimes committed over the years by his regime, while frequently exaggerated and not always unique, were very real. Yet Libya's most serious offenses, in the eyes of U.S. policymakers prior to the rapprochement during the previous decade, were not in the areas of human rights, terrorism, nuclear ambitions, subversion, or conquest, but in daring to challenge Western hegemony in the Middle East. Serving as an impediment to such American ambitions gave such regimes credibility and legitimacy they would not otherwise receive from large numbers of North African peoples resentful of such foreign domination, thereby strengthening these regimes' rule at home, as well as their influence throughout the Middle East and beyond. As a result, the intervention encouraged nationalist reaction that could play into Gadhafi's hands. It is no accident that Gadhafi chose as the backdrop to his bizarre and frighteningly belligerent speech on February 22 a building in Tripoli destroyed in the 1986 U.S. bombing. (And this history of U.S. intervention in Libya pre-dates the Gadhafi era – by 130 years: President Thomas Jefferson sent Lt. Stephen Decatur to attack the base of the Barbary Pirates, later referenced in the opening line of the Marine Hymn: "to the shores of Tripoli.")

Gadhafi eventually fell in October. Though the Libyan elections resulted in victories by relative moderates, the new government was unable to exert its power in the face of more than 200,000 militiamen under arms in a country with a population of barely six million. Scores of the militias have proclaimed themselves as "guardians of the revolution" and, in many cities, have more power than any government officials. Among the largest and well-equipped groups are made up of radical Islamists, including those who attacked the U.S. consulate in Benghazi in September 2012, killing the U.S. ambassador and three other Americans. Though partisan Republican Party efforts to turn the attack into a major scandal to discredit the Obama administration appear groundless, it raises the broader question as to whether intervention by the United States and other foreign powers in Libya's civil war did more harm than good in terms of advancing U.S. interests.

Given the chaos in the country and wariness in Washington to becoming too deeply involved in what appears to be a "failed state," the United States' ability to influence events in Libya remains limited. Security concerns led to a withdrawal of most U.S. diplomatic staff in April of 2013. In May of 2014, the State Department recommended the evacuation of virtually all Americans from the country. The following month, U.S. Special Forces conducted a raid in which they kidnapped Ahmed Abu Khatallah, a Libyan national and Al-Qaeda suspect; government officials denounced the U.S. Special Forces operation as a "brazen violation of Libyan sovereignty." Eight months earlier, another Libyan Al-Qaeda operative, Abu Anas al-Libi, was also captured by U.S. Special Forces in Tripoli and later died in custody. In June of 2015, U.S. air strikes killed Mokhtar Belmokhtar, an Algerian terrorist commander, and other leaders of the Al Qaeda-affiliated Ansar al-Shria in Ajdabya.

As an illustration of the decline of U.S. influence, air strikes by Egyptian and UAE forces in support of the Libyan government in August of 2014 took place without prior knowledge of the United States.[42] Still, the United States has continued to provide non-lethal military aid, training, advisors, and other assistance to the Libyan armed forces, and Americans are believed to be part of private security forces protecting oil installations and other sensitive areas. The United States also provided assistance in capacity-building efforts for government institutions, civil society groups, and elections, all of which are being coordinated with the United Nations Support Mission in Libya (UNSMIL), though with the recognized government no longer in control of most of the country, such efforts have been dramatically reduced. While such aid soared to $47 million in FY 2013, the subsequent chaos has resulted in subsequent allocations falling to around the $6 million level.

Egypt

Under British tutelage prior to the 1952 revolution led by nationalist army officers, and receiving large-scale Soviet support into the 1970s during most of the Nasser era, Egypt became closely allied with the United States under the regime of Anwar Sadat, formalizing its ties with the U.S.-facilitated Camp David peace agreement with Israel in 1978. The Camp David treaty included an annex with provisions for more than five billion dollars in military and economic aid to the two signatories. It was originally designed as a one-time payback to the two parties for agreeing to make peace. However, each year since, the United States has continued allocating this sizable military and economic assistance package to the Israeli and Egyptian governments. Since 1978, Egypt has received approximately $1.2 billion annually in military assistance. Concerns by pro-democracy groups in Egypt and human rights organizations in the United States that such aid was only making further repression possible was rejected by Washington. Despite the extreme unlikelihood that the Egyptian government, particularly under the staunchly pro-Western Mubarak, would initiate hostilities with the far more powerful Israel, the State Department continued to insist that such aid was necessary to advance the "peace process."[43]

As with the case of other autocratic allies in the region, U.S. military, economic, and diplomatic support for the regime continued through both Republican and Democratic administrations. There was some limited support – through the National Endowment for Democracy and other congressionally funded foundations – to civil society organizations addressing women's issues, working conditions, human rights, election monitoring, and other pro-democracy efforts. In 2004, the Bush administration began to press Mubarak on a number of human rights issues and Secretary of State Condoleezza Rice met with leading dissidents on a visit to Cairo. This effort was short-lived and never very substantive, however, and little was done or said regarding democracy and human rights in Egypt for the remainder of the Bush administration's time in office.

There was hope among pro-democracy activists that there might be a change in U.S. policy under the new administration of Barack Obama, and that the United States might finally apply real pressure on the regime. That hope did not last very long, however. On coming to office, in fact, Obama slashed funding for pro-democracy initiatives by 75 per cent. In the months prior to the uprising, Egyptian journalist Ibrahim Eissa complained that "Obama is not pressuring Mubarak at all" to end the repression, nor was Obama "realizing that society is going to implode on itself and destroy those regimes."[44] Particularly disappointing to pro-democracy activists was the administration's tepid response to the regime's blatantly fraudulent parliamentary elections in late November 2010, which were severely compromised by blatant acts of fraud, the refusal by the regime to allow independent monitors, and mass arrests and escalated media suppression just prior to the vote. Daniel Calingaert of Freedom House, in testimony before Congress, observed how the stolen elections posed "a clear-cut choice for the Obama administration – whether to side with the Egyptian government or with the Egyptian people."[45] The administration made its choice clear in successfully pushing for a renewal of the multibillion-dollar aid package to the Mubarak regime just weeks later.

Indeed, direct U.S. support for Egypt's armed forces, paramilitary units, and secret police remained at over $1.3 billion annually under Obama. Throughout Mubarak's nearly thirty years as Egypt's president, his regime received more aid than any other country except Israel. Despite the prodding of U.S.-based human rights groups, it was extremely difficult for anyone within Republican or Democratic administrations or on either side of the aisle on Capitol Hill to even raise questions about American support for the Egyptian dictatorship. For example, a proposed non-binding Senate resolution in 2010 calling on the Egyptian regime to liberalize and hold free elections was blocked by Senate Intelligence Committee chairwoman Dianne Feinstein.

When Obama visited Egypt in 2009, he did engage in a few symbolic efforts to demonstrate a concern for human rights. He didn't praise Mubarak from the podium in his University of Cairo speech, as is generally customary on such occasions. Nor did he physically embrace the dictator or otherwise offer visual displays of affection, as is also typical during such visits to leaders in that region. The Obama administration invited some leading critics of the regime, including both secular liberals and moderate Islamists, to witness his speech, and insisted that the regime allow them to attend. However, Kefaya, Egypt's leading grassroots pro-democracy group, boycotted the speech, demanding that Obama show his commitment to democracy in deeds, not words.

When the Egyptian uprising began on January 25, 2011, the U.S. government initially came to Mubarak's defense. Secretary of State Clinton insisted that the Mubarak regime was "looking for ways to respond to the legitimate needs and interests of the Egyptian people,"[46] despite the miserable failure of the regime in its nearly thirty years in power to do so. Asked whether the United States still supported Mubarak, White House spokesman Robert Gibbs said that Egypt remained a "close and important ally." Even when Clinton finally issued a statement, following the regime cutting off all cell phone and Internet communication on the third day of the uprising, urging "Egyptian authorities not to prevent peaceful protests or block communications including on social media sites,"[47] the administration simply called for the regime to reform from within rather than supporting pro-democracy protesters' demand that the dictator step down. As Clinton put it, "We believe strongly that the Egyptian government has an important opportunity at this moment in time to implement political, economic and social reforms to respond to the legitimate needs and interests of the Egyptian people."[48] As the protests grew over the next couple of days and the prospects that the regime might actually be facing a serious challenge, Vice President Joe Biden rushed to Mubarak's defense, rejecting calls that he step aside, simply saying that he needed to be "more responsive to some of the needs of the people out there" and expressing his belief that Mubarak "is going to respond to some of the legitimate concerns that are being raised." In addition, the vice president insisted, in response to a question by veteran journalist Jim Lehrer, "I would not refer to him as a dictator." And, despite explicit calls by the large and diverse protesters for the regime to step down, Biden claimed that they were simply "middle-class folks who are looking for a little more access and a little more opportunity."[49]

In the White House, aides were debating about how aggressively the United States should pressure Mubarak to resign or get serious about having free and early elections. There was a growing sense that Mubarak might be forced out but the United States would not want to be seen as trying to engineer a successor, particularly if the regime somehow survived. One senior administration official was quoted as saying, "It's just a very tough line to straddle. If he guts this out and stays, we're going to continue to need him and work with him, and he might not appreciate that we pushed. Bottom line, Egypt's destiny is Egypt's to decide, and we'll work with whoever emerges or is left standing." Another problem was the lack of any obvious successor. The official noted, "There isn't a natural successor. And if we were to embrace a particular person, it does more harm than good. It's a classic dilemma for America."[50] As a result, Obama's calls for democratic reforms still rested on the hope that needed changes could take place under President Mubarak, as when he noted how the Egyptian president "has a responsibility to give meaning" to his promises to build "a better democracy and greater economic opportunity" and to "take concrete steps and actions that deliver on that promise."[51]

On January 30, the fifth day of the Egyptian demonstrations, as the protests continued to gain momentum, the Obama administration started speaking in terms of an eventual transition to democratic rule and telling the regime that large-scale repression of nonviolent protesters – which would presumably be implemented with U.S.-supplied weaponry – would be unacceptable. As Marc Lynch, who advised the White House during the uprising, observed during that period, there was growing sense within the administration that "Mubarak's regime has been wounded at its core, and even if he survives in the short run the regime will have to make major internal changes to regain any semblance of normality. An Egyptian regime which spends the next years in a state of military lockdown will hardly be a useful ally."[52] It was at this point when Obama directed his aides to maintain close contact with Egyptian opposition activists and other leaders outside the government[53] and the Obama administration began speaking openly in terms of a transition to democracy.

The White House then announced that the president's position was that he wanted "an orderly transition to a government that is responsive to the aspirations of the Egyptian people." Recognizing the regional significance of these developments, Obama personally called on leaders of Great Britain, Turkey, Israel, and Saudi Arabia to discuss the situation. On January 31, the *Washington Post* reported, "The Obama administration firmly aligned itself on Sunday with the protest movement that has overtaken Egypt, calling for an 'orderly transition' to a more representative government." Fearing that such unrest could spread to other countries in the region, the article noted that "In telephone calls to Egyptian and regional leaders, President Obama and his top national security advisers tried to reassure them that their countries remain vital U.S. strategic partners, while warning that the political status quo is not sustainable."[54]

Indeed, though never explicitly calling on Mubarak to step down in public, President Obama became even more explicit regarding the shift in policy by announcing on February 1 that U.S. policy was for there to be "an orderly transition" of power in Egypt and that it "must be meaningful, it must be peaceful, and it must begin now."[55] To emphasize this sentiment still further, White House spokesperson Robert Gibbs said on February 2 – in response to Mubarak's promise to step down when his term expired in September – was that "now means yesterday" in terms of such a transition.

The change in the administration's approach likely came from the belated realization that nothing short of a Tiananmen Square-style massacre would probably stop the protests, and that such measures using U.S.-provided weaponry would inflame anti-Americanism throughout Egypt and the entire Arab world and could drive the anti-Mubarak resistance underground into the arms of violent extremists. The Obama administration made it clear to the Egyptian military that any large-scale repression would have seriously negative implications for the U.S.–Egyptian relationship, presumably meaning severing U.S. military aid and cooperation. It also began to press the military to force Mubarak to step down.

The pressure was met with great resistance, of course, as the regime continued to downplay the significance of the protests and exaggerate the threat from Islamists, but the administration persisted. While there was disappointment among pro-democracy activists and their American supporters that the Obama administration did not move earlier, some U.S. analysts, such as Lynch, defended the more gradualist approach, noting how Mubarak had been a U.S. ally for thirty years and "needed to be given the chance to respond appropriately. . . . Obama saying 'Mubarak must go' would not have made Mubarak go, absent the careful preparation of the ground so that the potential power-brokers saw that they really had no choice." However, as Lynch also noted, as the regime's desperation and its violence against the protesters escalated, it became both possible and necessary to increase the pressure.[56] The administration began working quietly on convincing leading military and civilian figures in the regime to distance themselves from Mubarak, negotiate with the opposition, and to consider drafting Constitutional revisions they could quickly push through the parliament.[57]

Quiet pressure from Washington and – more significantly – the massive and largely nonviolent resistance in the streets of Egypt increased over the next week and a half until Mubarak resigned on February 11, handing power over to the Supreme Council of the Armed Forces. U.S. support for the new regime continued, despite lessened but ongoing repression.

The narrow victory by Mohammed Morsi of the Muslim Brotherhood in the 2013 presidential election, while somewhat problematic in the eyes of Washington, did not result in a major crisis in U.S.–Egyptian relations. The Muslim Brotherhood leadership, despite its extreme antipathy toward Israel, was pragmatic enough not to threaten the Jewish state, given its vast military superiority. And, as a movement dominated by wealthy businessmen, the Brotherhood was quite willing to cooperate with U.S. economic interests and international financial institutions. More importantly, there was a clear sense that the U.S.-backed Egyptian military had enough leverage to keep the Brotherhood from doing much to hurt U.S. interests and would be willing and able to seize control if deemed necessary.

Though there is no evidence to suggest the United States was behind the July 2013 military coup, it was largely welcomed. The U.S. Senate defeated by an 86–13 margin a resolution to enforce U.S. law against providing military aid to regimes that seize power by military coups.[58] Aid continued to flow despite the massacre of over 1,200 Muslim Brotherhood supporters in August and a crackdown on democratic secular activists in subsequent months. As the regime's repression was escalating in January 2014, Congress approved an additional $1.3 billion in military assistance to Egypt, in addition to $200 million in economic aid. To get around the law prohibiting aid to any regime that overthrows a democratically elected government through a military coup, congressional leaders of both parties inserted language stating that the aid could flow "notwithstanding any provision of law restricting assistance for Egypt." Despite worsening repression, the Obama administration released all previously suspended military assistance at the end of March 2015.

The Maghreb: Regional entity within the framework of American foreign policy

As central as Egypt remains to U.S. policy in the greater Middle East, the United States has been giving increasing attention to the other states of the North African littoral. As should have been evident through the bilateral relations that the United States maintains with the Maghreb states, the main U.S. goal is to develop close political, military, economic, and security cooperation with the region. An examination of official statements, press conferences, and various government documents shows that the United States wishes to set up an economic alliance with the Maghreb by accelerating structural reforms within each country, by offering a greater role to the private sector, and by dismantling the intra-regional barriers, which represent obstacles for trade and investment. In the 1990s, the United States was intent on reigniting Maghreb integration through the Eizenstat Initiative (launched in 1999 as the U.S.–North Africa Economic Partnership), named after its main advocate Stuart Eizenstat, then undersecretary of state for economic, business, and agricultural affairs. The objective of this initiative – later renamed U.S.–North Africa Economic Program, and now part of the Middle East Partnership Initiative (MEPI) – was "to link the United States and the three countries of North Africa much closer together in terms of trade and investment, to encourage more trade between our countries, [and] to encourage more U.S. companies to invest in the region."[59] Implicit in this statement was a clear encouragement for the Maghreb countries to revive the moribund U.M.A. and for the reopening of the Algerian-Moroccan land border, closed since August 1994. Undoubtedly, from an economic perspective, the United States has made it plain that its business community prefers an integrated Maghreb, which now could include Libya, because it would constitute a much bigger market than the separate national markets. Recently, Eizenstat has been actively seeking to revive the UMA and has identified one of the major factors hindering the realization of an integrated market; in an effort to combat the terrorist threat, the countries of the region have tightened restrictions on the movement of people and goods at their borders, which has had the unintended consequence of further reducing cross-border commerce in the region and decreasing economic activity. The U.S. and EU likewise have encouraged the Maghreb countries to take antiterrorism measures, and economic development and integration have consequently been deemphasized. These countries are taking steps to enhance their cooperation on security matters; these efforts should go hand-in-hand with cooperation on economic matters in order to create greater long-term stability in the region.[60]

In July 2010, the deputy assistant secretary of state for Near Eastern Affairs, Janet Sanderson, expressed the willingness of the administration to reignite the Eizenstat Initiative to build an integrated Maghreb.[61] As noted earlier, however, one of the main obstacles to Maghreb regional integration remains the conflict in Western Sahara, which has aggravated the already tense relations between Algeria and Morocco, and the United States, along with France and Europe, has been instrumental in the persistence of the stalemate rather than part of the solution that would lead to Maghreb integration.[62]

Although it has failed to persuade the countries in the region to revive the Arab Maghreb Union, the United States is more interested in securing access to oil and natural gas (mainly in Algeria and Libya) and security. In this context, the conflict over Western Sahara has taken on a new dimension, given that its persistence remains a major obstacle in achieving one of America's regional policy objectives. This is why the United States insists on seeing a resolution of the conflict. But, the bias in favor of Morocco has in fact produced the opposite effect, a lasting stalemate which, though tolerable for the moment, has the potential of destabilizing the area. The persistence of the conflict has had a number of negative consequences: regional insecurity and the arms race; Algerian and Moroccan arms purchases at the expense of much-needed socioeconomic development; cyclical uprisings in the occupied territory accompanied by human rights violations against Sahrawis; a freeze of the Arab Maghreb Union; and limited security cooperation between Algeria and Morocco.

From "democratization" to securitization: U.S. security policy in the Maghreb-Sahel

After 9/11, democracy promotion in the Arab world became part of U.S. strategic interests. U.S. policymakers made explicit the correlation between democracy promotion and stability, on the one hand, and strategic interests, on the other. President Bush said in 2003:

> Sixty years of Western nations excusing and accommodating the lack of freedom in the Middle East did nothing to make us safe – because in the long run, stability cannot be purchased at the expense of liberty. As long as the Middle East remains a place where freedom does not flourish, it will remain a place of stagnation, resentment, and violence ready for export. And with the spread of weapons that can bring catastrophic harm to our country and to our friends, it would be reckless to accept the status quo.[63]

In fact, both the United States and the EU equated the "enduring security" of the American and European peoples with the promotion of "a world of democratic and well-governed states."[64] Furthermore, they both stressed their "shared commitment to promoting democracy" as "one of the fields where . . . [they] can do, and should do, even more together."[65] Nevertheless, this joint emblematic pledge never resulted in a cohesive, viable strategy. Despite the Wilsonian rhetoric, in practice realism prevailed. Indeed, in spite of his pro-democracy crusade, Bush never truly moved it forward. As Carothers noted, "Underneath [Bush's] lofty prodemocracy rhetoric and mild prodding of Arab counterparts, business as usual continued for the most part, that is, close U.S. security and economic ties with autocratic Arab allies like Saudi Arabia, the smaller Gulf States, Egypt, Jordan, and Morocco."[66]

Inevitably, the necessity of cooperation on counterterrorism resulted in rapprochement with, rather than distancing from, many authoritarian or semi-authoritarian regimes around the globe, particularly in the Middle East and North Africa. Thus, by 2006, democratization tended to take the backseat and is no longer mentioned today as a prerequisite for close cooperation with regimes in the south. In reality, security considerations have remained paramount. During her confirmation speech on January 13, 2009,[67] Secretary of State Hillary Clinton referred to the so-called "three Ds" (diplomacy, development, and defense) as the elements of U.S. power, but conspicuously absent was any reference to a fourth D – democracy. She did try to convince lawmakers that the United States had a "deep commitment to the cause of making human rights a reality for millions of oppressed people around the world." The "three D's" does not imply a rejection of democratization but seems to suggest a re-interpretation of democracy through development. In January 2010, Hillary Clinton made the link between development and democracy, stating that, "development also furthers a key goal of our diplomatic efforts: to advance democracy and human rights worldwide."[68] Although advancing development and linking it to democracy – albeit through the prism of realism – is quite essential, it does not seem, however, that the conduct of U.S. foreign policy has so far reflected that commitment, official statements to the contrary notwithstanding. Clearly, the heavier D relates to defense, interpreted in the broadest sense. Counterterrorism is paramount; this has remained evident as far as the Maghreb-Sahel is concerned.

The U.S. foreign and security policies shifted after 9/11 and the war in Iraq in 2003. The defense strategy was no longer centered on regions and structured around alliances but was now determined by key issues adapted to specific events and finally put into practice with tailor-made coalitions depending on the mission. In other words, the tendency was toward flexible coalitions for varying missions but always under U.S. overall command. Global issues such as the proliferation of WMD, terrorism, energy security, economic and political reforms, as well as what one might term "selective demands for democratization," led the list of priorities. U.S. policymakers suggested that since these phenomena are global in nature, the fight must be global, with appropriate regional applications. As George W. Bush announced in the U.S. National Security Strategy Report, 2002:

We will continue to encourage our regional partners to take up a coordinated effort that isolates the terrorists. Once the regional campaign localizes the threat to a particular state, we will help ensure the state has the military, law enforcement, political, and financial tools necessary to finish the task.

Regarding the southern Mediterranean, this meant setting new priorities, which had to be tackled with or without the help of partners. It is precisely this perspective that explains current U.S. involvement in the western Mediterranean, especially in the Maghreb-Sahel region.

As has been evident in the analysis of U.S. bilateral relations with Maghreb states, in the wake of 9/11 the key objective of the United States in the Maghreb has been to develop and/or strengthen closer military and security cooperation and economic partnerships with those states. The events reinforced the development of relations between the United States and the Maghreb authoritarian governments: Algeria (especially since 2001), Mauritania (since 2002), Morocco (since May 2003), Libya (after December 2003), and Tunisia (since 2002).

The U.S. interest in the Sahara-Sahel, a region where sub-Saharan Africa meets North Africa, covers both security/military and economic interests. Washington perceives the Sahel as a vulnerable region because of its low demographic density and its permeable borders. This region falls within the so-called "safe havens" that terrorists can use for mounting attacks against U.S. soil – as they did before 9/11 – and thus represents a genuine threat to the security of the United States.[69] There is evidently a correlation in U.S. strategic thinking regarding the notion of "safe havens" or "ungoverned spaces" and "failed states," a concept born during the Bush administration but which has continued under the current one. Failed states, like Somalia, were seen as the worst security threat to the United States. The current administration has supported this view. Indeed, Secretary of Defense Robert Gates declared that, "Dealing with such fractured or failing states is, in many ways, the main security challenge of our time."[70]

U.S. policymakers argue that terrorist groups – local as well as international – devote themselves to all kinds of smuggling, including weapons, and recruit new members among the local populations. According to Washington's senior security officials, Islamist terrorist groups – the most active being the Salafi Group for Preaching and Combat (GSPC), renamed Al-Qaeda in the Islamic Maghreb in 2007 – represent a threat to this area, which has more than 100 million inhabitants.[71]

The area has even been regarded as "the new front in the global war against terrorism." President Obama's appointment of General James Jones as the national security advisor was already a clear indication that, if anything, the Obama administration has subscribed to its predecessor's views on African security in general and on the Maghreb-Sahel in particular. Jones, prominent for his views on African security matters, made it obvious that "African security issues will increasingly continue to directly affect our homeland security" and that "North Africa and, in particular, the Pan-Sahel region of sub-Saharan Africa, provides opportunities to Islamic extremists, smugglers and other insurgent groups."[72] Therefore, the objective of the

United States has been since 2002 to assist cooperation among governments in the region (Algeria, Burkina Faso, Libya, Morocco, Tunisia, Mauritania, Mali, Niger, Chad, Senegal, and Nigeria) and reinforce their capacity to fight terrorist organizations, but also to purportedly inhibit terrorist groups from setting up bases in this region as they did in Afghanistan before 9/11. This is why at the end of 2002 the United States started the Pan Sahel Initiative (PSI) in order to train specialized troops in the fight against terrorism in Chad, Mali, Mauritania, and Niger. In 2003–2004, American Special Forces of the European Command (EUCOM) were detached to train the security forces of these nations. Later, indigenous forces of Chad and Niger fought the GSCPC members in their respective countries. Since the PSI program, completed in early 2004, was seen as a success, U.S. policymakers decided to create the Trans-Sahara Counterterrorism Initiative (TSCTI or TSCTP, partnership), to replace PSI. The objective of the TSCTI has been to reinforce local capacities to fight terrorism in the area, and to consolidate and institutionalize cooperation between the security forces across the region. TSCTP officially started in June 2005 with Exercise Flintlock 2005, which was repeated two years later as Flintlock 2007. In November 2008, fourteen nations participated in Flintlock 2009, "developed as a joint multinational exercise to improve information sharing at the operational and tactical levels across the Saharan region while fostering increased collaboration and coordination."[73] Flintlock 2010 was launched on May 3, 2010, and lasted until May 23, 2010. The mission now remains for U.S. special operations forces to provide training for their counterparts in Saharan countries, teaching military tactics, and to prevent alleged terrorists from setting up sanctuaries in that region. The most recent Flintlock was held in Niger in February 2014.

Undoubtedly, the Maghreb-Sahel region has inexorably become a strategic region for U.S. security interests, although other outside powers (such as Russia, as an arms supplier, or France, as a key economic actor) also play important roles. The underlying rationale for such U.S. presence is articulated in the "Report on Global Terrorism 2009" which was published in August 2010:

> Ongoing concern that extremists continued to seek safe havens and support networks in the Maghreb and Sahel – as well as recognition that al-Qa'ida and others were seeking to impose radical ideologies on traditionally moderate Muslim populations in the region – highlighted the urgency of creating an integrated approach to addressing current threats and preventing conditions that could foster persistent threats in the future.[74]

Some critics argue that not only is the U.S. presence in the region a destabilizing factor, but also that the United States has "fabricated" or greatly exaggerated the terrorist threat in order to maintain its presence – to be institutionalized through AFRICOM, the U.S. Command for Africa set up in 2007 – and to achieve its goals of controlling the region's hydrocarbon resources and warding off China's advance in mineral-rich Africa. As one expert observed, the United States is "making [Africa] into another front in its Global War on Terrorism, maintaining and extending access to energy supplies and other strategic raw material, and compet-ing with China and other rising economic powers for control over the continent's resources."[75] However, the United States would rather avoid direct military inter-vention and instead use friendly regimes, preferably those rich in natural resources, to serve as proxies for the United States. In sum:

> The hope that the Pentagon can build up African surrogates who can act on behalf of the United States is precisely why Washington is providing so much security assistance to these regimes and why it would like to provide even more in the future.[76]

In the Maghreb, Morocco and Tunisia continue to gain from an important level of security assistance from the United States. Morocco benefits from State Depart-ment programs, such as the ATA (Anti-Terrorism Assistance) and the TIP (Terrorist Interdiction Program). But, while security cooperation with Morocco and Tunisia is an ordinary one, cooperation with Algeria is one of the most important aspects of bilateral relations since 9/11. This cooperation is centered on the exchange of information, military cooperation, and the monitoring of the transfer of funds; the most recent ATA training was held in Algiers in July 2010.[77] The U.S. admin-istration has drawn some conclusions from its experience in Afghanistan and Iraq, where American soldiers face violent opposition from the local populations. U.S. officials under the Obama administration have carried on Bush's policy in Africa: instead of mobilizing a heavy U.S. military presence in given areas of intervention, the new program consists of dispatching Special Operations forces to countries like Mali and Mauritania in West Africa to train their soldiers and supply them with pickup trucks, radios, and global-positioning system equipment. According to General Jones, no U.S. forces have been committed to combat in Africa. U.S. deployment has primarily consisted of training and advisory teams. The hope, of course, is that American influence will be effective without being conspicuous. The U.S. Ambassador to Algeria, David Pearce, has confirmed this policy. In June 2009, he insisted that should the governments in the region solicit the United States, Washington would be willing to provide them with the necessary assistance in the fight against terrorism: "It's a huge, difficult region to control without regional cooperation."[78] This explains why the United States welcomed "the decision of the governments of Algeria, Burkina Faso, Chad, Libya, Mali, Mauritania, and Niger to meet on March 16 in Algiers to collectively confront the threat of terrorism."[79]

Obama and the question of Western Sahara: Continuity or change?

The Bush administration supported the Moroccan autonomy proposal despite its illegality and its ambiguity.[80] Owing to the principles that Obama upheld as presi-dential candidate, many anticipated that there would be a reversal of the U.S. posi-tion in this conflict under Obama, for there were some signs indicating that the

Obama administration might not be decidedly biased in favor of Morocco. Indeed, in June 2009, it appeared that the United States no longer supported unequivocally the Moroccan autonomy plan; Obama's avoiding mentioning the autonomy plan in his letter to King Mohammed VI was interpreted as an about-face in U.S. policy on the question. One passage in the letter was particularly revealing: "I share your commitment to the U.N.-led negotiations as the appropriate forum to achieve a mutually agreed solution. . . . My government will work with yours and others in the region to achieve an outcome that meets the people's need for transparent governance, confidence in the rule of law, and equal administration of justice."[81] Citing diplomatic sources, the report in which the letter was quoted suggested, "The United States no longer supports or endorses the Moroccan autonomy plan. . . . Instead, the administration has returned to the pre-Bush position that there could be an independent POLISARIO state in Western Sahara."[82] U.S. officials refused to confirm or deny such reports, stating only that the United States encourages the parties to engage in discussions under the United Nations' auspices.[83] Unquestionably, by referring to international legality (which in the case of Western Sahara would include the option of independence), Obama seemed to abide by the values he promised to uphold. Yet, in reality, there has not been any substantial shift in policy toward Western Sahara. What is apparent is that the administration seems torn between continuing to support a traditional ally, Morocco, and setting a new course that would contradict the interests of that ally. The conflicting pronouncements in Obama's letter and those issued by Hillary Clinton during her visit to Morocco in November 2009 highlight the policy constraints of the administration. During her visit to Marrakesh in November 2009 to attend the Forum for the Future, Hillary Clinton responded to the question as to whether the Obama administration had changed its position on the autonomy plan by saying that, "Our policy has not changed, and I thank you for asking the question because I think it's important for me to reaffirm here in Morocco that there has been no change in policy."[84] In another interview, she was asked what she meant by her affirmation that there was "no change in the Obama administration's position as far as the Moroccan autonomy plan in the Sahara is concerned." Her response was:

> Well, this is a plan, as you know, that originated in the Clinton Administration. It was reaffirmed in the Bush Administration and it remains the policy of the United States in the Obama Administration. Now, we are supporting the United Nations process because we think that if there can be a peaceful resolution to the difficulties that exist with your neighbors, both to the east and to the south and the west that is in everyone's interest. But because of our long relationship, we are very aware of how challenging the circumstances are. And I don't want anyone in the region or elsewhere to have any doubt about our policy, which remains the same.[85]

This being said, the United States displayed a tougher stand toward Morocco during the hunger strike of Aminatou Haidar, the Sahrawi human rights activist.

The United States was instrumental in resolving the case,[86] thus making it possible for Haidar to return from her imposed exile to her home in Western Sahara. But, as UN Security Council (UNSC) Resolution 1920 demonstrates, the United States has not changed its position and continues to use the same language that prolongs the stalemate in this conflict.[87] Human rights advocates raised hopes in late 2013, when the Obama administration – in sponsoring the semi-annual renewal of MIN-URSO's mandate – included authorizing human rights monitoring, similar to that of every other current UN peacekeeping force. Under pressure from the Moroccan regime, the Department of Defense, and some Congressional leaders, however, the administration backed down. Leaked documents reveal that in return for dropping the human rights monitoring provision, Morocco agreed to stop trying civilians in military courts, assist representatives from the UN High Commissioner for Human Rights to visit the occupied territory, and legalize banned Western Saharan organizations such as the Collective of Sahrawi Human Rights Defenders (CODESA). Morocco has failed to fulfill the final condition, however, with no public objections from Washington.

What is certain is that conflict in Western Sahara is low on the list of U.S. priorities, and it would be surprising if the U.S. government took any initiative to resolve the issue. Washington's agenda is pretty full. But, as paradoxical as it may seem, failing to resolve this conflict will sooner or later hamper U.S. security objectives in the region.

Conclusion

For the United States, the events of 9/11 changed the Maghreb's geopolitical importance, not only because it encouraged the bringing together of the Maghreb states with the United States, but also because it made the latter take a greater interest in the area, which, from a security point of view, now extends to the Sahel region. Undoubtedly, this is a significant region because, despite the poverty prevalent in some of the countries surrounding the Maghreb and the authoritarianism that characterizes practically all the incumbent regimes, it boasts valuable resources – not only hydrocarbons but also vital minerals. Furthermore, China's growing presence, as well as Russia's return as an important arms supplier in the Maghreb, particularly Algeria, provide the unspoken reason for the United States' increasing interest in containing what it perceives as genuine threats to its national security. This continued concern with security has raised the question as to whether the Obama administration is intent on promoting democracy. Although the debate is still ongoing, a preliminary analysis suggests that though the administration is concerned with democracy, it is searching for new formulas to overcome the dilemma that Obama himself raised before his election: "I recognize that our security interests will sometimes necessitate that we work with regimes with which we have fundamental disagreements; yet, those interests need not and must not prevent us from lending our consistent support to those who are committed to democracy and respect for human rights."[88]

So far, Obama's foreign policy reflects the first part of this realist statement rather than the second. Meanwhile, the authoritarian regimes continue to draw dividends from their antiterrorism cooperation with the United States.

Notes

1. Some sections draw from Yahia H. Zoubir, "The Maghreb: Strategic Interests," in Sharham Akbarzadeh, Ed., *Obama in the Middle East: Failure to Bring Change* (New York: Palgrave-Macmillan, 2011), pp. 105–132.
2. See Yahia H. Zoubir, "Les Etats-Unis dans l'espace Euro-Méditerranéen: Complémentarité, Rivalité et Réajustement d'influence," *Géoéconomie* 35 (2005): 65–83.
3. Office of the President, "National Security Strategy of the United States," The White House, May 2010, p. 37, www.whitehouse.gov/sites/default/files/rss_viewer/national_security_strategy.pdf. June 15, 2010.
4. Scott Wilson and Al Kamen, "'Global War on Terror' Is Given New Name: Bush's Phrase Is Out, Pentagon Says," *Washington Post*, March 25, 2009, www.washingtonpost.com/wp-dyn/content/article/2009/03/24/AR2009032402818.html. (Accessed on March 26, 2009).
5. "Egypt Protests: Hillary Clinton Urges 'Orderly Transition,'" *BBC News*, January 30, 2011, www.bbc.co.uk/news/world-uscanada-12319445. (Accessed January 31, 2011).
6. For U.S. relations with Morocco, see Yahia H. Zoubir, "The United States and Morocco: The Long Lasting Alliance," in Robert E. Looney, Ed., *Handbook of US–Middle East Relations: Formative Factors and Regional Perspectives* (London and New York: Routledge, 2009), pp. 237–248. On U.S.–Tunisian relations, see Yahia H. Zoubir, "The US and Tunisia: Model of Stable Relations," in Robert E. Looney, Ed., *Handbook of US–Middle East Relations: Formative Factors and Regional Perspectives* (London and New York: Routledge, 2009), pp. 249–261.
7. Assistant Secretary of State for Economic, Energy and Business Affairs, Jose W. Fernandez, travelled to the Maghreb in December 2010. After the conference held in Algiers, he went to Libya "to galvanize support for NAPEO [North Africa Partnership for Economic Opportunity] and to further economic engagement throughout the Maghreb region." U.S. Department of State, "Assistant Secretary Jose W. Fernandez Holds Press Briefing on His Travel to North Africa," Office of the Spokesman, Washington, DC, December 7, 2010, www.state.gov/r/pa/prs/ps/2010/12/152467.htm. (Accessed on February 12, 2011).
8. Yahia H. Zoubir, "Algerian-Moroccan Relations and Their Impact on Maghrebi Integration," *Journal of North African Studies* 5, no. 3 (2001): 43–74.
9. For an extensive account of U.S. policy toward the conflict in Western Sahara, see Stephen Zunes and Jacob Mundy, *Western Sahara: War, Nationalism, and Conflict Irresolution* (Syracuse, NY: Syracuse University Press, 2010).
10. See Yehudit Ronen, *Qaddafi's Libya in World Politics* (Boulder, CO: Lynne Rienner Publisher, 2009), chapter 2.
11. Tony Capaccio, "Lockheed Martin to Sell Morocco 24 New F-16s for $841 Million," *Bloomberg*, December 22, 2009, www.bloomberg.com/apps/news?pid=newsarchive&sid=aaF5gcH2t8H8. (Accessed on December 26, 2009); see also Global Security, "Royal Moroccan Air Force," www.globalsecurity.org/military/world/morocco/air-force.Html. (Accessed on August 8, 2010).
12. See the special dossier "Maghreb: Les Dessous d'une Course à l'Armement," *El Watan* (Algiers), May 21, 2009, pp. 1–4.
13. See Zunes and Mundy, *Western Sahara*.
14. Human Rights Watch, "Obama Should Press Morocco's King on Reforms," November 20, 2013, www.hrw.org/news/2013/11/20/us-obama-should-press-morocco-s-king-reforms. (Accessed on June 21, 2015).

15. The White House, "Joint Statement by the United States of America and the Kingdom of Morocco," November 22, 2013, www.whitehouse.gov/the-press-office/2013/11/22/joint-statement-united-states-america-and-kingdom-morocco. (Accessed June 21, 2015).
16. U.S. Department of State, "2012 Human Rights Reports: Western Sahara," April 19, 2013, www.state.gov/j/drl/rls/hrrpt/2012/nea/204390.htm. (Accessed June 21, 2015).
17. Ibid.
18. See Robert D. Kaplan, *Hog Pilots, Blue Water Grunts: The American Military in the Air, Sea, and on the Ground* (New York: Random House, 2007).
19. On this point, see Clement M. Henry, "Reverberations in the Central Maghreb of the 'Global War on Terror,'" in Yahia H. Zoubir and Haizam Amirah-Fernàndez, Eds., *North Africa: Politics, Region, and the Limits of Transformation* (London and New York: Routledge, 2008), 294–310.
20. UN Security Council, United Nations S/RES/1904 (2009), adopted by the Security Council at its 6247th meeting, December 17, 2009.
21. "Messahel: Lutte Antiterroriste, les Participants se Sont Engagés à Mettre en Œuvre les Conventions," Algerian Ministry of Foreign Affairs, March 21, 2010, http://193.194.78.233/ma_fr/stories.php?story=10/03/21/5613238. (Accessed on March 30, 2010).
22. See Philip J. Crowley, Assistant Secretary, Bureau of Public Affairs, U.S. Department of State, Washington, DC, March 16, 2010, www.state.gov/r/pa/prs/ps/2010/03/138370.htm. (Accessed on March 27, 2010).
23. "Bilateral Counterterrorism Contact Group Launched," Embassy of the United States in Algiers, March 3–4, 2011, http://algiers.usembassy.gov/daniel_benjamin2011.html. (Accessed April 15, 2011).
24. Ibid.
25. "La visite de John Kerry à Alger pour un plus grand élan aux relations USA-Algérie," Algérie Presse Service (APS), March 26, 2014, www.aps.dz/algerie/3551-la-visite-de-john-kerry-%C3%A0-alger-pour-un-plus-grand-%C3%A9lan-aux-relations-usa-alg%C3%A9rie. (Accessed March 29, 2014).
26. U.S. Energy Information Administration, "Algeria: Country Analysis Brief Overview," July 2014, www.eia.gov/countries/country-data.cfm?fips=ag. (Accessed October 15, 2014).
27. For instance, shortly after criticizing Tunisia, Powell praised the changes that were taking place there. See Colin Powell, Fox News Sunday, March 14, 2004, www.foxnews.com/story/0,2933,114159,00.html. (Accessed on March 17, 2004).
28. Scott Shane, "Cables from American Diplomats Portray U.S. Ambivalence on Tunisia," *New York Times*, January 15, 2011.
29. WikiLeaks, Cable reference id: #06TUNIS1673.
30. Hillary Rodham Clinton, interview with Taher Barake of Al Arabiya – Dubai, UAE, January 11, 2011.
31. Alexis Arieff, Congressional Research Service, "Political Transition in Tunisia," June 18, 2012.
32. Clinton, op. cit.
33. "US Embassy Cables: Tunisia – A US Foreign Policy Conundrum," *Guardian*, December 7, 2010.
34. Tim Lister, "Tunisian Protests Fueled by Social Media Networks," CNN, January 21, 2011.
35. Hillary Clinton, "Forum for the Future: Partnership Dialogue Panel Session," U.S. Department of State, January 13, 2011, www.state.gov/secretary/20092013clinton/rm/2011/01/154595.htm. (Accessed June 18, 2015).
36. Office of the Press Secretary, "Statement by the President on Events in Tunisia," The White House, January 14, 2011, www.whitehouse.gov/the-press-office/2011/01/14/statement-president-events-tunisia. (Accessed June 18, 2015).
37. Yahia H. Zoubir, "The United States and Libya: The Limits of Coercive Diplomacy," *Journal of North African Studies* 16, no. 2 (2011), pp. 275–297.

38. Willa Thayer, "Libya Awards Oil Contracts," Associated Press, December 20, 2006.
39. Ronald Bruce St. John, "A New U.S. Relationship with Libya?" *Foreign Policy in Focus*, March 27, 2009, www.fpif.org/articles/a_new_us_relationship_with_libya. (Accessed on March 28, 2009).
40. Ronald Bruce St. John, "'Libya Is Not Iraq': Preemptive Strikes, WMD, and Diplomacy," *Middle East Journal* 58, no. 3 (2004): 391–392.
41. "Arab League Criticizes Western Strikes on Libya," Agence France-Presse, March 20, 2011.
42. "Libya Crisis: U.S. 'Caught Off-Guard' by Air Strikes," *BBC News*, August 26, 2014.
43. Secretary of State Colin Powell, Testimony before the Senate Finance Committee, February 12, 2002.
44. David Lepeska, "Gag Time in Cairo: An Interview with Egyptian Journalist Ibrahim Eissa," *Columbia Journalism Review*, November 9, 2010.
45. Hearing before the Subcommittees on Africa, Global Health, and Human Rights of the Committee on Foreign Affairs, U.S. House of Representatives, 112th Congress, first session, December 8, 2011.
46. "US Urges Restraint in Egypt, Says Government Is Stable," *Reuters*, January 25, 2011.
47. "As Arabs Protest, U.S. Speaks Up," *The Washington Post*, January 27, 2011.
48. "U.S. Urges Restraint in Egypt, Says Government Is Stable," *Reuters*, January 25, 2011, www.reuters.com/article/2011/01/25/ozatp-egypt-protest-clinton-idAFJOE70O0KF20110125. (Accessed June 21, 2015).
49. Joe Biden, cited in PBS NewsHour, "Biden: Mubarak Is Not a Dictator, But People Have a Right to Protest," January 27, 2011.
50. Mike Allen, "White House Scrambles to Keep Up with Crisis," *Politico*, January 31, 2011.
51. Nicholas Johnson, "Obama Tells Mubarak He Must Stick to Pledge of Egyptian Reforms," *Bloomberg Business*, January 28, 2011, www.bloomberg.com/news/2011–01–28/obama-says-mubarak-must-take-concrete-steps-to-deliver-pledge-on-reforms.html. (Accessed June 18, 2015).
52. Marc Lynch, "Washington Eyes a Fateful Day in Egypt," *Foreign Policy*, January 28, 2011.
53. Hans Nichols, "Obama's Words Put to Test in U.S. Response to Egypt," Bloomberg Business, January 31, 2011.
54. Karen DeYoung, "Administration Aligns Itself with Protests in Egypt with Call for 'Orderly Transition,'" *Washington Post*, January 31, 2011.
55. Office of the Press Secretary, "Remarks by the President on the Situation in Egypt," The White House, February 1, 2011, www.whitehouse.gov/the-press-office/2011/02/01/remarks-president-situation-egypt. (Accessed June 18, 2015).
56. Marc Lynch, "Egypt Endgame," *Foreign Policy*, February 3, 2011.
57. David E. Sanger, "As Mubarak Digs In, U.S. Policy in Egypt Is Complicated," *New York Times*, February 5, 2011.
58. S.AMDT.1739, 113th Congress (2013–2014).
59. Stuart E. Eizenstat, Undersecretary for Economic, Business, and Agricultural Affairs, Third Annual Les Aspin Memorial Lecture, Washington, DC: Washington Institute for Near East Policy, March 8, 1999.
60. Stuart E. Eizenstat, "Prospects for Greater Global and Regional Integration in the Maghreb," remarks at Peterson Institute for International Economics, Washington, DC, May 29, 2008.
61. Ziad Salah, "Lutte Antiterroriste: Les Américains s'Alignent sur la Position Algérienne," *Le Quoitien d'Oran* (Algeria), July 22, 2010, www.lequotidien-oran.com/index.php?news=5140941&archive_date=2010–07–22. (Accessed on July 22, 2010).
62. Yahia H. Zoubir, "Conflict in Western Sahara," in David Sorenson, Ed., *Interpreting the Modern Middle East: Essential Themes* (Boulder, CO: Westview Press, 2010), pp. 303–336; Hakim Darbouche and Yahia H. Zoubir, "Conflicting International Policies and the Western Sahara Stalemate," *International Spectator* 43, no. 1 (2008): 91–105.
63. "President Bush Discusses Freedom in Iraq and Middle East," remarks by the President at the 20th Anniversary of the National Endowment for Democracy, Office of the White

House Press Secretary, November 6, 2003, www.ned.org/george-w-bush/remarks-by-president-george-w-bush-at-the-20th-anniversary. (Accessed June 18, 2015).

64. See, for instance, George W. Bush, "The National Security Strategy of the United States of America," March 2006, www.comw.org/qdr/fulltext/nss2006.pdf. (Accessed June 18, 2105); and European Council, "A Secure Europe in a Better World: The European Security Strategy," December 2003, www.consilium.europa.eu/uedocs/cmsUpload/78367.pdf. (Accessed on March 22, 2007).

65. Jose Manuel Barroso, EU-US Summit Press Conference, Vienna, June 21, 2006.

66. Thomas Carothers, "Democracy Promotion under Obama: Finding a Way Forward," Carnegie Endowment for International Peace, Policy Brief 77 (February 2009), p. 3.

67. Hillary Clinton, "Clinton Expresses Plans for New World Approach," Transcript of Clinton's Confirmation Hearing-In Depth: Clinton's Hearing, January 13, 2009, www.npr.org/templates/story/story.php?storyId=99290981. (Accessed on March 15, 2009).

68. Hillary Clinton, remarks on Development in the 21st Century at the Center for Global Development, Washington, DC, January 6, 2010, www.state.gov/secretary/rm/2010/01/134838.htm. (Accessed on February 15, 2010).

69. U.S. Department of State, Office of the Coordinator for Counterterrorism, "Terrorist Safe Havens: Strategies, Tactics, Tools for Disrupting or Eliminating Safe Havens," Country Reports on Terrorism, Chapter 5–5.1, April 30, 2008, www.state.gov/s/ct/rls/crt/2007/104103.htm. (Accessed on May 14, 2008).

70. As cited in Fareed Zakaria, "The Real Failed-State Risk," Newsweek, July 19, 2010, www.newsweek.com/2010/07/19/the- real-f ailed- state risk.html. (Accessed on July 25, 2010).

71. Statement of Assistant Secretary of State for African Affairs Johnnie Carson, Senate Foreign Relations Subcommittee on African Affairs, Hearing on Counterterrorism in Africa's Sahel Region, November 17, 2009, http://foreign.senate.gov/hearings/hearing/20091117. (Accessed on January 20, 2010); Testimony: Hearing on Counterterrorism in Africa's Sahel Region, November 17, 2009, cited in U.S. AFRICOM Public Affairs, www.africom.mil/getArticle.asp?art=3735. (Accessed on January 20, 2010).

72. Chris Scott, "Obama Announces James Jones as National Security Advisor," ONE, December 1, 2008, www.one.org/blog/2008/12/01/obama-announces-james-jones-as-national-security-advisor/. (Accessed on January 20, 2009).

73. For details, see Major Eric Hilliard, "Multinational Exercise Sparks Change for Africa," American Forces Press Service, November 20, 2008, www.defenselink.mil/news/newsarticle.aspx?id=52031. (Accessed on January 22, 2009).

74. U.S. Department of State, "Country Reports on Terrorism 2009," Washington, DC, August 2010, www.state.gov/s/ct/rls/crt/2009 /index.htm. (Accessed on August 10, 2010).

75. Daniel Volman, "Obama, Africom, and U.S. Military Policy toward Africa," Program of African Studies Working Paper no. 14 (Evanston, IL: Northwestern University, 2009), 7.

76. Ibid., 9.

77. U.S. Embassy in Algiers, "U.S. and Algeria Exchange Antiterrorism Expertise," July 25, 2010, http://algiers.usembassy.gov/event4.html. (Accessed on July 27, 2010).

78. Djamel Bouatta, "Plusieurs Fois Reporté, Le Sommet de la Sécurité au Sahel Maintenu," Liberté (Algiers), June 2, 2009.

79. Phillip J. Crowley, "Statement by Philip J. Crowley, Assistant Secretary of State for Public Affairs," Office of the Spokesman, March 16, 2010, www.america.gov/st/text transenglish/2010/March/20100316130306eaifas0.8310009.html. (Accessed on March 20, 2010).

80. Anna Theofilopoulou, "Western Sahara – How to Create a Stalemate," U.S. Institute of Peace Briefing, May 2007, www.usip.org/resources/western-sahara-how-create-stalemate. (Accessed on June 12, 2008).

81. Cited in "Obama Reverses Bush-Backed Morocco Plan in Favor of POLISARIO State," World Tribune, July 9, 2009, www.worldtribune.com/worldtribune/WTARC/2009/af_morocco0547_07_09.asp. (Accessed on July 14, 2009).

82. Ibid.
83. See www.elmuhajer.com/statedepartment.php.
84. Secretary of State Hillary Rodham Clinton, "Remarks with Moroccan Foreign Minister Taieb Fassi-Fihri," November 2, 2009, www.state.gov/secretary/rm/2009a/11/131229. htm. (Accessed on November 5, 2009).
85. Hillary Clinton, "Interview with Fouad Arif of Al-Aoula Television," Marrakech, Morocco, November 3, 2009, www.state.gov/secretary/rm/2009a/11/131354.htm. (Accessed on November 5, 2009).
86. Aboubakr Jamaï et Abdelkader Rhanime, "Enquête à Washington – Affaire Haidar Histoire d'un Ratage," *Le Journal*, January 22, 2010, www.lejournal-press.com/articles_plus. php?id=2195. (Accessed on January 25, 2010). Access to the article is no longer available as the Moroccan authorities shut down the newspaper since its publication, though they justified the closure on financial grounds.
87. Anna Theofilopoulou, "Western Sahara: The Failure of 'Negotiations without Preconditions,'" Institute of Peace United States Brief 22, U.S. Institute of Peace, April 23, 2010, www.usip.org/resources/westernsahara-the-failure-negotiations-without-preconditions. (Accessed on April 27, 2010).
88. "Illinois Senator Responds to Written Questions Submitted by the Washington Post – Q&A: Obama on Foreign Policy," *Washington Post*, March 2, 2008, www.washingtonpost .com/wp-dyn/content/article/2008/03/02/AR2008030201982_pf.html. (Accessed on March 3, 2008).

17

BARCELONA, TWENTY YEARS ON

George Joffe

In November 1995, at a major conference in the southern Spanish city of Barcelona – by then already the focus of Catalunyan aspirations for autonomy within the Spanish state, if not for full-blown independence from it – the European Commission spelled out how it anticipated its future relationship with the South Mediterranean region should develop. It sought, according to the Barcelona Declaration, which concluded the conference, to create a zone of shared peace, stability and prosperity throughout the Mediterranean basin.[1] This was to be achieved through recourse to two prior experiences; the construction of the European Union itself and the 1975 Conference on Security and Cooperation in Europe (CSCE), better known as the Helsinki Conference, which had ushered in the relatively brief period of *détente* during the Cold War. The European experience was to pinpoint the way in which peace and prosperity could be achieved whilst the CSCE process highlighted the role to be played by collective security in achieving regional stability.

The timing of the new policy was also significant for it emerged at the beginning of what was triumphantly expected to be a new era of hegemonic stability under the world's sole hyper-power.[2] Five years before, the United States, benefitting from its unrivalled global supremacy as a result of the end of the Cold War, had been able to openly intervene in the Middle East, forcing Iraq out of Kuwait, stationing American military forces permanently in Saudi Arabia and initiating a peace process between Israel and the Arab world. This geopolitical triumph was paralleled by geo-economics – a new approach to the global economy, based on liberalised markets reflecting the neoliberal vision of the Washington Consensus, as envisioned by the United States and international financial institutions such as the World Bank, the International Monetary Fund and the latest arrival, the World Trade Organisation, formally created the previous April. In this context, the European Union, created out of the European Economic Community as a result of the Maastricht Treaty in 1993, was in effect a regional version of this new global architecture.[3]

Yet it was also something more. In addition to its adoption of neoliberal principles in the organisation of its economic life, the Union also enunciated a set of normative concepts to govern its political structures.[4] In effect, it sought to abandon realist principles of international engagement for a set of rules that would govern such contacts, derived from legal and moral concerns, and would apply universally, irrespective of the relative power exercised by each of the states concerned. This normative vision was combined with a new approach to collective security in the wider sense of human security. This derived from the CSCE experience as elaborated in 1990 through a Spanish-Italian non-paper initiated by the then Italian foreign minister, Gianni de Michaelis, as the Conference for Security and Cooperation in the Mediterranean, an initiative also supported by France as a means of continuing engagement with its former colonial empire in North Africa.

The Euro-Mediterranean Partnership

The outcome of this process – the first initiative of the new Common Foreign and Security Policy (CFSP) of the Union – was to be the Euro-Mediterranean Partnership (EMP).[5] The EMP, often better known as the Barcelona Process, sought to create a series of bilateral agreements with Southern and Eastern non-European Mediterranean countries and the European Union that would be the basis through which the 'shared zone of peace, prosperity and stability' promised in the Barcelona Declaration would be achieved.[6] Each agreement would take substantially the same form which reflected both the Union's normative principles and its economic objectives. They would begin with a commitment to good governance and respect for human rights and then provide for three separate baskets of issues; one dealing with political issues and security, another with social and cultural concerns, and the third with issues of economic collaboration.

Implicit in the agreements was the view in Brussels that they would eventually encourage the integration of the Southern and Eastern Mediterranean region into its own single market to accelerate their economic growth potential. Implicit, too, was the belief in Europe that such development would end the migratory pressure within the region for access to the European labour market – a source of constant concern to major European economies, such as Germany, the Benelux countries, Britain, France, Italy and Spain. This was a European concern that stretched back over many years, after the initial post-war enthusiasm for migrant labour to help rebuild the European continent had dissipated in the face of indigenous European concerns over the social tensions attendant upon migration and the evolution of temporary workers into permanent minority communities. It had been a concern that had driven prior European policies towards the Mediterranean region, with the advent of collective association and cooperation agreements in the 1970s.

The most elaborate of the baskets was the basket devoted to economic issues, both because this mirrored the way in which the European Union itself had come into being and because it was key to the way in which Brussels hoped that the Southern and Eastern Mediterranean countries would eventually achieve their own path towards economic development. It anticipated the creation of a bilateral free trade zone in industrial goods between the Union and the partner-country concerned in which the reduction of tariff barriers between them would take place gradually over a period of twelve years. Agricultural free trade was deliberately excluded largely to protect the European Union's own Common Agricultural Policy because of the potential threat of exports from countries such as Morocco and Egypt to Europe's own producers. Over time, it was anticipated that agriculture, too, would be brought within the free trade provisions as well but not before 2000. The focus on industrial goods reflected the belief in Brussels that unrestricted competition with European industry and access to the European market would spur industrial development in the partner-countries and thus dramatically expand employment opportunities there.

It was acknowledged that, in the short term, there would be negative consequences of such unrestricted industrial competition – in Tunisia, for example, one-third of the industrial sector was expected to disappear, one-third to survive only with difficulty and only one-third would benefit from the competitive opportunities provided, whilst in Morocco, 60 per cent of the country's industrial base would be threatened without massive financial support. The long-term effects, however, were expected to be wholly beneficial as local industry was forced to adopt European and international standards in order to compete

TABLE 17.1 European Union MEDA support (allocations)

€ million	MEDA-1 (1995–1999)	MEDA-2 (2000–2004)	MEDA-1 & MEDA-2 (1995–2004)
Bilateral funding			
Algeria	164.0	232.8	396.8
Palestine	111.0	350.3	461.3
Egypt	686.0	353.5	1,039.5
Jordan	254.0	204.4	458.4
Lebanon	182.0	73.7	255.7
Morocco	660.0	677.1	1,337.1
Syria	101.0	135.7	236.7
Tunisia	428.0	328.6	756.6
Total bilateral	**2,586.0**	**2,356.1**	**4,942.1**
Regional funding	471.0	739.8	1,210.9
Total funding	**3,057.0**	**3,095.9**	**6,152.9**

Source: Europe Aid (2009), *Evaluation of the Council Regulation No 2098/2000 (MEDA II) and Its Implementation*, Brussels.

Note: According to the MEDA budget projections, funding under MEDA-1 (1995–1999) was set at €3,435 million, with an additional €4,808 million in soft loans from the European Investment Bank. Funding under MEDA-2 (2000–2006) will have totalled €5,350 million, with European Investment Bank loan funding up to 2007 of €6,700 million. The regulation instituting the MEDA programme can be found at:
http://europa.eu/legislation_summaries/external_relations/relations_with_third_countries/mediterranean_partner_countries/r15006_en.htm.

within the European single market and with European commodities within its own national market arena. It is worth noting, too, that issues of competivity and economies-of-scale were simply assumed to be automatically resolvable within the context of the basic economic principles that informed the agreement. In any case, European funding was to be made available to aid the process of transition; originally €4.85 billion was allocated for the first five-year period through the MEDA-1 funding proposal, followed by €5.3 billion for the subsequent five years, although, in practice the totals involved were slightly below these levels (see Table 17.1).

Statistical appendix

An inherent, albeit implicit, additional objective of the EMP was the European conviction that the Southern and Eastern Mediterranean would be impelled by the economic changes the policy would produce to integrate its national economies into a single market of its own. This would release the synergies innate in an amplified market size towards further endogamous economic growth, thus improving development without the need for additional external funding. This, in turn, would mitigate the explicit 'hub-and-spoke' concept that informed the original conception behind the EMP, which would otherwise ensure continued and expanding European economic dominance over the Mediterranean. Such market integration had been long seen as essential for viable regional economic development to occur. The advent of the Agadir Agreement for the integration of the Moroccan, Tunisian, Egyptian and Jordanian markets at the end of the 1990s was seen as the first spontaneous fruit of these aspirations although, in the event, they have proved to be premature.

The other two baskets were more aspirational in nature for they really sought to introduce European-style norms and security considerations into the political processes of the Mediterranean basin. Thus, the politics and security basket sought to encourage democratic good governance through direct engagement between government and the European Commission, along with the promise of a collective security arrangement throughout the Mediterranean basin – something that could not be achieved because of the unresolved Arab-Israeli dispute, despite concerted attempts made during the Nice EMP presidency summit in 2000. Direct military-based 'hard security' was, of course, beyond Europe's grasp as the Union had no integrated military mechanism available to it.[7] The social and cultural basket sought to address South Mediterranean concerns over migrant communities in Europe as well as seeking to encourage the development of civil societies in the non-European partner-states.

In reality both baskets remained largely unrealised because of geopolitical realities in the Mediterranean basin. Most partner-states were autocratic in nature and did not welcome interference in their domestic policies, quite apart from their resentments at European engagement at a regional level. This occurred, they felt, both in terms of ongoing disputes (the Western Sahara issue or the problem of Israel, for example) and at initiatives designed to weld their economies together into a single Southern market to enhance the beneficial consequences of cross-Mediterranean competition. The Algerian government, in particular, resented anything that seemed to infringe on its national sovereignty, especially as it was still in the throes of a civil war for which it held Europe partly responsible because of what it saw as liberal policies of European states on political asylum.

Behind these resentments lay two other fundamental issues that were eventually to seriously affect the outcome of the EMP. One was the fact that the whole EMP process was entirely driven by the European Union, which had deliberately sought to create a 'one-size-fits-all' policy approach. It had defined the nature of the policy and it managed the outcomes. Its dominant position in the foreign trade of all the Southern and Eastern Mediterranean countries ensured that it could do so (see Tables 17.2–17.4) and its determination to resolve the development issue in order to eliminate the migration issues that had resulted from earlier developmental failures – so troubling to European states – gave it the drive to push the policy

TABLE 17.2 ENPI (2007–2013)

Year	2007	2008	2009	2010	2011	2012	2013	Total 2007–2013
€ million (constant prices)	1,433	1,569	1,877	2,083	2,322	2,642	3,003	14,929

Source: Smith (2005), "The outsiders: The European Neighbourhood Policy", *International Affairs*, 81(4): 760.

Note: These figures combine both funds for the Mediterranean and non-member Eastern European states. They are therefore not comparable with MEDA funding. They can be compared with the budget for the East and the Mediterranean in 2004 (€1,420 million with €953 million for the Mediterranean).

TABLE 17.3 Evolution of EMP trade in goods and services (2008–2011)

	Trade in goods (€ billion)		
Year	EU imports	EU exports	Balance
2009	106.6	118.4	11.7
2010	131.9	147.6	15.7
2011	130.0	159.8	29.8
	Trade in services (€ billion)		
2008	33.1	23.9	−9.3
2009	29.8	22.0	−7.8
2010	40.8	28.1	−12.6

Source: Europe Aid (2009), *Evaluation of the Council Regulation No 2098/2000 (MEDA II) and Its Implementation*, Brussels.

TABLE 17.4 European oil and gas trade (2012)

European Union	Oil (b/d million)	Gas (billion cubic metres)		
		pipeline	LNG	Total
Consumption	12.796			443.9
Production	1.538			149.6
Imports	12.488	377.2	69.3	446.5
Exports	2.174	–	–	–
Imports from ME	2.261	7.5	31.1	38.6
Imports from NA	1.577	39.3	16.8	56.1
MENA total imports	3.838	46.8	47.9	94.7
% imports from MENA	30.7	12.4	69.1	21.2

Source: British Petroleum (2013), *2013 Statistical Review of World Energy* (London: BP Distribution Services).

forward, come what may. Conversely, however, this meant that the leaderships of the non-European partner-states were not engaged in the process beyond the need to respond to European insistence. By 2005, the tenth anniversary of the introduction of the EMP, their disaffection was evident. In the conference in Barcelona for the commemoration of the Barcelona Conference in 1995, only two heads-of-state from the non-European Mediterranean basin bothered to attend and the meeting was given over to an ill-tempered exchange over new measures to restrict international terrorism, led by European leaders.

Indeed, this highlighted the second problem, which was a reflection of quite different concerns that had arisen specifically as a consequence to the events in the United States of September 11, 2001. Even though European states had not been the target of the malevolence of *al-Qa'ida* as the United States had been, they nonetheless very rapidly endorsed the core vision of the subsequent 'war on terror'. In practice, this meant that the European Union securitised its policies towards the Southern and Eastern Mediterranean states.[8] Migration ceased to be merely a political problem in which non-European Mediterranean states could be co-opted as partners in its resolution – either by control measures or through economic development. Instead it now became associated with spillovers of threats to European security, including terrorism, from the Middle East and North Africa.[9] This approach, in turn, further increased Southern and Eastern Mediterranean resentment and sense of lack of ownership as a result of the exclusive control of policy exercised by European states and the European Commission in Brussels. In short, one of their major complaints over the new policy was that the free movement of capital and goods at the core of the Barcelona Process was now increasingly less likely to be matched by the concomitant free movement of people implicit in the concept of constructing a zone of shared peace, prosperity and stability in the Mediterranean basin.

European neighbourhood

In any case, by the mid-2000s, the European Commission had also become disillusioned by the prospect of achieving the objectives of the EMP and was casting around for an alternative. In 2004, the first group of Accession countries in Eastern Europe had successfully fulfilled the terms for their inclusion into the Union. Their accession had depended on their abilities to incorporate the European *acquis* – the complex legal and political regulations that governed the operation of the Union itself – into the process of governance. This was now seen as an alternative approach for the Southern and Eastern Mediterranean countries, which would also allow them to be partnered with Eastern European non-member states, thereby creating a 'circle of friends' around the European periphery, in the words of the then president of the European Commission, Romano Prodi, by granting them access to 'everything but the [European] institutions'.[10] This is what was to become the European Neighbourhood Policy (ENP) in 2004.

Indeed, even as early as December 2002, the Commission had begun to wonder how it could combine its experiences over Accession with the EMP, a process that had been partly driven by a parallel American policy innovation, the United States-Middle East Partnership Initiative (USMEPI), which was subsequently integrated into the Bush Administration's soft security counterpart to the 'war on terror', the Broader Middle East Initiative, introduced at the G7 Sea Island summit in 2004. This, in turn, had been partially driven by the deliberate exclusion of the United States, at French insistence, from the evolution of the EMP. USMEPI was to prove to be a much more modest policy than the EMP or any of its successors – funding for its four programmes of political, economic and educational development, together with women's empowerment, never totalled more than $100 million a year – but it did highlight the fact that the European Union could no longer assume that it alone would the arbiter of the geo-economic and geopolitical fate of the Mediterranean region.

The way in which the new policy was designed did little to address concerns within the Mediterranean basin itself towards Europe; it was still essentially decreed from Brussels, so added nothing to partner-state empowerment. Nor did it improve access to the European labour market or reduce the securitisation of the relationship across the Mediterranean basin. It also undermined the objective of removing the 'hub-and-spoke' nature of the original agreement, with its implications of European hegemony over the EMP, for the new arrangement actually intensified the hierarchical characteristics of the relationship and rendered them permanent. In theory, the new policy was intended to provide a mechanism for achieving the objectives of the association agreements at the heart of the original EMP, for it proposed that 'action plans' should be drawn up between the Commission and a partner-country.[11]

Each action plan should cover a three- to six-year period and delineate what objectives the country concerned would seek to achieve to improve its acquisition of the Copenhagen criteria-linked *acquis* related to what its association agreement would be during that period. The plans are based on a principle of positive conditionality (known in the rather peculiar vocabulary of the Commission as the 'more-for-more' principle), in that the degree of access to the institutions and processes of the Union depends on how successful the country concerned has been in fulfilling its action plan. The new policy's financial dimension, the European Neighbourhood and Partnership Instrument (ENPI), brought together the old TACIS (Eastern Europe) and MEDA (Mediterranean) programmes into a single initiative (see Table 17.5). Between 2007 and 2013, the ENPI provided €11.2 billion, a 32 per cent increase over the financing available under the old TACIS and MEDA programmes between 2000 and 2006 (see Table 17.2), together with over €13 billion worth of soft loans from the European Investment Bank (EIB), with additional facilities available from the European Bank for Reconstruction and Development (EBRD).[12]

After the Commission had reviewed the progress of the ENP in 2010–2011, it made specific facilities available under the 'more-for-more' principle. These included a new form of association agreement in terms of economic progress, the Deep and Comprehensive Free Trade Area (DCFTA), mobility partnerships in terms of improved personal visa access to Europe and improved financial facilities. These required progress in political and economic normative behaviour with the emphasis on political change in terms of the development of 'deep and sustainable' democratic governance.[13] At the same time, it also disaggregated the sixteen ENP partner-states concerned into what it called the Eastern Partnership, comprising Belarus, Moldova, the Ukraine and the Black Sea Synergy (Armenia, Azerbaijan and Georgia), alongside the ten Mediterranean EMP/MEDA-10 states, thus allowing a degree of specificity back into its globalised policy approach.

TABLE 17.5 Trade with MEDA-10 (2012)

€ million	Total trade		Imports from EU		Exports to EU		Total EU trade	
	Imports	Exports	value	%age total	value	%age total	value	%age total
Algeria	42,857	46,518	21,984	51.3	22,829	49.1	44,813	50.1
Egypt	66,078	34,754	16,216	24.5	7,333	21.1	23,548	23.4
Israel	56,697	49,933	19,535	34.5	13,341	26.7	32,876	30.8
Jordan	21,613	7,781	2,828	13.1	234	3.0	3,062	10.4
Lebanon	19,622	5,436	6,367	32.4	344	6.3	6,710	26.7
Morocco	38,325	16,838	15,848	41.4	8,442	50.1	24,290	44.0
OPT	–	–	–	–	–	–	–	–
Syria	23,093	16,738	1,232	5.3	240	1.4	1,472	3.7
Tunisia	21,693	14,609	11,812	54.4	8,494	58.1	20,305	55.9
Turkey	202,128	157,363	68,055	33.7	46.038	29.3	114,093	31.7
Total	469,013	349,970	149,282	31.8	107,295	30.7	256,577	31.3

Source: Europe Aid (2009), *Evaluation of the Council Regulation No 2098/2000 (MEDA II) and Its Implementation,* Brussels.

Union for the Mediterranean

The issue of a more targeted policy approach also arose amongst European member-states as well, an issue which reflected the changing power balance within the European Union itself. The key balance within the European Union has traditionally been that between Germany and France, as the two states that have determined pan-European objectives in place of their previous tradition of mutual hostility, with Germany as the junior partner. With the end of the Cold War and the growth in importance of Eastern Europe, as well as, beyond it, Russia and its surrounding states, the balance has gradually changed towards one in which Germany, given its over-whelming economic strength and access to the East, has become progressively more influential in European circles. France, on the other hand, has seen its relative economic strength weaken and its traditional arena of influence – Europe's Latin states, the Mediterranean basin and Africa – decline in Europe's hierarchical perceptions of its neighbours. These changes, which have increased in recent years as a result of the 2008 financial and economic crisis throughout Europe, were already evident before that crisis erupted.

As far as Europe's policies towards its periphery were concerned, these issues manifested themselves in the second half of the last decade in two quite specific ways. Firstly, European border policy became increasingly dominated by concerns over illegal migration, not just from neighbouring states but particularly as a result of security crises in Africa, the Middle East and Central Asia. One consequence of this was that countries, that had themselves been countries-of-origin for illegal migration and asylum-seekers (see Tables 17.6 and 17.7), now became countries-of-transit as well. Another was that, as the Justice and Home Affairs pillar of the Union became more integrated, so a greater European dimension emerged in the policies applied to prevent inward migration into Europe itself. This involved both intense inter- and trans-governmentalism between Europe and its neighbours and the externalisation of migration controls through European instruments such as FRONTEX, the Europe-wide border control agency located in Warsaw.[14] This was, in effect, an extension of European securitisation of its relationship with its neighbourhood – a direct contradiction of the normative values supposed to inform its interaction with its neighbour-states.

Furthermore, a wider implication followed from this, namely that Europe's normative agenda over good governance and human rights was merely rhetoric. The reality of Europe's engagement, therefore, reflected the acute self-interest of its states in ensuring effective barriers to migration – whether illegal or political – rather than in questions of appropriate patterns of governance. In short, stability and securitisation had become the rule in the place of representation and political engagement. In other words, Europe really sought 'illiberal democracies' which would cooperate in achieving its realist security objectives rather than 'deep and sustainable governance' as proposed under the ENP; in effect, the continuation of Middle Eastern and North African autocracy for the sake of political stability.[15] Both these tendencies intensified the 'hub-and-spoke' nature of the underlying

TABLE 17.6 Asylum-seekers (1980–2012)

Date	Europe total	Date	Europe total
1980	158,950	1996	276,240
1981	113,700	1997	312,970
1982	85,300	1999	386,889
1983	71,150	2000	405,812
1984	104,350	2001	416,023
1985	170,500	2002	407,394
1986	205,700	2003	339,619
1987	189,550	2004	268,565
1988	290,700	2005	227,425
1989	349,500	2006	201,000
1990	443,800	2007	229,100
1991	546,000	2008	239,150
1992	700,850	2009	247,330
1993	545,710	2010	240,410
1994	318,500	2011	277,800
1995	319,870	2012	296,690

Sources: www.unhcr.org/statistics/STATISTICS/3bfa31ac1.pdf (EU15 up to 1997).
http://ec.europa.eu/justice_home/doc_centre/asylum/statistics. /wai/doc_asylum_statistics_en.htm
(EU25 up to 2005).
www.unhcr.org/47daae862.html (EU25 2006–2007 – Bulgaria and Romania join on 1/1/2007).
http://unhcr.org/asylum_trends/UNHCR%20ASYLUM%20TRENDS%202012_WEB.pdf (EU27
2008).

TABLE 17.7 Ilegal migration (2002–2008)

Year	Illegal population (million)		%age Total population		%age Foreign population	
	minimum	*maximum*	*minimum*	*maximum*	*minimum*	*maximum*
EU15						
2002	3.1	5.3	0.80	1.40	14	25
2005	2.2	4.8	0.58	1.23	8	18
2008	1.8	3.3	0.46	0.83	7	12
EU27						
2008	1.9	3.8	0.39	0.77	7	13

Source: Morehouse & Blomfield (2011), *Illegal Migration in Europe*, Migration Policy Unit
(Washington, DC).

relationship between the European Union and its partner-states within European Neighbourhood Policy. Conversely, that situation, in turn, offered opportunities to any European state that overtly sought to alter that balance.

This was the opportunity that Nicolas Sarkozy sought to exploit during his 2008 presidential campaign with the objective of recovering France's leading role within

European Mediterranean policy, the traditional arena of French foreign policy dominance. The presidential candidate proposed the creation of a new 'Mediterranean Union', comprising all the littoral states of the Mediterranean basin, to address matters of regional concern in a collective manner. The proposal was unique in three ways: first, it sought to be truly collective and not merely dominated by European leadership and concerns, thus addressing the problem of 'co-ownership' of policy; secondly, the activities of the new initiative were to be entirely funded by the private sector; and, thirdly, it was the first time since the 1980s that the European Union as a collective unit had not been a partner in Mediterranean policy. This reflected the fragmentation of Mediterranean policy typical of the earlier era when a series of different groupings addressed security, developmental and governance issues.[16]

Despite French hopes, the imbalance of power within Europe soon reasserted itself after Nicolas Sarkozy emerged as victor in the presidential election. In July 2008, at a European summit in Paris, Germany made it clear that it would block the new president's Mediterranean initiative unless all twenty-seven European Union states were involved. By November 2008, under the title of 'Union for the Mediterranean' (UfM), the project had been re-engineered, away from French patronage and back into the hands of the European Commission. It also reintroduced the idea of a Mediterranean specificity in Europe's policies towards its neighbourhood by, in effect, reviving the EMP in a new guise and creating the Eastern Partnership for Eastern European non-member states and the Black Sea Synergy for the Caucasus. Membership was also expanded, for the twenty-seven members of the Union were now partnered by the original ten Mediterranean states and a new group made up of the Balkan states of Bosnia, Albania and Montenegro, together with Monaco and Mauritania. The Arab League joined Libya as an observer member of the new organisation.

In organisational terms, the principle of 'co-ownership' was preserved by ensuring that there were leadership institutions shared or duplicated across the Mediterranean, although the secretariat would be established in Barcelona – in a rhetorical nod towards the original EMP and the Barcelona Declaration that had started the whole process thirteen years earlier. There was also to be a cross-Mediterranean parliamentary assembly and a similar local government assembly but neither was to have legislative authority. The concept of regional activity was also preserved, as was the primacy of private sector funding, although both the European Neighbourhood and Partnership Initiative (ENPI) and the World Bank would contribute, the ENPI operating through the Infra-Med Infrastructure Fund. The funding was to be directed towards six regional projects, as delineated below:

- the de-pollution of the Mediterranean Sea, including coastal and protected marine areas;
- the establishment of maritime and land highways that would connect ports and improve rail connections so as to facilitate movement of people and goods;
- a joint civil protection programme on prevention, preparation and response to natural and man-made disasters;

- a Mediterranean solar energy plan that was to explore opportunities for developing alternative energy sources in the region;
- a Euro-Mediterranean University, inaugurated in Slovenia in June 2008, which was to mirror the Ana Lindt Foundation in Alexandria; and
- the Mediterranean Business Development Initiative, which would support small businesses operating in the region by first assessing their needs and then providing technical assistance and access to finance.[17]

Despite its elaborate infrastructure, however, the UfM was a pale shadow of its predecessor, the EMP, even though it addressed the issue of co-ownership. Unlike the EMP, it only addressed region-wide issues, for the ENP retained control of the bilateral Association and Cooperation Agreements; nor did it have its own funding line derived from the European budget, relying instead on the uncertain generosity of the private sector. Furthermore, even though it sought to be holistic in its approach, once again the ENP supervened over it, imposing its 'hub-and-spoke' vision as the priority, even dominating regional projects with its bilateral approach. The UfM, in short, was an irrelevance, a rhetorical nod in the direction of French and South Mediterranean sensibilities, for the ENP which had originally cannibalised the EMP still dominated the increasingly realist and securitised European policy agenda. This was to be underlined when the Arab world began its own crisis in 2011.

The Arab Awakening

The causes and consequences of the Arab Awakening are not a matter for discussion, as such, here.[18] The nature of the European Union's reactions to those events is of considerable significance, however, as it demonstrates the way in which the normative values and holistic approach which had informed its original policy initiatives have been progressively transformed into a set of fragmented, bilateral and realist policies instead, which are primarily concerned with security issues. There remains a profound irony, however, for the rhetoric of the original approach persists as the institutions through which it should have been reified have proliferated, but they are now ensconced within a discursive carapace of security concerns. In the Union's defence, however, it should also be added that the events of the Arab Awakening occurred at a moment when Europe was particularly vulnerable for its own domestic reasons and its reactions to the events of 2011 would, in consequence, be adversely affected.

As Frederica Bicchi pointed out, not only was Europe immersed in its own financial and economic crisis which had disproportionately affected Southern European states – normally the natural allies of the MEDA states – but the consequences of the Lisbon Treaty, which had institutionalised the CFSP into the European External Action Service (EEAS), were just beginning to be felt. This meant that the areas of relative competence for foreign policy between the new institution and the Commission still had to be demarcated. One obvious potential area of conflict is that, whilst the EEAS handles the CFSP, the Commission retains responsibility for its economic and financial aspects. In theory, the EEAS formulates policy but the Commission implements it; in practice the demarcation is not so clear, particularly over declaratory policy where the European Council and the European Union Council also have a voice! The Lisbon Treaty has also given much greater agency to the Union's delegations abroad, thus undermining the ability of Brussels to control policy and its implementation directly. The picture was further complicated by additional institutions: a special representative for the Southern Mediterranean and three task forces, one each for Egypt, Tunisia and Jordan, which were later expanded to include two more, one for the Gulf Cooperation Council and the other for Libya. The potential for confusion over policy development and implementation was, correspondingly, significantly intensified. Finally, not all European governments welcomed the likelihood of profound political change in the Southern and Eastern Mediterranean, preferring instead the certainties of the past. This dissuaded them from encouraging radical and innovative European Union responses to what was happening along Europe's southern periphery. This was particularly true of France, which had been leery about regional political change ever since the civil war in Algeria during the 1990s, with its attendant risks of extremist spillover into Europe, although the Sarkozy presidency was to prove to be quite willing to join Britain in achieving 'regime change' in Libya! There was a further problem, too: significant differences of opinion about the nature of the policies that should be adopted towards the non-Union member-states of the UfM which were undergoing transition. South European states, despite being profoundly weakened by their domestic financial problems, sought greater engagement with the southern region. Northern European states, however, sought ever greater compliance with the principles of economic liberalisation and conditionality contained in the economic dimension of ENP. There has, therefore, been no pressure of concerted and coherent new initiatives within the context of the CFSP.[19]

Yet, despite these hindrances, the Union did develop several initiatives designed to respond to the Arab Awakening and developed from its existing policies under the ENP. One was designed to improve governance and economic development and was christened by the EEAS as 'more-for-more' – in other words, the further a country extended political and economic liberalisation, the greater the support and cooperation it would receive from the European Union. The new initiative was specifically designed to respond in three fields: migration policy, market access and monetary support – the 'three Ms', as they were named by the EEAS's head, Catherine Ashton. Restrictions on legal migration were to be eased on a bilateral basis through 'mobility partnerships'; market access was to improved through new bilateral agreements for 'Deep and Comprehensive Free Trade Areas', designed to replace the old association agreements, which, in turn, would emphasise conditionality and regulatory convergence; and improved financial access as part of a new initiative for the South Mediterranean region called the SPRING programme, designed to encourage democratic transition, economic growth and the development of the concomitant institutions. The acronym stood for 'Support for

Partnership, Reforms and Inclusive Growth' and highlights the fragmentation of the ENP by establishing a specific policy arena for the Mediterranean as compared with Europe's neighbours to the East.

It is difficult to avoid the conclusion that the new policy initiatives really represented little more than tinkering at the edges of long-established policies, rather than reflecting a paradigm shift in the nature of cross-Mediterranean relationships.[20] In effect, the reforms proposed in response to the Arab Awakening simply reinforced the neoliberal economic principles established in the original EMP and intensified the regulatory framework that would lock the Mediterranean into the Union's single market. The one innovative development has been a revival of European interest in strengthening civil society in the South Mediterranean through the creation of a civil society facility linked to the European Endowment for Democracy.[21] This, of course, reflects a European concern over democracy promotion as part of the new agreements under the SPRING programme and may mark the abandonment of European preferences for the securitisation of its external policies towards the South Mediterranean, although this is still far from certain. In short, as Frederica Bicchi has remarked, the institutional response to the Arab Awakening has not even achieved its objective of 'more-for-more' but is rather 'less-than-before', thus underlining Europe's growing irrelevance to the political and economic future of the Mediterranean region and a betrayal of the original hopes of the Barcelona Process.[22]

Perhaps the most important arena for European response to the Arab Awakening has been that of financial support. The results of the engagement since 2011 have not been overly impressive, due in part, no doubt, to the financial crisis that European states have faced over the past seven years. The same has been true of parallel American efforts at engagement with the new states that have emerged in the Arab world, despite the G8's Deauville Programme, announced in 2008. Apart from security initiatives in Syria and Egypt, the Obama administration has been very cautious in responding to the profound changes that have taken place throughout the region. Indeed, promises – from both the United States and the European Union – have been far more impressive than their actual performance.

TABLE 17.8 Arab countries in transition – Financing needs

$ billion	Estimates		Projections	
	2011	2012	2013	2014
Current account deficit	26.5	31.0	28.0	29.4
External amortization	14.3	14.3	14.8	22.7
External gross financing needs	40.8	46.3	42.8	52.1
Budget deficit	37.1	46.9	55.7	61.1
Public external amortization	5.4	5.4	6.0	8.3
Fiscal financing needs	42.5	52.2	61.6	69.4

Source: International Monetary Fund (2013), *Arab Countries in Transition: Economic Outlook and Key Challenges* (Washington, DC)(October 2013).

Over the past four years, the Union has committed an additional €3.55 billion in loans or grants to the countries involved in the Arab Awakening, primarily to Egypt and other countries in North Africa. This included an increase of €1.2 billion in the ENPI to €6.9 billion for 2011 and 2012. The new budgetary allowance for ENPI between 2014 and 2020 will total €13.7 billion, equivalent to 20 per cent of the European External Action Service's total budget and a significant improvement on its predecessor. The United States, for its part, has contributed or committed $2.53 billion to North Africa, Jordan and Yemen, in addition to its normal provision of $1 billion in economic aid and $1.7 billion in military aid, whilst the G8's Deauville Partnership provided $2.8 billion up to the end of July 2013.[23]

These seem to be massive sums but they must be set against the funding needs of the countries involved in what the international community now terms the 'Arab countries in transition'. The IMF, in a paper prepared for the Deauville Partnership's meeting in October 2013, estimated that the cumulative shortfall in external financing in 2013 would be $48.2 billion and $61.6 billion in fiscal receipts (see Table 17.8). It goes on to point out that growth is low and unemployment is rising, with growth expected to have been 3 per cent in 2013 and 2014, compared with 2.5 per cent on average in 2012, whilst budget deficits will have averaged 9 per cent of GDP and public debt is of the order of 80 per cent of GDP. This must be set against the absolute declines in GDP in 2011 – -1.8 per cent in Tunisia and -0.1 per cent in North Africa overall – and sharply reduced growth elsewhere – 1.7 per cent in Egypt, for example, compared with 5.1 per cent growth in 2010. Unemployment has also grown, from 8.9 per cent in 2010 to 10 per cent in 2011.[24] In late 2013, the British bank HSBC estimated that, by the end of 2014, the GDPs of the seven countries most affected by the Arab Awakening – Egypt, Tunisia, Libya, Syria, Jordan, Lebanon and Bahrain – would be 35 per cent below what they would have been if the Arab Awakening had not occurred and that the direct costs of the Awakening would be $800 billion![25] Against circumstances such as these, the financial support offered by donors in the developed world seems less than impressive, despite IMF stand-by programme promises of $1.78 billion to Tunisia and $4.8 billion to Egypt, particularly when set against the $16 billion provided by the Gulf states to Egypt alone in 2013 and 2014.[26]

The implications

There seems little doubt that the European Union, despite its high-flown rhetoric, is no longer the normative power that it once so triumphantly claimed to be, at least as far as its external policies are concerned. As a result of the events of September 11, 2001, these have been securitised, with their underlying driver – migration – becoming the explicit target. This development alone has effectively transformed Europe from being a normative to a realist power in terms of its external relations, a development that has been further entrenched by the dramatic growth in migration flows from the Middle East and Africa during the last decade. In addition, these paradigmatic alterations in the nature of the Union's external relations have been reinforced by the consequences of the financial and economic crisis that erupted in Europe and the United States in 2008.[27]

In these circumstances, it could be argued that the European retreat from its normative ideals has been inevitable, even if the rhetoric has remained the same. As Jan Techau, the director of Carnegie-Europe, has recently pointed out in a penetrating analysis of the '3Ms' policy, the economic downturn caused by the Arab Awakening could hardly have been countered simply by the initiatives based on increased market access, mobility partnerships and improved financial provision, or, if they could have been, the costs to Europe would have been far greater than it could have borne. Concessions over access to the single European market for agricultural exports, textiles and low technology industrial goods would have been too small to make a significant difference to economic slowdown and the cost to Europe's Common Agricultural Policy and the European budget would hardly have been justified by the consequential benefits generated in the Arab world. Mobility partnerships would only impoverish non-European Mediterranean countries by removing their essential educated elites, thus further undermining their potential for economic development. And significant financial support would have been diverted by rent-seeking local elites, thus feeding corruption in the absence of effective measures to enforce conditionality. In short, more massive European intervention would not have altered local political relationships and would have further fed local resentment.[28]

That may be a plausible, if over-stated, scenario; it does not, however, eliminate the reality that Europe had over-reached itself in the triumphalist euphoria created by the end of the Cold War, not least in its claim to have invented a mode of political organisation that supervened over the Westphalian concept of the state as the primary mover in international relations. Its regionalist vision, allied to its claim to normative power, within a globalised world drove both the closed regionalism that characterised the European Union itself and the open regionalism behind the vision of the EMP.[29] Now that vision seems somewhat beleaguered as Europe itself, disillusioned by its own frailties over domestic economic policy and social integration, connives in reinforcing its periphery against the Hobbesian world around it rather than embracing the democratic transitions there that, earlier, it had professed to seek.[30]

Notes

1. Preamble (1995), Barcelona Declaration, November 28.
2. The original use of the term 'hyper-power' was by Peregrine Worsthorne in the *Daily Telegraph* in 1991. It was, however, revived in 1998 and popularised by Hervé Védrine, then French foreign minister, in a speech to the Association France-Ameriques in Paris on Monday, February 1, 1999. Geo-economics was very much an American vision, pushed by the Clinton administration and reflected the argument that factors related to economic globalisation would determine international relations, with the United States seeking to dominate the globalised world-economy. Allied to this, of course, was the Fukuyama argument that in the great ideological battle of the Cold War, Western concepts of democratic governance within free market economies had won a definitive victory. See Fukuyama (1989), "The end of history?" *The National Interest* (Summer).

3. John Williamson coined the term, the 'Washington Consensus'. See Williamson (1989), "What Washington means by policy reform," in Williamson, J. (ed.): *Latin American Readjustment: How Much has Happened?*, Institute for International Economics (Washington, DC). The term reflects the general agreement between the United States and international financial institutions in Washington that the path to economic success requires overcoming the inefficient allocation of national resources by opening an economy to realistic pricing policies reflected in global market prices. A secondary objective is to reduce the role of the state within an economy. Subsequently, market distortions were to be handled by the use of New Institutional Economics, importing transparency and accountability into the economic process. See Todaro (1989), *Economic Development in the Third World*, Longmans (London): 83. The European Union's policies towards the Mediterranean basin exemplify both the principles and the failures of this model of economic development.

4. Manners relates the values that define Europe as a normative power to key principles enshrined in the Union's *acquis* – peace, liberty, democracy, the rule-of-law and respect for fundamental individual rights and freedoms, together with a more implicit concept which is of some importance here, good governance. See Manners (2001), "Normative power Europe: The international role of the EU," European Communities Studies Association Panel 1D, Madison, May 31: 11; and Manners (2004), "Normative power reconsidered," *CIDEL Workshop: From Civilian to Military Power; the European Union Reconsidered*, Oslo, October 22–23. Sjursen and Smith argue that they are best represented by the Union's Copenhagen Principles, which determine the criteria for membership (a market economy, democratic governance and respect for human rights). See Sjursen and Smith (2001), "Justifying EU foreign policy: The logics underpinning EU enlargement," *Arena Working Papers*, WP1/01, Centre of European Studies, University of Oslo (Oslo).

5. The CFSP was the new foreign policy instrument of the Union, one of its three pillars as defined by the Maastricht Treaty. The other two were the Single Market and the integrated Justice and Home Affairs pillar. It is managed today by the Union's External Action Service. See Joffe (2012), "North Africa and Europe," in Adebajo, A, and Whiteman, K. (eds.), *The EU and Africa: From Eurafrique to Afro-Europa?* Hurst (London).

6. Eventually, all twelve non-European Mediterranean member-states, except Libya, were included. Turkey and Israel had more specific agreements, the first covering a customs union and the second a much wider free trade zone, as a result of prior agreements with the European Community. Malta and Cyprus became members of the Union in 2004, thus leaving only ten EMP member-states. Libya eventually engaged through a special observer status arrangement but never entered into an association agreement.

7. This raises the question of what the European Union's relationship with NATO should be and what NATO's relationship with the Southern and Eastern Mediterranean region might become, questions that have never been resolved. At present, NATO has engaged with the region since 1994 through the 'Mediterranean Dialogue', a consultative process that is supposed to occur only with democratic governments inside the region, and through the Istanbul Cooperation Initiative (ICI), signed in 2004, which allows for more substantive engagement along the lines of the 'Partnership for Peace' within the former Soviet space. For the ICI, see www.nato.int/cps/en/natohq/topics_52956.htm (accessed January 5, 2015) and www.nato.int/cps/en/natohq/topics_60021.htm (accessed January 5, 2015) for the Mediterranean Dialogue.

8. According to the terminology of the Copenhagen School's concept of security studies, the term 'securitisation', in this context, is taken to mean the process by which a policy tool or instrument becomes 'an instrument which, by its very nature or by its very functioning, transforms the entity . . . it processes into a threat' (Balzacq [2008], "The policy tools of securitization: Information exchange, EU foreign and interior policies," *Journal of Common Market Studies, 46*[1]). The instrument then becomes so all-important that its original significance is obscured as it conditions security discourse and seeks to determine new outcomes, with – in this case – migration being transformed into a key element in the context of trans-national threat. See also Balzacq (2005), "The three faces

of securitization: Political agency, audience and context," *European Journal of International Relations, 11*(2).

9. See Joffe (2008), "The European Union, democracy and counter-terrorism in the Maghrib," *Journal of Common Market Studies, 46*(1).

10. Prodi (2002), "A proximity policy as the key to stability: 'Peace, security and stability – international dialogue and the EU,'" *Sixth ECSA-World Conference, Jean Monnet Project*, Brussels, December 5–6.

11. http://eeas.europa.eu/enp/how-it-works/index_en.htm (accessed January 5, 2015).

12. http://ec.europa.eu/europeaid/how/finance/enpi_en.htm (accessed January 5, 2015).

13. http://eeas.europa.eu/enp/about-us/index_en.htm (accessed January 5, 2015).

14. Joffe (2008), "The European Union, democracy and counter-terrorism in the Maghrib," *Journal of Common Market Studies, 46*(1): 162–166.

15. This is the concept of an allegedly formal democratic process unleavened by liberal institutions, such as the rule-of-law or civil society, which are otherwise essential to guarantee viable democratic systems. See Zakaria (1997), "The rise of illiberal democracy," *Foreign Affairs, 76*(6) (Nov/Dec): 22–43.

16. These had included the 'Five-plus-Five' and the 'Mediterranean Forum', not to speak of NATO's 'Mediterranean Dialogue' and its later 'Istanbul Cooperation Initiative', or parallel discussions sponsored by the Western European Union and the Organization for Security and Cooperation in Europe (OSCE) network. The 'Five-plus-Five' group brought together France, Italy, Spain, Portugal and Malta with Libya, Tunisia, Algeria, Morocco and Mauritania in a security and development forum; the 'Mediterranean Forum' was an Egyptian-inspired initiative grouping the Arab littoral states of the Mediterranean with their European counterparts, including Greece, Turkey and Portugal for the same purposes.

17. http://eeas.europa.eu/euromed/index_en.htm (accessed December 13, 2014).

18. There are an increasing number of publications available that discuss events in the Arab world since 2011. One example that covers North Africa is Joffe (ed.) (2013), *North Africa's Arab Spring*, Routledge (London).

19. Bicchi (2014), "The politics of foreign aid and the European Neighbourhood Policy post-Arab Spring: 'More for more' or less of the same?" *Mediterranean Politics, 19*(3): 319.

20. Balfour (2012), *EU Conditionality after the Arab Spring*, IeMed – European Institute of the Mediterranean, Barcelona, June: 11–12.

21. Joffe (2014), "Regionalism, the European Union and the Arab Awakening," in Telo, M. (ed.), *European Union and New Regionalism* (3rd edition), Ashgate (Aldershot): 291.

22. Bicchi, op. cit., 325.

23. Greenfield, Hawthorne and Balfour (2013), *The US's and the EU's Lack of Strategic Visions: Frustrated Efforts towards the Arab Transitions*, Rafik Hariri Center for the Middle East, Atlantic Council – Washington, DC, September: 19–24, 35–36, 40–41.

24. Economic Commission for Africa (2013), *Economic and Social Conditions in North Africa: 2011–2012*, United Nations (New York): 8–10.

25. Reuters (Dubai), "Arab Spring to cost Middle East $800 billion, HSBC Estimates," October 9, 2013.

26. Kuwait $4 billion, Saudi Arabia $5 billion and the UAE $7.2 billion (Fitch [2014], "Gulf nations' sway rises in Egypt," *Wall Street Journal*, July 1).

27. The alterations are 'paradigmatic' in the sense that they represent a paradigm shift. The term originates with Tomas Kuhn who argued that, in science, progress occurs through radical shifts in structures of interpretation. Furthermore, such shifts are incommensurate – the new structure of meaning cannot be interpreted in terms of its predecessor. His concept has since been applied to the political and social sciences, although the requirement of incommensurability does not apply as different structures of meaning can and do coexist and can be interpreted, the new by the old. See Kuhn (1962 & 1969), *The Structure of Scientific Revolution*, University of Chicago Press (Chicago).

28. Techau (2014), "What if Europe had reacted strategically to the Arab Spring?" Carnegie-Europe, February 27, http://carnegieeurope.eu/publications/?fa=54672 (accessed January 5, 2015).

29. Open regionalism implies linkages between states that do not impinge directly upon their sovereign activities and rights. They therefore tend to be primarily economic in nature, even if the explicit objectives of such regional organisations may involve common security or diplomatic factors. Closed regionalism involves explicit common policies in all areas and thus diminishes the sovereign powers of constituent governments. (See Thomas [1998], "Globalisation versus regionalisation", in Joffe, G. [ed.], *Perspectives on Development: The Euro-Mediterranean Partnership*, Cass [London]: 63.)

30. These closing comments have been provoked by the fact that it seems now almost inevitable that Europe will achieve, instead, the pessimistic outcome forecast by Andrew Roberts in 1991 when he remarked that the developed world was now a 'Grotian one, observing norms of cooperation, and perhaps even [with] its Kantian element: a civil society of civil societies'. However, outside this normatively ideal focus, '. . . parts of the world beyond are still Hobbesian, with force still a very active final arbiter within and between countries, and sovereignty loudly proclaimed" (Roberts [1991], "A new age in International Relations?" *International Affairs* 67[3] [July]: 519).

References

Balfour, R. (2012), *EU Conditionality after the Arab Spring*, IeMed – European Institute of the Mediterranean, Barcelona, June 20.

Balzacq, T. (2005), "The three faces of securitization: Political agency, audience and context," *European Journal of International Relations, 11*(2).

Balzacq, T. (2008), "The policy tools of securitization: Information exchange, EU foreign and interior policies," *Journal of Common Market Studies, 46*(1).

Bicchi, F. (2014), "The politics of foreign aid and the European Neighbourhood Policy post-Arab Spring: 'More for more' or less of the same?" *Mediterranean Politics, 19*(3).

British Petroleum (2013), *2013 Statistical Review of World Energy*, London: BP Distribution Services.

Economic Commission for Africa (2013), *Economic and Social Conditions in North Africa: 2011–2012*, New York: United Nations.

Europe Aid (2009), *Evaluation of the Council Regulation No 2098/2000 (MEDA II) and Its Implementation* Brussels, June, available at http://ec.europa.eu/europeaid/how/evaluation/evaluation_reports/reports/2009/1264_vol1_en.pdf (accessed on June 17, 2015).

Fitch, A. (2014), "Gulf nations' sway rises in Egypt," *Wall Street Journal*, July 1.

Fukuyama, F. (1989), "The end of history?" *The National Interest* (Summer).

Greenfield, D., Hawthorne, A. and Balfour, R. (2013), *The US's and the EU's Lack of Strategic Visions: Frustrated Efforts Towards the Arab Transitions*, Rafik Hariri Center for the Middle East, Atlantic Council – Washington, DC, September.

International Monetary Fund (2013), *Arab Countries in Transition: Economic Outlook and Key Challenges*, Washington, DC, October.

Joffe, G. (2008), "The European Union, democracy and counter-terrorism in the Maghrib," *Journal of Common Market Studies, 46*(1).

Joffe, G. (2012), "North Africa and Europe," in Adebajo, A. and Whiteman, K. (eds.), *The EU and Africa: From Eurafrique to Afro-Europa?* London: Hurst.

Joffe, G. (ed.) (2013), *North Africa's Arab Spring*, London: Routledge.

Joffe, G. (2014), "Regionalism, the European Union and the Arab Awakening," in Telo, M. (ed.), *European Union and New Regionalism* (3rd edition), Aldershot: Ashgate.

Kuhn, T.N. (1962 & 1969), *The Structure of Scientific Revolution*, Chicago: University of Chicago Press.

Manners, I. (2001), "Normative power Europe: The international role of the EU," European Communities Studies Association Panel 1D, University of Wisconsin-Madison, May 31.

Manners, I. (2004) "Normative power reconsidered," *CIDEL Workshop: From Civilian to Military Power; the European Union Reconsidered*, Oslo, October 22–23.

Morehouse, C. and Blomfield, M. (2011), *Illegal Migration in Europe*, Migration Policy Unit, Washington, DC.

Preamble (1995), Barcelona Declaration, November 28. http://ec.europa.eu/com/external_relations/euromed/bd.htm (accessed January 3, 2015).

Prodi R. (2002), "A proximity policy as the key to stability: 'Peace, security and stability – International dialogue and the EU,'" *Sixth ECSA-World Conference, Jean Monnet Project*, Brussels, December 5–6.

Reuters (Dubai), "Arab Spring to cost Middle East $800 billion, HSBC Estimates," October 9, 2013, available at www.reuters.com/article/2013/10/09/mideast-economy-politics-idUSL6N0HZ2IT20131009 (accessed on June 17, 2015).

Roberts, A. (1991), "A new age in International Relations?" *International Affairs, 67*(3).

Sjursen H. and Smith K.E. (2001), "Justifying EU foreign policy: The logics underpinning EU enlargement," *Arena Working Papers*, WP1/01, Centre of European Studies, University of Oslo (Oslo).

Smith, K. (2005), "The outsiders: The European Neighbourhood Policy," *International Affairs, 8*(4).

Techau, J. (2014), "What if Europe had reacted strategically to the Arab Spring?" Carnegie-Europe, Brussels February 27. http://carnegieeurope.eu/publications/?fa=54672 (accessed January 5, 2015).

Thomas, G. (1998), "Globalisation versus regionalisation," in Joffe, G. (ed.), *Perspectives on Development: The Euro-Mediterranean Partnership*, London: Cass.

Todaro, M. (1989), *Economic Development in the Third World*, London: Longmans.

Williamson, J. (1989), "What Washington means by policy reform," in Williamson, J. (ed.), *Latin American Readjustment: How Much Has Happened?* Washington, DC: Institute for International Economics.

Zakaria, F. (1997), "The rise of illiberal democracy," *Foreign Affairs, 76*(6) (Nov/Dec).

18

CHINA IN NORTH AFRICA

A strategic partnership

Imen Belhadj and Degang Sun, with
the collaboration of Yahia H. Zoubir

The last two decades have witnessed China's success in establishing a strong presence in the African continent, particularly in terms of trade, investment and economic cooperation. The Sino-African trade volume had increased from less than $10 billion in 2003 to $210.2 billion in 2013, a remarkable leap forward. China's engagement in Africa has become one of the hottest debates in the world affairs. In this chapter, we shall explore the relationship between China and the North African region that will have a full spectrum of Chinese engagement.

We will first offer a thorough review of China's relations with the Maghreb countries and Egypt. We seek to understand how China's economic power has extended to North Africa, which has taken on added importance for China, not least because of the PRC's thirst for oil and markets available in the region. Based on the Chinese win-win cooperation philosophy, we assess the costs and benefits of the Sino-North African cooperation, and give some suggestions to push forward the relations between both sides.

China's strong presence in Africa is sometimes perceived as a "new colonialism"[1] in Africa, but officials in Beijing argue that China's economic presence serves the local peoples and governments as well, and it is a win-win cooperation totally different from modern Western colonialism. Incidentally, China is not a newcomer to Africa in general and to North Africa in particular; in fact, it has always maintained strong ties with the North African countries, especially with Algeria and Egypt, regarded as two pivotal states of China's diplomacy.

There are two dynamics driving China's policies towards North Africa: one is geopolitical, i.e., China's political rivalry in the region with other outside powers; the other is geo-economic, namely, China seeking economic opportunities, energy cooperation and investment destinations for its domestic oversupplied products and its modernization drive.

North Africa and China: Historical ties

China's first exchanges with the North Africa region started early in the 8th century. During the Tang Dynasty and the Baghdad-based Abbasid Empire, China and the Arab World had close trade relations through the Silk Road, the famous trade route linking China with the Arab World and Africa. At that time, the Arabs reached the western part of China, which constituted the major parts of the Silk Road under the control of the Arab Empire. Trade relations between China and the Arab Empire were fruitful for both sides: Arab traders imported Chinese goods, and helped China to introduce its "Four Great Inventions," namely papermaking, gunpowder, printing and the compass to Europe and the rest of the World through North Africa.

The interactions between China and the North African region were not limited only to trade relations. From the 12th century onward, there were frequent people-to-people relations between both sides. Chinese well-known traveler Du Huan (杜环) mentioned Morocco in his book[2] and Chinese historians estimated that he visited Morocco during his travel to Africa. During the Song Dynasty (960–1279), Zhao Rugua (赵汝适), the customs inspector of Quanzhou City, Fujian Province, wrote a two-volume book, titled *Zhufan Zhi* ("Records of Foreign Peoples"; 诸番志). This book is a catalog of foreign countries, with records and descriptions of the customs and trade goods produced in these countries. In this book, Zhao Rugua named the Maghreb region "Mulanpi" (木兰皮). He also described the goods produced in the region. Well-known Maghrebi traveler Ibn Battuta visited China from 1346 to 1349. He toured many Chinese cities, like Quanzhou, Guangzhou, Hangzhou, and Beijing. In 1336, the famous Chinese traveler and trader Wang Dayuan (汪大渊) visited Tangier. Wang Dayuan wrote his well-known book *Daoyi Zhilue* (岛夷志略) in which he described Tangier and its traditions.[3]

During the period of "closed-door policy" pursued by the Ming and Qing dynasties in the 14th and 15th centuries, and in modern times of the Western colonialism in Africa and China, Beijing's direct contact with the Maghreb region was interrupted, but its indirect trade with North Africa did not halt. Throughout the late Qing Dynasty and the Republic of China (1911–1949), the two sides gradually resumed contacts and exchanges via different channels, although exchanges were mainly sporadic.

From the establishment of the People's Republic of China (PRC) until the 1970s, China's relations with Asian, African and Latin American countries (AALA; 亚非拉) were essentially based on ideological claims. China was supporting AALA countries to fight against colonialism and imperialism. During the Bandung Conference held in Indonesia in 1955, Premier Zhou Enlai and President Gamal Abdul Nasser had a series of successful discussions which marked the beginning of Sino-Egyptian and Sino-North African relations. They called each other "brothers" in a united front against Western exploitation. Thereafter, the Chinese supported Algeria's revolution (1954–1962) against French colonialism. China was the first non-Arab and non-African country to recognize the Algerian provisional government (GPRA) in September 1958.

Egypt was the first African and Arab country to establish diplomatic relations with the PRC in 1956; Algeria and independent Morocco did so in 1958, while Tunisia established diplomatic ties with China in 1964. For its part, Mauritania and Libya recognized the PRC in 1978 and developed sound relations since then.

The good ties between China and North African countries were consolidated due to the prominent roles of Egypt, Algeria and Morocco. They helped China retrieve its permanent seat in the United Nations and the UN Security Council. In 1961 and during the 16th session of the United Nations General Assembly (UNGA), Morocco voted for the retrieval of China's permanent seat in the United Nations. Four years later in 1965, during the 20th session of the UNGA, Algeria was the first African country to submit an official proposal for the Chinese case, which was continuously supported by all North African countries during the following sessions of the Assembly. In 1971, during the 26th session of the UNGA, China successfully recovered its permanent seat with the majority of votes (76 approvals; 36 against; 17 abstentions). Among the approving votes, 26 were those of African states, including all North African countries.[4]

From 12 December 1963 to 10 February 1964, Premier Zhou Enlai, accompanied by Vice Premier Chen Yi, visited Egypt, Algeria, Morocco, Tunisia, Ghana, Mali, Guinea, Sudan, Ethiopia and Somalia. Zhou Enlai had talks with the leaders of these ten African countries. On that occasion, Premier Zhou declared the five principles of developing brotherly relations with African and Arab countries, as well as the eight principles of foreign aid. The five principles emphasized the support China provided to African and Arab governments to fight imperialism, colonialism and neocolonialism, to win their struggle for independence, to pursue a non-aligned policy of peace and neutrality, and to achieve unity and solidarity.

In the 1960s and 1970s, China did not have apparent economic interests in North Africa; China's motivation to provide aid to the newly independent African countries was to seek diplomatic recognition, and to compete with the Soviet Union and the United States in Africa politically and ideologically. But the distinctive part of the principles of Chinese foreign policy, which continued to play a very important role in shaping Chinese foreign cooperation, was the principle of non-interference and the protection of nations' sovereignty from any violations and interference, and settlement of disputes through peaceful negotiations. Beijing believed that such principles were opposite to the behavior of the old and new empires, the UK, France, the United States, and later the Soviet Union, dubbed the revisionist socialist empire.

The eight principles of foreign aid summed up the commitment of the Chinese government towards foreign countries and especially African countries, and emphasized the principle of equality, mutual benefit and assistance without political strings attached. The Chinese eight principles were the foundation of economic cooperation between China and North African countries in the 1960s and 1970s.

After the reform and opening up policy was launched in 1978, China's relations with the outside world became more pragmatic, less ideologically oriented, and development-based. The driving force of these relations was to promote

Sino-foreign economic cooperation to achieve Beijing's modernization drive, which was also the case with its relations with North African countries. From 20 December 1982 to 17 January 1983, Premier Zhao Ziyang visited Egypt, Algeria, Morocco, Guinea, Gabon, Zaire, Zambia, Zimbabwe and Kenya. On 13 January, he announced in a press conference in Dar-es-Salaam, Tanzania, the four principles of economic and technological cooperation between China and African countries, and summed it up as "equality, mutual benefit, practical results, diversity and common development." Different from Mao's ideology-driven "unconditional aid to the African brothers," his successor Deng Xiaoping highlighted mutual benefit and Chinese economic interests as top priorities.

After the "June 4" Tiananmen Square Incidents of 1989, Western powers unanimously decided to impose an embargo on China, and China's economic and political exchanges with the Western countries almost halted. To Beijing's delight, Egypt welcomed Chinese President Yang Shangkun in 1989, a gesture of breaking the Western blockade against China. Egyptian President Mubarak received his counterpart and asserted that the Western embargo against China was mistaken; foreign countries should not interfere in China's internal affairs.[5]

In the 1980s and 1990s, China's economic relations with North African countries witnessed steady progress in a multi-dimensional way. China and North African countries signed several economic and technological cooperation agreements in mining, fishing, agriculture and technology with Morocco; in energy, agriculture, water, transport and construction, the small and medium-sized industrial enterprises (SMEs) of Algeria had close-knit ties with their Chinese counterparts; and the phosphate and water industries of Tunisia have close relations with Chinese side as well. China established the Economic Joint Committee with Libya in 1982 and Mauritania in 1984. However, due to Libya's and Mauritania's backward political and economic conditions at that time, their economic and technological relations remained at a low level.

China's engagement in North Africa in the post-Cold War era

Since the end of the Cold War, China's engagement in North Africa has mainly focused on the economic dimension. Beijing's overseas interests in the region were two-fold: seeking natural resources and exploring markets for Chinese products. North Africa is an important region because it is the Northern gate of the continent with a total land area of 6,044,000 km^2 (including Western Sahara), with a population of more than 87 million people and more than 40% of the continent's proven energy reserves (48.59% of proven crude oil reserves; 43.72% of the proven natural gas reserves). The region is one of the richest in Africa and an attractive region for China's energy needs. The North African market as a whole has become attractive for Chinese companies and investments too. As part of the MENA region, it has emerged as an important market for Chinese goods, and Chinese companies are found across the region.[6] Over 50,000 Chinese are working in Algeria, and more than 30,000 Chinese workers were evacuated during the Libyan civil war in 2011.

Despite the remarkable economic ties between China and North Africa that developed recently compared with those during the Cold War period,[7] Chinese economic activities in North Africa in the first decade of the 21st century still remained limited in comparison with those with Sub-Saharan Africa. The trade volume between China and the whole of Africa has reached $126.9 billion, while Sino-Maghreb trade volume, for example, reached only 13.43% of China's total volume with Africa. Chinese investments in the Maghreb reached only 8.23% of China's total investments in Africa ($13.04 billion) in 2010. A report by the African Development Bank on China's trade and investments activities in Africa from 2003 to 2008 showed that 65% of Chinese FDI in Africa went to South Africa, while only 5% of its FDI went to Algeria.[8] The weak performance of the China–Maghreb economic interactions compared with the China–Sub-Saharan African economic relations underscores the strategic value of China for the Maghreb countries and vice-versa.

The Maghreb region's strategic value is more than its resources, but also its strategic position at the crossroads of the Arab World, Africa and the Mediterranean regions. China's economic performance is constantly growing and in the last several years, China has become the second largest economy in the world, and most experts inside and outside China expect it to be the largest economic power in the next ten years. Both China and North Africa have strategic value that pushes them to promote their economic cooperation.

China does not have an independent policy towards the Maghreb countries and Egypt in the 21st century; in fact, China's North African policy can be seen as a combination of China's African policy and its Arab policy. In the last 15 years, China began establishing mechanisms with Africa and the Arab world simultaneously. The Forum of China Africa Cooperation (FOCAC) and the China–Arab States Cooperation Forum (CASCF) were established in 2000 and 2004, respectively. Since the founding of these mechanisms, Beijing has drawn a clear policy of its engagement in Africa and the Arab World.

In January 2006, during the FOCAC Beijing Summit, the Chinese government issued an official white paper on "China's African Policy." In this paper, the Chinese government declared that it would enhance further cooperation with African countries based on its five principles of peaceful co-existence, such as mutual respect for each other's sovereignty and territorial integrity, non-aggression, non-interference in each other's internal affairs, equality, mutual benefit and peaceful co-existence. The policy paper has little concrete implications, but it included the mapping of Chinese policy for cooperation with Africa in the political, economic, cultural and social, as well as security, fields. For the first time throughout history, China has perceived Africa as a monolithic powerhouse and market, and has sought an all-round strategic relationship with the continent. On the political side, China has emphasized the importance of high-level visits, exchange visits of parliamentarians, exchanges between political parties, the establishment of consultative mechanisms, coordination in international affairs and close-knit exchanges between the Chinese local governments and their African counterparts. Since its market is basically saturated at home, Beijing has a strong desire to open African markets for its redundant and cheap products.

The Chinese policy is generally attractive for African countries and North African countries in particular, as it emphasized the equal partnership, mutual benefit and non-interference in each other's internal affairs. This policy has shown to the North African countries that Beijing is seeking cooperation in the region through a completely different philosophy from the one Westerners have.

Unfortunately, the attractive aspect of the Chinese model of cooperation with the African countries did not generate great interest from North Africans. If we take a look at North African countries' foreign policies, it is apparent that most of the countries are still focusing on their traditional partnership with European powers, especially with France, and have developed closer ties with the United States and the UK in recent years.

Following the Arab uprising in North Africa, some Maghreb countries like Morocco, Tunisia and Libya began to "Look East." However, instead of looking at the Far East, these countries are mainly looking at the rich Gulf monarchies, like Qatar and Saudi Arabia. Most of the Maghreb countries do not have a clear and long-term China policy. This can be explained by the very limited knowledge North Africans have about China, together with the phobia of the economic expansion of the "Chinese Giant." In recent years, North African countries have begun to appreciate China as a growing global economic power; yet, at the same time, they have no coherent policy to deal with China and have not drawn clear guidelines for their long-term cooperation with this rising developing country.

In terms of political relations between China and North African states, the latter have abided by some basic principles: they maintain their "One-China" policy to satisfy Beijing's demand. However, during the first decade of the 21st century, Libya was the only Maghreb country establishing de facto political and economic relations with Mainland China on the one hand and with Chinese Taiwan on the other hand. Relations between Taiwan and Libya, including Seif al Islam Qaddafi's visit to Taiwan, incensed the Chinese government's anger on many occasions.

Algeria, for its part, is aware of the strategic value of the economic cooperation with China, and attaches great importance mainly to the transfer of technology, which has potentially helped Algeria to boost its own industrial and economic development. Meanwhile, Algeria has sought to balance its relations with Europe and the United States, which is also the case of Tunisia and Morocco.

Mauritania seems to be the only North African country that promotes explicitly its partnership with China. In 2007, Mauritania's presidential candidate pledged to promote relations with China, which he depicted as "special" for the Mauritanian people, as China "takes up a unique place in their mind."[9] As Mauritania's foreign policy focuses mainly on searching for political protection, the state has suffered for a long time from national security dependence on outside powers. China has consistently followed its principles of non-interference and win-win cooperation, and it seems to be the best partner for Mauritanian leaders. China's FOCAC commitments towards the 26 less developed countries are much more attractive to

Mauritania than the US Millennium Challenge Corporation (MCC) program. This explains the dramatic development of political and economic relations between Mauritania and China.

Sino-Egyptian relations in the political dimension are sound with great momentum as well. In January 2004, President Hu Jintao paid a state visit to Egypt. During his visit, Hu had a cordial meeting in Cairo with the then Arab League Secretary General Amr Moussa and representatives from the 22 member states of the Arab League. During the meeting, Hu expounded China's overall vision for the establishment of CASCF.[10]

Since the establishment of the FOCAC and CASCF, economic relations between China and North African countries have witnessed a real takeoff: the trade volume has multiplied and Chinese investments have unprecedentedly rocketed in the North African region.

From 2005 to 2012, as Figure 18.1 shows, the trade volume between China and the Maghreb, for instance, has multiplied by four, and rose from $4.973 billion in 2005 to $23.706 billion in 2012. The increase of the trade volume between China and the Maghreb countries is explained by the surge of bilateral trade, which demonstrates the willingness of China to develop its trade relations equally with every single country on the one hand, and demonstrates also the interest of Maghreb countries to boost their trade relations with the Asian giant on the other.

Since the outbreak of the Arab Spring in late 2010, the political change that occurred in the region, especially the civil war in Libya, had a serious impact on the development of trade relations between China and North Africa. The trade volume has regressed by more than one billion dollars between 2010 and 2011. The trade volume between the two sides rose by $7.738 billion in 2012, and this augmentation is due to the rise of the trade volume between China and Libya, which has multiplied by four, from $2.783 billion in 2011 to $8.768 in 2012.

Figure 18.2 shows in details the increase of bilateral trade between China and the Maghreb countries. The trade volume between China and energy-rich countries namely, Algeria and Libya, is obviously higher than with Mauritanian and the non-energy-rich countries of Tunisia and Morocco. This is explained by the imports of oil, which is the main product imported from Algeria and Libya. China imports also phosphates, fisheries, mining and agricultural products from Morocco, Tunisia and Mauritania. The Maghreb countries import from China finished products like textiles, electronics, machineries and some agricultural products, such as tea and rice.

From 2005 to 2008, Algeria had the highest trade volume with China. Despite the impact of the civil war on China–Libya trade, Libya had surpassed Algeria and reached the highest trade volume ($8.768 billion) in 2012. It is important to mention that only Libya and Mauritania have trade surplus with China, which demonstrates the balance of Chinese economic policy in the Maghreb region between the rich and the less developed countries.

In 2010, as Table 18.1 illustrates, China surpassed France and Italy to become the largest trading partner of Mauritania; in the same year China became Libya's second

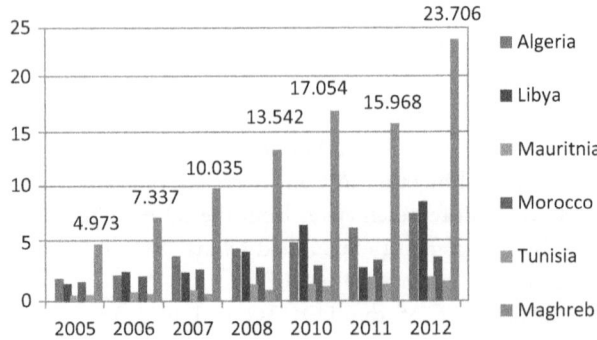

FIGURE 18.1 China's trade with the Maghreb (by year) (unit: Bn USD)

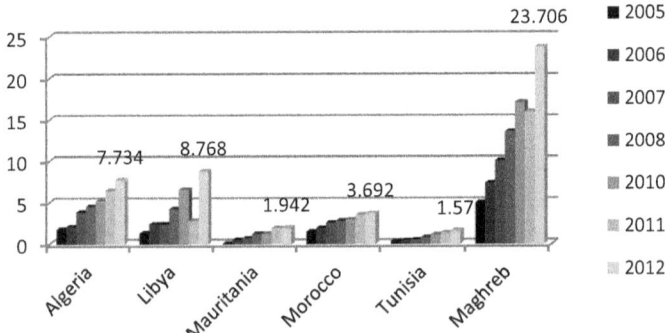

FIGURE 18.2 China's trade with Maghreb (by country) (unit: Bn USD)

TABLE 18.1 China's ranking in Maghreb top ten major trading partners in 2010

Maghreb Countries Ten Major Trade partners in 2010									
Algeria		*Libya*		*Mauritania*		*Morocco*		*Tunisia*	
1 EU	50%	EU	64.9%	EU	44.2%	EU	53.1%	EU	69.7%
2 US	16.5%	China	9.7%	China	12.3%	US	6.0%	Libya	4.4%
3 China	5.8%	US	4.2%	Brazil	4.5%	China	5.9%	China	3.1%
4 Turkey	4.3%	Turkey	3.8%	US	3.6%	Saudi Arabia	4.1%	Turkey	3.8%
5 Brazil	3.4%	S. Korea	2.6%	Malaysia	3.4%	India	3.2%	US	2.6%
6 Canada	3.4%	Tunisia	2.6%	Morocco	3.1%	Russia	2.7%	Algeria	2.4%
7 S. Korea	3.2%	Egypt	2.6%	Senegal	2.1%	Brazil	2.5%	India	1.5%
8 India	2.4%	India	1.3%	S. Africa	2.0%	Turkey	2.0%	Russia	1.4%
9 Japan	1.7%	Syria	1.1%	Egypt	2.0%	Algeria	1.9%	S. Korea	1.1%
10 Argentina	3%	Brazil	0.9%	Turkey	1.6%	Iraq	1.4%	Brazil	0.9%

Source: IMF (DoTS)

largest trading partner after the EU, and the third trading partner of the rest of the Maghreb countries, including Algeria, which has maintained a strategic partnership with China. In 2013, China became Algeria's main commercial supplier, surpassing France, which had traditionally been Algeria's main supplier (with $6.6 billion before year's end, while France, the traditional supplier, exported less than $5 billion); China remained number one in 2014, as well.[11]

Trade relations between China and the energy-rich countries (Algeria and Libya) focus on special types of products. The products imported by China are mainly energy products, like oil, mining products, steel and wood; the products imported by Algeria and Libya are mainly machinery, vehicles and clothing. According to the data provided by China's customs in 2010, Algeria mainly imported from China vehicles, nuclear equipment and steel products. The importation value of these products made up 45.8% of the total value. Libya has mainly imported nuclear equipment, electric and electronic products and clothing with an importation value reaching 40.16% of the total value. As for China, the energy products constitute the main imported products. The percentage of oil importation value reached 98.85% of exportation value from Libya to China, and 99.3% of exportation value from Algeria to China in 2010.

Trade relations between China and non-energy-rich countries are much more varied. For Morocco, the number of types of products imported and exported between China and Morocco increased from 1,306 types in 2000 to 3,004 types in 2008. The data provided by China's customs in 2010 revealed that China has mainly imported electrical goods and mining products, mainly phosphates, from Morocco and Tunisia.

Trade between China and Mauritania focuses on mining products exported from Mauritania to China (92.6% of exportation value). The top five products imported by Mauritania are tea, electrical and electronic products, chemical fibers, cotton and nuclear equipment.

As mentioned above, nuclear equipment has become common and one of the most important products imported by all Maghreb countries from China. This has highlighted Maghreb countries' import of Chinese technology in this field.

China has invested considerably in Algeria's infrastructure, to the dismay of France, Algeria's traditional trading partner. As Figures 18.3 and 18.4 show, China's investment in North Africa has increased significantly in recent years, exceeding one billion dollars in the Maghreb region.

Chinese investment in the energy-rich countries in the Maghreb, namely Algeria and Libya, focuses on energy and mining, and the majority of Chinese outward FDI stock in the Maghreb is located in Algeria (90.32%). According to the data provided by China's Ministry of Commerce, 81 state-owned Chinese enterprises have invested in Algeria from 2003 to 2013, and 32 state-owned enterprises invested in Libya from 2002 to 2012. As for the non-energy-rich countries of Morocco and Tunisia, Chinese investment is very limited and it mainly focuses on Morocco in the areas of fishing, motorcycle assembling, energy saving lights, plastics and printing. Twenty-nine state-owned enterprises invested there in 2012, according to

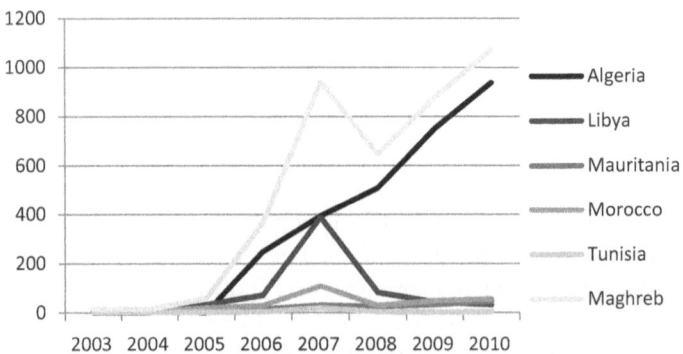

FIGURE 18.3 China's outward FDI stock in Maghreb (unit: M USD)

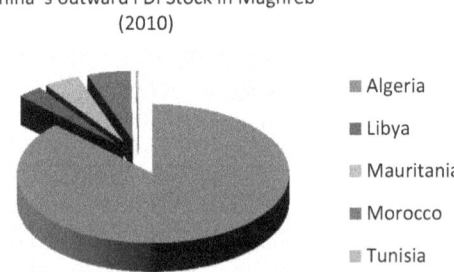

FIGURE 18.4 China's outward FDI stock in 2010

China's Ministry of Commerce. Chinese investment in Tunisia focuses on telecommunications, water resources and oil industry construction.

The economic takeoff of Chinese–Egyptian bilateral relations has been gradual, beginning in 1994 when a new investment agreement was signed that set the stage for increased economic activity. Chinese companies also started manufacturing electronics in the region. For instance, in 2008, Hisense, a Chinese company with a household name, opened its fifth production plant outside of China. Together with its Egyptian partner, Sun TV, Hisense is also producing 100,000 LCD TVs every year. As Table 18.2 shows, the total investment in the Egyptian economy, once all phases of the agreement are concluded, reached $60 million.[12] Egypt is the most populous country in North Africa with a huge market of 90 million people. Although the vast majority of Chinese investment in North Africa is in energy projects, it has some diversification, such as tourist and transport infrastructure, particularly in Egypt, where an agreement was signed in 2012 to build a high-speed train link between Cairo and Alexandria.[13]

In December 2014, Egyptian president Al-Sisi paid an important visit to Beijing and was warmly received by Chinese President Xi Jinping. The two leaders agreed

TABLE 18.2 2000–2012 China and Egypt trade (unit: Bn UDS)

	Trade		China exports		China imports	
	Value	%	Value	%	Value	%
2000	0.90	20.9	0.80	12.5	0.10	197
2001	0.95	5.1	0.87	8.4	0.08	-21.3
2002	0.94	-0.8	0.85	-2.3	0.09	14.4
2003	1.09	15.4	0.93	9.9	0.15	66.4
2004	1.57	44.7	1.38	48.3	0.18	23
2005	2.14	36.04	1.93	39.24	0.211	12.34
2006	3.19	49	2.97	54	0.217	3
2007	4.60	44	4.36	47	0.24	11
2008	6.23	33.5	5.81	31.1	0.42	78.6
2009	5.86	-7	5.11	-13.1	0.75	75.4
2010	6.96	19.07	6.04	18.29	0.918	24.5
2011	8.8	26.3	7.28	20.5	1.51	64.1
2012	9.54	–	–	–	–	–

Source: Chinese Ministry of Commerce: www.mofcom.gov.cn/aarticle/ae/ai/201007/20100706999141.html.

to promote bilateral relations to a strategic level; the two sides promised to jointly build the Silk Road of the 21st century, and will expand cooperation in antiterrorism, new energy, infrastructure and outer space.[14]

Challenges and opportunities of China–North Africa cooperation

Today, China and North African countries are facing a series of challenges to enhance further cooperation due to the vicissitudes of world politics, the economy in general and the North African internal changes in particular.

A. EU and US competition with China in North Africa

The North African region has been for a long time the most strategic region for Europe, and often perceived as the backyard of Europe. Concurrently, the Maghreb region is becoming a strategic partner of the United States, especially after the terrorist attacks of 9/11. EU and US engagement in North African markets began much earlier than Chinese economic engagement in the region; this has compelled Beijing to seek markets with lower competition risks in other parts of Africa.

B. Security and the political transformation of North Africa

The problem of security and instability, especially after the Arab uprisings that had swept through North Africa, is one of the major issues that North African countries are addressing today. This issue has also had an impact on China–North African economic relations, especially in those between China and Libya during the civil war in 2011. Chinese companies risk losing up to $6.6 billion in bilateral trade and almost $18 billion of infrastructure and assets should talks with the new Libyan government(s) collapse. China's leaders are exploring more efficient ways of securing national interests abroad and avoiding running the risk of suffering collateral damage caused by political movements.[15] The Chinese big loss in Libya's civil war forced Chinese decision-makers to focus on the security of its overseas interests, and some observers even started to ask if it was not time for Beijing to adjust its non-interference policy in order to protect its interests, including those in North Africa.[16]

C. New emerging powers' competition with China

China is not the only emerging country expanding its relations with North African countries; other emerging countries like Turkey, India and Brazil are also competing with China in the region. Turkey, India and Brazil have become significant trading partners of North African countries. For example Turkey became the fourth trading partner for Algeria, Libya and Tunisia, while in recent years Brazil became the Mauritania's third trading partner behind the EU and China.

D. North African countries' perception of China

China has a relatively positive image in the mindset of the North African people, and this image is partly due to the historical background of the two sides, and also due to the similar colonial experience that China and North African countries had experienced. China and North African countries offered each other political support and mutual understanding during their struggle against colonialism in the 1950s and 1960s.

Moreover, recent events, such as the alleged involvement of Chinese companies in corruption in Algeria and the conflicts between Chinese workers and Algerian locals, had a negative impact on China's image in North Africa. At the official level, China received some criticism from the African side regarding its engagement in the continent, especially regarding the impact of importing Chinese labor to Africa, the involvement of some Chinese companies in corruption, and the low and bad quality of Chinese products on the local economies.

During the fourth ministerial meeting of FOCAC held in Egypt (Sharm al-Shaykh, 8–9 November 2009), Libya's foreign minister sought to tone down criticism of China by praising its role in supporting African countries during their struggle against colonialism; but he raised concern about the impact of Chinese labor on unemployment in African countries. These issues have gotten the attention of the Chinese government, as they are affecting China's image in Africa in general and in North Africa in particular. However, the resolution of these problems will certainly require more effort and closer cooperation between China and

North African countries, because these issues have affected North African countries' internal conditions. Undoubtedly, North African governments share part of the responsibility for this situation, especially regarding the issues of corruption and the imports of bad quality products.

E. Language and cultural barriers

The language and cultural barriers between China and North African countries are also somehow impeding the development of relations between both sides. Despite the extension of the teaching of Chinese language in North African countries through the Confucius Institutes, cultural exchanges are still sparse compared with other countries in Africa. Moreover, the flooding of Chinese migrants in Maghreb region, especially in Algeria, revealed the cultural barriers and conflicts impeding people-to-people relations. At the official level, there is apprehension from the North African side regarding the promotion of relations with China. This fear derives from the limited knowledge North African governments have about contemporary China. They are not sure whether China regards Africa as a place to dump its cheap and bad-quality products; whether it plunders African resources like colonialists had done in the past.

However, some of the challenges that China and the North African region are facing today can be turned into opportunities to enhance further cooperation.

F. Political change in North Africa

The wave of political change that took place since late 2010 has influenced economic relations between China and North Africa. The political change that has taken place in North Africa, including the civil war in Libya, demonstrates the limits of China's political influence in North African affairs, due to China's "non-intervention" principle. Despite the loss that China has suffered from the civil war in Libya, the Asian dragon played a big role in the nation rebuilding of Libya. Regarding the chaotic security situation in the region, especially after the failure of Libya, security cooperation between North African countries should be a reset point to reboot the North African integration process, at least at the security level, using the successful example of ASEAN security cooperation as reference.

However, from a positive standpoint, the political change is also opportunity for the North African countries to build up stronger economic links and China is one of the most important emerging powers that could help North African countries to achieve this goal. As Chinese exports to Egypt surpassed those from the United States in 2011, Egypt can offer China economic and geopolitical influence in Africa and the Middle East. As a traditionally influential player in the Arab world, a closer relationship with Egypt could buy China political goodwill in the region, and may also facilitate concrete benefits, such as accelerated access to the Suez Canal for Chinese commercial vessels and warships.[17]

G. The world financial crisis and the Euro-zone crisis

Since 2007–2008, the world financial and the Euro-zone crises have directly affected developing economies, especially the North African countries, where European investments have decreased and unemployment rates have increased dramatically. This is an opportunity for both China and the North African region to enhance further economic cooperation. It is also an opportunity for North African countries to learn from the mistakes of their Euro-Mediterranean cooperation experience, and build up real and equal economic relations with China. A close analysis of the development of relations between North African countries and the EU within the framework of the Euro-Mediterranean Partnership clearly shows the imbalance of the benefits of such initiative in favor of EU countries, which impose political conditions on them. Euro-Mediterranean cooperation, to some degree, has served the European powers' political, security and economic interests much more than the southern neighbors. The failure of North African governments in establishing more balanced relations with the EU might be avoided with their cooperation with China within the framework of FOCAC, a mechanism of cooperation free of political conditions.

Conclusion

A grey zone, China perceives North Africa as the overlapping region of Africa, the Arab world and the Middle East. As the second largest economy in the world, China has increasingly complex and essential overseas interests in the region, including geopolitical and geo-economic interests. The former include Beijing's ambition to engage in North African political affairs through dispatching peacekeeping forces, setting up military training offices, establishing Confucius Institutes, sending more high-level delegations to the area to enhance China's voice; the latter includes the increase of China's economic presence of investment, energy projects and trade centers. In 2013, China's top five trading partners in Africa are: South Africa, Angola, Nigeria, Egypt and Algeria, and Sino-Egyptian bilateral trade reached $10.21 billion, an increase of 7%.[18]

Further and stronger ties between China and North Africa can hardly be achieved through the traditional way of cooperation, namely, a bilateral one. North African countries should work harder to realize their regional integration and pursue cooperation with China as a bloc. It is a formidable task for the North African countries to achieve such a goal, especially with the current volatile situation in the region, and the unsettled Western Sahara issue, which continue to impede the process of regional integration in North Africa.

However, the current situation is offering North African countries a golden opportunity to change the old way of thinking and handling regional issues as well. As the famous military strategist and political advisor Liu Ji of China's Yuan and Ming Dynasty said in his classic *The Master Who Sheds Light on Culture* ("Youlizi"): 蓄极则泄，闷极则达，热极则风，壅极则通 ("Excessive accumulation will lead to discharge; extreme annoyance will leave place to cheeriness; after extreme heat wind will breeze, and after extreme blockage circulation will release").[19] The general meaning of these old words is that "Crisis is an opportunity to turn for the better." As change is taking place in some parts of the region, North African people can achieve what their governments failed to do; the private sector could become one of the leading forces promoting genuine regional economic integration.

In the new era, Sino-North African all-round cooperation is unfolding, which is not driven by ideology, but by geo-economic consideration of improving the well-being of the sides. This will be beneficial not only for North African countries, but also for China, as it will give the opportunity to Chinese capital and investments to develop markets further, and benefit from the diversity of resource imports. From this point, it is essential to look at the political and economic situation in the North African region to position Chinese engagement in the region's political and economic affairs, and to assess the process of regional integration, mainly in the economic realm, and to get a better understanding of what needs to be done to achieve North African unity. In the foreseeable future, Sino-North African relations will continue to shift from "brotherhood" within the context of anti-Western neocolonialism, to new "business partners" in the age of economic globalization.

Notes

1. The Chinese government rebuked such accusations. See, for instance, 'Commentary: Win-Win Cooperation Disproves Accusation of "China's Neocolonialism in Africa"', *Xinhua*, 5 May 2014, available at: http://en.people.cn/90883/8617251.html.
2. 唐）杜环原著，张一纯笺注：《经行记笺注》，北京：中华书局，2000年，第19页.
   Du, H. (2000). *Jingxingji (Records of Travel)*, Beijing: Zhonghua Book Company, p. 19.
3. 夏吉生：《新中国与马格里布国家友好合作关系的发展》，载于 在于北京大学非洲研究中心编：《中国与非洲》，北京： 北京大学出版社，2000年，第117页。
   Xia, J. (2000). 'The Development of Friendly Cooperation Between New China and Maghreb Countries', in Peking University Center for African Studies, *China and Africa*, Beijing: Peking University Press, p. 117.
4. 夏吉生：《新中国与马格里布国家友好合作关系的发展》，载于 在于北京大学非洲研究中心编：《中国与非洲》，北京： 北京大学出版社，2000年，第120–121页。
   Xia, J. (2000). 'The Development of Friendly Cooperation Between New China and Maghreb Countries', in Peking University Center for African Studies, *China and Africa*, Beijing: Peking University Press, pp. 120–121.
5. An, H., 'Six Decades of China-Egypt Cooperative Relations', *Journal of Arab World Studies*, Vol. 30, No. 3, 2010, p. 3.
6. Breslin, S., 'China and the Arab Awakening', *ISPI Analysis*, No. 140, October 2012, pp. 1–8.
7. The trade and investment volume between China and Maghreb countries was very limited in the last century; for instance, in 1995, the trade volume between China and Algeria – "China's biggest partner in Maghreb" – was $79.53 million. The trade volume between both countries has jumped from $1.769 billion in 2005 to $8.19 billion in 2013.

8. Osei, B. and Mubiru, A.M., 'Chinese Trade and Investment Activities in Africa', *AfDB Policy Brief,* 2010, p. 8.
9. 'Mauritania's Presidential Candidates Hail Ties with China', *China Daily,* http://en.people.cn/200703/12/eng20070312_356522.html.
10. Ambassador Yao Kuangy, 'China-Arab States Cooperation Forum in the Last Decade', *Journal of Middle Eastern and Islamic Studies (in Asia),* Vol. 8, No. 4, 2014, pp. 4–8.
11. 'La Chine premier fournisseur de l'Algérie, loin devant la France', *Tout Sur l'Algérie, TSA,* 20 October 2014, www.tsa-algerie.com/2014/10/20/la-chine-premier-four nisseur-de-lalgerie-loin-devant-la-france/.
12. Alden, C. and Aggad-Clerx, F., 'Chinese Investments and Employment Creation in Algeria and Egypt', Economic Brief, African Development Bank, 2012, pp. 3–7.
13. Brown, K., 'Mixed Signals: China in the Middle East', *FRIDE,* Policy Brief, No. 190, December 2014, pp. 1–6.
14. 'President Xi Jinping Talks with Egyptian President Al-SiSi: The Two Sides Agreed to Enhance Sino-Egyptian Relations into an All-round Strategic Partnership', *People's Daily,* 24 December 2014, A.1. ("习近平同埃及总统塞西会谈：共同决定将中埃关系提升为全面战略伙伴关系，"载《人民日报》2014年12月24日，第1版).
15. Erian, S., 'China at the Libyan Endgame', *Policy,* Vol. 28, No. 1, autumn 2012, p. 49.
16. See Wang, Y., *Creative Involvement: A New Direction in China's Diplomacy,* Beijing: Peking University Press, 2011. (王逸舟：《创造性介入：中国外交新取向》，北京：北京大学出版社2011年版.)
17. Liu, T.C., 'China's Economic Engagement in the Middle East and North Africa', *FRIDE,* Policy Brief, No. 173, January 2014, p. 3.
18. Ministry of Commerce of the People's Republic of China, www.mofcom.gov.cn/article/i/jyjl/k/201401/20140100475432.shtml.
19. Translated by the authors.

Bibliography

Books:

Chinese:

1. 艾周昌，沐涛，《中非关系史》，上海： 华东师范大学出版社，1996年。
Ai, Z. and Mu, T. (1996). *The History of China Africa Relations,* Shanghai: East China Normal University Press.
2. 艾周昌，郑家馨，《非洲通史–近代卷》，华东师范大学出版社，1995年。
Ai, Z. and Zhen, J. (1995). *General History of Africa – Modern History Tome,* East China Normal University Press.
3. 陈玉来，肖克编：《中国非洲关系大事记》，北京： 中国社会科学院西亚非洲研究所，1986年。
Chen, Y. and Xiao, K. (1986). *Memorabilia of China-Africa Relations,* Beijing: West Asia and Africa Institute of the Chinese Academy of Social Science.
4. 中国非洲史研究会：《非洲通史》，北京师范大学出版社，1984年。
Chinese Society of African Historical Studies (1984). *General History of Africa,* Beijing: Normal University Press.
5. [荷]戴闻达著：《中国人对非洲的发现》，北京： 北京商务印书馆，1983年。
Duyvendak, J.J.L. (1983). *China's Discovery of Africa,* Beijing: Commercial Press.
6. 郭小凌，杨宁一主编，《北非各国》，北京： 北京语 北京： 言文化大学出版社，1998年。
Guo, X. and Yang, N. (1998). *North African Countries,* Beijing: Beijing Language and Cultural University Press.
7. 郭应德著，《阿拉伯史纲：610–1945》，北京： 中国社会科学出版社，1991年。

Guo, Y. (1991). *A Survey of Arab History: 610–1945,* Beijing: Chinese Academy of Social Science Press.

8. 江淳，郭应德，《中阿关系史》，北京：北京经济日报出版社，2000年。

Jiang, C. and Guo, Y. (2000). *The History of China-Arab Relations,* Beijing: Beijing Economic Daily Press.

9. 李安山，安春英，李忠人主编，《中非关系与当代世界》，太原：非洲史研究会论文集之一，太原，2008年。

Li, A., An, C. and Li, Z. (2008). *China-Africa Relations and the Contemporary World,* Taiyuan: Chinese Society of African Historical Studies.

10. 刘文鹏，吴宇虹，李铁匠：《古代西亚北非文明》，福州：福建教育出版社，2008 年。

Liu, W., Wu, Y. and Li, T. (2008). *The Old History of West Asia and North African Civilization,* Fuzhou: Fujian Education Press.

11. 陆廷恩，彭坤元，《非洲通史-现代卷》，上海：华东师范大学出版社，1995 年。

Lu, T. and Peng, K. (1995). *General History of Africa – Modern History Tome,* Shanghai: East China Normal University Press.

12. 纳忠主编，《阿拉伯通史》上、下卷，北京：商务印书馆，1997年。

Na, Z. (1997). *General History of the Arab World – Tomes 1 and 2,* Beijing: Commercial Press.

13. 潘光，朱威烈主编，《阿拉伯非洲历史文选》，上海：华东师范大学出版社，1992年。

Pan, G. and Zhu, W. (1992). *Collected Works of the History of African Arab Countries,* Shanghai: East China Normal University Press.

14. 彭树智主编，《阿拉伯国家简史》，福建人民出版社，1991年。

Peng, S. (1991). *A Brief History of Arab Countries,* Fuzhou: Fujian People Press.

15. 沈福伟，《中国与非洲关系——中非关系二千年》，北京：中华书局，1990 年。

Shen, F. (1990). *China and Africa Relations: Two Thousands Years of History,* Beijing: Zhonghua Book Company.

English:

1. Barbour, N. (1959). *A Survey of North West Africa (The Maghrib),* London: Oxford University Press.
2. Otman, W. and Karlberg, E. (2007). *The Libyan Economy: Economic Diversification and International Repositioning,* New York: Springer.
3. Zoubir, Y. and Amirah-Fernandez, H. (2008). *North Africa: Politics, Region and the Limits of Transformation,* New York: Routledge.

Collections:

Chinese:

1. 北京大学非洲研究中心编：《中国与非洲》，北京：北京大学出版社，2000 年。

Center for African Studies of Peking University (2000). *China and Africa,* Beijing: Peking University Press.

2. 《中国与非洲共同发展》，国际学术研讨会，北京，2006年12月18–19日。

China and Africa Common Development, International Conference, Beijing, 18–19 December 2006.

English:

China in North Africa: Oil & Diplomacy in the Maghreb Region, *The China Monitor,* Issue 51, CCS, May 2010.

Papers:

Chinese

1. 白国瑞，栗云生：《马格里布首脑们的首次会晤》，《瞭望》，1988年第30期，第45–46页。

Bai, G. and Jia, Y. (1988). 'The First Meeting of Maghreb Leaders', *Outlook Weekly,* No. 30, pp. 45–46.

2. 陈淑仁，《北非区域集团化浅析——试谈马格里布联盟成立及其发展》，《国际贸易》，1991年4期，第24–27页。

Chen, S. (1991). 'Simple Analysis on the Collectivization in North Africa: Establishment and Development of the Arab Maghreb Union', *International Trade,* No. 4, pp. 24–27.

3. 楚树龙：《北非中东局势与中国》，《现代国际关系》，2011年第3期，第25–26页。

Chu, S. (2011). 'Situation in the MENA and China', *Contemporary International Relations,* No. 3, pp. 25–26.

4. 傅政罗：《中国同北非国家的经贸合作与前景展望》，《西亚非洲》，1996年，第5期，第64–66页。

Fu, Z. (1996). 'The Economic Cooperation Between China and North African Countries and Its Prospective', *West Asia and Africa,* No. 5, pp. 64–66.

5. 高潮：《阿尔及利亚：非洲最具投资潜力的资源大国》，《中国对外贸易》，2009年，第1期，第78–81页。

Gao, C. (2009). 'Algeria: Big Energy Rich Country with the Highest Investment Potential in Africa', *China's Foreign Trade,* No. 1, pp. 78–81.

6. 胡盛霞，董有德：《中国对非洲直接投资特点及其原因分析》，《对外经贸实务》，2008年第12期。

Hu, S. and Dong, Y. (2008). 'Analysis on the Characteristics of the Chinese Direct Investment in Africa and Its Origin', *Practice in Foreign Relations and Trade,* No. 12, pp. 76–79.

7. 黄泽全：《开拓中非合作新思路》，《国际经济合作》，2002年第2期，第21–23页。

Huang, Z. (2002). 'Exploring New Ideas on China-Africa Cooperation', *International Economic Cooperation,* No. 2, pp. 21–23.

8. 李录：《马格里布事业》，《世界知识》，1983年第12期，第26页。

Li, L. (1983). 'The Maghreb Project', *World Affairs,* No. 12, p. 26.

9. 李铁立，朱思全：《中东北非变局中的中国出路》，《大经贸》，2011年第4期，第68–71页。

Li, T. and Zhu, S. (2011). 'China's Way in the MENA Revolution', *Foreign Trade and Economy,* No. 4, pp. 68–71.

10. 李献兵，郭玉华：《我国中小企业在非洲的投资策略研究》，《中国流通经济》，2009年第3期。

Li, X. and Guo, Y. (2009). 'Research on the Investment Strategies Applied by Chinese SMEs into Africa', *Chinese Circulation Economy,* No. 3, pp. 71–73.

11. 李珍石：《马格里布的新形势》，《世界知识》，1983年第15期，第5–6页。

Li, Z. (1983). 'The Maghreb New Situation', *World Affairs,* No. 15, pp. 5–6.

12. 李智彪：《北非政局动荡，中国如何应对?》，　《社会观察》，2011年第5期，第60–61页。

Li, Z. (2011). 'Instability in North Africa: How China Deals with It? ', *Social Outlook*, No. 5, pp. 60–61.

13. 梁玎玎：《当前马格里布地区形势缕述》，《西亚非洲》，1998年，第6期，第22–26页。

Liang, D. (1998). 'Statement on the Actual Situation in Maghreb', *West Asia and Africa*, No. 6, pp. 22–26.

14. 刘塞君：《马格里布联盟成员国加强经济合作》，《瞭望》， 1991年第40期，第43页。

Liu, S. (1991). 'The Countries of the AMU Strengthening Economic Cooperation', *Outlook Weekly*, No. 40, p. 43.

15. 马宏：《北非政局对中国国际石油合作的影响与对策》，《非洲贸易研究》，2011年第9期，第20–22页。

Ma, H. (2006). 'The Impact of North African Revolution on the Chinese International Oil Cooperation and Its Countermeasures', *Studies on African Economic Relations*, No. 9, pp. 20–22.

16. 卡罗尔·马特莱克：《马格里布的崛起》，《商业周刊》，2009年，第4期，第58–60页。

Matlack, C. (2009). 'The Emerging Maghreb', *Business Week*, No. 4, pp. 58–60.

17. 墨翰：《马格里布一体化的最早构想及其尝试》，《阿拉伯世界研究》，1996年第3期，第61–62页。

Mo, H. (1996). 'The Early Conception of the Maghreb Integration and Its Attempts', *Arab World Studies*, No. 3, pp. 61–62.

18. 朴英姬：《中国对非洲直接投资的国别、路径及策略选择》，　《西亚非洲》，2009年第7期，第55–60页 。

Piao, Y. (2009). 'Receiving Countries, Pathways and Policy Choices of Chinese Direct Investment in Africa', *West Asia and Africa*, No. 7, pp. 55–60.

19. 王莉莉：　《摩洛哥外贸大臣马阿祖兹(Mr. Abdellatif Maazouz): "'北非花园'欢迎中国客人"》，　《中国对外贸易》， 2009年第11期，第10–11页。

Wang, L. (2009). 'Moroccan Foreign Trade Minister Mr. Abdellatif Maazouz: North African Garden Welcome Chinese Guests', *China's Foreign Trade*, No. 11, pp. 10–11.

20. 魏仁苗：《马格里布加速一体化进程》，《瞭望》，1990年第32期，第37页。

Wei, R. (1990). 'The Maghreb Accelerating the Process of Integration', *Outlook Weekly*, No. 32, p. 37.

21. 夏吉生：《新中国与马格里布国家友好合作关系的发展》， 载于 在于北京大学非洲研究中心编：《中国与非洲》， 北京： 北京大学出版社，2000年，第117–128页。

Xia, J. (2000). 'The Development of Friendly Cooperation Between New China and Maghreb Countries', in Peking University Center for African Studies, *China and Africa*, Beijing: Peking University Press, pp. 117–128.

22. 谢绑定：《中国与突尼斯建交的前前后后》，《百年潮》，2006年第11期，第15–18页。

Xie, B. (2006). 'The Whole Story of the Establishment of Diplomatic Relations Between China and Tunisia', *Hundred Year Tide*, No. 11, pp. 15–18.

23. 张晶星：《中国石油企业对非洲投资的区位选择分析》，《黑龙江对外经贸》，2009年第1期，第52–54页。

Zhang, J. (2009). 'Analysis on Chinese Oil Companies Investment Choices in Africa', *HLJ Foreign Economic Relations and Trade*, No. 1, pp. 52–54.

24. 张历历：《中国全力从利比亚大撤侨分析》，《当代世界》，2011年第4期，第21–23页。
Zhang, L. (2011). 'China's All-Out Evacuation of Her Nationals from Libya: An Analysis', *Contemporary World*, No. 4, pp. 21–23.

25. 张小峰，玄兆娟：《中国对北非阿拉伯国家直接投资动因分析及策略选择》，《阿拉伯世界研究》，2010年，第3期，第51–58页。
Zhang, X. and Xuan, Z. (2010). 'Analysis of Chinese Direct Investment in North African Countries and Its Policy Choices', *Arab World Studies*, No. 3, pp. 51–58.

26. 张迎新：《马格里布地区油气资源形势》，《国土资源情报》，2002年第9期，第19–27页。
Zhang, Y. (2002). 'The Situation of Oil and Natural Gas Resources in the Maghreb', *Land and Resources Information*, No. 9, pp. 19–27.

27. 张颖：《中国对非洲阿拉伯国家的"伙伴外交"》，《阿拉伯世界研究》，2009年，第5期，第34–40页。
Zhang, Y. (2009). 'China's "Partnership Diplomacy" toward African Arab Countries', *Arab World Studies*, No. 5, pp. 34–40.

28. 赵慧杰：《浅析马格里布地区一体化进程》，《西亚非洲》，2008年，第10期，第41–45页。
Zhao, H. (2008). 'Simple Analysis on Maghreb Regional Integration', *West Asia and Africa*, No. 10, pp. 41–45.

English:

1. African Development Bank (2012). 'Chinese Investments and Employment Creation in Algeria and Egypt', *AfDB Economic Brief*. http://www.afdb.org/fileadmin/uploads/afdb/Documents/Publications/Brochure%20China%20Anglais.pdf, accessed 10 July 2015.

2. Bräutigam, D. and Tang, X. (2011). 'African Shenzhen: China's Special Economic Zones in Africa', *Journal of Modern African Studies*, Vol. 49, No. 1, pp. 27–54.

3. Castel, V., Mejia, P.X. and Kolster, J. (2011). 'The BRICs in North Africa: Changing the Name of the Game?' *AfDB North Africa Quarterly Analytical*, No. 1, p. 1–16.

4. Hilal, Khalid (2010). 'China's Relations with North Africa', *CCS the China Monitor*, May, pp. 4–8.

5. Jewell, J. (2011). 'A Nuclear-Powered North Africa: Just a Desert Mirage or Is There Something on the Horizon?' *Energy Policy*, No. 39, pp. 4445–4457.

6. Keenan, J.H. (2006). 'Security & Insecurity in North Africa', *Review of African Political Economy*, Vol. 33, No. 108, pp. 269–296.

7. Li, A., Liu, H., Pan, H., Zeng, A. and He, W. (2012). 'FOCAC Twelve Years Later: Achievements, Challenges and the Way Forward', *Nordic Africa Institute Discussion Paper*, No. 74.

8. Nadi, D. (2008). 'Chinese State-Owned Enterprises Engagement in Algeria', in *Expert Meeting Report: Chinese State-Owned Enterprises and Stability in Africa*, The Hague: Clingendael Institute, p. 1–14.

9. Osei, B. and Mubiru, A.M. (2010). 'Chinese Trade and Investment Activities in Africa', *AfDB Policy Brief*, Vol. 1, No. 4, pp. 1–11.

10. Shichor, Y. (2009). 'Libya Cautions China: Economics Is No Substitute to Politics', *China Brief*, Vol. 9, No. 24, pp. 5–7.

11. Volman, D. and Klare, M. (2006). 'The African "Oil Rush" and US National Security', *Third World Quarterly*, Vol. 27, No. 4, pp. 609–628.

French:

1. Abid, Z. (2008). 'La Chine à l'assaut du Maghreb: La région possède une valeur stratégique pour la Chine', *Afkar/Idées*, No. 16, pp. 21–24.

2. Vairon, L. (2010). 'La Chine en Méditerranée, l'émergence d'une nouvelle puissance', *Confluences Méditerranée,* Vol. 3, No. 74, pp. 39–52.

3. Wade, A. (2006). 'Maroc-Chine: La Muraille invisible', *Aujourd'hui le Maroc,* No. 1145, http://www.aujourdhui.ma/une/focus/maroc-chine-la-muraille-invisible-41118# .VaOxa2cVjX4 (Accessed July 12, 2015).

Theses:

1. 李宁：《北非地区石油勘探开发项目风险规避研究》，　　　中国石油大学硕士论文，2008年。
Li, N. (2008). *Study on Risk Circumvention of Petroleum Exploration and Development Projects in North Africa Area,* Master Thesis, China University of Petroleum.

2. 刘洋：《论阿拉伯马格里布联盟一体化的进程与前景》，上海外国语大学外交学硕士论文，2008年。
Liu, Y. (2008). *Discussing the Process and the Future of Regional Integration in Arab Maghreb,* Master Thesis, Shanghai International Studies University.

3. 杨红梅：《中国石油企业投资非洲的动因分析》，对外经济贸易大学硕士论文，2007 年。
Yang, H. (2007). *Analysis on the Investment Motivation of Chinese Petroleum Companies in Africa,* Master Thesis, The University of International Business and Economics.

Electronic Papers:

1. Pairault, T. (2012). 'La chine en Afrique: Le cas du Maghreb', *Forum des économistes tunisiens,* Hammamet, 7–9 Juin, http://www.pairault.fr/sinaf/index.php/statistiques/325-la-chine-en-afriquen-le-cas-du-maghreb (Accessed March 27, 2013).

2. 张宏明：《中国对非经济政策的回顾与思考》，《海外投资与出口信贷》，2006 年第3期。
Zhang, H. (2006). 'Rethinking the Chinese Economic Policy Towards Africa', *The Exim Bank of China: Overseas Investments and Exports Credits Magazine,* No. 3. URL: www .eximbank.gov.cn/topic/hwtz/2006.shtml.

Internet Sources:

1. Ministry of Commerce of the People's Republic of China: www.mofcom.gov.cn.
2. Ministry of Foreign Affairs of the People's Republic of China: www.fmprc.gov.cn.
3. US Energy Information Administration: www.eia.doe.gov.

19

THE ROLE OF THE GCC IN NORTH AFRICA IN LIGHT OF THE 'ARAB SPRING'

Elena Maestri

Introduction

Popular demonstrations and uprisings of the so-called "Arab Spring", while leading in the Maghreb region to the toppling of Zine al-Abidine Ben Ali in Tunisia, and to the overthrow and killing of Muammar Qaddafi in Libya, opened up new challenges and prospects in the relationships of North Africa with the Gulf Cooperation Council (GCC) member states. The GCC tried to adapt to the transformations sweeping across the Middle East and the Mediterranean, by reformulating its strategic goals and by assuming a major unprecedented role in regional and global affairs. Such a role has been increasingly founded on assistance programs and donations and, when possible, on political mediation efforts. Tunisia, Libya and Morocco in North Africa on the one hand, and Yemen in the Arabian Peninsula on the other, well exemplify this new Gulf Arab pro-activism largely motivated by the political willingness to promote stabilization.[1]

The aim of this chapter is to deal with the rising involvement of the GCC in the Maghreb region. Within the emerging lively dynamism of three GCC actors in particular – namely Qatar, Saudi Arabia and the United Arab Emirates (UAE) – Islam and business come to the fore. These are two main factors, which can be properly grasped only against the background of the evolving structural reality of the GCC region itself, with its specific political-cultural-religious-social-economic traits, and in light of the challenges that North Africa countries are facing at this delicate stage of difficult reorganization, marked by uncertainties and risks.

Within this framework, the "Islam factor" can assume a positive role, if it intertwines with the creation of better prospects for business and with initiatives aimed at achieving sustainable development. The growing influence of some Gulf Arab countries puts even more emphasis on the importance of dialogue with Islam and within Islam. Specifically, the Saudi state, as both the cradle of Wahhabism and Custodian of the two Holy Mosques, has huge responsibility in this direction: strengthening its developing "flexible approach" to the thought of Ibn Abd al-Wahhab seems to be the only way to boost a confidence-building process with its Arab and foreign partners and to build vital economic ties. Both processes are deeply interlinked. The improvement of the regional business environment, through the development of a more appropriate regulatory framework, which is consistent with constructive Islamic values also affecting the economic sphere, is more and more seen by most business circles in the Gulf as an essential step to enhance the growth of entrepreneurship and its impact beyond the region. Financial barriers that Small and Medium Enterprises (SMEs) often face in the MENA are a major hindrance to entrepreneurs, among whom one should not ignore the female component. The latter has been emerging as a very dynamic force in the Gulf in the last few years: limited access to external funding and to bank loans is a fact for SMEs in the whole region, and GCC countries are no exception, despite their generally large availability of funds. Special funds are requested to address the problem of adequate access to finance for SMEs: the availability of funds in the hands of many GCC female citizens and a still limited investment of such funds in productive domains, for instance, is a main contradictory issue to be addressed, against the backdrop of the growing Islamic finance sector and of its beneficial potential to bolster such entrepreneurship.

This is a new delicate phase, in which coordinated political and institutional support from all the actors is urgently needed for the promotion of fruitful initiatives aimed at enhancing sustainability in the region. That would certainly be to the interest of North Africa, of the GCC, and of all the parties looking for security and stability from the Gulf to the Mediterranean.

Mutual knowledge and confidence-building as a new key to re-balancing relationships

It is well-known that throughout history, Gulf ties with the Maghreb have been weaker than with the closer Mashreq territories. Religious ties are certainly a relevant fact, but nobody can deny the existence of important cultural differences between North Africans and Gulf Arabs. Some distrust among them is no secret: on the one hand, the stereotype of Gulf Arabs as "very wealthy people, but with little culture and history" tends to prevail in the Maghreb (Zoubir 1993: 81) and, on the other, the idea of North Africans marked by a combination of cultural influences going beyond the Arab ones, often inspired by Turkish and colonial Western models, leads Gulf Arabs to perceive them as quite far from the most authentic Arabian-Islamic cultural context of the cradle of Islam.

The historical evolution in the Maghreb is certainly marked by its ethnic, cultural and Islamic religious specificities – including Berbers, Turkish elements, Islamic brotherhoods and Sufis. Islam has largely retained its Arab-Berber traits here and the Turkish component, with the exception of Morocco, has affected both the ethnic composition and the cultural environment. Thus, one can agree with

Francesco Gabrieli, who noted that in North Africa there is no significant evidence of a clear and strong pure Arab identity consciousness until modern–contemporary times (Gabrieli 1997: 163). In the Maghreb, even more than in the Mashreq, the great revival of Arabism and the development of Arab nationalism were deeply influenced by European colonialism, and they emerged as direct reactions to it. On the other side, Gulf Arabs were not so deeply affected by European colonialism during the last century, and their history is not marked by invasions and migrations, as it happened in neighboring countries: largely isolated from the outside world, they generally kept clear awareness of the continuity of their history, of their pattern of society and statehood, in which Arabian tribalism, tradition and Islam have been merging in a paradigm, which is quite unique in its internal mechanisms.

The first successful development phase in the Gulf, following the oil-boom in the 1970s, can be largely ascribed to the flexibility of the system, in spite of its weaknesses and fragilities. In the most recent past, within the typical Islamic-tribal paradigm pertaining to this region, bureaucracy contributed to transforming a society based on a community-order into a political-social systemic structure based on a post-traditional, but not yet modern, order. In this sense, neo-traditionalist methods in the Gulf's post-traditional liberalized autocracies give the political, institutional and social evolution of the area a distinct flavor amongst the variegated Arab and Islamic panorama (Nonneman 2006: 4). All that can put some light on the reasons why the resulting internal dynamics in the political, social and economic fields have been quite different from the ones in the Maghreb, both in republics like Tunisia and in a monarchy like Morocco, where the state paradigms that emerged were deeply affected by the decolonization process. The Algerian Armed Forces, after assuming a crucial role in the war for independence, were involved in politics, but in Tunisia, Morocco and Libya, the ruling elites deliberately marginalized the military, while giving more importance to other security institutions, namely, the intelligence services (*mukhabarat*), the police and the *Kata'ib* (brigades), as was the case in Libya under Qaddafi's rule (Zoubir and Dris-Aït-Hamadouche 2013: 21). The security sector had traditionally been less strong in all the Gulf Arab monarchies, where co-optation of political opponents often served to neutralize them much more than sentencing them. If the general absence of free debates in the media was certainly a trait that Gulf Arab countries shared with Mediterranean Arab countries, one cannot ignore that in the Gulf the largely respected tradition to hold regular meetings in domestic spaces, referred to as *diwaniyyah* or *jalsah*, somehow helped, throughout the years, long before the ICTs revolution, to nourish constant debates on political issues as well, although largely limiting them to private domains (Tétreault 2000: 118).

As for the monarchical system, the monarchy in Morocco is very peculiar compared to Gulf Arab monarchies, the Saudi one included: no royal family in the Gulf enjoys special authority in Islam, and only the Saudi king, as "Custodian of the two Holy Mosques", has a well-defined religious role, which, nevertheless, does not allow him to bypass religious authorities – the *'ulama* – officially, as far as issues directly pertaining to Islam and Islamic jurisprudence are concerned.

The Moroccan dynasty of the Alawids, on the contrary, adopted the title of *Amir al-Mu'minin* (Commander of the Believers) in the 17th century, after ascending the throne. The institution of *Imarat al-Mu'minin* (Command of the Believers), tracing back in Islamic history to the second Caliph 'Umar, never disappeared in Morocco's contemporary history, and it was even revitalized in the 1990s by King Hassan II, who, through his self-attributed right to enter into Islamic jurisprudence issues, reformed the family law (*Mudawwanah*) and tried to strike a balance between Islamic and Westernized models; all that gave the king the final say on crucial issues concerning Islam in his country and, according to some Moroccan groups and analysts, that was a step forward both towards modernization and towards the con-solidation of an authoritarian model (Buskens 2003: 83).

While it is difficult to contest the assumption that the link between the political system and control of economic resources is by and large still very strong in the GCC region, one cannot ignore that, within an Arab world generally marked by an underdeveloped bourgeoisie, the Gulf Arab states represent a quite significant exception, as the merchants – the *tujjar* – have always represented a social force here, often reaching a high degree of autonomy from the state, and not rarely imposing itself as a "national bourgeoisie", claiming a political role as well. That is a well attested regional reality, though acquiring specific nuances in each country: the Kuwaiti merchants, for instance, at the beginning of the oil era, ended up clash-ing with the government and became the core of the opposition, while in Saudi Arabia the origin of the state itself, since the 18th century, refers both to the crucial alliance between the religious and military/political power (*din wa dawlah*) and the merchants' economic power, which gained from the protection of the *dawlah* (tribal state) and never entered in serious conflict with it (Luciani 2005: 157).

Against this backdrop, it is clear that differences in systemic-structural realities and leadership cannot be overlooked in any assessment, although the evolving Gulf Arab special relationship with Morocco undoubtedly refers to a series of con-vergences in terms of political interests between monarchies: it is well-known, in fact, that in the 1980s Saudi Arabia provided Rabat with strong financial support to pursue "anti-Polisario activities" in Western Sahara (Barbier 1982: 370), and in 1990 King Hassan II sent to Saudi Arabia one thousand troops to bolster it, after the Iraqi invasion of Kuwait, although these troops did not enter the Kuwaiti ter-ritory. The presence of well-trained hired troops from Morocco within the police force of the UAE and, most recently, in the aftermath of the "Arab Spring", Rabat's expression of solidarity with Bahrain against "Iranian interference" and its support, as a non-permanent member of the UN Security Council, to foreign intervention in Syria, in line with the Saudi and Qatari positions, are just confirmation of a con-solidated line of foreign policy largely converging with Gulf Arab interests. And yet mutual suspicion, as expressed by public opinion of both sides, is still quite strong.[2]

The conservatism of Gulf Arab societies is another aspect to be evaluated within its own framework. It is often connected by external observers to the Saudi Wah-habi influence, even if conservatism in the Gulf has not really prevented that in internal debates; tradition, socio-economic development and modernity drive the need to come to terms with new models, paradigms and discourses, such as political reform and human rights in Islam. Each society is seen as striving to preserve its cultural-religious heritage and transmit it to the members of its social group, or at least to those who belong to certain strata of the population. In the eyes of the GCC leaderships, it is exactly this cultural-religious heritage which, by leveraging growing economic interests and networks, can also contribute to promoting political change, without, however, leading to social and political chaos. This belief is not simply rooted in the desire for regime protection; it has deep roots in the Arabian-Islamic-tribal political and religious culture shared by the GCC member states, an aspect which is often neglected both in the West and in North Africa.

The "Arab Spring" in the Maghreb, while skipping stagnant Algeria, brought about important changes, though in very different ways and degrees in Tunisia, Libya and Morocco. As such, GCC leaderships could not but rethink their policies towards the region. The "Islam factor" and a pragmatic approach aimed at creating better prospects for business emerge as the two main drivers of GCC foreign policies in the Mediterranean. In view of this, the Gulf Arab states have become more exposed than others to being perceived as an intrusive foreign power in North Africa. If cultural differences are a natural fact, the need to avoid serious frictions is crucial at this stage, in which re-balancing relationships cannot be decoupled from a mutual confidence-building process.

The post-Arab Spring Mediterranean is increasingly seen as a potentially more important region in a GCC perspective, as attested by the new dynamics. Diplomatic, economic and socio-cultural contacts have distinctly become more intense. With reference to Tunisia, for instance, notable in this respect are the official visits of the Emir of Qatar to Tunis, of the Tunisian Minister of Foreign Affairs to the Emirates, and of the Tunisian Prime Minister to Riyadh between January and February 2012. Alongside this, there have been a series of agreements and memorandums of understanding aimed at enhancing GCC development assistance to the area.[3] And yet, the challenge is to go beyond aid programs. Both North Africa and the GCC region are confronted with great challenges and there are priorities to be considered. The promotion of a vital cooperative approach able to re-shape relationships and create effective partnerships cannot be conceived without the involvement of other crucial actors, namely Europe, and within it, more specifically, European Mediterranean countries, Turkey and the US: securitization implies reduction in the number of weapons circulating among militant groups, in particular in Libya and neighboring territories, and sustainability implies enhancement of human and economic development.

Engagement, in this sense, needs to go beyond official people, along the lines of dialogue and real mutual knowledge. Trustworthy organizations able to expand innovative capabilities of human resources, by canalizing the flow of positive energies along the lines of concrete and coherent joint projects, are still quite lacking, but they would certainly help to move from present uncertainty to constructive change, against the growing threats of extremist Islamists and the dangers of an enduring state of chaos (*fawda*) (Pellitteri 2011–2012: 238).

The "Islam factor": Ideational influence and networks

Islam is a key factor in the foreign policy of the GCC states and above all of Saudi Arabia, which, having the custodianship of the two Holy Mosques, has been strongly re-affirming its leadership role in the Islamic world. The relations with North Africa clearly reflect this reality as well, referring at one and the same time to the variegated series of links between the Maghreb and the Arabian Peninsula throughout the centuries. The Hejazi merchant class, through the pilgrimage (*hajj*), had largely contributed to building relations with near and far-away Arab and Muslim countries many centuries before the establishment of the Kingdom of Saudi Arabia and the emergence of the Wahhabi variant of Salafi Islam: religion and trade often intermingled in relations and North Africa was no exception. The approach of 'Allal al-Fassi, one of the leaders of the independence movement in Morocco, and among the authors of the *Mudawwanah* (codification of the family law) in 1958, for instance, seems to be deeply rooted in a well-established network directly linking the Maghreb to the Hejazi pre-Wahhabi Salafi environment. In this sense, considering that *Salafiyyah* is far from a monolithic movement of Sunni fundamentalism, we can argue that nowadays religious, humanitarian and political aspects in Gulf–North African relations are expressions of official government policies, on the one hand, and of a series of historical Islamic transnational networks on the other, often re-emerging in the non-official channels of the growing Gulf Arab Islamic charity sector.

Southern Mediterranean Arab countries, affected by deep social disparities and serious economic mismanagement, coupled with high corruption levels, have witnessed the progressive expansion of a complex Islamic network of Gulf Arab-supported charitable activities in the last decade. This has intertwined with rising popular support for some Islamist groups and the strengthening of political Islam throughout the region (Salzman 2011: 152). On the one hand, funding from GCC member states and, above all from Saudi Arabia, cannot be decoupled from the growing ideological influence of the already hinted religious-political thought generally defined as *Salafiyyah*. On the other hand, however, one cannot forget the relevance of other kinds of locally rooted Islamist thought, such as the Muslim Brotherhood and, in the case of Libya, the Senussi Sufis.

Since 2011 events, Saudi Arabian foreign policy has been strongly re-affirming the leadership role of the Kingdom within the Islamic world, through the support gained by major Islamic organizations, such as the Organization of the Islamic Conference (OIC), the non-governmental *Rabitah al-'alam al-islami* (Islamic World League), and the Fiqh Muslim Congress. Most surprisingly, the small and wealthy Qatar has been positioning itself as the second most active GCC supporter of a Salafi-inspired Islamic framework and network, followed closely by the UAE and Kuwait. Despite their traditional tribally-rooted competition, Saudi Arabia and Qatar seem to proceed both towards enhanced ideological Salafi convergence, confirmed by the rising personal contacts between Qatari and Saudi scholars and preachers in the last few years, and towards a careful "division of labour" in post-Arab Spring environments (Colombo 2012: 9). Within this perspective, in the meantime, one cannot neglect that the custodianship of the two Holy Mosques keeps affecting the foreign policy of the Kingdom. In view of that, it is maybe easier to understand why Saudi Arabia has to be officially more cautious than Qatar at the international level, while sharing some interest in achieving certain goals.

A knowledge-based Islamic thought, which is developing stronger links with a peaceful wing of *Salafiyyah*, has been emerging as one of the determinants of the events in post-Arab Spring environments. With reference to North Africa, the financial and political support to an Islamic *nahdah* (renaissance) by Gulf Arab forces and powers, as an expression of *Salafiyyah* and Hanbalism – the most traditionist juridical school in Sunni Islam – is well exemplified by Qatar's initiatives at the start of the state-building process in post-Qaddafi Libya. These initiatives have to be understood in the context of the Islamic reformist discourse, which is developing as a means to find appropriate formulas to combine modernity and democracy with Islamic teachings. In the light of the substantial ideological Saudi-Qatari convergence within the *Salafiyyah*, the support of a certain local Salafi group or another is often determined by the contacts of the members. The personal relations of the exiled Libyan cleric Ali Al-Sallabi with this *Salafiyyah* network in Qatar, for instance, are among the factors explaining Qatar's support for Salafi elements in the new Libya. That support, translated into an indirect supply of weapons to certain Islamist groups, was soon openly criticized by some secular members of the National Transitional Council, and it has been leading Qatar in North Africa to a quite risky involvement in a more and more uncontrollable network, in which extremism, far from "transforming into civilian life", as expected by the Emir of Qatar, ended up hurting GCC interests too (Khatib 2013).

That is a reality shedding light on the importance of more far-sightedness on the part of Gulf Arab states, when interacting with other environments in Arab and Islamic countries. In the case of Qatar, in particular, one can agree with those arguing that pragmatism can essentially explain much more than ideology its external engagement;[4] nevertheless, Qatar's clear lack of monitoring capacity in a theater like Africa seems to have contributed to fomenting rumors accusing this state of funding some African militias, such as Ansar al-Din in Mali. "Qatar has become quite accustomed to hearing such malicious propaganda against it", said the Prime Minister, *shaykh* Hamad bin Jassem bin Jabor Al Thani, in January 2013, while emphasizing that there is no evidence for such allegations.[5] All the same, it is more evident that the country's leading role, in order to have positive effects in the long-term, needs to be re-thought and founded on solid bases of direct knowledge and expertise on the territory, rather than on mere co-optation of local elements, who can use charity organizations' aids for their own interests and purposes quite unscrupulously, opening up extremely dangerous scenarios in the end (Coates Ulrichsen 2012: 26).

It is a fact that Gulf Arab rulers have always mistrusted organized political and militant Islam, and Qatar, in spite of its support to some North African members of the Muslim Brotherhood and of Salafi groups, who lived in the country for some time as exiles, is no exception. There is no doubt that the *Salafiyyah* in the Muslim world – in its multiple incarnations – represents new dimensions of knowledge, and it leads to new forms of social organization espousing both modern know-how and traditional knowledge. As an intellectual-dogmatic-religious-juridical movement, the "peaceful *Salafiyyah*" in the Gulf is very different from the militant *Salafiyyah* opposition, which spread to the Middle East from Syria and Jordan in the 1960s and early 1970s. During the very last years of the 20th century, the Arab world witnessed the strengthening of the moderate reformist wing within the composite *Salafiyyah* movement. This wing, propounding knowledge, education (*tarbiyyah*) and culture as the true way to encourage all Muslims (even the most tepid) to respect the principles of Islam, has been developing increasingly closer links with GCC societies, both at the official level and among influential and rich men and women in the private sector. These segments of society are viewed as being more likely to react in a constructive way both to Western policies towards the Muslim world, in particular after 9/11, and to the threats posed by violent militant groups (Fiorani Piacentini 2003: 146). The "peaceful Salafi thought" has been gaining further support from the Saudi government and other Gulf Arab states, as an interpretation that makes it possible to contrast the more radical and militant organizations and to fight terrorism, while remaining true to "the purest form of Islam".

When assessing divergent Gulf Arab reactions to the evolving situation in the Arab world, one cannot ignore that some parallel factors have been interacting with the official line, while concurring to rising complexity in ties and relations between the Gulf and post-Arab Spring environments. The Maghreb is no exception. Qatar's persistent large dependency on Arab expatriate human resources in some pivotal sectors, like the media, certainly had an impact on its political approach to transition processes in North Africa as well, throughout 2012 and 2013. In the eyes of all the Gulf Arab rulers, the transnational Sunni Muslim Brotherhood (MB) network has never been so different from the transnational Shia network, as they both pose a threat to their system. Under the pressure of internal demographic and labor market anomalies, Qatar tried to get around the problem, by giving leading MB representatives an extraordinary outlet through *Al Jazeera*, in order to appease the movement's members among its expatriates and to divert their ideological engagement out of the country at the same time. In the light of all that, the Qatari stance certainly resulted in strengthening the MB transnational network from the Gulf to the Maghreb after 2011 events. Against this backdrop, the UAE in 2013, although sharing with its neighbors similar demographic anomalies and challenges, decided to strengthen the Gulf Arab long-established confrontational attitude towards the Muslim Brothers, by arresting several Egyptian members of the network in the country.

The complexity of the Islamist field in Saudi Arabia is another relevant factor, despite and beyond the official line. No doubt, the Saudi leadership has never been on good terms with the Muslim Brotherhood, which inevitably had an impact also on the uneasy development of relations with the Al-Nahda government in Tunisia.

Not surprisingly, the Saudi press started involving rising numbers of Tunisian secularists to put emphasis on human rights violations in the North African country since 2011 (Al-Rasheed 2013: 31). Nevertheless, strong support to al-Nahda came from the Saudi movement of Islamic Awakening (*al-Sahwah al-Islamiyyah*), a hybrid of the religious views of *Salafiyyah* and the Muslim Brotherhood's ideology (Lacroix 2010). Therefore, increasing polarization in Islamism in the Gulf has inevitably been affecting ties with the Maghreb as well.

The emergence and consolidation of Salafi groups as political actors and, alongside with them, of extremist Salafi-Jihadi militants has led to further diversification in the North African Islamist camp since 2011. At one and the same time, Gulf Arab Islamic capitalism, as an expression of a well-defined Salafi ideological dimension, clashing with the Islamic socialist thought of the reformist wing of the Muslim Brotherhood, started being more and more mistrusted by certain groups in the region. Within this perspective, some Salafi networks have also been indicated as the main supporters of Gulf Arab "intrusiveness" within the economic sphere. And yet, one cannot ignore that a number of North African exiles in the Gulf, although associated with the Muslim Brothers, have been developing links with Gulf Arab Salafi scholars as well, leading to the strengthening of a conservative wing within the Muslim Brotherhood, which is quite close both to some Salafi elements and powerful Gulf Arab business circles.

Transitional processes in the Maghreb are certainly affected by such rising complexity in ties and relations with the Gulf. Some of these ties certainly contributed to the rise of puritanism and radicalism, often in sharp contrast with local Sufism. The rising number of Salafi preachers in North Africa is a fact: some of them tend to endorse the official puritan religious interpretations of the Saudi Mufti and of the Saudi Higher Council of Ulama, as often absorbed during the pilgrimage (*hajj*) to Mecca throughout the last decades, whereas others are brainwashed by radical preachers heard in mosques built in the region through unchecked funds coming from Gulf Salafi charities and NGOs. Nonetheless, that is only one aspect of a radicalization process, which has been combining with much more worrying ties with Pakistani and Afghani preachers, already linked to jihadist groups and Al Qaeda (Zoubir and Dris-Aït-Hamadouche 2013: 101–102). Not surprisingly, the appeal of military jihad has been rising in the region, and in particular in Libya, where Islamist militias started extending their control to the majority of the territory outside Tripoli after the fall of Qaddafi. Libyan Islamist groups, such as the *Ansar al-Shari'a* (Protectors of Islamic Law) based in Benghazi, tend to refuse elections as "un-Islamic", and vow to remain armed until a strict version of the Islamic Law is implemented across the country (Wagner and Cafiero 2013): they are an expression of an extremist and violent *Salafiyyah*, and yet their approach and their language seem to evoke very clearly the "doctrine of armed jihad", as expressed in a treatise published in Cairo in 1913 by the head of the Senussiyah brotherhood, al-Sayyid Ahmad al-Sharif, at that time. Political circumstances in Libya were certainly different, but the inclusion among the *murtaddun* (apostates) of those Muslims who do not accept armed jihad against non-Muslim enemies was a turning point then (Fiorani Piacentini 2003: 85). It is obvious that, despite the heterogeneity of jihadist groups and militias, their differences in nature and origin, they all share a "doctrine of violence" largely nourished by political and economic frustrations.

Beyond the existing disruptive elements, post-Arab Spring environments in the Maghreb, as in the rest of the Arab world, need to buttress their transition processes: an evolving Islamic thought along constructive lines is pivotal in this direction. Such a thought has certainly been developing also within the newly built transnational networks between the Gulf and the Maghreb. Within this orientation, connecting Islamic authenticity with contemporary issues, there is a lively debate on some institutionalization of collective *ijtihad* (interpretation of the Qur'an and of the Tradition of the Prophet, or *Sunnah*), a crucial point in any reform process within a Sunni Islamic context. During his exile in Qatar, Yusuf Al-Qaradawi, a prominent Egyptian Islamic scholar originally linked to the Muslim Brotherhood, contributed to the creation of an integrated network of Islamic scholars, who engaged in the above-mentioned debate. This network started reaching out to North Africa from the Gulf, through exiles living between the GCC and Europe. Al-Qaradawi's promotion of the International Union of Muslim Scholars (IUMS) in 2004 was also in line with the flexible and moderate Salafi approach, which had been strengthening at government levels in Qatar with Sheikh Hamed, and in Saudi Arabia with King Abdullah. The latter, with other Saudi authorities, started supporting a flexible interpretation of Ibn Abd al-Wahhab's thought, against the most rigid and restrictive line (Niblock 2006: 24). Against this backdrop, IUMS, while representing the multifarious voices of the Islamic world,[6] was certainly conceived as a forum striving to bridge gaps through dialogue, a fact that led Qatar to back it and, at one and the same time, to get some winning cards in its growing activism as international mediator, and in its involvement in Mediterranean affairs (Zaman 2010: 118). IUMS's rising opposition against reactionary forces, which would refuse any change and reform in the Muslim world, anticipated in a way al-Qaradawi's open support to uprisings in Tunisia, Egypt and Libya, as expressed from the Qatari satellite channel *Al Jazeerah*. A series of factors, as already hinted, contributed to differentiate Qatari political reactions from the rest of the GCC, as far as transitions were concerned. Qatari boldness certainly contrasted Saudi caution on several occasions, and yet such caution did not prevent the Kingdom to adapt quite rapidly to some political changes in North Africa, as confirmed by the recognition of the new Muslim Brotherhood's leadership in Tunisia: despite the asylum given to Ben Ali, the Kingdom officially prevented him from engaging in seditious activities from its soil against the new Tunisian government, which was soon promised financial help (Obaid 2012: 24).

The growing role of Saudi Arabia in the Southern Mediterranean seems to be more and more shaped by the official flexible line of interpretation of Wahhabi thought after 2011 events. Within this perspective, dialogue becomes an essential preliminary step to oppose violence, to pursue stabilization efforts and to improve human development and economic relations.[7] As expressed by the Secretary

General of the Vienna-based King Abdullah bin Abdulaziz International Center for Interreligious and Intercultural Dialogue (KAICIID), the activities of this Center can be seen as part of a process of institutional planning aimed at guaranteeing sustainability, by building trust between Saudi Arabia and Muslims, on the one hand, and Europe and the West, on the other. A major possible outcome of this process is also its positive contribution to the establishment of a successful Euro-Med partnership (Bin Muammar 2013: 123).

No doubt, the Gulf Arab media concurred to strengthen the image of the GCC in post-Arab Spring environments, while aids coming from Gulf Arab charities and NGOs have been growing in parallel with official governments' financial packages to Islamic institutions and groups within the composite local Islamic panorama. The possible combination of humanitarian and religious goals with the support to some extremist elements also led to some allegations of abuse, driving the attention, for instance, on the banking system in Qatar and in the UAE, which seems to be less strictly regulated than the Saudi one after 9/11, and yet it is undeniable that the use of cash couriers, bypassing the banking system, is much more common everywhere among private charities. All that opened up heated debates. Although much emphasis is put on the large official foreign aid programs from the Gulf governments, with the Saudi one in the forefront (at $10 to $15 billion per year),[8] the existing independent charities cannot be neglected nor can they be decoupled from the rising awareness in the GCC region of the need to regulate their activities and enhance their transparency, in order to avoid implication of Gulf Arab funds to supporting violent militant groups abroad. That is an issue particularly relevant in all post-Arab Spring environments, and the Maghreb is no exception: the fact that, in 2012, 90 per cent of Saudi charity organizations were contested not to be transparent stressed in the Kingdom the need for strengthening relations among charity societies, their sponsors, their beneficiaries and the media.[9]

Developments within Islamist forces in the region have definitely been shaping more clearly official GCC policies towards North Africa since 2011, but they have also been shedding light on the need to address the roots of the existing problems in a more responsible way. Al-Nahda's electoral victory in Tunisia and the election of Abdelillah Benkirane of the Islamic Justice and Development Party as Prime Minister in Morocco have been referring to the urgency of an Islamic approach more responsive to modern and global issues, beyond possible intellectual, political and doctrinal differences, against radicalization and sectarianism. All that deals with culture and the growth of civil societies and not only with politics.[10]

The pragmatic logic of business

The unprecedented economic and human development witnessed in the GCC countries within a relatively short period spurred them to open up to both developed and emerging economies and to enhance quite rapidly their integration with the global economy, as attested by capital transfer and trade movement. The importance of entrepreneurship as a diversification strategy has been attracting more and more attention, in light of the challenges facing most GCC economies and labor markets, with Saudi Arabia, Bahrain and Oman in the forefront. The most pressing unemployment problem and the provision of job opportunities for nationals in the private sector require the adoption of different patterns of growth more founded on productivity (Gubash 2010: 41). The emphasized need to identify and implement an integrated system of economic development, while bearing in mind that economic aspects had often prevailed in terms of Gulf Arab cooperation during the last decade, cannot be neglected after 2011 events. The shared perception by GCC leaderships of very concrete threats to security and stability, posed by the most recent political developments in the Arab world, once again, after the early 1990s, has been stressing the importance to enhance coordination on foreign policy and security issues in the region. And yet, present challenges at the regional and international level in the GCC cannot but shed new light on the multidimensional concept of state sustainability and on the crucial role of further cooperation initiatives in the economic sphere, involving post-Arab Spring environments as well. Within this perspective, the unprecedented vision for greater unity supported by the Kingdom of Saudi Arabia sheds new light on re-defining relations within the GCC and between the GCC and Arab Mediterranean countries, both on multilateral and bilateral bases.

On the flip side of the religious/ideological drive underpinning Gulf Arab engagement with the Maghreb are mundane and highly pragmatic business interests. The failure of most regional groupings in the Arab world that emerged during the last century can largely be ascribed to the fact that they were more ideologically than business oriented. Development and economic issues, however, have never been neglected in the evolution of the GCC, and have contributed to the member states' more pragmatic and flexible approach to both domestic and foreign policy. In spite of a general reluctance to embark upon political liberalization, the Gulf has openly embraced economic globalization (Al-Issa 2005: 117), thanks to the last oil boom, which provided them with some of the largest Sovereign Wealth Funds (SWFs) and foreign exchange reserves in the world (see Figure 19.1 and Table 19.1).

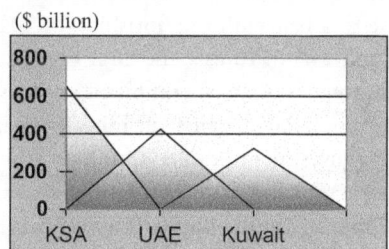

FIGURE 19.1 Top GCC foreign exchange reserves
Source: elaborated on data from KFCRIS

TABLE 19.1 The Largest GCC Sovereign Wealth Funds

Assets under management $ billion	
UAE – *Abu Dhabi Investment Authority*	$627
Abu Dhabi International Petroleum Investment Company	$58
Abu Dhabi Mubadala Development Company	$27.1
Dubai Investment Corporation	$70
Ras Al-Khaimah Investment Authority	$1.2
Saudi Arabia – *SAMA Foreign Holdings*	$532.8
Kuwait – *Kuwait Investment Authority*	$296
Qatar – *Qatar Investment Authority*	$85
Bahrain – *Mumtalakat Holding Company*	$9.1
Oman – *State General Reserve Fund*	$8.2

Source: SWF Institute

The interest in exploring investment opportunities beyond Western markets spurred Gulf Arabs to look more and more at Asia as a favorite destination of investment flows in the financial, real estate, tourism and agribusiness sectors, due to its greater absorption capacity. At the same time, at the dawn of the new century, the GCC started turning to the Mediterranean as well, increasingly seen as a potentially profitable destination of its external economic activities. The political desire to counterbalance the Gulf's turn towards Asian markets – in particular China and India – can also explain the extraordinary rise in Gulf FDIs towards various Arab Mediterranean countries, included in the so-called Med 11 group, in 2006 (see Tables 19.2 and 19.3).[11]

The Maghreb, after the Mashreq, had started being perceived as a potentially business-friendly environment by the GCC: Tunisia and Morocco were in the forefront. And yet, Gulf investment flows towards the region, though expanding from hydrocarbon and real estate to manufacturing and financial services, were somehow put off by low standards of transparency, red tape and high rates of corruption. This meant that beyond a generally growing interest, GCC economic involvement in the Southern Mediterranean has been rather discontinuous, with peaks in investments flows between 2005 and 2007 and significant drops in the following years.

On the eve of the "Arab Spring", new investment initiatives had been announced, but they obviously came to a halt with the uprisings. In 2010, for instance, only a few months before the upheaval in Tunisia, the Gulf Finance House of Bahrain, an investment bank which provides *Shari'ah* compliant services, had made its biggest FDI announcement to launch Africa's first offshore financial center in the Tunis Financial Harbor, with an investment of €2,100 million and a specific plan to create 16,000 jobs and attract Arab and European business; Qatar Telecom (Qtel) had also invested €1,100 million in Tunisia. In 2010, Libya had attracted the attention both of the Qatar Investment Authority and of Qatari Diar, which had planned an investment of €657.7 million in the country to redevelop the waterfront in Tripoli. Also in Libya, UAE's Al-Maabar had launched the joint venture development

TABLE 19.2 Net FDIs flows from the GCC region into Med 11 (2006–2010)

	(€ million)					
	2005	*2006*	*2007*	*2008*	*2009*	*2010*
Bahrain	61	1,518	408	128	945	642
Kuwait	1,610	4,292	2,802	2,182	790	511
Qatar	219	844	1,331	917	724	1,840
KSA	2,356	4,039	2,581	1,233	1,935	492
UAE	2,823	9886	11,874	3,751	2,355	1,861
Oman	–	–	–	373	–	–
GCC	**7,069**	**20,579**	**18,996**	**8,584**	**6,749**	**5,346**

Source: Data available at ANIMA-MIPO Observatory, http://www.animaweb.org.

TABLE 19.3 Net FDIs flows by GCC country of origin into Maghreb (between 2006 and 2009)

	(€ Million)
Bahrain	1,585
Kuwait	3,488
Qatar	1,083
KSA	1,617
UAE	9,347
Oman	365
Total GCC	**17,485**

Source: Data available at ANIMA-MIPO Observatory, http://www.animaweb.org.

project of Al-Waha, with an investment of €132 million (De Saint-Laurent, Lapujade and Luçon 2011: 68).

The role played by Qatar and the UAE in NATO's operation in Libya, Qatar's contextual decision to assimilate Libya's reduced oil production into its own for export to give further financial support to the rebels' forces, and the following proactive Qatari role at the dawn of post-Qaddafi Libya point to the fact that the Gulf's economic clout in North Africa is increasingly intertwined with political and security interests (Anthony 2012: 76). All of this is confirmed by the unanimous recognition of the GCC's main strategic objectives in 2012: (1) to protect member-states against all internal and external threats and risks; (2) to achieve sustainable economic growth and promote human development; and (3) to reinforce Gulf Arab presence at the international level to effectively confront international threats.

In view of this, the southern Mediterranean countries have become part of a complex regional context that requires concerted efforts by the GCC alongside the EU, Turkey and the US. Boosting security and preventing chaos from spreading have been repeatedly indicated as major goals by top GCC officials.

Gulf Arab states, which committed billions of dollars to post-Arab Spring environments, are realizing that the challenge is now to go beyond foreign aid programs, and give business a more positive role in re-shaping relationships with the countries of the region. It is not by chance that, in April 2012, Qatar decided to purchase the Bank of Commerce and Development in Libya and the UAE re-iterated its support to rebuilding Libya via trade and economic institutions, confirming its help to make the country join the World Trade Organization and to assist it in the implementation of infrastructures and technology projects. That is an orientation confirmed by the UAE-based Al Ghurair Group's announcement to plan an investment of $1.5 billion to expand a refinery in the country.

With reference to Morocco, the GCC decision to consider including the country in the organization with Jordan came in May 2011 in a surprise announcement that inevitably generated skepticism as well as new hopes in the region. While there seems to be a clear rationale for Jordan's membership, given its geographic contiguity with Saudi Arabia, Morocco's membership was immediately considered far more questionable, and the idea of a "privileged partnership" has been prevailing. In fact, there is clear awareness that an enlargement of the GCC to the Arab Mediterranean would be ill-advised without taking into consideration specific economic and labor market issues directly affecting Gulf Arab interests. In this sense, achieving greater economic union among the six GCC members requires a rigorous process of accountability and consolidation within the Council so as to avoid the risk of weakening the economic bloc itself. And yet, the invitation to Morocco, while being politically driven, cannot be decoupled from some economic considerations as well: on the one hand, the rising levels of trade and investment between the two sides spur towards the establishment of an evermore stable and sustainable business environment, and on the other, structural economic weaknesses both of Morocco and of the Gulf Arab states represent clear deterrents. A GCC projection towards the Mediterranean, through stronger strategic economic ties both with Arab partners and with the EU and Turkey, can actually represent a crucial factor of growth, sustainability and stability.[12] It should come as no surprise, then, that the GCC recommended a five-year development plan to Morocco in September 2011.[13] The implementation of this plan was presented as a precondition for any process aimed at building a "privileged partnership" with a country whose economy is recognized by Gulf Arab operators as being one of the most open and with the highest potential in the Maghreb, in spite of its persisting structural imbalances, still hindering really sustainable economic performance (Colombo 2011: 171).

Within this framework, some important steps were taken between 2011 and 2012: in November 2011, Qatar's Sovereign Wealth Fund and Rabat agreed to establish a 50–50 investment joint venture worth $2 billion that aims to fund major development projects, within a multilateral accord signed between Qatar, Morocco, Kuwait and the UAE on the creation of a tourist investment fund in Morocco; in December 2011, the GCC decided the establishment of a special Gulf development fund worth $2.5 billion aimed at providing support to development projects in Morocco (and in a similar way in Jordan); and in October 2012, the visit of King Muhammad VI to Saudi Arabia, Qatar, the UAE and Kuwait just re-affirmed the crucial importance of Gulf Arab support to development projects in this North African country.

As for Tunisia, the GCC looked with rising concern at the deteriorating situation in the country in 2012: the new government's ability to promote real growth, to foster the emergence of a collaborative democratic society and to counter social tensions is seen as a prerequisite for creating an attractive business environment to GCC interests too; in 2012 that is also attested by the UAE's call upon international donors to provide coordinated financial aid and technical support to Tunisia and all the countries affected by the "Arab Spring", so as to attract foreign investments and provide greater employment opportunities and basic services for the citizens.

"Securing markets" is in fact viewed as a precondition by GCC economic operators for their investments and support to development projects locally; uncertainty over the outcome of the transition process in Tunisia, and even more in Libya, and the persistence of major obstacles to the establishment of real economic cooperation in North Africa, as a first step towards real integration, proved to be major hindrances to further involvement of GCC business in the region throughout the last few years. The Arab Maghreb Union (AMU), in spite of the recent interests of the member states to revive it, is still trapped by serious fundamental political obstacles, such as the Western Sahara question (Zoubir 2012: 97); besides, it has rarely paid the proper attention to the economic benefits of an enlarged market, which is quite discouraging for developing business and wider economic partnerships within a real perspective of sustainability.

The role that investments from the GCC region can play in boosting soft security (human development) in North Africa cannot be decoupled from the ability of North African governments to create a more business-friendly environment in the region: the revival of the AMU might give some positive contribution in this direction as well. Beyond the large-scale projects involving the banking and finance sectors and major industries – petroleum refining, petrochemicals and metals' extraction and processing – the role of Small and Medium Enterprises (SMEs) in key sectors such as agribusiness, gas, renewable energy and textiles becomes crucial in Gulf–Mediterranean relations. A cooperative approach aimed at translating human, material and financial potential into economic power is recognized as a major challenge within Gulf business circles too at this stage, while more socially responsible investments are debated as an essential key to addressing human and environmental needs in the region. The mega urban projects supported by GCC investors in the past proved totally unable to respond to local needs of economic sustainability and largely fueled criticism of Gulf capitalist initiatives from Tunis to Rabat. The Dubai urban model was unscrupulously promoted by some Gulf companies, often aggressively adapting to local levels of corruption. In this respect, Tunisia, before 2011, with Ben Ali's laissez-faire model, was more negatively affected than Morocco, which instead was apparently able to insert greater regulation in the management of these projects (Barthel 2006: 2).

Different attitudes are requested on the part of both businessmen and institutions, in view of the importance to strengthen business networks founded on more socially responsible projects. GCC investments in agricultural and manufacturing sectors, for instance, have already proved to be quite promising in Turkey, one of the top recipients of Saudi investments in these fields. Food-security and water-balance will indeed be among the priorities in the Gulf in the coming years, with Saudi Arabia already being a major food exporter to the other GCC states. Pursuing sustainable agriculture can certainly enhance Gulf involvement in Mediterranean agriculture markets, considering that Saudis in particular seem to be quite interested in "integrative partnerships" – joint triangular, multilateral initiatives – to develop and manage agricultural investments in various strategic crops: the potential of North Africa in terms of agricultural land is just there to be developed (see Table 19.4).[14]

Power transmission and interconnections linking national electricity grids beyond the GCC with those of Middle Eastern and North African countries is an equally important issue discussed in the Gulf. Achieving integrative partnerships here means to develop synergies within a crucial multilateral approach which, in this field, would make it possible to set up a continuum of interconnections from the Gulf to Europe through a Mediterranean electricity grid. This would have a major impact on sustainable growth for all the parties involved, as markets can exploit hourly and seasonal differences in energy peak load demand (Abi Aad 2011: 9). Cooperation in renewable energies, and most specifically solar energy, with an involvement of both Tunisia and Algeria, is another aspect, which would have a major impact on sustainable growth and is seen with greater interest. In this sense, the fact that Algeria signed with Qatar a series of accords, covering joint projects in the steel industry, in energy, mining and maritime transport, for a total cost of around $5 billion, is another important complementary step which cannot be overlooked.

TABLE 19.4 Agricultural land in the Arab Mediterranean countries and in Turkey

(Year 2005)
(Square km)

Algeria	**411,500**
Egypt	35,200
Jordan	10,120
Lebanon	3,880
Libya	**155,850**
Morocco	**303,950**
Palestine	3,720
Syria	140,080
Tunisia	**97,690**
Turkey	412,230

Source: OIC

Finally, tourism remains a crucial sector for cooperation in the area, and Morocco is certainly better positioned at the moment to attract more Gulf investments, as attested by the already hinted signature of new agreements in this direction by SWFs from Abu Dhabi, Qatar and Kuwait, pledging almost $3 billion to help Rabat fund major development projects in tourism, and providing around $2.5 billion in Wessal Capital for the establishment of a Moroccan-led investment firm to fund investment opportunities proposed under Morocco's tourism development plan by 2020. As for Tunisia, regaining the investors' confidence in this critical sector of its economy is a major challenge. The Al-Nahda government, while trying to charm the West by insisting on its moderate Islamism, decided to sell $500 million worth of treasury bills to Qatar, and the visit to Tunis of the Qatari Crown Prince in July 2012 inaugurated a series of new investments on well-defined development projects in the country, such as energy and infrastructures. Further GCC involvement in Tunisia seems to depend largely on the present government's ability to promote real economic growth to foster the emergence of a collaborative democratic society and to counter social tensions.

Conclusion

Regional and international stabilization emerges as the main goal of the GCC at the current juncture. Gulf Arab leaderships' support to new governments in North Africa is therefore linked to the perception that new economic-financial forces can help stabilize the political and security contexts in the region. Business increasingly intertwines with the "Islam factor", leading to a new form of Islamic capitalism. Such capitalism emanates from the growing and increasingly global Gulf Arab Islamic financial institutions, which seek further opportunities in the Southern Mediterranean, a region still considered underdeveloped both in terms of Islamic finance and of infrastructure, but rich in natural and human resources.[15] Shari'ah compliant project finance is seen as having the potential to contribute effectively to North Africa's infrastructure development: being recommended by the Jeddah-based Islamic Development Bank, it seems to attract more attention (African Development Bank 2011: 27).

Against this backdrop, the rising international dynamism of Gulf Arab state and non-state actors in the Southern Mediterranean could more effectively contribute to development and sustainability, provided that an "integrative partnership model" is adopted in coordination with the EU and Turkey, as well as the US. All these parties share an interest in ensuring that economic growth in the region can help the political transition process: the GCC role as a prominent financial Islamic power in the Southern Mediterranean is a reality which cannot be ignored, and yet it needs to be accompanied by the other actors able to provide know-how and training in relevant sectors for economic development. The existing opportunities to deepen multilateral cooperation within broader economic ties between all the involved parties should not be missed at this crucial and extremely delicate stage and need the support both of the EU and the US. Therefore, the implementation and securitization of sustainable development projects at this stage in North Africa is strictly connected with the pursuance of a strategic dialogue among all the parties that have a direct crucial role to play. The establishment of joint initiatives, starting from business and investment, might help to create new convergences.

Gulf Arab pro-activism in the Southern Mediterranean could translate into a more constructive approach only within a synergic dimension. In this direction, besides the large-scale projects involving top industries, SMEs have a positive role to play as well, in spite of all the constraints they may face. Agri-food, for instance, is emerging with other micro-sectors, such as medicine, engineering, tourism, real estate and textiles, as a promising field for multilateral approaches, considering its growth potential both in terms of FDI and partnerships. The main areas where GCC expertise could be useful are certainly represented by the petrochemical sector, where the Saudi Arabian Basic Industries Corporation (SABIC) has gained a global role, and the growing Islamic banking sector, both in terms of wealth management and retail banking. Going beyond aid packages to pursue socially responsible investment projects becomes a great challenge as well as an essential clue for those human and environmental needs, which, if properly answered, can have a highly positive impact on growth and sustainability from the Mediterranean to the Gulf.

Notes

1. See Keynote Address by H.E. Maj. Abdellatif Al-Zayani, GCC Secretary General, The 2012 Gulf Research Meeting, University of Cambridge, July 2012.
2. Suspicion and distrust were soon re-expressed by public opinion both in the Gulf and in Morocco at the proposal to include Morocco in the GCC: the sex trafficking market which has been growing between Morocco and the Gulf is considered one of the issues contributing to rising misconceptions. For further details see Errazzouki (2012).
3. See *Gulf Times*, 14.01.2012, "Red Carpet Welcome for Qatar's Emir in Tunis"; *Khaleej Times*, 21.01.2012, "UAE for Fruitful, Progressive Ties with Tunisia".
4. *The Economist*, 5.11.2011, "The Rise of Qatar. Pygmy with the Punch of a Giant. The Burgeoning Influence of Qatar in the Arab World Arouses Admiration, Suspicion and Puzzlement. But Its Motives Are Mainly Pragmatic".
5. *The Peninsula*, 30.01.2013, PM denies meddling in Mali, http://thepeninsulaqatar.com/news/qatar/223824/pm-denies-meddling-in-mali-, accessed on 16.06.2015.
6. IUMS members include Rashid al-Ghannushi, the Islamist leader of the Tunisian Al-Nahda party; Salman al-Awda, a Saudi Salafi who opposed the Saudi regime in the 1990s; Muhammad Husain Fadl Allah, a prominent Shi'a religious authority in Lebanon; and Jalal al-Din Haqqani, a key figure in the Taliban movement. The importance of mediation in Islam traces back to the time of the Prophet Muhammad and early Islam, when settling disputes by arbitration was considered a great value for the community of believers (*ummah*), a principle further elaborated by the classical orthodox doctrine.
7. Most recently this line of interpretation has been leading Saudi Arabia to pursue some officially dialogue-oriented policies, both at the national level, through the King Abdulaziz Center for National Dialogue, and at the international level, through the King Abdullah International Center for Interreligious and Intercultural Dialogue, inaugurated in Vienna in 2012. The establishment of an Inter-Muslim Dialogue Center in Riyadh is another priority, according to this line supported by King Abdullah.
8. Estimates given by Nawaf Obaid in Obaid (2012).
9. H. Dammam, "Expert Says Most Charity Societies Not Transparent", *Arab News*, 8.05.2012, available at www.arabnews.com/node/412618, accessed on 15.06.2015.

10. As observed by Ghassan Charbel in "The Post-Spring Pangs" in *Al-Hayat*, 2.05.2013, "There are legitimate questions that present themselves and urgently so. Are the ballot boxes sufficient to ensure smooth transition from one regime to another? Are elections results enough to draft constitutions hastily and take electoral mandates further than society can bear? . . ." Available at www.sauress.com/en/alhayaten/479558, accessed on 15.05.2015.
11. Med-11 indicates the 11 Mediterranean countries neighboring Europe and included in the EU's Mediterranean policy platforms: Algeria, Egypt, Israel, Jordan, Lebanon, Morocco, Palestinian Authority, Syria, Tunisia, Libya and Turkey.
12. This perception clearly emerged in the Workshop *The EU and the GCC Countries in the Southern Mediterranean* at the Gulf Research Meeting 2011, University of Cambridge, 6–9.07.2011.
13. A similar development plan was submitted to Jordan as well.
14. As shown in Table 19.4, according to the estimates of the Organization of Islamic Countries (OIC), the total agricultural land of Libya, Tunisia and Morocco combined is about 557,490 square km against 412,230 square km in Turkey.
15. Islamic finance in North Africa is underdeveloped both in comparison to the GCC region and South East Asia and, surprisingly, in comparison to the United Kingdom as well.

References

Abi Aad, N. (2011). 'Energy in the Mediterranean. Synergies Between Europe and the Gulf', paper presented at the Gulf Research Meeting, Cambridge, 6–9 July.

African Development Bank (2011). *Islamic Banking and Finance in North Africa. Past Development and Future Potential*. Accessed at www.afdb.org.

Al-Issa, S.Y. (2005). 'The Political Impact of Globalisation on the Arab Gulf States', in The Emirates Center for Strategic Studies and Research (ECSSR) (ed.), *The Gulf. Challenges of the Future*, Abu Dhabi: ECSSR.

Al-Rasheed, M. (2013). 'Saudi Arabia: Local and Regional Challenges', *Contemporary Arab Affairs*, 6:1.

Anthony, J.D. (2012). 'The Future Significance of the Gulf Cooperation Council', in The Emirates Center for Strategic Studies and Research ECSSR (ed.), *Global Strategic Developments. A Futuristic Vision*, Abu Dhabi: ECSSR.

Barbier, M. (1982). *Le conflit du Sahara Occidental*, Paris: L'Harmattan.

Barthel, P.-A. (2006). *Tunis en projet(s). La fabrique d'une métropole au bord de l'eau*, Rennes: Presses universitaires de Rennes.

Bin Muammar, F.A. (2013). 'Saudi-Italian Relations. A History of Political and Cultural Cooperation', in S. Colombo (ed.), *Italy and Saudi Arabia Confronting the Challenges of the XXI Century*, Roma: Edizioni Nuova Cultura.

Buskens, L. (2003). 'Recent Debates on Family Law Reform in Morocco: Islamic Law as Politics in an Emerging Public Sphere', in *Islamic Law and Society*, 10:1, *Public Debates on Family Law Reform Participants, Positions, and Styles of Argumentation in the 1990s*. Accessed at www.jstor.org/stable/3399220.

Coates Ulrichsen, K. (2012). 'A European Perspective on the GCC Involvement in the Mediterranean in Light of the Arab Spring', in S. Colombo, K. Coates Ulrichsen, S. Ghabra, S. Hamid, and E. Ragab (eds.), *The GCC in the Mediterranean in Light of the Arab Spring*, Washington, DC: GMF-IAI Mediterranean Paper Series.

Colombo, S. (2011). 'Morocco at the Crossroads: Seizing the Window of Opportunity for Sustainable Development', in S. Colombo and N. Tocci (eds.), *The Challenges of State Sustainability in the Mediterranean*, Roma: Edizioni Nuova Cultura.

Colombo, S. (2012). *The GCC Countries and the Arab Spring. Between Outreach, Patronage and Repression*, Roma: IAI Working Papers 1209.

De Saint-Laurent, B., Lapujade, J., and Luçon, Z. (2011). 'The Mediterranean Between Growth and Revolution. Foreign Direct Investments and Partnerships', in ANIMA

Investment Network, *MED Countries in 2010, Study no. 21*. Gémenos, http://www.ani-maweb.org/en/mediterranean-between-growth-and-revolution-foreign-direct-invest ments-and-partnerships-med (Accessed July 13, 2015)..

Errazzouki, S. (2012). 'A Monarchical Affair: From Morocco to the Arabian Peninsula', *Jadaliyya*, 10 April. Accessed at www.jadaliyya.com/pages/index/4980/a-monarchical-affair_from-morocco-to-the-arabian-peninsula.

Fiorani Piacentini,V. (2003). *Islam. Logica della fede e logica della conflittualità*, Milano: Franco-Angeli.

Gabrieli, F. (1997). *Maometto e le grandi conquiste arabe*, Milano: Newton Compton Editori.

Gubash, S.G. (2010). 'Economic Development and the Challenges Facing the GCC Labor Market', in The Emirates Center for Strategic Studies and Research ECSSR (ed.), *Education and the Requirements of the GCC Labor Market*, Abu Dhabi: ECSSR.

Khatib, L. (2013). 'Qatar's Involvement in Lybia: A Delicate Balance'. World Peace Foundation, Tuft University. Accessed at http://sites.tufts.edu/reinventingpeace/2013/01/07.

Lacroix, S. (2010). *Awakening Islam: A History of Islamism in Saudi Arabia*, Cambridge, MA: Harvard University Press.

Luciani, G. (2005). 'From Private Sector to National Bourgeoisie: Saudi Arabian Business', in P. Aarts and G. Nonneman (eds.), *Saudi Arabia in the Balance*, London: Hurst.

Niblock, T. (2006). *Saudi Arabia, Power, Legitimacy and Survival*, London: Routledge.

Nonneman, G. (2006) 'Political Reform in the Gulf Monarchies: From Liberalisation to Democratisation? A Comparative Perspective', Sir William Luce Fellowship Paper No. 6, Durham Middle East Papers No. 80.

Obaid, N. (2012). *Saudi Arabia: The Kingdom in a Post 'Arab Spring' Environment*, Riyadh: King Faisal Center for Research and Islamic Studies (KFCRIS).

Pellitteri, A. (2011–2012). 'La cosiddetta primavera degli Arabi: alcune definizioni tra riferimenti storico-culturali ed attualità', in *Civiltà del Mediterraneo*, 20–21 June.

Salzman, P.C. (2011). 'When They Proclaim "Islam is the Answer," What Is the Question? The Return to Political Islam', *The Journal of the Middle East and Africa*, 2:2.

Tétreault, A.M. (2000). *Stories of Democracy. Politics and Society in Contemporary Kuwait*, New York: Columbia University Press.

Wagner, D. and Cafiero, G. (2013). *Implication of the Rise of Radical Muslim Groups in Libya*, INEGMA, 23 January.

Zaman, M.Q. (2010). 'Bridging Traditions. Madrasas and Their Internal Critics', in A. Shryock (ed.), *Islamophobia Islamophilia. Beyond the Politics of Enemy and Friend*, Bloomington: Indiana University Press.

Zoubir, Y.H. (1993). 'Reactions in the Maghreb to the Gulf Crisis and War', *Arab Studies Quarterly*, 15:1 (winter 1993).

Zoubir, Y.H. (2012). 'Tipping the Balance Towards Intra-Maghreb Unity in Light of the Arab Spring', *The International Spectator: Italian Journal of International Affairs*, 47:3.

Zoubir, Y.H. and Dris-Aït-Hamadouche, L. (2013). *Global Security Watch – The Maghreb: Algeria, Libya, Morocco, and Tunisia*, Santa Barbara: Praeger.

Newspapers and magazines:

Al-Hayat
Al-Watan
Arab News
Gulf Times
La Lettre de la Méditerranée
Middle East Online
The Economist
The Peninsula

20

PERSPECTIVES: NORTH AFRICA'S ENERGY CHALLENGES

John Hamilton and Hakim Darbouche

Introduction

The past decade can generally be characterized as a period of declining optimism in the prospects for increased energy output from Algeria, Libya and Egypt, North Africa's main hydrocarbon producing countries. It is arguably no accident that the failure of the attempts to revive the oil and gas sectors in Libya and Algeria in particular, and to create a new era of exploration in Egypt can be directly attributed to the parallel failures of attempts to prolong and to introduce generational change within the ruling elites. This attempt in Libya came to a violent conclusion in February 2011 with the "Arab Spring" uprising against the regime of Colonel Muammar Qadhafi and eight months of civil war resulting in the downfall of the regime. The transition to a replacement system has become deadlocked in faction fighting. In Algeria, the situation is considerably more complex, with the question of where power may lie in the future still apparently unresolved, but revolution remains one of the least likely scenarios. The major question, then, is whether the politics of North Africa over the next period will provide anything like the conditions necessary to make a new and perhaps more reasonable and more commercial attempt to allow new exploration and production of oil and gas. The signs from the current political changes are far from promising.

These essentially unsatisfactory political conditions leave Algeria, Libya and Egypt ill-equipped to deal with the challenges facing their oil and gas sectors – and many other economic and social challenges besides. In terms of supply, the main existing fields that have been the bedrock of output for the past decades are beginning to decline. Large and sophisticated redevelopments are necessary to increase recovery rates and sustain production plateaus. Even then, the discovery and development of new fields to replace output is now essential. While geologists are optimistic that new significant resources will be discovered in these countries, recent exploration results have been disappointing. The development of discovered fields has also been massively delayed for a combination of bureaucratic, political and commercial reasons.

At the same time domestic energy consumption continues to grow at an alarming rate across the region. This is partly a result of demographics, and also of shifting social and consumer trends. But it is also the penalty paid for the failure of governments in these countries to reform or phase out generous subsidy schemes. Populations are rapidly expanding and, thanks to the availability of cheap imports, now expect to live with air-conditioning and every other type of standard household appliance. But there is no matching expectation to pay a realistic price for the electricity they consume. Diesel and gasoline are also sold at subsidized prices, although at present this currently manifests itself as a fiscal problem rather than a direct call on hydrocarbons resources, because a high proportion of refined products are imported.

The example of Egypt, which, having become a net importer of oil a few years ago, is now faced with the prospect of becoming a net importer of gas as well, is a stark warning of the fate which both Libya and Algeria will be forced to confront many years before the absolute limits of their resources make it strictly necessary. The challenges facing North Africa's energy sector are not new and have emerged gradually over the past period. But while senior industry executives and officials in these countries clearly understand the threats, their ability to gather enough political momentum to avert the worst-case outcome must be questioned.

The fact that – in Algeria especially – the public debate over resources has been almost entirely given over to the country's potentially vast unconventional resources is an indication of the unreality which still envelops these questions. Whether or not these resources are in fact commercially viable, there is no prospect that the thousands of wells necessary for their testing and exploitation can be drilled under the existing conditions. As Algeria's Energy and Mines minister Youcef Yousfi himself commented, it may well be another 40 years before they are put into production. However, even this more "realistic" view masks a delusion about the present. The authorities are failing to extract and monetize their existing conventional resources in the most effective way possible, and lack the courage to rein in domestic energy demand through pricing reform. Under these circumstances, the promise of shale gas is first and foremost a comfort blanket against the prospect of a too-rapidly advancing "post-hydrocarbons" future.

A tale of a lost opportunity

To understand how a region so rich in hydrocarbon resources has failed to realize its potential, and to get a clear picture of what regional governments should do over the next period to rectify this, it is necessary to glance back over the history of the past decade, which began as a period of great optimism for the North African energy sector.

In Libya the signing of the final contracts under the EPSA-III model in 2003 was followed by four EPSA-IV licensing rounds introduced by the then National

Oil Corporation (NOC) chairman Shukri Ghanem in 2004, plus the signing of a number of major bilateral agreements under the same framework. After a long period when it had not been counted as a major zone of hydrocarbons exploration because of the international sanctions imposed on the Qadhafi regime during the late 1980s and the 1990s, Libya had come back. More than 30 international oil companies (IOCs) took on new exploration risk in the country over this period.

Algeria was enjoying a similar renaissance. Even though the bloody conflict of the 1990s had not damaged oil and gas production – in fact hydrocarbon production and exports had seen phenomenal growth during this period – the settling of the country in its aftermath facilitated a number of licensing rounds starting in 2000 which had provided a way for a number of IOCs to enter the country and to carry out successful exploration campaigns. In 2005, Energy and Mines minister Chakib Khelil introduced major reforms to the Hydrocarbons Law which appeared to put the country on track for a further major expansion in exploration. Khelil also launched a major campaign of expanding and developing Algeria's gas export infrastructure with plans to build new liquefied natural gas (LNG) export terminals at Arzew and the rebuilding of the damaged plant at Skikda, the building of the Medgaz pipeline to Spain and the proposed Galsi pipeline to Italy – all with the aim to increase gas exports from 60 billion cubic meters (Bcm) in 2000 to 85 Bcm in 2009 and 100 thereafter. He also signed agreements for a substantial expansion of Algeria's petrochemicals sector.

In Egypt, despite declining oil production, the country's gas production saw a marked increase from around 20 Bcm in 2000 to over 60 Bcm by the end of the decade. Egypt joined the ranks of gas exporters in 2003, with its first shipment of gas through the Arab Gas Pipeline to Jordan, and in 2005 became North Africa's newest exporter of LNG, having built the world's largest LNG production unit at the time. The country had plans to continue expanding gas production for continued use in power generation domestically and to export through expanded pipeline and liquefaction capacity.

However, it did not take long for these plans to falter. In Libya, as the EPSA-IV licensing process continued up until the end of 2007, IOCs in their excitement to access territories bid increasingly aggressive production shares. Ultimately, the results of exploration and much higher than expected operating costs failed to justify these bids. From the entire exploration effort, only six or seven new discoveries have been made – none of them substantially large. Meanwhile, after the Algerian parliament had passed Minister Khelil's hydrocarbons law in 2005, but before it had been published in the *Journal Officiel*, it was withdrawn and subjected to major amendments which altered its character completely. By the time it was re-passed and published in 2006 its liberal provisions were stripped out and it was transformed into a much more restrictive law, reflecting the prevailing preferences and prejudices of the country's leadership. Tellingly, out of a total of 36 perimeters offered in the three bid rounds held since 2006, only eight were successfully bid for by and awarded to international oil companies.

Similarly, gas production in Egypt saw a marked slowdown since 2006, growing on average by 4.6% per year compared to a compound average growth rate of 12.2% between 1989 and 2006. And, in 2010, Egypt's gas output fell for the first time, declining by over 2%, and did not recover since. Upstream licensing rounds held since 2008 have been largely disappointing with foreign investors reserving muted responses to the acreage and the commercial terms offered by the Egyptian authorities.

In all three countries, it became apparent that the desire to attract IOCs into the upstream was not backed up by a willingness to tackle the lingering issues hampering commerciality for foreign investors and to recognize and take account of the shifts taking place in global energy markets (recession, falling demand in Europe, growing US supply, emergence of new hydrocarbon provinces in Latin America, the Eastern Mediterranean, sub-Saharan Africa, etc.). Combined with the growing trend of resource nationalism, and increasingly difficult operating environments, delays in decision-making and rising costs quickly took the shine off most of the exploration activity that was going on. In three countries IOCs showed less and less interest in licensing rounds, until the authorities simply decided to abandon them.

Unpromising political outlook

In spite of changes in political personnel across the region, it is by no means certain that resource nationalism has had its day in these countries. The ruling elites still appear to be committed to nationalist ideologies in terms of resource management. Secondly, the problems of corruption with the sector are far from resolved. In Algeria's case, this means that traumatic investigations into past deals could continue. The effect of this has been to gum up decision-making as managers at all levels work under conditions of extreme paranoia. In Libya, lack of trust between the various factions currently vying for power means that achieving consensus over the control and management of hydrocarbons resources will be extremely difficult.

Meanwhile, the security situation has significantly deteriorated since early 2011 across the entire region. Even if terms, commercial arrangements, contracts and decision-making are all in place to encourage IOCs to explore, concerns about the ability of the authorities to provide a secure environment – particularly in the southern desert – may yet keep them out.

The other major problem is that of hydrocarbons legislation. Up to five attempts have been made to overhaul Libya's 1955 law, which has been amended many times but never replaced. A draft replacement under the guidance of the then NOC chairman, the late Shukri Ghanem, was partly formed in the months immediately prior to the 17 February 2011 uprising. A new committee to rewrite the legislation was formed in March and will soon start consultations for the writing of a strategic white paper.

The authorities have made numerous positive statements about their willingness to do this, their desire to be flexible and the fact that they expect it to be done soon. However, with no constitution in sight, and the chances of a body being put together that is capable of writing a basic law acceptable to the vast majority of the population also receding, it seems almost impossible that fundamental decisions about the exploitation of hydrocarbons are going to be reasonably resolved in the foreseeable future. Changes to the now discredited EPSA-IV model contract will also be very difficult to introduce. One of the major problems this leaves Libya with is that there is no proper legislation to incentivize and manage the exploitation of gas. This is also one of the major priorities for the development of the sector.

Algeria's situation with regard to legislation is different, as the authorities during 2012 and the first part of 2013 made strenuous efforts to review and reform the country's hydrocarbons legislation. A major process of consultation went ahead, finally resulting in revisions to the 2006 law, which were introduced in February 2013. The main thrust of the revisions was to introduce better fiscal terms for certain classes of resources and also to make it easier for companies that have made discoveries but have not started to develop them to achieve better profits if their resources could be classed as unconventional or frontier. However, these changes have yet to be tested, and until a licensing round is held their effect on foreign investor interest in Algeria's upstream sector post-In Amenas will remain uncertain. Many companies appeared underwhelmed by the impact of the changes, particularly as many of the discoveries which could be developed under the improved terms, or indeed, likely to be found in new exploration, are marginal or on their way towards being unconventional. However it does not appear that the authorities are yet willing to make the really fundamental changes necessary to realize the full potential of their hydrocarbon sector.

Declining existing resources

Both Algeria and Libya are reliant on aged and declining fields for most of their production. The historic peak of Libya's oil production was reached in the 1970s when output was about 3.5 million (mb/d). During the latter years of the Qadhafi regime, the authorities liked to claim that production capacity was in the 1.7–2 mb/d range, although output was restricted to about 1.5 mb/d because of OPEC quotas. According to Tripoli University's Dr Ahmed Urayet, 18 billion barrels (bbls) of recoverable reserves remain from an estimated 48 billion bbls of total oil reserves.[1] Twelve billion bbls of these are proven reserves and the remaining 6 billion bbls are probable or possible reserves. He estimates that it will be possible to maintain 1.5 mb/d oil production until 2030 or 2035 if further discoveries are made before 2020. Under the best scenario, production could increase to 2.1 mb/d for a period.

The maximum output achieved since the February 2011 revolution has been 1.55 mb/d. In 2013, even before the drastic blockades of most export terminals in the east (which started in July and showed no signs of being lifted in October), output had anyway started to fall. This was partly due to some more minor strikes and blockades, but was also caused by electricity supply problems at the Sarir and Messla fields – the mainstays of Arabian Gulf Oil Company's 400,000 b/d production.

Providing security, budget and decision-making bottlenecks are eventually resolved, some increases in both gas and oil production are possible. In the short term, new output will come from offshore developments around existing production at Bahr Es-Salam and the NC41 reserves. The onshore Wafa fields may also be developed. NOC subsidiary Arabian Gulf Oil Company (Agoco) can also produce associated gas from the Hamada fields. In the Sirte Basin, there is a large quantity of associated gas being flared. Projects are being considered to capture and feed 6 cm (thousand cubic meters) of this into the network.

In late September 2013, oil and gas minister Abdelbari Laroussi publicly maintained that once the terminal blockades in the east were lifted, output would return to 1.6 mb/d in a matter of weeks. NOC chairman Dr Nouri Berouin has also said that the shutdown in production in the Sirte Basin has not damaged fields and wells. However, these, and similar assertions made in the past, have been questioned by some industry participants. Without pointing to specific examples, some engineers have expressed concerns that the failure to invest properly in fields during the sanctions period or in the decade that followed, combined with the unplanned outage of almost all production during the 2011 civil war and the inability to service or maintain equipment both during the war and in the following two years, followed by another extended production outage, will cause some damage to both facilities and fields.

In Algeria both gas and oil output is likely to fall in the medium term. The IEA's Medium-Term Oil Market Report, published in May 2013, forecast a 0.4% decline in Algeria's crude oil production capacity in the period 2012–2018. With gas developments also likely to be further delayed over this period because of new security concerns, it is probable that gas output will also fall. Production declined in 2013. According to one analyst, exports to Italy in 2013 had fallen by 40% and LNG exports in general were 30% down. The authorities' own estimates do not reflect these concerns. Figures published in May 2013 by the IMF, based on Algerian data, forecast stable oil exports of 1.3 mb/d until 2017, while gas exports were projected to slowly increase from 50.4 Bcm in 2012 to 52.1 Bcm in 2017.

There has for many years been considerable speculation about the status of the vast Hassi R'mel gas field, the mainstay of Algerian production since 1961 and historically responsible for approximately half the country's total gas production. According to one Sonatrach internal estimate,[2] it produced 91.6 Bcm in 2009. Total gross gas production that year, excluding condensates, was probably about 150 Bcm. There is some doubt whether production has actually begun to decline since then, and if so at what rate, with rumours of water incursion into the field widespread but not officially confirmed.

Part of the expected decline in gas output could be met by pending developments. There is a potential 13 Bcm/yr of production waiting to be developed in a handful of fields in south-west Algeria. But developments have been delayed repeatedly owing to difficulties in establishing commercial terms between Sonatrach and its international partners, and Sonatrach's own delays in building the pipeline necessary to connect the group of fields to the Hassi R'mel hub. First gas had been expected in 2014 and will now not happen until 2016 at the earliest.

The decline in Egypt's gas production has been imputed to the depletion of mature fields in the Nile Delta and offshore Mediterranean and to the marked slowdown in exploration and production activity since 2006. Indeed, Egypt is not short of gas resources. Estimates of its gas reserves range from 78 to 102 Tcf. However, with over 75% of this reserve base located in the offshore Mediterranean and with production moving gradually to the deeper, costlier areas, the investment terms offered by the government within the existing production-sharing regime have become less attractive for international upstream investors.

IOCs have to sell up to two-thirds of their share of the gas (cost gas + profit gas) to the Egyptian gas holding company EGAS at a fixed price of $2.65/MMBtu. But rising upstream costs, coupled with slow decision-making and delayed receivables payments from EGAS, meant that foreign investors have seen their margins squeezed and have in many cases been unable to justify spending on existing production facilities, let alone engage in fresh exploration, particularly in offshore concessions.

Recognizing the need to offer improved pricing terms to keep investors interested in Egyptian gas upstream opportunities, the government decided in 2008 to offer higher prices on a case-by-case basis depending on the concession agreement and the position of the acreage. The West Mediterranean Deepwater concession, held by BP and RWE, was the first to be awarded a new pricing arrangement, but it remains unclear how far the new government will go in increasing prices and applying them to other concessions.

Over-optimistic plans for future exploration?

The authorities in both Algeria and Libya have said they expect to hold licensing rounds in the near future. Libya's plan was to write a new hydrocarbons law and a new model EPSA-V contract in time to hold a round in the middle of 2014. Most observers regarded this as being an extremely optimistic programme. Leaving aside the question of whether a new constitution would be in place and therefore whether the hydrocarbons law will appear sufficiently permanent and reliable to give confidence to investors, it was will be difficult to get a strong workable piece of legislation and all the related regulations and contracts ready in that time.

Algeria is in a better position having passed amendments to its inadequate hydrocarbons law in February 2013. In September 2013, IOCs were still waiting to see the detailed regulatory decrees, which will show how the new taxation and production was sharing conditions contained in the law will be implemented. Guidance is particularly needed about which resources will be classified as unconventional and therefore eligible for more generous terms. As many of the expected undiscovered or undeveloped gas resources in Algeria are expected to be of a "tight" or unconventional nature, companies are hoping that they will be classified together with shale resources.

This matters not only for resources which come up in future licensing rounds, but also for certain discoveries which have not yet been developed and which could therefore qualify for improved terms. France's Total, for instance, will only proceed with the 4 Bcm/yr Ahnet development if its resources are reclassified as unconventional.

Increasing pressure from domestic demand

The unpromising supply situation of the region is exacerbated by the pressure from uncontrolled growth in domestic energy demand driven by fast population growth and greater per head energy consumption. In Libya, demand for electricity has been growing at approximately 7% per year. According to Tripoli University's Urayet, domestic consumption of oil products is currently about 180–190,000 b/d oil and increasing at 3.6% per year. At this rate, and with an expected decline in crude output from 2030, he argues that Libya will become a net oil importer in 2045. The reduction of the rate of increase in consumption to 2.4% via the adoption of good energy efficiency, conservation and renewables policies would put back this date to 2048. The discovery of a further 6 billion bbls of reserves would enable Libya to keep exporting until 2055.

In Algeria electricity demand has grown in recent years at 14% per annum.[3] In its July 2013 report, the International Energy Agency (IEA) reported that Algerian fuel imports had increased by 50% over a three-year period while domestic production of refined products fell 35% over the same period. Fuel demand is growing at 10% per year.

Demand for diesel and gasoline may well be growing more quickly in both countries thanks to the massive incidence of cross-border smuggling into Tunisia, Morocco, Egypt and, in the case of Libya, also to Malta. Anecdotal evidence from the international market suggests that imports of refined products into Libya may have increased by as much as 40% since the revolution, a situation made worse by credible allegations of the outright theft and re-export of refined products.

In Egypt, the pressure from domestic demand has tended to express itself most acutely in the gas the sector. Indeed, domestic gas consumption has grown solidly, doubling every ten years since 1991 and reaching over 52 Bcm in 2012. Demand for gas in Egypt is driven primarily by the power sector (56% of demand), which has been growing at an average annual rate of 8–10% in recent years, followed by the industrial sector. Like the other two countries, Egypt's fast-growing energy needs are the result of sustained economic and demographic growth, as well as the artificially low prices at which energy products are provided to consumers by the government.

Going forward, demand for gas-to-power is expected to continue growing at a sustained rate, based on the forecast that the size of the population is set to reach over 90 million and the number of households almost 28 million by 2020, with the bulk of this increase being concentrated in the urban centres. Furthermore, government plans for increasing of the country's power generation capacity consist of adding over 12,000MW in the five years from 2012–13 to 2017–18, most of which will be gas-fired.

Of course, the present limited domestic refining capacity in the region means that unrestrained fuel demand is more of a financial burden than a direct restraint on crude oil exports. Significant amounts of the revenue earned from crude sales goes towards buying diesel and gasoline on the international market. However, all three countries have ambitious plans to construct new refineries. Sonatrach has plans to build six new refineries over the coming period, with the objective of doubling refining capacity to more than 60m tonnes. The Libyan authorities are considering plans for the upgrade of the refineries at Az-Zawiya and Ras Lanuf, which together have a maximum production capacity of about 340,000 b/d. NOC also wants to build two or three more plants, ultimately enabling it to process about half its total crude production. In Egypt, plans for new refining capacity are mostly led by the private sector, such as the Citadel-led Egypt Refining Company which plans to build a $3.7 billion refinery with a capacity of 4.2 million tons per annum.

More gas usage from domestic power sector expansion

Additionally, the proposed expansion of power generation capacity in both countries will restrict the amount of gas available for export. Algeria's plans are the most ambitious. A recent contract signed with GE for the supply of turbines with total capacity of 8,400MW means the addition of power equivalent to 70% of the country's current installed capacity of approximately 12,000MW. Libya is also planning several new power stations. This is necessary as probably more than one-quarter of the nominal installed capacity of 5,270MW is out of service. In summer of 2013 the authorities expected a shortfall in generation capacity of about 1GW from the peak load. Blackouts were widespread. General Electric Company of Libya (Gecol) has hired 450MW of diesel-fired temporary power to plug the gap. Even so, the country already lacks sufficient gas to supply its under-performing power sector in spite of the fact that Eni's gas importing subsidiary Snam is currently not taking its full allocation via the Greenstream pipeline, meaning an extra 2 Bcm/yr is available for domestic consumption.

Algeria is already feeling the pressure on gas availability and reacting to that pressure. In August 2013, The Autorité de Régulation des Hydrocarbures (ARH) notified the Fertial fertilizer production joint venture that supply of gas to its complexes in both Annaba and Arzew would be reduced by 30%. Similar pressure has been applied to other joint ventures in the fertilizer sector. Sorfert, a joint venture between Sonatrach and Orascom Construction Industries, recently resolved a dispute over gas supply. Sonatrach is also trying to increase the contractually agreed price at which the Algerian-Omani Fertilizer Company, which is majority-owned by Oman's Suheil Bahwan Group, will pay for gas feedstock.

In the face of the country's growing gas deficit, the Egyptian authorities decided to turn to LNG imports as a stopgap measure aimed at allowing it to satisfy domestic needs and export commitments until the coming on stream of new domestic supply from 2015–16. The original plan was to import 5–7 million tons per annum of LNG through a floating regasification facility from the second half of 2013, but political and commercial hurdles have since prevented its implementation. In the meantime, the government has decided to halt imports to Israel while reducing its shipments of gas to Jordan to negligible amounts.

Subsidies failure

One of the key policy failures in every North African country over the past period has been the reluctance of politicians to tamper with unaffordable subsidies arrangements. Possible changes to generous government support for energy and other commodity prices have been mooted in almost every capital city. However, in the years prior to the 2011 uprisings when regimes and governments across the region were attempting to engineer complex schemes for the transition of power to new generations within the elite, it was not considered propitious to adopt unpopular measures of this sort.

Since the fall of the regimes in Libya, Tunisia and Egypt, the transitional authorities have suggested that subsidy reform is back on the agenda, while taking no actual steps towards it. In Libya, subsidies on fuel cost the government $9.1 billion in 2012, while electricity subsidies cost it $0.9 billion. Together their cost was equivalent to 7.2% of GDP. According to research published by the IMF, the "elimination of petroleum subsidies in Libya would be likely to lead to a reduction in gasoline consumption of 33.1 to 48.8%."[4] The fact that most Libyans do not pay at all for electricity, combined with the fact that there are huge inefficiencies in generation, mean that the actual cost to the state is probably higher. Subsidy reform, if enacted, could achieve important domestic energy savings, thus improving the long-term prospects for oil and gas exports significantly. However, the political cost would be substantial. The Algerian authorities have also toyed with the possibility of subsidy reform for many years but have never shown any real inclination to actually enact even modest reforms in this direction.

In Egypt, where energy subsidies are highest in absolute as well as in relative terms, the issue has had the most devastating effect on energy sector development and government finances. Subsidies have encouraged wasteful use of energy products while benefiting the rich at the expense of the poor, and have diverted substantial public financial resources away from vital sectors such as health and education. Yet, despite repeated statements from policymakers, under both the old and new regimes, the issue remains a political "hot potato", with many vested interests preventing the implementation of sustainable pricing reform.

Conclusion

Traditionally, the view of North Africa has been that of a region rich in energy resources and an important source of supply for international oil and gas markets. While undoubtedly the region is home to large conventional and unconventional (including renewable) energy resources, its ability to develop its potential and bring new energy supplies to market is less certain. On the one hand, this is due to the region's own growing energy needs, which over the last decade or so have been growing at an average of 6–8% per annum. Such strong demand growth in North Africa, both in the energy-rich countries of Algeria, Egypt and Libya, and net energy importers Morocco and Tunisia, has been driven by sustained economic and demographic expansion, as well as by government policies of keeping domestic energy prices at artificially low levels. On the other hand, investment in oil, gas and renewable energy production requires stable and attractive political and institutional frameworks, which is a factor that has generally been lacking in North Africa in recent years and will, in the wake of the "Arab Spring" events, continue to be elusive.

Notes

1. Interview with the authors, Tripoli, 13 May 2013.
2. John Hamilton and Jon Marks, *Algeria's Energy Future*, London: Cross Border Information, 2011, p. 8.
3. www.genewscenter.com/Press-Releases/GE-and-Sonelgaz-Affiliate-SPE-Sign-Contracts-Valued-at-2-7-Billion-to-Help-Power-Algeria-42c2.aspx.
4. *Libya: Selected Issues*, IMF, 2 May 2013, p. 5, www.imf.org/external/pubs/ft/scr/2013/cr13151.pdf.

CONTRIBUTORS

Ahmed Aghrout is a Research Fellow at the University of Salford in England. He specializes in the politics and economics of Euro-Maghrebi relations and has published articles in journals such as *The Journal of Modern African Studies*, the *British Journal of Middle Eastern Affairs* and the *European Union Review*. He is the author of *From Preferential Status to Partnership – The Euro-Maghreb Relationship* (Ashgate, 2001).

Ibrahim Awad is a Professor of Public Policy and Global Affairs and the Director of the Center for Migration and Refugee Studies (CMRS) at the School of Global Affairs and Public Policy (GAPP) at the American University in Cairo (AUC). He is the author of numerous articles and book chapters on migration politics and democratic transitions in the MENA.

Imen Belhadj is a post-doctoral candidate in the School of Foreign Languages of Peking University. She obtained her PhD in International Politics from the School of International Studies and her Master's Degree in Chinese Contemporary Literature from the Department of Chinese Literature, both at Peking University. She has published numerous articles in Chinese academic journals. In 2012, she won a fellowship to conduct research at the Nordic Africa Institute in Uppsala, Sweden, where she also lectures on Chinese policy in Africa.

Miloud Chennoufi teaches International Relations at the Canadian Forces Colleges, where he also chairs the Department of Security and International Affairs. He is the author of *Grandes puissances et islamisme (Great Powers and Islamism)* (Éditions El-Ikhtilef, 2003).

Hakim Darbouche is Research Associate with the Oxford Institute for Energy Studies (OIES). He has been with OIES since 2009, where he has worked as a

Research Fellow and published extensively on North African energy issues and MENA gas markets. He is now a practising professional in the oil & gas industry, working in the exploration and production division of a mid-cap European energy group. He holds a PhD from the University of Liverpool and a BA from Sussex University.

Abdoulaye Diagana is a Researcher in political geography. Currently a consultant in the Cross-Border Cooperation in West Africa Project: Mapping Policy Networks 2015–2016 West African Futures (WAF) Program in the Sahel and West Africa Club at the Organization of Economic Cooperation and Development, Paris. His publications focus on decentralization, local development and the state in Mauritania and West Africa in journals such as *Hommes et migrations*.

Gonzalo Escribano is Professor of Applied Economics at the Spanish Open University (UNED), and research fellow at the Elcano Royal Institute of International Studies. He has several publications on different aspects of North African political economy in journals that include *Mediterranean Politics, Energy Policy* and *Renewable and Sustainable Energy Reviews*.

Irene Fernández Molina is a Research Fellow at the European Neighbourhood Policy Chair of the College of Europe, Natolin campus (Warsaw). Her latest publications are *Moroccan Foreign Policy under Mohammed VI, 1999–2014* (Routledge, 2015) and "Protests under Occupation: The Spring inside Western Sahara" (*Mediterranean Politics*, 2015). She has previously worked as PhD research fellow at the Universidad Complutense de Madrid, a Schuman fellow at the Directorate-General for External Policies of the European Parliament (Brussels), and a visiting research fellow at Centre Jacques Berque and the Institut Marocain des Relations Internationales (in Morocco) and IREMAM (France).

John Hamilton is a Director of the Africa and Middle East-focused business intelligence consultancy and publisher Cross-Border Information, and is a contributing editor at the industry newsletter *African Energy*. He has spent the past eight years monitoring and analysing commercial and political risks in the countries of North Africa and their energy industries. He frequently comments on Libyan affairs in the international media and at specialist conferences. Earlier in his career, he spent five years as a freelance journalist in Bulgaria. His travel memoir, *The Good Balkans*, was published in 2007. He speaks, reads and writes Arabic, French and Spanish and is fluent in Bulgarian.

Miguel Hernando de Larramendi is a Professor of Politics and Society in the Contemporary Arab World at the Universidad de Castilla-La Mancha in Toledo, Spain. He is an associate researcher at the Mediterranean International Studies Workshop at the Universidad Autónoma de Madrid, where he is a supervisor in the PhD program. His books include: *La política exterior de Marruecos* (1997, translated into Arabic in 2005); *La política exterior española hacia el Magreb. Actores e intereses* (2009, with Aurelia Mañé); *España, el Mediterráneo y el mundo arabomusulmán. Diplomacia e historia* (2010, with Bernabé López García) and *Mohamed VI. Política y cambio social en Marruecos* (2011, with Thierry Desrues).

George Joffe teaches at the Department of Politics and International Studies in the University of Cambridge. He was previously the Deputy-Director of the Royal Institute of International Affairs (Chatham House) and is also the founder and co-editor (with Phillip Naylor and Gregory White) of the *Journal of North African Studies*. He has just completed participation in a major study of Tunisia's media after the revolution in 2011.

Lina Khatib is the Director of the Carnegie Middle East Center in Beirut. Previously, she was the co-founding head of the Program on Arab Reform and Democracy at Stanford University's Center on Democracy, Development, and the Rule of Law. She is the author of *Image Politics in the Middle East: The Role of the Visual in Political Struggle* (I.B. Tauris, 2013) and co-editor (with Ellen Lust) of *Taking to the Streets: The Transformation of Arab Activism* (Johns Hopkins University Press, 2014).

Azzedine Layachi is a Professor of Political Science at St. John's University. He received a PhD and Master's Degree in Political Science from New York University, and a Bachelor's Degree from the Institut des Etudes Politiques of the University of Algiers, Algeria. He is also a consultant to private and public institutions and the author of several books, book chapters and articles, including *Economic Crisis and Political Change in North Africa; State, Society and Liberalization in Morocco: The Limits of Associative Life;* "Algeria: The Untenable Exceptionalism in the Spring of Upheavals"; "Meanwhile in the Maghreb: Have Algeria and Morocco Avoided North Africa's Unrest?"; and "The Changing Geopolitics of Natural Gas: The Case of Algeria."

Elena Maestri is a tenured Researcher and Adjunct Professor of History and Institutions of the Muslim World at the Faculty of Political and Social Sciences of the Università Cattolica del Sacro Cuore (UCSC), Milan, Italy. She is the author of *La regione del Gulf Cooperation Council (GCC). Sviluppo e sicurezza umana in Arabia* [The Gulf Cooperation Council Region (GCC) Region. Development and Human Security in Arabia] (Rome: Franco Angelli, 2009) and co-editor of a forthcoming volume on *Arab Women and Media in Changing Landscapes: Realities and Challenges*.

Jennifer Miller-Gonzalez received her PhD in Political Science from the University of Michigan. She is currently a Research Fellow at the Weiser Center for Emerging Democracies at the University of Michigan.

Emma C. Murphy is a Professor of Political Economy and Head of School in the School of Government and International Affairs, Durham University. Her writings have covered the Israeli and Palestinian political economies, economic and political reform in the Arab region, Tunisian politics, and issues of contemporary Middle Eastern political economy. Since the Arab Spring, she has been researching the Tunisian political transition and the political economy of Arab youth.

Alison Pargeter is a Senior Research Fellow at the Royal United Services Institute. She is a specialist on North Africa with a particular focus on Libya, and on political Islam and radicalization. Her books include *Libya: The Rise and Fall of Gaddafi; The Muslim Brotherhood: The Burden of Tradition;* and *The New Frontiers of Jihad: Radical Islam in Europe.*

Eduard Soler i Lecha is a Senior Research Fellow and research coordinator at CIDOB, the Barcelona Centre for International Affairs. He has published extensively on Euro-Mediterranean relations, Turkey's foreign and domestic politics, North African and Middle Eastern political dynamics and security cooperation in the Mediterranean. Two of his recent papers are "Can the EU Still Inspire Integration in the Gulf" (published by the Gulf Research Center) and "The Future of Multilateral Security Dialogue in the Mediterranean: Lessons Learnt, Opportunities and Choices" (published by the Istituto Affari Internazionali).

Degang Sun is a Professor and the Deputy Director of Middle East Studies Institute, Shanghai International Studies University, China. His latest articles (with Yahia H. Zoubir) are, "China's Response to the Revolts in the Arab World: A Case of Pragmatic Diplomacy," in *Mediterranean Politics,* and "China's Economic Diplomacy Towards the Arab Countries: Challenges Ahead?" in *Journal of Contemporary China.* He is also the co-editor with Yahia H. Zoubir of *Building a New Silk Road: China and the Middle East in the 21st Century* (World Affairs Press, 2014).

Mark Tessler is Samuel J. Eldersveld Professor of Political Science at the University of Michigan. His most recent books include *Islam and Politics in the Middle East: Explaining the Views of Ordinary Citizens* (Indiana University Press, 2015) and *Public Opinion in the Middle East: Survey Research and the Political Orientations of Ordinary Citizens* (Indiana University Press, 2011). He is the recipient of a recent Carnegie Scholar Award and the past president of the American Institute for Maghreb Studies.

Gregory White is the Mary Huggins Gamble Professor of Government at Smith College. He is the co-editor-in-chief of the *Journal of North African Studies.* His work focuses on North African politics, environmental security and migration studies. He is the author most recently of *Climate Change and Migration: Borders and Security in a Warming World* (Oxford University Press, 2011). His current book project focuses on Morocco's tourism sector and its hydrological and sustainability challenges in the context of climate change.

Michael J. Willis is a Fellow in Moroccan and Mediterranean Studies at St Antony's College at the University of Oxford. Before taking up his current post in Oxford he taught politics at Al Akhawayn University in Ifrane, Morocco, for seven years from 1997–2004. His research focuses on the politics, modern history and international relations of the central Maghreb. He is author of *Politics and Power in the Maghreb: Algeria, Tunisia and Morocco from Independence to the Arab Spring* (Hurst & Co and Oxford University Press, 2012) and co-editor (with Adam Roberts, Timothy Garton-Ash and Rory McCarthy) of *Civil Resistance in the Arab Spring: Triumphs and Disasters* (Oxford University Press, 2015).

Alice Wilson is a Social Anthropologist, with research interests in the political and economic anthropology of North Africa and the Middle East. She holds a PhD in social anthropology from the University of Cambridge and is currently Addison Wheeler Research Fellow at Durham University. Her research interests centre on sovereignty, state power and tribes, explored through the case of the government-in-exile of Western Sahara's liberation movement.

Yahia H. Zoubir is a Professor of International Relations and International Management, and Director of Research in Geopolitics at KEDGE Business School, Marseille, France. His latest (co-authored) book is, *North African Security* (2013). He is co-editor of *North Africa: Politics, Region, and the Limits of Transformation* (2008); the editor and main contributor of *North Africa in Transition—State, Society & Economic Transformation in the 1990s* (1999); co-editor of *L'Islamisme Politique dans les Rapports entre l'Europe et le Maghreb* (1996); and co-editor and main contributor of *International Dimensions of the Western Sahara Conflict* (1993). His publications have appeared in major US, Canadian and European scholarly journals and as chapters in edited volumes, as well as in various encyclopedias.

Stephen Zunes is a Professor of Politics and International Studies at the University of San Francisco, where he serves as coordinator of the program in Middle Eastern Studies. He serves as a senior policy analyst for the Foreign Policy in Focus project of the Institute for Policy Studies and as co-chair of the academic advisory committee for the International Center on Nonviolent Conflict. His most recent book (co-authored with Jacob Mundy) is *Western Sahara: War, Nationalism and Conflict Irresolution* (Syracuse University Press, 2010).

INDEX